TIBULLUS I

TIBULLUS I

A Commentary on the First Book of the Elegies of Albius Tibullus

PAUL MURGATROYD

Bristol Classical Press

First published by University of Natal Press, 1980

Reprinted, with permission, 1991, 2001 by
Bristol Classical Press
an imprint of
Gerald Duckworth & Co. Ltd
61 Frith Street
London W1D 3JL
e-mail: inquiries@duckworth-publishers.co.uk
Website: www.ducknet.co.uk

A catalogue record for this book is available from the British Library

ISBN 1-85399-175-9

TIBULLI CARMINA TIBULLO

PREFACE

This work, which will, I hope, soon be followed by a commentary on the second book of Tibullus, began its life in 1971 as a Ph.D. thesis for the University of London. It was not until 1974 (with the bulk of the groundwork already completed) that I had access to Putnam's *Tibullus: A Commentary*, and a year later Guy Lee's *Tibullus: Elegies* appeared. Inevitably there have been some coincidences in opinion, but where I have incorporated ideas taken from them I have always done so with due recognition. I have followed the same (standard) practice with other scholarly works on Tibullus as well, discussing, with acknowledgement, important points of interpretation, but simply taking over (after sifting) parallel passages and general references. Almost invariably I have added extra parallels for greater elucidation and a better understanding of Tibullan variations and innovations. To avoid inordinate bulk, I have in the main cited and discussed only theories which have contributed significantly towards our appreciation of Tibullus or which have become widely accepted and so deserve some mention, if only for refutation.

With a poet who writes at such length it is difficult to produce a commentary that is both detailed and easy to follow. Accordingly I have confined more general discussion of the individual elegies to introductory essays and I have included notes on whole sections of the poems, in which I give a résumé of the passage and cover any major themes in it. For the same reason I have tried to be selective in what I have to say, aiming at comment that is broad and full, but not encyclopaedic. There is some textual criticism, but only in the case of points that substantially affect the interpretation of the elegies, and, because I felt that such discussion tended to clog an already bulky commentary, I have revived the institution of the Critical Appendix. There is also some literary criticism, which I regard as essential for a proper understanding of poetry, but again I have restricted my remarks. On questions of imitation, genre and themes, which are so vital in the case of a *doctus poeta*, and on matters of interpretation

I have allowed myself some scope. But I have generally refrained from commenting on points of style, unless I consider them to be of importance in the appreciation of a particular passage or poem, and similarly with regard to assonance, alliteration and kindred metrical effects, a controversial subject, I have only pointed out the most striking examples, and I have only ventured further comment when I feel that a particular emotion is already evident in the words and sound seems to reinforce it. Such remarks are couched in tentative terms because they are highly subjective.

The primary purpose of the structural schemes in the introductory essays is to reduce these long compositions to shorter parts and thereby facilitate comment and comprehension. I would emphasize that these schemes are not to be regarded as rigid divisions. They merely show where I feel the main breaks in the poems occur, as Tibullus moves on to a new idea, theme or character. It seemed desirable to deal with the unity of the elegies because the myth of the poet's penchant for digressions is not yet extinct and because Tibullus would be a lesser author if he were guilty of irrelevance and an inability to manipulate successfully material on the scale he has chosen. In my opinion the technique of composition is an important part of the poet's *ars*. These discussions also reflect my findings on the function of a poem's individual parts, which generally assists understanding of the poem as a whole. The examination of verbal repetition as a binding device in Tibullus was suggested to me by Elder *Critical Essays on Roman Literature I: Elegy and Lyric* (ed. Sullivan, 1962), 100f. (cf. also Lee op. cit. 12f.), and I believe that the process is deliberate since it is discernible in all the elegies of the first book. It is not always easy to decide when Tibullus is consciously repeating a word (cf. Introduction sect. 7), and so I have restricted myself to words which are connected with the main theme(s) of the elegy, which appear with particular frequency and which recur later in the poem with some definite (and presumably deliberate) twist.

On the difficult question of the amount of fact and fiction in the poetry I have been careful not to commit myself one way or the other. This is a problem which cannot be solved with any certainty and which I regard as outside the scope of a commentary. At any rate, for the purpose of the poems the characters and events are real enough, and when in the notes I talk of, for instance, situations or emotions, I mean those shown in the elegies.

There remains the pleasant duty of recording my many debts of thanks. My first real introduction to Tibullus came in Cambridge, when as an undergraduate I listened to Guy Lee's sensitive lectures on this underrated author, and I fear that my commentary may unconsciously reflect more of his ideas than I have acknowledged. My thesis was supervised by Dr J.B. Hall, whose scholarship, thoroughness and patience over a lengthy period have improved this work immeasurably. I was very fortunate to have as my external examiner Professor H.D. Jocelyn, and I have benefited greatly from his shrewd, searching and stimulating criticism. D.S. Raven read through the penultimate draft with care and made a number of helpful comments and penetrating suggestions. I would also like to acknowledge the kind permission of the Oxford University Press to base my text on the Oxford Classical Texts edition of *Tibullus* by J.P. Postgate (2nd ed., 1915), and I would like to thank Professor G.C. Galinsky for generously allowing me to quote his *sigla* in the Critical Appendix. Particular gratitude is due to my family: to my parents for very real aid and encouragement over the years, to my sister-in-law for typing at an early stage, and to my wife for prolonged help in many departments and very great understanding. Finally, I would like to record my thanks to Tibullus, to whom this book is aptly dedicated, for standing on my papers and sitting on my knee.

28 February 1978 P. M.

Now that this book has been finally accepted for publication under conditions which I can satisfy, I have two further debts to record. I wish to acknowledge the generous financial assistance of the Human Sciences Research Council towards the publication of this work. Of course, opinions expressed in this work, or conclusions reached, are my own and not those of the Human Sciences Research Council. Finally, I would like to thank most sincerely my head of department, Professor M.M. Henderson, for his invaluable support at a critical time.

6 December 1979 P. M.

CONTENTS

INTRODUCTION

1 The Sources for constructing a Biography of Tibullus.

The sources are the *vita*, the epigram of Domitius Marsus, Horace *C.* 1.33, *Epist.*1.4, Ov. *Am.*1.15.27f., 3.9, *A.A.*3.333f., 535f., *Rem.* 763ff., *Tr.* 2.445ff., 4.10.51ff., 5.1.15ff., Vell.Pat.2.36.3, Quint. *Inst.* 10.1.93, Stat. *Silv.*1.2.250ff., Mart.4.6, 8.70, 8.73, 14.193, Apul. *Apol.*10, Diomedes 484.17ff.(K), Sidon.Apoll. *C.*9.259ff., *Epist.*2.10.6 (all these passages are quoted in Smith 173ff. and Lenz & Gal. 171f., 176ff.). Unfortunately there is some controversy over the credibility of the *vita* and the identity of the person addressed in the Horatian poems, so that any biography must be preceded by discussion of these pieces.

The *vita* probably contains extracts from a lost work of Suetonius on T. (Rostagni *RF* n.s. XIII (1935), 25ff., *Suetonio 'De Poetis' e biografi minori* (Turin, 1944), 134ff., Avery *CPh* LV (1960), 24ff.), although Suetonius himself would have been writing a century and more after T., and it is impossible to tell exactly how much has been taken from him.

Postgate (*Selections* Appendix A) maintained that the *vita* contains nothing which could not have been based on the epigram of Marsus, the Horatian pieces or T. himself. However, to begin with minor points, although T.'s friendship with Messalla is mentioned in his poetry, Horace and Marsus do not mention his patron's name, and T. himself refers to him only as Messalla, so that the *vita*'s *Corvinum Messalam* is not taken from any of Postgate's sources. The same applies to the remark in the *vita* that many regarded T. as the foremost elegist, as Postgate himself admits. Both these points would probably have been common knowledge, but they do indicate some measure of independence. More important, the *vita* says of T. *cuius* [*Messallae*] *et contubernalis Aquitanico bello militaribus donis donatus est*, words which have a factual ring and are without exact parallel in the suggested sources. Postgate says that these remarks 'may be nothing more than an amplification of the words "*non sine me est tibi partus honos*"

1.vii.9', but his own hesitancy betrays the speculative nature of his argument. Finally, the *vita* calls T. an *eques,* a detail which is not mentioned at all in Marsus, Horace or T. and which concerns not only his financial position but also his social status. Postgate's explanation of this remark as a compromise between T.'s claim of *paupertas* and Horace's attribution to him of *divitias* at *Epist.*1.4.7 seems unlikely, especially since Horace redefines *divitias* as a modest standard of living at line 11 (see below).

These four points tend to invalidate Postgate's argument. In addition, there seems no reason for doubting the veracity of these remarks: the first two we know to be true; the third seems quite likely, since we are told at 1.7.9 that T. accompanied Messalla on the Aquitanian campaign, while a detestation of war is not incompatible with bravery in the field and is often based on actual experience of war; as to the fourth, the other Roman elegists were probably *equites* also (Taylor *TAPhA* XCIX (1968), 479ff.), and both Propertius and Ovid also complain of lack of money. The fact that Marsus, T. himself and Horace do agree with the remainder of the *vita* does not invalidate those remarks in the *vita* but actually provides corroborating evidence. There seems, then, no reason to doubt the credibility of the *vita.*

The Horatian poems are addressed to a poet called Albius. The resemblances to T. are considerable: T. wrote *miserabiles elegi*; he is described as handsome in the *vita*; he was fond of the countryside; he could well be described as *sapiens* and *bonus*; he had *gratia* and *fama*, and there is no reason to suppose that as a general rule he did not also have *valetudo*; his *nomen gentile* was Albius (see section 3).

Certain objections have been raised against this identification (see Postgate *Selections* Appendix A, *AJPh* XXXIII (1912), 450ff., and cf. Ullman *AJPh* XXXIII (1912), 149ff., 456ff.). Postgate maintained that there was a discrepancy between T.'s claim of *paupertas* and Horace's attribution to him of *divitias* at *Epist.*1.4.7. However, *divitiae* is a relative term (cf.e.g. Prop.3.13.26, Stat. *Silv.*1.2.255), and Horace defines it at line 11 as *mundus victus non deficiente crumina.* To judge from his use of *mundus* at *S.*2.2.65 and *C.*3.29.14 (cf. also *Epist.*2.2.199), Horace is here envisaging a modest standard of living (similar to that described in T.1.1: see section 3). Postgate also expressed disbelief that Horace would ask the famous T. if he was writing something to surpass the minor productions of Cassius Parmensis (according to the scholiasts on *Epist.*1.4.3, a dilettante who wrote among other things elegies and tragedies). Here Postgate seems to have ignored completely the tone of the piece. Either Horace fears that in his present melancholy state T. may turn to tragedy or, more likely, this is a gently teasing remark which would not give offence to a poet with an established reputation but would do to a literary amateur (Postgate's interpretation of Horace's Albius).

To turn to *C.*1.33, Postgate objected that nowhere in his poetry does T. mention a younger rival or anyone called Glycera. It is possible that T. did have an affair with a Glycera, was supplanted by a younger rival and wrote a few elegies about it which were subsequently destroyed (because they were too mournful?) or simply lost. However, Nisbet & Hubbard (on Hor. *C.*1.33) offer the most likely interpretation of the ode, namely that it is a teasing criticism of T.'s poetry, using the elegist's own imagery and situations: Glycera, a common name for hetaerae (Nisbet & Hubbard on *C.*1.19.5), is merely imaginary, and the rival who is younger and outshines T. (no elegist would have admitted this) is an example of Horace teasing T., as he probably does in *Epist.* 1.4.

It would appear, then, that the Albius of Horace is very similar to T. It seems most unlikely that there could have been at the same time another elegist of the same name and with the same characteristics and circumstances. If such a person did exist, one wonders who he could have been. If he was a rich literary amateur, as Postgate maintains, it seems odd that Horace should devote two whole poems to him but comparatively little to Virgil. If, on the other hand, he was a serious and successful professional, it is strange that he receives no mention in Ovid's or Quintilian's lists of elegists, or anywhere else. It seems scarcely conceivable, then, that the Albius of Horace can be anyone but T.

2 Birth and Death.

Ovid at *Tr.* 4.10.51-4 gives the succession of the elegists as follows: *Vergilium vidi tantum nec amara Tibullo/ tempus amicitiae fata dedere meae./ successor fuit hic tibi, Galle, Propertius illi,/ quartus ab his serie temporis ipse fui.* He states expressly that this order is chronological (*serie temporis*), but it is impossible to be certain about the exact ref. here. The passage has been cited as proof that T. was born before Propertius, but Ovid could equally well be thinking of some sort of literary succession. Although Propertius' first book probably preceded T. I (see section 6) and although most of Prop.'s works were written while T. was still alive, Ovid could mean that T. wrote and recited some poetry before Prop. did or that until his death T.'s reputation was the greater and he was regarded as the leading elegist of the day (cf. Marsus and the *vita*). The passage of Ovid, then, seems to be of no help in establishing the date of T.'s birth.

Marsus tells us that T. died a *iuvenis* and the *vita* that he died an *adolescens,* citing Marsus as evidence. *Adolescens* is often used as a synonym for *iuvenis* (e.g. Livy 2.3.2, 2.33.5, 22.53.3, 6), a term which is applied to people from the age of 16 to 45 (1.8.31-2n., Varro in Censorinus 14.2, Plin. *Epist.*8.14.7, Manil.3.610). As T. died in either 19 or 18 B.C. (see below), 64 B.C. is the earliest possible date for his birth.

However, there are a number of considerations in favour of assuming a late date for T.'s birth. Love-poetry at that time was usually started by poets when they were young (book I was completed in 27 or 26 B.C.: see sect.5), and an early death would help explain the reason for such a comparatively small output by T. Similarly, at *Am.* 3.9.49ff. Ovid tells us that T.'s mother and sister survived him (admittedly Ovid is there paying a tribute to T. by a reminiscence of 1.3.5ff., but he would hardly have said this if they were dead). It appears likely, then, that he was born a good deal later than 64 B.C. Beyond this further speculation seems useless.

The date of T.'s death can be determined with more certainty, on the testimony of Domitius Marsus, but before considering his epigram it is necessary to discuss the evidence for the date of T.'s death suggested by Avery (*CJ* LV (1960), 205ff., LVI (1961), 229ff.) and Buchheit (*Philologus* CIX (1965), 104ff.). A thorough criticism of these proposals and a good discussion of the subject in general is offered by McGann in *Latomus* XXIX (1970), 774ff.

Avery argued that the fact that T. alone of the poets in Ovid *Am.* 1.15.9-30 is addressed in the vocative indicates that he alone was alive when it was written, and that, as *Aeneiaque arma* (25) is a definite ref. to the *Aeneid* in published form, T. was alive after the publication of the *Aeneid.* McGann points out that the vocative has been explained by considerations of metre and variety (in fact Ovid is at pains throughout these lines to avoid structural and verbal monotony) and that, as the point of the whole passage is to show that poetry is superior to death (31f.), it is inconceivable that a living poet should be present, and placed between Virgil and Gallus at that. He also adds that line 25 contains too vague a ref. to prove that the *Aeneid* already existed in published form.

Avery also argued that the tenses in Ovid *Am.* 3.9 show that it was written at the time of T.'s death and that lines 13, 14 and 27 prove Ovid's acquaintance with the *Aeneid,* so that the *Aeneid* was published before T.'s death. However, as McGann points out, the present tenses merely indicate that Ovid is depicting a dramatic situation – himself mourning beside T.'s pyre. It should also be noted that elsewhere Ovid speaks of the funeral in the past tense (41-6, 49-54). As for Ovid's alleged acquaintance with the *Aeneid* in published form, Avery's evidence is neither extensive nor esp. convincing: *fratris . . . Aeneae* in 13 is supposed to hark back to *Aen.* 1.667, but more probably harks back to T. 2.5.39; *pulcher Iule* in 14 is said to be taken from

Virgil's *pulcher Iulus* (*Aen.* 5.570 etc.), which is possible, although it may be simply a variation on Ovid's own *formosus Iulus* (*Her.* 7.83), and it hardly proves knowledge of the *Aeneid* in published form; line 27 he derives from *Aen.* 6.429 = 11.28 (*dies* is the only point in common, and *mersit* perhaps partially) and *Aen.* 2.324 (*summa dies* only).

Buchheit claimed that there are certain passages in T. 2.5 which show a knowledge of the whole *Aeneid* that could only have been acquired after it was published. In general his claim is not well supported and there is little that could not have been suggested by previous poets or readings from the *Aeneid* (rather than the whole work in published form). He compares T. 2.5.41f. with *Aen.* 8.38f., maintaining that the idea of Italy welcoming the Trojans was a Virgilian innovation. However, this kind of idea was common enough (e.g. Aesch. *Supp.* 23ff., Soph. *O.T.* 1391, *O.C.* 772f.), and, as McGann points out, it could easily have occurred to both poets that someone who could not promise a welcome from the inhabitants of Italy would stress a welcome from the land itself. Buchheit also claimed that T. 2.5.55f. was inspired by *Aen.* 8.347f., since the contrast between pastoral Rome and the greatness to come was not found before the *Aeneid.* However, the Romans, who were aware of their pastoral origins (McGann compares Varro *R.R.* 2.1.9), had only to look around them to see the contrast with their present circumstances. In fact, this contrast had already been suggested at Cic. *Re pub.* 2.10, and the antithesis between present magnificence and former simplicity had already been pointed out at Sall. *Cat.* 12.3 and implied at T.1.10.19ff. Finally, Buchheit held that behind T. 2.5.48 was the idea that the death of Turnus was a precondition of settlement in Italy by the Trojans and that at T.2.5.47f. the final combat between Aeneas and Turnus is preceded by the Trojan burning of Laurentum in T. as in the *Aeneid* (12.554ff.). However, McGann reasonably remarks that line 48 is not explicit enough to justify such an interpretation and Turnus' rôle in T. is similar to that in Cato's *Origines,* while *Rutulis castris* at 2.5.47 cannot refer to a Latin town, a point that Virgil constantly emphasizes. It should also be noted that there are textual difficulties at 2.5.47.

So we must turn to the epigram of Marsus for establishing the date of T.'s death. Here there is some dispute over the meaning of the words *Vergilio comitem . . . / . . . misit.* In the passages cited by *Thes.L.L.* (III.1774.58ff.) where *comes* is applied to the dead or dying most frequently the word is used of a person who dies at the same time or shortly after another (cf. e.g. Virg. *Aen.* 4.677f., 12.881, Ov. *Met.* 4.152, *Ex P.* 3.1.109, Val.Fl.6.213, Sil.It.5.467), and when a person is described as a *comes* of another and motion is implied, as here, the word always means 'fellow-traveller'. In answer to the objection that with the meaning 'fellow-traveller' the genitive would be expected, it may be pointed out that in Augustan usage of *comes* as 'fellow-traveller' in a general sense the dative is more common of the person accompanied (*Thes. L. L.* III.1772.29ff.), and in the passages on the dead and dying the only possible ex. of the genitive of the person accompanied is Ov. *Ex P.* 3.1.109, and there the genitive may well depend on *Manes* (as McGann suggests). The sense of *Vergilio comitem . . . / . . . misit,* therefore, is almost certainly 'sent as a fellow-traveller', and there is a close parallel at Virg. *Aen.* 12.362 (*huic comitem Asbyten coniecta cuspide mittit*).

In any case, exactly what the meaning of the epigram would be, if not that two great poets died within a short period of time, is not clear, as McGann rightly comments. Avery suggested that 'Tibullus and Virgil are *comites* after death because both were poets in life, albeit of two distinct genres', but Marsus would then be using a particularly pointed form (epigram) to make a quite pointless remark, and surely other poets (e.g. Calvus, Catullus and Gallus, as at Ov. *Am.* 3.9.61ff.) would be better candidates for such *comites* of T.

It seems certain, then, that the epigram means that T. died at about the same time as Virgil, and this coincidence may also be implied by the juxtaposition of the two poets at Ov. *Tr.* 4.10.51f. Most probably T. died a few days or weeks after Virgil, but his death may have been later still. Exactly how long an interval of time would elapse before the two deaths could not be associated is not an easy question, but about a year would seem the most likely outside limit. Virgil died in Sept., 19 B.C., and so it seems probable that T. died some time afterwards in 19 or in 18 B.C.

3 Name, Family and Circumstances.

The poet's *nomen gentile* was Albius: it is given as such in the *vita* (there is no reason for doubting the statements in the *vita,* and if it was derived from Suetonius, as seems probable, one would expect that the poet's name at least would still be remembered about a century later: see section 1); the Horatian pieces are addressed to a poet called Albius who was almost certainly Tibullus (see section 1); cf. also Acro on *Epist.* 1.4.1, Acro and Porphyrio on *C.* 1.33.1, Diomedes 484.17ff.(K), the Horatian and Tibullan mss. The poet's *praenomen* is unknown. His *cognomen* was Tibullus according to his own words (1.3.55, 1.9.83; cf. also all the passages cited at the beginning of section 1 except Ov. *A.A.* 3.535f. and the Horatian poems).

Horace at *Epist.* 1.4.2 speaks of T. residing *in regione Pedana,* and so it is possible that the location of T.'s ancestral estate was at Pedum, in Latium. T. tells us that his mother and sister were alive during his lifetime (1.3.5ff.) and Ovid that they survived him (*Am.* 3.9.49ff.: see section 2). T.'s father is mentioned neither by T. nor by Ovid, and, as T. depicts himself as in charge of the family estate and performing religious functions for it in 1.1, 1.10 and 2.1, it seems likely that he was dead.

T. says that his ancestral estate had formerly been large and prosperous (1.1.19, 21, 41f.) but by the time he was writing had been reduced (1.1.19, 22, 33). The reason for this reduction is not given, but two possibilities suggest themselves: either some of the property was lost in the land-confiscations of the period, as happened to Virgil and Propertius, or his father squandered it (see Ullman *AJPh* XXXIII (1912), 160f.). In any case, this reduction appears to have left him with a modest fortune, but one sufficient to satisfy his needs (1.1.25, 77f., Hor. *Epist.* 1.4.11). As for the complaints of actual poverty (e.g. 1.5.61ff.), they may be largely conventional (cf. 1.4.61-2n.), or the beloved may be supposed to have made excessive demands on the poet. The *vita* tells us that T. was an *eques*, which is compatible with this estimate (see section 1).

4 Main Characters of Book I.

Delia is the name given to T.'s mistress in book I and she is mentioned in poems 1, 2, 3, 5 and 6. According to Apuleius (*Apol.* 10) the name was a pseudonym: *eadem igitur opera accusent . . . Tibullum, quod ei sit Plania in animo, Delia in versu.* The name may have been used, like Prop.'s Cynthia, because it suggested the sister of Apollo, god of poetry, or because δῆλος is the Greek for *planus*. At any rate, the number and quantity of the syllables in the names agree, which seems to have been a general requirement for these pseudonyms (see Bentley on Hor. *C.* 2.12.13).

The general view that Delia was not depicted as a married woman has been recently challenged by Williams (*Tradition and Originality in Roman Poetry* (Oxford, 1968), 535ff.). His main arguments are as follows: (i) in 1.2 and 1.6 she is credited with a *coniunx*, a word which he takes to mean 'husband'; (ii) the meaning of 1.6.67-8 is 'teach her to behave as if she were married to me, although her relationship to me is not one of marriage'; (iii) Ovid envisaged Delia as a married woman and her *coniunx* as her husband (*Tr.* 2.457-66).

In reply the following observations may be made: (i) *coniunx* does not invariably mean 'husband': at Catull.64.123 and 182 (see 139ff.) and at Ov. *Her.* 9.118 (see 131ff.) the word is applied to lovers who are merely potential husbands; at Ov. *Am.* 1.10.2 (of Helen, *coniugibus belli causa duobus erat*) the term is applied to husband and lover; D. S. Raven brings to my attention Virg. *Ecl.* 8.66, where *coniunx* probably denotes a lover. In 1.2 and 1.6, then, *coniunx* could easily denote simply 'the man in possession'; (ii) the literal meaning of 1.6.67-8 is 'teach her to keep away from other men, although she does not have the characteristic dress of the Roman matron': the most obvious implication here is 'teach her to behave like a married woman, although she is not one' (not married to me or anyone else). That *castitas* was equated with the married state is shown by e.g. Ov. *A.A.* 1.31, *Tr.* 2.247-52, *ExP.* 3.3.51-6. Such a remark by T. is not without point (1.6.67-8n.). It is hard to see how Williams gets the idea 'although her relationship *to me* is not one of marriage' out of the Latin. Certainly when T. says *sit modo casta, doce* he is thinking primarily of his own interests, but that does not mean that in the rest of the couplet he must be thinking only of her relationship to him. The Latin of *sit modo casta, doce* does not mean 'teach her to confine herself to me' or 'teach her to be faithful to me', but it simply means 'teach her to stop being promiscuous': T. is not specific in any part of the couplet. Williams also remarks that in 1.6 'the dramatic situation requires a male who has actual rights over Delia and can say 'Yes' or 'No': such rights come from marriage': I am not sure exactly which 'rights' Williams is thinking of here, but if he means the 'right' to place a guard on Delia (and to grant T. that position), I would point out that such a 'right' was hardly confined to husbands (cf. e.g. Ov. *A.A.* 3.613ff.); (iii) the only relevant line in *Tr.* 2.457-66 is 457 *denique ab incauto nimium petit ille marito* (462 does not imply that Delia was married, merely that T.'s precepts about deception could be used by married women). *Incauto . . . marito* obviously refers to T. 1.6.15 *coniunx incaute,* but does not provide firm enough evidence that Delia's *coniunx* was her husband. Firstly, *maritus* does not always mean 'husband': at Virg. *Aen.* 4.35 (and possibly 536) it is used of potential husbands (Dido's suitors), and so could perhaps be used, like *coniunx,* to mean 'the man in possession'; secondly, even if Ovid is using *maritus* in the sense of 'husband', this line comes in a passage in which Ovid is trying to represent his predecessors in as bad a light as possible, and so a distortion of the facts must have been quite tempting (cf. section 5 and Critical Appendix on 1.5.69); in any case, the precise relationship of Delia to her *coniunx* was probably unknown to Augustus, so that a deal of exaggeration seems likely here, while there is no particular reason to believe that Ovid himself necessarily knew their relationship (cf. e.g. *Tr.* 4.10.51f.); (iv) T. 1.6.18 is also relevant, where T. talks of Delia's garment revealing her breasts. If Delia were a married woman she would naturally wear the *stola,* which did not show the breasts or much else (cf. e.g. Hor. *S.* 1.2.94f., 99). Her interest in Isis may also be pertinent (see 1.3.23-4n.). It would appear, then, that the old view of Delia as a courtesan is correct.

Beyond this little is clear about Delia. As Lee (p. 14) points out, she may have been a Roman citizen, if Apuleius' statement that her real name was Plania is correct (only Roman citizens had gentile names). However, Apuleius was writing almost two centuries later and may only be reflecting the literary gossip of the day, while a *gens Plania* is unknown. Delia, as she appears in T.'s poetry, differs little from the mistresses of other love poets: she is beautiful (1.5.43-4n.), but lying, unfaithful and mercenary, although T. does mention her tenderness (1.1.61ff.).

Marathus appears with certainty in 1.4(81ff.) and 1.8. It is generally assumed (without discussion) that the unnamed boy in 1.9 is Marathus. It is probable, but not certain, that T. is writing about the same character in all three elegies. There are physical similarities between the unnamed boy and Marathus (1.8.9ff. cf. 1.9.13ff.), and both employ the trick of crying to get their own way (1.8.67f., 1.9.37f.). More significant, both are said to be in love with a girl, which is most unusual for a *puer delicatus* (see intro. essay to 1.8), and Pholoe in 1.8 behaves as T. wishes the boy's girlfriend in 1.9 to behave (1.9.40). In addition, it would considerably heighten the humour in the contrasts between 1.8 and 1.9 (see intro. essay to 1.9) if the unnamed boy was supposed to be Marathus.

'Marathus' is a real name (cf. Suet. *Aug.* 79.2, 94.3), but, as in the case of Delia and Pholoe, it may well be a pseudonym (cf. Apul. *Apol.* 10) chosen for particular point. Smith mentions the suggestion that the name is connected with μαραίνω, and the verb's meaning 'to wear out, to make waste away' agrees well with *lento me torquet amore* (1.4.81), where the name first appears. Perhaps more likely is the connection with fennel (*marathrum*, μάραθρον, μάραθον, μάραθος). Primarily one thinks of Prometheus stealing fire in fennel (e.g. Hes. *Theog.* 565ff.), which gives the name an appropriate background of furtiveness and deceit. Possibly also suggested is a connection with fire (of love), as fennel was used for carrying fire (see above and cf. also Pliny *N.H.* 13.126). The idea of pain may be present as well, as fennel was used as a cane (Mayor on Juv. 1.15), again a notion which agrees with 1.4.81.

Marathus exhibits a number of characteristics of the *puer delicatus* in literature (beardless, pretty, effeminate and cruel), and the elegies concerning him contain a number of conventional situations. However, there are also some unusual features. In 1.8 (and probably in 1.9: see above) Marathus is in love with a girl. This is a rare occurrence for the *puer delicatus,* and even more unusual is his lack of success and maltreatment by her in 1.8, while T. takes an amused stance and speaks on behalf of the boy, an uncommon attitude for the paederast (see intro. essay to 1.8).

In 1.8 (and possibly at 1.9.39ff.) Marathus is having some sort of an affair with a girl called Pholoe. A girl of the same name and similar character appears in Horace (*C.* 1.33.7, 2.5.17, 3.15.7). The name also occurs at Virg. *Aen.* 5.285 (cf. Serv. ad *Aen.* 1.316) of a Cretan slave, and at Stat. *Silv.* 2.3.10 of a fleeing nymph. Again 'Pholoe' may be a pseudonym: it is not attested outside poetry and may symbolize ruggedness, after the mountain of the same name (see Nisbet & Hubbard on Hor. *C.* 1.33.7).

M. Valerius Messalla Corvinus (64 B.C. – 8 A.D.) is mentioned by T. at 1.1.53, 1.3.1, 56, 1.5.31, 2.1.31, 33, 2.5.119, while his achievements are celebrated at length in 1.7, and the admission of his son Messalinus to the *XVviri sacris faciundis* is the subject of 2.5. Both T.'s poems and the *vita* testify to his affection for his patron.

After earlier supporting Brutus and Cassius, and then Antony, Messalla eventually joined Octavian, fought a number of campaigns for him and took part in the battle of Actium (Appian *B.C.* 4.38). After this came two expeditions (Eastern and Aquitanian), in which T. himself was involved to a varying degree (see below). Unfortunately the chronology of these expeditions is not certain, but it does seem likely that the Eastern was the earlier of the two. When Dio (51.7.7), speaking of the year 30 B.C., says of the gladiators in the East καὶ οἱ μὲν ὑπὸ τοῦ Μεσσάλου ὕστερον ἀπατηθέντες, he probably means that Messalla dealt with them later in that same year, in view of Octavian's usual swift action in such matters, and, if the Eastern expedition did take place first this would provide a simple and obvious explanation for Messalla not celebrating his Aquitanian triumph until 27 B.C. (see Hammer *Prolegomena to an Edition of the Panegyricus Messallae* (Columbia, 1925), 46ff.). At any rate, it is likely that in 1.3 T. is referring to the Eastern expedition, on which it appears that he was left behind at Corcyra through illness. Beyond the reference to the gladiators in Dio the reasons for and events of this expedition are uncertain, but a list of places in some way connected with the expedition is given at 1.7.13ff. The Aquitanian campaign was to quell a revolt of the Celts (Appian *B.C.* 4.38), and for his victory Messalla celebrated a triumph on the 25th of September, 27 B.C. (*CIL* 1^2 p.50). T. himself was present in Gaul (1.7.9), and the *vita* tells us *cuius [Messallae] contubernalis Aquitanico bello militaribus donis donatus est.* The exact details of the campaign are unclear, but Messalla won a victory at the Atur (1.7.4), and T. cites other places too as witnesses of the glory that his patron won (see 1.7.11-2n.).

Messalla was also a statesman: he was *praefectus urbi* (although he resigned the post after a short period), *curator aquarum* and a member of the College of Augurs. He reconstructed part of the *via Latina* (1.7.57-8n.) and various public buildings. He was also a man with literary interests (esp. in points of grammar and style) and was himself a distinguished orator and writer (Cic. *ad Brut.* 1.15.1, Tac. *Dial.* 18,

Sen. *Contr.* 2.4.8, Quint. *Inst.* 1.7.35, 10.1.113). But it is as a literary patron that he is best remembered: he gathered around himself a group of poets including T., the other authors of the *Corpus Tibullianum* and possibly Valgius (4.1.179f.).

This is perhaps also the place to comment on T.'s failure to include a particular character in book I (and II). The fact that T., in contrast to his contemporaries, does not openly praise Augustus or the new régime has led to speculation that he was actually hostile. The omission is noteworthy, but there is no concrete evidence of any hostility. It may reflect nothing more than a degree of independence on the poet's part in the choice of subject-matter, and, in fact, there are suggestions that he was favourably disposed. In general (apart from his patron) he has little to say about contemporary figures or events, and he may well have felt unhappy about writing 'official' poetry. It should be pointed out that he does pay an allusive compliment to the régime in 1.7 (see 1.7.5-8n.), his longest elegy (2.5) is an expression of national feeling which would have been favourably received by Augustus, and he had already proved his patriotism by fighting and distinguishing himself in Aquitania (see above). It should also be noted that he seems to hold a number of sentiments in common with Augustus: a liking for the native Italian gods is in line with Augustus' attempts to restore the ancient Italian religion; his remarks about greed and wealth are in accord with Augustan sumptuary laws; his praise of rustic life fits in with Augustus' concern for agriculture; and, finally, a poet who says that he detests war so violently might be expected to be sympathetic to the *princeps* who put an end to civil wars and closed the gates of Janus.

5 The Chronology of Book I and Arrangement of the Elegies.

Elegy 7 was written around the time of Messalla's birthday, some time after his Aquitanian triumph in September, 27 B.C. (see intro. essay to 1.7), and the whole book must have been published shortly afterwards. Ovid at *Tr.* 2.463f. says of T. *non fuit hoc illi fraudi, legiturque Tibullus / et placet, et iam te principe notus erat.* Here Ovid is obviously referring to general access to T.'s work for the public such as could only have been possible from a published edition. Owen (on *Tr.* 2.464) points out that the title *princeps* come into use as a designation of Augustus from January, 27 B.C., but Ovid was writing the *Tristia* much later and, in any case, would not be so fastidious over precise chronology (especially if it made his argument stronger). He must mean little more than very early in Augustus' principate. It is clear that T. I preceded Propertius' second book (see 1.10.61-4n.), which was probably published in 26 or 25 B.C. (see Camps *Propertius Elegies Book II* (Cambridge, 1967), p.1). We may take it that T. I was published soon after the composition of elegy 7, late in 27 or possibly early in 26 B.C.

In view of the above it seems almost certain that T. himself was responsible for the arrangement of the poems, and investigation shows that they have been carefully positioned to produce correspondence, contrast and overall symmetry and variety.

The book as a whole can be divided into a simple pattern, a series of single elegies divided by pairs of elegies (the same division on similar principles has also occurred to Lee, p. 13):

1 The poet's ideal existence in contrast to the soldier's life; main emphasis on country and morality.
2+3 Heterosexual love: separation from Delia and hints of rivals.
4 Homosexual love: Priapus' lecture.
5+6 Heterosexual love: Delia has taken up with a rival and is not averse to further infidelity.
7 Non-amatory: Messalla's birthday and exploits.
8+9 Homosexual love: the boy has taken up with another; theme of venality present.
10 The poet's ideal existence in contrast to the soldier's life; main emphasis on country and morality.

Elegy 1 forms a good introduction to the whole collection (see intro. essay to 1.1). The second poem continues the situation of 1.1.56 (and 73f.), and at 65ff. it briefly picks up from 1 the opposition of an ideal rustic existence with the mistress to the soldier's life (see notes ad loc.). However, unlike its predecessor, it is concerned with the city. Although 3 forms a pair with 2, there is still antithesis: the pleas to Delia to be unfaithful (to her *coniunx*) in 2 contrast with the plea to her to be faithful (to T.) at 3.82ff., and the condemnation of the man who left Delia for war at 2.65ff. is neatly turned in 3, where T. himself has gone off on an expedition. The fourth elegy concerns homosexual love, and its light, ironic attitude is opposed to the seriousness of the third. With the fifth poem we are back to heterosexual love and an earnest tone. Although 6 is to be grouped with 5 because of similarity of situation, its insults and intimidation are in marked contrast to the *obsequium* and *blanditia* of the preceding piece. The non-amatory subject-matter and 'official' character of the seventh elegy come as a complete change. In 8 the subject is again amatory, and the tone is now amused and humorous. The partner poem, the ninth, contains extensive antithesis to 8 (see intro. essay to 1.9). Elegy 10 forms a final contrast in themes and has only a few lines on love (heterosexual and not subjective). Its numerous similarities to the first poem (see intro. essay to 1.10) mean that 1 and 10 form a frame and give the whole first book unity and balance.

6 The Relative Dating of Propertius I and Tibullus I.

This is a difficult problem and one that it is impossible to solve with complete certainty, but there are certain indications that Prop. I was probably earlier. The only datable elegy in Prop.'s first book is the sixth: it refers to the proconsulship in Asia of L. Volcacius Tullus in 30 – 29 B.C. In T.'s first book the seventh elegy concerns Messalla's triumph in Sept., 27 B.C., and it seems likely that the whole book was published shortly afterwards (see section 5). Although Prop. 1.6 need not be one of the latest elegies in that book, and so show that his first book preceded T.'s first book, these dates do at least provide a pointer in that direction.

To turn to metrical matters, it is very noticeable that non-disyllabic pentameter endings in Prop. II are far less frequent than in his first book (the figures given by Platnauer (p.17) are 36% for I and 10.5% for II). It is possible that Propertius independently came to favour the disyllabic ending, but it may well be the case, as has sometimes been suggested, that T. was responsible for this drastic drop (25.5%) in Prop.'s non-disyllabic pent. endings. In his first book T.'s use of non-disyllabic pent. endings is only 6.6%, and, if T. I came out after Prop. I, this low percentage in T. provides an obvious and plausible explanation for the change in Prop.'s second book. Incidentally, it should be pointed out that in T. II the percentage of such non-disyllabic endings is 8.37 (only slightly higher than in T. I), so that it could hardly be argued that Prop.'s greater number of non-disyllabic pent. endings in his first book influenced T. and that Prop. I therefore appeared after T. I.

The impression that Propertius' first book was the earlier of the two is also given by an examination of parallel passages in T. and Propertius, where imitation of one poet by the other seems likely. Similarity to Prop. I is evident in the following places in T. (for refs. see the commentary): 1.1.43, 53-8, 61-8, 69-70, 75, 1.2.10, 13-14, 43-44, 74, 75-8, 1.4.39ff., 1.5.45, 59f., 1.8.3-6, 7-8, 9 (see also intro. essay to 1.8). In many of these passages it is hard to be sure exactly who is imitating whom, but there are four places where it seems very probable that Propertius was the model. In general it would be fair to say that when T. and Prop. handle the same subject independently there is a simpler approach from T. and a more intense and more complex treatment by the flamboyant Propertius. Accordingly, when in similar versions of the same theme by the two poets we find more detail and pointedness, extra complexity and originality in T., it seems reasonable to conclude that T. has taken Propertius as his model and tried to expand and improve upon him. By the same token Prop.'s comparative simplicity would be best explained as due to a first attempt at the theme, and, if T. had in fact handled the subject first, one would not expect a pale imitation and a shortened version by Prop., esp. since it is clear from a number of refs. to Tibullan passages in Prop. II, III and IV that when he picked up ideas from T. he usually tried to improve or comment on them (see e.g. 1.10.61-4n.). These observations are applicable to the four parallel passages mentioned above.

At 1.1.61-8 T. gives a description of his own funeral, as he imagines it will be. This theme was as yet rare in early Latin elegy, appearing elsewhere only at Prop.1.17.21-4 (quoted in intro. essay to 1.1). In both passages the emphasis is on dutiful observance and mourning at the poet's funeral. T. underlines this idea by two details not found in Prop.'s version (the mourning of the youth of Rome at 65f. and the appeal to the mistress not to grieve excessively at 67f., where *parce . . . / crinibus* may be intended to outdo Prop.1.17.21). These two details look like an attempt to improve on Propertius.

Again, at 1.1.75 after excusing himself from a campaign on the grounds of his love for Delia T. contrasts his own type of (amatory) warfare with the real thing in the words *hic ego dux milesque bonus.* The excuse is similar to that found in Prop.1.6 (see intro. essay to 1.1), and Propertius makes a similar contrast at line 30 with the statement *hanc me militiam fata subire volunt.* Prop.'s use of the word *militia* is by no means new in *militia amoris* (cf. Plaut. *Pers.* 232, *Truc.* 230), but T.'s phrase is highly original (see 1.1.75-6n.). Again we seem to see in T. a progression from Prop., and it seems unlikely that Prop. would offer the tame old *militia* after T.'s innovation.

At 1.2.75-8 T. rejects wealth for happiness in love, pointing out that all the luxury of an expensive bedroom cannot bring sleep to a man who is unhappy in love. There is a similar treatment of the same theme at Prop.1.14.15ff. (quoted in 1.2.75-6n.). In both passages emphasis is placed on the extravagance of the bedroom and the unhappiness of its occupant, but these points are brought out particularly well by some details found only in T. (*Tyrio* 75, *fletu* 76, which may be improvements on Prop.'s *ostrino* (20) and *miserum* (21), *plumae* 77 and *sonitus . . . aquae* 78). The Propertian passage's relative simplicity seems best explained by taking it to be an earlier version of the theme.

Finally, at 1.8.3-6 T. contrasts his erotic knowledge with prophecy in lines reminiscent of Prop.1.9.5ff. (quoted in 1.8.5-6n.). The exx. of types of divination given by T. are wider than those in Prop., and he expresses the pain of love (which led to his erotic knowledge) by means of a picturesque image which has additional connotations. Again the comparative colourlessness of Prop. seems best explained as a first attempt at the idea, and, if Prop.'s lines were modelled on T., they would be a rather weak and insipid imitation.

I would add that if one accepts that Propertius I came first, the same process of adaptation and variation by T., although to a less marked degree, can be seen in most of the other parallel passages cited above (see the commentary ad loc.).

This discussion of datable refs., metre and parallel passages has shown that there is some indication that Propertius book I should be dated prior to T.'s first book. The decision cannot be made with absolute certainty, but the evidence is clearly in favour of this conclusion. Consequently, throughout the commentary below I have assumed that this is the correct relative dating of the two books.

7 Tibullus and the Analogistic Grammatical Theory.

Bürger (*Beiträge zur Elegantia Tibulls*, 'Χάριτες, *F. Leo, zum sechzigsten Geburtstag dargebracht*' (Berlin, 1911), 371ff.) first propounded the theory that T. was an analogist, claiming in support of his contention that where a word exists in two different forms and where two (or more) words are available to express one idea, T. shows a marked preference for one over the other(s). So, for instance, he points to T.'s preference for *seu* to *sive* (never occurs), *neu* to *neve, atque* to *ac, nec* to *neque,* his general use of *e* and *a* before consonants, but *ex* and *ab* before vowels, and the comparative frequency of *quod* as opposed to *quia.* Similarly he notes that T. always uses *nam(que)* (never *enim*), *sic* (not *ita*), *quamvis* (not *etsi, quamquam*), *cinis* (not *favilla*), *rogus* (not *bustum*), *aetas* (not *aevum*), *ventus* (not *aura*), *gaudium* (not *laetitia*), *ara* (not *altaria*), *fessus* (not *lassus*), *timere* (not *metuere*), *sinere* (not *pati*), *amare* (not *diligere*), *audere* (not *conari*), *temptare* (not *experiri*), *ire* (not *ambulare* or *vadere*), and so on.

Although initially rather attractive, Bürger's theory does not stand up well under scrutiny. Axelson (chap. 5 = p.114ff.) produces a number of cogent and convincing objections. He shows at length that to a great extent much of T.'s usage is merely in line with the practice of other poets (esp. the other elegists and Augustans) and that often metrical or linguistic considerations influence T.'s attitude to words (e.g. in the case of *atque* (p.82), *quamvis* (p.123f.), and see also p.127). He reasonably points out that a personal preference for particular words, as found in other authors, may well play a part. His censure of Bürger's somewhat cavalier attitude to textual criticism in his attempt to remove exceptional usages which contradict his theory and his often-voiced warning of the need to keep in mind the smallness of T.'s output are also pertinent. Finally, he does much to discredit the analogistic theory by citing exx. of alternative forms to be found in T. (p.130): so we find the perfect forms in *-erunt*, *-ere* and *-runt* (cf. 1.5.47-8n.), *caeruleus* and *caerulus, vinculum* and *vinclum, senecta* and *senectus, deorum* and *deum* and *quibus* and *quis.*

In support of the last observation of Axelson, it may be added that T. does actually use synonyms: e.g. he shows little or no marked preference in the cases of *anguis* and *serpens* (1.4.35-6n.), *umens* and *umidus* (1.9.37-8n.), *porto* and *veho* (1.3.93-4n.) or *coma, capillus* and *crinis* (1.4.3-4n.). In any case, there are yet more ways of explaining why T. repeats himself. Luck (*The Latin Love Elegy* (2nd. ed., 1969), p.72) points out that T. tends to ignore much of conventional erotic terminology. The fact that amatory expressions that occur with frequency in Plautus, Terence, Catullus, Virgil *Ecl.*, Horace *Epod.* and Prop. I are not found in T. suggests that a number of repetitions are due to an attempt to avoid more obvious and somewhat hackneyed phraseology rather than to the implementation of analogist principles. So, for instance, T.'s avoidance of *ardeo, ardor, ignis, depereo* and *pereo* used in an amatory context must inevitably bring about a restriction in erotic vocabulary, and the absence of *lux, vita, deliciae* and *amica* applied to the mistress means that the proper name, *domina* and *puella* occur with greater frequency. Often the repetition of a word seems to be deliberate (see the lists of verbal echoes in the intro. essays, and N.B. esp. *revocare*, which occurs only at 1.8.41 and 78; see 1.8.77-8n.). Sometimes such repetition is due simply to coincidence or carelessness (cf. Postgate *Selections* xxviii f.: the most striking exx. are *despuo* at 1.2.54 and 96 only and *odi* at 1.8.69 and 75 only).

While T. does from time to time repeat himself, there are other ways of accounting for this than that of assuming the application of analogist theory, and the fact that he is not averse to employing alternative forms and synonyms is hardly compatible with strict adherence to the principles of analogism.

8 Abbreviations etc.

Periodicals are abbreviated as in *L'Année philologique*. The following abbreviations are also used:

André	J. André *Tibulle Élégies Livre Premier* (Paris, 1965).
Axelson	B. Axelson *Unpoetische Wörter, ein Beitrag zur Kenntnis der lateinischen Dichtersprache* (Lund, 1945).
Cartault	A. Cartault *Tibulle et les auteurs du Corpus Tibullianum* (Paris, 1909).
Dissen	L. Dissen *Albii Tibulli Carmina* (Gottingae, 1835).
Gild.-Lodge	B. L. Gildersleeve and G. Lodge *Latin Grammar* (London, 1895).

Kühner-Stegmann	R. Kühner and C. Stegmann *Ausführliche Grammatik der lateinischen Sprache* (Darmstadt, 1955, rev.).
Lee	A. G. Lee *Tibullus: Elegies* (Cambridge, 1975).
Lenz & Gal.	F. W. Lenz and G. C. Galinsky *Albii Tibulli Aliorumque Carminum Libri Tres* (Leiden, 1971).
Leumann-Hofmann-Szantyr	Leumann-Hofmann-Szantyr *Lateinische Grammatik* (Munich, 1963).
Luck (Artemis ed.)	G. Luck *Properz. Tibull. Liebeselegien* (Zurich, 1964).
Müller	L. Müller *De Re Metrica* (Leipzig, 1861, repr. 1967).
Némethy	G. Némethy *Tibulli Carmina* (Budapest, 1905).
Neue	F. Neue and C. Wagener *Formenlehre der lateinischen Sprache* (Leipzig, 1902).
OLD	*Oxford Latin Dictionary* (1968–).
Otto *Sprichwörter*	A. Otto *Die Sprichwörter und sprichwörtlichen Redensarten der Römer* (Leipzig, 1890, repr. 1962).
Pauly	Pauly-Wissowa *Real-Encyclopädie der classischen Altertumswissenschaft* (Stuttgart, 1893–).
Pichon	R. Pichon *Index Verborum Amatoriorum* (Hildesheim, 1966, repr.).
Platnauer	M. Platnauer *Latin Elegiac Verse* (Cambridge, 1951).
Ponchont	M. Ponchont *Tibulle et les auteurs du Corpus Tibullianum* (Paris, 1955, 4th. ed.).
Postgate *Selections*	J. P. Postgate *Selections from Tibullus and Others* (London, 1903).
Postgate (OCT)	J. P. Postgate *Tibulli Aliorumque Carminum Libri Tres* (Oxford, 1915, second ed.).
Putnam	M. C. J. Putnam *Tibullus A Commentary* (Norman, 1973).
Ramsay	G. G. Ramsay *Selections from Tibullus and Propertius* (Oxford, 1900, third ed.).
Roby	H. J. Roby *A Grammar of the Latin Language* (London, 1871).
Smith	K. F. Smith *The Elegies of Albius Tibullus* (New York, 1913).

T.	Tibullus.
Thes. L. L.	*Thesaurus Linguae Latinae* (Leipzig, 1900–).
Woodcock	E. C. Woodcock *A New Latin Syntax* (London, 1959).

A full bibliography containing all the references (and more) that the student of Tibullus could wish for (up to 1970) is provided by H. Harrauer *A Bibliography to the Corpus Tibullianum* (Hildesheim, 1971). I list below only general works additional to those mentioned in the Abbreviations that I have found particularly helpful in the preparation of this commentary. Select bibliographies of articles and books dealing with a single poem or passage are included in the intro. essays to the individual elegies.

A. Della Casa	*Le Concordanze del Corpus Tibullianum* (Genova, 1964).
S. Govaerts	*Le Corpus Tibullianum. Index Verborum et relevés statistiques* (Univ. de Liège, 1966).
G. Luck	*The Latin Love Elegy* (London, 1969).
E. N. O'Neil	*A Critical Concordance of the Tibullan Corpus* (Ithaca, 1963).
M. Schuster	*Tibull-Studien* (Vienna, 1930).
J. P. Sullivan (ed.)	*Critical Essays on Roman Literature I: Elegy and Lyric* (London, 1962).

VARIANTS FROM THE OXFORD TEXT

1.25–32	follow line 6
1.25	*iam modo iam*
1.9	*spes*
1.15	*fit*
1.17	*donatur*
1.35	*hic*
1.38	no dash at end of line
1.40	no dash at end of line
1.48	*igne*
1.60	*te*
1.78	*despiciam dites*
2.7	comma after *domini*
2.40	*rabido*
3.12	*triviis omina*
3.64	*Amor*
4.9	*ne*
4.27	semi-colon after *errabis* and colon after *aetas*
4.28	no exclamation mark after *cito*
4.44	*admittat* and no obeli
4.46	comma at end of line
4.48	full stop at end of line
5.20	*sed*
5.42	*et pudet et . . .*
5.47	comma after *mihi* and colon at end of line
5.69	*fata*
5.76	*nat*
6.7	*tam multa*
6.42	† *stet procul aut alia stet procul ante via* †.
6.76	no lacuna after this line
7.4	*Atur*
7.49	*centum ludis Geniumque*
7.53	comma after *venias*

8.35	*invenit*
9.25	*lene*
9.36	*puras fulminis*
9.69	*ista haec*
10.37	*pertusisque*
10.45 and 47	*Pax*
10.49	dash after *nitent*
10.50	no full stop after *situs*
10.52	no dash at end of line
10.68	*perfluat*

TEXT

1

DIVITIAS alius fulvo sibi congerat auro
   et teneat culti iugera multa soli,
quem labor adsiduus vicino terreat hoste,
   Martia cui somnos classica pulsa fugent:
me mea paupertas vita traducat inerti,
   dum meus adsiduo luceat igne focus. 6
iam modo iam possim contentus vivere parvo 25
   nec semper longae deditus esse viae,
sed Canis aestivos ortus vitare sub umbra
   arboris ad rivos praetereuntis aquae.
nec tamen interdum pudeat tenuisse bidentem
   aut stimulo tardos increpuisse boves; 30
non agnamve sinu pigeat fetumve capellae
   desertum oblita matre referre domum. 32
ipse seram teneras maturo tempore vites 7
   rusticus et facili grandia poma manu:
nec spes destituat sed frugum semper acervos
   praebeat et pleno pinguia musta lacu. 10
nam veneror, seu stipes habet desertus in agris
   seu vetus in trivio florida serta lapis:
et quodcumque mihi pomum novus educat annus,
   libatum agricolae ponitur ante deo.
flava Ceres, tibi fit nostro de rure corona 15
   spicea, quae templi pendeat ante fores;

pomosisque ruber custos donatur in hortis
terreat ut saeva falce Priapus aves.
vos quoque, felicis quondam, nunc pauperis agri
custodes, fertis munera vestra, Lares.
tunc vitula innumeros lustrabat caesa iuvencos:
nunc agna exigui est hostia parva soli.
agna cadet vobis, quam circum rustica pubes
clamet 'io messes et bona vina date.'
at vos exiguo pecori, furesque lupique,
parcite: de magno praeda petenda grege.
hic ego pastoremque meum lustrare quot annis
et placidam soleo spargere lacte Palem.
adsitis, divi, neu vos e paupere mensa
dona nec e puris spernite fictilibus.
fictilia antiquus primum sibi fecit agrestis
pocula, de facili composuitque luto.
non ego divitias patrum fructusque requiro,
quos tulit antiquo condita messis avo:
parva seges satis est; satis est, requiescere lecto
si licet et solito membra levare toro.
quam iuvat immites ventos audire cubantem
et dominam tenero continuisse sinu
aut, gelidas hibernus aquas cum fuderit Auster,
securum somnos igne iuvante sequi!
hoc mihi contingat: sit dives iure, furorem
qui maris et tristes ferre potest pluvias.
o quantum est auri pereat potiusque smaragdi,
quam fleat ob nostras ulla puella vias.
te bellare decet terra, Messalla, marique,
ut domus hostiles praeferat exuvias:
me retinent vinctum formosae vincla puellae,
et sedeo duras ianitor ante fores.
non ego laudari curo, mea Delia: tecum
dum modo sim, quaeso segnis inersque vocer.

te spectem, suprema mihi cum venerit hora,
te teneam moriens deficiente manu.
flebis et arsuro positum me, Delia, lecto,
tristibus et lacrimis oscula mixta dabis.
flebis: non tua sunt duro praecordia ferro
vincta, nec in tenero stat tibi corde silex.
illo non iuvenis poterit de funere quisquam
lumina, non virgo sicca referre domum.
tu manes ne laede meos, sed parce solutis
crinibus et teneris, Delia, parce genis.
interea, dum fata sinunt, iungamus amores:
iam veniet tenebris Mors adoperta caput;
iam subrepet iners aetas, nec amare decebit,
dicere nec cano blanditias capite.
nunc levis est tractanda venus, dum frangere postes
non pudet et rixas inseruisse iuvat.
hic ego dux milesque bonus: vos, signa tubaeque,
ite procul, cupidis vulnera ferte viris,
ferte et opes: ego composito securus acervo
despiciam dites despiciamque famem.

2

ADDE merum vinoque novos compesce dolores,
occupet ut fessi lumina victa sopor:
neu quisquam multo percussum tempora baccho
excitet, infelix dum requiescit amor.
nam posita est nostrae custodia saeva puellae,
clauditur et dura ianua firma sera.
ianua difficilis domini, te verberet imber,
te Iovis imperio fulmina missa petant.
ianua, iam pateas uni mihi victa querellis,
neu furtim verso cardine aperta sones.

et mala si qua tibi dixit dementia nostra,
ignoscas: capiti sint precor illa meo.
te meminisse decet quae plurima voce peregi
supplice cum posti florida serta darem.
tu quoque ne timide custodes, Delia, falle.
audendum est: fortes adiuvat ipsa Venus.
illa favet seu quis iuvenis nova limina temptat
seu reserat fixo dente puella fores:
illa docet molli furtim derepere lecto,
illa pedem nullo ponere posse sono,
illa viro coram nutus conferre loquaces
blandaque compositis abdere verba notis.
nec docet hoc omnes, sed quos nec inertia tardat
nec vetat obscura surgere nocte timor.
en ego cum tenebris tota vagor anxius urbe,
. . . .
nec sinit occurrat quisquam qui corpora ferro
vulneret aut rapta praemia veste petat.
quisquis amore tenetur, eat tutusque sacerque
qualibet; insidias non timuisse decet.
non mihi pigra nocent hibernae frigora noctis,
non mihi cum multa decidit imber aqua.
non labor hic laedit, reseret modo Delia postes
et vocet ad digiti me taciturna sonum.
parcite luminibus, seu vir seu femina fiat
obvia: celari vult sua furta Venus.
neu strepitu terrete pedum neu quaerite nomen
neu prope fulgenti lumina ferte face.
si quis et imprudens aspexerit, occulat ille
perque deos omnes se meminisse neget:
nam fuerit quicumque loquax, is sanguine natam,
is Venerem e rabido sentiet esse mari.
nec tamen huic credet coniunx tuus, ut mihi verax
pollicita est magico saga ministerio.

hanc ego de caelo ducentem sidera vidi,
fluminis haec rapidi carmine vertit iter,
haec cantu finditque solum manesque sepulcris
elicit et tepido devocat ossa rogo:
iam tenet infernas magico stridore catervas,
iam iubet aspersas lacte referre pedem.
cum libet, haec tristi depellit nubila caelo:
cum libet, aestivo convocat orbe nives.
sola tenere malas Medeae dicitur herbas,
sola feros Hecatae perdomuisse canes.
haec mihi composuit cantus, quis fallere posses:
ter cane, ter dictis despue carminibus.
ille nihil poterit de nobis credere cuiquam,
non sibi, si in molli viderit ipse toro.
tu tamen abstineas aliis: nam cetera cernet
omnia: de me uno sentiet ille nihil.
quid credam? nempe haec eadem se dixit amores
cantibus aut herbis solvere posse meos,
et me lustravit taedis, et nocte serena
concidit ad magicos hostia pulla deos.
non ego totus abesset amor, sed mutuus esset,
orabam, nec te posse carere velim.
ferreus ille fuit qui, te cum posset habere,
maluerit praedas stultus et arma sequi.
ille licet Cilicum victas agat ante catervas,
ponat et in capto Martia castra solo,
totus et argento contextus, totus et auro,
insideat celeri conspiciendus equo;
ipse boves mea si tecum modo Delia possim
iungere et in solito pascere monte pecus,
et te dum liceat teneris retinere lacertis,
mollis et inculta sit mihi somnus humo.
quid Tyrio recubare toro sine amore secundo
prodest cum fletu nox vigilanda venit?

nam neque tunc plumae nec stragula picta soporem
nec sonitus placidae ducere posset aquae.
num Veneris magnae violavi numina verbo,
et mea nunc poenas impia lingua luit?
num feror incestus sedes adiise deorum
sertaque de sanctis deripuisse focis?
non ego, si merui, dubitem procumbere templis
et dare sacratis oscula liminibus,
non ego tellurem genibus perrepere supplex
et miserum sancto tundere poste caput.
at tu, qui laetus rides mala nostra, caveto
mox tibi: non uni saeviet usque deus.
vidi ego qui iuvenum miseros lusisset amores
post Veneris vinclis subdere colla senem
et sibi blanditias tremula componere voce
et manibus canas fingere velle comas:
stare nec ante fores puduit caraeve puellae
ancillam medio detinuisse foro.
hunc puer, hunc iuvenis turba circumterit arta,
despuit in molles et sibi quisque sinus.
at mihi parce, Venus: semper tibi dedita servit
mens mea: quid messes uris acerba tuas?

3

IBITIS Aegaeas sine me, Messalla, per undas,
o utinam memores ipse cohorsque mei!
me tenet ignotis aegrum Phaeacia terris:
abstineas avidas Mors modo nigra manus.
abstineas, Mors atra, precor: non hic mihi mater
quae legat in maestos ossa perusta sinus,
non soror, Assyrios cineri quae dedat odores
et fleat effusis ante sepulcra comis,

Delia non usquam quae, me cum mitteret urbe,
dicitur ante omnes consuluisse deos.
illa sacras pueri sortes ter sustulit: illi
rettulit e triviis omina certa puer.
cuncta dabant reditus: tamen est deterrita numquam
quin fleret nostras respiceretque vias.
ipse ego solator, cum iam mandata dedissem,
quaerebam tardas anxius usque moras.
aut ego sum causatus aves aut omina dira
Saturnive sacram me tenuisse diem.
o quotiens ingressus iter mihi tristia dixi
offensum in porta signa dedisse pedem!
audeat invito ne quis discedere Amore,
aut sciat egressum se prohibente deo.
quid tua nunc Isis mihi, Delia, quid mihi prosunt
illa tua totiens aera repulsa manu,
quidve, pie dum sacra colis, pureque lavari
te, memini, et puro secubuisse toro?
nunc, dea, nunc succurre mihi (nam posse mederi
picta docet templis multa tabella tuis)
ut mea votivas persolvens Delia voces
ante sacras lino tecta fores sedeat
bisque die resoluta comas tibi dicere laudes
insignis turba debeat in Pharia.
at mihi contingat patrios celebrare Penates
reddereque antiquo menstrua tura Lari.
quam bene Saturno vivebant rege, priusquam
tellus in longas est patefacta vias!
nondum caeruleas pinus contempserat undas,
effusum ventis praebueratque sinum,
nec vagus ignotis repetens compendia terris
presserat externa navita merce ratem.
illo non validus subiit iuga tempore taurus,
non domito frenos ore momordit equus,

non domus ulla fores habuit, non fixus in agris
qui regeret certis finibus arva, lapis.
ipsae mella dabant quercus, ultroque ferebant
obvia securis ubera lactis oves.
non acies, non ira fuit, non bella, nec ensem
immiti saevus duxerat arte faber.
nunc Iove sub domino caedes et vulnera semper,
nunc mare, nunc leti mille repente viae.
parce, pater. timidum non me periuria terrent,
non dicta in sanctos impia verba deos.
quod si fatales iam nunc explevimus annos,
fac lapis inscriptis stet super ossa notis:
HIC IACET IMMITI CONSUMPTUS MORTE TIBULLUS,
MESSALLAM TERRA DUM SEQUITURQUE MARI.
sed me, quod facilis tenero sum semper Amori,
ipsa Venus campos ducet in Elysios.
hic choreae cantusque vigent, passimque vagantes
dulce sonant tenui gutture carmen aves;
fert casiam non culta seges, totosque per agros
floret odoratis terra benigna rosis;
ac iuvenum series teneris immixta puellis
ludit, et adsidue proelia miscet Amor.
illic est, cuicumque rapax Mors venit amanti,
et gerit insigni myrtea serta coma.
at scelerata iacet sedes in nocte profunda
abdita, quam circum flumina nigra sonant:
Tisiphoneque impexa feros pro crinibus angues
saevit et huc illuc impia turba fugit;
tum niger in porta serpentum Cerberus ore
stridet et aeratas excubat ante fores.
illic Iunonem temptare Ixionis ausi
versantur celeri noxia membra rota;
porrectusque novem Tityos per iugera terrae
adsiduas atro viscere pascit aves.

Tantalus est illic, et circum stagna: sed acrem
iam iam poturi deserit unda sitim;
et Danai proles, Veneris quod numina laesit,
in cava Lethaeas dolia portat aquas.
illic sit quicumque meos violavit amores,
optavit lentas et mihi militias.
at tu casta precor maneas, sanctique pudoris
adsideat custos sedula semper anus.
haec tibi fabellas referat positaque lucerna
deducat plena stamina longa colu;
at circa gravibus pensis adfixa puella
paulatim somno fessa remittat opus.
tunc veniam subito, nec quisquam nuntiet ante,
sed videar caelo missus adesse tibi.
tunc mihi, qualis eris longos turbata capillos,
obvia nudato, Delia, curre pede.
hoc precor, hunc illum nobis Aurora nitentem
Luciferum roseis candida portet equis.

4

'SIC umbrosa tibi contingant tecta, Priape,
ne capiti soles, ne noceantque nives:
quae tua formosos cepit sollertia? certe
non tibi barba nitet, non tibi culta coma est;
nudus et hibernae producis frigora brumae,
nudus et aestivi tempora sicca Canis.'
sic ego: tum Bacchi respondit rustica proles
armatus curva sic mihi falce deus.
'ne fuge te tenerae puerorum credere turbae:
nam causam iusti semper amoris habent.
hic placet, angustis quod equum compescit habenis;
hic placidam niveo pectore pellit aquam;

hic, quia fortis adest audacia, cepit: at illi
virgineus teneras stat pudor ante genas.
sed ne te capiant, primo si forte negabit,
taedia; paulatim sub iuga colla dabit.
longa dies homini docuit parere leones,
longa dies molli saxa peredit aqua;
annus in apricis maturat collibus uvas,
annus agit certa lucida signa vice.
nec iurare time: veneris periuria venti
inrita per terras et freta summa ferunt.
gratia magna Iovi: vetuit Pater ipse valere,
iurasset cupide quidquid ineptus amor:
perque suas impune sinit Dictynna sagittas
adfirmes, crines perque Minerva suos.
at si tardus eris errabis; transiet aetas:
quam cito non segnis stat remeatque dies.
quam cito purpureos deperdit terra colores,
quam cito formosas populus alta comas.
quam iacet, infirmae venere ubi fata senectae,
qui prior Eleo est carcere missus equus.
vidi iam iuvenem, premeret cum serior aetas,
maerentem stultos praeteriisse dies.
crudeles divi! serpens novus exuit annos:
formae non ullam fata dedere moram.
solis aeterna est Baccho Phoeboque iuventas:
nam decet intonsus crinis utrumque deum.
tu, puero quodcumque tuo temptare libebit,
cedas: obsequio plurima vincet amor.
neu comes ire neges, quamvis via longa paretur
et Canis arenti torreat arva siti,
quamvis praetexens picta ferrugine caelum
venturam admittat imbrifer arcus aquam.
vel si caeruleas puppi volet ire per undas,
ipse levem remo per freta pelle ratem,

nec te paeniteat duros subiisse labores
   aut opera insuetas atteruisse manus.
nec, velit insidiis altas si claudere valles,
   dum placeas, umeri retia ferre negent.
si volet arma, levi temptabis ludere dextra;
   saepe dabis nudum, vincat ut ille, latus.
tunc tibi mitis erit, rapias tum cara licebit
   oscula: pugnabit, sed tibi rapta dabit.
rapta dabit primo, post adferet ipse roganti,
   post etiam collo se implicuisse velit.
heu male nunc artes miseras haec saecula tractant:
   iam tener adsuevit munera velle puer.
at tua, qui venerem docuisti vendere primus,
   quisquis es, infelix urgeat ossa lapis.
Pieridas, pueri, doctos et amate poetas,
   aurea nec superent munera Pieridas.
carmine purpurea est Nisi coma: carmina ni sint,
   ex umero Pelopis non nituisset ebur.
quem referent Musae, vivet, dum robora tellus,
   dum caelum stellas, dum vehet amnis aquas.
at qui non audit Musas, qui vendit amorem,
   Idaeae currus ille sequatur Opis,
et tercentenas erroribus expleat urbes
   et secet ad Phrygios vilia membra modos.
blanditiis vult esse locum Venus ipsa: querellis
   supplicibus, miseris fletibus illa favet.'
haec mihi, quae canerem Titio, deus edidit ore:
   sed Titium coniunx haec meminisse vetat.
pareat ille suae: vos me celebrate magistrum,
   quos male habet multa callidus arte puer.
gloria cuique sua est: me, qui spernentur, amantes
   consultent: cunctis ianua nostra patet.
tempus erit, cum me Veneris praecepta ferentem
   deducat iuvenum sedula turba senem.

eheu quam Marathus lento me torquet amore!
deficiunt artes, deficiuntque doli.
parce, puer, quaeso, ne turpis fabula fiam,
cum mea ridebunt vana magisteria.

5

ASPER eram et bene discidium me ferre loquebar:
at mihi nunc longe gloria fortis abest.
namque agor ut per plana citus sola verbere turben
quem celer adsueta versat ab arte puer.
ure ferum et torque, libeat ne dicere quicquam
magnificum post haec: horrida verba doma.
parce tamen, per te furtivi foedera lecti,
per venerem quaeso compositumque caput.
ille ego cum tristi morbo defessa iaceres
te dicor votis eripuisse meis:
ipseque te circum lustravi sulpure puro,
carmine cum magico praecinuisset anus;
ipse procuravi ne possent saeva nocere
somnia, ter sancta deveneranda mola;
ipse ego velatus filo tunicisque solutis
vota novem Triviae nocte silente dedi.
omnia persolvi: fruitur nunc alter amore,
et precibus felix utitur ille meis.
at mihi felicem vitam, si salva fuisses,
fingebam demens, sed renuente deo.
rura colam, frugumque aderit mea Delia custos,
area dum messes sole calente teret,
aut mihi servabit plenis in lintribus uvas
pressaque veloci candida musta pede.
consuescet numerare pecus; consuescet amantis
garrulus in dominae ludere verna sinu.

illa deo sciet agricolae pro vitibus uvam,
pro segete spicas, pro grege ferre dapem.
illa regat cunctos, illi sint omnia curae:
at iuvet in tota me nihil esse domo.
huc veniet Messalla meus, cui dulcia poma
Delia selectis detrahat arboribus:
et, tantum venerata virum, hunc sedula curet,
huic paret atque epulas ipsa ministra gerat.
haec mihi fingebam, quae nunc Eurusque Notusque
iactat odoratos vota per Armenios.
saepe ego temptavi curas depellere vino:
at dolor in lacrimas verterat omne merum.
saepe aliam tenui: sed iam cum gaudia adirem,
admonuit dominae deseruitque Venus.
tunc me discedens devotum femina dixit,
et pudet et narrat scire nefanda meam.
non facit hoc verbis, facie tenerisque lacertis
devovet et flavis nostra puella comis.
talis ad Haemonium Nereis Pelea quondam
vecta est frenato caerula pisce Thetis.
haec nocuere mihi, quod adest huic dives amator:
venit in exitium callida lena meum.
sanguineas edat illa dapes atque ore cruento
tristia cum multo pocula felle bibat:
hanc volitent animae circum sua fata querentes
semper, et e tectis strix violenta canat:
ipsa fame stimulante furens herbasque sepulcris
quaerat et a saevis ossa relicta lupis;
currat et inguinibus nudis ululetque per urbes,
post agat e triviis aspera turba canum.
eveniet; dat signa deus: sunt numina amanti,
saevit et iniusta lege relicta Venus.
at tu quam primum sagae praecepta rapacis
desere: nam donis vincitur omnis amor.

pauper erit praesto tibi semper: pauper adibit
primus et in tenero fixus erit latere:
pauper in angusto fidus comes agmine turbae
subicietque manus efficietque viam:
pauper ad occultos furtim deducet amicos
vinclaque de niveo detrahet ipse pede.
heu canimus frustra nec verbis victa patescit
ianua sed plena est percutienda manu.
at tu, qui potior nunc es, mea fata timeto:
versatur celeri Fors levis orbe rotae.
non frustra quidam iam nunc in limine perstat
sedulus ac crebro prospicit ac refugit
et simulat transire domum, mox deinde recurrit
solus et ante ipsas exscreat usque fores.
nescio quid furtivus amor parat. utere quaeso,
dum licet: in liquida nat tibi linter aqua.

6

SEMPER ut inducar blandos offers mihi vultus,
post tamen es misero tristis et asper, Amor.
quid tibi, saeve, rei mecum est? an gloria magna est
insidias homini composuisse deum?
nam mihi tenduntur casses: iam Delia furtim
nescio quem tacita callida nocte fovet.
illa quidem tam multa negat, sed credere durum est:
sic etiam de me pernegat usque viro.
ipse miser docui, quo posset ludere pacto
custodes: heu heu nunc premor arte mea.
fingere tunc didicit causas ut sola cubaret,
cardine tunc tacito vertere posse fores:
tunc sucos herbasque dedi quis livor abiret
quem facit impresso mutua dente venus.

at tu, fallacis coniunx incaute puellae,
me quoque servato, peccet ut illa nihil,
neu iuvenes celebret multo sermone caveto
neve cubet laxo pectus aperta sinu,
neu te decipiat nutu, digitoque liquorem
ne trahat et mensae ducat in orbe notas.
exibit quam saepe, time, seu visere dicet
sacra Bonae maribus non adeunda Deae.
at mihi si credas, illam sequar unus ad aras:
tunc mihi non oculis sit timuisse meis.
saepe, velut gemmas eius signumque probarem,
per causam memini me tetigisse manum:
saepe mero somnum peperi tibi, at ipse bibebam
sobria supposita pocula victor aqua.
non ego te laesi prudens: ignosce fatenti.
iussit Amor: contra quis ferat arma deos?
ille ego sum, nec me iam dicere vera pudebit,
instabat tota cui tua nocte canis.
quid tenera tibi coniuge opus? tua si bona nescis
servare, frustra clavis inest foribus.
te tenet, absentes alios suspirat amores
et simulat subito condoluisse caput.
at mihi servandam credas: non saeva recuso
verbera, detrecto non ego vincla pedum.
tum procul absitis, quisquis colit arte capillos,
et fluit effuso cui toga laxa sinu:
quisquis et occurret, ne possit crimen habere,
†stet procul aut alia stet procul ante via†.
sic fieri iubet ipse deus, sic magna sacerdos
est mihi divino vaticinata sono.
haec, ubi Bellonae motu est agitata, nec acrem
flammam, non amens verbera torta timet:
ipsa bipenne suos caedit violenta lacertos
sanguineque effuso spargit inulta deam,

statque latus praefixa veru, stat saucia pectus,
   et canit eventus quos dea magna monet.
'parcite quam custodit Amor violare puellam,
   ne pigeat magno post didicisse malo.
attigerit, labentur opes, ut vulnere nostro
   sanguis, ut hic ventis diripiturque cinis.'
et tibi nescio quas dixit, mea Delia, poenas:
   si tamen admittas, sit precor illa levis.
non ego te propter parco tibi, sed tua mater
   me movet atque iras aurea vincit anus.
haec mihi te adducit tenebris multoque timore
   coniungit nostras clam taciturna manus:
haec foribusque manet noctu me adfixa proculque
   cognoscit strepitus me veniente pedum.
vive diu mihi, dulcis anus: proprios ego tecum,
   sit modo fas, annos contribuisse velim.
te semper natamque tuam te propter amabo:
   quidquid agit, sanguis est tamen illa tuus.
sit modo casta, doce, quamvis non vitta ligatos
   impediat crines nec stola longa pedes.
et mihi sint durae leges, laudare nec ullam
   possim ego quin oculos appetat illa meos;
et si quid peccasse putet, ducarque capillis
   immerito pronas proripiarque vias.
non ego te pulsare velim, sed, venerit iste
   si furor, optarim non habuisse manus.
nec saevo sis casta metu, sed mente fideli:
   mutuus absenti te mihi servet amor.
at quae fida fuit nulli, post victa senecta
   ducit inops tremula stamina torta manu
firmaque conductis adnectit licia telis
   tractaque de niveo vellere ducta putat.
hanc animo gaudente vident iuvenumque catervae
   commemorant merito tot mala ferre senem:

hanc Venus ex alto flentem sublimis Olympo
spectat et infidis quam sit acerba monet.
haec aliis maledicta cadant: nos, Delia, amoris
exemplum cana simus uterque coma.

7

HUNC cecinere diem Parcae fatalia nentes
stamina, non ulli dissoluenda deo:
hunc fore, Aquitanas posset qui fundere gentes,
quem tremeret forti milite victus Atur.
evenere: novos pubes Romana triumphos
vidit et evinctos bracchia capta duces:
at te victrices lauros, Messalla, gerentem
portabat nitidis currus eburnus equis.
non sine me est tibi partus honos: Tarbella Pyrene
testis et Oceani litora Santonici,
testis Arar Rhodanusque celer magnusque Garunna,
Carnutis et flavi caerula lympha Liger.
an te, Cydne, canam, tacitis qui leniter undis
caeruleus placidis per vada serpis aquis,
quantus et aetherio contingens vertice nubes
frigidus intonsos Taurus alat Cilicas?
quid referam ut volitet crebras intacta per urbes
alba Palaestino sancta columba Syro,
utque maris vastum prospectet turribus aequor
prima ratem ventis credere docta Tyros,
qualis et, arentes cum findit Sirius agros,
fertilis aestiva Nilus abundet aqua?
Nile pater, quanam possim te dicere causa
aut quibus in terris occuluisse caput?
te propter nullos tellus tua postulat imbres,
arida nec pluvio supplicat herba Iovi.

te canit atque suum pubes miratur Osirim
barbara, Memphiten plangere docta bovem.
primus aratra manu sollerti fecit Osiris
et teneram ferro sollicitavit humum,
primus inexpertae commisit semina terrae
pomaque non notis legit ab arboribus.
hic docuit teneram palis adiungere vitem,
hic viridem dura caedere falce comam:
illi iucundos primum matura sapores
expressa incultis uva dedit pedibus.
ille liquor docuit voces inflectere cantu,
movit et ad certos nescia membra modos:
Bacchus et agricolae magno confecta labore
pectora tristitiae dissoluenda dedit:
Bacchus et adflictis requiem mortalibus adfert,
crura licet dura compede pulsa sonent.
non tibi sunt tristes curae nec luctus, Osiri,
sed chorus et cantus et levis aptus amor,
sed varii flores et frons redimita corymbis,
fusa sed ad teneros lutea palla pedes
et Tyriae vestes et dulcis tibia cantu
et levis occultis conscia cista sacris.
huc ades et centum ludis Geniumque choreis
concelebra et multo tempora funde mero:
illius et nitido stillent unguenta capillo,
et capite et collo mollia serta gerat.
sic venias, hodierne: tibi dem turis honores,
liba et Mopsopio dulcia melle feram.
at tibi succrescat proles quae facta parentis
augeat et circa stet veneranda senem.
nec taceat monumenta viae, quem Tuscula tellus
candidaque antiquo detinet Alba Lare.
namque opibus congesta tuis hic glarea dura
sternitur, hic apta iungitur arte silex.

te canet agricola, a magna cum venerit urbe
serus, inoffensum rettuleritque pedem.
at tu, Natalis multos celebrande per annos,
candidior semper candidiorque veni.

8

NON ego celari possum, quid nutus amantis
quidve ferant miti lenia verba sono.
nec mihi sunt sortes nec conscia fibra deorum,
praecinit eventus nec mihi cantus avis:
ipsa Venus magico religatum bracchia nodo
perdocuit multis non sine verberibus.
desine dissimulare: deus crudelius urit,
quos videt invitos succubuisse sibi.
quid tibi nunc molles prodest coluisse capillos
saepeque mutatas disposuisse comas,
quid fuco splendente genas ornare, quid ungues
artificis docta subsecuisse manu?
frustra iam vestes, frustra mutantur amictus
ansaque compressos colligat arta pedes.
illa placet, quamvis inculto venerit ore
nec nitidum tarda compserit arte caput.
num te carminibus, num te pallentibus herbis
devovit tacito tempore noctis anus?
cantus vicinis fruges traducit ab agris,
cantus et iratae detinet anguis iter,
cantus et e curru Lunam deducere temptat,
et faceret, si non aera repulsa sonent.
quid queror heu misero carmen nocuisse, quid herbas?
forma nihil magicis utitur auxiliis:
sed corpus tetigisse nocet, sed longa dedisse
oscula, sed femori conseruisse femur.

nec tu difficilis puero tamen esse memento:
persequitur poenis tristia facta Venus.
munera ne poscas: det munera canus amator,
ut foveat molli frigida membra sinu.
carior est auro iuvenis, cui levia fulgent
ora nec amplexus aspera barba terit.
huic tu candentes umero suppone lacertos,
et regum magnae despiciantur opes.
at Venus invenit puero concumbere furtim,
dum timet et teneros conserit usque sinus,
et dare anhelanti pugnantibus umida linguis
oscula et in collo figere dente notas.
non lapis hanc gemmaeque iuvant, quae frigore sola
dormiat et nulli sit cupienda viro.
heu sero revocatur amor seroque iuventas
cum vetus infecit cana senecta caput.
tum studium formae est: coma tum mutatur, ut annos
dissimulet viridi cortice tincta nucis:
tollere tum cura est albos a stirpe capillos
et faciem dempta pelle referre novam.
at tu dum primi floret tibi temporis aetas
utere: non tardo labitur illa pede.
neu Marathum torque: puero quae gloria victo est?
in veteres esto dura, puella, senes.
parce precor tenero: non illi sontica causa est,
sed nimius luto corpora tingit amor.
vel miser absenti maestas quam saepe querellas
conicit et lacrimis omnia plena madent!
'quid me spernis? ait. 'poterat custodia vinci:
ipse dedit cupidis fallere posse deus.
nota venus furtiva mihi est, ut lenis agatur
spiritus, ut nec dent oscula rapta sonum;
et possum media quamvis obrepere nocte
et strepitu nullo clam reserare fores.

quid prosunt artes, miserum si spernit amantem
et fugit ex ipso saeva puella toro?
vel cum promittit, subito sed perfida fallit,
est mihi nox multis evigilanda malis.
dum mihi venturam fingo, quodcumque movetur,
illius credo tunc sonuisse pedes.'
desistas lacrimare, puer: non frangitur illa,
et tua iam fletu lumina fessa tument.
oderunt, Pholoe, moneo, fastidia divi,
nec prodest sanctis tura dedisse focis.
hic Marathus quondam miseros ludebat amantes,
nescius ultorem post caput esse deum;
saepe etiam lacrimas fertur risisse dolentis
et cupidum ficta detinuisse mora:
nunc omnes odit fastus, nunc displicet illi
quaecumque opposita est ianua dura sera.
at te poena manet, ni desinis esse superba.
quam cupies votis hunc revocare diem!

9

QUID mihi, si fueras miseros laesurus amores,
foedera per divos, clam violanda, dabas?
a miser, et si quis primo periuria celat,
sera tamen tacitis Poena venit pedibus.
parcite, caelestes: aequum est impune licere
numina formosis laedere vestra semel.
lucra petens habili tauros adiungit aratro
et durum terrae rusticus urget opus,
lucra petituras freta per parentia ventis
ducunt instabiles sidera certa rates:
muneribus meus est captus puer. at deus illa
in cinerem et liquidas munera vertat aquas.

iam mihi persolvet poenas, pulvisque decorem
   detrahet et ventis horrida facta coma;
uretur facies, urentur sole capilli,
   deteret invalidos et via longa pedes.
admonui quotiens 'auro ne pollue formam:
   saepe solent auro multa subesse mala.
divitiis captus si quis violavit amorem,
   asperaque est illi difficilisque Venus.
ure meum potius flamma caput et pete ferro
   corpus et intorto verbere terga seca.
nec tibi celandi spes sit peccare paranti:
   scit deus, occultos qui vetat esse dolos.
ipse deus tacito permisit lene ministro
   ederet ut multo libera verba mero:
ipse deus somno domitos emittere vocem
   iussit et invitos facta tegenda loqui.'
haec ego dicebam: nunc me flevisse loquentem,
   nunc pudet ad teneros procubuisse pedes.
tunc mihi iurabas nullo te divitis auri
   pondere, non gemmis, vendere velle fidem,
non tibi si pretium Campania terra daretur,
   non tibi si Bacchi cura Falernus ager.
illis eriperes verbis mihi sidera caeli
   lucere et puras fulminis esse vias.
quin etiam flebas: at non ego fallere doctus
   tergebam umentes credulus usque genas.
quid faciam, nisi et ipse fores in amore puellae?
   sit precor exemplo sit levis illa tuo.
o quotiens, verbis ne quisquam conscius esset,
   ipse comes multa lumina nocte tuli!
saepe insperanti venit tibi munere nostro
   et latuit clausas post adoperta fores.
tum miser interii, stulte confisus amari:
   nam poteram ad laqueos cautior esse tuos.

quin etiam attonita laudes tibi mente canebam,
  at me nunc nostri Pieridumque pudet.
illa velim rapida Vulcanus carmina flamma
  torreat et liquida deleat amnis aqua.
tu procul hinc absis, cui formam vendere cura est
  et pretium plena grande referre manu.
at te qui puerum donis corrumpere es ausus
  rideat adsiduis uxor inulta dolis,
et cum furtivo iuvenem lassaverit usu,
  tecum interposita languida veste cubet.
semper sint externa tuo vestigia lecto
  et pateat cupidis semper aperta domus:
nec lasciva soror dicatur plura bibisse
  pocula vel plures emeruisse viros.
illam saepe ferunt convivia ducere baccho,
  dum rota Luciferi provocet orta diem:
illa nulla queat melius consumere noctem
  aut operum varias disposuisse vices.
at tua perdidicit: nec tu, stultissime, sentis,
  cum tibi non solita corpus ab arte movet.
tune putas illam pro te disponere crines
  aut tenues denso pectere dente comas?
ista haec persuadet facies, auroque lacertos
  vinciat et Tyrio prodeat apta sinu?
non tibi sed iuveni cuidam vult bella videri,
  devoveat pro quo remque domumque tuam.
nec facit hoc vitio, sed corpora foeda podagra
  et senis amplexus culta puella fugit.
huic tamen accubuit noster puer: hunc ego credam
  cum trucibus venerem iungere posse feris.
blanditiasne meas aliis tu vendere es ausus,
  tune aliis demens oscula ferre mea?
tum flebis, cum me vinctum puer alter habebit
  et geret in regno regna superba tuo.

at tua tum me poena iuvet, Venerique merenti
fixa notet casus aurea palma meos:
HANC TIBI FALLACI RESOLUTUS AMORE TIBULLUS
DEDICAT ET GRATA SIS, DEA, MENTE ROGAT.

10

QUIS fuit, horrendos primus qui protulit enses?
quam ferus et vere ferreus ille fuit!
tum caedes hominum generi, tum proelia nata,
tum brevior dirae mortis aperta via est.
an nihil ille miser meruit, nos ad mala nostra
vertimus, in saevas quod dedit ille feras?
divitis hoc vitium est auri, nec bella fuerunt,
faginus astabat cum scyphus ante dapes.
non arces, non vallus erat, somnumque petebat
securus varias dux gregis inter oves.
tunc mihi vita foret vulgi nec tristia nossem
arma nec audissem corde micante tubam.
nunc ad bella trahor, et iam quis forsitan hostis
haesura in nostro tela gerit latere.
sed patrii servate Lares: aluistis et idem,
cursarem vestros cum tener ante pedes.
neu pudeat prisco vos esse e stipite factos:
sic veteris sedes incoluistis avi.
tunc melius tenuere fidem, cum paupere cultu
stabat in exigua ligneus aede deus.
hic placatus erat, seu quis libaverat uvam
seu dederat sanctae spicea serta comae:
atque aliquis voti compos liba ipse ferebat
postque comes purum filia parva favum.
at nobis aerata, Lares, depellite tela,
. . . .
hostiaque e plena rustica porcus hara.

hanc pura cum veste sequar myrtoque canistra
vincta geram, myrto vinctus et ipse caput.
sic placeam vobis: alius sit fortis in armis,
sternat et adversos Marte favente duces,
ut mihi potanti possit sua dicere facta
miles et in mensa pingere castra mero.
quis furor est atram bellis accersere Mortem?
imminet et tacito clam venit illa pede.
non seges est infra, non vinea culta, sed audax
Cerberus et Stygiae navita turpis aquae:
illic pertusisque genis ustoque capillo
errat ad obscuros pallida turba lacus.
quin potius laudandus hic est quem prole parata
occupat in parva pigra senecta casa!
ipse suas sectatur oves, at filius agnos,
et calidam fesso comparat uxor aquam.
sic ego sim, liceatque caput candescere canis
temporis et prisci facta referre senem.
interea Pax arva colat. Pax candida primum
duxit araturos sub iuga curva boves:
Pax aluit vites et sucos condidit uvae,
funderet ut nato testa paterna merum:
pace bidens vomerque nitent – at tristia duri
militis in tenebris occupat arma situs –
rusticus e lucoque vehit, male sobrius ipse,
uxorem plaustro progeniemque domum.
sed veneris tunc bella calent, scissosque capillos
femina, perfractas conqueriturque fores;
flet teneras subtusa genas: sed victor et ipse
flet sibi dementes tam valuisse manus.
at lascivus Amor rixae mala verba ministrat,
inter et iratum lentus utrumque sedet.
a lapis est ferrumque, suam quicumque puellam
verberat: e caelo deripit ille deos.

sit satis e membris tenuem rescindere vestem,
   sit satis ornatus dissoluisse comae,
sit lacrimas movisse satis: quater ille beatus
   quo tenera irato flere puella potest.
sed manibus qui saevus erit, scutumque sudemque
   is gerat et miti sit procul a Venere.
at nobis, Pax alma, veni spicamque teneto,
   perfluat et pomis candidus ante sinus.

COMMENTARY

1

Jacoby *RhM* LXIV (1909), 601ff., LXV (1910), 22ff.; Reitzenstein *Hermes* XLVII (1912), 60ff.; Martin *WJA* 2(1947), 361ff.; Hanslik *WS* LXIX (1956), 297ff.; Fisher *Latomus* XXIX (1970), 765ff.; Lee *Quality and Pleasure in Latin Poetry* (ed. Woodman and West, 1974), 94ff.

In 1.1 there seems to be some pressure on T., probably from Messalla, to go off on another campaign (25-6n., 53ff.), but he is unwilling to do so and describes the existence that he would rather lead, contrasting it with various aspects of the soldier's way of life (on these contrasts see the commentary: I acknowledge a partial debt to Fisher and Lee (*Quality and Pleasure in Latin Poetry*) here). T.'s ideal is a modification of his present situation: no longer absent on frequent campaigns (cf. 25f.), he would spend all his time on his small ancestral estate, relaxing, working and revering the country-gods (11-44n.), and, at last successful in his affair with Delia (cf. 55ff.), he would enjoy there a life of love with her until his final hour. *Pace* Lee (*Quality and Pleasure in Latin Poetry*) I believe that T. does envisage his ideal life with Delia in the country, not in the city. That love is to be part of his longed-for rustic existence is made clear at 45ff. (lines still set in the country), and it seems highly unlikely that his *domina* there would be anyone other than Delia. So at 1.2.71ff. and 1.5.21ff. he imagines a similar rural life with Delia, while in 2.3 Nemesis has actually gone off to the country with a lover. Nor are the details at 73f. inconsistent with such an interpretation: cf. the similar passage at 1.10.53ff. (see 1.10.45-68n.), the locked doors at 2.3.73ff. and the quarrels at Theoc. *Id.* 14.31ff., T.2.5.101ff. (so too Propertius at 2.5.21ff. (probably based in part on 1.1.73f.: see 1.10.61-4n.) describes such behaviour as that of a *rusticus*).

The whole poem is not an excuse to Messalla, as has been sometimes suggested: it is not addressed to him, he is not mentioned until the second half (and then only briefly), nor is he even the only person apostrophized in it (at 33f., 37ff., and 57ff. there are prayers and appeals to others on whom the fulfilment of T.'s ideal depends). It should also be pointed out that there is no strong evidence in the poem to support the various theories (see e.g. Dissen, Ramsay, Hanslik) about which particular campaign T. is refusing to go on here. Nor is the setting of the elegy entirely certain, although it seems to me that it is most probably T.'s estate (*hic* (*ego*), rather than *illic*, at 35; the claim that 55f. show that T. is at Rome seems based on a rather literal interpretation of imagery, while Hanslik's suggestion that T. is writing while on campaign (from 26 and 75f.) appears unlikely in view of 55f.).

Concerning the structure of 1.1 much of the groundwork has been done by Martin, Fisher and Lee (*Quality and Pleasure in Latin Poetry*). My own schema is as follows (for the transposition of 25-32 to follow line 6 see Critical Appendix on 25-32):

1-44	Farming side of T.'s ideal: preface (1-6): wealth, greed and hardships of soldier rejected; elaboration: (25-32, 7-10) rustic relaxation and occupations, (11-24, 33-44) piety and modest means.
45-52	Transition: love introduced into T.'s ideal.
53-74	Amatory side of T.'s ideal: preface (53-58): hardships and glory of soldier rejected; elaboration: (59-68) T.'s death and funeral, (69-74) T.'s life of love with Delia.
75-78	Conclusion.

It will be seen that the elegy falls into two main halves (farming and amatory), but overall unity is achieved. In fact, both halves present the same ideal rustic existence (see above), but with a different emphasis, and in both the hardships of the soldier are rejected for *inertia*. Throughout the poem there is contrast with the soldier, and the same general sentiment (condemnation of warfare) is present. Great care is taken over the passage that makes transition from the first to the second half (45-52n.) and over the conclusion, which draws together the main themes of the poem. In addition, verbal echoes bind the various sections together: see 45-52n., 75-6n., 77-8n. and N.B. also *paupertas/pauper* (5, 19, 37), *parvus* (25, 22, 43), *rusticus* (8, 23), *iners* (5, 58, 71), *terreo* (3, 18: see 17-18n.) and *decet* (53, 71: see 71-2n.).

The themes and models of 1.1 require detailed discussion, since the poem has been accused of being merely derivative (see Jacoby and Reitzenstein loc. cit.). In fact, none of the main themes of 1.1 is original. For the overall theme of the elegy, condemnation of war, cf. e.g. Hes. *Opera* 13ff., 145f., 161, Theogn.885f., Eur. *Hel.* 1151ff., Aristoph. *Lys.*, *Acharn.*, *Pax*. So too in the first half of the poem we find the old themes of the rejection of wealth (Archil.22D, Theogn. 83ff., 227ff., 523f., Anac.8D, Aristoph. *Plut.* 559ff., Menand.1099K, Hor. *S.* 1.1.38ff., *Epod.* 1.23ff.) and the praise of *paupertas* (Hes. *Opera* 694, Solon 4D, Pind. *Pyth.* 11.50ff., *Nem.* 11.47f., Aristoph. *Plut.* 551ff., Menand.6, 588, 666K, Lucr.5.1118f., Virg. *G.* 4.125ff., Hor. *S.* 1.1.92f., 106f., 2.2.1ff., 2.6.1ff.). The obvious contrast between wealth and *paupertas* had already been made (Theogn.145f., 1155f., Aesch. *Ag.* 378ff., Eur. *Io.* 485ff., Lucr.2.20ff., Cic. *De Off.* 1.69ff., Hor. *S.* 1.1.73ff.), and had more recently been developed into the rejection of the wealth won by warfare in favour of a life of rustic *paupertas* similar to that led by the early Romans (Virg. *G.* 2.458ff., esp. 532ff., Hor. *Epod.* 2).

In the first half of the elegy T. seems to be particularly indebted to Hor. *Epod.* 2, and the number of similarities between the two poems is too large for coincidence. In Horace also we find an ideal life of rustic *paupertas* similar to that of former times (2), with the farmer performing the tasks (3, 9ff.) and offerings to the gods (21f.) himself. In addition, there are a number of minor details common to both (see esp. notes on interruption of sleep 4, hearth 6, taking shade 27f., Terminus 11f., offerings to Silvanus 13f. and Priapus 17f., Lares 19f.). However, T. nowhere reproduces the language of Horace, and omits many of his details of rustic life, while introducing new ones of his own. There is also a great difference in emphasis: Horace does make the contrast with the soldier (5), but this is only one among others, whereas in T. the contrast is with the soldier alone. This in turn explains his concentration to a far greater extent than Horace on the relaxation, inactivity and piety of his life as a farmer. Finally, the tone in T. is not at all the same as that in Horace: T. is talking about his own ideal existence with apparent sincerity, while *Epod.* 2 is not subjective and is highly ironical. In addition, the Horatian piece is comparatively short and contains little real profundity (basically it is merely in praise of country life), but in T. this passage is only part of a long poem and it makes some serious points by opposing the piety and *paupertas* of his ideal to the immorality and wealth of the soldier. T. has taken Horace merely as the basis of his more ambitious poem, and by his concentration on the inactivity and morality of his ideal life as a farmer he has made a significant variation on the whole theme of rustic *paupertas* preferable to the wealth won by warfare.

In this first half the influence of Virgil is also evident (on the language and expression): in 4 *Martia (classica)* may be a reminiscence of *G.* 4.71 *Martius ille aeris rauci canor*; in 15 *flava Ceres* comes from *G.* 1.96 (where this adjective is first applied to the goddess); in 16 *spicea* is taken from *G.* 1.314 *spicea . . . messis* (the adjective first appears there in Latin literature); 18 may be based on *G.* 1.156 *et sonitu terrebis aves*;

in 19f. *felicis quondam, nunc pauperis agri / custodes* is probably a combination of *Ecl.* 1.74 *ite meae, quondam felix pecus, ite capellae* and 7.34 *custos es pauperis horti.* In each case, however, there is a subtle alteration or new application (cf. Lee (*Quality and Pleasure in Latin Poetry*) 100f.).

In the second half of the elegy T.'s main theme, the rejection of war in favour of love, occurs perhaps as early as Catull.45.22 (see Quinn ad loc.). The combination of love with a rustic life is an old idea (e.g. Theoc. *Id.* 11.42ff., 65f., Virg. *Ecl.* 2.28ff., T.1.5.21ff.) and had been contrasted with the soldier's life at Virg. *Ecl.* 10.35ff. (cf. also T.1.2.71ff.). However, by the adaptation of Propertian passages on the lover's death and the lover opposed to the man of action T. makes a contrast between the inactive and inglorious lover and the hardships and glory of the soldier's life, which represents an original contribution to this theme also.

In this half T.'s indebtedness to Propertius is evident. Lines 53-8 and 75 are based on Prop.1.6.: *non ego nunc Hadriae vereor mare noscere tecum, / Tulle, neque Aegaeo ducere vela salo, / cum quo Rhipaeos possim conscendere montis / ulteriusque domos vadere Memnonias; / sed me complexae remorantur verba puellae, / mutatoque graves saepe colore preces.* (1-6) . . . *tu patrui meritas conare anteire securis, / et vetera oblitis iura refer sociis.* (19-20) . . . *me sine, quem semper voluit fortuna iacere, / hanc animam extremae reddere nequitiae.* (25-6) . . . *non ego sum laudi, non natus idoneus armis: / hanc me militiam fata subire volunt.* (29-30). Apart from the obvious verbal similarities, once again we find the lover unable to go on a journey with his friend because of love, and there is contrast between the lover and the man of action. However, T.'s passage is much more compressed, and there are obvious differences in the exact circumstances. T. also gives his lines originality by his use of *servitium amoris* in 55f. and by his variation on Propertius' *militia amoris* in 75. Prop.1.6 is basically a rejection of his friend's invitation. T.'s lines do make a similar rejection, but they also perform the important function of contrasting the lover with the soldier, a contrast which in the following lines is elaborated at much greater length than in Propertius, where there are merely hints of this idea.

Lines 61-8 were suggested by Propertius 1.17.21-4: *illa meo caros donasset funere crinis, / molliter et tenera poneret ossa rosa; / illa meum extremo clamasset pulvere nomen, / ut mihi non ullo pondere terra foret.* This is the first detailed description in love-poetry of the poet's own funeral, and, as in T., we find dutiful observance by the poet's mistress. However, there is no similarity in diction, and the actual details of the observance in T. are different (unless *parce . . . / crinibus* 67f. is an improvement on Prop.1.17.21), while the appeal to his mistress to avoid excessive mourning is a progression from

Propertius. In addition, T. uses his funeral for a special purpose, to contrast with the soldier's funeral, an idea which is wholly absent from Propertius. T. also adds to the picture the grief of the young men and women (65f.), which is itself probably an adaptation of Prop.1.7.23f. *nec poterunt iuvenes nostro reticere sepulcro / 'Ardoris nostri magne poeta, iaces'*, where the idea first appears, with some similarity in language.

Finally, lines 69-70 are based on Propertius 1.19.25-6: *quare, dum licet, inter nos laetemur amantes: / non satis est ullo tempore longus amor.* Here the same sentiment occurs after the mention of the poet's death, and the language is similar. However, again T. makes an advance upon Propertius by the striking picture of Death and the addition of old age at 71-2, and again the sentiment is used differently by him, not as the conclusion of his poem, but to form a transition to the activities of the lover.

Thus, although T. is extensively influenced by other poets here, his variations on and use of his models preclude charges of plagiarism, and, although none of the themes of 1.1 is new, his elaboration and extended treatment of these themes ensure that the poem has originality, while his combination of them is novel and makes his ideal an interesting mixture, consisting of the traditional life of the old Roman farmer and the unconventional (by contemporary standards: cf. e.g. Ov. *Am.* 1.15) choice of love in preference to military glory.

The elegy stands first in the book, and, as is often the case in Roman poetry with poems in such a position, it contains a deferential reference to an important friend (cf. Catull.1, Hor. *S.* 1.1, *Epod.* 1, *C.* 1.1, *Epist.* 1.1, Prop.2.1, T.2.1). T. also prefaces this collection with a lengthy allusion to his mistress, as Propertius does in 1.1, although, unlike Propertius, he does not mention her until late in the poem and she does not exclusively form the subject. T.'s first elegy is not strictly a programme-poem (for instance, it contains no ref. to homosexual love or the affair with Marathus, topics which occupy 1.4, 1.8 and 1.9), but it does contain many sentiments, characters and themes which later recur throughout this first book of his elegies. The poem exhibits many similarities in themes and details to 1.10 (see intro. essay to 1.10), and this correspondence gives the first book unity and balance.

1.1 is an attractive piece. The wistfulness, the gentleness and tenderness of sentiment have always appealed to readers. Similarly the sensitive rejection of the military way of life and the delightful picture of T.'s ideal of love and country-living have been rightly praised. But there is more to the poem than this, much of it underlying the surface simplicity. A large part of the elegy is subtly allusive and contains implicit contrasts to various aspects of soldiering. Throughout there is skilful and ingenious use of language, to underline the antithesis to the soldier or to produce pointed echoes and verbal play. So too the structure is ambitious, rather complex and ordered with great care. There is also significant thematic variation and a high degree of *doctrina* (esp. literary). This is an elegy whose charm, whose learning and whose subtle cleverness and elegance make it particularly worthy of a leading position in Tibullus' first book.

1–6 These lines form a preface to the first half of the elegy (1-44), rejecting certain aspects of soldiering and stating a preference for the farming side of T.'s ideal. The rejection operates on an intellectual and a practical level: to the wealth that the soldier may win and his avariciousness (1f.) T. opposes a more modest and moral existence (*paupertas, focus*: see 5-6n.), and to the (mental and physical) hardships of the soldier (3f.) he opposes a way of life that is not warlike, but inactive, relaxed and comfortable (*inerti, igne*: see 5-6n.). These features of T.'s ideal are elaborated in the following lines. For the influence of Hor. *Epod.* 2 and Virgil in this first half see intro. essay.

1–2 See Critical Appendix.

For the definition of wealth as land and gold cf. Pind. *Nem.* 8.37f. χρυσὸν εὔχονται, πεδίον δ'ἕτεροι / ἀπέραντον, Theogn.719f., Hor. *Epod.*4.13, 15.19f., *S.*1.1.41ff., 1.2.13, T.1.9.31-2n., 2.2.13f. From the various exx. of riches (e.g. 2.3.41ff.) T. has chosen these two because they are conventional and would represent the aim of the average soldier, and for contrast with his own situation: instead of a heap of gold T. wants a heap of produce (9, 77), and instead of many acres he possesses only a few (22).

Gold here obviously typifies military booty (51-2n.), and the many acres are probably an investment for the soldier's booty (cf. 2.3.41f.). The idea that there is a ref. here to land-confiscations seems unlikely, since in general these confiscations did not make veterans esp. rich (cf. e.g. Suet. *Aug.* 13).

fulvo . . . auro: *fulvus* is first here applied to gold (*aera fulva* occurs at Enn. *Ann.* 454V): cf. Virg. *Aen.* 7.279, 10.134, Ov. *Tr.* 1.5.25, 1.7.7.

The ablative may be one of material going with *divitias* or instrumental with *congerat.*

Fulvo and *congerat* are picturesque touches.

3–4 labor: signifies fighting (Caes. *B.G.* 7.41.2), marching (Livy 44.3.9), digging and similar tasks (Caes. *B.C.* 3.63.3, Livy 21.27.6).

adsiduus: this word and the plurals in 4 indicate that T. is thinking here of a continuous process, all the more unpleasant for the lack of respite (contrast 29).

vicino hoste: emphasizes the danger by describing the enemy as no distant threat but near at hand.

Martia cui somnos classica pulsa fugent: *somnos . . . fugare* is an original phrase (cf. Plin. *N.H.* 14.117, 32.116, Val.Max.1.7.7) and apt because of the military connotations of *fugo*, which also brings out the violence of the awakening. The interruption of sleep (cf. Bacchyl.fr. 4.75ff. Snell, Plut. *Nic.* 9, Hor. *Epod.* 2.5, Luc.4.394f., Sen. *Contr.* 1.8.2, Sen. *Epist.* 51.12, Sil.It.15.48) contrasts with the pictures of 27f. and 43ff. (esp. *somnos . . . sequi*: 47-8n.).

Martia is possibly a reminiscence of Virgil (see intro. essay). Here the epic tone of the word suggests epic dangers and hardships.

Classica pulsa is an unusual phrase: *classicum* denotes a trumpet-call in classical lit., and *pello* here means 'give forth, emit' (cf. Stat. *Theb.* 6.218f. *horrendum pepulere fragorem / arma,* Calpurn. *Ecl.* 6.24 *expellis male singultantia verba*). For the idea behind *pello* cf. also Luc.7.475f., Sen. *Oed.* 733f. The verb was probably chosen here to express the violence with which the call is emitted.

The subjunctives in this couplet are jussive, as in 1f.

The idea that the aim of warfare is the acquisition of wealth was common, esp. in T. (1.10.7-8n.). Ramsay (who was Professor of Humanity at Glasgow University) comments by way of illustration: 'The Celtic races have never known but two motives to war – plunder and revenge. The Scottish Celt was able to live up to his principles till put down by the strong arm of England in the middle of last century.'

5–6 me mea paupertas vita traducat inerti: *paupertas* means not 'want' or 'poverty', but 'modest means' and has moral overtones (cf. Livy *praef.* 11, Sen. *Epist.* 87.39ff., Mart.11.32.8, Varro ap. Non.43M (p.60 Müller), Porph. on Hor. *Epist.* 2.2.199 *nam paupertas etiam honestae parsimoniae nomen est et usurpatur in fortuna mediocri*). For T.'s concept of *paupertas* cf. 25, 9f., 77f.

Inerti (see 1-6n.) means both 'inactive' and 'unwarlike' (*Thes.L.L.* VII_1.1309.1ff.).

Vita traducat is an original variation on the more usual *traducere vitam.* For *traduco* 'lead' with an ablative of route cf. Livy 23.24.7 *silva . . . qua exercitum traducturus erat*, Tac. *Hist.* 4.68. Note the military connotations of the verb.

dum meus adsiduo luceat igne focus: see Critical Appendix.

This is a homely touch. The fire is a symbol of rustic *paupertas* (48, Virg. *Ecl.* 7.49f., Ov. *F.* 4.510, Pers.1.72, *Moret.* 37), and the hearth has religious overtones (e.g. Hor. *Epod.* 2.43). The mention of the fire here also suggests relaxation, and *adsiduo* contrasts the continuous comfort of the fire with the *labor adsiduus* of the soldier in 3.

The glow of the fire (*luceat*) is in opposition to the gleam of gold (*fulvo*, 1).

25–10 For the transposition here (and the transition) see Critical Appendix on 25-32.

A charming picture of the relaxation and occupations in T.'s rustic existence. The point of view is optimistic (cf. 1.5.21ff.), and the poet foresees no trouble or difficulties and ignores the toil involved (1.9.7-8n.). Since T. is to take part in the work himself (29-30n.), just as in the next section he performs the religious rites himself (35-6n.), the ideal life which he envisages is that of the Roman farmer of former days. For this desire for the old days at this time see intro. essay, 1.10.15-32n. and cf. also Hor. *S.* 2.2.89ff.

The section also elaborates the rejection of soldiering, esp. on practical grounds (1-6n.), and after 25f. contrast with the soldier is implicit (underlined by the use of words with military connotations: see 29-30n., 9-10n.). T.'s ideal existence as a farmer is the antithesis to the soldier's hardships both physically (he is to enjoy relaxation and comfort, his occupations are to be less frequent and less energetic) and mentally (he is to be free from fear and to have peace of mind).

25–26 This couplet virtually re-states 1-6 (in reverse order) and indicates that T. himself has experienced the hardships of 3f. *Longae . . . viae* is an example of *labor* (3-4n.), since the phrase refers to the long journeys which were necessary for soldiers securing and maintaining a large empire (cf. 52, 1.3.14, 56, 2.6.3, Tac. *Ann.* 2.14). It would appear that T. has served as a soldier himself but now wishes to retire from the army (see Introduction sect.4).

iam modo iam possim contentus vivere parvo: see Critical Appendix.

For the emotional repetition of *iam* Lee (*Quality and Pleasure in Latin Poetry*) cites Sen. *Dial.* 4.29.3, Val.Fl.8.108; cf. also Virg. *Aen.* 12. 178f. *tu Saturnia coniunx, / iam melior, iam, diva, precor.*

This may be an appeal to Messalla, but the whole poem is not an excuse to him (see intro. essay).

On *modo* used in a wish see *OLD* s.v. 1c, Roby 1594.

For the expression *contentus vivere parvo* cf. Cic. *Tusc.* 5.89, Hor. *S.* 2.2.1, 110, *C.* 2.16.13. For rustic peace of mind cf. 48, 77, Virg. *G.* 2. 467 *secura quies*, Hor. *Epod.* 2.1, *C.* 2.18.14.

deditus: 'fully occupied in, given over to', a strong word (cf. Lucr. 4.996 *fugae . . . dedita*, Cic. *Fin.* 1.61, Ov. *Met.* 13.920f. *ante tamen mortalis eram, sed, scilicet altis / deditus aequoribus, tantum exercebar in illis*). There may be a play here on the military sense of the word ('surrender'), as Putnam suggests.

27–28 Taking the shade, a conventional pastime of rustics (Virg. *Ecl.* 1.1 *Tityre, tu patulae recubans sub tegmine fagi*, 51f., *G.* 2.435, 470, Hor. *Epod.* 2.23, *C.* 3.29.21f., anon. *A.P.* 16.227), here is an example of rustic relaxation and comfort. T. can escape from the heat, which is a hardship of a journey (1.4.41f., 1.9.15f.) that the soldier must endure.

Canis aestivos ortus: the Dog-star (Sirius) occurs elsewhere in T. at 1.4.6, 42, 1.7.21. For its intense heat and destructive nature cf. Hom.

*Il.*22.26ff., Virg. *G.*4.425, *Aen.*10.273ff., Hor. *S.*1.7.25f., Prop.2.28. 3f. T. here refers to a specific period in the year (Plin. *N.H.*3.117, 31. 51), in July, when the weather was extremely hot (Ov. *F.*4.939f. *est Canis, Icarium dicunt, quo sidere moto / tosta sitit tellus*, Plin. *N.H.* 2.107, 123, 12.58), and so an even greater hardship for the soldier.

ad rivos praetereuntis aquae: the sound of running water was considered pleasant, and even soporific (1.2.77-8n., cf. esp. Hor. *Epod.*2. 27f.): as such it would add to T.'s peace of mind (contrast 4 and cf. 43ff.). The plural may be a genuine one, or it may stand for a single stream (cf. Hor. *C.*3.13.7).

29–30 pudeat: cf. *pigeat* (31): unlike many of his 'civilised' contemporaries, T. is to work on his own farm, like an old Roman farmer (cf. Hor. *Epod.*2.2, Col. *R.R.*12.*praef.*10).

tenuisse . . . / . . . increpuisse: the perfect infinitive was used in early Latin after verbs of wishing or prohibiting (Kühner-Stegmann 1.133f.). The Augustans extended this usage of the perfect infinitive for metrical convenience and because of its archaism and similarity to the Greek aorist (the perfect tense was already used in prose to express the Greek aorist: see Roby 1473). The perfect infinitive can, of course, express a past action, but often it is simply used as an alternative for the present infinitive. The mixture of perfect and present (*referre* in 32) is frequent (e.g. 45-6, 73-4).

Increpo is first used here of physical rather than verbal correction: cf. Ov. *Am.*3.15.17 *corniger increpuit thyrso graviore Lyaeus*, *Met.* 14.820f., Stat. *Theb.*3.431, 10.462. The verb is used elsewhere in a military context (e.g. Livy 3.63.3, 10.35.8).

31–32 A delightful detail. Carrying a lamb or kid is an undignified but necessary task (2.3.17f., Hor. *Epist.*1.13.13, Calpurn. *Ecl.*5.39ff., Stat. *Theb.*7.397), esp. in view of T.'s single shepherd (35).

non: for *nec* (29) followed by *non* see 1.6.45-6n.

desertum oblita matre: cf. Virg. *Ecl.*1.14f. *hic inter densas corylos modo namque gemellos / spem gregis, a! silice in nuda conixa reliquit.* The repeated *a* may be intended to suggest the sound of bleating.

7–8 Again T. is to take part in the work himself, a true countryman (*ipse . . . / rusticus*, both words in emphatic positions): cf. Virg. *G.* 4.112ff. *ipse thymum tinosque ferens de montibus altis / tecta serat late circum, cui talia curae: / ipse . . .*, Hor. *Epod.*2.3ff., Prop.3. 17.15ff., Ov. *ExP.*1.8.51ff., 1.2.71-4n.

Note the variation in the arrangement of accusatives and ablatives and the contrast between *teneras . . . vites* and *grandia poma* (as Postgate *Selections* points out, the fruit trees are larger and stronger than the vines: cf. Virg. *G.*2.362ff., 426ff.).

facili: 'expert, nimble': cf. Prop.2.1.9f. *sive lyrae carmen digitis percussit eburnis, / miramur, facilis ut premat arte manus*, Ov. *A.A.*

1.160, *F.* 3.536. Such changes in adjectives from passive to active and vice versa are common: for other exx. in T. see notes on *piger* 1.2.29, *tardus* 1.3.16, *angustus* 1.4.11, *sobrius* 1.6.28, *fertilis* 1.7.22, *inexpertus* 1.7.31, *tristis* 1.8.28, *gratus* 1.9.84.

poma: 'fruit trees' (cf. Cato *Ag. Cult.* 28.1, Virg. *G.* 2.426).

9–10 nec spes destituat: see Critical Appendix.

For the connection between hope and the farmer cf. 2.6.21f. *Spes destituat* (cf. Livy 1.41.1) is an original variation on the more usual phrases *destituere spem* and *destitui* (*a*) *spe.* The absolute use of *destituo* was not common (cf. Livy 1.41.1, 37.7.9, Luc.5.298, Sen. *Contr.* 2.1.1, Sen. *Ben.* 4.39.4, Sil.It.3.251, Val.Max.2.6.7, Cels.4. 31.4). As Putnam points out, the verb has military connotations (*Thes. L. L.* V_1.764.19ff.).

frugum . . . acervos: in view of the various types of work mentioned in the previous lines and the various kinds of food in the following lines *frugum* probably refers not to corn alone but to produce in general.

Acervos (like *musta* below) is probably distributive, referring to a process repeated year by year (cf. the singular *acervo* at 77).

pleno pinguia musta lacu: *pinguis* here means 'rich', and is also applied to *mustum* at Col. *R.R.* 10.432, Manil.3.153, 663.

Lacu refers to the vat in which the fresh wine (*mustum*) is stored (2.3.64, 2.5.86). On the vintage see 1.5.21-4n.

Note the optimism here (*semper, acervos, pleno*).

The alliteration of s and p is striking.

11–44 *Nam* (11) makes the transition: his habitual piety is the reason why his hopes for success should come true (9f.).

The emphasis now shifts onto piety and humble simplicity. Apparently what T. is wishing for here is the ability to give up campaigning (cf. 41-4n.) and to devote all his time to the way of life that he leads at present when not away on campaigns (cf. 25f.), revering the country-gods and enjoying modest circumstances in the future (23f., 33f., 41ff.), as now (11ff.).

This section elaborates the rejection of soldiering, esp. on intellectual grounds (1-6n.), and opposition to the soldier is implicit throughout (underlined by the military connotations of *custos* 17, *custodes* 20, *caesa* 21, *cadet* 23, *praeda* 34; N.B. also 18 recalls 4). Religion is an integral and enjoyable part of country-life for T., and on it depends his all-important *paupertas*, but T.'s emphasis on religion here and the close interweaving of it with *paupertas* indicates that religion forms a part of this intellectual rejection. There is an obvious contrast between the *divitiae* of the soldier and T.'s *paupertas*, but the concentration on religion suggests a further contrast, between the morality of T.'s existence and the immorality (greed) of the soldier's.

At 41ff. T. smoothly closes the first half of the poem: the repetition of *divitias* (41, cf. 1) and of the themes of *paupertas*, religion and relaxation recalls lines 1-6 and provides a neat ring-structure.

11–12 In general the worship of trees and stones was widespread (see Smith, Enk on Prop.1.4.24). If T. is thinking of any particular god here, the ref. is probably to Terminus (cf. Ov. *F.* 2.641f. *Termine, sive lapis, sive es defossus in agro / stipes, ab antiquis tu quoque numen habes*), the god who presided over boundaries, and whose function it was to keep property the same size. So Terminus would be instrumental in maintaining T.'s small farm: cf. Ov. *F.*2.659f. *tu populos urbesque et regna ingentia finis, / omnis erit sine te litigiosus ager.* The god's annual festival, the Terminalia, took place on the 23rd of February and consisted of a sacrifice and feast by neighbours (Hor. *Epod.* 2.59, Ovid loc.cit., Fowler *The Roman Festivals of the Period of the Republic* (London, 1899), 324ff.). For the offering of flowers to Terminus (*florida serta*) cf. Ov. *F.* 2.644.

This is a well-constructed couplet: anaphora of *seu*, parallelism of *desertus in agris* and *vetus in trivio* and contrast between lonely fields and more busy crossroads.

13–14 The practice of offering firstlings and firstfruits was ancient (Hom. *Il.* 9.533ff., Ov. *F.* 2.515ff., Plin. *N.H.* 18.8) and was widespread (Frazer *Golden Bough* (London, 1949), 2.373ff., Hastings *Encyclopaedia of Religion and Ethics* (New York, 1908), s.v. 'First-fruits').

educat: 'nurtures, matures' (Catull.62.41, 50, Ov. *ExP.* 1.3.51 *non ager hic pomum, non dulces educat uvas*).

annus: 'season' (cf. Virg. *G.* 2.516, Hor. *Epod.* 2.29 *tonantis annus hibernus Iovis*, *C.* 3.23.8).

libatum agricolae ponitur ante deo: *agricola* used as an adjective first appears here and is not common (*Thes. L. L.* I.1422.2ff.).

Agricolae . . . deo is a vague phrase (cf. 1.5.27, 2.1.36), perhaps deliberately so. If any particular god is meant, there are two possibilities. Postgate *Selections* suggests Vertumnus and for the offering compares Prop.4.2.11ff. Perhaps more likely is Silvanus, who is probably designated by this phrase at 1.5.27 (see notes ad loc.). He is described as one of the *deos . . . agrestis* at Virg. *G.* 2.493f. (cf. *Aen.* 8.600f.), and he (not Vertumnus) is offered firstfruits at Hor. *Epod.* 2.19ff. (quoted on 17-18).

Ponitur ante stands for *anteponitur* (cf. Cic. *Off.* 3.71, Hor. *S.* 1.3.92) and is the only ex. in elegy of such tmesis.

15–16 See Critical Appendix.

flava Ceres: Ceres was an old Italian corn-goddess, generally identified with Demeter (e.g. Cic. *N.D.* 2.67, Ov. *F.* 4.393ff.). Elsewhere she is mentioned by T. at 2.1.4, 2.5.58, 84.

The adjective is first applied to her at Virg. *G.* 1.96 (cf. ξανθὴ

Δημήτηρ at Hom *Il.* 5.500 etc.), later at Ov. *Am.* 3.10.3, *F.* 4.424 etc. On the attribution to deities and heroes of blond hair see Pease on *Aen.* 4.590.

nostro de rure: for *rus* meaning 'farm, estate' cf. Cic. *Rosc.Am.* 133, Virg. *G.* 2.412f. *laudato ingentia rura, / exiguum colito.*

Nostro probably includes T.'s family (1.2.11-12n.).

corona / spicea: the adjective is from Virgil (see intro. essay). The crown was in thanks for a good harvest (1.5.28, 1.10.22, Hor. *C.S.* 29f., Ov. *Met.* 10.433 *primitias frugum dant spicea serta suarum*).

17–18 See Critical Appendix.

Priapus, the god of fertility and the countryside, was frequently represented as a statue, painted red and holding a sickle, whose function was that of a scarecrow or, as Ramsay would have it, a tatie-bogle, to frighten away birds (and thieves): see 1.4.1-2n.

pomosisque: the word first appears here and is rare in classical Latin. It suggests that the offerings are firstfruits (cf. *Priap.* 84, 85, *A.P.* 6.102 (Philippus), esp. Hor. *Epod.* 2.19ff. *ut gaudet insitiva decerpens pira / certantem et uvam purpurae, / qua muneretur te, Priape, et te, pater / Silvane, tutor finium*).

terreat ut saeva falce Priapus aves: *terreat* and *saeva* are mock-heroic (cf. *Priap.* 11.2, 20.6 *at me terribilem mentula tenta facit*, 30.1, 56.4, 63.9, *Copa* 24). The humour is increased by the postponement of the object of all his menacing – mere birds. The line may be intended to recall 3 (esp. *terreat*), contrasting the humorous 'terror' of the countryside with the real terrors of war.

The language may be based on Virgil (see intro. essay).

19–20 The origin of the Lares is uncertain: ancient authors give various stories (Varro *L.L.* 9.61, Ov. *F.* 2.599ff., Plin. *N.H.* 36.204), while modern scholars maintain that they were originally ghosts of the dead (e.g. Samter *Familienfeste der Griechen und Römer* (Berlin, 1901), 105ff.) or gods of the farmland (e.g. Wissowa in Roscher *Lexicon der griech. und röm. Mythologie* II.1868ff.). The fact that T. here describes them as *agri / custodes* and at 21-4 (see n.) makes a sacrifice to them to promote fertility, attended by the country-people, tends to support Wissowa's theory (cf. also Cic. *Leg.* 2.19 *lucos in agris habento et Larum sedes*, 2.27). The functions of the Lares came under four main headings: *praestites* (tutelary spirits of Rome), *compitales* (protectors of cross-roads), *viales* (guardians of travellers) and *familiares* (guardians of the household). See also 1.3.33-4n., 1.10.15-16n., 21-2n., 25, 2.1.60, 2.4.54, 2.5.20, 42. They are also mentioned at Hor. *Epod.* 2.66.

felicis quondam, nunc pauperis agri / custodes: probably based on Virgil (see intro. essay). Note the chiasmus.

On the reduction of T.'s estate see Introduction sect.3.

fertis: 'receive' (cf. Ov. *Am.* 3.6.66 *munera promissis uberiora* *feres*).

21–24 That the Lares were believed to have the power to promote fertility is shown by the song of the Arval Brothers *e nos lases iuvate* [*e*] *nos lases iuvate e nos lases iuvate* (Dessau *Inscript. Lat. Sel.* No. 5039). Cf. also Hor. *C.* 3.23.

There is emphasis on T.'s *paupertas* here: the contrast between *tunc vitula innumeros* and *nunc agna exigui*, the presence of *parva* and the repetition of *agna*.

hostia: see 1.2.61-2n.

agna cadet vobis: for the lamb as a poor man's offering cf. Hor. *C.* 2.17.32, Ov. *Tr.* 1.10.43f., *ExP.* 3.4.81f. *haec facit ut veniat pauper quoque gratus ad aras, / et placeat caeso non minus agna bove.* On offerings to the Lares see 1.10.21-2n.

cadet . . . / clamet: for similar shifts in moods and tenses cf. 61, 1.5.29ff., 1.7.8, 2.4.43, 2.6.1ff. *Cadet* is graphic: in his mind's eye T. suddenly pictures the continuation of this customary sacrifice in his ideal life. *Clamet* is jussive subjunctive.

quam circum: postposition of prepositions is frequent in poetry and is found occasionally in prose, mainly with disyllables. For postposition of disyllabic preps. in T. see 1.2.21, 1.3.68, 1.5.11, 51, 1.6.57, 65, 1.7.25, 2.5.66, 2.6.35, and for monosyllabic preps. see 1.4.26, 2.1.74.

'io messes et bona vina date': note the graphic *io* (cf. 2.4.6, 2.5.118) and quotation.

Bona agrees with the nearest noun, but probably should be taken with *messes* also.

A short open vowel at the end of the pentameter is rare (Platnauer 64ff.). In T. I and II there are only 27 cases, usually ending, as here, in -e.

33–34 For the fear of thieves and wolves cf. Virg. *Ecl.* 3.16ff., *G.* 3.406ff. *numquam custodibus illis / nocturnum stabulis furem incursusque luporum / aut impacatos a tergo horrebis Hiberos*, Hor. *Epod.* 2.60, T.2.5.88, 4.1.187, Ov. *Tr.* 4.1.79f.

Parcite and *de magno* (in contrast to *exiguo*) are emphatic by position.

Any losses to the flock would affect T.'s *paupertas*, in that he would lose even this meagre possession and the means of ensuring good harvests and vintages (21ff.).

de magno praeda petenda grege: on the omission of *est* see 1.3.43-4n.

For the expression cf. Virg. *G.* 1.130 *praedarique lupos iussit*, Ov. *Am.* 1.8.56 *plena venit canis de grege praeda lupis.*

35–36 See Critical Appendix.

This couplet gives the reasoning behind 33f. The sense is: 'seek your prey elsewhere: (for) here Pales protects my flock'. *Hic* means 'here' and is in contrast to *magno . . . grege* (34), which implies somewhere else, the connecting link being understood. The ref. in 35f. is to the

Palilia, and one of the purposes of this festival was to ensure protection of the animals by Pales, which is here implied in *placidam* (see below).

Pales was an old Roman deity of flocks and shepherds, usually, as here, female (2.5.28, Virg. *G.*3.1, 294, *Culex* 20, Serv. ad *Ecl.* 5.35), but occasionally male (Serv. ad *G.* 3.1). Her festival, the Palilia (Varro *L.L.* 6.15) or Parilia (Festus s.v. *Pales*), was celebrated annually on the 21st of April. For a fuller account see T.2.5.87ff. (and Smith ad loc.), Ov. *F.* 4.721ff. (and Frazer ad loc.). The purpose of the festival was the purification of sheep and shepherds (Ov. *F.* 4.735ff., 786) and the protection of the flock (T.2.5.88, Ov. *F.*4.747f. *'consule,' dic, 'pecori pariter pecorisque magistris: / effugiat stabulis noxa repulsa meis'*, 765f.).

T. personally performs the religious rites here and presumably all the other rites mentioned (as 37ff. implies), again like the old Roman farmer (see 29-30n., and cf. 1.10.23, 27f., Cato *Ag.Cult.* 143 *scito dominum pro tota familia rem divinam facere*).

pastoremque meum: only one shepherd is a further indication of T.'s *paupertas.*

placidam: may be a complimentary epithet, but in view of the reciprocal nature of the religious ref. it is most probably proleptic.

soleo spargere lacte Palem: for the offering of milk to Pales cf. Ov. *F.* 4.746 *silvicolam tepido lacte precare Palem*, Probus on Virg. *G.* 3.1. For the sprinkling of the statue with milk cf. 2.5.27f.

37–38 For the request for the presence and participation of the deity cf. e.g. Sappho 1D, Virg. *G.* 1.347, T.2.2.5, Ov. *Tr.* 5.3.43. The many spondees here give an air of solemnity.

For the apology for humble adornment cf. 1.10.17ff. The simplicity and frugality of early Roman religion had to an extent been replaced by a more lavish expenditure, and earthenware had been largely supplanted by more costly materials (e.g. Livy 34.4.4, Juv.11.116 and Mayor ad loc., Persius 2.59f.). The gods, however, were not supposed to require extravagance in adornment or gifts (Cic. *Leg.* 2.25, Hor. *C.* 3.23, Ov. *ExP.* 3.4.81f. (quoted on 21-4), 4.8.37ff., Persius 2.61ff.).

e puris . . . fictilibus: the adjective may refer to the ritual purity required in religious ceremony (1.3.25-6n.), but probably means 'unadorned' (Cic. *Verr.* 2.4.49, Juv.9.141), and so even humbler and poorer (another ex. of *paupertas* and parallel to *paupere* in 37).

The noun first appears here.

For the tendency of the elegists towards disyllabic pentameter endings see Platnauer 17 and Postgate *Selections* 1ii. My figures for T.I and II are closer to Postgate's: 5-syllable 2 cases (1.2.42, 1.4.84), 4-syllable 21 cases, 3-syllable 22 cases. The percentage of disyllabic endings is 92.5, with 27 non-disyllabic endings in I and 18 in II. Note also 4 cases of elided *est* forming a disyllabic word-group (1.4.4, 1.10.4, 2.6.10,

44). See also *CQ* XLII (1948), 68ff., *CR* XXXIV (1920), 168, Introduction sect. 6.

39–40 On the punctuation see Critical Appendix.

For the antiquity of earthenware see Ov. *F.* 5.522, Sen. *Ep.* 31.11, Juv. 6.342ff., Plin. *N.H.* 35.157 (of earthenware statues) *hae enim tum effigies deorum erant lautissimae, nec paenitet nos illorum, qui tales eos coluere.* T.'s defence of earthenware on the grounds of antiquity is based on the fact that for him and for the Roman mind in general antiquity was synonymous with real piety and morality (Ter. *Ad.* 442, Cic. *Re Pub.* 3.8, Sall. *Cat.* 7, 9, Hor. *S.* 2.7.23, T.1.10.17ff.). So *antiquus* is an emotive word with laudatory connotations (*Thes. L. L.* II.179.24ff.).

de facili composuitque luto: i.e. *deque facili composuit luto.* Displacement of the enclitics *-que* and (less frequently) *-ve* and *-ne* is generally common in elegy (for metrical convenience). T. introduced the practice, which is also popular with Ovid, but only occasional in Prop. The postponement is usually to the second half of the pentameter, where the enclitic is commonly attached to a quadrisyllable (most often a verb). Postponed enclitics in the hexameter are much rarer (in T.I and II only at 1.10.51, 2.4.27), while for the first half of the pent. Platnauer (91f.) cites only Prop.4.8.44. In T.I and II *-ne* is never postponed, *-ve* twice (2.3.12, 2.6.52), *-que* fifteen times (*sec. loc.* 1.4.2, 26, 1.7.62, 1.10.54, 2.3.54, 2.4.27, 54, 2.5.22, 86, 90, 2.6.16; *tert. loc.* 1.1.40, 1.3.38, 1.10.51; *quart. loc.* 1.6.54). For *-que* joined to the preceding word see 1.7.49-50n. For further exx. of word-displacement see 21-4n., 1.4.23-4n.

41–44 The second defence for the poor adornment is that he does not want much in return – only a small harvest (the basis of his *paupertas*: cf. 9, 77f.) and rest in his own bed (i.e. not the life of a soldier: see below).

avo: in view of *antiquo* probably a synonym for *patrum* (sing. for plural).

parva: emphatic by position.

requiescere lecto: probably taken from Prop.1.8(b).33 *illa vel angusto mecum requiescere lecto.*

solito membra levare toro: emphatically repeats and expands upon *requiescere lecto.*

For *levo* meaning 'rest' in this connection cf. Ov. *Am.* 1.5.2, *Rem.* 205f. *nocte fatigatum somnus, non cura puellae, / excipit et pingui membra quiete levat*, *F.* 6.328.

For the pleasure of one's accustomed bed, a touch of homeliness and stability, cf. Catull.31.10, Ov. *Tr.* 3.3.39 (cf. also T.1.2.72). A contrast with the soldier is implied: T. is to sleep in a bed, his own as always, and to be rested, whereas the soldier often has no bed, must sleep in various places and does not enjoy such rest.

Every line since 40 has ended in -o: for the homoeoteleuton see 53-4n.

45–52 The mention of the bed at 43f. is picked up by *cubantem* (45) and naturally (for an elegist) suggests a mistress.

These lines form a transition from the first to the second half of the poem. With themes they look backwards and forwards: the hardships, wealth and greed of the soldier are again rejected for T.'s ideal rustic life with its relaxation, comfort and peace of mind, but love is introduced into this life at 46 briefly, and repeated at 51f. for emphasis, and the unmanliness of the lover is suggested at 46. There are also a number of verbal echoes and pointers: *iuvat* 45 (48, cf. 74), *tener* 46 (cf. 7, 64, 68), *sinu* 46 (cf. 31), *somnos . . . sequi* 48 (cf. 4), *igne* 48 (cf. 6), *dives* 49 (cf. 1, 41), *maris* 50 (cf. 53), *auri* 51 (cf. 1), *fleat* 52 (cf. 61, 63), *puella* 52 (cf. 55), *vias* 52 (cf. 26).

45–46 For the sentiment and the delightfully cosy scene cf. Alcaeus 90D, Virg. *Ecl.* 7.49ff. *hic focus et taedae pingues, hic plurimus ignis / semper et adsidua postes fuligine nigri: / hic tantum Boreae curamus frigora, quantum / aut numerum lupus aut torrentia flumina ripas*, Ov. *Her.* 19.79ff. See also 3-4n., 1.2.71-4n. There is a contrast here with the soldier, who must endure such weather (49f.) without female companionship.

dominam: the slave's name for his mistress (picked up at 55f.). For *servitium amoris* see 1.5.5-6n. This use of *domina* had become common (Catull.68.68, 156, Prop.1.1.21, 1.3.17, 1.4.2, 1.7.6 etc.; cf. also *era* at Catull.68.136). The term appears elsewhere in T. at 1.5.40, 2.3.5, 79, 2.4.1, 19, 25, 2.6.41, 47 and was subsequently very frequent.

tenero continuisse sinu: the adjective contrasts with *immites* and suggests the unmanliness of the lover (1.4.39-40n.), in contrast to the manliness of the soldier.

The verb means 'to hold tightly': cf. Cic. *Arat.* 86 *pressu duplici palmarum continet Anguem*, Ov. *A.A.* 1.544 *vix sedet, et pressas continet arte iubas.* This is not a common usage of the word: possibly it is chosen here because of its military use (of hemming in troops etc.: see *Thes.L.L.* IV.703.23ff.).

47–48 See Critical Appendix.

The contrast with the soldier's hardships is skilfully underlined: juxtaposition of *gelidas hibernus*, opposition of *gelidas . . . aquas* to *igne*, emphatic position of *securum* and the juxtaposition of *securum somnos.*

aquas cum fuderit Auster: cf. Ov. *ExP.* 2.1.26 *fuderit adsiduas nubilus Auster aquas*, and *effundo* at Virg. *G.* 2.352, 4.312.

Auster is often associated with cold and rainstorms: cf. Lucr.5.745, Virg. *G.* 1.462, 3.278f. *unde nigerrimus Auster / nascitur et pluvio contristat frigore caelum*, 4.261, Hor. *C.* 3.3.4f., Prop.2.26.36, Ov.

Met. 1.65f.

The tense here seems to reflect the idea that the pouring precedes the actual falling of the rain on the earth.

securum: see 25-6n.

somnos . . . sequi: an original phrase (cf. the use of *petere* at 1.10.9, Virg. *Aen.* 7.88, Ov. *Met.* 13.676). It is probably here because of the use of *sequi* in military contexts (e.g. *signa, hostes sequi*).

igne: looks like a deliberate echo of *igne* in 6. See 5-6n.

49–50 *Furorem / . . . maris* indicates that here and in the preceding lines T. is thinking of the soldier's discomforts on sea-journeys, while *terra . . . marique* (53) suggests that he has in mind land-journeys also. For the dangers of sea-faring see 1.3.37-8n. The soldier took to sea both for battles (53) and for journeys to various parts of the empire (1.3).

Furorem (in emphatic position) and *tristes* (1.2.49-50n.) are strong words, underlining the soldier's hardships (cf. *immites* (45) and 47-8n.).

51–52 The usual order is: *o quantum est auri smaragdique pereat potius quam* . . . For the displacement see 39-40n. and 1.7.49-50n.

The phrase *quantum est* is uncommon (see Smith and cf. also Cic. *Verr.* 2.3.45) and emphatic.

With *auri* and *smaragdi* T. is thinking of soldiers' wealth again, since gold and gems were typical booty (1, Livy 27.49.6, Prop.3.5.3f., etc.).

For the lover leaving his mistress to go away on a campaign see 1.2. 65-6n. For the choice of love rather than the possession of wealth see 1.2.75-6n.

smaragdi: only found before here in Lucr. (2.805, 4.1126), the noun signifies various types of emeralds and green gem-stones (Plin. *N.H.* 37.62ff.).

Note that the word does not lengthen the preceding syllable (cf. 2.4.27, Prop.2.16.43, Ov. *Am.* 2.6.21, and see Platnauer 62f.).

nostras: stands for *meas* (1.2.11-12n.).

53–58 The themes of the soldier's hardships and booty in 49ff. are continued at 53f. (but here in a respectable light), and the mention of a *puella* at 52 is picked up at 55ff.

T.'s present situation (55f.) is in strong contrast to the more vigorous and respectable way of life that the soldier may lead (53f.), but T. accepts this and the only change that he would have for his ideal is to be successful in his love (57f.).

These lines form a preface to the second half of the elegy (53-74), rejecting again certain aspects of soldiering and stating a preference for the amatory side of T.'s ideal life. Again the rejection operates on a practical and an intellectual level: to the hardships of the soldier (53, esp. in view of 45ff.) he opposes the unwarlike and inactive existence of the lover (*retinent* 55, *sedeo* and the whole situation of 56; picked up by *segnis inersque vocer*, 58), and to the glory of the soldier (54) he opposes the inglorious lover (the *servitium amoris* in 55f.; picked up by *non ego laudari curo*, 57).

These features of T.'s ideal are elaborated in the following lines. For the influence of Propertius in this half of the poem see intro. essay.

53–54 For Messalla see Introduction sect. 4. For the complimentary ref. to an important friend and the brief excuse to him here see intro. essay.

ut domus hostiles praeferat exuvias: unlike the greedy soldier, Messalla wins spoil (a clever connection between the two halves of the poem) for the glory of his family and himself (cf. 2.1.33f.). So his motives are correct (*decet*), again in contrast to the greedy soldier. Spoil won from the enemy by the Roman general was carried in the triumph and fixed in front of his house (cf. Prop.3.9.26, Ov. *Tr.* 3.1.33f., Livy 10.7.9, 38.43.10 *spolia eius urbis ante currum laturus et fixurus in postibus suis*, Plin. *N.H.* 35.7, Sil.It.6.434f., Suet. *Nero* 38).

Exuvias forms a third rhyming pentameter-ending. On this phenomenon, which is not common in Roman poetry, see Smith and Müller p.567ff. For similar homoeoteleuton in T. cf.40-44, 1.2.68-70, 1.7.17f., 1.9.14, 1.10.40. The most common type of rhyme in elegy is internal rhyme in the pentameter (see Platnauer 49), which is occasionally found with the same rhyme in the hexameter (e.g. 1.2.68-9, 1.5.43-4, 1.9.25-6, 49-50. Cf. also 1.7.13-14, 1.7.49-54n.). See also *TAPhA* XXXIV (1903), xxviii ff.

55–56 me retinent vinctum formosae vincla puellae: see Critical Appendix.

Me is opposed to *te* in 53 (both in emphatic positions).

Retinent has point: the word is used of holding back troops (e.g. Caes. *B.G.* 7.47.3, 52.1, Livy 40.35.7). So too *sedeo* below, as Lee (*Quality and Pleasure in Latin Poetry*) points out, is also often used of being inactive, esp. in a military context (Lewis and Short s.v. IB2).

On *formosae* see 1.5.43-4n.

The use of *servitium amoris* picks up *dominan* (46), but here describes the harshness of his present situation. The figure is first found here in elaborated form in Latin elegy (1.5.5-6n.), and the originality in ideas and expression brings out the lover's ingloriousness.

T.'s bondage is emphasized by *vinctum* in conjunction with *vincla.* Chains are first used here explicitly in the figure (probably taken from the fetters of love common in epigram); subsequently they are very common: e.g. 1.2.90, 1.6.38, 1.9.21-2n., 79, 2.3.80, 2.4.1ff., Prop. 3.15.10, Ov. *Am.* 3.11.3 *scilicet adserui iam me fugique catenas.*

ianitor: more emphatic than *ut ianitor.* In 55 T. describes himself as chained, and in 56 he informs us that he is an *exclusus amator* (for this figure see intro. essays to 1.2 and 1.5). He combines the image of 55 with the situation of 56 and describes himself as the *ianitor*, the slave chained to his post (Ov. *Am.* 1.6.1, Col. *R.R.* 1.*praef.* 10). The idea of the lover performing servile tasks is not new (cf. Call. *Hymn.* 2.47ff., Ter. *Phorm.* 144, T.1.5.59ff., 1.9.41f. and notes, 2.3.11ff., 79f., Ov. *Am.* 3.11.17f., *A.A.* 2.209ff.), but this is the first time that the lover is depicted as a *ianitor* (cf. Ov. *Am.* 1.6.45ff., 3.11.12 *excubui clausam servus ut ante domum*). There is added piquancy in that the *ianitor* usually refused the lover entry and was regarded as an enemy (e.g. Ov. *Am.* 1.6).

duras . . . fores: the door is made of wood, but is *durus* esp. because it is closed against him (cf. 1.2.6, 1.8.76, Prop. 1.16.18, Ov. *Am.* 2.1.22, 3.1.53). It is not clear whether T. means that Delia has herself locked him out, or that a guard has been placed on her (as in 1.2).

57–58 *Laudare* and *laus* are frequently, as here, used in a military sense (e.g. Virg. *Aen.* 10.449, Livy 3.12.5). So too *segnis* (e.g. Virg. *Aen.* 9.787, Livy 29.1.6) and *iners* (cf. 5 and see n.) have military connotations here ('unwarlike' as well as 'inactive').

For Delia see Introduction sect. 4.

tecum: (doubly) emphatic by position.

59–68 The lines continue the idea of *non ego laudari curo* in 57 (see below), and *te* (59, 60) picks up *tecum* (57).

A tender and poignant picture of the poet's death in Delia's presence and of his funeral. The idea seems to be that in his ideal T. wishes to be with Delia always and visualizes their mutual love enduring until his final hour (and beyond). However, since at present T. is locked out (55f.), the lines also form an appeal to his mistress' emotions (prior to the actual exhortation at 69ff.).

This section elaborates the rejection of soldiering, esp. on intellectual grounds (53-8n.), and opposition to the soldier is implied throughout. Here there is a significant variation from the ex. of glory in 54: another form of glory for the soldier was death (Tyrtaeus 6.1f. D, Hor. *C.* 3.2.13 *dulce et decorum est pro patria mori*), and, apart from the fact that this ex. is easier to attack (esp. in view of Messalla), death was probably the way in which most ordinary soldiers won any glory and the end which T. would have feared most for himself. The glorious death of the soldier was one facing the enemy (Tyrtaeus 8.19f., 9.23-6 D), but afterwards he received a mass funeral without mourning and the presence of loved ones, perhaps no funeral at all (esp. Luc. 5.277-82 *en improba vota: / non duro liceat morientia caespite membra / ponere, non anima galeam fugiente ferire, / atque oculos morti clausuram quaerere dextram, / coniugis illabi lacrimis, unique paratum / scire rogum*, T.1.3.5ff., Livy 22.52.6). In contrast T. imagines his death as one facing Delia, and afterwards he is sure of a private funeral with (possibly excessive) mourning and the presence of his loved one (and others).

The contrast between the soldier's glorious death and T.'s inglorious end as a lover is clear, as pointed out by Lee (*Quality and Pleasure in Latin Poetry*). With regard to T.'s funeral, Fisher (loc. cit. intro. essay) maintains that there is a contrast with the lack of piety in the soldier's funeral. This idea may be in T.'s mind, but there is no open ref. to piety at 61ff. and no mention that such mourning is required by religion. Rather the emphasis is on sentiment as the cause of grief (63f., 65 *non . . . poterit*). So it seems that T. is here rejecting the 'manly' insensitivity and callousness of soldiering, making clear his preference for a funeral marked by emotion and feeling. For this reason (and to heighten the appeal to Delia) he underlines the mood of tenderness and pathos in this passage (see below).

59–60 See Critical Appendix.

T. wishes to die ingloriously, facing Delia and comforted by her (cf. Ov. *Am.* 1.3.17f., 3.9.58, *Met.* 4.145f., 7.860f., Stat. *Silv.* 2.1.148ff., Damagetus *A.P.* 7.735).

Note the pathos in *deficiente* and the emphatic positioning and repetition of *te*, picking up *tecum* in 57 (to underline the contrast with the soldier and heighten the appeal to Delia).

The theme of the poet's own death and funeral is not found in such an elaborated form in love poetry until Prop. 1.17 (for T.'s use of Prop. here see intro. essay). It subsequently occurs in elegy at 1.3, 3.2, Prop. 2.13.17ff., 3.16.23ff.

The alliteration (s, t and m) and assonance (esp. e) in this couplet are striking.

Those interested in how old Voltaire was when he wrote his verses to Madame du Deffant will find Smith relevant here.

61–62 The scene becomes clearer and Delia's devotion more certain – hence the shift to the future indicative (see 21-4n.).

Tears and kisses are the conventional offerings to the dead (Hom. *Il.* 24.712ff., *A.P.* 7.476 (Meleager), Prop. 2.13.29, Ov. *ExP.* 1.7.29), and are here important to T. as a sign of Delia's love (cf. Prop. 1.19.3f. *sed ne forte tuo careat mihi funus amore, / hic timor est ipsis durior exsequiis*, 2.8.17ff., 3.16.21ff., 4.7.23ff., Petron. *S.* 42).

Flebis and *tristibus* are given emphasis by their positions.

lecto: 'bier' (cf. e.g. Cic. *Leg.* 2.60 and see *Thes.L.L.* VII_2.1098. 78ff.).

63–64 The repetition of *flebis* (emphasized by position and sense-pause), the contrast between *duro* and *tenero* and the double image of lack of feeling (with *ferro* and *silex* in emphatic positions) underline Delia's tenderness.

For stone and iron as images of lack of feeling cf. Hom. *Od.* 23.172 ἦ γὰρ τῇ γε σιδήρεον ἐν φρεσὶν ἦτορ, Hes. *Opera* 147, *Theog.* 239, Aesch. *P.V.* 244, Cic. *Tusc.* 3.12, Prop. 1.9.31, 1.16.29f., T. 1.10.2,

59, Ov. *Her.* 10.107, 12.183, *Met.* 9.614, *Tr.* 1.8.41f., and see Nisbet & Hubbard on Hor. *C.* 1.3.9. Novelty is achieved here by the play *praecordia – corde* and the use of *vincta* (i.e. 'bound': cf. 1.9.69f., Ov. *Am.* 2.15.1 of a ring around a finger, Virg. *Aen.* 1.337 of a boot enclosing the leg). The idea is that the heart is not inaccessible (*ferro / vincta*) and not unfeeling itself (*silex*).

stat: the monosyllabic sound suggests immobility (cf. Virg. *Aen.* 6. 471 *stet Marpesia cautes*, Prop.4.11.4 *non exorato stant adamante viae*).

65–66 The young men and women mourning increase the pathos. Their grief will be heightened by the fact that T. is a love poet (cf. Prop.1.7. 23f. (which probably inspired this couplet: see intro. essay) *nec poterunt iuvenes nostro reticere sepulcro: / 'Ardoris nostri magne poeta, iaces'*).

lumina . . . referre domum: an unusual phrase (cf. Catull 10.11, Hor. *Epod.* 16.50, Virg. *Ecl.* 4.21f. *ipsae lacte domum referent distenta capellae / ubera*).

67–68 Loosening, rending and cutting of hair, along with the scratching of cheeks, were customary signs of grief: cf. Hom. *Il.* 24.711f., Eur. *Or.* 128, *A.P.* 7.489 (Sappho), Prop.1.17.21, T.1.3.8, Ov. *Her.* 11.115f., Virg. *Aen.* 4.673 and Pease ad loc., Petron. *S.* 111.

For the request to refrain from grief cf. Plato *Menex.* 248B, *A.P.* 7. 667 (anon.), Prop.4.11.1, Ov. *F.* 2.505f., *Tr.* 3.3.51 *parce tamen lacerare genas, nec scinde capillos*, Stat. *Silv.* 2.1.153, 5.1.179ff. As well as for the usual reason given, that such grief does not benefit, but may even hurt the dead, T. makes the plea in order to spare Delia's beauty (*teneris:* cf. 1.5.43-4n.). Thus the couplet represents the climax of the appeal to Delia and of the contrasts with the soldier (in that T. even has to ask for a restraint of grief).

ne laede: *ne* with the first form of the imperative was frequent in early and colloquial Latin and common in poetry (Woodcock 128 n.2).

parce . . . / . . . parce: repetition for emphasis.

69–74 *Interea* (69) makes the transition (cf. 1.10.45, Virg. *G.* 3.40, Prop. 2.13.41).

A brief sketch of the joyous life of love with Delia that T. wishes for before the onset of death and old age. The description of this ideal takes the form of an exhortation to his mistress (see 59-68n.).

The section also elaborates the rejection of soldiering, esp. on practical grounds (53-8n.), and contrast with the soldier is implicit (underlined by the use of words with military connotations: see 69-70n., 73-4n.). As at 25ff., T.'s activities as a lover are opposed to the hardships of the soldier both physically (less energetic) and mentally (they involve no fear for him, and are actually enjoyable: *iuvat* 74). The treatment here is short (the theme has already been handled) but enlivened by some pointed use of language.

Iners (71, cf. 58), *decebit* (71, cf. 53) and the mention of the door (73, cf. 56) recall lines 53-8, and so neatly round off the amatory half of T.'s ideal existence.

69–70 The sentiment, based on the rapid passing of time, that one should enjoy oneself while one can, was an old one, esp. in the amatory sphere (1.4.27-8n.). Here T. achieves novelty by the impressive description of Death and the reversal of the chronological sequence (death here precedes old age).

iungamus amores: for the expression cf. Catull.64.372, 78.3, T.1.9.76 and n. Quite possibly the phrase here is intended to recall the military expressions *iungere exercitum* etc. (Virg. *Aen.* 2.267, Vell.2. 113.1, Front. *Strat.* 1.2.9), to underline the contrast with the soldier.

iam veniet tenebris Mors adoperta caput: *iam* is emphatically placed. *Tenebris* seems best taken with *adoperta.* Darkness was traditionally associated with Death's person and apparel (1.3.3-4n.). As Dissen points out, T. may be thinking here of the Cap of Hades (Hom. *Il.* 5.844f. *αὐτὰρ Ἀθήνη / δῦν' Ἄϊδος κυνέην, μή μιν ἴδοι ὄβριμος Ἄρης*, Hes. *Scut.* 226f. *δεινὴ δὲ περὶ κροτάφοισιν ἄνακτος / κεῖτ' Ἄϊδος κυνέη νυκτὸς ζόφον αἰνὸν ἔχουσα*), or possibly the cloud of mist used by the gods for concealment (Austin on Virg. *Aen.* 1.411, 412, Nisbet & Hubbard on Hor. *C.* 1.2.31), but there is no exact parallel for this description. The picture is mysterious and striking for the originality of thought (and expression: *adoperta* first appears here, cf. 1.9.44), suggesting well the gloom and unseen approach of Death (see 1.10. 33-4n).

71–72 iam subrepet iners aetas: there is emphasis in the position and repetition of *iam.*

For old age creeping cf. Cic. *Sen.* 4, 38, Virg. *G.* 3.67 *subeunt morbi tristisque senectus*, Sen. *Dial.* 10.9.4, Juv.9.129.

For the inactivity of old age cf. Cic. *Sen.* 34f., T.1.10.40, Ov. *Tr.* 4.8.3 *iam subeunt anni fragiles et inertior aetas. Iners* is chosen here for verbal play: the actions of the lover in the next couplet are vigorous when compared with the inactivity of old age, but themselves inactive (cf. *iners* 58) when compared with the soldier. So T. is making a double contrast: what he says is that such actions are just vigorous enough for him.

nec amare decebit, / dicere nec cano blanditias capite: *decebit* looks like a pointed echo of *decet* in 53. The implication is that now such behaviour is fitting for the poet (cf. *non pudet* in 74; both expressions are emphatically placed). T. here seems to be giving his own (elegiac) views on what activities are correct for himself and to be playing on the unconventional nature of his ideal.

For the shamefulness of love in old age cf. Menand.509K, Plaut. *Merc.* 305, Ov. *Am.* 1.9.4 *turpe senilis amor* (see also 1.2.89ff. and notes). For blandishments and the old lover see 1.2.91-4n.

73–74 **nunc levis est tractanda venus**: *levis* (for the application cf. 1.7.44, Ov. *Am.* 3.1.41, *F.* 4.100) has the sense 'swift, active', which contrasts well with *iners* (71); the word is common in love poetry with a variety of meanings ('gay', 'trifling', 'fickle'), all of which may also be present here.

The activity and fittingness of such behaviour in youth is opposed to the description of old age in the last couplet, while the military connotations in the vocabulary emphasize the contrast with the hardships of the soldier (*tractanda venus* is a variation on *bellum tractare* and similar phrases (e.g. Livy 23.28.4, Tac. *Ann.* 1.59); see also below).

frangere postes: the action of the *exclusus amator.* For the military undertones here cf. Ov. *Am.* 1.9.20 *hic portas frangit, at ille fores*, Luc. 2.444, *OLD* s.v. *frango* 9.

rixas inseruisse: see Critical Appendix.

This is a difficult phrase. It could mean either literally 'to introduce brawls', i.e. into the house (cf. Lucr.2.115 of the sun's rays *inserti fundunt radii per opaca domorum*), or 'to include brawls', i.e. among other actions (cf. Tac. *Hist.* 1.23 of Otho trying to win popularity with the soldiers *alios agnoscere, quosdam requirere et pecunia aut gratia iuvare, inserendo saepius querelas et ambiguos de Galba sermones*).

Rixas here denotes brawls between the lovers, probably as a result of the broken door (see 1.10.53-6 and n.).

75–78 Transition is made by means of *hic* (in the field of love, not battle), and the military vocabulary of the previous couplet is picked up.

In these concluding lines T. draws together the main themes and recalls the opening lines of the elegy, thereby forming a neat ring-structure and ensuring the unity of the whole poem.

75–76 **hic ego dux milesque bonus**: *bonus* agrees with the nearest noun but applies to both.

For *militia amoris* see 1.10.53-6n. For the expression here cf. Hom. *Il.* 3.179, Xen. *Mem.* 3.2.2, Plut. *Mor.* 331C, Caes. *B.G.* 5.33.2, Sall. *Cat.* 60, *Carm. Epig.* 1525.2B: it suggests all-round prowess and activity, and it is a variation on Prop.1.6.30 (see intro. essay), possibly inspired by Plaut. *As.* 656 *amorisque imperator*, the only place where the term 'general' is used in *militia amoris* before here. The description of the lover as a general and soldier is first found here (cf. Prop.2.22.34, Ov. *Am.* 2.12.8, 13f. *me duce ad hanc voti finem, me milite veni*; / *ipse eques, ipse pedes, signifer ipse fui*). *Militia amoris* is of greater importance here than a mere conceit, in that it is used in the expression of the contrast between love and real warfare and is thereby incorporated within T.'s overall philosophy (rejection of warfare), a use of the figure not found until the Roman elegists (cf. Prop.1.6.29f., 2.7.13ff., 3.5.1f.).

signa tubaeque: suggests the hardships of the soldier. *Tubae* recalls *classica* (4).

cupidis vulnera ferte viris: the adjective refers to the two aims of soldiers mentioned in the poem (eager for both *vulnera* and *opes*), since wounds are an ex. of the soldier's glory (Tyrt.9.23-6D, Cic. *Rabir.* 36, Ov. *Am.* 2.10.31f.).

77–78 **ferte et opes**: recalls the greed of the soldier.

composito . . . acervo: the verb (of literally heaping up: cf. Virg. *Aen.* 7.6) calls to mind *congerat* (1), and the noun echoes *acervos* (9).

securus: recalls peace of mind, an integral part of T.'s ideal existence (25-6n., 48).

despiciam dites despiciamque famem: see Critical Appendix.

Dites here echoes 1,41 and 49.

For this expression of *paupertas* cf. Hes. *Opera* 363, Theogn. 559f., Virg. *G.* 2.498f. *neque ille / aut doluit miserans inopem aut invidit habenti*, Prop.1.14.23f., Hor. *C.* 2.10.5ff. There is forcefulness here in the emphatic positioning and repetition of *despiciam* (cf. 1.4.82, 1.7.64, 2.5.100, 105) and in the alliteration.

2

Wilhelm *RhM* LVII (1902), 599ff.; Vretska *WS* LXVIII (1955), 20ff.; Copley *Exclusus Amator* (Am.Phil.Assoc.Phil.Monogr., 1956); Solmsen *Hermes* XC (1962), 314ff.; Williams *Tradition and Originality in Roman Poetry* (Oxford, 1968), 496ff., 500f.

1-6 T.'s unhappiness (Delia's door is locked) and determination to drown it in drink.

7-14 Curse and pleas directed at the door.

15-40 T. advises Delia of Venus' aid: 15-24 she approves of *furtivus amor* and teaches lovers stealth; 25-32 she protects lovers from harm; 33-40 she punishes informers.

41-64 The magic charm to ensure concealment and reasons for believing in its efficacy.

65-78 Attack on Delia's *coniunx*: 65-6 preface: he left her for war and booty; 67-70 rejection of military glory; 71-74 T.'s preference for a life with Delia in the country; 75-78 vanity of wealth without happiness in love.

79-86 Promise of atonement for any impiety.

87-96 Threat of nemesis for mocker.

97-98 Final appeal to Venus.

Opinions vary over the mise en scène: some maintain that the action is imagined at Delia's door, others that T. is drinking with his friends and unfolding his story to them, while more recently Vretska (loc.cit.) held that the poem was a monologue by the poet in his rooms (full refs. for these views are given by Vretska: note also that Williams inclines towards Vretska's interpretation, while Copley places the action before Delia's door).

It seems to me that the most obvious and natural setting is before the door, and an examination of the poem shows that the weight of the evidence supports this view. The direct addresses to the door (7ff.) and to Delia (15ff.) and the way in which the reader is returned to the door throughout the elegy (note esp. the graphic *non labor hic laedit* at 31 and the immediacy of *iam pateas* at 9) all suggest this setting. In addition, the poem contains many features that are common in the παρακλαυσίθυρον, i.e. the addresses just mentioned, nemesis, *furtivus amor* (see below) and the various details at 7-14 (see notes). Nor are there any details in the poem which invalidate this interpretation. The presence of the slave in line 1 is not without parallel (see below on the address to the slave, and cf. also Plaut. *Curc.* 2). For the *exclusus amator* bringing wine with him cf. schol.ad Aristoph. *Plut.* 179 (τὰ πρόθυρα αὐτῆς οἴνῳ ἔρραινεν, where the ref. is most probably to locked-out lovers) and Plaut. *Curc.* It is not possible to prove conclusively on the basis of *Curc.* 82-5 that it would not be unusual for the lover to drink the wine (the lines may be meant humorously), but, in any case, T. may well be giving this detail of wine a new twist (like the garlands: see 13-14n.). Similarly in falling asleep on the doorstep (3f.) T. would only be doing what other lovers in his situation had done before him (e.g. *A.P.* 5.23 (Callimachus), Prop. 1.16.22). Finally, although the address to the mocker at 87ff. is strictly an innovation in the παρακλαυσίθυρον, the presence of a third party is not uncommon (e.g. the hag at Aristoph. *Eccl.* 960ff., the *custos* in Plaut. *Curc.*, the doorkeeper in Ov. *Am.* 1.6 and the rival lovers who are described as usual hazards at Plut. *Mor.* 753B).

Vretska's arguments against this interpretation are groundless. *Novos . . . dolores* (1) need not mean 'einen neuen, bisher noch nicht dagewesenen Schmerz'. The *dolores* are simply additional, complementing former ones (see *OLD* s.v. *novus* 5 and 8). Vretska's argument that *ille* (65) must mean the *coniunx* and that the *coniunx* is present at 41 and absent at 65, a contradiction supposedly unthinkable in a real παρακλαυσίθυρον, is also invalid (see the discussion of the *coniunx* below). Similarly his claim that the address to Venus does not provide a conclusion to a παρακλαυσίθυρον is misplaced (cf. Aristoph. *Eccl.* 966ff.).

In opposition to Vretska's own theory it may be pointed out that the addresses to the slave (1) and the mocker (87) indicate that T. intended to depict an actual dramatic situation in a definite location, as he usually does. There are no indications in the poem that it is a monologue. The parallels given by Vretska for his interpretation of the command in 1 being addressed to a *puer* not present do not convince (this is a direct address, and from lines 5f. and 57 it seems obvious that T.3.6.62 is being addressed to a *puer* who is present). Nor, as Williams implies, does this theory alone give the 'heterogeneous collection of themes the unity of a poem': if taken as a παρακλαυσίθυρον the poem has at least equal cohesion (see below).

The *convivium*-theory also seems unlikely: 1ff. and 87ff. need not imply a *convivium*, and no connection between these two passages is stated, while elsewhere in the poem there are no hints or indications whatsoever of a *convivium* or of the presence of any friends.

The scene, then, seems to be as follows: Delia's *coniunx* (see Introduction sect. 4) has put her under guard and her door is barred (7-8n., Critical Appendix on 7); T. arrives at her door and calls for more wine, to drink himself into a stupor; meanwhile he tries appeals, and, when a bystander shows amusement, he turns on him; he closes the poem with a despairing appeal to Venus.

This is apparently not the first time that T. has tried to gain entry, since in this elegy he has not made complaints to the door (9), nor spoken to it at length in suppliant tones, nor decorated it with garlands (13f.). However, his former attempts have been unsuccessful (otherwise, of course, he would not be trying again, and, in any case, the *exclusus amator* only leaves garlands at his mistress' door when he has failed: 13-14n.). T. is not the only one vying for Delia's favours (9-10n., 57-8n.), but her attitude is one of extreme caution, based on fear of detection by the guards and of information being given to her *coniunx*. The exact situation of the *coniunx* is not clear: opinions vary over whether he is supposed to be present in Rome or absent on an expedition. It is impossible to determine whether he is in Rome or not at the time of the elegy from the lines which definitely refer to him (7, 41, 55-8), and lines 65ff., which probably concern him, are of little help, since the ref. there may be to an expedition from which he has already returned or is on the point of returning (65-6n.).

The progression of thought is logical and transitions are smooth. The immediate situation is seldom lost sight of for long, and all sections are addressed to or for the benefit of the various participants. There are also verbal repetitions in connection with the main themes: the door (*ianua* 6, 7, 9; *postis* 14, 31, cf. 86; *limen* 17, cf. 84; *fores* 18, 93), *furtivus amor* (*furtim* 10, 19; *sono / sonus* 10, 20, 32; *fallo* 15, 53; *nox* 24, 29, cf. 61, 76) and the power of Venus (*Venus* 16, 34, 40, 79, 90, 97).

The locked-out lover's serenade is found in basic form as early as Alcaeus 65D. Other surviving exx. are Aristoph. *Eccl.* 960ff., Theoc. *Id.* 3, 23, *Alexandrian Erotic Fragment* (= Powell *Coll.Alex.* 177ff.), *A.P.* 5.23 (Callimachus), 103 (Rufinus), 145, 164, 189 (Asclepiades), 191 (Meleager), 12.118 (Callimachus), 252 (Strato), Plaut. *Curc.* 147ff., Catull.67, Prop.1.16.17ff., T.1.5, Hor. *C.*1.25, 3.10, Ov. *Am.* 1.6, *A.A.* 3.581. For full refs. and discussions see Copley op.cit. and *TAPhA* LXXIII (1942), 96ff., Canter *AJPh* XLI (1920), 355ff., Cairns *Generic Composition in Greek and Roman Poetry* (Edinburgh, 1972), index s.v. Komos.

1.2 is the longest existing ex. of the locked-out lover's serenade. It also surpasses all preceding versions in complexity and variety. The number of different addresses in the poem is remarkable: to the slave (1: unusual: *Alex.Er.Frag.* 25, cf. *A.P.* 12.116.1 anon.), to the door (7ff.: a common Latin feature: 7-14n.), to the mistress (15ff.: very common in Latin and Greek), to himself (79ff.: unusual: Theoc. *Id.* 3.37ff., *A.P.* 5.189 (Asclepiades), T.1.5.67f., Ov. *Am.* 1.6.49ff.), to the mocker (87ff.: entirely original), and to Venus (97f.: unusual: Aristoph. *Eccl.* 966f.). In addition to the fact that two of these addresses are uncommon and one is unique, further originality lies in the combination of so many addresses.

Apart from a number of new details and refinements in detail (see commentary below), entirely new themes in this *παρακλαυσίθυρον* are the rejection of the wealth and glory of the soldier in favour of a life with Delia in the country (65ff., cf. 1.5.19ff.) and T.'s fear that his misfortunes may be a punishment for impiety (79ff.). The threat of nemesis (87ff.) is not a new feature, but this threat was usually addressed to the mistress and was a warning of the rapid advent of old age (cf. Theoc. *Id.* 23.28ff., *A.P.* 5.23 Callimachus, 164 Asclepiades). Here it is given a new turn by being addressed to the mocker and taking the form of the loveless mocker himself in love. So the mention of magic at 41ff. (cf. Theoc. *Id.* 3.31ff., T.1.5.9ff., 41ff., 49ff.) and the background of *furtivus amor* (common in Roman versions since Plautus) are not innovations, but both themes are handled at much greater length and are far more elaborated than in previous versions. Again the combination is remarkable.

1.2 shows adroit, and frequently ingenious, manipulation of genre, with innovation and variation in evidence both formally and thematically. T. also gives this version of the locked-out lover's serenade life and interest by a number of vivid and realistic details and by its breadth, as he combines in one poem many motifs which other poets would have handled individually – and his treatment of them is often very effective (esp. the picture of lovers as divinely favoured and divinely protected personages at 15ff., the lines on the witch's powers at 43ff. and the sketch of the loveless mocker fallen in love at 89ff.). The length of the elegy also makes for depth, as it captures and explores a particular stage in the love-affair and the reactions of the lover. The poem is a good example of the pleading of the unhappy *exclusus amator*, in particular of variety in types of appeal and tone adopted with them, as all possible sources of help are tried (obstinate door, timid mistress beyond it and, more remote, unhelpful goddess of love). Dejection and misery are evident esp. at the beginning and end, and the poet twice reveals a nagging fear of rivals (9-10n., 57-8n.). The bulk of the elegy is taken up by earnest entreaties. With the door T. hastily stifles an outburst of temper and becomes wheedling and apologetic. He bases his exhortation to Delia on lengthy arguments (both explicit and implicit), producing an exalted passage on Venus' aid to lovers, awe-some lines on the witch and her charm to ensure concealment and a spirited attack on Delia's *coniunx* for his lack of love for her (implying that she should rather consider the poet, who does love her). So carried away is he that during this apostrophe he twice seems to go too far and corrects himself by means of compliments to her (31-2n., 63-4n). To Venus he shows deep humility and supplication, turning an attack on an amused bystander into yet another plea and closing with a hurt, despairing complaint. In forms of appeal, in tone, and in addresses and themes too, variety is the keynote of this lively *παρακλαυσίθυρον*.

1–6 These lines sketch briefly the background-situation (although the scene is not yet made clear) and prepare the way for T.'s appeals. The poet's unhappiness (*dolores* 1, *infelix* 4, *saeva* 5, *dura* 6) and his grim determination to drown it in drink (*compesce* 1, the imagery in 2f., *multo* 3) are in evidence here.

1–2 adde merum vinoque novos compesce dolores: T. calls for more wine. For *addo* of serving drinks cf. 3.6.62, Mart.9.93.1, 10.98.1, 14. 170.2. On the address to the slave and the detail of wine in the *παρακλαυσίθυρον* see intro. essay.

For the use of wine to drown sorrows (esp. amatory sorrows) see 1.5.37-8n. Neat wine induces sleep more quickly: 1.6.27, Ov. *Am.* 1.4.51f., Sen. *Dial.* 1.3.10 *mero se licet sopiat. Compesco* is a strong word (cf. Nisbet & Hubbard on Hor. *C.* 1.16.22).

Dolor and *doleo* occur in an amatory context 6 times in T.I and II. The words are variously used of the generally painful process of being in love, including harsh treatment by the mistress (2.4.7, 2.5.110, Prop.1.18.3, 13, 26), and more specifically of the anguish of the lover spurned (2.3.73, Prop.1.16.21, 25, 35), fooled (1.8.73, Ov. *Am.* 2.5. 59) or separated from his mistress through desertion or some other cause (Catull.96.2, T.1.2.1, 1.5.38, Ov. *Her.* 10.33).

For the sense of *novos* see intro. essay.

occupet ut fessi lumina victa sopor: for the use of *occupo* and *vinco* cf. Virg. *G.*4.190, Prop.3.17.42, Ov. *Her.*16.102, *Rem.*500, *Met.* 7.634f.

Fessi probably reinforces the verbs (i.e. 'so that I will be tired'), although it may refer to an already existing fatigue (as a result of his *dolores*: cf. Prop.3.24.17, Ov. *Am.*3.11.2 *cede fatigato pectore, turpis Amor*).

The combination of expressions here also indicates the totality and forcefulness of the desired possession by sleep.

3–4 neu quisquam multo percussum tempora baccho / excitet: see Critical Appendix.

For the request cf. Theogn.469f. *μηδ᾽ εὕδοντ᾽ ἐπέγειρε, Σιμωνίδη, ὅντιν᾽ ἂν ἡμῶν / θωρηχθέντ᾽ οἴνῳ μαλθακὸς ὕπνος ἕλῃ*. Here it is made because T. is free from his troubles when asleep. The spondees suggest gravity and seriousness.

Percussum continues the military imagery in 2: cf. *percussit* (Plaut. *Cas.*640), *saucius* (Mart.3.68.6), *saucio* (Ennius ap.Fulg.117, 11f. Helm), *quassus* (Ov. *Rem.* 146), *ictus* (Hor. *S.* 2.1.24), *τιτρώσκω* (Hom *Od.*21.293, Eur. *Cycl.*422), *οἰνοπλήξ* (*Trag. Graec. Frag. Adesp.* 238N) and *μεθυπλήξ* (Call.fr.544Pf., Leonidas *A.Plan.* 306.5).

Baccho means 'wine' (Nisbet & Hubbard on Hor. *C.*1.7.22, *OLD* s.v. *Bacchus* 2b).

infelix dum requiescit amor: T. may refer to himself here (for *amor* = *amator* cf. e.g. 1.4.24, Prop.1.16.19 *cur numquam reserata meos admittis amores*, 2.28B.39). Alternatively T. may neatly represent his love as sleeping also: cf. Ibycus 6.6-7D, *A.P.*5.212.3, 215.1f., 12. 49.1f. (Meleager) *Ζωροπότει, δύσερως, καὶ σοῦ φλόγα τὰν φιλόπαιδα / κοιμάσει λάθας δωροδότας Βρόμιος*, Catull.2.7.

Note the emphatic position of *infelix*.

5–6 *Nam* introduces the reason why T. is unhappy and so eager to drink himself to sleep. The exact situation is made clear by the next couplet: it is Delia's *coniunx* who is responsible for the guard.

For guards see 1.6.9-10n.

There is emphasis in the parallel *saeva* and *dura* (1.1.55-6n.).

7–14 *Ianua* (7) picks up *ianua* (6), as T. turns to deal first with the door.

The address to the door is a Latin feature of the *παρακλαυσίθυρον* (Plaut. *Curc.* 147ff., Catull.67, Prop.1.16.17ff., Ov. *Am.* 1.6.73f., *A.A.* 3.581). T. avoids cliché by adapting and adding details.

In the first couplet T. gives vent to his temper, but then there is an abrupt change to wheedling and apology. There is also a hint of fear of rivals (9).

7–8 ianua difficilis domini: see Critical Appendix.

Domini means 'householder' and is qualified by *difficilis* (1.8.27-8n.).

This παρακλαυσίθυρον is delivered not by a lover who has been locked out by his mistress, as is usually the case, but by one who is excluded on the orders of her *coniunx* (cf. Plaut. *Curc.*147ff., where Planesium is guarded by the slave of the pimp Cappadox). So the ref. to the *coniunx* in *difficilis domini* is unusual (cf. Catull.67, where the householders are mentioned also).

te verberet imber, / te Iovis imperio fulmina missa petant: the abuse of the door first appears in Latin versions of the παρακλαυσίθυρον: see Plaut. *Curc.*153f. *hoc vide ut dormiunt pessuli pessumi / nec mea gratia commovent se ocius*, Prop.1.6.17 *ianua vel domina penitus crudelior ipsa*, Ov. *Am.*1.6.73f., *A.A.*3.581, and cf. also *A.P.*12.252 (Strato). T.'s abuse takes the form of a curse of bad weather to which the door would be esp. vulnerable. Such a curse on the door is not found elsewhere, but is possibly deliberately opposite to Catull.67.2 (*salve, teque bona Iuppiter auctet ope*) and represents a pointed reversal of rôles, since usually it is the lover himself who has to endure such bad weather (*A.P.*5.23 (Callimachus), 189 (Asclepiades), Prop.1.16.23f., 2.9.41, Hor. *C.*3.10.1ff., 19f., Ov. *Am.*2.19.21f.).

Verbero is a strong word, suggesting strong feelings: cf. Virg. *Aen.* 9.667ff. *pugna aspera surgit: / quantus ab occasu veniens pluvialibus Haedis / verberat imber humum.*

Iovis imperio is a grandiose and awesome touch (cf. Virg.*Aen.*5.726, 747, 784, 8.381, 9.716). For the invocation of Jupiter and his thunderbolt in prayers and curses cf. Soph. *O.T.*202 ὦ Ζεῦ πάτερ, ὑπὸ σῷ φθίσον κεραυνῷ, Virg. *Aen.*4.25, 5.691f., Ov. *Ibis* 327f., 469ff. For similar divine approval on the highest level see 1.4.23-4n.

9–10 **ianua, iam pateas uni mihi**: this abrupt change of tone from abuse to pleading is apparently an inversion of Plaut. *Curc.* 147ff. A similar course of action is recommended (*A.A.*3.582, *Rem.* 35f.) and put into practice (*Am.* 1.6) by Ovid.

The second person of the present subjunctive used in a command is rare in classical prose and mainly poetic, except when the subject is indefinite. Elsewhere it appears in T. at 1.1.37, 1.2.57, 1.3.4, 5, 83, 1.4.40, 1.7.53, 1.8.67, 1.9.51. This usage was frequent in Old Latin and was colloquial. *Ne* with the present subjunctive (*neu . . . sones* in 10) is also mainly poetic, except when the subject is indefinite (elsewhere in T. at 1.4.41, 1.6.75, 1.8.29, 2.6.28). See Leumann-Hofmann-Szantyr 335f., Woodcock 126 (ii).

Iam suggests immediacy (see intro. essay), and *uni mihi* implies rivals (cf. 57f.).

victa querellis: cf. 1.5.67, Prop.1.16.36. The ref. is to past complaints (see intro. essay).

neu furtim verso cardine aperta sones: the creak of the door (or absence of it) is another feature found only in Roman versions of the παρακλαυσίθυρον (Prop. 1.16.25f. *tu sola humanos numquam miserata dolores / respondes tacitis mutua cardinibus*, Ov. *Am.* 1.6.49f.). T. cleverly adapts this detail by asking the door to open without creaking, so as not to alert the guards (note the emphasis in *neu . . . sones* and *furtim*).

The ancient door (*foris* = one of the folding doors, *fores* = *ianua* (cf. 1.4.75-8n.) = θύρα) was usually opened by means of pivots at the top and bottom fitted into sockets. These pivots were most often made of hard wood, or even of metal, so that they creaked when the door was opened (cf. Plin. *N.H.* 16.210, Theophr. *Hist. Plant.* 5.3.5, 5.5.4, Serv. ad *Aen.* 1.449). For the specification of creaking *cardo* cf. Plaut. *Curc.* 94, 158, Ov. *Am.* 1.6.49. On means of avoiding creaking see 1.6.11-12n.

11–12 The retraction of abuse in the παρακλαυσίθυρον is an innovation (note the self-denigration in *dementia* and the emphatic positions of *ignoscas* and *meo*).

dixit dementia nostra: i.e. *dixi ego demens*. This type of metonymy is not common in T. (see Smith).

The use of *nos / noster* for *ego / meus* goes back as far as Ennius (*Ann.* 377V) and is found in poetry and prose, esp. Cicero's letters (Kühner-Stegmann 1.87f., Leumann-Hofmann-Szantyr 19f.). In T. I and II definite exx. are as follows: (*nos*) 1.9.48, 1.10.25, 67, 2.4.52, 2.6.44; (*noster*) 1.1.52, 1.2.5, 11, 1.3.14, 1.4.78, 1.5.44, 1.6.53, 1.9.43, 75, 1.10.14, 2.1.35, 2.3.34. Smith is probably correct in thinking that *noster* at 1.1.15 may include the family. So too at 1.2.87 T. may mean 'us lovers', at 1.3.93 he may include Delia and at 2.1.18 the company. But Smith incorrectly sees distinctions at 1.1.52, 1.3.14 (surely tears only for T.'s journeys), at 2.1.35 (N.B. *mihi* in 35 and *cano* in 37), and at 2.3.34 (surely an attack on T. personally). This use of *nos / noster* is at times found in proximity to *ego* and *meus* (1.2.11f., 1.3.14f., 1.4.77f., 1.9.48, 75, 2.1.35, 2.4.51f.). For 1st pl. instead of 1st sing. in verbs cf. 1.3.53, 1.5.67, 2.3.79, 2.4.5 (next to 1st sing.).

capiti sint precor illa meo: for the expression cf. Aristoph. *Pax* 1063, *Acharn.* 833, *Plut.* 526, Plaut. *Poen.* 645, Ov. *Her.* 20.127f., *A.A.* 1.340, *Ibis* 448, Sen. *Thy.* 996. Here the imprecation is a witty touch, since *illa* probably refers to the curse of bad weather in 7f., which normally fell on the locked-out lover's head, and this imprecation thus also represents a reversal of a reversal (7-8n.).

13–14 These actions were performed in the past (see intro. essay). The argument of past kindness (there is emphasis here in the superlative and the position of *supplice*) is first found in the παρακλαυσίθυρον at Prop. 1.16.35ff. *sed tu sola mei, tu maxima causa doloris, / victa meis numquam ianua muneribus* etc. Cf. also Ov. *Am.* 1.6.19f. (to the *ianitor*).

supplice: the usual attitude of the *exclusus amator* (e.g. *A.P.* 5.191.6

(Meleager), Prop.1.16.14, Hor. *C.*3.10.16, Ov. *A.A.*2.527 *postibus et durae supplex blandire puellae*).

cum posti florida serta darem: garlands (at times drenched with tears and occasionally accompanied by a few lines of poetry) are often left behind by the *exclusus amator* when unsuccessful, either laid on the step or hung on some part of the door (here the door-post). Elsewhere this dedication of garlands is mentioned in the παρακλαυσίθυρον itself only at *A.P.*5.145 (Asclepiades), 191 (Meleager) and Ov. *Am.*1.6.67ff., but it is described as a characteristic act at Lucr.4.1177ff. and Plut. *Mor.*753B. For refs. to garlands in connection with the *exclusus amator* see Smith and Copley *TAPhA* LXXIII (1942), 99f. The garlands are usually an indication of the lover's vigil for his beloved to see in the morning, but here they are given a new twist by being viewed as gifts to the door.

15–24 After the door, which does not open, T. naturally addresses his mistress beyond the door. The transition is helped by *tu quoque* (i.e. 'I address you too and say that . . .': cf. 2.1.11), which picks up *te* (13), and by *custodes*, which picks up *custodia* (5).

The first part of the section on Venus' aid (15-40) concerns her approval of *furtivus amor* and her teaching of stealth to lovers. There is a circular argument in the section: be brave, and Venus will help you; and (implicitly) in view of the very useful and extensive assistance she will give, you have every reason for being brave. Apart from their message for Delia, lines 15-40 show remarkable grandness for love-poetry in their lofty conception of lovers as figures enjoying divine favour and exalted above other mortals (cf. Solmsen loc. cit. intro. essay).

The appeal is expressed forcibly (the emphasis on the need for daring at 15f., picked up at 23f., the insistent anaphora of *illa* in emphatic positions at 17ff.), and with dignity and elegance (the period and repetition at 17ff., anaphora of *seu* in 17f., the balance in couplets at 17-24, the ring-structure). After stating his main point that Venus aids the brave at 15f., T. gives exx. of this help in the next three couplets. The first couplet is esp. relevant to their present situation, the second is of a more general nature but still has some relevance, while the third has no real bearing on their present circumstances but represents a progression in audacity. The following couplet restates the idea of the opening.

15–16 ne timide custodes . . . falle: for the construction see 1.1.67-8n. On the duping of guards see 1.6.9-10n.

fortes adiuvat ipsa Venus: an original adaptation of the Roman proverb *fortes fortuna adiuvat* (see Otto *Sprichwörter* s.v. *fortuna* 9). For similar variations see Ov. *Her.*19.159 *auso Venus ipsa favebit*, *A.A.* 1.608 *audentem forsque Venusque iuvat.* For the original proverb used in amatory situations cf. Ov. *F.*2.782, *Met.*10.586.

This is a carefully constructed couplet: there is emphasis in the triple repetition of the idea of boldness, in the urgent terseness of *audendum est* and in the positions of *audendum, fortes* and *ipsa Venus*, and the repetition of d (esp. dē) seems insistent.

17–18 For lovers tampering with doors see 1.6.11-12n., 1.8.59-60n.

illa: for the repetition (*illa* recurs at 19, 20, 21) cf. Cic. *Sest.* 133, *Top.* 66 and (5 times) Ov. *F.* 4.91-7.

nova: 'new, unfamiliar', and therefore more difficult.

fixo dente: most commentators take the ref. here to be to a key pushed in, and for this use of *dens* compare Germ. *Arat.* 196. This interpretation is possible, but the phrase then seems rather otiose. It is more likely that *fixo dente* describes *fores. Dens* is used of various tooth-like objects (cf. 1.9.67-8n.), and here probably refers either to the *pessulus* (bolt at base of each *foris* pushed into socket in sill: cf. Marcell. *De Med.* 17.48) or the *sera* (bar placed across door and inserted in sockets on each side of doorway: cf. Fest. s.v. *adserere*). The idea of a locking mechanism seems more relevant here, and this emphasis on the difficulty of opening the door balances well with *nova*.

19–20 This is the first elaborated ex. of a love-deity as a *praeceptor amandi* (cf. 1.8.5f., 35ff., 55f., 2.1.75ff., 4.6.12, and on the subject in general see intro. essay to 1.4). The idea of Eros as a *praeceptor* had been very briefly handled at Moschus fr. 3.8 (Gow) καὶ ποταμὸν διὰ φίλτρον Ἔρως ἐδίδαξε κολυμβῆν, Bion fr. 10.13 (Gow) ὅσσα δ' Ἔρως με δίδαξεν ἐρωτύλα πάντα διδάχθην and Prop. 1.1.5f. *donec me docuit castas odisse puellas / improbus, et nullo vivere consilio*. Cf. also Ov. *Am.* 1.6.7f.

For the vivid details of slipping stealthily from bed / bedroom and walking silently cf. Aristoph. *Thesm.* 482, Nonn. *Dionys.* 16.265f., *A.P.* 5.294 (Agathias Scholasticus), T. 2.1.75ff., Ov. *Am.* 1.6.7f., 3.1.49ff., *F.* 1.425f., 2.331ff., 6.337f., Maxim. 3.27ff. As Dissen points out, T. may be thinking of the lover or the mistress here.

molli furtim derepere lecto: see Critical Appendix.

The meaning of the rare *derepere* is 'to crawl, creep down' (*Thes. L.L.*, *OLD* s.v.), so that the ref. here may be either to crawling down from the bed itself (cf. Ov. *Am.* 3.1.51 *delabique toro*) or to creeping down (by the stairs or on a rope) from the place where the bed is situated (cf. Prop. 4.7.15ff.).

For compounds of *repo* applied to the lover see 1.8.59, Petron. *S.* 87 *irrepsi tamen et male repugnanti gaudium extorsi*, Apul. *Met.* 9.5, 21 *videt sub lectulo soleas incognitas quibus inductus Philesitherus irrepserat*, and cf. also *A.P.* 5.294.12 (Agathias Scholasticus) γαστέρι συρόμενος.

For *molli . . . lecto* see 55-6n.

The alliteration and internal rhyme make the pentameter a pleasantly musical line.

21–22 Nods and sign-language are often found together: cf. Naevius 75R, Plaut. *As.* 784, Ov. *Am.* 1.4.17ff., 2.5.15ff., 3.11.23f., *A.A.* 1.137f., *Met.* 4.63, *Tr.* 2.453f.

For the pre-arranged sign see esp. Ov. *Am.* 1.4.21ff. and cf. also 2.5.19f. *sermonem agnovi, quod non videatur, agentem / verbaque pro certis iussa valere notis.*

Signs were given by making marks, gesturing, double entendre, using a verbal code etc.: see above and cf. also Ter. *Heaut.* 372f. *inversa verba, eversas cervices tuas, / gemitus, screatus, tussis, risus*, Plaut. *As.* 792ff., Kost on Musaios *Her. et Leand.* 102, Ov. *Her.* 17.75ff., *A.A.* 1.569ff.

viro coram: 'even before the husband / boyfriend himself'. For the postponement of *coram* see 1.1.21-4n.

nutus conferre: 'exchange nods': apparently an adaptation of *sermonem / sermones conferre* (*Thes. L. L.* IV.179.16ff.).

23–24 As the point of 15-24 is the need for boldness and courage, *inertia* here probably means 'want of spirit / enterprise' (*OLD* s.v.2b), rather than 'idleness', and so balances *timor* in the pentameter. For the lover's lack of fear and spiritlessness cf. *A.P.* 5.25 (Philodemus), Ov. *Am.* 1.6.9ff. *at quondam noctem simulacraque vana timebam: / mirabar tenebris quisquis iturus erat; / risit, ut audirem, tenera cum matre Cupido / et leviter 'fies tu quoque fortis' ait. / nec mora, venit amor: non umbras nocte volantis, / non timeo strictas in mea fata manus*, 1.9.5f., *A.A.* 2.233f.

obscura . . . nocte: this is, of course, the time for *furtivus amor.*

25–32 The lines are a natural progression in situation and ideas (*tenebris* picks up *obscura . . . nocte*, 24).

The second part of the section on Venus' aid (15-40) concerns her protection of lovers from harm, whether from man (25-28) or the elements (29f.) or sufferings as an *exclusus amator* (31f.). The figure of the lover receives even greater elevation (the lover appears here first in Latin as a divinely protected, sacred person). The appeal to Delia continues (esp. 27f., which have obvious application to her too) and culminates in flattery (the proviso at 31f., which implies even more power than Venus has).

25 For the lacuna after this line see Critical Appendix (probably we are missing a single pentameter to the effect that Venus protects T. from danger).

tota vagor anxius urbe: in view of the lacuna it is hard to tell exactly what the ref. is here, but *anxius* seems to denote amatory worry (cf. Catull. 64.203, 68.8, Prop. 2.20.2, Ov. *Her.* 17.214, *A.A.* 3.727), and the wandering may well be because T. is distraught (cf. Virg. *Aen.* 4.68f. *uritur infelix Dido totaque vagatur / urbe furens*). In any case, this is a vivid detail.

25a–26 The lover in his nocturnal comings and goings was esp. vulnerable to such dangers: see on 27-8 and cf. also *A.P.* 5.213 (Posidippus), Hor. *S.* 1.2.42f. *fugiens hic decidit acrem / praedonum in turbam, dedit hic pro corpore nummos*, Prop.3.16, Ov. *Am.* 1.6.9ff., *Eleg. in Maec.* 1.29f. The sense of danger is heightened throughout this passage by the use of words often found in a military connection (*occurrat, ferro, vulneret, rapta, praemia, insidias*).

For the thieves and cut-throats in Rome and Italy by night cf. Petron. *S.* 82, Juv.3.278ff., 10.19ff., Tac. *Ann.* 13.25, Suet. *Nero* 26, Plin. *N.H.* 8.144. Clothes-stealing (*rapta . . . veste*) was common in antiquity and usually took place in the street (or the baths), the favourite time being nightfall: cf. Petron. *S.* 12 (street at night) and Plat. *Res Pub.* 575B, Xen. *Mem.* 1.2.62, Plaut. *Rud.* 382ff., Catull.33, Petron. *S.* 30.

sinit occurrat: the imperative of *sino* without *ut* is found in poetry and prose, but with finite forms of *sino* this omission is not common and is mainly poetic (e.g. Plaut. *Miles* 54, T.1.4.25f., Virg. *Aen.* 12.828, Ov. *Met.* 3.377). In general with verbs of desiring or demanding T. prefers to omit *ut* (*ut* at 2.3.34, but omitted at 1.2.63f., 1.9.49f., 69f., 84, 2.3.32, 2.6.36; at 1.2.12, 1.3.5, 83, 1.6.56, 1.9.40 the subjunctive is jussive in parataxis to *precor*: 1.3.5-8n.).

27–28 For the lover's protection by the love-gods cf. *A.P.* 5.213 (Posidippus), 12.115 (anon.), T.1.5.57f., 1.6.51, 4.3.4, Prop.3.16.11ff., Ov. *Her.* 15.213ff. T. has added to this theme by the vivid details of the previous couplet, and here he elaborates further by saying that the lover may go anywhere (*qualibet* in emphatic position) and by describing him as sacrosanct (since he is consecrated to Venus). The sacrosanctity of the lover (cf. also 1.3.83f.) is picked up at Prop.3.16.11ff. *nec tamen est quisquam, sacros qui laedat amantis: / Scironis media sic licet ire via. / quisquis amator erit, Scythicis licet ambulet oris, / nemo adeo ut noceat barbarus esse volet* etc. Cf. also Hor. *C.* 1.22, where he may have this passage of T. in mind (see *Latomus* XXVIII (1969), 575ff.).

quisquis amore tenetur: for this use of *teneo* cf. Virg. *Aen.* 1.675, Ov. *Am.* 2.10.10 *dividuumque tenent alter et alter amor, Her.* 15.12, 21.125f., *Rem.* 529.

On hexameter caesuras in T. see Smith ad loc., and on hexameter (and pentameter) caesuras in elegy generally see Platnauer 4ff. Note that 2w + 3w (rather than 3s) is rare: elsewhere in elegy only at 1.2.63, Prop.2.33.9, 3.8.23, 4.7.41 (Platnauer 5f.). D. S. Raven points out to me that here we have 1w + 2w + 3w, which is even odder.

tutusque sacerque: on this use of *que . . . que* (which heightens the tone) see 1.5.35-6n.

29–30 Venus' protection also applies against the elements (*A.P.* 12.115. 3f. anon.). For the lover's exposure to bad weather cf. *A.P.* 5.120 (Philodemus), T.1.4.41ff., Prop.2.26.35ff., Ov. *Am.* 1.9.11ff., *A.A.*

2.231f., 235f.

Note the emphasis here on the unpleasantness of the weather (*pigra*, the juxtaposition *hibernae frigora, multa . . . aqua*) and the insistent anaphora of *non mihi* (and *non* in 31).

pigra: 'that makes sluggish, numbing': cf. Lucr.5.746f. *tandem bruma nives adfert pigrumque rigorem / reddit hiemps*, T.1.10.40, Lucan 4.50, and see 1.1.7-8n.

multa decidit imber aqua: abl. of attendant circumstances. For the pleonasm cf. esp. Virg. *Aen.* 5.696 *turbidus imber aqua*, and in general see 1.7.49-50n.

31–32 For the graphic *labor hic* (his present sufferings before Delia's door) see intro. essay. To say that these sufferings do not harm him seems to be going too far and likely to spoil his chances of making Delia open up – hence the apparently hasty correction by means of a highly complimentary proviso (see intro. essay).

ad digiti . . . sonum: a good detail. It is not clear exactly what action is meant here, but it is obviously intended to attract T.'s attention without rousing the guards. It may be a snapping of the fingers (Mart. 3.82.15), a scratching (Aristoph. *Thesm.* 481), or a gentle tap on the door (Ov. *Am.* 2.19.39f. *incipe, quis totiens furtim tua limina pulset, / quaerere*). For a similar stealthy signal see 1.5.71-4n.

33–40 These lines may refer to T.'s present situation (outside Delia's door), but, as he is throughout trying to persuade Delia to open the door, it seems more likely that the lines pick up the dramatic situation of the last couplet (Delia opening up), and 55-6 tend to confirm this interpretation. Lines 33-36 are addressed to any man or woman who may come across T. and Delia together.

The third part of the section on Venus' aid (15-40) concerns her punishment of informers. The divine protection of lovers is further elaborated, as T. issues a solemn warning as the privileged mouthpiece of Venus and speaks of the more dreadful aspect of the goddess. The lines are aimed at Delia's fear of betrayal, and, to remove this, T.'s warning covers men and women and intentional and unintentional witnesses of their affair.

33–34 **parcite luminibus**: 'do not look' (cf. Prop.4.9.53, Ov. *Met.* 5.248).

celari vult sua furta Venus: for the love-gods' desire for concealment cf. *A.P.* 5.4 (Philodemus), Ov. *A.A.* 2.607f. The same idea is behind *A.P.* 5.252 (Paulus Silentiarius), Ov. *Am.* 2.2.41ff., Petron. *S.* 20. Here there is a new application and fuller elaboration than previously. *Celari* and *Venus* are emphatic by position.

Furta meaning amatory 'intrigues' is first found at Catull.68.136, 140 and is common in elegy (see Smith). This type of expression was frequent in Greek and goes back as far as Homer: Il.6.161 κρυπταδίῃ φιλότητι μιγήμεναι, Mimnerm.1.3, *A.P.* 5.120.1 (Philodemus), 219.1,

221.1 (Paulus Silentiarius), 267.6 (Agathias Scholasticus). See also 1.8.57-8n.

35–36 These are vivid and realistic details.

neu strepitu terrete pedum: for sounds causing fear cf. Soph. fr. 58N, Ap.Rhod.3.954f., Dio Cass.63.28.2, Virg. *Aen.*2.727f., Luc.8.5f., Sil. It.6.58f., Claud. *Eutrop.* 2.452f.

neu quaerite nomen: for the questioning cf. Petron. *S.* 82, Juv.3.290ff.

neu prope fulgenti lumina ferte face: see 1.9.41-2n.

The sound of this couplet is remarkable: the (emphatic) repetition of *neu*, frequency of e, t and p (possibly onomatopoeic, as André suggests) at the start of the hexameter, alliteration of f in the pentameter.

37–40 perque deos omnes: a very solemn and earnest oath.

nam fuerit quicumque loquax: for the displacement see 1.4.23-4n.

is sanguine natam / is Venerem e rabido sentiet esse mari: see Critical Appendix.

The harsh and punitive aspects of Venus are often mentioned in poetry (1.9.19-20n.) and often illustrated in mythology (e.g. Hippolytus, Smyrna, Atalanta, the women of Lemnos). As Smith points out, the most apposite legend here is that of Anchises, who for boasting (cf. *loquax*) of his intercourse with Venus was enfeebled, blinded or killed by a thunderbolt (Serv. ad *Aen.* 1.617, 2.649, Hygin. *Fab.* 94).

This is a deliberately awesome and impressive ref. to Venus (note too the hissing of s and x in these four lines). T. here alludes to one of the most common versions of Venus' birth, that she grew from the white foam that spread around the genitals of Uranus when severed and thrown into the sea (e.g. Hes. *Theog.* 188ff.).

Venus was born of violence (*sanguine* abl. of origin) and so of a violent nature (cf. Ov. *Met.* 1.160ff. *sed et illa propago / contemptrix superum saevaeque avidissima caedis / et violenta fuit: scires e sanguine natos*). Similarly those sprung from the sea were proverbially cruel: cf. Hom. *Il.* 16.34, Catull.64.154f. *quaenam te genuit sola sub rupe leaena? / quod mare conceptum spumantibus expuit undis . . .*, Ov. *Her.* 7.39f., 10.131f., T.3.4.85, Sil.It.1.638, Gell.15.21.

For *rabidus* applied to the sea cf. Stat. *Silv.* 3.2.85, Sil.It.15.784. The adjective brings out Venus' own cruelty.

For similar remarks about the birth and innate characteristics of the love-deities cf. Theogn.1231f., Theoc. *Id.* 3.15f., *A.P.* 5.180 (Meleager), Sen. *Phaed.* 274 *diva non miti generata ponto.*

41–64 After the warning to informers, T. strengthens his argument by claiming that Delia's *coniunx* will not believe an informer anyway (*huic* = *is* of 39f.).

T. maintains that a witch's charm will ensure this disbelief (41f.), and cites the feats which the witch can perform (43-52); he then gives details of the charm (53-8), and cites her ability even to free him from his love (59-64). Thus T. twice tries to win credibility for the witch and her charm. The solemnity of the previous lines is still in evidence, but here it is of a more mysterious and awesome nature. T. also reveals fear of rivals again (57f.) in the middle of his appeal.

The list of magic feats was esp. common in Roman poetry. T.'s predecessors were Ap.Rhod.3.531ff., Virg. *Ecl.* 8.69ff., Hor. *Epod.* 17.76ff., Prop.1.1.19ff. T. elaborates, adds new details to the list and extends the witch's powers from heaven to earth and to the Underworld (to make her more impressive for Delia). Note also the solemn anaphora and the balance and contrast evident throughout these lines. For other exx. of the list cf. 1.8.19ff., Virg. *Aen.* 4.487ff., Prop.4.5.9ff., Ov. *Am.* 1.8.5ff., 2.1.23ff., 3.7.31ff., *Her.* 6.83ff., *Med.Fac.* 39ff., *Rem.* 253ff., *Met.* 7.199ff., Petron. *S.* 134, Sil.It.8.498ff., Val.Fl.6.441ff., Apul. *Met.* 1.8, 2.5, Claud. *In Ruf.* 1.145ff.

41–42 verax: the position of the word gives it emphasis.

pollicita est magico saga ministerio: the ablative is instrumental (with *pollicita est*) and refers to the charm of 53ff.

For the pentameter ending see 1.1.37-8n.

Magic seems to have been mainly the province of women in Greece and Rome: the most famous exponents (e.g. Circe, Medea, Erichtho) were women, and the female sex was widely believed to possess particular abilities in this field (cf. Plin. *N.H.* 25.10). Often, esp. in elegy, the witch also engaged in other professions, such as *meretrix*, *lena* and poisoner (1.5.59, Prop.4.5, Ov. *Am.* 1.8, Mart.9.29.10, Plin. *N.H.* 30.15, 17, Non. 23.1M.).

43–44 de caelo ducentem sidera: charming down stars (and the moon: 1.8.21-2n.) was one of the more common magic feats (esp. connected with Thessalian witches): cf. Hor. *Epod.* 5.45f. *quae sidera excantata voce Thessala / lunamque caelo deripit*, 17.5, Prop.1.1.23f., Luc.6. 499f., Quint. *Decl.* 10.15, Apul. *Met.* 1.3.

vidi: the poet himself as a witness lends greater credibility (cf. Hor. *S.* 1.8.23, 1.4.33-4n.).

fluminis haec rapidi carmine vertit iter: *vertit* may mean 'turns' (i.e. alters the course of) or 'turns back' (cf. Ov. *ExP.* 4.6.45f.). Magical incantation had the power to do both these feats: cf. (change course) Prop.1.1.23f. *tunc ego crediderim vobis et sidera et amnis / posse Cytaeines ducere carminibus*, which possibly inspired this couplet, Val. Fl.6.443, and (turn back) Ov. *Am.* 2.1.26, *Med.Fac.* 40, Luc.6.473f., Apul. *Met.* 1.3, Claud. *In Ruf.* 1.159f. (cf. also, with incantation not specified, Ov. *Am.* 1.8.6, *Met.* 7.199f., Sen. *Med.* 762).

Rapidi (and the swift, dactylic movement of the pent.) underlines the difficulty of the feat.

For further powers of magic in these fields see Pease on Virg. *Aen.*

4.489.

45–46 For the theme of necromancy, the magic ceremony in which ghosts are called up and asked questions, see esp. Hom. *Od.* 10.504ff., 11.1ff., Phrynicus *Bekk.An.* 73.13 (Aeschylus' Ψυχαγωγοί), Aesch. *Pers.* 619ff., Aristoph. *Aves* 1553ff., Hor. *S.* 1.8, Luc.6.419ff., Sen. *Oed.* 530ff., Apul. *Met.* 2.28ff. For the actual practice of necromancy cf. Cic. *Div.* 1.132 (see Pease ad loc., and on *Aen.* 4.490), Plin. *N.H.* 30.18.

haec cantu finditque solum: cf. Ov. *Am.* 1.8.17f. *evocat antiquis proavos atavosque sepulcris / et solidam longo carmine findit humum*, *Rem.* 253f., Virg. *Aen.* 4.490f. The purpose was to allow the ghosts to come up to the witch (Sen. *Oed.* 571ff., Luc.6.728ff., Sil.It.1.95ff. *immugit tellus, rumpitque horrenda per umbras / sibila . . . / tum magico volitant cantu per inania manes / exciti*).

manesque sepulcris / elicit: cf. Virg. *Ecl.* 8.98, Ov.loc.cit., *Met.* 7.206.

Elicio is the regular word in this connection (*Thes.L.L.* V_2.366. 56ff.).

et tepido devocat ossa rogo: the verb here means 'summon away from' or 'summon down from', i.e. the pyre (see *OLD* s.v.), which is quite different from merely stealing (Smith's interpretation). It would appear that just after cremation (*tepido*) the witch revives the remains and makes them come to her. Context suggests that she makes the dead body live again (for the feat cf. Hor. *Epod.* 17.79 *possim crematos excitare mortuos*, Claud. *In Ruf.* 1.155f.), so that its soul will answer her questions (cf. Luc.6.619ff., Apul. *Met.* 2.28ff.).

47–48 iam tenet infernas magico stridore catervas: she holds the ghosts against their will (cf. Sen. *Oed.* 562f. *decantat ore quidquid aut placat leves / aut cogit umbras*, 621ff., Apul. *Met.* 2.29). Ghosts were believed to return to earth only for specific reasons, e.g. vengeance (1.5.51-2n.), guilt (Isid. *Orig.* 8.11.101), bad burial (Plin. *Epist.* 7.27.5ff.) – hence the unwillingness here. Broukhusius mentions the *synochitis* (Plin. *N.H.* 37.192), a rather useful stone which had the power of holding ghosts.

Catervas denotes large numbers, and so highlights the witch's powers.

Stridor is also applied to magic incantations at Sil.It.8.502. In this connection the word seems to refer to a sound esp. like that made by screech-owls: cf. esp. Ov. *F.* 6.139ff. *est illis strigibus nomen; sed nominis huius / causa, quod horrendum stridere nocte solent. / sive igitur nascuntur aves, seu carmine fiunt / naeniaque in volucres Marsa figurat anus.* Incantations consisted of words (1.5.43-4n.), but the words were indistinct (*murmur* and *demurmuro* at Ov. *Met.* 7.251, 14.58) and generally abnormal, alien and hard to understand (Lucian *Dial.Mer.* 4.5, Ov. *Met.* 14.57, Plin. *N.H.* 28.20). The tone in which they were delivered frequently, as here, made them resemble various sounds of nature: cf. Petron. *S.* 63, esp. Luc.6.685ff., and the use of *illatro* at Luc.6.729, and *ululo* / *ululatus* at Hor. *S.* 1.8.25, Ov. *Met.* 7.190, 14.405, which are also used of animals howling (e.g. Enn. *Ann.* 342V, Virg. *Aen.* 6.257, Petron. *S.* 62).

iam iubet aspersas lacte referre pedem: milk was a placatory offering to the dead (used in both summoning and dismissing them): Hom. *Od.* 10.519, Aesch. *Pers.* 610f. (and Broadhead ad loc.), Sen. *Oed.* 565f., Stat. *Theb.* 4.453, 543ff. For the sprinkling of milk over ghosts cf. esp. Stat. *Theb.* 4.543ff. *Argolicas magis huc appelle precando / Thebanasque animas; alias avertere gressus / lacte quater sparsas maestoque excedere luco, / nata, iube.*

49–50 The idea that the weather could be controlled by magic goes back in literature as far as Homer (*Od.* 5.268, 10.19f., 11.7f.). Magic was supposed to have the power to cause storms (Val.Fl.8.351f.) and to lay them (Hdt.7.191), to control winds (Ov. *Met.* 7.202, Petron. *S.* 134) and even the thunderbolt (Claud. *In Ruf.* 1.158). See esp. the various powers listed at Luc.6.461ff.

haec tristi depellit nubila caelo: for magic control over clouds cf. Ov. *Am.* 1.8.9 *cum voluit toto glomerantur nubila caelo, Met.* 7.201f., 14.368, Luc.6.465ff., Diod.Sic.5.55.3.

For *tristis* cf. Plin. *N.H.* 2.13 *caeli tristitiam.* The adjective may mean 'lowering' or 'saddening' (because connected with bad weather). For *tristis* similarly applied to celestial phenomena cf. Virg. *G.* 4.235, Hor. *Epod.* 10.10, *C.* 1.3.14, T.1.1.50, Ov. *Met.* 6.690.

aestivo convocat orbe nives: for the production of snow in summer, an unusual detail, cf. Diod.Sic.5.55.3 (of the Telchines). For similar inversion of seasons cf. Sen. *Med.* 759f. *temporum flexi vices: / aestiva tellus floruit cantu meo, / coacta messem vidit hibernam Ceres.* Cf. also Luc.6.478f. (thawing of snow in winter).

Orbis here means 'sky': cf. Ov. *Am.* 1.8.10, *Ciris* 38 *sidera caeruleis orbem pulsantia bigis.*

51–52 The mention of the most famous witch and the goddess of witchcraft herself forms a fitting climax to the list of feats.

sola tenere malas Medeae dicitur herbas: Medea was the witch par excellence, renowned for her cunning and knowledge (πολυφάρμακος Pind. *Pyth.* 4.233, Ap. Rhod. 4.1677, πολυκερδής Ap. Rhod. 3.1364), and taught by Hecate herself (Ap.Rhod.3.528ff.). For her herbs see e.g. Ov. *Met.* 7.224ff., Sen. *Med.* 705ff., Val.Fl.7.349ff. They represented maximum effectiveness (T.2.4.55, Prop.2.4.7f., esp. Theoc. *Id.* 2.15f. φάρμακα ταῦτ' ἔρδοισα χερείονα μήτε τι Κίρκης / μήτε τι Μηδείας μήτε ξανθᾶς Περιμήδας), so that sole possession of them means supreme power.

Malas . . . herbas is possibly a variation on Homer's κακὰ φάρμακα

(*Od.* 10.213 etc., cf. Virg. *Aen.* 2.471 *mala gramina*). For *malus* meaning 'noxious, harmful' cf. Virg. *G.* 1.129, Hor. *S.* 2.1.56, *Epod.* 3.7.

Dicitur denotes renown.

sola feros Hecatae perdomuisse canes: for Hecate see esp. Roscher *Lex. der griech. und röm. Mythologie* s.v. She first appears at Hes. *Theog.* 411ff. (the genuineness of the passage is disputed) as a great and beneficent deity in many departments of life. She was of triple form (Luna, Diana, Proserpina: Serv. ad *Aen.* 6.118; cf. *triformis, triceps* at e.g. Ov. *Met.* 7.94, 194). As her worship was esp. connected with the places where three roads met, she was also called Trivia (1.5.15-16n.). A more respectable cult of her did exist (Farnell *Cults* ii.501ff.), but she was connected with sorcery from at least as early as the time of Euripides (cf. *Med.* 395ff.), and she was invoked and worshipped by witches (Ap.Rhod.3.528f., Theoc. *Id.* 2.10ff., Ov. *Her.* 12.168, *Met.* 7.194f., 14.405, Sen. *Med.* 750f.) and controlled ghosts (Eur. *Hel.* 569f., Apul. *Met.* 11.2).

The hounds of Hecate were always with her when she appeared on earth and announced her approach by howling (Serv. ad *Aen.* 6.257). An exaggerated description of them is given at Lucian *Philops.* 24. For further refs. see Smith. The taming of her hounds, like the possession of Medea's herbs, implies great power. The hounds were commonly identified with the Furies (Acro ad Hor. *S.* 1.8.35, schol. ad Luc.6. 733, Serv. ad *Aen.* 6.257), and so for a similar feat cf. Luc.6.730ff.

The witch's power here is emphasized by the positions and repetition of *sola*, and by *malas, feros* and *perdomuisse* (intensifying prefix).

The verb *perdomo* is only found at Sall. *Hist.* 1.11 before here. The perfect tense is fully felt (1.1.29-30n.).

53–54 T. returns to the charm and situation of 41f. For the charm cf. Prop.4.5.15f. *posset ut intentos astu caecare maritos, / cornicum immeritas eruit ungue genas*, perhaps Juv.6.610ff. The plurals (*cantus, quis, carminibus*) may be plural for singular or they may denote a charm that consisted of more than one verse.

haec mihi: the juxtaposition suggests a close relationship between poet and witch.

ter cane, ter dictis despue carminibus: odd numbers were considered powerful, esp. the number three (Virg. *Ecl.* 8.75 and Serv. ad loc., Plin. *N.H.* 28.23 *cur inpares numeros ad omnia vehementiores credimus*?). Cf. also 1.5.15-16n. Charms and prayers are often repeated three times (Ap.Rhod. 4.1668f., Ov. *F.* 4.551, Plin. *N.H.* 28.21, Marc.Emp.28.74), and spitting three times is also common (Theoc. *Id.* 6.39, Petron. *S.* 131, Plin. *N.H.* 24.172, 25.167, 28.36).

Spitting was in general considered a powerful charm and averter of witchcraft and misfortune (cf. 95-6n.). We find spitting during magic rites and spells (*Ciris* 372f., Marc.Emp.15.101, 26.70 and see above) and after them (Varro *R.R.* 1.2.27, Petron. *S.* 131). The purpose was to avert disaster from the reciter (Gow *CR* LVI (1942), 109 n..1) and to render the charm more effective (Plin. *N.H.* 28.36 *ita effectus adiuvare*).

All this ritualistic detail seems intended to impress Delia.

The frequency of c, t and d in the couplet is striking.

55–56 For the blind husband or boyfriend see 53-4n. and cf. also Catull. 17 esp. 20f. *tantundem omnia sentiens quam si nulla sit usquam, / talis iste meus stupor nil videt, nihil audit*, T. 1.6.15ff., 1.9.53ff., Ov. *Am.* 2.2.51ff., Apul. *Met.* 9.5.ff., 17ff.

Cuiquam is left until the end of the line for emphasis.

For the earnest elaboration of 56 (to convince Delia) cf. Ov. *Am.* 2.2.57f., 3.14.43f., esp. *Her.* 4.145f. *tutus eris mecum laudemque merebere culpa, / tu licet in lecto conspiciare meo.* Note the emphatic position of *non sibi.*

molli . . . toro: *mollis* is a frequent epithet for beds in elegy (e.g. 19, Prop. 1.3.34, 2.4.11, Ov. *Am.* 2.4.14, *A.A.* 2.712).

57–58 The sudden addition of this strongly expressed warning (*cetera . . . / omnia* and *de me uno . . . nihil* in emphatic positions and strong contrast, the triple alliteration in the hexameter) is a further indication of T.'s nagging doubts about Delia (cf. 9). T. himself does not explain why the charm relates to him alone. However, it was generally supposed that if in the course of a charm mention was made of the name of the person for whom the charm was intended, then the charm would relate to that person alone and to no-one else. It seems likely that T. is supposed to have acquired a charm in which his name was mentioned. The context suggests that his fear of rivals led him to do this. For this practice in charms against diseases cf. Plin. *N.H.* 22.50, 23.103 *radix eorum circumscripta terra manu sinistra capitur, ita ut qui id faciet dicat quare capiat et cuius causa*, 26.116, and for charms in love magic cf. Lucian *Dial.Mer.* 4.5 (of the lover's boots) ταύτας κρεμάσασα ἐκ παττάλου ὑποθυμιᾷ τῷ θείῳ, πάττουσα καὶ τῶν ἁλῶν ἐπὶ τὸ πῦρ. ἐπιλέγει δὲ ἀμφοῖν τὰ ὀνόματα καὶ τὸ ἐκείνου καὶ τὸ σόν. For further refs. see Heim *Incantamenta Magica Graeca Latina* (Lipsiae, 1892), 471f.

abstineas: for the amatory use of the verb cf. Catull. 61.136, Ov. *Her.* 17.98, *A.A.* 1.327, 380, Hor. *C.* 3.7.18, *Ars Poet.* 414.

59–60 Delia may have her doubts about this charm because of its rather unusual nature, and so, to forestall these doubts, T. cites the witch's claim to be able to do something even more difficult (remove his love for Delia) and mentions the strange and impressive ceremony that she held. This interpretation seems more likely than that of Smith (*quid credam*? etc. denotes real doubt on the poet's part about the witch's powers), which ruins the whole point of the section on magic.

nempe haec: for the rare elision see 1.7.61-2n.

se dixit amores / cantibus aut herbis solvere posse meos: for the removal of love by magic see below and cf. Theoc. *Id.* 2.90f., Prop. 1.12.9f., Ov. *Rem.* 249f., 259f.

Solvere is used of removing love by magic, as here, at Hor. *Epod.* 5.71, 17.45, *C.* 1.27.21f., Virg. *Aen.* 4.479, 487, and of removing love without the use of magic (where the ref. is probably to *Veneris vincla:* 1.8.5-6n.) at 1.9.83, Prop.1.4.15, Ov. *A.A.* 2.385 etc. There is no indication here, as Smith suggests, that T. suspects that his love for Delia was caused by magic, and the statement of such a suspicion would hardly endear him to Delia or incline her to open up. So in the following lines the magic details are too vague to support Smith's theory that the ref. is to a reversal of the moon-charm.

Cantibus aut herbis suggests that the witch has various methods at her disposal and regards the task as an easy one.

61–62 **me lustravit taedis**: fire had purgatory powers (Serv. ad *G.* 2.389, Ov. *F.* 4.785). For its use in this connection cf. Nemes. *Ecl.* 4.62ff. *quid prodest, quod me pagani mater Amyntae / ter vittis, ter fronde sacra, ter ture vaporo, / incendens vivo crepitantes sulphure lauros, / lustravit, cineresque aversa effudit in amnem, / cum sic in Meroen totis miser ignibus urar*? Sulphur may also be used here (cf. Ov. *Rem.* 260), since *taedae* were often coated with sulphur (Juv.2.157f., Claud. *Paneg. VI Cons.Hon.*324f.). For sulphur in the rite of lustration see 1.5.11-12n.

nocte serena: night was the usual time for magic rites, and the presence of the moon (another aspect of Hecate) as witness and helper was often required (Theoc. *Id.* 2.10f., Hor. *Epod.* 5.51ff., Ov. *Met.* 7.180ff., Sen. *Med.* 6f. *tacitisque praebens conscium sacris iubar / Hecate triformis*).

For *serenus* meaning 'clear, bright' cf. e.g. Enn. *Ann.* 396V, Cic. *Re Pub.* 1.15.23 *quod serena nocte subito candens et plena luna defecisset*, Virg. *G.* 1.426.

hostia pulla: *hostia* usually denoted the smaller sacrificial animals, such as sheep, and *victima* the larger ones, such as cattle (Char. *Gramm.* 403.28B *victima maior est, hostia minor*). As a general rule white victims were sacrificed to the gods of heaven and black ones to the gods of the Underworld (*magicos . . . deos*): cf. Euseb. *Praep.Evang.* 4.9.2, Arnob. *Adv.Nat.* 7.19 *quae in coloribus ratio est, ut merito his albas, illis atras conveniat nigerrimasque mactari*? etc. (on the principle of similarity, because they were dark gods: cf. Serv. ad *G.* 2.380 *victimae numinibus aut per similitudinem aut per contrarietatem immolantur: per similitudinem, ut nigrum pecus Plutoni*). So animals of a ruddy colour were sacrificed to fire-deities. Cf. also the general rule of a male animal for a god and a female for a goddess (Arnob.7.19).

The purpose of the sacrifice is probably to invoke the aid of the gods (cf. Ov. *Met.* 7.238ff., Luc.6.706ff.). For a discussion of the precise details in such sacrifices see Headlam *CR* XVI (1902), 52ff.

magicos . . . deos: also found at Luc.6.577, the phrase refers to the gods of the Underworld, esp. Hecate, Night, Dis, Erebus and the Furies (cf. Ov. *Met.* 7.192ff., 14.404f., Virg. *Aen.* 4.510f., Sen. *Med.* 740f., Luc. 6.695ff., Apul. *De Mag.* 31).

63–64 The witch had started the ceremony, but T. stopped her and continually asked her instead to make Delia love him. The correction represents a compliment to Delia and an attempt to restore the credibility of the witch (elsewhere in the poem it appears that T.'s love for Delia has not been removed). T. had gone too far in trying to ensure belief in the charm (see intro. essay).

On the power of magic to inspire love see 1.8.17-18n. For T.'s request cf. Prop. 1.1.21f. *en agedum dominae mentem convertite nostrae, / et facite illa meo palleat ore magis*, T.4.5.6, 13ff., 4.6.7f., Ov. *Met.* 14.23f., *A.P.* 5.88 (Rufinus). *Mutuus amor* was an old theme: see Leo *Plaut. Forsch.* 145 and cf. also Theoc. *Id.* 12.15f., Plaut. *Miles* 100f.

For 2w + 3w in the hexameter see 27-8n.

nec te posse carere velim: cf. Ov. *Am.* 3.11.39, *A.A.* 2.454 *quo sine non possit vivere, posse velit*, Mart.12.46.

For the omission of *ut* see 25a-26n.

65–78 T. contrasts himself, who would not wish for the ability to do without Delia (63f.), with the man who actually preferred to do without her (*posset habere* in 65 echoes *posse carere* in 64).

T. now attacks Delia's *coniunx* (65-6n.). A short criticism of his action in leaving Delia for war and booty is followed by a fuller discussion in a series of neat contrasts. In two couplets T. rejects military glory, in the next two he states his preference for a simple life in the country with Delia and the happiness that this life would bring him, and in the final two he points out that when one is not happy in love wealth is useless.

The attack on the *coniunx* and protestations of the poet's love represent a further (implicit) argument: Delia should show consideration for T., who loves her, rather than for her *coniunx*, who obviously does not. The tone changes from strong disapproval and contempt to longing to rather superior scorn.

The theme of 1.1, the opposition of an ideal rustic existence with his mistress to the soldier's life (see intro. essay to 1.1), is here repeated briefly, and there are actual echoes of 1.1.45ff., but here it is happiness in love as much as *paupertas* that is the contrast to the soldier's wealth, and the main ex. of the soldier's glory (here rejected with sarcasm) is not death but the rôle of the conquering hero. So the soldier's lack of sleep is here due to unhappiness in love rather than the rigours of military life, a topic which is totally absent from the present passage. The fact that this theme has already been handled partly explains the brevity here, but this curt dismissal of glory and wealth is in fact most effective.

65–66 See Critical Appendix.

The reference here may be to an imaginary person (*fuit* meaning 'he would have been': cf. e.g. Cic. *Verr.* 2.4.28 *hic tibi in mentem non venit iubere ut haec quoque referret HS VI milibus D se tibi vendidisse? . . . fuit tanti, mihi crede*), or to a rival (cf. 9-10n., 57-8n.). Most probably, however, T. is thinking of the *coniunx*. No rival has been definitely identified in the poem, and it is the *coniunx* rather than a rival who has been uppermost in T.'s mind since line 41, so that *ille* here (as at 55 and 58) most naturally refers to him. The whole of the succeeding passage has more point if directed against the *coniunx*, since he is T.'s main opponent for Delia's affections and it is supposed to be fear of him that most restrains Delia from opening up. The expedition may be one from which he has already returned or is about to return (hence the futures at 41 and 55ff.).

For iron as an image of lack of feeling see 1.1.63-4n. The application of *ferreus* to a soldier seems particularly apt (cf. 1.10.1-4n.). This word and the balancing *stultus* in the pentameter indicate intense disapproval of his action.

The motif of the lover / husband being separated from his mistress / wife due to a military campaign or similar official business was common in Roman poetry, and, as here, the tone is usually one of disapproval and the implication is often that the man was influenced by desire for booty: cf. esp. Prop.3.12.1ff. *Postume, plorantem potuisti linquere Gallam, / miles et Augusti fortia signa sequi? / tantine ulla fuit spoliati gloria Parthi, / ne faceres Galla multa rogante tua? / si fas est, omnes pariter pereatis avari, / et quisquis fido praetulit arma toro.* Cf. also Catull.68.79ff., Virg. *Ecl.* 10.44ff., T.1.1.51ff., 1.3, 2.6.1ff., Prop. 1.6, 3.20, 4.3, Ov. *Her.* 1, 13. This situation was also a theme of Roman and Attic comedy (e.g. Ar. *Pax* 439f., 865ff., Plautus *Amphitruo*).

67–70 A mock-heroic sketch of the glory which the *coniunx* may win and the brave figure he may cut. The sarcasm may be reinforced by the frequency of hard c and t sounds.

ille licet Cilicum victas agat ante catervas: *Cilicum* is probably a ref. to Messalla's Eastern expedition (1.7.15f.).

This action is suggestive of an epic hero (e.g. Hom. *Il.* 16.293, 394ff., 21.1ff., Virg. *Aen.* 5.265 *Demoleos cursu palantis Troas agebat*). *Catervas* denotes large numbers.

ponat et in capto Martia castra solo: the adjective seems mock-heroic (cf. 1.1.3-4n.). As Dissen points out, *ponere castra* here is the action of a general.

Capto . . . solo balances *victas . . . catervas*: note the emphasis on victory.

totus et argento contextus, totus et auro: as *contexo* can be used of making something by joining etc. or by weaving, it is not clear whether the ref. here is to gold and silver armour or to a voluminous cloak with much gold and silver woven into it (the former is more extravagant and so more pointed). In either case the tone is mock-heroic, suggesting an epic hero's arms (Hom. *Il.*6.235f., Lucian *Dial.Mer.* 13.3) or cloak (Virg. *Aen.* 5.250, 8.167). Also mock-heroic is the description of the warrior as *conspiciendus* and his horse as *celeri* in the pent.

This use of *totus* (adjective for adverb) is frequent in poetry and prose. Note the emphatic positions and repetition.

conspiciendus: appears here first as an adjective (cf. 2.3.52, 4.6.4).

For rhyme see 1.1.53-4n. Here there is rhyme in -as (67) and internal rhyme in -o (68, 69), while *equo* in 70 makes a third line ending in -o.

71–74 **ipse boves mea si tecum modo Delia possim / iungere**: *ipse* contrasts with *ille* (67), but also underlines T.'s personal involvement in the work (cf. 1.1.7 and note).

The (slow) *boves* are in contrast to the *celeri . . . equo* of 70.

in solito pascere monte pecus: for the touch of homeliness and stability cf. 1.1.43f. and n.; for the pastoral idyllic scene cf. Theoc. *Id.* 2.65f., Virg. *Ecl.* 2.28ff.

et te dum liceat teneris retinere lacertis: for the situation and the expression cf. 1.1.45-6 and notes.

mollis et inculta sit mihi somnus humo: for *mollis . . . somnus* cf. Enn. *Ann.* 368-9V, Catull.68.5, Lucr.3.112, Virg. *G.* 2.470, 3.435, Ov. *Met.* 1.685. The phrase comes from the Homeric *μαλακῷ δεδημένοι ὕπνῳ* (*Il.* 10.2 etc.).

For the idea compare 1.1.45-8, Sen. *Epist.* 90.41, Alciphron.2.4.10 *κἂν πέτραν οἰκῶμεν, εὖ οἶδα ἀφροδίσιον αὐτὴν τὸ εὔνουν ποιήσει.*

The line seems to be an adaptation of Prop.1.18.28 *inculto tramite dura quies. Incultus* when applied to the ground normally means 'uncultivated', but here, as André points out, the word suggests 'unadorned', in contrast to the comfortable bed with its rich coverlets in the following lines.

For elision in T. see Smith ad loc., Kent *TAPhA* LIV (1923), 68ff. and Platnauer 72ff. Estimates of the frequency of elision in T.I and II vary: 10.4% (Smith), 15% (Kent), 14% (Platnauer). I count 181 elisions (109 in I, 72 in II), which gives a frequency of approx. 14.5%.

75–76 For the choice of happiness in love rather than the possession of wealth cf. Theogn.1063ff., Theoc. *Id.* 8.53ff., Plaut. *Curc.* 178ff., T.1. 1.51f., 1.8.33-4n., 1.8.39f., 1.9.71f., 3.3, Hor. *Epist.* 1.6.65f., Alciphron 2.3.12f. In particular the influence of Prop.1.14.15ff. is evident here: *nam quis divitiis adverso gaudet Amore? / nulla mihi tristi praemia sint Venere! / . . . illa neque Arabium metuit transcendere limen / nec timet ostrino, Tulle, subire toro / et miserum toto iuvenem versare cubili: / quid relevant variis serica textilibus? / quae mihi dum placata aderit, non ulla verebor / regna vel Alcinoi munera despicere.* Here T. follows Prop.'s thought closely, but integrates the passage within his argument by the addition of another passage (71-4n.), changes the expression and adds new details (*Tyrio* 75, *fletu* 76, *plumae* 77, *sonitus . . . aquae* 78), which bring out even more the extravagance of the bedroom and the unhappiness of its occupant.

In the moralists too we find the idea that a luxurious bedroom is useless when the occupant is unsuccessful in love (Sen. *Prov.* 3.10, Mart. 14.147), and when fears for his wealth keep him awake (Sen. *Epist.* 90.41f., Mart.9.92, 14.162 *fraudata tumeat fragilis tibi culcita mula. / non venit ad duros pallida cura toros*).

Tyrio . . . toro: the adjective suggests wealth and luxury (1.9. 69-70n.). The ref. is to purple coverlets (cf. Catull.61.165 and see 77-8n.).

cum fletu nox vigilanda venit: for the unhappy lover's sleepless nights see 1.8.63-4n.

On this use of *venio* for *esse* see Smith and Enk on Prop.1.4.10.

77–78 On these details of the wealthy bedroom see esp. Sen. *Prov.* 3.10 (of Maecenas unhappy in love) *mero se licet sopiat et aquarum fragoribus avocet et mille voluptatibus mentem anxiam fallat, tam vigilabit in pluma quam ille* [Regulus] *in cruce.*

For feathers (used for stuffing mattresses and pillows) cf. Prop. 3.7.50, Sen. loc.cit., Pliny *N.H.* 10.54, Juv.1.159, 6.88, 10.362, Mart.9.92.4, 12.17.8.

For embroidered (*picta*) and purple (*Tyrio*, 75) coverlets cf. Lucr. 2.35, Sen. *Epist.* 90.41, Pliny *N.H.* 8.196, Juv.6.88f. *sed quamquam in magnis opibus plumaque paterna / et segmentatis dormisset parvula cunis*, Mart.2.16, 12.17.8, 14.147, Clem.Alex. *Paed.* 2.9, p.216.

The sound of running water was considered soporific (e.g. Hor. *Epod.* 2.28), and so a stream was sometimes passed through the bedroom to induce sleep: cf. Sen. *Dial.* 1.3.10, *Epist.* 100.6, Celsus 3.18.15, Stat. *Silv.* 1.3.37.

stragula: the noun occurs only at Cic. *Tusc.* 5.61 and Varro *L.L.* 5.167 before here.

soporem / . . . ducere: 'to bring sleep' (Hor. *Epod.* 14.3 *pocula Lethaeos . . . ducentia somnos, C.* 3.1.21, Ov. *Met.* 2.735).

The frequency of initial n, p and s in the couplet is remarkable, and the pentameter is an aptly rapid, dactylic line.

79–86 The transition of thought is subtle. Despite his devotion to Delia (in contrast to her *coniunx*) T. is still unhappy in love, and the fact that Venus (presumably) caused the unhappiness of the lover in the previous lines suggests that she may be responsible for his own misery. Possibly, as Dissen suggests, we are to imagine a dramatic situation here: this outburst results from the fact that the door has not been opened after the previous section.

These lines bring us back sharply to T.'s present situation. In the first two couplets T. wonders if he is guilty of impiety (he thinks it is unlikely: *num* 79, 81; cf. also *si merui* 83), and in the next two states that he is fully prepared to atone. His respect is also shown by the reverence and humility of the language employed (*Veneris magnae violavi numina* 79, *impia* 80, *incestus* 81, *sanctis* and *sancto* 82, 86, *sacratis* 84, *supplex* 85, *miserum* 86). The appeal operates on a divine and human level, since this section would also indicate to Delia the extent of his love for her (in that he is prepared to go through all this to ensure success with her). The tone is one of uncertainty and humility.

79–80 For fear of impiety cf. *A.P.* 12.140 (anon.), 141 (Meleager), Prop.2.28.9ff., T.3.5.7ff., Ov. *Her.* 21.47f., 151ff., 177ff., esp. Plaut. *Cas.* 616ff. *qua ego hunc amorem mi esse avi dicam datum / aut quot ego umquam erga Venerem inique fecerim, / quoi sic tot amanti mi obviam eveniant morae?*, Lucr.5.1222ff. *non populi gentesque tremunt, regesque superbi / corripiunt divum percussi membra timore, / nequid ob admissum foede dictumve superbe / poenarum grave sit solvendi tempus adultum?*

T. is not exact, but among the more common verbal impieties of lovers were blasphemy because of an unhappy love-affair, which seems most likely here (cf. Ov. *Am.* 3.3), perjury (1.9.2), and inordinate praise of one's mistress (Ov. *Am.* 3.2.60).

For *magnus* of deities see 1.6.47-50n.

81–82 It is not clear whether the ref. here is to two separate actions (defiling temples and stealing garlands) or to one and the same action (entering temples and then stealing garlands; *incestus* then would mean 'wicked(ly)': cf. Hor. *C.* 3.2.30). T. probably means the theft of garlands to provide gifts for Delia or (cf. 14) to be hung on her door (see 2.4.21ff.).

feror: with this meaning ('I am said') the first person is poetic but not uncommon: cf. Catull.63.68, Prop.3.9.60, T.4.7.10, Ov. *Her.* 2.82, 6.114, Stat. *Theb.* 9.436, Mart.9.28.6, Claud. *Cons. Stil.* 2.288.

Note the alliteration of s and d.

83–86 If guilty, T. would not hesitate to show the deepest humility and repentance.

procumbere: cf. Lucr.5.1198ff. *nec pietas ullast . . . procumbere humi prostratum*, Prop.3.8.12, 3.17.1, Ov. *ExP.* 2.2.122, Stat. *Silv.* 5.1.73, 163, *Theb.* 9.637f., 10.49ff., Arnob.1.49.

dare . . . oscula liminibus: cf. Cic. *Verr.* 2.4.94, Livy 45.44.20 *cum veniret in curiam, summisisse se et osculo limen curiae contigisse*, Arnob.1.49.

tellurem genibus perrepere: cf. Sen. *Vit.B.* 27.8, Cass.Dio 43.21.2, Juv.6.524ff. *inde superbi / totum regis agrum nuda ac tremibunda cruentis / erepet genibus.*

The verb first occurs here.

tundere ... caput: a sign of grief (here for his impiety): cf. Cic. *Tusc.* 3.62, Livy 25.37.9 *flere omnes repente et offensare capita*, Suet. *Aug.* 23, Lucian *De Luctu* 12.

On the arrangement of words in 86 see 1.7.25-6n.

87–96 Continuing with the theme of his present misfortunes and the idea that they may be caused by divine anger, T. turns on a bystander who is amused by them and by the poet's outburst in the previous lines and warns him that he may thus incur divine anger and similar misfortunes himself. The transition is helped by the echo of *miserum* (86) in *miseros* (89).

This is an angry attack, but the lines also show a knowledgeable dignity. The ex. of nemesis is not, as is usually the case in the *παρακλαυσίθυρον*, for the benefit of the mistress, but for a bystander who laughs at the poet. T. could hardly thus attack Delia, as she has not locked him out, and this ex. has a more general application (for anyone who slights Venus), and so fits in with the ubiquitous sentiment of the power of Venus.

Nemesis occurs elsewhere in T. at 1.4.67ff., 1.5.69ff., 1.6.77f., 1.8.71f., 77f., 1.9.11f., 13ff., 40, 53ff., 79ff. (see notes ad loc.). For this particular ex., the loveless scoffer himself in love, cf. *Hom. Hymn.* 5.45ff., *A.P.* 5.234 (Paulus Silentiarius), 12.23, 101 (Meleager), Prop. 1.7, 1.9. T.'s version takes the form of a graphic and well observed sketch. He adds novelty by making the mocker an old man (cf. Paulus Silentiarius *A.P.* 5.234), and so more ridiculous, and by details that bring out the humour of the situation. As usual in T., the punishment is apt, but here the aptness is twofold. The mocker in the ex. does all that those he mocked did and becomes an object of attention and humiliation himself. In addition, the man who laughs at T. does so because he is an *exclusus amator*: the ex. of nemesis that T. cites is that of a mocker himself locked out, the obvious implication being that this is the position in which the man who taunts T. may well find himself. For similar complexity, a progression from earlier exx. of nemesis, see intro. essay to 1.8.

87–88 See Critical Appendix.

For the advice to the mocker see 1.5.69-70n., and for the presence of the bystander in the *παρακλαυσίθυρον* see intro. essay.

caveto: see 1.8.49-50n. for the form.

non uni saeviet usque deus: for the rare dative with *saevio* cf. Plaut. *Rud.* 825, Ov. *Her.* 4.148.

Deus is probably general, but possibly refers to Venus (*deus* for *dea* is not uncommon: see *Thes.L.L.* V_1.890.16ff., and cf. 1.6.43, 1.8.7 and notes).

For the turning of the tables cf. Soph. *Trach.* 129ff., T.1.5.69ff. (and n.), Prop.1.9.23f., 2.18.21f. *saepe Cupido / huic malus esse solet, cui bonus ante fuit*, 2.25.27.

Note the solemn spondees and the emphatic positions of *caveto, mox tibi* (at end of clause and at start of line) and *non uni*.

89–90 For *vidi* and the ex. based on personal experience see 1.4.33-4n. T. depicts a common figure, the unsuccessful and ridiculous old lover: cf. Anac.5D, Aristoph. *Eccl.* 876ff., Demipho in Plaut. *Mercator*, Nicobulus and Philoxenus in Plaut. *Bacc.* V.ii, Hor. *Epod.*5.55ff., *C.* 3.15, 4.13, *A.P.* 5.234 (Paulus Silentiarius). This figure illustrates the common sentiments that love is shameful in old age (1.1.71-2n.) and worse the later it comes (Menand.235K, Prop.1.7.26, 1.13, 2.34.25ff., Ov. *Her.* 4.19). Note the emphatic position of *senem* here.

iuvenum miseros lusisset amores: see Critical Appendix.

Veneris vinclis subdere colla: on *servitium amoris* see 1.5.5-6n. For slavery to Venus see below on 97-8, and for the ref. to chains see 1.1.55-6n. (cf. esp. Prop.3.15.9f. *nec femina post te / ulla dedit collo dulcia vincla meo*).

In older authors the masc. form *collus* appears, and (according to *Thes.L.L.* III.1658.80f.) the neut. sing. *collum* does not occur until Cic. *Brut.* 313 and the pl. *colla* until Catull., Cic. *Nat.D.* and Varro *R.R.* The use of the pl. (*colla*) for sing. was frequent in poetry and first occurs at Virg. *G.* 3.421, Hor. *S.* 2.7.92. For the use of the word in imagery see *Thes.L.L.* III.1662, 67ff.

91–94 et sibi blanditias tremula componere voce: for blandishments cf. 1.1.72 and see Ov. *A.A.* 1.439ff. (on tablets), 571f. (traced in wine), 619ff. (spoken). Smith (on 1.1.72) notes the use of Greek in this connection. For the rehearsal, a good point of detail, cf. Lucr.4.1182 *et meditata diu cadat alte sumpta querela.*

Tremula neatly ridicules (cf. Hor. *C.*4.13.5f. *cantu tremulo pota Cupidinem / lentum sollicitas*).

et manibus canas fingere velle comas: *fingere* means 'arrange, groom' (cf. Plaut. *Truc.* 287, Ov. *A.A.* 1.306). For the lover's attention to his hair see 1.6.39-40n., 1.8.9-10n., and cf. esp. Hor. *Epod.* 5.57f. *senem, quod omnes rideant, adulterum / latrent Suburanae canes, / nardo perunctum.* The humour is brought out well by *canas* (cf. 1.1.72, Plaut. *Merc.* 305), and so *velle* may simply mean 'eager to', but quite possibly means 'attempt to' (cf. Cic. *Div.* 1.35, Ov. *F.* 2.262), i.e. at his age this was not easy.

stare nec ante fores puduit: i.e. he should have been ashamed (cf. 1.1.71f., 2.1.73f., Hor. *C.* 3.15.7ff. *non, si quid Pholoen, satis / et te, Chlori, decet: filia rectius / expugnat iuvenum domos*).

ancillam . . . detinuisse: for the situation cf. Ov. *Her.* 20.131f. Maids were useful for carrying messages (Ov. *Am.* 1.11, 1.12.3ff., 2.19.41, 3.1.55f.) and could lend other assistance also (Ov. *A.A.* 1.357ff., Ach.Tat.2.4.2), and so their aid was frequently sought by lovers (Ter. *Heaut.* 300f., Ov. *A.A.* 1.351ff., 2.251ff.).

medio . . . foro: i.e. in full view of everyone.

95–96 **hunc puer, hunc iuvenis turba circumterit arta**: see Critical Appendix.

The verb occurs here only in Latin literature. For *tero* so used of a crowd cf. Stat. *Silv.* 1.2.234 *omnis plebeio teritur praetexta tumultu.*

The boys and youths (sing. for pl.) throng around to get a better view (cf. Hor. *Epod.* 5.57, *C.* 4.13.22ff. *sed Cinarae breves / annos Fata dederunt, / servatura diu parem / cornicis vetulae temporibus Lycen, / possent ut iuvenes visere fervidi / multo non sine risu / dilapsam in cineres facem*). Here the old man is now himself an object of attention for the young, which is an apt reversal of situations.

despuit in molles et sibi quisque sinus: *molles . . . sinus* means 'soft clothing' (Catull.65.21, *Ciris* 250).

Spitting (esp. into the bosom) was supposed to avert evil in general (Pliny *N.H.* 28.35ff., Nicolson *HSPh* 8.23ff.), and so was done to avoid the bad omen in anything said (Plaut. *As.* 39), to protect oneself when reciting charms (53-4n.), to ward off nemesis (Theoc. *Id.* 6.39 and Gow ad loc.), to avoid contagion from lunatics and epileptics (Theophr. *Char.* 16 Ussher, Plaut. *Capt.* 550, Pliny *N.H.* 10.69, 28.35, Apul. *De Mag.* 44) and to avoid bad luck (Pliny *N.H.* 28.36). Here the spitting may be to ward off bad luck, but there is much more point if it is to avoid contagion from a lunatic (this takes the reversal of situations one stage further: more insulting and humiliating than simply laughing at the old man, the boys and youths view such behaviour at his age as that of a lunatic).

97–98 In contrast to the mocker of the above example, who scorned Venus and deserved his unhappiness, T. complains that he has never scorned her, but is nevertheless made unhappy by her. So he picks up the dominant thought of the previous lines and turns the attack on the bystander into a plea. Hurt and unable to understand, he closes the poem with a despairing supplication. It is a good touch that even now T. tries a final appeal.

For the address to Venus in the *παρακλαυσίθυρον* see intro. essay.

semper tibi dedita servit / mens mea: *servit* is in emphatic position and is reinforced by *dedita* (see 1.1.25-6n.). *Servitium amoris* (1.5.5-6n.) shows the totality of his subjection to Venus. For slavery to the love-gods cf. Eur. *Troad.* 950 (of Zeus' relationship to Aphrodite) κείνης δὲ δοῦλός ἐστι, *A.P.* 5.100 (anon.), Catull.45.14, T.1.2.90, 1.8.5f., 2.3.29f., 2.4.3f., Ov. *Am.* 1.2.17f. Here T.'s continual slavery (*semper* in emphatic position) is in contrast to the late slavery of the mocker (*post* and *senem*, 90).

quid messes uris acerba tuas?: i.e. 'why destroy your own property?' For the idea cf. Ov. *Am.* 2.9.3ff. (addressed to Amor) *quid me, qui miles numquam tua signa reliqui, / laedis, et in castris vulneror ipse meis? / cur tua fax urit, figit tuus arcus amicos?* For the expression (which looks proverbial) cf. *Frag. Com. Graec. Adesp.* 564K, Hor. *Epist.* 2.1.220 *ut vineta egomet caedam mea.* The use of *messis* at Ov. *Her.* 20.143 is similar.

Acerba brings out the cruelty of Venus: for the application of the word to her cf. 1.6.84, and for the idea see 1.9.19-20n.

3

Leo *'Zu augusteischen Dichtern' Phil. Unters. II* (Berlin, 1881), 23ff.; Elter *RhM* LXI (1906), 267ff.; Schuster *Tibull – Studien* (Vienna, 1930), 9ff., 25ff.; Hanslik *'Tibulls 1.3' Forschungen zur lat. Lit. I Festschrift K. Büchner*, 138ff.; Eisenberger *Hermes* LXXXVIII (1960), 188ff.; Wimmel *Der frühe Tibull* (München, 1968), 175ff.; Bright *Arethusa* Vol.4. No.2 (1971), 197ff.

Despite the reluctance and anxiety felt by Delia and himself, T. has accompanied Messalla on an expedition to the East as a member of his *cohors*, and he has fallen seriously ill at Corcyra. The expedition is probably that alluded to at 1.7.13ff. (see Introduction sect. 4). The poem takes the form of a series of reflections, recollections and rêveries prompted by this situation. In the first half (1-52) T. is mainly concerned with the past and the present, and gives an examination of the situation and how it arose, along with recollections of the past and prayers for safety. T. concludes that his misfortunes (and possible death) are due to the fact that because of the nature of the present age he had to go off on an expedition and thus disobey Love (21-2n., 53-6n.). In the second half (57-94) T. switches his attention to the future and imagines the happiness he will enjoy in death or life and the misery that his rival(s) will endure.

1-9 The sick poet bids farewell to Messalla and prays to Death for mercy.

9-22 Lesson to be drawn from events prior to his departure: 9-14 Delia's unwillingness for him to go; 15-20 His own unwillingness to go; 21-22 Moral.

23-34 Isis-section: 23-26 Complaint of inefficacy; 27-32 Prayer for aid; 33-34 Hope of recovery and return.

35-48 The Golden Age.
49-52 The present age and prayer for mercy to its ruler.
53-56 Transition: T.'s epitaph.
57-66 Elysium: 57-58 As a lover, T. assigns himself a place there; 59-66 Description of the place and its inhabitants.
67-82 Tartarus: 67-80 Description of the place and its inhabitants;
81-82 Any enemy of T.'s love is consigned there.
83-94 T.'s homecoming.

All sections directly refer to or arise out of the background-situation (Schuster's 'Keimzelle'), and transitions are made with care. Although the elegy falls into two main parts (see above), the transitional passage provides a strong link (53-6n.), and the sections on Elysium and Tartarus (see notes ad loc.) pick up a number of points from the Golden Age in the first part. In addition, the themes of death, travel and love recur throughout (with verbal echoes: *Mors* 4, 5, 55, 65, *ossa* 6, 54; *unda* 1, 37, cf. 78, *terra* 3, 39, 56, cf. 62, 75, *mitto* 9, 90, *via* 14, 36, cf. 50, *mare* 50, 56; *Delia* 9, 23, 29, 92, *Amor* 21, 57, 64, cf. 81, *Venus* 58, 79).

The propempticon, a poem or group of lines wishing the traveller bon voyage, is found in basic form from earliest times (Hom. *Od.* 5. 203ff., 15.125ff., Sappho 25.1f., 96.7f. D., Theognis 691f., Aristoph. *Eq.* 498ff.). The first fully developed exx. do not occur until the Hellenistic period (Callim. fr. 400Pf., Theoc. *Id.* 7.52ff., Erinna fr. 1 = Athen. 283D), and the genre was taken up by the Augustans (Prop.1.8, Hor. *Epod.* 10, *C.* 1.3, 3.27, Ov. *Am.* 2.11; so too Stat. *Silv.* 3.2). For fuller refs. and discussion see Quinn *Latin Explorations* (London, 1963), 239ff., Nisbet & Hubbard's introduction to Horace *C.* 1.3, Cairns *Generic Composition in Greek and Roman Poetry* (Edinburgh, 1972), index s.v. propempticon.

With the exception of Statius, no latin version is a propempticon pure and simple: Propertius and Ovid combine the genre with love-poetry, and Horace adds a tirade on inventiveness (*C.* 1.3), a cautionary tale (*C.* 3.27) and in *Epod.* 10 completely reverses the normal sentiments by wishing the traveller a bad journey. T.1.3 is another example of this adaptation of the usual form.

The poem begins with a brief, conventional propempticon addressed to Messalla (1-2n.). However, in the rest of the poem also there are details frequently connected with the propempticon whose number is too large for coincidence but must mean a conscious and deliberate adaptation.

It was normal in the propempticon to make some mention of the feelings and actions of the person left behind, but here the poem is almost totally devoted to this person (i.e. Tibullus), and many features of the propempticon are applied to his situation. So the reference to signs for the voyage (Hor. *Epod.* 10.1, *C.* 3.27.1ff., Stat. *Silv.* 3.2.51f.) is made concerning T.'s own voyage to Corcyra (11ff.), and the diatribe against navigation (Horace *C.* 1.3.9ff., Ov. *Am.* 2.11.1ff., Stat. *Silv.* 3.2.61ff.: probably belongs to the traditional σχετλιασμός, see Nisbet & Hubbard p. 43) is delivered with regard to this same journey (37ff.). So, instead of the customary description of the hazards of the voyage facing the traveller (Hor. *Epod.* 10.3ff., *C.* 3.27.17ff., Prop. 1.8.1ff., Ov. *Am.* 2.11.7ff., Stat. *Silv.* 3.2.71ff.), T. concentrates on the dangers facing himself (illness and death), and, instead of the prayer to deities to help the traveller (Sappho 25.1f.D, Theognis 692, Aristoph. *Eq.* 499f., Hor. *Epod.* 10.21ff., *C.* 1.3.1ff., Prop. 1.8.17f., Ov. *Am.* 2.11.33ff., Stat. *Silv.* 3.2.1ff.), T. begs divine aid for himself (27ff., 51). Similarly in place of the voyager's homecoming (Sappho 25.1D, Aristoph. *Eq.* 500ff., Ov. *Am.* 2.11.39ff., Stat. *Silv.* 3.2.127ff.) we find T. wishing for a happy return for himself (33f., 89ff.). T. has realized the poetic possibilities inherent in the background-situation of the poem (one that is unique in surviving elegy), in which he has just made a voyage himself and is experiencing the fears and hopes usually felt by a person at sea. So the propempticon is adapted and applied to the person being left behind, and T. produces an original reversal of the propempticon, which contrasts with the brief, conventional propempticon at the opening of the poem.

There does seem to be allusion to Odysseus in 1.3, but not as extensively as some scholars maintain (see Eisenberger, Bright loc. cit.). T.'s circumstances are similar to those of the hero (in Corcyra while on military service, and separated from his family and beloved), a fact which probably explains in part the use of *Phaeacia* for Corcyra (3-4n.). So too at 83ff., when T. pictures his return to Delia, he may have in mind Odysseus' νόστος and Penelope (Delia's occupation is the same as Penelope's during her husband's absence (e.g. Hom. *Od.* 1.356f.), and Delia also is to remain chaste and not give in to rivals). But the allusion goes no further. Other suggested similarities (see esp. Bright) are coincidental, insignificant or fanciful, and there are too many details in the elegy which do not fit in with an extended parallel.

At 23ff. we find the first mention in T. of oriental divinities (Isis). The others to which he refers are Cybele (1.4.67ff.), Bellona (1.6.45ff.), Astarte (1.7.17f.) and Osiris (1.7.27ff.). T.'s interest in them declines rapidly: they appear in four poems only and are never mentioned again after 1.7. The passage on Isis suggests mixed feelings: T. shows scepticism but represents himself as so desperate for help that he will accept it from any quarter, although his personal preference is for his native gods. So at 1.7.27ff., where he again seems to come quite close to accepting an oriental divinity, the inventions that he credits Osiris with are the same as those ascribed to the *ruris deos* of 2.1, and he identifies Osiris with Bacchus. That passage is rather literary, contains echoes of Callimachus and is included for poetical effect rather than as a tribute to the god (see intro. essay to 1.7). So at 1.7.17f. T. uses Astarte to make a learned allusion, and at 1.4.67ff. the passage on Cybele-worship is probably derived from Callimachus. He makes similar use of Bellona at 1.6.43ff. (to give a warning to rivals and frighten Delia). Literary reminiscence plays an important part in T.'s refs. to these oriental deities, and they are used to add interest and variety to his poetry.

T.'s version of the Golden Age (35-48) should be compared with 1.10.1ff. and 2.3.69ff. The earliest account of the Ages occurs in Hesiod, who gives five (Gold, Silver, Bronze, Heroes and Iron), but the most common version was of four (the metals), although the number was sometimes reduced to two, as here (49-52n.). Refs. to the Ages occur in most genres of poetry (Hes. *Opera* 109ff., Telekleides fr.1K, Aratus *Phaen.* 108ff., Virg. *Ecl.* 4, *G.* 1.125ff., 2.536ff., Ov. *Am.* 3.8.35ff., *Met.* 1.89ff., 15.96ff., *Aetna* 9ff., Juv.6.1ff., Sen. *Phaed.* 525ff., *Med.* 309ff., *Oct.* 395ff., Manil.1.66ff., 77ff., Claud. *Ruf.* 1.380ff., *Rapt. Pros.* 3.19ff.), are not uncommon in philosophers and moralists (Emped.128D, Plat. *Polit.* 271Cff., cf. Lucr.5.925ff., Sen. *Epist.* 90.36ff.), and occur even in historians (Dion.Hal.1.36, Diod.Sic.5.66, Justin.43.13). T.'s version contains ideas found in various accounts (see commentary), but he adds a few innovations (the absence of tamed horses and doors). On its relevance to the poem see 35-48n.

Critics have seldom failed to be charmed and moved by this elegy: Dissen, for instance, refers to it as a '*pulchrum carmen*', while Ponchont remarks 'une de ses plus belles oeuvres . . . Poésie profondément humaine en somme, par cette tristesse et cette inquiétude . . . ' Certainly the sections on the Golden Age, Elysium and T.'s return to Delia are delightful vignettes, and the opening lines with their sad music also have their own beauty (cf. Lee 10f.). So too this is a poem of mood and atmosphere, a poem of feeling: along with the grim realities of the present, there is wistfulness for the past and uncertainty as to the future (even regarding Delia); melancholy, angst, doubt and fear are evident, as well as reproach, hope and yearning; the poem is constantly punctuated by wishes, appeals and prayers (2, 4, 5, 27f., 33f., 51, 53f., 81, 83ff., 93f.). Yet 1.3 has qualities of a more technical nature too. The whole elegy is an interesting and ingenious innovation in genre. The passages on the Golden Age, Elysium and Tartarus, in addition to their descriptive merits, have subtle point and undertones (see notes ad loc.). The poem is also noteworthy for its scholarship, exhibiting literary, religious and mythological *doctrina* to an extent unusual in T. Several whole sections are full of such learning, while the accounts of Isis and Elysium are both firsts in Roman poetry (see notes ad loc.). These various details (and the emotions mentioned above) form a colourful and piquant mixture, and there is a careful arrangement to produce antithesis and correspondence: esp. (within the compass of one poem) contemporary Roman funeral and divinatory procedures, the rites of oriental Isis, various Graeco-Roman deities and personifications, the traditional Italian household-gods, Graeco-Roman notions about the Ages and eschatology; parallelism between the prayers to Death, Isis and Jupiter (4f., 27ff., 51); parallelism between the Golden Age and Elysium (57-66n.); contrast between Tartarus and both the former passages (67-82n.); contrast between the opening and conclusion of the elegy (83-94n.); contrast again between the first part of the poem, concerned mainly with the past and present, and the second half, concerned mainly with the future (see above). Thus 1.3 is a delicate combination of scholarship and sensitivity.

1–9 This section gives the background-situation: while accompanying Messalla on an expedition T. has fallen ill on Corcyra and fears for his life. It opens the poem with a mood of anxiety, gloom and desolation (esp. Death, T.'s funeral and the absence of loved ones to mourn him), reinforced by anaphora (*abstineas . . . Mors* 4, 5; *non . . . quae* 5f., 7, 9) and by assonance and alliteration (i, ae, m, a at 1-5).

1–2 These lines form a miniature version of the propempticon (see intro. essay) and contain two common features of the genre: the speaker is being left (so always, but here because T. is ill) and asks to be remembered (cf. Sappho 96.7-8D, Ov. *Am.* 2.11.37, Hor. *C.* 3.27.14 *et memor nostri, Galatea, vivas*).

ibitis: plural because Messalla's *cohors* is also included: cf. Hom. *Od.* 2.310, Virg. *Aen.* 9.525 and see Fordyce on Cat.39.20.

o utinam memores ipse cohorsque mei: for *o utinam* cf. Prop. 1.3.39, 1.8.9, 1.16.27, Ov. *Am.* 2.5.7, *Met.* 1.363, Val.Fl. 1.113, 7.135, 8.439. Hiatus after interjections is common in elegy (Platnauer 57).

This omission of the verb is not unusual: cf. Ter. *Ad.* 518, Cic. *Fam.* 12.25.5, *Att.* 13.22.4, Stat. *Silv.* 4.6.17, Tac. *Ann.* 1.58.

For the recurrence of wishes etc. see intro. essay.

On the uses of *cohors* see *Thes. L. L.* III.1552.57ff., *OLD* s.v. 4 and 5, Fordyce on Cat.10.10. The *cohors* (*praetoria, praetoriana, praetoris*) was originally the bodyguard of a Roman general (Paul.ex Fest.223 *praetoria cohors est dicta, quod a praetore non discedebat. Scipio enim Africanus primus fortissimum quemque delegit, qui ab eo in bello non discederent et cetero munere militiae vacarent et sesquiplex stipendium acciperent*). The term was extended to refer also to the retinue of friends attached to a provincial governor (Cic. *Q. Frat.* 1.1.12 *quos . . . ex domesticis convictionibus aut ex necessariis apparitionibus tecum esse voluisti, qui quasi ex cohorte praetoris appellari solent*). Here by a further extension *cohors* seems to be applied to the retinue of friends attached to a person travelling abroad in some other official capacity (Messalla's exact status here is not clear): cf. Hor. *Epist.* 1.3.6, 1.8.14 (of the retinue of Tiberius Claudius, sent by Augustus to place Tigranes on the throne of Armenia), Suet. *Galba* 7 (the emperor's *cohors amicorum*). Men of literary tastes included poets and writers in their *cohors* (Catull. 10, Hor. *Epist.* 1.3, 1.8).

3–4 **Phaeacia**: Corcyra was identified as the land of the Phaeacians (cf. Thuc. 1.25, Pf. on Call. *Aet.* fr. 13 and 14, Pliny *N.H.* 4.52 *Corcyra . . . Homero dicta Scheria et Phaeacia*). The word first appears here in Latin, and the mythological ref. stands out because such refs. are rare in T. The similarity of the background-situation to that of Odysseus probably suggested the use of *Phaeacia* here (see intro. essay). The mythological term, rather than the more mundane geographical name, also tends to make Corcyra seem more remote (Eisenberger loc. cit. intro. essay).

abstineas avidas Mors modo nigra manus: see Critical Appendix. *Abstineas* is jussive (1.2.9-10n.). For *modo* meaning 'only, just' in commands or requests see *OLD* s.v. 1b and cf. Cic. *Orat.* 136 *tantum modo notetur locus*, T.3.6.9 *vos modo proposito dulces faveatis amici.*

For *niger* as an epithet of *Mors* see Stat. *Theb.* 9.851 (cf. also Sil. It. 13.560). Darkness is traditionally associated with Death and 'black' is a common epithet: Pind. *Pyth.* 11.56f. *μέλανος ὅγ' ἐσχατιὰν / καλλίονα θανάτοι' ἔσχεν*, Eur. *Tro.* 1315, *A.P.* 7.646.3f. (Anyte), 5-8n. So parts of Death's person and apparel are black (Eur. *Alc.* 843, Hor. *S.* 2.1.58, Ov. *Am.* 3.9.20; cf. 1.1.69-70n.).

For the greed of Death cf. *A.P.* 7.476.7f. (Meleager), T.1.3.65, Sen. *Oed.* 164f. *Mors atra avidos oris hiatus / pandit.*

The prayer has parallels at 27f. and 51f. (see intro. essay).

T.'s concentration throughout on the dangers facing him is similar to the description of the traveller's hazards in the propempticon (see intro. essay).

5–8 For this fear of death in a foreign land, alone and unmourned by loved-ones, cf. *A.P.* 7.259 (Plato), Catull. 68.93ff., Ov. *Her.* 10.119ff., *Tr.* 3.3.37ff., *ExP.* 1.2.57f.

For the poet's own funeral see 1.1.59-60n. When the pyre was burnt down, it was extinguished with water or wine. The chief mourners collected the bones and ashes, sprinkled them with wine and milk, dried them in a linen cloth and placed them in an urn or box with perfumes and spices. The urn was then placed in a sepulchre, or a monument was raised above it (see 3.2.9ff., Prop. 2.13.17ff., 2.24.35, 50, 4.1.127, Ov. *Tr.* 3.3.65, 69, Suet. *Calig.* 15). For the bones gathered in the folds of dress cf. T.3.2.18, Luc. 9.60, and for weeping see 1.1.61-2n. On loosing of hair see 1.1.67-8n.

See Introduction sect. 3 for T.'s mother and sister.

abstineas: jussive (1.2.9-10n.) in parataxis to *precor*. For the construction cf. Hor. *C.* 1.3.7, Ov. *F.* 4.247 and see Handford *The Latin Subjunctive* 24ff., 42f., 49ff. Elsewhere in T. the construction occurs at 1.2.12, 1.3.83, 1.6.56, 1.9.40.

atra: an emotive word, with connotations of 'ill-omened' and 'terrible', frequently applied to Death (1.10.33, Hor. *C.* 1.28.13, Stat. *Theb.* 4.528, Sen. *Oed.* 164; cf. Hor. *S.* 2.1.58).

non hic mihi mater: on hex. endings see Smith. Note also that on ten occasions in I and II a monosyllable is found at the end of the hex. (usually *est* in elision making a disyllabic or trisyllabic word-group). Once (1.4.63) *ni sint* occurs at the end, where the two monosyllables combine to form a disyllabic word-group.

in maestos . . . sinus: either 'sorrowing bosom' (cf. Ov. *Am.* 2.6.5, *F.* 4.854) or 'funeral dress' (cf. Prop.3.6.13). The latter meaning is perhaps more likely in view of the imitation at 3.2.17f.

Assyrios cineri quae dedat odores: *Assyrios* stands for *Syrios* (Catull. 66.12, 68.144, Virg. *Ecl.* 4.25, Hor. *C.* 2.11.16). For the perfumes of Syria see Gow on Theoc. *Id.* 15.114, Ellis on Catull.6.8. There were Italian and Greek perfumes, but the finer and more costly ones were imported from the East, where the main centres of the perfume industry were (cf. Plin. *N.H.* 13.1ff.). So the adjective implies quality and expense, as is fitting for a loved one.

Dedat here is used rather strangely. The meaning seems to be 'give, assign' (cf. Plaut. *Most.* 498 *hic habito, haec mihi dedita est habitatio, Bacc.* 1150, Mart.4.64.34 *uni dedite Setiam colono*), although there is no parallel for *dedo* with this sense used in the context of a funeral.

ante sepulcra: *sepulcrum* can be used of a pyre (Ter. *Andr.* 128) as well as a tomb. Either meaning is possible here (*ante . . . rogum* occurs at 3.2.12). *Sepulcra* may be plur. for sing. (Smith compares 1.1.67 and *funera* at Prop.2.1.56), but, if *sepulcra* means 'tombs', the plural may be genuine and refer to ancestors' tombs.

9–22 Delia is mentioned last for emphasis and to facilitate transition (which takes place smoothly within a line), and her forebodings here pick up T.'s anxiety and circumstances in the opening section.

Reminiscences about Delia's (6 lines) and his own (6 lines) behaviour at the time of their separation lead to a conclusion on the cause of his present misfortune (21-2). There is a contrast between the favourable predictions of T.'s return that she was given and the unfavourable signs that T. invented, but a clear parallelism between the unwillingness of both of them for the journey to take place. The reminiscences reflect T.'s own uncertainty as to his future (hope of return combined with anxious apprehensiveness).

9–10 For the lover separated from his mistress on official business see 1.2.65-6n.

Delia non usquam: *Delia* is emphatic by position, and *non usquam* picks up and intensifies *non hic* (5).

mitteret: 'let me leave' (cf. Catull.64.221, 66.29 *maesta virum mittens*).

dicitur: i.e. her behaviour was noticed and commented upon.

omnes: in her anxiety to make sure. There is emphasis on the optimism of all the predictions (cf. *ter*, 11, *cuncta* and the imperfect, 13) – her fear despite this shows the extent of her love for T.

11–12 Lot was one of the most common methods of divination in Italy (also found in Greece: Eur. *Hipp.* 1057 and schol.) and was connected with various temples, esp. those at Praeneste (Cic. *Div.* 2.85), Caere (Livy 21.62.5), Falerii (Livy 22.1.11), Clitumnus (Pliny *Ep.* 8.8.) and near Patavium (Suet. *Tib.* 14). There were wandering *sortilegi* (Apul. *Met.* 9.8), and in Rome they plied their trade esp. in the Circus (Cic. *Div.* 1.132, Hor. *S.* 1.6.114, Juv.6.582f.). The lots were made of various materials, including wood and metal, with ambiguous signs or words inscribed on them (e.g. Livy 22.1.11 *Mavors telum suum concutit*, Apul. *Met.* 9.8 *ideo coniuncti terram proscindunt boves, / ut in futurum laeta germinent sata*). They were shuffled in a container, drawn out individually and interpreted by the *sortilegus*. In the present passage Delia herself draws out the lots (cf. Juv.6.582f., schol. on Pind. *Pyth.* 4.337), but elsewhere a boy is employed for this purpose (Cic. *Div.* 2.86; cf. Lucian *Hermot.* 57).

sacras . . . sortes ter sustulit: for the verb used of drawing lots see Pease on Cic. *Div.* 2.86.

Three was a sacred and lucky number (1.2.53-4n.), and so *ter* (like *sacras*) emphasizes the solemnity and reliability of the drawing of the lots.

illi / rettulit e triviis omina certa puer: see Critical Appendix.

The words *e triviis . . . puer* are generally taken together. Némethy explains this phrase as '*puer qui in triviis vaticinari solet*', but, as is shown by the paraphrase itself, *in triviis* would be more normal than *e triviis.* Otherwise the phrase is explained as a synonym for *ignotus*, but this seems an odd way of expressing the idea. In any case, the intrusion of two words between *e triviis* and *puer* makes the expression even more obscure, and, if any qualification at all of *puer* is desirable, it most probably would have been made in line 11, when the *puer* was first mentioned. *E triviis*, then, should not be taken with *puer.*

It seems more likely that the boy reported clear omens (an *omen* was a sign taken from utterances or actions: Cic. *Div.* 1.102ff., 2.83f.) that he had picked up at the *trivia* (the *trivia* presumably because they were crowded places full of people talking). The boy may have been sent there to pick up omens, as Dissen suggests (for the deliberate seeking of *omina* cf. Cic. *Div.* 1.104 and Pease ad loc.), or he may simply mention some omens that he happened to pick up there.

The mention of such signs here and in the following lines is similar to references to signs for the voyage common in the propempticon (see intro. essay).

13–14 See Critical Appendix.

cuncta dabant reditus: on *cuncta* see 1.4.75-8n. Note the emphatic position.

For *dare* meaning 'promise' cf. Lucan 5.107f. (of an oracle) *saepe dedit sedem totas mutantibus urbes, / ut Tyriis.* Note the continuous force of the imperfect.

Reditus is either plural for singular (cf. Hor. *C.* 3.5.52) or distributive plural (cf. Ov. *F.* 1.279).

numquam: the word may pick up the idea at 10ff. of the many consultations and predictions of a safe return, or it may be an emphatic negative ('by no means': cf. Ter. *Ad.* 528, Virg. *Ecl.* 3.49). The word is emphatic by position.

quin: for *quin* with *deterreo* see *Thes. L.L.* V_1.808.13ff.

fleret . . . respiceretque: apparently a ὕστερον πρότερον.

For *respicio* meaning 'view with alarm' cf. Caes. *B.G.* 8.27, *B.C.* 1.5.2, Cic. *Planc.* 38.91, Sen. *H.O.* 656, Tac. *Ann.* 1.31.5.

nostras: stands for *meas* (1.2.11-12n.).

vias: military (1.1.25-6n.).

15–16 ipse ego solator . . . / quaerebam: note the emphatic position of *ipse ego. Solator* first occurs here and is rare (cf. Stat. *Silv.* 5.5.40 *ille ego lugentum mitis solator*).

For phrases combining agent noun and finite verb to express the force of two verbs (here *solabar et quaerebam*) cf. 1.6.27f., Ov. *Met.* 5.137f. *torquet in hunc hastam calido de vulnere raptam / ultor Abantiades, Ibis* 154 *et tendam gelidas ultor in ora manus*, Val.Fl.3.308, Petron. *S.* 122 v.168, Sil.It.16.621.

cum iam mandata dedissem: i.e. on the very point of leaving, since *mandata* are the final instructions prior to departure (Ov. *Her.* 13.7, 15.105, *Tr.* 1.3.59).

quaerebam tardas anxius usque moras: for the lover's excuses for delay cf. Ov. *Her.* 5.49, *Rem.* 213ff., *Met.* 11.461, the arguments employed by Dido at *Her.* 7.73ff., 169ff.

Tardas is active (1.1.7-8n.).

The imperfect and *usque* (cf. *quotiens*, 19) underline T.'s continuous attempts to delay.

17–18 aut ego sum causatus aves aut omina dira: see Critical Appendix.

The first *aut* goes with the second *aut*, not with line 16.

For *causatus* ('gave as an excuse') cf. Prop.4.4.23, Ov. *Met.* 9.767f.

For omens when starting a journey (including birds) cf. Ov. *Met.* 10. 452f., Val.Max.1.4.2, esp. Hor. *C.* 3.27.1-16. T. may be referring to omens that bode ill in general for the journey, or specifically to signs of bad weather (cf. Cic. *Div.* 1.14f. and Pease ad loc., Virg. *G.* 1.373ff.), or to both.

Saturnive sacram me tenuisse diem: see Critical Appendix.

Teneo here means 'detain, hold back'.

Saturni . . . diem is the first Latin ex. of the expression from which the English 'Saturday' is derived (cf. Frontin. *Strat.* 2.1.17, Tert. *Apol.* 16, Marc. *Med.* 2.13; in Greek *Κρόνου ἡμέρα*: Dio.Cass.37.16.2, 37.17. 3, 49.22.4, 66.7.2).

The reason why this day might compel T. to stay is usually explained in terms of Jewish belief: the Sabbath was the day on which Jews refrained from work, and some Romans followed this practice (Juv.14. 96, 105f., Porph.ad Hor. *S.* 1.9.69), or at least regarded it as an unlucky day (Hor. *S.* 1.9.69, Ov. *A.A.* 1.415f., *Rem.* 219f., Pers.5.184).

However it is also possible that T. has in mind astrology. Astrologers divided the sidereal month of 28 days into 4 weeks of 7 days. Sun, Moon, Mars, Mercury, Jupiter, Venus and Saturn were supposed to be rulers of the first 7 of the 24 hours of a day and thereafter of each successive set of 7 hours in turn. Each day was named after the planet that ruled its first hour, thus producing the 7 day planetary week. Saturn in astrology was a malefic influence, and when he ruled hours and days everything was supposed to be unlucky and dubious and journeys to turn out badly. See Prop.4.1.84, Hor. *C.* 2.17.23, Lucan 1. 652, Juv.6.569f., Boll, Bezold & Gundel *Sternglaube und Sterndeutung* (Darmstadt, 1974), 179ff., F. H. Colson *The Week* (1926).

19–20 A progression from the previous lines: here T. has actually started his journey (a real last second delay).

Stumbling in general was considered a bad omen (Cic. *Div.* 2.84 *quae si suscipiamus, pedis offensio nobis et abruptio corrigiae et sternumenta erunt observanda*, Val.Max.1.4.2), but esp. so at the threshold or, as here, city gate when setting off (see Pease on Cic.loc.cit. and Austin on *Aeneid* 2.242).

tristia . . . / . . . signa: for *tristis* used of warning signs and omens cf. Sen. *H.F.* 688, Tac. *Ann.* 15.7, Sil.It.2.54, 9.258, 16.271.

21–22 By a neat personification of the feelings of Delia and himself prior to his departure T. finds an explanation for his present misfortunes and points a moral (picked up at 49ff.: see intro. essay). Delia was afraid for T.'s safety (9ff.) and he was unwilling to leave (15ff.) because they were in love, i.e. Love was unwilling that the journey should take place. Therefore in making the journey T. was disobeying Love, and his present situation is described as a punishment for this bold disobedience, since Love is a god and must be obeyed (1.6.29-30n.). This idea is underlined by the balance between *invito . . . discedere Amore* and *egressum . . . prohibente deo* (*deo* left to the end for emphasis). For the lover's misfortunes viewed as a result of divine punishment cf. 1.2.79-80n.

23–34 *Nunc* points to the main connection in thought, T.'s present illness (implied in 21f.), and T. continues with recollection (still with reference to Delia) and blame of a deity.

The section on Isis consists of a series of contrasts: firstly T. complains that Delia's worship of Isis in general has been useless (23-6), then he himself prays to the goddess to help him, in view of a particular vow for his safety made by Delia (27-32), and finally he voices the wish to return home and worship his household-gods, in contrast to Delia's worship of Isis (33-4).

The section adds colour to the poem (see intro. essay: this is the first detailed mention of Isis in Latin poetry), and its forceful expression, contrasts and fluctuations of mood are expressive of the poet's psychological state.

23–24 For oriental gods in T. see intro. essay. For Isis see esp. Plut. *De Iside et Osiride*, Apul. *Met.* 11 (with the commentary of Griffiths = *The Isis-Book* Leiden, 1975) and Witt *Isis in the Graeco-Roman World* (London, 1971). In Egyptian mythology Isis was the wife and sister of Osiris and the mother of Horus. Her names and functions were infinite, and she was identified with many Greek and Roman goddesses, esp. Io (Apul. *Met.* 11.2, 5, 25, Witt op.cit. chap. 9). Her worship entailed much abstinence and purification (see below). There were two daily services (31-2n.) and two annual festivals: the *Isidis navigium* on March 5th, in which after a procession to the sea the sacred ship was launched, and the autumn festival, in which the loss of Osiris was mourned and his recovery celebrated (Plut. *Is. et Os.* 39, Juv. 8.29ff. and schol.). Isis was introduced at Rome *sub illis Syllae temporibus* (Apul. *Met.* 11.30), where after initial official opposition she eventually became a favourite with later Roman emperors (Witt op.cit. chap. 17). To judge from the frequent refs. to her in elegy she particularly attracted women, but it is not until Joseph. *Ant.* 18.66ff., Juv. 6.489, 526f. that we hear of Roman noblewomen and ladies showing interest in her. The other elegists' mistresses were devotees (25-6n.) and at this period Isis seems to have appealed to the demi-monde.

Note the vigorous repetitions of *quid* (also in 25), *tua* and *mihi*, and the juxtaposition (*Isis mihi*).

illa tua totiens aera repulsa manu: *aera* (see 1.8.21-2n.) probably refers to the *sistrum* or 'rattle', in view of Ovid's ref. to these lines at *Am.* 3.9.33f. (*quid nunc Aegyptia prosunt / sistra?*). The rattle was usually made of brass (Apul. *Met.* 11.4, 10) and was shaped like a tennis-racquet, with a circular top through which were passed bars which made a rattling and tinkling noise when shaken (Witt op.cit., plate 39, Plut. *Is. et Os.* 63). It was a characteristic symbol of Isis and was carried by her (Apul. *Met.* 11.4, Serv. ad *Aen.* 8.696), by her priests (Pers. 5.186,

Apul. *Met.* 11.6, 12) and by devotees (Ov. *A.A.* 3.635 *cum sedeat Phariae sistris operata iuvencae*, Apul. *Met.* 11.10).

The *sistrum* was shaken, not struck. By a slight extension of meaning *repello* is applied to this action: the verb is used in the sense of 'push away' (in view of *totiens* the prefix probably does not have iterative force: cf. Ov. *Met.* 2.157, 6.661, 9.164), which is basically the movement repeated when shaking a rattle.

25–26 With *quidve* supply *prodest* (from *prosunt* in 23), on which *lavari* and *secubuisse* depend. The rueful *memini* is parenthetical. There is probably no distinction between the tenses of the infinitives (1.1. 29-30n.).

Bathing was undertaken both by devotees (Apul. *Met.* 11.23 *sueto lavacro* and Griffiths ad loc.) and by priests (Hdt. 2.37).

The verb *secubo* is only found at Catull. 61.101 before here. The ref. is to the period of sexual abstinence lasting ten days and nights (Prop. 2.33.1f. *tristia iam redeunt iterum sollemnia nobis: / Cynthia iam noctes est operata decem*, Juv. 6.535f., Apul. *Met.* 11.30, Griffiths op. cit. p. 290, 355f.), which is mentioned elsewhere in elegy at Prop. 2.33, 4.5.34, Ov. *Am.* 1.8.74, 3.9.34.

Purity (note the emphasis in *pureque . . . / . . . puro*) was a prime requirement in Isis-worship (Plut. *Is. et Os.* 4f.) and in religious ceremonial in general (e.g. Hom. *Il.* 1.449, 6.266, 9.171, 24.302ff., Hes. *Opera* 724f., Soph. *O.C.* 469f. (and Jebb ad loc.), T. 1.10.24, 27, 2.1. 11ff., Livy 1.45.6).

27–28 The prayer to Isis is parallel to those to Death (4f.) and Jupiter (51). For the recurrence of prayers etc. see intro. essay. For a Roman of this period (esp. such an apparent champion of old Italian deities as T.) to appeal to Isis for personal help suggests desperation (see intro. essay; reinforced by the repetition of *nunc* and the alliteration esp. of n and t). T.'s prayer here is similar to the prayer for aid for the traveller in the propempticon (see intro. essay).

Isis was renowned for her omniscience in pharmacology and her great powers of healing. Mythological exx. of these powers are Osiris and Horus. See also Diod. Sic. 1.25.2, Ov. *Am.* 2.13.7ff., Witt op. cit. chap. 14.

(nam posse mederi / picta docet templis multa tabella tuis): with *posse* supply *te*. The ref. is to votive paintings hung up in her temples as thank-offerings for cures. Similar paintings are mentioned elsewhere and, as here, used as proofs of the particular deity's power (Cic. *Nat. D.* 3.89 and Pease, Ov. *F.* 3.268 and Frazer). Juvenal alludes to the great number of votive paintings to Isis at 12.28 (*pictores quis nescit ab Iside pasci?*), and many exx. of these and similar representations have been found (Witt op. cit., p. 196).

29–30 Rather than hymns of praise, which are mentioned at 31, most probably *votivas . . . voces* refers to prayers (cf. Virg. *G.* 4.505 *quo fletu*

Manis, quae numina voce moveret?). A *votum* was a promise to the gods to do a particular thing or things for them, if a particular favour is granted (see *Oxford Classical Dictionary* s.v. *votum*): here Delia had apparently promised prayers to Isis in return for T.'s safety (probably prayers in thanksgiving, as Némethy suggests), as well as hymns of praise (*tibi dicere laudes / . . . debeat*, 31f.). For the promise to a deity of something in return for a service see 1.4.1-2n.

Linen was worn by Isis herself (Ov. *A.A.* 1.77, *ExP.* 1.1.51f., Apul. *Met.* 11.3), and by her priests (Hdt.2.37, Juv.6.533, Mart.12.29.19) and devotees (Apul.*Met.* 11.23, 24 *byssina quidem sed floride depicta veste conspicuus*), again for the sake of purity (Plut. *Is. et Os.* 4).

A sitting position was normal for worshippers of Isis (see Postgate *Selections*), but here, since daily services took place within the temple (for refs. see on *bisque die*, 31-2), the ref. seems to be either to Delia waiting outside for the opening of the temple in her eagerness (cf. Apul. *Met.* 11.20 *sic anxius et in proventum prosperiorem attonitus templi matutinas apertiones opperiebar*), or to her saying her prayers outside, to give public testimony to the power of the goddess (cf. Ov. *ExP.* 1.1.51ff. *vidi ego linigerae numen violasse fatentem / Isidis Isiacos ante sedere focos. / . . . talia caelestes fieri praeconia gaudent / ut sua quid valeant numina teste probent*).

On the arrangement of words in the hex. see 1.7.25-6n.

31–32 **bisque die**: there were two regular daily services, one in the morning (Apul. *Met.* 11.20) and one in the afternoon (Mart.2.14.8, 10.48.1).

resoluta comas: the general rule in service to the gods (see Pease on Virg. *Aen.* 4.509).

insignis: because of her beauty.

Pharia: a learned epithet, first found here. Pharos was an island near the entrance to the harbour of Alexandria, so the adjective means 'Egyptian'. Subsequently the word is often applied to Isis-worship: cf. Ov. *A.A.* 3.635, *ExP.* 1.1.38, Mart.10.48.1, Stat. *Silv.* 5.3.244f. *ut Pharios aliae ficta pietate dolores / Mygdoniosque colunt* (cf. also *Phariacus* at Apul. *Met.* 2.28).

33–34 *At mihi* is probably in contrast to Delia, although *at* may simply add urgency and emphasis (for this use of *at* in prayers, invocations, imprecations etc. see Jocelyn on Ennius *Trag.* frag.150, Austin on Virg. *Aen.* 2.535).

T. desires to come home and live on (*Lar* and *Penates* are often used as synonyms for 'home' (e.g. Cic. *Pro Quinct.* 26.83, Apul. *Met.* 11.17), and *celebro* suggests repeated action, as Smith points out), and he also states his preference for Roman religion (*patrios . . . Penates* is in contrast to Egyptian Isis, the simple monthly offering of incense to the more exotic and frequent worship of Isis, and *antiquo . . . Lari* to the more recently arrived goddess). For the recurrence of wishes etc. see intro. essay. The mention of a homecoming is a conventional feature of the propempticon (see intro. essay).

This is a particularly poignant appearance of the household-gods, as Putnam points out. *Lari* refers to the *Lar familiaris* (cf. Plaut. *Aul.*2). The *Lar* was guardian of the household (1.1.19-20n.), while the *Penates* were gods of the store-cupboard (*penus*) in charge of the family's food. These household-gods were worshipped in close connection and are often mentioned together (e.g. Plaut. *Merc.* 834, 836, Cic. *Re Pub.* 5. 7.). For *patrius* and *antiquus* applied to them cf. 1.10.15, Prop.4.1.91, Ov. *Her.* 3.67, *Tr.* 4.8.22.

For the offering of incense cf. Plaut. *Aul.*24, 385f., Hor. *C.* 3.23.2ff. *nascente luna, rustica Phidyle, / si ture placaris et horna / fruge Lares.* Offerings were made to the Lares at fixed periods of the month, and also on holidays and on any special domestic occasion: cf. Cato *Ag. Cult.* 143 *Kalendis, Idibus, Nonis, festus dies cum erit, coronam in focum indat, per eosdemque dies lari familiari pro copia supplicet*, Hor. loc. cit., Prop. 4.3.53f.

Reddo is often used of offerings to the gods (e.g. Virg. *G.* 2.194, Ov. *F.* 6.476).

Reddereque is the only ex. in love-elegy of *-que* preventing elision of a dactylic infinitive. Smith cites 1.6.48, 1.10.26, 3.2.10, 4.3.10 for *-que* performing a similar function with nouns and adjectives. See also Platnauer 93 on the general avoidance of words ending in *-ĕque* (esp. when *-que* is unelided) by the elegists.

35–48 This section picks up the suggestion of former happiness and simplicity in *antiquo . . . Lari*, 34 (cf. 1.1.37ff., 1.10.15ff.). T. immediately ensures relevance to his present circumstances by the mention of travel and ships, and the description of the Golden Age by means of almost continual negation recalls throughout the contemporary situation (note too the verbal echoes: *via* 36, 14; *unda* 37, 1; *ignotis . . . terris* 39, 3).

For the theme of the Golden Age and T.'s treatment of it see intro. essay. In his present state it seems natural that T. should dilate wistfully on the blessings of the past, and he produces a charming sketch of life then. But the passage is not, as is often suggested, an ex. of T.'s supposed fondness for picturesque digression. The opening (absence of seafaring) and conclusion (absence of war) are highly relevant to the background-situation of the poem. The middle of the section is of a more general nature but is not irrelevant: it suggests that there was no pressure to do what one did not want to (41f.), nor were there any restrictions on doing what one wanted to (43f.), but life was easy and carefree (45f.). T. is here expressing a yearning for the complete antithesis to the present (hence the repetition of negatives throughout, usually in emphatic positions): he wishes for the freedom to do not what others want, but what he desires, and to enjoy life (i.e. to be a lover and not to be forced to sail away on expeditions).

35–36 Saturno . . . rege: in Greek versions of the Ages Cronus was the supreme god of the Golden Age, later deposed by Zeus at the close of the period (Hes. *Opera* 111, Plat. *Polit.* 271C, 272B, 276A τὴν ἐπὶ Κρόνου βασιλείαν). The Romans identified with Cronus their Saturn, who ruled over Italy at an early period (cf. Virg. *Aen.* 8.319ff., Ov. *F.* 1.235ff.) – hence the designation of the Golden Age as the period of Saturn's reign (Virg. *Ecl.* 4.6, 6.41 *Saturnia regna*, *G.* 2.536ff., Ov. *Am.* 3.8.35, *Met.* 1.113f., Juv.6.1 *Saturno rege*, Mart.12.62.1ff., Sen. *Oct.* 396, Claud. *Rapt. Pros.* 3.20f.) and the association of it with the primaeval history of Italy (Dion.Hal.1.36, Justin.43.1.3).

priusquam / tellus in longas est patefacta vias: the ref. in *vias* is not specifically military, although this idea is present. Men stayed in their own countries and there was no travel to distant parts of the world (the vague *vias* may include travel by land and sea, but the circumstances of the poem, the progression in the next lines and the parallels cited below suggest that T. is thinking primarily of sea-travel). This idea seems to be a development from the detail of no ships: cf. Virg. *Ecl.* 4.38, Ov. *Am.* 3.8.44, *Met.* 1.94ff., Sen. *Med.* 331f., 335f., 369ff. *terminus omnis motus et urbes / muros terra posuere nova, / nil qua fuerat sede reliquit / pervius orbis.*

For the expression cf. Ov. *Am.* 2.16.16 *in longas orbem qui secuere vias*, 18 *si fuit in longas terra secanda vias*.

37–38 nondum caeruleas pinus contempserat undas: Aratus (*Phaen.* 110f.) is the first to mention the absence of seafaring in the Golden Age, and this feature became common in later accounts (Lucr.5.1000f., Virg. *Ecl.* 4.31f., *G.* 1.136f., Ov. *Am.* 3.8.43, *Met.* 1.94f., 132ff., Sen. *Phaed.* 530, *Med.* 311f.).

The sea was notoriously dangerous (see Smith, and Mayor on Juv. 12.58), esp. due to the winds (cf. *ventis* in 38): cf. Hes. *Opera* 620f., 645, 674ff., Hor. *C.* 1.3.9ff., Prop.3.7.35, Ov. *Am.* 2.11.25f., Sen. *Med.* 304, 1.7.19-20n. Therefore to voyage on the sea was an act of boldness and scorn: cf. *A.P.* 7.264, 266 (Leonidas), 9.131 (anon.), Ov. *Am.* 2. 11.3, Sen. *Med.* 301, 607, Stat. *Silv.* 3.2.61ff., *Theb.* 6.19f. *ausurae trans alta ignota biremes, / seu Tyrrhenam hiemem, seu stagna Aegaea lacessant.*

Pinus standing for *navis* is common enough, but in some accounts the first ship was made of pine (Catull.64.1f., Hor. *Epod.* 16.57 (of the Argo), Ov. *Met.* 1.95), and *pinus* may also be preferred here to suggest the unnaturalness of the process, the antithesis between land and sea emphasized by *caeruleas* (cf. Virg. *Ecl.* 4.38 *nautica pinus* and Coleman ad loc., Ov. *Met.* 1.133f. *quaeque prius steterant in montibus altis, /*

fluctibus ignotis exsultavere carinae).

For the treatment of the sea as a person here cf. *A.P.* 7.264.3 (Leonidas of Tarentum) *μεμφέσθω μὴ λαῖτμα κακόξενον*, Luc.3.193, Stat. *Theb.* 6.19f.

praebueratque: on the postposition of *-que* see 1.1.39-40n. For *nondum . . . -que* cf. Virg. *Aen.* 4.698f., Val.Fl.1.110f.

These lines are similar to the diatribe against navigation common in the propempticon (see intro. essay).

39–40 T. alludes to the common idea that the motive for navigation is greed for gain: cf. Hes. *Opera* 684ff., Eur. *I.T.* 408ff., Prop.3.7.1ff., 37, Ov. *Met.* 1.130ff., Sen. *Med.* 361f. The trader was synonymous with greed (cf. Hor. *C.* 1.1.18, 3.24.35ff., *Pers.* 5.132ff.), but greed was unknown in the Golden Age (Ov. *Met.* 1.128ff., Sen. *Phaed.* 540f., *Oct.* 422ff., *Epist.* 90.38). So there were no traders then: cf. Arat. *Phaen.* 111, Virg. *Ecl.* 4.38f. (of the return of the Golden Age) *nec nautica pinus / mutabit merces.*

vagus: cf. Hor. *Ars Poet.* 117, Manil.1.87 *et vagus in caecum penetravit navita pontum*, Stat. *Silv.* 3.1.4.

ignotis repetens compendia terris: it is obvious that *compendia* means 'gain, profit' (*OLD* s.v.1) and that the *externa . . . merce* of the pent. picks up and comes from these *ignotis . . . terris*. Hence *repetens* may mean 'bringing' (Sen. *Oed.* 61) or 'bringing back' (Caes. *B.C.* 3. 76), and *ignotis . . . terris* may be separative; or the verb may mean 'seeking' (Sil.It.14.41) or 'seeking again' (Virg. *Aen.* 2.178), and the abl. may be local.

Ignotis and *externa* suggest the strangeness and unnaturalness of the action.

ratis: although elsewhere used merely as a synonym for *navis*, the word often means 'raft', so that here it may reflect the idea of danger in the previous couplet (cf. 1.7.20).

41–42 illo non validus subiit iuga tempore taurus: a further connection with the previous couplet lies in the idea of desire for gain as the motive for agriculture as well as navigation (cf. 1.9.7ff.).

At Hes. *Opera* 109ff. ploughing is conspicuous by its absence, but Plato (*Polit.* 272A) is the first to state openly that there was no ploughing then. Aratus depicted the men of the Golden Age as living by means of agriculture (*Phaen.* 112f.), but subsequent accounts disagreed, maintaining that agriculture was unnecessary, as the earth gave ample produce untilled or men subsisted on acorns and water: see on 45-6 and cf. also Lucr.5.933ff., Virg. *Ecl.* 4.39ff., *G.* 1.125ff. *ante Iovem nulli subigebant arva coloni; / . . . in medium quaerebant, ipsaque tellus / omnia liberius, nullo poscente, ferebat*, T.2.3.69f., Ov. *Am.* 3.8.39ff., *Met.* 1.101ff., *Aetna* 10f., Claud. *Ruf.* 1.381f.

non domito frenos ore momordit equus: in view of the hexameter the horse is probably for domestic use, although T. may also have in mind war-horses. This detail of horses not champing the bit (*frenos . . . momordit*: cf. Luc.6.398) first occurs here in connection with the Golden Age: cf. (of primitive man) Aesch. *P. V.* 465f. ὑφ᾽ἅρμα τ᾽ἤγαγον φιληνίους / ἵππους, Lucr.5.1297ff. *et prius est armatum in equi conscendere costas / et moderarier hunc frenis dextraque vigere / quam biiugo curru belli temptare pericla*, T.2.1.42, (of early Arcadians) Ov. *F.* 2.297 *nullus adhuc erat usus equi.*

Note the alliteration of t and the frequency of o in the couplet.

43–44 non domus ulla fores habuit: another new feature in the Ages theme. Doors were unnecessary because there were no thieves (Juv.6. 17f.), as everything was held in common (see below). This lack of doors also meant that lovers were not locked out (T.2.3.73f.). The usual tradition represented people as living without houses in caves, woods or in the open air: cf. Plat. *Polit.* 272A, Lucr.5.948ff., 970, 982ff., Ov. *Met.* 1.121ff., Sen. *Phaed.* 538f., *Epist.* 90.41, Juv.6.2f.

non fixus in agris / qui regeret certis finibus arva, lapis: a feature of Roman accounts of the Ages (cf. Virg. *G.* 1.126, Ov. *Am.* 3.8.42, *Met.* 1.136, Sen. *Phaed.* 528f. *nullus in campo sacer / divisit agros arbiter populis lapis*, Claud. *Ruf.* 1.380f., Just.43.1.3).

The absence of doors and boundary-stones reflects the common idea that all property and possessions were shared in the Golden Age: cf. Virg. *G.* 1.125ff., Ov. *Met.* 1.135f., Sen. *Epist.* 90.36, *Oct.* 403 *communis usus omnium rerum fuit*, Claud. *Ruf.* 1.380, Justin.43.1.3.

With *fixus* understand *est*. In general the omission of *esse* is a feature of epic style and is relatively rare in elegy and lyric (Leo *Senecae Tragoediae* i. p. 185). In particular the omission of *esse* with participles in independent sentences is uncommon in elegy (and in lyric, Virg. *Ecl.*, *G.*): Leo (p. 188) cites only 2.1.43, 57 (in the latter case there are textual difficulties) elsewhere in T.; 18 times in Prop.; 39 times in Ovidian elegy.

Rego was the technical word for marking out boundaries (Cic. *Mur.* 22, *Leg.* 1.55, *Top.* 43).

45–46 Note the graphic imperfects, the variation from the negative statements and the balance between *ipsae . . . dabant* and *ultroque ferebant* (both *ipsae* and *ultroque* emphatic by position).

One of the most frequently mentioned features of the Golden Age was the lack of cultivation (41-2n.) and the abundance and automatic production of food: cf. Hes. *Opera* 117f., Plato *Polit.* 271D, Virg. *Ecl.* 4.18ff., *G.* 1.127f., Ov. *Am.* 3.8.39, *Met.* 1.101ff., *Aetna* 12ff., Sen. *Phaed.* 537f., *Oct.* 404f., *Epist.* 90.40, Claud. *Rapt. Pros.* 3.24ff. A land of milk and honey was a symbol of abundance (cf. Eur. *Bacc.* 142f., 708ff., Plat. *Ion* 534A, Hor. *C.* 2.19.10ff., Ov. *Met.* 1.111f.). The two details by which T. expresses this idea are found only in Roman versions of the Ages.

ipsae mella dabant quercus: for *ipse* meaning 'of one's own accord' cf. Virg. *Ecl.* 4.21, 7.11, *G.* 2.10.

For oaks producing honey in this connection cf. Virg. *Ecl.* 4.30, *G.* 1.131, Ov. *Am.* 3.8.40, *Met.* 1.112, *Aetna* 13f., Claud. *Rapt. Pros.* 3.25, *Ruf.* 1.383 and (Isles of the Blest) Hor. *Epod.* 16.47. Honey in the Golden Age was found in the hollows of trees (Hor. *Epod.* 16.47 (Isles of the Blest), Ov. *Am.* 3.8.40 *in quercu mella reperta cava*; presumably because there were in fact beehives there: Hes. *Opera* 232f., Virg. *G.* 2.452f.). There was also a common idea that honey fell from the sky as dew and collected on leaves (see Smith, Virg. *G.* 1.131 *mellaque decussit foliis*, Page on Virg. *G.* 4.1). It is unclear to which idea T. here refers.

ultroque ferebant / obvia securis ubera lactis oves: this detail in connection with the Golden Age is found elsewhere only at Virg. *Ecl.* 4.21f. (of goats) *ipsae lacte domum referent distenta capellae / ubera.* Cf. also Hor. *Epod.* 16.49f. (Isles of the Blest).

For *securis* cf. Hes. *Opera* 112f. ὥστε θεοὶ δ' ἔζωον ἀκηδέα θυμὸν ἔχοντες / νόσφιν ἄτερ τε πόνων καὶ ὀιζύος, 118f., T.1.10.10, Ov. *Met.* 1.100, Diod. Sic. 5.66.

For *ubera lactis* ('udders full of milk') cf. Lucr. 1.887, 2.370 *ad sua quisque fere decurrunt ubera lactis.*

47–48 The asyndeton, repetition of negatives, build-up of important words in 47 and juxtaposition (*immiti saevus*) in 48 give emphasis and forcefulness.

non acies, non ira fuit, non bella: for the absence of war in the Golden Age cf. Hes. *Opera* 143ff., Teleklid fr.1.2K, Virg. *Ecl.* 4.32f., *G.* 2.539f., T.1.10.7ff., Ov. *Met.* 1.97ff. *Acies* suggests the sophisticated order and strategy of contemporary armies: for the absence of such sophistication then cf. Lucr. 5.999f., 1.10.9-10n.

Ira was the usual cause and concomitant of war: cf. Hor. *C.* 4.15.19f. *ira, quae procudit enses / et miseras inimicat urbes*, Virg. *Aen.* 12.331ff., Sen. *Ag.* 596ff., Sil.It.4.438f. For its absence in the Golden Age cf. Aratus 108f., Sen. *Phaed.* 549.

nec ensem / immiti saevus duxerat arte faber: in versions of the Ages the absence of the sword is first found at Aratus *Phaen.* 131f. (of the Bronze Age) οἳ πρῶτοι κακόεργον ἐχαλκεύσαντο μάχαιραν / εἰνοδίην, and subsequently occurs at Cic. *N.D.* 2.159, Virg. *G.* 2.539f., Ov. *Met.* 1.99, Sen. *Phaed.* 548. Cf. also 1.10.1-4n.

The prosaic *gladius* is far less common in elegy than *ensis* (also at 1.10.1; *gladius* never occurs in T.). *Ensis* is more common in poetry generally, esp. in epic and tragedy, so that here the word heightens the tone (Axelson 51).

For *duxerat* ('had drawn out, moulded') cf. Lucr. 5.1264f. *tenuia*

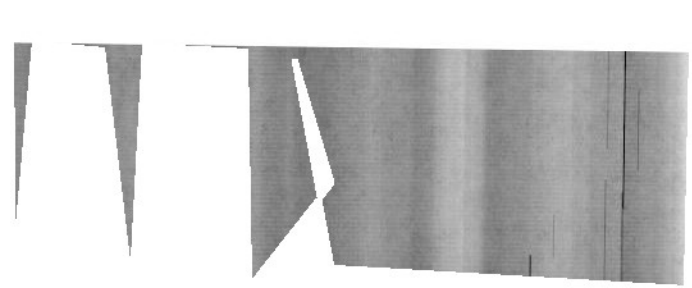

posse / mucronum duci fastigia procudendo, Virg. *Aen.* 7.634.

On the arrangement of words in the pent. see 1.7.25-6n.

49–52 To facilitate transition (by means of contrast) T. follows the tradition of only two ages, the Golden Age under Saturn and the present one under Jupiter (cf. Plat. *Polit.* 272B, Virg. *G.* 1.121ff., Claud. *Rapt. Pros.* 3.19ff.), and mentions war in the hexameter as a feature of his own period (absent in the Golden Age: 47f.). The bellicosity and sudden death of Jupiter's age brings T. back to his misfortunes and suggests that they may be a punishment from Jupiter – hence the hurried prayer to him (parallel to the prayers to Death (4f.) and Isis (27f.): for the recurrence of prayers etc. see intro. essay).

49–50 For the attack on the present age in this connection cf. Hes. *Opera* 174ff., T.1.10.1ff., Ov. *Am.* 3.8.47ff.

T.'s expression here is vigorous (repetition of *nunc*, asyndeton, emphatic position of *semper* and the forceful *mille*).

nunc Iove sub domino: for *dominus* applied to the gods see *Thes. L. L.* V_1. 1931.10ff.

nunc mare, nunc leti mille repente viae: see Critical Appendix. *Repente* acts as an adjective and goes with *viae* or *leti*: for this use of the word cf. Livy 1.13.6 *ex bello tam tristi laeta repente pax*, 22. 17.3 *quo repente discursu, furtim* at T.2.5.53.

Mille means 'innumerable', as always in T. (2.3.44, 2.4.60).

For *leti . . . viae* cf. Lucr.2.918, T.1.10.4, Hor. *C.* 1.28.16. The phrase means either 'the road by which death comes' (Prop.2.27.2) or 'the road to death' (Hor. *C.* 1.28.16 and Nisbet & Hubbard ad loc.).

51–52 For the fear that one's misfortunes may be due to divine punishment (and for similar possible crimes) see 1.2.79-80n. This fear and the appeal to Jupiter (for the recurrence of appeals etc. see intro. essay) suggest well an agitated state of mind.

parce, pater: i.e. Jupiter (cf. 1.4.23).

timidum non me periuria terrent: for the expression cf. Prop.3.8.15 *seu timidam crebro dementia somnia terrent*, Virg. *Aen.* 12.875 *ne me terrete timentem.* The meaning here seems to be: 'I am afraid, but it is not guilt that frightens me (but fear of death)'.

non dicta in sanctos impia verba deos: André points out the careful arrangement of adjectives and nouns, and the expressive juxtaposition (*sanctos impia*).

53–56 The progression of thought is: 'but if my prayer is unavailing and my death fated . . . .' This section makes a transition from the preoccupation with the present and the past in the first half of the poem to thoughts about the future which dominate the second half, and it looks both forwards and backwards: by the suggestion of T.'s death it leads into the description of Elysium, while the epitaph recalls the mention of Messalla and Death in the opening lines. The heavily spondaic nature of these lines reinforces the tone of solemnity and sadness.

fatales . . . annos: for a person's destined span see 1.7.1-2n.

fac lapis inscriptis stet super ossa notis: for the not uncommon omission of *ut* see Smith and cf. my note on 1.2.25a-26. The request is apparently addressed to Jupiter (cf. Prop.3.16.25; here perhaps not unreasonably, since T. regards himself as a victim of Jupiter's age: see below), although it may be intended for Messalla, who was apostrophized at 1 and would naturally perform this duty. For the recurrence of requests etc. see intro. essay.

Lines 55-6 contain the first ex. in elegy of the poet's own epitaph (for the poet's own death see 1.1.59-60n.): cf. T.3.2.29f., Prop.2.13. 35f. *QUI NUNC IACET HORRIDA PULVIS, / UNIUS HIC QUONDAM SERVUS AMORIS ERAT*, Ov. *Tr.*3.3.73ff. *HIC EGO QUI IACEO, TENERORUM LUSOR AMORUM, / INGENIO PERII NASO POETA MEO. / AT TIBI QUI TRANSIS NE SIT GRAVE QUISQUIS AMASTI / DICERE NASONIS MOLLITER OSSA CUBENT.* For exx. of other epitaphs in elegy see Prop.4.7.85f., Ov. *Am.*2.6.61f., *Her.*2.147f., 7.195f., 14.129f. *F.*3.549f. T.'s epitaph contains no mention of his love or his poetry, but is a simple statement of his death while on an expedition, thus stating clearly that he is victim of the present age (the idea is also underlined verbally: *IMMITI* cf. *immiti* 48, *TERRA . . . MARI* cf. *terris* 39 and *mare* 50). For the connection with 21f. see intro. essay.

IMMITI in 55 is normally translated as 'cruel', but the basic meaning of the word is 'bitter, sour' (of unripe fruit), so that the sense 'premature' (Lee: 'UNTIMELY') is suggested here (see *Thes. L.L.* $\text{V}11_1$.467.15ff.).

For the displacement of *-que* in 56 see 1.7.49-50n.

57–66 A natural progression to the condition of his soul after death (*me* 57, in contrast to *ossa* 54).

T. here presents a pleasant vignette of Elysium, selecting features which appeal to him as a lover, poet and rustic. Note too that this is the first detailed description of Elysium in Latin literature, and that T. is the first to concentrate on lovers in Elysium, rather than heroes or the pious (57-8n.).

Elysium is T.'s means of achieving happiness through death, and again T. depicts longingly a happy existence in which it is possible to do exactly what one wishes without hindrance. The description of Elysium is a positive statement of the Golden Age: again there is ease and freedom from cares, the automatic gifts of the earth (61f., cf. 41, 45f.), and no restraint (59 *passimque vagantes*, cf. 41f.), while the battles of love (64) recall the absence of real warfare at 47f.

57–58 Elysium, often identified with the Isles of the Blest (e.g. Serv. ad *Aen.*5.735), was originally the place where those favoured by the gods went, and divine family-connections were the qualifications for entry (esp. Hom. *Od.* 4.561ff.). However, the idea of recompense for a good life appears later: Plat. *Axioch*.371C ὅσοις μὲν οὖν ἐν τῷ ζῆν δαίμων ἀγαθὸς ἐπέπνευσεν, εἰς τὸν τῶν εὐσεβῶν χῶρον οἰκίζονται, Virg. *Aen.* 6.660ff., Serv.loc.cit., Val.Fl.1.843, 851. The position of Elysium in early versions is at the end of the earth in the far West (Hom.loc.cit., cf. Hes. *Opera* 167ff.), but Virgil places it in the Underworld (*Aen.* 6. 637ff.) and others situate it in the heavens (Serv.loc.cit., Luc.9.1ff. and schol.). For the idea of lovers in Elysium cf. Prop.4.7.59ff., *Culex* 261ff. So lovers are placed in the Isles of the Blest by Lucian (*Ver. Hist.* 2.19, 25ff.). In Virgil those who die of love occupy the *Lugentes Campi* in the Underworld (*Aen.* 6.441ff.).

quod facilis tenero sum semper Amori: *facilis* means 'susceptible, compliant'. The word in this sense is often applied to a mistress in elegy (e.g. 2.6.27).

For *tener* applied to Amor cf. 2.6.1, Ov. *Am.* 2.18.4, 19, 3.15.1.

ipsa Venus campos ducet in Elysios: for the reason given in 57 (cf. 1.2.97f.) Venus herself (*ipsa Venus* emphatic by position) replaces Mercury, the usual ψυχοπομπός. For this novel touch cf. *Carm. Epig.* B.1108.19ff. (esp. *nam me sancta Venus sedes non nosse silentum / iussit et in caeli lucida templa tulit*), Pind. *Ol.* 2.79f. (Thetis leads Achilles to the Isles of the Blest). T. is also placed in Elysium by Ovid (*Am.* 3.9.60) and Marsus in his epigram.

59–60 hic choreae cantusque vigent: for the scansion of *choreae* (usually the e is long, as at 1.7.49) cf. Prop.2.19.15, Virg. *Aen.* 6.644, Auson. 393.50, *Carm. Epig.* 1282.8.

For song and dance in Elysium cf. Aristoph. *Ran.* 155, Plat. *Axioch.* 371C, Virg. *Aen.* 6.644, 656f., Val.Fl.1.845f., Lucian *Ver. Hist.* (Isles of the Blest) 2.5, 15, 18. The song and dance may be in honour of the gods, as Smith suggests, but need not be so (cf. Lucian loc.cit.).

dulce sonant tenui gutture carmen aves: this is the first mention of birds in Elysium. Ovid hopes that Corinna's parrot will go there to join other birds (*Am.* 2.6.49ff.). There are birds in the Isles of the Blest also (Lucian *Ver. Hist.* 2.5, 14, 15).

For *tenuis* meaning 'narrow, slender' cf. Virg. *Ecl.* 1.2, 6.8 (shepherd's pipe), Ov. *Am.* 1.13.8 *et liquidum tenui gutture cantat avis.* The word suggests gracefulness and charm, and *tenuitas* is a quality that would naturally appeal to an elegist (cf. Prop.3.1.8, Ov. *Tr.* 2.327, of elegiac writing).

The assonance, alliteration and jingle (*-que vigent . . . -que vagantes*) make this an aptly musical couplet.

61–62 fert casiam non culta seges: produce is ample and appears automatically (cf. Hes. *Opera* 172f., Plat. *Axioch.* 371C, Lucian *Ver. Hist.* 2.13).

Casia here is probably the more exotic κασία (a type of cinnamon), rather than the common Italian herb of the same name (see Coleman on Virg. *Ecl.* 2.49, Page on *G.* 4.30). *Casia* first occurs here in connection with Elysium, but the abundance of flowers and spices is mentioned elsewhere: cf. Pind.fr.114 Bowra, Plat. *Axioch.* 371C, Greek Epitaph Kaibel 649.3, *Carm. Epig.* B.525.5, Stat. *Silv.* 5.1.257, and (Isles of the Blest) Pind. *Ol.* 2.72f., Lucian *Ver.Hist.* 2.5, 14.

For *seges* meaning 'field, ground' cf. e.g. Virg. *G.* 4.129.

totosque per agros: *totus* may signify entirety (its original sense) or do duty for *omnis* (a predominantly late usage): see Löfstedt *Philologischer Kommentar zur Peregrinatio Aetheriae* (Uppsala, 1911), 69, *Late Latin* (Oslo, 1959), 22. Elsewhere in T. I and II *totus* signifies entirety (1.2.25, 63, 69, 1.5.30, 1.6.32, 2.2.13).

floret odoratis terra benigna rosis: for *benignus* 'bountiful, fertile' cf. 3.3.6, Ov. *Am.* 1.10.56, Plin. *N.H.* 18.1, 33.2.

For roses in Elysium cf. Pind.loc.cit., Prop.4.7.60, Lucian *Ver. Hist.* 2.5, 6, 26. The flower is appropriate here, as it was sacred to Venus and is often found in connection with love and lovers (see Gow on Theoc. *Id.* 10.34, Gow and Page on *A.P.* 5.136.5 = Meleager XLII).

This is another pleasantly musical couplet (esp. frequency of o and the internal rhyme in 62).

63–64 Souls generally pursued their former occupations and retained the same tastes in Elysium (cf. Virg. *Aen.* 6.653ff. *quae gratia currum / armorumque fuit vivis, quae cura nitentis / pascere equos, eadem sequitur tellure repostos*) and in the Isles of the Blest (Lucian *Ver. Hist.* 2.17, 22, 23, 25). So in the *Lugentes Campi* those who have died of love still feel the pangs: Virg. *Aen.* 6.442ff. *hic, quos durus amor crudeli tabe peredit, / secreti celant calles et myrtea circum / silva tegit; curae non ipsa in morte relinquunt.*

ludit: the verb can be used of dancing, but this action has already been mentioned at 59. Probably the word here refers to amatory 'play' (cf. e.g. Catull.17.17, Prop.1.10.9, Ov. *Am.* 1.8.43, Hor. *C.* 3.15.5).

adsidue proelia miscet Amor: see Critical Appendix.

For the military phrase cf. Livy 28.30.11, 28.33.14, Ov. *Met.* 5.156. So too *immisceo* is often used in a military context: see Lewis & Short s.v.1c (note the play *immixta – miscet*). For *militia amoris* see 1.10.53-6n. As in life (e.g. 1.1.73ff., 1.10.53ff.), so in Elysium love's warfare continues. Simple refs. to battles in *militia amoris* are common and go back as far as lyric (Anac.34D ἀστραγάλαι δ᾽Ἔρωτος εἰσιν μανίαι τε καὶ κυδοιμοί, Hermesianax 7.83f. (Powell *Coll. Alex.*), Plaut. *Pers.* 25, Ter. *Eun.* 59ff., Catull.37.13, T.1.10.53, Prop.2.1.45, Ov. *Am.* 1.9.45).

65–66 illic est, cuicumque rapax Mors venit amanti: the participial force may or may not be present in *amanti* ('those who died of love' or 'dead lovers').

For the greed of Death see 4n.

et gerit insigni myrtea serta coma: for myrtle in Elysium cf. Aristoph. *Ran.* 156, Pherecrat. 108.25K, Lucian *Ver. Hist.* 2.5. So too there is a myrtle wood in the *Lugentes Campi* (Virg. *Aen.* 6.443f.). Here it is worn by the lover because it is sacred to Venus (cf. Ov. *F.* 4.139ff., Serv. ad *Ecl.* 7.62, ad *G.* 2.64). So *insigni* means distinguished by the wearing of the myrtle (as a worshipper of Venus).

67–82 Continuing the Underworld theme, by contrast T. turns to Tartarus, as often happens in such accounts (e.g. Pind. fr. 114 Bowra, Aristoph. *Ran.* 145ff., Plat. *Axioch.* 371, Virg. *Aen.* 6.540ff.). A further connection is made at 81f. (see below).

In this selective and well-constructed passage T. dwells on Tartarus in malicious detail and emphasizes the grimness and unpleasantness because, just as Elysium is the place for T. the lover (57f.), so Tartarus is the place for T.'s enemy in love (81f.). He consigns him/them to the antithesis of his own yearnings. Tartarus is in strong contrast to Elysium and the Golden Age: in general the unhappiness of the existence and the unpleasantness of the place and its inhabitants; also a number of of minor details, esp. sounds (68, 72, contrast 59f.), hostility of animals (69, 71f., 76, contrast 45f., 59f.), restriction on movement (71f., contrast 59) and doors (72, contrast 43).

The list of sinners at 73-80 has caused difficulty for perceptive critics. The passage would have more point and be more relevant to the profaner of the poet's love (81f.), if all the sinners were guilty of crimes in love (also the contrast with Elysium would be sharper). Ixion, Tityos and the Danaids fit into this category (see notes below), but scholars have been unable to find any such crime on the part of Tantalus. If T. had not had in mind an amatory sin of Tantalus, he could easily have omitted him (as he does Sisyphus), and his inclusion would have been rather careless and sloppy. For the solution of the problem we have to thank Lee (p. 106): according to Orosius *Hist.* 1.12.4 (citing Phanocles, the Hellenistic poet) Tantalus abducted Ganymede (for further refs. see Phanocles fr. 4 Powell = *Coll. Alex.* p. 108).

67–68 A sombre couplet, with darkness in the hexameter balanced by darkness in the pentameter.

Tartarus was originally the prison of the Titans (Hom. *Il.* 8.477ff., Hes. *Theog.* 713ff.), but became also a place of punishment for sinners (Aristoph. *Ran.* 145ff., Plato *Axioch.* 371E, *Gorg.* 526B, Virg. *Aen.* 6. 563ff.; for amatory sinners cf. Aristoph. *Ran.* 148, Prop. 4.7.55ff.). It lay far beneath the earth, a terrible place from which none could escape (Hom. *Il.* 8.13ff., Hes. *Theog.* 720ff., Virg. *Aen.* 6.577ff.).

at scelerata iacet sedes in nocte profunda / abdita: *scelerata . . . sedes* stands for *sedes sceleratorum* (cf. Cic. *Cluent.* 171), and is also applied to Tartarus at Ov. *Met.* 4.456 (cf. also *Ibis* 174, Virg. *Aen.* 6.563). For the personification cf. Virg. *Aen.* 6.441 (*Lugentes Campi*).

On the darkness of Tartarus see Hom. *Il.* 8.13, Hes. *Theog.* 119, 721, 726f., 729, 736, 807, Aesch. *P. V.* 221f., 1050f., *Eum.* 72, Lucr.3.966, Virg. *Aen.* 6.577f., Ov. *Met.* 1.113.

quam circum flumina nigra sonant: Tartarean rivers first occur in surviving literature at Pind.fr.114 Bowra (cf. also Sen. *H.F.* 889). In Virgil (*Aen.* 6.551) and Seneca (*Phaed.* 1227) Phlegethon surrounds Tartarus. The underground rivers were said by some to flow from and back into Tartarus (Plat. *Phaed.* 112f., Virg. *Aen.* 6.295 and Serv. ad loc., Sen. *H.F.* 709ff.).

For black infernal rivers cf. Pindar loc.cit. (unspecified), Virg. *G.* 4. 478, *Aen.* 6.132, Hor. *C.* 2.14.17f. (Cocytus), and Stat. *Theb.* 4.521-3 (various, including Phlegethon).

69–70 The Furies appear as punishers of sinners after death in the Underworld as early as Homer *Il.* 19.259f. So later they are particularly connected with Tartarus (Virg. *Aen.* 6.570ff., Ov. *Ibis* 183ff., *Met.* 4. 455f.). In Roman poetry Tisiphone usually takes the leading rôle, as here (Virg. *Aen.* 6.555, 570ff., Ov. *Met.* 4.474f., Stat. *Theb.* 4.486).

Tisiphoneque impexa feros pro crinibus angues / saevit: see Critical Appendix.

Impexus may mean 'entangled, unkempt' without any idea of combing felt (Virg. *Aen.* 7.667 of a lion's mane). Alternatively, the word may mean 'uncombed': combing snaky locks is only one stage further than Tisiphone tossing snakes away from her face (Ov. *Met.* 4.475) and Discordia wearing *vittae* on her snaky locks (Virg. *Aen.* 6.281), and there is a parallel for such combing at Claud. *Eutrop.* 2.111 of Bellona *Illyricis pingues pectebat stragibus hydros* (cf. also Ov. *Met.* 4.454 *deque suis atros pectebant crinibus angues*).

Feros pro crinibus angues is a striking expression for a striking picture: the words all form one idea (cf. 2.5.103). Aeschylus was said to be the first to represent the Furies with snakes in their hair (Paus.1. 28.6, Aesch. *Cho.* 1049f.); cf. also Virg. *G.* 4.482, Ov. *Met.* 4.454, 475, Stat. *Theb.* 11.65f. For snakes in place of hair, as here, cf. Catull.64. 193f. *Eumenides, quibus anguino redimita capillo / frons*, Claud. *Rapt. Pros.* 1.39f., Serv. ad *Aen.* 6.572. In a number of passages it is difficult to tell exactly which idea is present (Prop.3.5.40, Virg. *Aen.* 7.329, 346, *Culex* 218, Sen. *H.F.* 984f.).

For the use of *anguis* see 1.4.35-6n.

Saevit is given emphasis by its position.

The sigmatism (and the x in *impexa*) suggests the hissing of snakes (continued in the next couplet).

huc illuc impia turba fugit: for the picture cf. Apollod.2.5.12, T.1. 10.37f., Virg. *Aen.* 6.490f. *ut videre virum fulgentiaque arma per umbras, / ingenti trepidare metu: pars vertere terga*, Stat. *Theb.* 1.93f.

71–72 tum niger in porta serpentum Cerberus ore / stridet: i.e. the crowd of sinners (fleeing from Tisiphone) are stopped from leaving by Cerberus. Note the balance with the previous couplet: like Tisiphone, Cerberus is endowed with snakes and terrifies the wicked. For Cerberus frightening shades and preventing egress from the Underworld cf. Hes. *Theog.* 769ff., Sen. *H.F.* 782f. *hic saevus umbras territat Stygius canis / qui terna vasto capita concutiens sono / regnum tuetur*, Stat. *Theb.* 4.486f., Quint. Smyrn. 6.261ff. Cerberus' more usual position was at the far side of Charon's crossing (e.g. Virg. *Aen.* 6.417f.), but the topography of the Underworld was vague, and Cerberus is elsewhere referred to as the dog of Tartarus (Sen. *H.F.* 649, *Ag.* 751, *H.O.* 1770, Mart. 5.34.4).

For 'black' applied to Cerberus cf. Hor. *C.* 2.13.34f., Sen. *H.O.* 23, Stat. *Theb.* 2.28f. Again darkness in Tartarus is emphasized.

The phrase *serpentum Cerberus ore / stridet* means that Cerberus makes the snakes that form part of him emit hisses from their mouths. The dog's head and neck bristle with snakes (Apollod. 2.5.12, Hor. *C.* 3.11.17f., Virg. *Aen.* 6.419, *Culex* 221, Ov. *Met.* 10.21f., Sen. *H.F.* 785ff.), as does his tail (Apollod. loc. cit., Sen. *H.F.* 787, Sil. It. 13.594); for his snakes hissing cf. Sen. loc. cit., Sil. It. 6.177f. This is an unusual expression of the idea, for which Dissen compares Virg. *Aen.* 7.447 *tot Erinys sibilat hydris*. Here *ore* is singular for plural (cf. Virg. *G.* 3.273, 4.201, T.4.1.71); its combination with the plural *serpentum* is odd (Postgate *Selections* compares Virg. *Aen.* 10.334f. of weapons *steterunt quae in corpore Graium / Iliacis campis*).

On the use of *serpens* see 1.4.35-6n.

aeratas . . . fores: cf. Hom. *Il.* 8.15, Hes. *Theog.* 732f. θύρας δ'ἐπέθηκε Ποσειδέων / χαλκείας. Bronze was noted for its strength and durability (e.g. Lucr. 5.1270, Hor. *C.* 3.30.1).

73–74 The list of sinners in Tartarus is a common literary theme (Hom. *Od.* 11.576ff., Plat. *Axioch.* 371E, Lucr. 3.978ff., Virg. *Aen.* 6.580ff., Ov. *Ibis* 175ff., Sen. *Ag.* 15ff., *H.F.* 750ff.). Note throughout the predominance of spondees conveying suitable solemnity.

When Ixion tried to assault Hera, Zeus shaped a cloud to resemble her, and as a punishment had Ixion bound to a wheel in the Underworld which never ceased to revolve (Pind. *Pyth.* 2.21ff. θεῶν δ'ἐφετμαῖς Ἰξίονα . . . / . . . ἐν πτερόεντι τροχῷ / παντᾷ κυλινδόμενον, Hygin. *fab.* 62, Lucian *Dial. Deor.* 216-19). He is bound by chains of bronze (Ap. Rhod. 3.62) or snakes (Serv. ad. *G.* 3.38) and, according to some, the wheel is on fire (schol. ad Eur. *Phoen.* 1185). Here *celeri* reflects the traditional detail of πτερόεντι, and by emphasizing the speed of the revolutions brings out the unpleasantness of the punishment.

temptare: of an amatory attempt (cf. Hor. *C.* 3.4.71, Ov. *A.A.* 1.389, 394).

75–76 Tityos tried to rape Leto and was killed by one or both of her children (Hom. *Od.* 11.580f., Pind. *Pyth.* 4.90ff., Ap.Rhod. 1.759ff., Apollod. 1.4.1) or by Zeus (Hygin. *fab.* 55). As a punishment he was stretched out in the Underworld (esp. Hom. *Od.* 11.576ff.). Being a giant, he covered nine acres (*novem . . . iugera*): cf. Hom.loc.cit., Lucr. 3.988f., Prop. 3.5.44, Virg. *Aen.* 6.596, Ov. *Met.* 4.457f., *Ibis* 181, Paus. 10.4.5, Claud. *Rapt. Pros.* 2.339, Hygin. *fab.* 55. In Homer two vultures (cf. the plural here) feed on his liver (Virgil loc.cit. mentions one, and there is disagreement over this point in Roman accounts: see Smith). The liver in later versions grows again and provides a meal for the birds constantly (*adsiduas*): cf. Plat. *Axioch.* 371E, Lucr. 3.990f., Ov. *ExP.* 1.2.39f., Sen. *Ag.* 18, *Thy.* 9ff., *H.F.* 756, esp. Virg. *Aen.* 6. 597ff. *rostroque immanis voltur obunco / immortale iecur tondens fecundaque poenis / viscera, rimaturque epulis, habitatque sub alto / pectore, nec fibris requies datur ulla renatis.*

The devouring of the liver was an apt punishment, since it was regarded as the seat of the passions (*Thes. L. L.* VII_1.245.71ff.).

atro viscere: it seems likely in view of the specification of the liver in the myth (see above) that *viscere* is used as a general and indefinite term for *iecur* (Virgil loc.cit.), in which case *atro* may refer either to the naturally dark colour of the human liver, or to its discolouration by blood due to the birds gnawing (cf. Aesch. *P. V.* 1025 κελαινόβρωτον δ'ἧπαρ ἐκθοινάσεται; for *ater* of objects dark with blood see *OLD* s.v. 3b).

77–78 The crimes usually ascribed to Tantalus are: (1) he divulged the counsels of Zeus which had been told to him in confidence (Hygin. *fab.* 82); (2) he served up his son Pelops as a meal to the gods (Serv. ad. *Aen.* 6.603); (3) he stole nectar and ambrosia for his friends (Pind. *Ol.* 1. 60ff.); (4) the golden dog which guarded Zeus' temple in Crete was stolen by Pandareus and entrusted to Tantalus, who subsequently refused to give it up and swore that he had never received it (Eustath. ad *Od.* 19.518); (5) most relevant here, he abducted Ganymede (67-82n.).

There is a similar multiplicity of punishments: (1) he stands in the middle of a lake which always retires when he tries to drink (as here); (2) branches laden with fruit hang near him but when he tries to eat are always blown out of his reach; (3) a huge boulder hangs over his head always threatening to crush him. The first two occur in surviving literature as early as Homer (*Od.* 11.582ff.) and the third first in Archilochus (Paus. 10.31.12). For further refs. see Smith. For the present punishment cf. esp. Hom. *Od.* 11.582ff.

acrem: either 'fierce' or 'eager', as Putnam points out. The word is in emphatic position.

iam iam poturi deserit unda sitim: *iam iam* (see *Thes. L. L.* VII_1. 119.57ff.) and the juxtaposition (*unda sitim*) bring out well the torture of the water deserting his lips at the very last moment.

79–80 Aegyptus quarelled with his brother Danaus and, as a gesture of peace, proposed that his fifty sons should marry Danaus' fifty daughters. Danaus was suspicious and fled with his daughters, but, after capture, agreed to the marriages, instructing his daughters to murder their husbands, an order which was carried out by all except Hypermestra (Apollod.2.1.4ff., Hor. *C.*3.11.25ff., Serv. ad *Aen.* 10.497, Hygin. *fab.* 168). The murder of their husbands was an affront to Venus (*Veneris quod numina laesit*), and their punishment was to spend eternity in futile attempts to fill a leaking vessel with water (Plat. *Axioch.* 371E Δαναΐδων ὑδρεῖαι ἀτελεῖς, Lucr.3.1008f. *aevo florente puellas / quod memorant laticem pertusum congerere in vas, / quod tamen expleri nulla ratione potestur*, Ov. *Ibis* 177f., Sen. *H.F.* 757).

As Dissen shrewdly remarks, the mention of the Danaids here may well be a passing hint and covert warning for Delia, should she prove unfaithful (so Horace at *C.*3.11 uses the Danaids to give a similar warning to Lyde). This interpretation seems likely in view of the injunction in 83, the presence of the duenna at 83ff. and the sudden arrival of T. at 89. If it is correct, the poet's doubts about his mistress would be another indication of a disturbed state of mind.

proles: see 1.4.7-8n.

laesit: see 1.9.5-6n.

in cava Lethaeas dolia portat aquas: for *cavus* 'full of holes' cf. Manil. 5.150 (pumice-stone), Plin. *N.H.* 11.188 (lungs).

Lethaeas does not refer esp. to Lethe but to the Underworld in general (cf. Hor. *C.*4.7.27, T.3.3.10, 3.5.24, Lucan 6.685).

On *porto* see 93-4n.

81–82 At first sight it seems that there is a contradiction between *violavit amores* here and *at tu casta precor maneas* (83), but closer examination shows that there is in fact no contradiction. It is possible that *violavit amores* means that actual infidelity has occurred and refers not to Delia but to previous mistresses (and/or boyfriends), with T. praying in 83 that his present mistress, Delia, will not be like the others.

However, *lentas . . . militias* surely has more point and relevance if it refers to the Eastern expedition, and the transition in 83 to Delia is easier if she is referred to in *violavit amores*. In this case, as *at tu casta precor maneas* (83) means that no actual infidelity has occurred yet, *violavit amores* must refer to an attempt to steal the affections of Delia. *Violo* in an amatory context need not refer to infidelity (at Ov. *Her.* 7.57 Dido uses the phrase *violasse fidem* of Aeneas' desertion of her), and it does not seem unreasonable that a love-poet should describe an endeavour to seduce his mistress as a 'profanation'. At Ov. *Her.* 17.1ff. Helen says of Paris' attempt to win her over *nunc oculos tua cum violarit epistula nostros, / non rescribendi gloria visa levis. / ausus es hospitii temeratis, advena, sacris / legitimam nuptae sollicitare fidem.* There is similar reasoning behind Ov. *Am.* 3.4.3f. *siqua metu dempto casta est, ea denique casta est; / quae, quia non liceat, non facit, illa facit* (later picked up at Sen. *Ben.* 4.14.1). At Calp. *Ecl.* 3.88 (*ilice, quae nostros primum violavit amores*) T.'s phrase is applied to a tree, beneath which the speaker's girl merely sat and sang in company with another man (*Ecl.* 3.26f.).

On the recurrence of wishes etc. see intro. essay.

For the sanctity of love and lovers cf. 83 (*sanctique pudoris*), 1.2. 27-8, 1.6.51-2 and notes.

The vague *quicumque* could refer to one or more rivals.

Amores here may mean 'love' (1.1.69 etc.) or 'the loved one' (1.6. 35-6n.

T. suspects that his prolonged separation from Delia may have been due to someone having wished it upon him (another indication of T.'s disturbed state of mind). *Opto* is frequently so used: cf. e.g. Cic. *Prov. Cons.* 4, *Tusc.* 1.44.107, *Pis.* 20.46 *haec ego semper de vobis expetivi, haec optavi, haec precatus sum*, Mart. 8.61.9, Tac. *Hist.* 1.84.

For *lentus* meaning 'slow, long-lasting' see 1.4.81-4n. Note the predicative position of the word.

83–94 For the transition see 81-2n.

The final section is T.'s picture of happiness in his lifetime, as Elysium was happiness in death, and the joy is increased by the contrast with the section on Tartarus. Although 83f. suggest that he may be thinking of a homecoming, this is postponed for dramatic effect until 89. For possible allusion to Odysseus and Penelope here see intro. essay.

The description of the group of spinners was a frequent motif (cf. Catull.64.303ff., Virg. *G.* 4.333ff., Ov. *Met.* 4.32ff., Claud. *Paneg.Prob.* 177ff.). For the lover arriving to find his beloved spinning, as here, cf. Ter. *Heaut.* 275ff., Prop.3.6.15ff., Ov. *Met.* 4.214ff. and the story of Lucretia (Livy 1.57.7ff., Ov. *F.* 2.725ff.). The point here is that spinning, although often a task of the poor (1.6.77-84n.), was also one of the ways in which the respectable unattached woman earned a living (Ter. *Andr.* 74f.). T.'s sketch is simple, homely and full of pictorial detail, and he gradually builds up a quiet, sleepy scene to be interrupted by his sudden arrival.

This concluding section is in sharp contrast to the opening of the poem: in place of the gloom and anxiety there, with T. seriously ill and stranded far from his loved ones, here there is happiness and optimism, with T. fully recovered and home again, re-united with Delia (note too the antithesis between the brightness at 93f. and the darkness at 4f.).

83–84 at tu casta precor maneas: for the injunction to remain faithful and the temptations when one partner is absent cf. Catull.68.27ff., Prop.1.11, 3.12, 4.3, 4.8, T.4.3, Hor. *C.* 3.7. On the recurrence of appeals etc. see intro. essay.

On the sudden arrival to check up see 83-94n. and cf. also Prop. 2.29. 23f., 4.8.49ff.

For *castus* 'abstinent from other men' cf. e.g. 1.6.67, 75, 3.1.23, Prop. 1.11.29.

sanctique pudoris / adsideat custos sedula semper anus: on the sanctity of love and lovers see 1.2.27-8, 1.6.51-2 and notes.

For the duenna cf. Plaut *Curc.* 76, *A.P.* 5.262 (Paulus Silentiarius), 289, 294 (Agathias Scholasticus). Here her identity is uncertain: she may be Delia's mother (cf. 1.6.67) or her nurse (cf. Prop.4.3.41).

85–86 **haec tibi fabellas referat**: when spinning or weaving the time was often passed by singing (Hom. *Od.* 5.61f., 10.221f., Virg. *G.* 1.293f., 4.348f.) or telling stories (Eur. *Ion* 196f., *I.A.* 787f. *παρ' ἱστοῖς / μυθεῦσαι τάδ' ἐς ἀλλήλας*, Ov. *Met.* 4.39ff.).

positaque lucerna: 'when the lamp is set down': cf. Ov. *Her.* 19.151 *sternuit et lumen – posito nam scribimus illo* (so *pono* is used of serving up at table at Hor. *S.* 2.2.23 etc.). The late hour implies tiredness (cf. 88) and shows Delia's assiduity: cf. Virg. *G.* 1.291ff., Livy 1.57.9 *nocte sera deditam lanae inter lucubrantes ancillas in medio aedium sedentem inveniunt*, Ov. *F.* 2.741ff. This is, of course, also the time when Delia would be most likely to be with a lover.

deducat plena stamina longa colu: on spinning see 1.6.77-80n. For the forms of *colus* see Neue 1.969f.

Plena and *longa* (like the story-telling above) suggest the tedium of the work (also helped by the concentration of slow spondees in 86-8).

87–88 **at circa gravibus pensis adfixa puella**: the *pensum* was the amount of wool to be spun in a day. *Gravibus* is literal (cf. Virg. *Aen.* 8.411f., Ov. *Her.* 10.90, esp. Prop.4.7.41 *et graviora rependit iniquis pensa quasillis*) and brings out the boredom of the task.

For *adfixus* 'intent on, absorbed in' cf. Virg. *Aen.* 5.852f. *clavumque adfixus et haerens / nusquam amittebat*, Sil.It.7.362ff. *adfixus caelo sub nocte serena, / fluctibus e mediis sulcator navita ponti / astra videt.*

Puella is sing. for plur. and refers to maids (it can hardly refer to Delia, as Putnam suggests, in view of *circa* and *tibi* at 85 and 90).

paulatim somno fessa remittat opus: a good point of detail, emphasizing the drowsiness and quiet. The maids are sleepy esp. because spinners are early risers (Ov. *Am.* 1.13.23f., Virg. *Aen.* 8.407ff.).

89–92 T. gives himself a very dramatic entrance (esp. as he has not referred to himself as anything but dead since 53): its suddenness (at a late hour and unannounced) and the excitement with which it is received (91f.) are in sharp contrast to the quiet scene of the previous lines (underlined by the flurry of dactyls at the start of 89 and the contrast between *subito* in 89 and *paulatim* in 88).

The mention of the homecoming is a conventional feature of the propempticon (see intro. essay).

nec quisquam nuntiet ante: on the custom of having one's arrival announced in advance cf. Plaut. *Amph.* 195, Ter. *Hec.* 314, Ov. *A.A.* 3.245, Plut. *Quaest.Rom.* 9. Here, of course, T. arrives unannounced to surprise Delia at whatever she is doing and gauge her reaction.

caelo missus: a proverbial expression for a sudden unexpected appearance (usually welcome): see Otto *Sprichwörter* s.v. *caelum* 8 and cf. also Livy 8.9.9f. *in equum insiluit ac se in medios hostes immisit . . . sicut caelo missus.*

Delia's casual appearance in 91f. is desirable because it shows that she is not expecting or entertaining a lover, but it would also be attractive in itself to T. (cf. Ov. *Rem.*350). In her excitement and haste to embrace T. (*curre*) Delia is not to attend to her hair or put on her sandals.

nudato . . . pede: for *nudatus* in the sense of *nudus* (rare) cf. Catull. 64.17 *nudato corpore nymphas*, Prop.3.14.13, Sen. *H.O.* 1357, Sil.It. 10.605. For participles and the notion of activity and passivity see 1.4.11-12n.

93–94 T. ends with a fervently optimistic prayer (for the recurrence of prayers etc. see intro. essay): note the emphasis in *hoc . . . hunc*, and the brightness and colour (*nitentem* and the neatly juxtaposed *roseis candida*). Cf. Ov. *Am.* 2.11.55f., *Tr.* 3.5.55f., *ExP.* 1.4.57f., *Consol. ad Liv.* 281f.

Hunc illum . . . Luciferum means 'this day (*hunc*), the one I have been describing (*illum*)'. For this uncommon use of *hic ille* cf. Cato *Ag. Cult.* 132.1, Cic. *Pro Flac.* 52, Virg. *Aen.* 7.255, 272, Tac. *Ann.* 14.22.

Lucifer is used in the sense of 'day': cf. Prop.2.19.28, Ov. *F.* 1.45f. *ne tamen ignores variorum iura dierum, / non habet officii Lucifer omnis idem.*

For *Aurora . . . / . . . candida* cf. Hom. *Il.*24.785, *Od.*4.188 Ἠοῦς . . . φαεινῆς, *Hom.Hymn.*2.51, Sen. *Oct.* 1f. The adjective also contains connotations of joy, beauty and good fortune (cf. 1.7.64, 1.10.45-6n., Catull.8.3, Prop.2.15.1, Virg. *Aen.*5.571, Serv. ad *Ecl.* 5.56), as does *nitentem* (cf. Catull.2.5, 61.189, Hor. *S.* 2.5.12, T.4.1.183).

The horses of Dawn occur as early as Homer (*Od.* 23.244ff.). *Roseus* is also applied to them at Ov. *Am.* 1.8.4, *F.*4.714, Virg. *Aen.*6.535, 7.26, Val.Fl.2.261 (probably suggested by Homer's stock epithet for Dawn, ῥοδοδάκτυλος).

Porto is generally avoided by the better prose authors and is possibly colloquial, although used freely by poets. In T. I and II *porto* occurs 8 times (a high percentage), *veho* 5 times. See Axelson 30f.

4

Hubner *Hermes* XIV (1879), 307ff.; Karsten *Mnemosyne* XV (1887), 230ff.; Schuster *Tibull-Studien* 29f.; Dawson *AJPh* LXVII (1946), 1ff.; Luck *The Latin Love Elegy* 92ff.; Solmsen *Hermes* XC (1962), 320ff.; Wimmel *Der frühe Tibull* 17ff.

The elegy takes the form of an imaginary dialogue between the poet and a statue of Priapus (in the opening lines (esp. 5f.) Priapus is referred to as a statue exposed to the elements rather than a fully mobile god able to avoid them at will, and the promise of covering at 1f. could only be an inducement aimed at a statue). In reply to T.'s query about the god's technique for catching boys Priapus launches into a lengthy speech praising *παιδικὸς ἔρως* and listing various *praecepta.* T. then states that the god's advice was really asked on behalf of Titius, but, as Titius has an awkward wife, he will pass it on to maltreated boy-lovers. At the end, however, he admits that it was for himself and states that it is useless in the case of his love for Marathus. For this gradual revelation see 73-84n., and cf. Smith on 73-4 and Wimmel op.cit. The same process is to be found in 1.5, 1.8 and 1.9.

1-8	*Introduction*:	main speaker and topic.	
9-72	*The speech of Priapus*:	9-14	general recommendation of παιδικὸς ἔρως.
		15-20	patience required.
		21-26	perjury permissible.
		27-38	necessity of swift action.
		39-56	success the result of obsequiousness.
		57-72	obsequious poetry preferable to gifts of money.
73-84	*Conclusion*:	73-80	T. as a *praeceptor amandi.*
		81-84	inefficacy of his teachings in Marathus' case.

The progression of thought in 1.4 (esp. in the second part) has been questioned, and various transpositions have been suggested (for full refs. and discussions see Karsten and Hubner loc.cit.). In fact, the order of the lines in the mss. is unexceptionable. The progression in the first part is perfectly logical, and the lines form an obvious introduction to 9-72, while the transition is carefully made at 7f. In the speech of Priapus, apart from the obvious connection in that all the various groups of lines after the general recommendation are erotic *praecepta*, they all have in common the idea of the need for qualities such as humility, patience, endurance and perseverance, an idea which forms the basis of the advice. Transitions from precept to precept are handled in the commentary, but a short summary of the advice will show that the progression is natural: 'do entrust yourself to boys, but, having done so, don't expect immediate success; you must be patient and persevere, using even perjury to gain your ends; this does not mean that you should take a long time about winning over the boy, but rather that you should put up with various discomforts for his sake without becoming discouraged; so too the poems which you send the boy (rather than money) should be obsequious.' Careful transition is made to the final part of the elegy (73), which develops the *praeceptor* idea of 9-72. Although there are a number of unexpected turns here, these are all deliberate (73-84n.), and any transpositions would ruin the effect of the poem.

Verbal echoes also help to bind the elegy together: in connection with boys *puer* (9, 39, 58, 61, 76, 83) and *tener* (9, 14, 58); with skill and teaching *ars* (57, 76, 82), *doceo* (17, 59, cf. 61) and *magister* (75, cf. 84); with attraction *formosus* (3, 30, cf. 36), *capio* (3, 13, cf. 15) and *placeo* (11, 50).

The influence of the Alexandrians is particularly evident in 1.4 (see esp. Dawson and Luck), and the main character, the form, the main theme and possibly some of the secondary material of the poem are derived from them.

Priapus is frequently mentioned by Catullus and the Augustans: cf. Catull.47.4, fr.1, Virg. *Ecl.* 7.33ff., *G.* 4.110f., *Copa* 23f., Hor. *S.* 1.8, *Epod.* 2.21, T.1.1.17f., 1.4, Ov. *F.* 1.391ff., 6.319ff., *Met.* 9.347, 14. 640, *Tr.* 1.10.26, and cf. also the *Carmina Priapea.* His worship originated in Lampsacus in the Hellespont and thereabouts, and, after Alexander, spread to Greece and eventually to Italy (cf. Paus.9.31.2, Strabo 587, Serv. ad Virg. *G.* 4.111). He was esp. popular in the Hellenistic period, when he was included in Ptolemy Philadelphus' procession (Athen.201 C-D) and he first appears in literature (cf. Strabo loc.cit.). To judge from the remnants he must have appeared often: cf. Theoc. *Id.* 1.21, 81ff., *Epigr.* 3, 4, Moschus 3.27 Gow, *A.P.* 6.292 (Hedylus), 10.2 (Antipater of Sidon), 16.236 (Leonidas), 237 (Tymnes), 261 (Leonidas), Demosthenes Bithynus fr.11 (Powell *Coll. Alex.*), Sotades Πρίηπος. In addition, the selection of Priapus in particular as *praeceptor* shows Alexandrian influence (see below).

For the form of the dialogue involving the poet in elegy cf. Catull.67, T.3.1, Prop.4.1, Ov. *Am.* 1.1, 3.1, 3.5, *Rem.* 1ff. and *Fasti* passim (e.g. 1.99ff., 3.167ff.). The particular fictions of a talking statue and of a dialogue with such a statue were not Alexandrian innovations (they appear in early epigram: see Rose *CR* XXXVII (1923), 162f.), but they do appear to have been common in that period, and were handled then more fully than was possible in epigram: see Dawson *YClS* XI (1950), 82f. and cf. Call. *Epigr.* 24 Pf. (statue of Hero speaks), fr. 197 Pf. (statue of Hermes speaks), fr. 114 Pf. (dialogue between a statue of Apollo and an unknown person, possibly the poet himself) and fr. 199 Pf. (see below). Not only the length of the treatment suggests Alexandrian influence here: the talking statue of Priapus originated with the Alexandrians (*A.P.* 10.2 Antipater of Sidon, 16.236, 261 Leonidas, 237 Tymnes), and the subject under discussion, παιδικὸς ἔρως, is first found in such a dialogue at Call. fr. 199 Pf. (a lover of boys holds a conversation with an ithyphallic statue of Hermes).

This is not the first appearance in Roman elegy of the *praeceptor amandi* and amatory precepts (cf. Prop. 1.7, 1.9, 1.10, 1.20), and at 39ff. T. adopts one of Prop.'s precepts (see 39-40n.). The theme recurs in T. 1.6 and 1.8 (cf. also 1.2.19-20n.), and was common in elegy (cf. esp. Prop. 2.4, 4.5, Ov. *Am.* 1.4, 1.8, *A.A.*, *Rem.*). For the influence of 1.4 on Ovid see Wilhelm *Satura Viadrina* (Breslau, 1896), 48ff.: 9-14 cf. *A.A.* 3.381ff.; 15-20 cf. *A.A.* 1.469ff.; 21-26 cf. *A.A.* 1. 631ff.; 27-38 cf. *A.A.* 3.59ff.; 39-52 cf. *A.A.* 2.177ff.; 53-56 cf. *A.A.* 1.663ff.; 57-72 cf. *A.A.* 2.261ff., 3.533ff. (it seems unlikely that T. and Ovid were jointly following any preceding *artes amatoriae*, since one would have expected Ovid to mention their existence in his defence in *Tristia* 2). On the subject in general see Wheeler *CPh* V (1910), 440ff., VI (1911), 56ff. and Cairns *Generic Composition in Greek and Roman Poetry* (Edinburgh, 1972) index s.v. erotodidaxis.

Wheeler maintained that the source of erotodidaxis in Roman elegy was Greek New Comedy. In Plautus and Terence instruction is given by a *lena, meretrix* or *peritus adulescens*, and fragments of Menander suggest that this element may have been present in him too (e.g. 258, 541, 566, 646K), but in basic form the didactic attitude and claim of expertise may be traced back even further (e.g. Theogn. 1353ff., Aristoph. *Eccl.* 893ff.). However, in the case of 1.4 again we may detect Alexandrian influence.

Praecepta for παιδικὸς ἔρως are first mentioned at Call. fr. 571 Pf. (Erchius is a teacher of boy-love). Similarly at Moschus 3.83 Gow Bion is described as teaching kissing of boys, and at Bion fr. 13 Gow an old man teaches a boy about love. The claim by the poet himself to be a *praeceptor amandi*, which Wheeler maintained was an adaptation by the elegists of the part played in comedy by the *lena, meretrix* and *peritus adulescens*, had already been made at Moschus fr. 2 Gow, and the actual designation of such advice as 'teachings' at Moschus fr. 2.7 Gow (cf. also Moschus fr. 3 and Bion fr. 10 Gow, where there is play on the idea of Love teaching). In addition, the choice of Priapus as the amatory expert seems to have been based on the Alexandrian concept of him.

He was suited for the rôle as a son of Aphrodite (7-8n.) and as a lustful god of fertility and lover of boys (Theoc. *Epigr.* 3, schol. ad Theoc. *Id.* 1.81, *A.P.* 16.240 (Philippus), 241 (Marcus Argentarius), 243 (Antistius), Lucian *Dial.Deor.* 273-5, *Priap.* 3,5,6,13 etc.). He actually appears as adviser on matters of love to Daphnis at Theoc. *Id.* 1.81ff., his aid is sought by a lover at Theoc. *Epigr.* 4, and he acts as a judge in a beauty-contest at *A.P.* 6.292 (Hedylus). So Ovid attributes to him erotic skills at *F.* 1.417ff.

Dawson and Luck suggest a number of passages in which T. directly imitates Callimachus. Of Dawson's parallels only the curse on the venal lover seems really likely (67-70n), although the topics of the poor poet and poetry versus wealth may have been inspired by Callimachus (61-2n.). Of the additional parallels cited by Luck the only one which seems at all possible is the combination of the yoke image and the idea of perseverance (15-16n.). Elsewhere ideas are not exclusively Callimachean and there is no close verbal similarity. I would add that Call. *Iamb.* 3 may just have suggested the attack on the venality of the present age in connection with boy-love (57-8n.).

It should be pointed out that although the influence of the Alexandrians in 1.4 is extensive, T. does not merely imitate them. His main debt to them is simply the framework for the poem. Most of the secondary material derives from the common stock of love poetry, and is elaborated and presented from a new angle (didactic), while the tone and technique ensure individuality and originality.

On the overall interpretation of the elegy cf. Smith on 9-56 and Solmsen loc.cit. The following account is largely an elaboration of their views. Evidence for my statements will be found in the commentary.

Lines 1-8 act as a signpost: the description of Priapus here as a figure lacking in dignity and even rather laughable is to put the reader on his guard against taking too seriously the god's appearance as a *praeceptor* in the following lines.

The second part (9-72) is highly ironical: the subject is a humble one, and the remarks upon it put in Priapus' mouth are commonplace, but presented with complete seriousness and with the pose of a dignified, dogmatic and learned professor. This attitude is to be seen in the orders and prohibitions, the structural precision and the lists of exx. and full discussion which are given to each precept with parallels from nature and personal experience. Even when this calm and logical attitude is abandoned (57ff.), it is only to soar into the heights of poetry. The extraneous material that is introduced is seldom entirely new, but seems intended to enhance the god's and the subject's dignity (e.g. the refs. to time's universal laws at 15ff. and 27ff., the claim of divine support at 21ff., and the elaboration of the theme of immortality conveyed by poetry at 61ff.). *Doctrina* is also in evidence, esp. literary reminiscence (often to heighten the tone). So the language is generally poetic and elevated, with many new or unusual forms and words, and stylistically the elegance seems a little overdone (e.g. the various metrical effects, the frequent use of anaphora, the contrasts, correspondences, climax, word-play and artistic arrangement of words).

In the final part (73-84) the pose of instructor is taken over by T. himself, and he shows similar seriousness and self-importance, depicting himself as a detached and uninvolved figure. However, at 81ff. comes the unexpected climax to the whole poem, and the present impinges: we are told that all the logical precepts are useless in the face of T.'s love for Marathus, and T.'s pose becomes laughable.

In 1.4 there are two sets of contrasts, the second mirroring the first: Priapus appears initially as the usual comic and undignified figure, but then is shown in a serious and learned pose; so T. appears next in the same dignified pose, but is finally reduced to a laughing-stock. The irony at the expense of Priapus and the self-irony introduced by the conclusion give the whole poem the tone of a gentle skit on the rationalizing *praeceptor amandi* and his *praecepta* (so the poem closes with the words *vana magisteria*, 84). The humour is heightened by the way in which T. until the very end misleads the reader over the person for whom the god's advice is supposed to be intended and by the positioning of the elegy between two serious pieces.

This is intellectual and accomplished poetry. Scholarship and sophistication are combined with rather irreverent wit, and the whole is handled with an elegant lightness of touch and dexterity of technique. T. has produced the most detailed and most amusing version of this theme until Ovid, and, apart from thematic considerations, the elegy exhibits many features and qualities normally associated with T.'s sparkling successor.

1–8 An introduction to the main speaker and the main topic. Priapus is here described as a weatherbeaten statue, unattractive, naked and rustic (i.e. undignified and rather comic). Various poetic devices (esp. balance, alliteration and anaphora) help the bantering tone, and the lines thus warn against taking too seriously the pose as an instructor shortly to be attributed to Priapus.

1–2 The prayer is to a statue of Priapus (see intro. essay), which, as usual, is treated as a living being with appropriate feelings and powers, and it takes the form of a benefit which will be conferred on the god on condition that he grants the petitioner's wish. For such prayers to Priapus cf. Theoc. *Epigr.* 4.13ff., Virg. *Ecl.* 7.35f., *Priap.* 50, and for this use of *sic* and the subjunctive as an introduction to a request for information cf. Virg. *Ecl.* 9.30ff., Ov. *Met.* 8.857ff.

Priapus, god of fertility and the countryside, protected livestock and property against birds and thieves (Virg. *Ecl.* 7.34, *G.* 4.110f. *et custos furum atque avium cum falce saligna / Hellespontiaci servet tutela Priapi*, T.1.1.17f., Paus.9.31.2, *Priap.* 35, Mart.6.49, 8.40). He was often represented as a statue (as early as Theoc. *Epigr.* 4), made of various types of wood (Theoc. loc.cit., Mart.6.49, *Priap.* 6.1f.) or occasionally of marble (Virg. *Ecl.* 7.35). He had enormous genitals and a sickle, and was often painted red (7-8n., Hor. *S.* 1.8.1ff., Virg. *G.* 4.110f., T.1.1. 17f., Ov. *F.* 1.415, 6.319, 333, *Priap.* 1.5). Statues of Priapus usually stood in the open air all year round (*Priap.* 84, 85.6ff.), exposed to all kinds of weather (5-6, *Priap.* 61.5ff., 63.1ff.). Hence the promise of shade here. Priapus is occasionally given some cover by trees (Theoc. *Epigr.* 4, *Priap.* 83.6f.) or a small chapel (*Priap.* 82.2, Myrinus *A.P.* 6.254.8).

soles . . . nives: distributive plurals: sun every day in the summer and various falls of snow in the winter (cf. Lucr.5.252, Hor. *C.* 3.24.39).

Note the neat balance between *ne . . . soles* and *ne . . . nives*, the alliteration of n and the internal rhyme in the pentameter.

3–4 The amusingly careful order avoids offence by mentioning success and cleverness first and adding lack of beauty almost as an afterthought. For Priapus as a lover of boys and for his *sollertia* see intro. essay.

Priapus was generally represented as a rude and ugly figure (cf. Theoc. *Epigr.* 4.1ff., *Priap.* 10, 39.5 *me pulcra fateor carere forma*), and in his exposed position his hair and beard were unlikely to be in good condition: cf. Hor. *S.* 1.8.37f. *mentior at si quid, merdis caput inquiner albis / corvorum*, *Priap.* 63.5f., 83.9ff. (for good grooming as a sign of beauty cf. 1.6.39-40n., and on the beard see Austin on Cic. *Pro Caelio* 33.25). Hence the conclusion that Priapus' success with boys is due not to beauty but to cleverness (cf. Ov. *F.* 1.419ff.).

formosos: substantive (cf. the Greek καλοί): cf. 1.9.6, Prop.4.4.52, Ov. *A.A.* 2.117, Sen. *Phaed.* 781. The fem. subst. is more common (2.3.65 etc.).

cepit: the verb in an amatory context is used of *artes*, gifts etc. (1.9.11, 19, Ov. *Am.* 1.8.70, 2.19.10, *A.A.* 1.265) and of physical attractions (Prop.1.1.1, 2.3.9, T.1.4.13, Ov. *Am.* 1.10.10, 2.4.13).

non tibi barba nitet: the verb and its derivatives are usually applied to the sheen on hair, whether produced by oil (Hor. *C.* 2.7.7) or natural (Virg. *G.* 4.337). Perhaps the connotation of 'elegant, neat' (cf. Cic. *Cat.* 2.10.22 *pexo capillo, nitidos*, Sen. *Epist.* 115.2) is also present here.

non tibi culta coma est: prodelided *est* at the end of the pent. is not uncommon in the elegists (Platnauer 40), but in T. I and II there are only 4 exx., all following a disyllable in -a (1.4.4, 1.10.4, 2.6.10, 44). The only other ex. in the *Corp. Tib.* is 4.4.16 (*tibi est*). For the practice in hexameters see 63-4n.

On words for hair in Latin poetry see Axelson 51. In the loftier genres the prosaic *capillus* is rare (apart from Ovid), while *coma* and *crinis* are more frequent: Virgil 2: 28: 30; Sen. *Trag.* 4: 61: 20; Lucan 2: 27: 20; Val.Fl.2: 18: 25; Sil.It.2: 24: 27; Statius 4: 90: 84; Ov. *Met.* 64: 32: 38 (Lucr. has *coma* only, once). In comedy and satire, on the other hand, *capillus* is generally more common than the other two words: Plautus 8: 0: 3; Terence 4: 0: 0; Hor. *S.* 2: 0: 0; Persius 1: 0: 0; Juvenal 5: 5: 7. In lyric also *capillus* is quite common: Catull. 2: 5: 4; Hor. lyric 11: 10: 12. So too in elegy, where *coma* is most frequent and *crinis* least common: T. 12: 26: 8; Prop. 15: 29: 8; Ovid 98: 128: 30.

Crinis, the collective singular, is rare in elegy (T. 1.4.38 only, Prop. never, Ov. *Her.* 15.140, *Am.* 3.6.71, *A.A.* 3.250, 783, *F.* 3.257, 4.318, 6.441) and lyric (Catull. never, Hor. twice), being mainly confined to the loftier genres (e.g. never in Plautus, Terence, Lucilius, Hor. *S.*, Pers., Lucr., but Sen. *Trag.* 16 exx., Ov. *Met.* 15, Sil.It. 13, Val.Fl. 9, Virg. 8 – all in *Aen.*). *Caesaries* in elegy occurs only once (Ov. *Am.* 3.1.32), but the word was not often used in poetry (e.g. Ov. *Met.* 7 exx., Virg. 5, Sil.It. 4, Catull. 1, Hor. 1, Juv. 1, Val.Fl. 1, Sen. *Trag.* 1).

Note the alliteration, and the balance and anaphora in the pentameter.

5–6 Statues of Priapus were conventionally *nudus* (*Priap.* 1.6, 9.1, 14.8, 16.8), which meant that they had a weatherbeaten appearance (1-2n.), and that the enormous genitals were exposed to view, a fact that seems to have aroused mirth (*A.P.* 16.86 (anon.), 243 (Antistius), *Priap.* 10.7f. *nimirum tibi salsa res videtur / adstans inguinibus columna nostris*).

producis: 'pass, spend' (with the idea of a long period of time): cf. Ter. *Ad.* 591 *cyathos sorbilans paullatim hunc producam diem*, Mart. 2. 89.1, Stat. *Theb.* 8.219.

Canis: for the Dog-star see 1.1.27-8n. Priapus complains about it at *Priap.* 63.2.

Note the emphatic anaphora and the contrast between hex. and pent.

7–8 Bacchi . . . rustica proles: in most accounts Bacchus is Priapus' father (*A.P.* 10.15.7f. (Paulus Silentiarius), 10.2.7f. (Antipater of Sidon) ταῦθ' ὁ Πρίηπος / ὔμμιν ἐνορμίτας παῖς ἐνέπω Βρομίου), his mother being either Aphrodite (Paus. 9.31.2, Diod.Sic. 4.6.1, schol. ad Ap. Rhod. 1.932-3, Serv. ad *G.* 4.111) or a nymph (Strabo 13.1.12, schol. ad Theoc. *Id.* 1.21).

Proles is here mock-solemn. The word was archaic and later had a solemn and poetic tone (Cic. *De Or.* 3.153, Norden on *Aen.* 6.784). *Proles* occurs 5 times in T. I and II, and, apart from the present instance, adds a touch of real solemnity (1.3.79, 1.7.55, 1.10.39, 2.2.21).

For *rusticus* applied to Priapus cf. *Priap.* 68.1, 81.1, *ruricola* at Ov. *Tr.* 1.10.26, ἀγροιώτης at *A.P.* 6.22.5 (anon.) and *ruris numina* at *Priap.* 14.7.

armatus curva sic mihi falce deus: for military language in connection with Priapus cf. *Priap.* 9.14, 11.2, 55.4, *Copa* 23f. *est tuguri custos,* *armatus falce saligna, / sed non et vasto est inguine terribilis.* The tone is usually mock-serious (underlined here by the concentration of spondees in the couplet).

For Priapus' sickle see Virg. *G.*4.110, *Copa* 23, T.1.1.18, Ov. *Met.* 14.640, Mart.11.18.21, *Priap.*6.2, 11.2, 30.1, 33.6, 55.1.

Sic here goes with *respondit* in 7 (the only ex. of postponed *sic* in the *Corp. Tib.*). *Sic mihi* balances *sic ego* (7).

9–14 The speech of Priapus has been carefully introduced by the preceding couplet.

For the irony of the pose as *praeceptor* attributed to Priapus see intro. essay. A brief recommendation of boy-love, based on the great variety of attractions in boys, prefaces the *praecepta*. This section may well be modelled on the openings of didactic works where complimentary remarks are made about the subject under discussion (e.g. Cic. *De Or.* 1.30ff., *Nat.D.* 1.7ff.). The structural neatness and verbal play which characterize Priapus' speech are evident here: the basic statement (2 lines) is followed by 4 exx. (4 lines); in the exx. there is balance in the expression (*hic placet . . . quod . . . / hic . . . / hic, quia . . . cepit: at illi / . . .*); the exx. are skilfully arranged (11f. concern sporting activities (manly skill contrasted with beauty, and land with water), 13f. concern character (boldness contrasted with modesty), and in both couplets the masculine aspect in the hex. is opposed to the feminine aspect in the pent.).

9–10 ne fuge te tenerae puerorum credere turbae: see Critical Appendix.

For *ne* with the first form of the imperative see 1.1.67-8n.

The imperative of *fugio* for the more common *noli* is rare and poetic: it is first found in poetry at Lucr.1.1052, and later only at Hor. *C.* 1.9.13, 2.4.22, Pers.6.65, Stat. *Theb.*9.139. Other forms of *fugio* (and *fugito*) with an infinitive, probably modelled on the Greek φευγειν, are found in poetry and prose (e.g. Cic. *Or.* 3.153, *Att.* 10.8.5, Virg. *Aen.*9.199f.).

For *credo* see 1.6.23-4n.

See 1.9.15-16n. on the delicacy of the *puer delicatus.*

nam causam iusti semper amoris habent: for *iustus* 'having good cause, justified' cf. e.g. Cic. *Brut.*158 *plena iusti doloris oratio* and see *OLD* s.v.5.

There may be an attempt at quasi-legal solemnity here, as in general *causa* and *iustus* have obvious legal connotations, and in particular both the phrase *causam habere* and *iustus* 'justified' are found in legal writings (Julian *Dig.*40.9.7.1, Gaius *Inst.*3.160; cf. also *iusta causa* at Gaius *Inst.* 4.36, Ulp. *Dig.*4.6.1.1, 10.3.7.3 etc.).

Amoris refers to the observer's feeling of love.

For the different attractions of various boys (and women) cf. *A.P.* 5.232 (Paulus Silentiarius), 12.5 (Strato), 87 (anon.), 93 (Rhianus),

198, 244 (Strato), Prop. 2.22, 2.25.39ff., Ov. *Am.* 2.4, 2.10.

11–12 For the observation of young men engaged in sporting activities and the admiration of their manliness, dexterity and uncovered bodies leading to love cf. Cic. *Pro Cael.* 36, *A.P.* 12.123 (anon.), Ov. *Her.* 4.67ff. The ref. may be general here, but, if confined to Roman youths, it will be to the Campus Martius and the Tiber (*placidam . . . aquam*, cf. Ov. *A.A.* 3.386, Virg. *Aen.* 2.782), where such sports took place (Nisbet & Hubbard on Hor. *C.* 1.8.4 and 8).

hic placet, angustis quod equum compescit habenis: *placeo* in an amatory context is common: cf. Plaut. *Merc.* 103, Prop. 1.2.26, T. 1.4. 50, 1.8.15, 2.5.35, 51, 4.13.3, Hor. *C.* 3.7.24, Ov. *Am.* 2.2.14 etc.

Angustus with an active force first appears here and is rare (mainly later prose): cf. Ov. *Met.* 5.410 *angustis inclusum cornibus aequor.* Verbal adjectives and participles in -tus were originally passive in force, but some of them eventually acquired an active signification (cf. *inexpertus*: 1.7.31-2n.): see Stolz-Schmalz *Lat. Gramm.*[4] (Munich, 1910), 300, 415f., Sommer *Handbuch der lat. Laut-u. Formenlehre* (Heidelberg, 1902), 637ff.

Horse-riding involves manliness and skill: cf. esp. Ov. *Her.* 4.79f. *sive ferocis equi luctantia colla recurvas, / exiguo flexos miror in orbe pedes.* For this sport see Nisbet & Hubbard on Hor. *C.* 1.8.6.

hic placidam niveo pectore pellit aquam: swimming is no less manly, but *niveo* shows the real attraction here, the uncovered body. Whiteness was generally considered improper and effeminate in a man, since he should be sunburnt, esp. by exercise such as that in 11 (Eur. *Bacc.* 457ff. and Dodds ad loc., Lucian *Anachars.* 25, Ov. *A.A.* 1.513, 723ff.), but was found attractive in women (1.5.66, Hor. *C.* 1.19.5, 2.5.18, Ov. *Met.* 13.789, Mart. 1.115.2f.) and in the *puer delicatus* (*A.P.* 12.5.1, 244.1 (Strato), Mart. 6.39.12, 11.22.1).

The line may be a reminiscence of Enn. *Ann.* 230V *poste recumbite vestraque pectora pellite tonsis* (Putnam's suggestion), as though Priapus were trying to elevate the theme.

The contrast with 11 is heightened by *placidam*, which suggests a more graceful and less strenuous scene. Note too the echoing *hic plac-* at the start of each line, the alliteration of p in the pentameter and the way in which in the word-order, as in the action, the *placida aqua* encloses the *niveum pectus*.

13–14 hic, quia fortis adest audacia, cepit: for this attraction see 11-12n.

Quia occurs here only in T., but is not uncommon elsewhere in elegy (9 exx. in Prop. (8 with indicative), 100 exx. in Ovid, 1 ex. in Catullan elegiacs). For the present indicative cf. Prop. 1.18.17f.

On the use of *capio* see 3-4n.

at illi / virgineus teneras stat pudor ante genas: for this attraction cf. Plat. *Charm.* 158, Theoc. *Id.* 30.7ff., *A.P.* 12.96, 99 (anon.), Mart. 8.46.

For *virgineus* and *tener* in connection with the *puer delicatus* see 1.9.15-16n.

Stat . . . ante is a unique phrase in this connection. The *pudor* may be regarded as a sort of covering: for the expression cf. Suet. *Nero* 48.1 *ante faciem optento sudario*, and for the idea cf. Stat. *Theb.* 2.231 *candida purpureum fusae super ora pudorem*. Possibly the military use of the phrase is in point here ('take a stand before, guard': e.g. Livy 36.45.6): cf. Hor. *C.* 4.13.7f. (of Love) *Chiae / pulchris excubat in genis.* This idea would pick up the military connotations in *fortis . . . audacia* and contrast amusingly with *virgineus teneras.* It is also possible that *stat . . . ante* contains an allusion to the *antistes* (guardian, overseer of a temple), i.e. the *pudor* guards the cheeks. For this idea also cf. Hor. loc. cit., and for *antistes* in an extended sense meaning 'protector' cf. Ov. *Tr.* 3.14.1.

Note the contrast between *fortis . . . audacia* and *virgineus . . . pudor* (underlined by the juxtaposed *teneras*), and the order of words in the pent. (1.7.25-6n.).

15–20 The connection in thought is: 'having entrusted yourself to boys (following on from 9), don't expect to be successful straight away' (*sed ne* picks up *ne* in 9).

The first of the *praecepta*: 'don't be put off if you do not have immediate success' (i.e. humility, patience, endurance and perseverance are necessary). Again we find neatness of structure and expression: again the basic statement (2 lines) is followed by 4 exx. (4 lines); in the exx. the anaphora of *longa dies* (with gnomic perfects) is balanced by that of *annus* (with present tenses); in 17f. there is a contrast between animate and inanimate, and in 19f. between terrestrial and celestial. The exx. are close parallels to the situation under consideration, and most of them are original, if merely variations on preceding exx.

15–16 sed ne te capiant, primo si forte negabit, / taedia: for the sentiment cf. Theogn. 1283ff., *A.P.* 12.99 (anon.), 101 (Meleager), 149 (Callimachus), Prop. 1.1.9ff., Hor. *C.* 2.5, Ov. *A.A.* 1.469ff., 2.177ff., Nemes. *Ecl.* 4.56ff.

The locution *aliquid aliquem capit* is found throughout Latin prose and poetry, and occurs as early as Ennius (*Trag.* fr. 222 Jocelyn *cupido cepit miseram nunc me proloqui*): see *OLD* s.v. *capio* 21b. *Capiant* here humorously picks up *cepit* (13).

Primo is emphatic by position (so too the contrasting *paulatim* in the pentameter).

Nego in an amatory context is common: cf. 2.6.27, Prop. 2.14.20, Ov. *Am.* 2.8.25 etc.

paulatim sub iuga colla dabit: the image of the yoke was often used of marriage in Greek tragedy (Eur. *Med.* 242, 673 etc.) and of love in erotic poetry (Theogn. 1357f., Theoc. *Id.* 12.15, 27.21, 30.28f., *A.P.*

5.22.2 (Rufinus), Hor. *C.*1.33.10f., 2.5.1f., 3.9.18, Prop.2.5.14, 3.11.4, 3.25.8, Ov. *Her.*6.97, 9.6, *Rem.* 90). For the beloved compared to an untamed animal cf. esp. Anac.88D, Hor. *C.*2.5, 3.11.9f.

These lines may have been inspired by Callimachus (*A.P.*12. 149), where the sentiment and the image are combined, as here: *'ληφθήσῃ, περίφευγε, Μενέκρατες·' εἶπα Πανήμου / εἰκάδι, καὶ Λώου τῇ – τίνι; τῇ δεκάτῃ / ἦλθεν ὁ βοῦς ὑπ' ἄροτρον ἑκούσιος. εὖγ' ἐμὸς Ἑρμῆς, / εὖγ' ἐμός· οὐ παρὰ τὰς εἴκοσι μεμφόμεθα.*

17–18 longa dies homini docuit parere leones: in line with the pose as *praeceptor, docuit* (like *peredit* in 18) is a gnomic perfect (1.8.35-6n.).

For *longa dies* 'a long time, length of time' cf. Plaut. *Epid.* 544, Virg. *Aen.* 5.783, 6.745, Ov. *Met.* 1.346, Juv.10.265.

In other versions of the subjugation of animals theme the ox and the horse are more common (e.g. Prop.2.3.47f., Ov. *A.A.*1.471f., 2.184, *Tr.*4.6.1ff.), and this is the first time that the lion is so used (cf. Ov. *A.A.* 2.183, *Tr.*4.6.5f. *tempore Poenorum compescitur ira leonum, / nec feritas animo, quae fuit ante, manet*, Sen.*Ben.*1.2.5, Maxim.1.271). Smith cites Uncle Remus.

Tamed and trained lions were exhibited in Greece as early as the fourth century B.C. (Isoc. *Antidosis* 213). For Roman times cf. Plut. *Ant.*9, Plin. *N.H.* 8.55, Mart.1.6, 14, 22, 2.75, Stat. *Silv.*2.5, Sen. *De Ira* 2.31.6.

The lion is chosen here as a symbol of extreme ferocity (e.g. Juv. 8.36f.) – hence the position of *leones*. The lion and lioness are often used to express the savagery of humans, esp. lovers (Eur. *Med.* 1342, *Or.* 1555, Catull.60.1, 64.154 *quaenam te genuit sola sub rupe leaena*?, T.3.4.90). The implication is that, like the lion, the boy's ferocity will be overcome.

longa dies molli saxa peredit aqua: for the proverbial wearing away of stone by water see Otto *Sprichwörter* s.v. *gutta* (2), Bion fr.4 Gow, Plut. *Mor.* 2D. The rock is the prime ex. of hardness (e.g. Ov. *A.A.*1.475) and is often used as an image for lack of feeling in humans, esp. lovers (1.1.63-4n.). The suggestion is that in the same way the boy's indifference will be worn away.

The verb *peredo* is poetic, and before here is applied to water's effect on stone only at Lucr.1.326 (*vesco sale saxa peresa*), so that the present phrase is probably a Lucretian reminiscence, as Putnam suggests (again to heighten the tone).

Note the juxtaposition (*molli saxa*) and the emphatic position of *aqua*.

19–20 annus in apricis maturat collibus uvas: the ex. of the ripening grape is first found here in such remarks on time's nature and power: cf. Ov. *Tr.*4.6.9f. *tempus ut extensis tumeat facit uva racemis, / vixque merum capiant grana quod intus habent*. The grape is often used in erotic imagery to describe the immaturity and bitterness of the young beloved: cf. *A.P.* 5.20 (Honestus), 304 (anon.), 12.205 (Strato), Hor. *C.* 2.5.9f. *tolle cupidinem / immitis uvae.* So here the effect of the sun on the grape provides an obvious symbol of the boy maturing into ripeness for love.

The line seems to be modelled on Virg. *Ecl.* 9.49 *duceret apricis in collibus uva colorem.*

annus agit certa lucida signa vice: this ex. of the constellations occurs here only in this connection, and it concludes the list, implying the immutability of the law and the inevitability of change (so too the boy must change). Here Priapus is giving another, and a supreme, ex. of the wonders that time brings to pass. For the idea of the fixed movements of the constellations cf. Cic. *N.D.* 2.51, Sen. *Med.* 402 *nitidusque certas mundus evolvet vices*, Manil. 1.110, 474ff., 2.207, 3.71 *certasque vices. Vicis* is also used of changes in love (Prop. 3.25.15, Ov. *Met.* 4.191, cf. Hor. *Epod.* 15.24), which makes the parallelism all the more obvious.

The phrase *lucida signa* is a reminiscence of Lucr. 5.518, as Putnam points out, and is another ex. of Priapus' elevated language.

21–26 *Nec* picks up *sed ne* (15). Continuing with the idea of the need for patience and perseverance, Priapus' advice is to use even perjury to gain one's ends (i.e. among various devices), and, taking up the idea of humility, to bind oneself with oaths to the boy (cf. Plat. *Symp.* 183A, where this action is included among the various servile acts of lovers).

The second of the *praecepta*: 'use any oath to gain your object, since the gods do not punish lovers' perjuries'. Again the basic statement (2 lines) is followed by 4 lines (this time elaboration rather than exx.); in the elaboration there is balance between divine approval on the highest level (23f.) and on the most unlikely level (25f.); there is verbal play in *iurare, periuria* (21) and *iurasset* (24) and in *perque suas* . . . / . . . *perque* . . . *suos* (25f.).

21–22 The idea that lovers' perjuries go unpunished is very common from Hesiod (23-4n.) onwards: see Smith and cf. also Ov. *Am.* 1.8.85f., 3.3.11f., 43f. *si deus ipse forem, numen sine fraude liceret / femina mendaci falleret ore meum.* It appears here first in surviving Latin literature, as Lee (p. 106) points out. For T.'s expression of this idea here see 1.5.35-6n.

nec iurare time: *nec* with the imperative is mainly poetic (Leumann-Hofmann-Szantyr 2.340).

per . . . freta summa: 'over the top of the sea'. For *freta* of the sea in general cf. Virg. *Aen.* 1.607, 10.147, Hor. *C.* 1.15.1, and for *summus* meaning 'the top of' in this connection cf. Virg. *Aen.* 1.110, 5.819 *caeruleo per summa levis volat aequora curru*, 6.357.

23–24 Probably there is learned allusion here to the story, first in Hesiod (fr. 124 Merk. and West), that Zeus seduced Io, but, when detected by

Hera, changed Io into a white heifer and swore that he had never touched her: ἐκ τοῦ δ' ὅρκον ἔθηκεν ἀποίνιμον ἀνθρώποισι / νοσφιδίων ἔργων πέρι Κύπριδος (schol. ad Plat. *Symp.* 183B, Apollod.2.1.3, Hesychius s.v. ἀφροδίσιος ὅρκος). The allusion is amusingly indelicate in the mouth of Priapus. For Jupiter's approval here cf. 1.2.8, 3.6.49f., Prop.2.16. 47f., Ov. *A.A.* 1.631ff., and for another case of divine approval on a high level cf. 1.6.43ff.

gratia magna Iovi: an ambiguous phrase, perhaps deliberately so. The following translations are possible: (i) 'many thanks to Jupiter' (cf. Ov. *Tr.* 4.10.117 for the dative and the omission of *esse*; cf. Cic. *Marc.* 33 for the use of *magnus*); (ii) 'great is the kindness of Jupiter', i.e. towards lovers (for *gratia* cf. Ov. *Her.* 7.41); (iii) 'great is the friendship of Jupiter', i.e. towards lovers (for *gratia* cf. Caes. *B.G.* 1.35.4); (iv) even 'great is the favouritism of Jupiter', i.e. towards lovers (for *gratia* cf. Cic. *Q.Frat.* 1.2.10); and perhaps (v) 'great is the popularity of Jupiter', i.e. in the eyes of lovers (for the dative cf. Plin. *N.H.* 14.73; for the use of *magnus* cf. Cic. *Att.* 5.11.6).

Pater: i.e. Jupiter (cf. 1.3.51).

iurasset cupide quidquid ineptus amor: for the displacement of the compound pronoun cf. (*quisquis*) 2.2.15 and (*quicumque*) 1.2.39, 1.4.39, 1.10.59, 2.2.13. *Iurasset* represents a future perfect indicative in *oratio recta* (chronologically prior to *valere*).

On *amor* see 1.2.3-4n.

For *ineptus* applied to love cf. Plaut. *Rud.* 1204 *nimi' paene inepta atque odiosa eius amatiost*, and for *ineptus* and *ineptire* applied to lovers cf. Plaut. *Merc.* 381, Catull.8.1, T.4.10.2, Ov. *A.A.* 1.306.

25–26 Just as Jupiter allows perjury, so do other gods: cf. *A.P.* 5.6 (Callimachus), Ov. *Am.* 1.8.85f., 3.3.11ff., *A.A.* 1.631f. Here Diana and Minerva are chosen for emphasis but with comical exaggeration: as chaste and virgin goddesses, they would be the last to overlook lovers' misdemeanours, and lovers would be unlikely to swear by them in any case. The remark is even funnier in the mouth of another god.

Oaths were sometimes sworn by the favourite weapons or other attributes of the gods. For the former cf. Ov. *Am.* 2.7.27 (Cupid's arrows), *Her.* 2.39f. (Cupid's bow and torch), *F.* 2.157f. (Diana's arrows), Juv. 13.78ff. (Diana's arrows and many more). Arrows were a favourite weapon of Diana (*Hom.Hym.* 5.18, Call. *Hym.* 3.2, 8). Minerva was proud of her hair (Serv. ad *Aen.* 6.289), but I can find no exact parallel for an oath by her hair: cf. Zeus' head (*Hom.Hym.* 4.274), Caesar's head (Ov. *ExP.* 3.3.68), the sun's rays (Ov. *Met.* 1.768, Juv.13.78), the song of the Fates (Prop.4.7.51).

sinit . . . / adfirmes: for the omission of *ut* see 1.2.25a-26n.

Dictynna: a learned allusion (she was a Cretan nymph or goddess of the wild, generally identified with Diana: Eur. *Hipp.* 145 and Barrett ad loc., Ov. *Met.* 2.441).

crines perque Minerva suos: on postponement of prepositions in T. see 1.1.21-4n. For the postponement of *-que* see 1.1.39-40n.: this is the only ex. in T. of a postponed enclitic attached to a monosyllable, and there are only 8 other exx. in the whole of elegy (Platnauer 92).

27–38 The need for patience and perseverance is restated for clarification: to be slow (in making use of perjury etc.) is a mistake (because the lover will soon be too old for love: cf. 1.1.71-2n., 1.8.29-30n.). The correct application of the idea is given at 39ff.

The third of the *praecepta*: 'don't be slow, or your youth will pass you by'. Again the basic statement is given in two lines and is followed by four exx. (this time occupying six lines), and there is also a brief complaint (four lines). There is verbal play in the anaphora of *quam cito* (28ff.), picked up by *quam iacet* (31). The section exhibits a series of contrasts: in 27f. *tardus* is opposed to *quam cito non segnis*; in the exx. the first pair are inanimate (1 line each), representing the speed of change, while the second pair are animate (2 lines each), concentrating on old age; in the complaint the non-human snake's renewed youth is followed by the human's fleeting youth, which is followed by divine everlasting youth.

27–28 See Critical Appendix.

For the phenomenon of allowing syllables to remain closed before an initial vowel (*eris*) see 1.10.13-14n.

transiet: a rare form, but not unique in the classical period (Sen. *N.Q.* 3.10.4, Apul. *Ascl.* 28 = p.314 Hildebrand all mss.). Cf. also *redies* (Apul. *Met.* 6.19 all mss.), *iniet* (Sen. *Ben.* 2.1.2 N Hosius), *inietur* (Cic. *Leg. Agr.* 2.25.67 most mss.), *exiet* (Sen. *Epist.* 17.9 oldest mss.), *exient* (Iulius Modestus, quoted by Pliny ap. Charis. *Gramm.* 1.125K). These forms are occasionally found in later authors and are frequent in biblical writings and church Latin (Neue 3.327f.).

aetas: may mean (1) 'youth' (1.8.47, Ov. *A.A.* 3.65, 571), (2) 'life' (Cic. *Div.* 2.141, *Tusc.* 5.5), or even (3) 'time' (Cat. 68.43, Hor. *C.* 4.9.10). In view of the drift of the following lines (esp. *serior aetas* 33 and *iuventas* 37) 'youth' seems most likely here.

There is urgency and emphasis in the brief phrases in the hexameter.

non segnis stat remeatque dies: there are three possible ways of taking the phrase. *Stat* means 'stand still' (Hor. *C.* 3.28.6), while *dies* may mean 'daylight', 'day' (singular for plural) or 'time in general'. Firstly, as *remeare* most frequently means 'to come back', 'daylight / day does not sluggishly linger and (sluggishly) return'. Secondly, as *remeare* can also mean 'go back' (of receding water at Tac. *Hist.* 1.86, Plin. *N.H.* 2.212), 'daylight / day does not sluggishly linger and (sluggishly) recede'. In either case the idea is that day follows day in rapid succession (cf. Hor. *C.* 2.18.15, Sen. *Ep.* 24.26, Petron. *S.* 41). Thirdly, *remeare* may again be used in the sense of 'come back' and *dies* may refer to 'time in general': 'time stands not idle and does not return' (for the idea cf. Cic. *Sen.* 19.69, Virg. *G.* 3.284, Ov. *Met.* 15.179ff.). This interpretation seems the most likely in view of Ovid's imitation at *A.A.* 3.64 *nec, quae praeteriit, hora redire potest.*

Note the fullness and emphasis in *quam cito non segnis*.

For the sentiment that youth and beauty are short-lived (due to the rapid passing of time) cf. Mimnerm.2, 5D, Theogn.1305f., Theoc. *Id.* 27.8, 29.25ff., *A.P.* 5.79 (Plato), 12.29 (Alcaeus), 32 (Thymocles), Hor. *C.* 2.14, Ov. *Am.* 1.8.49f. *labitur occulte fallitque volubilis aetas, / et celer admissis labitur annus equis*. Hence one should enjoy oneself while still able (frequently in an amatory context, as here): cf. Theogn. 983ff., 1299ff., *A.P.* 5.12 (Rufinus), 72 (Palladas of Alexandria), 85 (Asclepiades), Catull.5.1ff., T.1.1.69ff., 1.8.41ff., Hor. *C.* 1.9.15ff., 1.11, Prop.2.15.21ff., 4.5.59f., Ov. *A.A.* 3.59ff., Sen. *Phaed.* 446ff., 761ff.

29–30 See Critical Appendix.

Youth and beauty were often compared to various products of nature (*A.P.* 5.20 (Honestus), 124 (Philodemus), 304 (anon.), 11.36 (Philippus) etc.) and their passing to the short life of these products. For beauty as short-lived as the flowers see Smith and cf. also Ov. *A.A.* 3.67f., *A.P.* 5.118 (Marcus Argentarius). For the passing of youth and beauty compared to the short life of the leaf see Smith and cf. also Nemes. *Ecl.* 4. 23f. *nec longum tenet uva comas nec populus umbras: / donum forma breve est nec se quod commodet annis.*

There is verbal emphasis on the similarity between these natural exx. and the human situation (as Smith points out): *purpureus* is also used in connection with humans (eyes Val.Fl.3.179; lips Cat.45.12, Hor. *C.* 3.3.12, Ov. *Am.* 3.14.23; complexion Virg. *Aen.* 11.819; bloom of youth Virg. *Aen.* 1.591), *formosus* and *altus* are equally applicable to humans, *color* can signify both flower and complexion (esp. Virg. *Aen.* 11.819 *purpureus . . . color*), *comae* can designate either leaves or hair, and the personification in *deperdit* helps. The idea is that (like the earth) humans quickly lose their *purpureos . . . colores* and (like the poplar) their *formosas . . . comas* (through it turning white, dropping out or being cut off: cf. Ov. *A.A.* 3.73ff., Sen. *Phaed.* 761ff.: Smith).

Note the intensifying prefix in *deperdit.*

For *colores* of flowers cf. Cat.64.90, Virg. *G.* 4.306, Prop.1.2.9, *Culex* 71, Val.Fl.6.492.

Poplars were renowned for their height (e.g. Hor. *Epod.* 2.10, Plin. *N.H.* 13.141). In view of the emphasis on the similarity with humans in the couplet the *populus alta* here suggests the tall and straight figure of a youth.

Note the internal rhyme and the chiastic arrangement of nouns and adjectives in the pentameter.

31–32 The ex. is relevant because humans were compared to horses (Hom. *Il.* 22.22f., Alcman 1.46ff., Anac.88D), and in particular old humans were compared to old horses: cf. Ibycus 7D, Plato *Parm.* 137A, Plut.*Mor.*785D, Enn.*Ann.* 374-5V, Hor.*Epist.* 1.1.8f. *solve senescentem mature sanus equum, ne / peccet ad extremum ridendus et ilia ducat*, and (from a different point of view) Soph. *Electra* 25ff. The similar failure of human strength and powers in old age is the clear parallel.

iacet: well chosen. The word is often used of weakness and sickness (T.1.5.9, 2.5.109, Stat. *Theb.* 11.743) and here also suggests the horse's fall from former eminence and its inability to stand. Emphasis is given by the juxtaposed *infirmae.*

venere: for the archaic tone of the form see 1.5.47-8n.

fata senectae: *fata* does have point, since it suggests inevitability and calamity, but the periphrasis also seems intended as a dignified and lofty mode of expression.

qui prior Eleo est carcere missus equus: this use of *prior* (adjective for adverb) is found in poetry and prose: cf. Caes. *B.C.* 1.66.4, Prop. 4.5.42, Ov. *A.A.* 2.218.

Eleo refers obliquely to the Olympic games (cf. Virg. *G.* 3.202, Prop. 3.9.17, Hor. *C.* 4.2.17), as Elis was a district in the western Peloponnese with a capital of the same name, near Olympia. An Olympian victory is often used as an ex. of the supreme athletic achievement (e.g. Virg. *G.* 3.49, Prop.3.9.17, Hor. *C.* 1.1.3ff.) and the Olympic victor as an ex. of supreme happiness (Plat. *Res Pub.* 465D, Cic. *Tusc.* 1.111, *Pro Flac.* 31 etc.). Yet the Olympic games do not occur commonly in metaphor (Lucian *De Merc. Cond.* 13, Plut. *Mor.* 790F) or simile: cf. Enn. *Ann.* 374V, Ov. *Her.* 18.165 (of Leander's arms) *protinus illa valent, atque ad sua praemia tendunt, / ut celer Eleo carcere missus equus.*

33–34 A human ex., based on personal experience, of the unhappiness of a man who has let time pass him by and has missed his opportunities for love (*stultos*). The use of such an ex. goes back as far as Homer (e.g. *Il.* 1.254ff.) and is characteristic of didactic poetry and the didactic attitude (see Smith and cf. also Lucr.4.577f., 6.1044f., Virg. *G.* 1.316ff.). Elsewhere in T. this type of ex. occurs at 1.2.89f., 1.8.71f. For this use of *vidi*, introducing an ex. to illustrate a general statement or maxim, see also Fraenkel *Horace* (Oxford, 1957), 245.

Significant words paint the picture black (*premeret, maerentem, stultos*).

35–36 crudeles divi: for this common complaint (here amusingly in the mouth of another god) see Leo *Plaut. Forsch.* 113ff. Here the ref. must be to the deities of Fate (cf. *fata*, 36), who were generally regarded as being in control of the ageing process in humans (e.g. Mimnerm.2. 5ff. D, Theogn. 767f., Hor. *C.* 4.13.22ff., Juv.10.250ff.).

serpens novus exuit annos: for the snake's sloughing of its skin, which is often used as an ex. of renewed youth, see Smith and cf. also Ov. *Met.* 7.237, Plin. *N.H.* 8.99, 111, 9.95. So Pliny refers to the old skin as *senectus* (*N.H.* 29.101, 122, 137). Ovid uses this ex. in the same way at *A.A.* 3.77-9 *anguibus exuitur tenui cum pelle vetustas, / nec faciunt cervos cornua iacta senes: / nostra sine auxilio fugiunt bona.*

Serpens here is in emphatic position (as is the contrasting *formae* in the pentameter).

For the use of *novus* cf. Virg. *G.* 3.437, *Aen.* 2.473, Ov. *Met.* 9.266.

Exuo is applied to this action before here only at Lucr.4.60f. (*cum lubrica serpens / exuit in spinis vestem*), so that there may well be another Lucretian reminiscence here.

A suitable tone of solemnity and sadness is conveyed by the concentration of spondees in this couplet (and in 37-8).

Anguis is mainly found in poetry (cf. *Thes.L.L.* II.51.76ff.), while *serpens* is common in both prose and poetry. Even in poetry *anguis* was common only in Virgil, Ovid, Val.Fl. and Statius. *Anguis* is generally preferred to *serpens* in comedy and satire (Plaut.8: 0; Ter.1: 0; Lucil. 1: 0; Hor. *S.* 0: 3; Pers.1: 0; Juv.2: 8; Petron.2: 0), but in other genres there is no distinct preference and the choice seems to depend on the author's individual taste: e.g. *anguis* is more popular in Ovid (57: 43), Virgil (21: 13), Val.Fl. (17: 3), Statius (29: 15), but less popular in Catull. (0: 1), Lucr. (1: 5), Hor. (3: 5), Sil.It. (9: 24), Lucan (7: 24) and Sen. *Trag.* (11: 28). For elegy the figures are T. 2: 2 (*anguis* at 1.3.69, 1.8.20: *serpens* at 1.3.71, 1.4.35), Prop. 2: 3, Ovid's elegy 31: 10.

37–38 *Nam* introduces either the grounds for the attribution of eternal youth to Bacchus and Apollo ('for, as a matter of fact, both gods have long hair, which suits them') or a semi-parenthetical remark ('for, as a matter of fact, both gods look fine with long hair').

Bacchus and Apollo were in poetry the prime exx. of eternally young gods (but *solis* here is an exaggeration, as they were not the only gods with eternal youth): cf. Ov. *Met.* 1.564f. (Apollo) *utque meum intonsis caput est iuvenale capillis, / tu quoque perpetuos semper gere frondis honores*, 4.17f. (Bacchus), Sen. *Phaed.* 754 (Bacchus) *intonsa iuvenis perpetuum coma.* In art and literature they are constantly represented with long, unshorn hair: for Bacchus cf. Ov. *Met.* 4.13, *ExP.* 2.9.31, Sen. *Phaed.* 754; for Apollo cf. Hom. *Il.* 20.39, *Hom.Hymn.* 3.134, T.2.3.12, 2.5.121, 3.4.27, 4.4.2, Virg. *Aen.* 9.638, Ov. *Met.* 1.450f., 564, 12.585, *Priap.* 36.2. In Greece it was the general custom to cut boys' hair when they reached the age of majority (Pamphilus ap. Athen. 11.494F, Eustath. ad *Il.* 23.141), so that unshorn hair is a symbol of eternal youth (Ov. *Met.* 1.564, Sen. *Phaed.* 754). These two gods are often so paired (Ov. *Am.* 1.14.31f., *Met.* 3.421, Mart.4.45.7f. etc.).

intonsus: the word is confined mainly to poetry and later prose (see *Thes.L.L.* V11$_2$.29.50ff.).

crinis: the collective singular is rare in elegy and appears mainly in the loftier genres (3-4n.): this is another ex. of the elevated language in the speech of Priapus.

39–56 Picking up from *errabis* (27), these lines give the correct application of the main idea of the need for patience, perseverance, humility and endurance (for the obvious connection between these qualities and *obsequium* cf. Ov. *A.A.* 2.177ff.).

The fourth of the *praecepta*: 'you will gain your ends by obsequiousness'. Again the basic statement is given in two lines, and is followed by four exx. (this time occupying 12 lines), and an additional four lines (here a conclusion on the success of the precept). Of the exx. the first concerns a land-journey (4 lines), in contrast to the second, which concerns a boating-trip (4 lines), while the final two both refer to sport, with hunting (2 lines) balanced by fencing (2 lines). The conclusion contains a careful climax: kisses are at first allowed to be snatched with a fight (53-5), then are given on request (55), and finally comes the boy's voluntary embrace (56). Throughout the section there is alternation between positive and negative statement, and the usual verbal play is evident (*ire* 41, 45; *nego* 41, 50; *quamvis* 41, 43; *si* 45, 49, 51; *volo* 45, 49, 51, 56; *nec* 47, 49; *rapias* and *rapta dabit* 53, 54, 55; *primo* and *post* 55, 56).

39–40 tu, puero quodcumque tuo temptare libebit, / cedas: note the expressive juxtaposition (*tu, puero*) and the emphatic position of *cedas*.

For the displacement of *quodcumque* see 23-4n.

On the form of command here (mainly poetic) see 1.2.9-10n.

obsequio plurima vincet amor: *obsequio* is emphatic by position. Obsequiousness (cf. Prop.1.8.40, Ov. *Am.* 3.4.12), the sort of behaviour shown by the exx. which Priapus cites below, was the standard attitude of the lover (Theogn.1341ff., Plat. *Symp.* 183A, *Phaedr.* 255A, Lucr. 4.1121f., intro. essay to 1.5) and found its most ready expression in *servitium amoris* (1.5.5-6n.). However, the first time obsequiousness appears as a precept is at Prop.1.10.21ff. *tu cave ne tristi cupias pugnare puellae, / neve superba loqui, neve tacere diu; / neu, si quid petiit, ingrata fronte negaris, / neu tibi pro vano verba benigna cadant. / irritata venit, quando contemnitur illa, / nec meminit iustas ponere laesa minas: / at quo sis humilis magis et subiectus amori, / hoc magis effectu saepe fruare bono. / is poterit felix una remanere puella, / qui numquam vacuo pectore liber erit.* T. accepts Propertius' precept and the reason for it (T.1.4.39-40 and 53-6 = Prop.1.10.27-8), but gives it a fuller treatment with different exx. The precept of obsequiousness is also given at Prop.2.23.23f., Ov. *A.A.* 2.177ff., 511ff., and is put into practice by T. in 1.5, 1.9.41ff., 2.3.5ff., 79f.

The elegiac lover is conventionally a weak and unmanly type (e.g. 1.1.46, 58, 1.2.73, 2.3.9f., 4.3.7ff., Prop.1.5.21f., 4.3.23f., Ov. *A.A.* 1.733ff., *Tr.* 1.5.71ff.): the 'toil' involved in the activities mentioned in the following lines would seem to him to be considerable, and so there is deliberate exaggeration and irony.

For the *militia amoris* ref. see 1.10.53-6n.

The expression here looks like a roguish adaptation of Virg. *Ecl.* 10.69 *omnia vincit amor* (cf. also Ov. *Am.* 3.4.12).

41–44 Accompany him on a trip by land. The contrast is between a long walk in hot weather (41-2) and any walk when a downpour is imminent (43-4). Both instances would show the lover's obsequiousness because of the extremes of weather involved. For these hardships of the lover cf. Ov. *Am.* 1.9.9ff., *A.A.* 2.223ff., Sen. *Phaed.* 613ff., 700ff. (Phaedra to Hippolytus) *te vel per ignes, per mare insanum sequar / rupesque et amnes, unda quos torrens rapit; / quacumque gressus tuleris hac amens agar.*

neu . . . neges: for the construction (mainly poetic) see 1.2.9-10n.

via longa: the adjective is probably an exaggeration: the trip seems long to the unmanly lover (39-40n.).

Canis: see 1.1.27-8n. and cf. Ov. *A.A.* 2.231 *nec grave te tempus sitiensque Canicula tardet.* This looks like a deliberate echo of line 6.

arenti torreat arva siti: note the emphatic juxtaposition. For this application of *arens* (first found here) cf. Ov. *Her.* 4.174, Sen. *Thy.* 4f. (*arida* at Ov. *Met.* 11.129): this looks like a reminiscence of Lucretius' *sitis arida* (3.917, 6.1175; the only places where *aridus* is applied to *sitis* before here).

On the text of 43-4 see Critical Appendix.

praetexens picta ferrugine caelum: *ferrugo* and *ferrugineus* denote various dark colours, including greenish-blue (see Fordyce on Cat.64. 227, André *Étude sur les termes de couleur dans la langue Latine* (Paris, 1949), 105ff.), so that the ref. here seems to be to a rainbow (*arcus* 44) in which the darker colours prevail (*picta ferrugine* could refer to the sky (= 'with its darkness coloured', i.e. by the rainbow), but this seems an unlikely way to express the idea, esp. in view of the juxtaposed present participle).

Ferrugo occurs only at Cat.64.227 and Virg. *G.* 1.467 before here.

For *pictus* here cf. (of Iris) Ov. *Met.* 14.838 *pictos delapsa per arcus,* Sen. *Oed.* 317 *picto nuntiat nimbos sinu.*

venturam admittat imbrifer arcus aquam: *admittat* here must mean 'allow in, receive', alluding to the common idea of the rainbow drinking to feed the clouds (Plaut. *Curc.* 131, Virg. *G.* 1.381, Prop.3.5.32, Ov. *Met.* 1.270, Lucan 4.81, Sen. *N.Q.* 1.8.8, Stat. *Theb.* 9.405f., *Ach.* 1. 220). A parallel for the expression occurs at Mart.12.29.6 *casuras alte sic rapit Iris aquas.*

Imbrifer is found before here only at Virg. *G.* 1.313. The word is elsewhere applied to rainbows at Sen. *Oed.* 315, Stat. *Silv.* 3.3.81, *Theb.* 7.427, 9.405 (cf. also Rutil.Nam. *De Red. Suo* 1.98).

The final syllable of *admittat* remains closed before the initial vowel of *imbrifer.* This practice is not uncommon in elegy and usually occurs, as here, at the main caesura (for the pentameter cf. Prop.2.8.8, 2.24.4; for the hexameter see 1.10.13-4n.). For a final syllable in *-at* remaining closed before an initial vowel cf. Ov. *Tr.* 5.7.23. After a description of the people of Tomis Ovid says (21ff.): *vivit in his heu nunc lusorum oblitus amorum, / hos videt, hos vates audit, amice, tuus. / atque utinam vivat et non moriatur in illis, / absit ab invisis et tamen umbra locis.* The mss' *et non* in 23 gives excellent sense: 'and may he live on amongst them, rather than die, but (when he does die) may he escape from this hateful place as a shade'. Heinsius' transposition (*non et*) is inappropriate and unnecessary.

45–46 For the punctuation of 46 see Critical Appendix.

Accompany him on a boating-trip, and, instead of just sitting there, actually row the boat yourself (*ipse* in emphatic position), to show *obsequium.*

In 46 *levem . . . ratem* must mean a small rowing-boat, but *freta* may refer to the sea (21-2n.) or to a river or lake (Virg. *G.* 1.386, 2.164), *caeruleus* is a common epithet of the sea (André *Étude sur les termes de couleur dans la langue Latine* (Paris, 1949), 165), but is also applied to rivers (1.7.14), while both *ratis* and *puppis* may denote sea-going vessels (Ov. *Her.* 13.97) or river-craft (Caes. *B. G.* 6.35, Prop.1.14.4, Virg. *Aen.* 6.302, 410). So the following interpretations are possible: (1) row him out to a sea-going ship anchored in deep water, (2) quite straightforward: take him for a trip in a rowing-boat on a river, lake or at sea, (3) with humorous exaggeration: take him on a trip in a rowing-boat (46), with 45 suggesting an ocean-voyage, which is what the trip seems to the unmanly lover (39-40n.). The third interpretation fits best with the tone of this section.

For the motif of the boat-journey cf. Prop.2.26.29ff. *seu mare per longum mea cogitet ire puella, / hanc sequar, et fidos una aget aura duos* etc., Ov. *Am.* 1.9.13f. (of the lover) *nec freta pressurus tumidos causabitur Euros / aptaque verrendis sidera quaeret aquis*, Sen. *Phaed.* 700.

47–48 Commentators generally take the ref. here to be to agricultural labour. However, there is no mention of the country in this couplet (neither *labores* nor *opera* is specifically agricultural), something which one would expect, esp. when switching from the water-activity in the previous distich and when the blisters mentioned here could be caused by such an activity. Nor is it made clear here exactly how agricultural labour would constitute *obsequium.* This interpretation also leaves 41-6 rather lop-sided, with four lines on land-journeys and their hardships but only two lines on water-travel, in contrast to the structural precision evident elsewhere in the speech of Priapus.

It also seems unlikely that this couplet is a generalization on the various *labores* expected of the lover: the pentameter points to specifically manual labour, and, in any case, this is hardly the point for such a generalization.

Most obviously the ref. is to the boating-trip in 45f. (48 = blisters from rowing, picking up *ipse* in 46), and the expansion here on the toil involved means that 41-4 are now matched by 45-8. Accordingly my punctuation differs from that of Postgate (OCT): see Critical Appendix.

For the vivid detail of blisters cf. 2.3.9f., 4.3.7f., Prop.4.3.23f.

duros subiisse labores: another ex. of ironical exaggeration (39-40n.).

insuetas: 'unaccustomed to' (hard work). The word in this sense is used absolutely first here, but subsequently this use was not uncommon (e.g. Virg. *Aen.* 8.92, Livy 21.35.3, 38.21.6, Stat. *Theb.* 5.91, 11.94).

atteruisse: this is the only ex. in surviving literature of this form of the perfect of *tero* or its compounds apart from Apuleius and the Itala (Neue 3. p. 394). The validity of this form is also vouched for by Charis. 1.248.4 and Vel.Long.7.74.5 (who describes it as archaic).

Note the neat balance in the arrangement of adjective, perfect infinitive and noun in hexameter and pentameter.

49–50 Take a part in sport with him, and, to show particular obsequiousness, when he goes hunting don't just accompany him but actually carry the nets for him: this was a tedious and tiring task (cf. Sen. *Phaed.* 44f.) – hence *negent.* For this motif cf. 4.3.11f., Ov. *Her.* 5.19 *retia saepe comes maculis distincta tetendi, A.A.* 2.189, *Met.* 10.171. So in mythology the lover often develops an interest in the beloved's hunting (Eur. *Hipp.* 215ff., Ov. *Her.* 4.37ff., *Met.* 10.529ff.). Cf. also Plut. *Mor.* 52B.

insidiis: i.e. *venatorum* (Cic. *Fam.* 2.11.2, Virg. *Aen.* 7.478 *insidiis cursuque feras agitabat Iulus*).

altas: the adjective is probably another ex. of exaggeration (39-40n.).

placeas: for this amatory use of the verb see 11-12n.

51–52 Fence with him and, to show obsequiousness, let him win often (*saepe* in emphatic position). For this motif (here only in an amatory context) cf. Suet. *Calig.* 32.2 *Murmillonem e ludo rudibus secum battuentem et sponte prostratum confodit ferrea sica ac more victorum cum palma discurrit.* Cf. also (of running) Plut. *Mor.* 471E, (of games) Ov. *A.A.* 2.203ff.

For the pastime of fencing cf. Cic. *Sen.* 58, Ov. *Tr.* 3.12.19 (of characteristic Roman sports) *lusus equi nunc est, levibus nunc luditur armis.*

levi temptabis ludere dextra: the adjective may mean 'light', so as not to hurt the boy and to let him appear the better fencer (see *OLD* s.v. 5). Alternatively *levis* may mean 'frail' (cf. Ov. *ExP.* 3.1.96), of the unmanly lover (39-40n.), with *temptabis* implying that he is not really suited to such a manly pursuit.

The future indicative for the imperative (so too *dabis* in the pent.) is found in poetry and prose (Roby 1589, Gild.-Lodge 243). It occurs here only in T. and is in line with the pose as instructor attributed to Priapus.

nudum: 'unprotected, defenceless' (Sall. *J.* 107.1 *nudum et caecum corpus ad hostis vortere*, Livy 5.45.3).

53–56 The result of the obsequiousness: note the climax.

For snatched kisses cf. Cat.99.1, 16, T.1.8.58, Hor. *C.* 2.12.27f., Ov. *Am.* 2.4.26, *Her.* 15.44, 17.27f., *A.A.* 1.667, *Met.* 4.358, *A.P.* 5.219 (Paulus Silentiarius).

For the token resistance, soon abandoned, cf. Theoc. *Id.* 27, Hor. *C.* 2.12.25ff., Prop.2.15.5f., Ov. *Am.* 1.5.13ff. *deripui tunicam – nec multum rara nocebat; / pugnabat tunica sed tamen illa tegi. / quae cum ita pugnaret, tamquam quae vincere nollet, / victa est non aegre proditione sua, A.A.* 1.663ff., *A.P.* 12.200 (Strato).

mitis: 'compliant' (in the amatory sense also at Hor. *C.* 3.10.18, Ov. *Am.* 2.17.5, *A.A.* 2.178).

cara . . . / oscula: cf. Ov. *ExP.* 1.4.50, *Culex* 293. The adjective here and the emphatic positioning of *oscula* suggest enthusiasm and encouragement.

pugnabit: a basic ref. to *militia amoris* (cf. Catull.62.59f., Ov. *Am.* 1.5.14f., *A.A.* 1.665f., and see 1.10.53-6n.).

sed tibi rapta dabit: see Critical Appendix.

Rapta dabit must mean here 'allow you to snatch kisses': as Smith points out, although elsewhere this phrase is applied to the snatcher (Ov. *Am.* 2.4.26, *Her.* 15.44), in such circumstances there is little real difference between giving and receiving kisses. There may even be a play on this idea: i.e. he will give you what you snatch (cf. Ov. *A.A.* 1.664 of kisses *illa licet non det, non data sume tamen*).

post etiam collo se implicuisse velit: for this type of embrace cf. Prop.1.13.15 *vidi ego te toto vinctum languescere collo*, 3.12.22, T.3.6.45, Ov. *Am.* 1.4.6, 35, 2.18.9, 3.7.7f., *Her.* 2.93, 5.48, 13.106, 16.167, 18.164, 19.103, 20.58, *A.A.* 2.457.

The potential subjunctive indicates a touch of uncertainty about such a great show of spontaneous affection.

For monosyllabic elision see Platnauer 78, and for the rare position of the elided *se* here see Platnauer 87f.

57–72 At first sight it is hard to grasp what the actual precept here is, the tirade against the venality of boys and the praise of poetry at 57-70 seem irrelevant and look like a digression, while the connection with the preceding section is not clear.

In fact, the basic precept is contained in 71-2 and is that the lover should send obsequious poems as presents to his boy (that 71-2 refer to poems rather than actual *blanditiae, querellae* and *fletus* is suggested by context and confirmed by the fact that the latter would have no point there; the type of poem sent to the beloved would commonly contain *blanditiae, querellae* and *fletus*, and these terms and similar ones are frequently applied to such poetry: see 71-2n.).

Although, generally speaking, there is no reason why Priapus should not digress (for variety or parody), to take 57-70 as a digression here would leave one sole couplet (71-2) as the precept, giving an abrupt and sloppy structure which hardly fits with the rest of Priapus' speech and which provides a poor ending for the lecture. In fact, 57-72 do form one section, which is concerned with the nature of presents. The advice is to send poems, but the contemporary situation, in which more expensive gifts are demanded, naturally also receives discussion (so too at Ov. *A.A.* 2.273ff.). In effect Priapus' opinion is that it is wrong to ask for more costly gifts and that poems are preferable to them, but instead of a calm discussion he produces a passionate outburst (*heu* 57, curses, appeal), in which he claims that poems are superior (because they confer immortality on their subjects) and curses the contemporary practice and the man who introduced it. So, it is as arguments against more expensive gifts and in favour of poems as presents that the tirade against the venality of boys and the praise of poetry are relevant. The consideration that the influence of money would be so opposed to the *sollertia* attributed to Priapus and would make the subject such an emotive one for the speaker could explain why the section does not begin with the precept, but launches straight away into an attack on the contemporary state of affairs, but this postponement also adds variety and heightens the effect of the precept (which in this position sums up), while the exhibition of passion provides a good climax to the whole lecture.

As these lines are concerned with the sending of presents, the progression from the *obsequium* of the previous section seems natural enough (so too at Ov. *A.A.* 2.261ff.), esp. since the type of poem sent is itself to be obsequious (71-2n.), although the actual connection is made by way of contrast (unpleasant present opposed to the pleasant fantasy of 53-6).

The complaint of boys' venality (57f.) acts as a brief general introduction to the section, which then proceeds by way of contrast, as remarks attacking venality (59-60, 67-70) alternate with remarks in praise of poetry (61-6, 71-2). As usual, verbal play is in evidence: *munera* (58, 62), *puer* (58, 61), *venerem / amorem vendere* (59, 67), *Pierides* (61, 62), *carmen* (63), *Musae* (65, 67), *dum* (65, 66) and *qui* (67).

57–58 For the venality of boys see intro. essay to 1.9. The attack on the mercenary present age in this connection may have been inspired by Call. *Iamb.* 3 (= fr.193 Pf.), in view of its probable influence elsewhere in the poem (see 61-2n., 67-70n.): the Diegesis (VI.34f.) tells us that Callimachus καταμέμφεται τὸν καιρὸν ὡς πλούτου / μᾶλλον ἢ ἀρετῆς ὄντα.

Note the emotional emphasis in *heu male . . . miseras.*

artes: it is amusing to find that boys too have their *artes* (cf. 76) and a teacher (59).

tener: for the delicacy of the *puer delicatus* see 1.9.15-16n.

59–60 For the inventor see Leo *Plaut.Forsch.* (ed.2), 151ff., Nisbet & Hubbard on Hor. *C.* 1.3.12, and cf. T.1.7.19f., 29ff., 1.10.1, 45f., 2.1.37ff. For the cursing of the inventor cf. Soph. *Ajax* 1192f., Eur. *Hipp.* 407f., Aristoph. *Lys.* 946, Eubul.72K, Menand.154K, Callim. *Aetia* 110.48ff., Catull.66.48ff., Prop.1.17.13f., 2.33.27f., T.1.10.1f., esp. *A.P.* 12.212.7f. (Strato) ἀλλ' ἤδη πρὸς κέρδος ἔχεις φρένας. ὡς ὁ διδάξας / τεθνάτω· οἷόν μου παιδίον ἠφάνικεν.

The present curse is a reversal of the prayer *sit tibi terra levis* (cf. 2.4.49f.), which is first found at Eur. *Alc.* 463f. and was subsequently very frequent (see Lattimore *Themes in Greek and Latin Epitaphs* (Urbana, 1962), 65ff.). For this reversal cf. *A.P.* 7.204.7f. (Agathias Scholasticus), 394.5f. (Philippus of Thessalonica), 401 (Crinagoras), Sen. *Phaed.* 1279f., Tert. *De An.* 4. The curse reflects the idea that the dead are affected by what happens to them after death (1.1.67-8n., 1.10.37-8n.). The hissing of s and x in the pentameter suggests anger.

at: adds urgency and emphasis to the curse (1.3.33-4n.).

venerem: 'sexual charm, attractiveness' (1.5.7-8n.) or (esp. sexual) 'love' (cf. 67).

infelix: 'that brings misfortune, trouble': the word is also used in curses at *CIL* IV.1329, Prop.4.11.28 *infelix umeros urgeat urna meos.* Cf. also Ov. *Am.* 2.16.15 *solliciti iaceant terraque premantur iniqua.*

61–62 These lines contain two themes which began with the Alexandrians and were subsequently common, esp. in elegy. For the poor love poet cf. *A.P.* 5.30 (Antipater of Thessalonica), 32 (Marcus Argentarius), 50, 12.90 (anon.), 148 (Callimachus), 212 (Strato), Hor. *Epod.* 11.11f., T.1.5.61ff., 2.4.21f., Ov. *Am.* 1.3.5ff. and see below. For poetry versus wealth cf. Theoc. *Id.* 16, Prop.1.8.27ff., 4.5.53ff., T.1.5.67f., 2.4.13f., Ov. *Am.* 1.8.57ff., 1.10.57ff., 3.8, *A.A.* 2.273ff., 3.531ff.

It is possible that the present passage was influenced in particular by Call. *Iamb.* 3 (= fr.193 Pf.), where Call.'s love for a boy is hindered by lack of money and he seems to contrast poetry with wealth (see Dawson *AJPh* LXVII (1946), 8, 11f.).

Pieridas: Lee (p.107) comments: '*Pierides* was a title of the Muses from Hesiod *Scutum* 206 onwards; they were born in Pieria, a district of S.W. Macedonia (Hesiod *Theogony* 54).' Here *Pieridas* stands for 'poetry' (Ov. *Tr.* 3.7.4, 5.1.34).

doctos: the epithet is often applied to poets and poetry (see *Thes. L.L.* V_1.1757.12ff., 1758.17ff.) and is probably a translation of the Greek *σοφός* applied to poets (see Smith on 4.6.2). In Augustan times it referred esp. to literary and mythological learning. Often the connotation of taste and elegance is present (cf. Catull.35.17 and Quinn ad loc., Ov. *Am.* 2.4.17f.), so a further contrast may be implied (between the refined poet and the boorish *dives amator*). The echo of *docuisti* (59) seems deliberate.

aurea . . . munera: 'gifts consisting of gold', and so of the most expensive kind (cf.1.9.17f., 31f.).

This is a suitably learned and elegant couplet (the ref. in *Pieridas*, the alliteration of p, the arrangement of key words at the beginnings and ends of lines, the repetition of *Pieridas* as first and last word of the distich (see Smith and Munari on Ov. *Am.* 1.9.1f. for similar devices) and the antithetical juxtaposition *munera Pieridas*).

63–64 The exhortation of 61f. is backed up by the claim of the immortality bestowed by poetry on its subjects (cf. Theoc. *Id.* 16.29ff., Ov. *Am.* 1. 10.59ff. and see below). The claim was often supported by exx. of people who were famous through poetry: cf. Pind. *Pyth.* 3.112ff., Theoc. *Id.* 16.34ff., 17.118ff., Ov. *Am.* 1.3.21ff., 3.9.29ff., *ExP.* 4. 8.51ff., Hor. *C.* 4.8.25ff. Similarly the negative form of the claim, obscurity without poetry, was common: cf. Pind. *Nem.* 7.12ff., *Ol.* 10.91ff., Theoc. *Id.* 16.42ff., Catull.68.41ff., Hor. *C.* 4.8.20ff., 4.9. 25ff., Prop.3.1.25ff., Ov. *ExP.* 4.8.53f. There is emphasis here in the combination of the positive and negative forms.

Myths are chosen which had been mentioned at an early stage in poetry and which received lengthy or frequent treatment, esp. at the hands of other Augustan poets (so they are good exx. of the influence of poetry). Note also that these are tall stories that largely depend on poetry for their survival.

The myth of Nisus first occurs in surviving lit. at Aesch. *Choeph.* 613ff. and was covered in detail at Ov. *Met.* 8.1ff. (cf. also Virg. *Ecl.* 6.74ff., *G.* 1.404ff., Prop.3.19.21ff., Ov. *A.A.* 1.331f., *Rem.* 67f.; at Nemes. *Cyneget.* 44 the story is said to be trite). Nisus was a king of Megara and, when Minos besieged the city, his own daughter, Scylla, brought about his death by pulling out his purple hair on which his life depended. As punishment she was either drowned by Minos (Apollod. 3.15.8) or, in the form of a bird or fish, pursued by her father, who had been changed into an eagle (Virg. *G.* 1.404ff., Ov. *Met.* 8.1ff., Hygin. *fab.* 198).

The myth of Pelops in surviving lit. appears as early as Pind. *Ol.* 1. 46ff. Virgil (*G.* 3.7) describes it as a popular subject and Lucian (*Salt.*

54) as a favourite theme of the drama. At *C.* 1.6.4ff. Horace includes it among conventional mythology, and it is mentioned by Ovid at *Met.* 6. 403ff. The most common version was that Pelops was killed by his father Tantalus and served up to the gods. They, however, realised what the meal was and refused to eat it, except for Demeter, who, distraught with grief for the loss of Persephone, ate the shoulder. The gods then ordered Hermes to put Pelops' limbs into a cauldron and restore him, and an ivory shoulder was supplied in place of the one eaten by Demeter (Pind. and Ov. loc.cit., Hygin. *fab.* 83).

carmina ni sint / . . . non nituisset ebur: in early Latin the present subjunctive in conditional sentences could refer to present time as well as to future time. This usage of the pres. subj., either in both clauses or with an imperfect (1.8.22) or pluperfect, as here, continued throughout classical prose and verse (Woodcock 198, Handford *The Latin Subjunctive* (London, 1947), 121f.).

The only other exx. in the *Corp. Tib.* of a monosyllable at the end of a hexameter are 4.10.1 and 4.11.5, where they are preceded by another monosyllable so as to make a disyllabic word-group, as here. More common is prodelided *est*: 1.6.3, 7, 1.8.49, 51, 1.9.51, 2.3.31, 2.4.11, 33, 2.5.49, 3.1.19, 3.6.25, 4.10.5. For this ending in the pent. see 3-4n.

This is another learned and elegant distich (the mythological refs., the repetition of *carmen* (in emphatic positions), the alliteration of n and c, the jingle *Nisi . . . ni sint*).

65–66 For similar expressions of the immortality bestowed and enjoyed by poetry cf. Virg. *Aen.* 9.446ff., Hor. *C.* 3.30.8ff., Ov. *Am.* 1.15.9ff. *vivet Maeonides, Tenedos dum stabit et Ide, / dum rapidas Simois in mare volvet aquas; / vivet et Ascraeus, dum mustis uva tumebit, / dum cadet incurva falce resecta Ceres* etc., *Tr.* 3.7.51f., Luc. 9.980ff.

This type of expression of perpetuity (i.e. so long as the natural order of things remains unchanged) was common: see Smith and cf. also *A.P.* 7.153.2 (Homer or Cleobulus of Lindos) ἔστ' ἂν ὕδωρ τε νάῃ, καὶ δένδρεα μακρὰ τεθήλῃ, 716.6 (Dionysius), Sen. *Oed.* 504ff., *H.O.* 1576f., *Med.* 401ff., Stat. *Silv.* 1.1.93f., Claud. *Ruf.* 2.526f.

Note the repetition of *dum* and the zeugma.

67–70 For oriental religion in T. see intro. essay to 1.3. The Roman goddess Ops was generally regarded as the wife of Saturn (Varro *L.L.* 5.57, Ov. *Met.* 9.498), and so was identified with Rhea, wife of Cronus. Rhea in turn was identified with Cybele (Eur. *Bacc.* 59 and Dodds ad loc., Ov. *F.* 4.201f.). So, as Mt. Ida was a seat of Cybele-worship (Strabo 469), *Idaea . . . Ops* is a learned allusion to Cybele (cf. *Idaea mater* at Lucr. 2.611, Livy 29.10.5).

Cybele was a mother-goddess of Anatolia whose chief sanctuary was at Pessinus in Phrygia (Dio Cass. 17.61). She was commonly represented with a turreted crown and a lion-drawn chariot (Lucr.2. 600ff., Ov. *F.* 4.215ff.). The priest of Cybele was known in 4th century Athens (cf. e.g. Aristot. *Rhet.* 3.2.10), and Cybele was officially brought to Rome in 204 B.C. (Ov. *F.* 4.247ff., Livy 29.10f.), but limited to her temple on the Palatine and served only by oriental priests until the time of Claudius (Dio.Hal.2.19.3-5).

The eunuch priests of Cybele (Galli) toured cities (Babrios 141 Crus., Phaedr.4.1, Dio.Hal.loc.cit., Lucr.2.624ff.). In their processions they followed the image of the goddess in a chariot (Lucr.2.601f. and Bailey ad loc., Virg. *Aen.* 6.784f., Ov. *F.* 4.185f.) amid a great din of drums and flutes (esp. Phrygian: Lucr.2.618ff., Frazer ad Ov. *F.* 4. 181f.), begging for alms (Lucr.2.624ff., Ov. *ExP.* 1.1.39f.) and slashing their persons with weapons (Lucr.2.629ff.). Romans often mentioned their self-mutilation (Prop.2.22.15f., Juv.2.115f., Mart.9.2.13f., 11.84.3f., Stat. *Theb.* 10.170ff., Val.Fl.8.241f. *quis modo tam saevos adytis fluxisse cruores / cogitet*?) and their mendicancy (Cic.*Leg.* 2.9.22, 2.16.40, Ov. *F.* 4.350ff.). In general they were despised as effeminate and worthless (Juv.8.171ff., Mart.14.204, Aug. *C.D.* 7.26).

So, as usual in T., the curse fits the crime: it attacks the boy's personal attributes (cf. 1.9.13ff.), which were formerly so lucrative; instead of making money and being loved he is to become a despised beggar; and he is to be exposed to dangers to which his nature (previously so attractive and lucrative) does not suit him (cf. esp. *A.P.* 6.217 (Simonides), 218 (Alcaeus), 219 (Antipater), 220 (Dioscorides), 237 (Antistius) for the wanderer's hazards in this connection); so too the boy's inability henceforth to make sexual use of his penis (through castration) is a symmetrical repayment for not allowing the love-poet to use his penis sexually (through lack of money). It is also a neat touch that Priapus, famed for the size and activeness of his genitals, should curse someone with castration (a common motif in the *Priapea*: cf. 15.3, 26.2, 37.4, 55.5f.).

Clearchus (in Athen.541E) mentions such a fate as a bad end, and the same curse occurs at Ov. *Ibis* 453f. The curse here was probably inspired by Callimachus. In the third *Iambus* he complains of his poverty (in contrast to his rich rivals) and declares that in an age that does not value poetry he may as well be a worshipper of Cybele or Adonis (fr. 193.34ff. Pf.), just as this curse is reserved for the venal boy who is an enemy of poetry. There is possibly a verbal reminiscence of Φρύγ[α] πρ[ὸς] αὐλὸν (fr. 193.36Pf.) in *ad Phrygios . . . modos* (cf. Prop.2.22.16, Ov. *Ibis* 454, Mart.11.84.4 for this phrase).

et tercentenas erroribus expleat urbes: this use of adverb and distributive was frequent in poetry (often for metrical reasons) and was also found in prose (e.g. Plaut. *Pseud.* 345 (*quater quinis*), Lucr.5.1300 (*bis . . . binos*), Varro *R.R.* 3.9.10 (*bis deni*), Virg. *Ecl.* 1.43 (*bis senos*);

see Kühner-Stegmann 1.661, Neue 2.341). *Tercentenus* first appears here and is not common (cf. Mart.2.1.1). It is used (like *mille*: 1.3. 49-50n.) for any large number (Wölfflin *ALL* ix. 177ff.).

Expleat is a bold extended usage. The word is used of completing, and so covering, a circle (Virg. *Aen.* 12.763; cf. *compleo*, T.2.4.17f.) or a journey (Suet. in Isid. *Nat.* 3.3): so here it seems to be used in the sense 'cover, traverse'. Cf. the use of *impleo* at Ov. *F.* 2.223 (*vallem latis discursibus implent*) and πληρόω and similar words (Kannicht on Eur. *Hel.* 1570).

vilia membra: 'worthless' in the speaker's eyes (cf. Ov. *Ibis* 454) and in the boy's own eyes – hence the mutilation (Ov. *F.* 4.244).

The solemnity of the many spondees in 67-69 gives way to the aptly musical and fast-moving line 70 (assonance, alliteration and dactyls).

71–72 See Critical Appendix.

The use of *blanditiae, querellae* and *fletus* in verse (see 57-72n.) was the love poet's traditional method of winning over the beloved: cf. 1.5.67ff., 2.4.19f., Prop.1.8.39f. *hanc ego non auro, non Indis flectere conchis, / sed potui blandi carminis obsequio*, 2.8.11f., Hor. *C.* 3.11.7f., Ov. *Am.* 2.1.21f., 3.1.45ff.

This is a carefully constructed couplet, emphasizing the method favoured by the love poet (*blanditiis* by position, *querellis / supplicibus, miseris fletibus* by (chiastic) juxtaposition) and the approval of Venus herself (*ipsa* and *favet* by position): thus it is stressed that if money prevails over such poetry, the very goddess of love is thwarted.

73–84 Transition from Priapus' speech is made with care in 73.

The conclusion of the elegy. For the effect of this section on the poem as a whole see intro. essay. Some unexpected turns build up to and improve the climax at 81ff. So far in the poem T. has tried to mislead the reader over the person for whom Priapus' advice is supposed to be intended: 1-56 suggest that T. wants general information on παιδικὸς ἔρως; 57-72 'poetry versus wealth' suggests that he may have asked for his own use; 73 tries to allay this suspicion: T. says that the advice was really asked on behalf of another poet; in 74 comes another turn: this poet apparently cannot use it because of his wife; therefore (75-80) T. says that he will pass it on to other lovers (it seems that he still wanted general information only); at 81-4 comes the unexpected climax: T. says that he did need it for himself after all and that it proves useless. The climax is made more effective by T. himself taking over Priapus' pose as *praeceptor*, showing similar self-importance and representing himself as detached and uninvolved, only to state at 81ff. that the pose is laughable and the *praecepta* worthless in the case of his love for Marathus.

73–74 haec mihi, quae canerem Titio, deus edidit ore: *edere ore* is a solemn phrase, found in epic (Virg. *Aen.* 7.194, Ov. *Met.* 1.637, 8.703,

12.577, Sil.It.6.457). It seems a little too impressive for Priapus' speech.

The sudden appearance of Titius is the first of the unexpected turns. T. now represents himself as having asked Priapus for advice to give to Titius (rather than for himself): for dramatic effect and to trick the reader, this detail has been suppressed until this late stage in the elegy.

Titius' primary function is to enable T. to pretend that he did not ask advice for himself and to maintain the pose long enough and embroider on it in sufficient detail to give the climax its maximum force. Unless we are to assume that T. forgets that it is Priapus who is supposed to be speaking at 57ff. and voices his own opinions (an extremely unlikely idea in view of the care and subtlety evident elsewhere in the poem), it follows that, for T. to pretend that the advice was more fitting for someone else and allay the suspicions raised at 57ff., he must choose a poet for that person. It is unlikely that Titius is an entirely fictitious character, since the reason for his inclusion would then not be at all clear. Lucius Titius was often used in law for 'citizen A' or 'citizen B' (Pauly s.v. Titius 10) and at Juv. 4.13 Titius on its own is so used, but there are objections to this interpretation here: if we assume that Priapus has been taken in by this request for advice for 'citizen A', then the mention of poetry at 57ff. is irrelevant; if we assume that Priapus has seen through this blind and is in fact addressing T. himself, the real petitioner, at 57ff., then an unlikely and difficult convolution of plot is added, which spoils the climax of 81ff. To avoid ruining the climax and to keep the poem intelligible, T. must be referring here to a reasonably well-known poet. There is a poet of the same name mentioned by Horace (*Epist.* 1.3.9ff. *quid Titius, Romana brevi venturus in ora? / Pindarici fontis qui non expalluit haustus, / fastidire lacus et rivos ausus apertos*), and it is possible that he is referred to here. The attribution to Titius of a wife at 74 suggests that he is an authentic character, and the identification is chronologically possible, since the date of *Epist.* 1.3 is 20 B.C. (see Wilkins ad loc.). If Horace's Titius is the Titius of 73f., another reason for his inclusion here would be the opportunity to mention a fellow-poet and have a joke at his expense.

sed Titium coniunx haec meminisse vetat: the remark suggests that Titius was recently married. The injunction to forget other sexual interests was common around the time of marriage: cf. Ter. *Andr.* 189 *nunc hic dies aliam vitam defert, alios mores postulat*, Catull.61.134ff., Mart.11.78. If Titius had been married for a long time, one would hardly expect T. to make such a damaging disclosure about his tastes (there seem no grounds for suspecting any enmity: the passage is light-hearted in tone rather than an attack).

In the loftier genres of poetry *coniunx* for 'wife' is far more common than the prosaic *uxor*, but in the shorter poems of Catullus and in elegy there is no marked preference for either word. Elsewhere in T. I and II *coniunx* for 'wife' does not occur, but *uxor* is so used at 1.9.54, 1.10. 42, 52, 2.2.11. In T. neither word is restricted to a particular context. See Axelson 57, Adams *Glotta* L (1972), 252ff.

Note the chiastic order *haec . . . Titio . . . / . . . Titium . . . haec.*

75–78 **pareat ille suae**: neatly disposes of Titius. For *suae* cf. 1.9.65.

vos me celebrate magistrum: *celebro* here may mean 'come flocking to' or 'praise' or even 'honour'.

This use of *magister* comes from the Alexandrian use of διδάσκω and δίδαγμα in this context (see intro. essay). *Magister* and similar terms are often so used in Ovid (e.g. *A.A.* 1.1ff., 2.161, 173, 497, 3.341, 812, *Rem.* 55). There seems to be humour here, since, of course, normally a *magister* taught *pueri*, as Putnam points out.

quos male habet multa callidus arte puer: note the emphasis in the phrase *multa callidus arte*, which has various shades of meaning, as *callidus* can denote here 'expert', 'clever' or 'crafty', and *ars* can refer to 'skill' as something acquired by practice, 'technique', 'crafty action' or 'craftiness' (*OLD* s.v. *callidus* and *ars*). On the boy's *ars* see 57-8n.

Male habere ('harass, trouble') is not colloquial, as Smith suggests: he cites Plaut. *As.* 844, Ter. *And.* 436, 940, *Hec.* 606, Caes. *B.C.* 1.63, but cf. also Pacuv. *Trag.* 277R, Lucr.3.826, Sen. *Epist.* 95.3.

gloria cuique sua est: possibly a proverbial expression (for similar phrases cf. Plaut. *Stich.* 693, Catull.22.20, Virg. *Aen.* 10.467, Quint. 10.2.22), or, at any rate, a typical learned phrase (cf. Cic. *Opt. Gen. Or.* 1.1 *poematis enim . . . suum cuiusque est, diversum a reliquis*, Hor. *Ars Poet.*92). T.'s vocabulary throughout also suggests that he is adopting the pose of the expert.

For synaloephe of *est* in T. see Smith.

me, qui spernentur, amantes / consultent: for the amatory use of *sperno* cf. Virg. *Ecl.* 3.74, T.1.8.55, 61, Prop.2.18.7, Hor. *C.* 1.9.16, Ov. *Am.* 3.6.65, *Her.* 4.168, *Met.* 3.393, *F.* 3.553.

Consulto, considering the subject, is rather a grand word (it is used esp. of asking advice of seers, oracles and gods).

cunctis ianua nostra patet: like the wise man or expert whom people visit to ask advice or listen to opinions (e.g. Plut. *Pericl.* 24.3, Cic. *De Or.* 3.133, Hor. *S.* 1.9.9f.). Humour may be intended here, with T. contrasting his door, which is open to all (*cunctis* in emphatic position), with the closed door of the *puer delicatus* (implied in *spernentur*).

Cunctis means 'all together' (cf. Ps. Ascon. in Caec. p. 100 Baiter, Serv. ad *Aen.* 1.518, Paul. ex Fest. p. 50.15 Müll. *cuncti significat quidem omnes, sed coniuncti et congregati*).

On the use of *fores* and *ianua* as synonymous terms for 'house-door' see *Thes.L.L.* VI$_1$.134.1ff. After the older authors (who all prefer *fores*) *fores* is more common in archaizing or poeticising authors in prose and, generally speaking, in poetry (of course, *ianua*, except for nom. and voc. sing., is impossible unless elided in dactylic metres). So *fores* is more frequent in elegy (T.15: 8; Prop.12: 11; Ovid 55: 34; *ostium* for 'house-door' never occurs) and in most other dactylic authors (e.g. Lucr., Virgil, Ov. *Met.*, Val.Fl., Statius). But *ianua* is more common in Juvenal (6: 2) and in Catullus (7: 0), while in Hor. *C. fores* and *ianua* occur 3 times each (in *S. fores* 2: *ianua* 1).

79–80 tempus erit, cum me Veneris praecepta ferentem: the periphrasis (cf. Virg. *Aen.* 2.268) seems pompous here. T. will be like the philosopher dispensing wisdom as he walks around (e.g. Diog.Laert.2.21) or the expert whose advice is sought in the street (Cic. *De Or.* 3.133).

deducat iuvenum sedula turba senem: such an escort was accorded to old men as a sign of respect (Cic. *Sen.* 63, Aul.Gell.2.15.2). This was a phenomenon which T. probably witnessed himself, and so Callim. fr.41 Pf. probably did not inspire the idea here (there is no close similarity of expression either).

For similar appreciation envisaged by the love poet cf. Prop.1.7.23f., 3.9.45f., Ov. *A.A.* 2.733ff.

81–84 The present suddenly impinges with the dramatic and pained *eheu* (emotional involvement and disturbance are also suggested by the appeal in 83f. and perhaps reinforced by the alliteration (of m, d, p and f) in these two couplets).

For the device of the sudden switch to the present cf. 1.5.35f., Hor. *Epod.* 2.67ff., *C.* 3.26.9ff. For its effect here see intro. essay.

On Marathus see Introduction sect. 4.

lento amore: the adjective has two possible meanings here: 'prolonged, lingering' (cf. Ov. *A.A.* 3.573, Hor. *C.* 1.13.8, 3.19.28) or 'cold, unresponsive' (cf. T.2.6.36, Prop.1.6.12).

deficiunt artes, deficiuntque doli: for the order see 1.1.77-8n.

fabula: an object of gossip, and the chief figure in stories illustrating 'others he saved, himself he cannot save' (cf. Hor. *Epod.* 11.8, T.2.3.31f., Ov. *Am.* 3.1.21 for this use of the word in an amatory context).

cum mea ridebunt vana magisteria: Callimachus (fr. 195.30 Pf.) shows a similar inability to deal with his beloved (ἆ, μή με ποιήσῃς γέ[λω]), which may have inspired T., but there is no close similarity of expression and the situation of the lover being laughed at is not unusual (cf. *Hor. Epod.* 5.57, T.1.2.87, 89, Prop.3.25.1). For horror at being a cause of laughter in general cf. Soph. *O.C.* 902f., Hdt.3.29, Hor. *S.* 1.4.34f., *Epist.* 1.1.8f., *Ars Poet.* 381.

Magisterium ('teaching, precepts') in this sense only occurs at Plaut. *Bacc.* 148, *Most.* 33 before here, and is not common until later authors (*OLD* s.v. 3).

Vana magisteria here is an ironical echo of 75, and the words are deliberately left until the very end of the poem (see intro. essay).

For the pentameter ending see 1.1.37-8n.

5

Oppenheim *WS* XXX (1908), 146ff.; Copley *Exclusus Amator* (Am. Phil. Assoc. Phil. Monogr. 1956); Elder *Critical Essays on Roman Literature. 1* (ed. Sullivan, 1962), 75ff., 84, 95ff.

T. gives the following background-situation: there has been a separation, for which apparently a *lena* was to blame, turning Delia against the impoverished T. by her mercenary advice (57f.); Delia is quite content: she has a rich lover and apparently does not look with disfavour on another man who is waiting his chance; T. has tried various ways to forget Delia, but his infatuation has proved too great and in the poem he begs for a reconciliation – unsuccessfully. It is not entirely clear whether the rich lover is supposed to have arrived on the scene before or after the separation, and the witch of 12 and *lena* of 48ff. may be entirely different people or they may be the same person (in which case she may have won Delia's regard by her help during her illness). This background-situation is not revealed in its entirety until the final lines, and successive pieces of new information help keep the reader interested throughout. For this process see intro. essay to 1.4.

1-6	Submission to punishment for former misbehaviour.
7-18	Plea for mercy on grounds of past kindness.
19-36	Dream of happiness, enclosed by present unhappiness (19f., 35f.).
37-46	Unsuccessful attempts to forget Delia.
47-58	Curse on the *lena*.
59-66	Recommendation of the poor lover.
67-76	Failure of the appeals and parting advice to rival.

Transitions are made with care, and all sections are concerned with the characters and incidents of the background-situation, and, apart from 67-76, all represent appeals to Delia in one way or another. Verbal echoes also help to ensure unity (cf. Elder op.cit. p. 101): in connection with the contrasts between past and present (see below) *nunc* and *iam* (2, 17, 35, 39, 69, 71); words from the opening recur at the end whose number seems too large for coincidence: *celer* (4, 70), *versare* (4, 70), *verbum* (6, 67, cf. also 43), *furtivus* (7, 75), *amor* (17, 75, cf. also 60), *uti* (18, 75); also deliberately repeated are *noceo*

(13, 47: see 47-8n.) and *felix* (18, 19: see 19-36n.).

That the elegy is another version of the παρακλαυσίθυρον (see intro. essay to 1.2 and Copley op.cit.) becomes evident at 67-8, where T. clearly places himself outside Delia's door and describes the previous part of the poem as an attempt to make Delia open up. This is not just a convenient image of rejection, as is shown by the way in which T. goes on in the following lines to keep the scene outside the door (71ff. do not, as it might first appear, show that T. would be some distance from the door: see 71-4n.). The addresses to Delia and the rival imply a dramatic situation, and the concentration on the door at the close of the elegy and the number of points throughout the poem in common with 1.2 (see below) suggest strongly that the poem is a locked-out lover's serenade. The argument that the setting of the elegy is the locale of the symposium seems unlikely: there is nothing in the poem to suggest this, and the remark at 37f. means that such a setting is most improbable.

1.5 is the second-longest surviving example of the παρακλαυσίθυρον (shorter only than 1.2). T. is careful to ensure that this poem is not just a pale repetition of 1.2 and that it has individuality and originality of its own. Structurally the main difference lies in the point at which it is made clear that the poem is a παρακλαυσίθυρον (in 1.2 at the very beginning, but in 1.5 in the closing lines: such a late revelation is an innovation). The background-situation is not the same either: here T. depicts himself as locked out by Delia herself (not on the orders of her *coniunx*) and trying to overcome her greed for the gifts of a rich lover (not her fear of detection), and a *lena* lurks in the background. T. omits a number of the addresses of 1.2 (to the slave, the door, the mocker and Venus) and adds a new one. Three people are addressed in 1.5: his mistress (1-66: very common: see intro. essay to 1.2), himself (67-8: unusual: see intro. essay to 1.2) and his rival (69-76: new). Entirely original themes in the παρακλαυσίθυρον are the attempts to fall out of love (37ff.), the rich rival (47), the *lena* and the curse on her (48ff.) and the poor lover (61ff.). Some themes are present which also figure in 1.2 (for these see intro. essay to 1.2), but they are generally presented with a different emphasis or a new twist: the argument of past kindness is addressed to the mistress (9ff., cf. 1.2.13f.), the ideal life in the countryside with Delia is treated at greater length and with the emphasis on Delia's part (21ff., cf. 1.2.71ff.), the witch appears twice, the second time as the poet's enemy (12, 48ff., cf. 1.2.41ff.), and the ex. of nemesis is here for the benefit of the rival and takes a different form (69ff., cf. 1.2.87ff.).

As in the case of 1.2, variation and innovation are here evident on both a formal and a thematic level. 1.5 is also another interesting and and varied παρακλαυσίθυρον, due to the presence of some vivid details, the range of mood and tone (cf. Elder op.cit. p.99f., and see commentary), the combination in one poem of a number of motifs (which are skilfully handled: see esp. the charming and poignant dream at 19ff. and the terrible curse on the *lena* at 49ff.) and the contrasts between past and present, happiness and misery (2, 17, 19, 35, 47, 67). This elegy too captures a particular stage in the love-affair, as the figure of the unhappy *exclusus amator* is again set before us. But this time there are different circumstances, which call for a different approach. The poet's problem here is his mistress' resentment of his former insolence and her venality. So there is concentration on Delia, and *obsequium* is particularly in evidence, as the poet fawns, wheedles and cajoles, employing humility, flattery, pathos and protestation. Hence the opening apology, the submissiveness and self-abasement (esp. 1ff., 61ff.), the various compliments (esp. 43ff.), the affirmation of the misery that the separation causes him and the emphasis throughout on the extent of his love and on what he has done and would do for her. So obsequious is he that he never openly criticizes or attacks Delia for her behaviour (complaints and warnings are indirect and come in passing), and he in fact tends to shift the blame from her (onto himself at 1ff. and onto the *lena* at 47ff.). Even when for once he is not coaxing but gives vent to anger (49ff.), it is the *lena* whom he attacks, and even when his appeals fail for the present (67ff.), he still does not recant his subservient attitude but shows restraint and resignation (perhaps mindful of his chances in the distant future: see 67-76n.). Such obsequiousness seems clearly aimed at the psychology of the *domina* (see also 19-36n. for similar ploys), and so too to desist from angry complaint and criticism and instead to appear miserable and contrite can be an effective way of making another relent. This is a carefully thought out παρακλαυσίθυρον and an excellent example of the *arguta blanditia* of the locked-out lover.

1–6 A general introduction: T. and Delia have parted, but his love for her has proved so uncontrollable that he expresses horror at his former boasts of indifference and professes willingness to endure the most extreme punishment in his desire to achieve a reconciliation. The mood is one of humble apology, helplessness and self-abasement.

1–2 For the situation cf. 2.6.11ff., Prop.2.2.1f. *liber eram et vacuo meditabar vivere lecto; / at me composita pace fefellit Amor.* For the contrast between past and present see intro. essay.

loquebar: may be vivid or may denote repeated boasts (to taunt or convince Delia).

at mihi nunc longe gloria fortis abest: for *longe . . . abest* cf. Caes. *B.G.* 1.36, Prop.1.7.17, Virg. *Aen.* 12.52 *longe illi dea mater erit*, Ov. *Met.* 4.649f.

Note the military connotations in *gloria fortis* ('brave boast', 'boast of bravery'). *Fortis* is also used of a resolute fight against love at Ov. *Met.* 7.76.

3–4 For the top-simile cf. Hom. *Il.* 14.413, Aristoph. *Av.* 1461f., Virg. *Aen.* 7.378ff. *ceu quondam torto volitans sub verbere turbo, / quem pueri magno in gyro vacua atria circum / intenti ludo exercent (ille actus habena / curvatis fertur spatiis; stupet inscia supra / inpubesque manus, mirata volubile buxum; / dant animos plagae), non cursu segnior illo / per medias urbes agitur populosque ferocis*. Here for the first time it is applied to a mental state rather than to physical movement. At its most basic level the simile represents T. as hopelessly driven by his passion, but the expansion here gives it added implications. *Plana . . . sola* and *celer* indicate ease and rapidity of movement, and so bring out the intensity of T.'s emotional disturbance. *Verbere* suggests pain and servile punishments (as he is Delia's slave), and his wish for reconciliation is play on the idea of a flogging). Line 4 implies that T. is being expertly manipulated (*adsueta . . . ab arte*), and *puer* suggests that Amor is the manipulator (*celer* is a not unsuitable epithet for the god: cf. Ov. *Her.* 16.203, *A.A.* 2.98, *Met.* 9.482).

turben: see Critical Appendix.

Probably because of his different sources Charisius is not consistent about this word (at p.64.26ff.K he says that *turbo* is the correct form, but at p.145. 8K he prefers *turben* and quotes this line reading that form). The validity of the form *turben* is defended by Commentator Cruquii on Hor. *Ars Poet.* 380 and Serv. ad *Aen.* 7.378. It is formed by analogy with words like *carmen, pecten* and *fulmen* (Serv. loc. cit., Leumann-Hofmann-Szantyr 1.259).

ab arte: *ab* with *arte* for the simple ablative of manner is mainly poetic and is first found here in poetry (see Smith; elsewhere in T. at 1.9.66, 2.1.56).

5–6 ure ferum et torque: his unruly behaviour deserves the harshest of servile punishments (as he is Delia's slave), and his wish for reconciliation makes him willing to suffer anything. For such punishment of slaves see 1.9.21-2n. The use of fire included branding (Mart. 2.29.9f., Petron. *S.* 105f.), *lamina* (Prop. 4.7.35, Sen. *Epist.* 78.19) and pitch, either on the head (Plaut. *Capt.* 597) or in the *tunica molesta* (Mayor on Juv. 8.235). Such punishments were regarded as extreme (Petron. *S.* 115 (of burning) *immo hanc poenam gravissimam credimus, ubi servis irascimur*, Juv. 14. 15ff.).

For *servitium amoris* see Copley *TAPhA* LXXVIII (1947), 285ff. He points out its importance in the Hellenistic poets (other exx. occur in Meleager *A.P.* 12.81 and Dioscorides 12.169), but fails to stress its origin in the pre-Alexandrian period (Soph. *Ant.* 756, Eur. *Troad.* 950, Plat. *Symp.* 183A, Xen. *Mem.* 1.3.11, Menander 338, 541K), and its presence through the Republican period down to elegy (e.g. Lucilius 1106, 1168, Ter. *Eun.* 1026f., *Phorm.* 144, Catull.45.14, 68.68, 136, 156). In T. there are refs. to slavery to the love-gods (1.2.97-8n.), the mistress as *domina* (1.1.45-6n.), chains (1.1.55-6n.), servile tasks (1.1.55-6n.) and servile punishments (1.6.37f., 1.8.5f., 1.9.21f. and notes, 2.3.79f., 2.4.1ff., 2.6.5). T.'s original contributions to the figure are chains, servile punishments and some new exx. of servile tasks.

Ferus is also used of one who fights against love at 2.6.5 and Sen. *Phaed.* 240. The connotation of 'warlike, fierce' (*OLD* s.v. 5) picks up *fortis* (2).

horrida verba: 'rough, angry words' (*Thes. L. L.* VI$_3$. 2993.28ff.) or 'dreadful words' (*OLD* s.v. *horridus* 6).

Note the emphasis given (by position) to T.'s crime (*magnificum, horrida*) and its harsh punishment (*ure, doma*).

7–18 Continuing with the theme of punishment, T. now abruptly begs for mercy. As justification for the plea he cites his behaviour during Delia's illness, bringing out the importance of his help (9f.) and the extent of his loving concern and devotion (repetition in emphatic positions of words underling his personal contribution (*ille ego, ipseque, ipse, ipse ego*) and listing of his services in full (and graphic) detail). In the final couplet there is another abrupt change: despite all his efforts she now prefers another. Thus the tone changes from pleading to indirect (and pathetic) complaint. The section is in effect an appeal for reinstatement (esp. 17f.) as much as for mercy.

7–8 Oaths and appeals by the head were frequent (e.g. Catull.66.40, Mart. 9.48.2), but the mention of the bed here points to Homeric influence. As Smith points out, the appeal was inspired by the oath at *Il.* 15.36ff. (Hera to Zeus) ἴστω νῦν τόδε γαῖα καὶ οὐρανὸς εὐρὺς ὕπερθε / καὶ τὸ κατειβόμενον Στυγὸς ὕδωρ, ὅς τε μέγιστος / ὅρκος δεινότατός τε πέλει μακάρεσσι θεοῖσι, / σή θ' ἱερὴ κεφαλὴ καὶ νωΐτερον λέχος αὐτῶν / κουρίδιον, τὸ μὲν οὐκ ἂν ἐγώ ποτε μὰψ ὀμόσαιμι. T. adapts this passage to his situation, appropriately making it more elegiac in tone (he substitutes *compositumque caput* for ἱερὴ κεφαλή, *furtivi... lecti* for λέχος ... κουρίδιον and adds *per venerem*). Note the forcefulness in the triple appeal and the frequent alliteration.

For similar appeals by the bed cf. Soph. *Ajax* 493, Ov. *Am.* 3.11.45 *per o lecti socialia iura, Her.* 5.101, 9.159 *per iura sacerrima lecti, Met.* 7.852 *per nostri foedera lecti.*

On the common displacement of the pronoun see Kühner-Stegmann 1.584f., 2.593 (elsewhere in *Corp. Tib.* at 3.1.15f., 4.5.7f.).

furtivi: see 1.2.33-4n.

foedera: see 1.9.1-2n. Primarily *foedus* denotes an agreement or treaty establishing friendly association and alliance between states, and so a compact of partnership between private persons, and then the marriage-bond and other sexual unions (*Thes.L.L.* V1$_1$.1004.80ff.). For the phrase *foedera lecti* cf. Prop.4.3.69, Ov. *Her.* 5.101, *A.A.* 3.593, *Met.* 7.710, 852, *Ibis* 15.

venerem: 'love' or 'charm' (cf. Brink on Hor. *Ars Poet*. 42, 320), here, as the context suggests, specifically 'sexual charm' (cf. 1.4.59 and n., Hor. *C.* 4.13.17, Ov. *Am.* 2.4.40, Petron. *S.* 126).

compositumque caput: 'your head that has laid by mine'. The idea seems to be of the lovers' heads next to each other in bed: cf. Prop.2. 14.22 *mecum habuit positum lenta puella caput* (certainly in bed: 9, 28) and Ov. *Her.* 3.107 *perque tuum nostrumque caput, quae iunximus una* (99f. suggests that bed is meant). The Plautine phrase *caput limare* (lit. 'to rub heads') is rather similar and also suggests the location of the bed (cf. *Poen.* 292, *Merc.* 537 *neuter stupri caussa caput limaret*). Those interested in horticulture or Arabian eroticism should consult Smith here.

9–10 For the theme of past kindness cf. Catull.72, 73, 76 and see intro. essay. The motif of illness was common in elegy, the reactions of the other partner being an obvious test of his or her feelings: cf. 1.3, 4.4, 4.11, Prop.2.9.25ff., 2.28, Ov. *Am.* 2.13, 2.14, *Her.* 20, 21, *A.A.* 2.315ff.

Exact definition of the illness here is not possible: Smith maintains that Delia has malaria, but *defessa* (9) could refer to the debilitating effects of most illnesses, and, even if *somnia* (14) does refer to delirium (see 13-14n.), this symptom is not confined to malaria.

The seriousness of Delia's illness, and thereby the importance of T.'s help, is emphasized (*tristi, defessa,* the dramatic *eripuisse* and the grave spondees throughout).

ille ego . . . dicor: *ille* is in apposition to *ego* ('I, the famous one'). The idea is probably that T.'s devotion was so great that it has drawn attention and he is generally regarded as the one who saved Delia.

iaceres: for *iaceo* in the context of illness see 1.4.31-2n.

votis: defined at 15f. For vows (indicative of love and concern) in such passages cf. 4.4.11ff., Prop.2.9.25, 2.28.43, 59f., Ov. *Am.* 2. 13.23f., *A.A.* 2.327.

11–12 ipseque te circum lustravi sulpure puro: i.e. such was his love and devotion that he himself performed the normal function of the witch (Ov. *A.A.* 2.329f. *et veniat quae lustret anus lectumque locumque / praeferat et tremula sulpur et ova manu*). For the rite of lustration see 1.2.61-2n. and cf. Prop.4.8.83ff., Ov.loc.cit., Nemes.4.62ff., Claud. *VI Cons. Honor.* 324ff., Serv. ad *Aen.* 6.229. As Smith points out, the Romans deified diseases (Plin. *N.H.* 2.15) and *lustratio* was a sort of exorcism (Plaut. *Amph.* 775ff. (Sos.) *quaeso quin tu istanc iubes / pro cerrita circumferri*? (Amph.) *Edepol qui facto est opus; / nam haec quidem edepol larvarum plenast*).

Sulphur was a disinfectant (Hom. *Il.* 16.228) and had curative powers (Plin. *N.H.* 35.176). So it was commonly used in purification and lustration: cf. Hom. *Od.* 22.481, 23.50, Theoc. *Id.* 24.96, Prop.4.8.86, Ov. *F.* 4.739f., *Met.* 7.261, Juv.2.157f., Plin. *N.H.* 35.177.

For *puro* ('purifying') cf. Theoc. *Id.* 24.96 (and see Gow ad loc.) καθαρῷ δὲ πυρώσατε δῶμα θεείῳ, perhaps Prop.4.8.84 *pura limina tergit aqua.*

praecinuisset: 'chanted a spell beforehand'. The women who performed this function were known as *praecantrices* (Plaut. *Mil.* 693, Varro apud Non. 8.494M, Porph. ad Hor. *C.* 1.27.21). For the witch see 1.2.41-2n. and intro. essay.

13–14 ipse procuravi ne possent saeva nocere / somnia: *procuro* was the technical word for nullifying the effects of prodigies (Cic. *Div.* 1.3 and Pease ad loc., Livy 40.2.3, 4). The first syllable is usually long, but for this quantity cf. Ov. *A.A.* 1.587, *F.* 3.343. The verb occurs only in these three places in elegy and is not common in poetry, apart from Plautus (10 exx.).

Saeva . . . / somnia are frightening dreams (because ill-omened). For *saevus* here cf. Val.Fl.1.329f. *quam saeva insomnia curis / prospicio*, Soph. *Elec.* 500 (δεινός), Ap.Rhod.3.618 (ὀλοός). These dreams may be ordinary nightmares or they may be produced by delirium (either of malaria, as Smith thinks, or of some other illness). They are probably Delia's dreams: if they were T.'s nightmares (cf. e.g. Ov.*A.A.* 2.328) the expiation would not be unusual, but if they were Delia's *ipse* would again have point, since the rite was usually performed by the person who had the dream or by a witch (cf. Mart.7.54.4, 11.49.8 and see below).

For the motif of bad dreams cf. Aesch. *Pers.* 176ff., Eur.*I.T.* 42ff., Cic. *Div.* 2.119ff., T.2.6.37ff., 3.4, Macrob. *Comm. in Somn. Scip.* 1.3.

ter sancta deveneranda mola: see Critical Appendix.

Deveneror appears here only in Latin, unless it is to be restored at Ov.*Her.* 2.18, which may be spurious. For the passive force of the deponent cf. esp. the gerundives *venerandus* (1.7.56, Cic. *Agr.* 2.95, Virg. *G.* 3.294), *precandus* (Tac. *Ann.* 4.7) and *deprecandus* (Cic. *Fam.* 12.24.2). Context suggests as the most probable meaning for the verb here 'to ward off by rites', and on the analogy of *deprecor* ('ward off by prayers') from *precor* ('pray') comes *deveneror* ('ward off by worship / rites') from *veneror* ('worship / perform rites to': cf. Virg. *Aen.* 5.745 *farre pio et plena supplex veneratur acerra*).

For the number three see 1.2.53-4n.

For *mola* (i.e. *salsa*) used in religion and magic (it was sprinkled over the sacrificial victim and over the altar) cf. e.g. Virg. *Ecl.* 8.82, Plin. *N.H.* 12.83, 18.7, 31.89 *maxime tamen in sacris intellegitur auctoritas, quando nulla conficiuntur sine mola salsa*, and see Pease on Virg. *Aen.*

4.517. For its use in this particular connection see 3.4.10, Plaut. *Amph.* 740, Mart. 7.54.5.

For *sancta* see 11-12n. (on *puro*) and cf. T.3.4.10, Serv. ad *Ecl.* 8.82 *far enim pium, id est mola casta, salsa.*

15–16 ipse ego velatus filo: again *ipse* shows devotion, since a less-concerned lover could have employed a witch here.

The covering of the head was common in religion (for the woollen fillet here cf. Varro. *L.L.* 5.84, Livy 1.32.6 etc.); for this practice in magic cf. Sen. *Med.* 802f. *tibi funereo de more iacens / passos cingit vitta capillos*, Hosid.Get. *Med.* 334.

tunicisque solutis: the general rule in both religion and magic (Servius on *Aen.* 4.518 *in sacris nihil solet esse religatum*, Pease ad loc., Ov. *Her.* 6.89, *Met.* 7.182). Cf. also 1.3.31-2n.

vota novem Triviae nocte silente dedi: for the requirement of night and silence in magic ceremonies see 1.2.61-2n. and Gow on Theoc. *Id.* 2.38.

On the analogy of *preces dare* = 'pray' (Ov. *ExP.* 4.9.130 etc.) and since *omnia persolvi* (17) means 'I paid all my vows', *vota dare* here probably means 'make, utter vows'.

Nine was a powerful number (three multiplied by three: 1.2.53-4n.), frequently found in connection with magic (e.g. Ov. *F.* 5.439, *Met.* 14. 58, *Ciris* 371f., Sen. *Med.* 772). It is not clear whether T. means that he made a vow on nine separate nights or on one night made nine vows.

Trivia was a name of Hecate (cf. *τριοδῖτις*, e.g. Charicleides ap. Athen. 325D): the places where three roads met were considered eery (Plat. *Leg.* 933b) and were esp. connected with Hecate (55-6n., Theoc. *Id.* 2.36 and schol., Virg. *Aen.* 4.609 *nocturnisque Hecate triviis ululata per urbes*).

As to the exact purpose of the vows, there are various possibilities: this may be a prayer to Hecate to avert Delia's disease, since the moon (one of Hecate's forms: 1.2.51-2n.) was regarded as able to cause and influence diseases (Plin. *N.H.* 2.110, Macrob. *Sat.* 1.17.11); he may be praying to her as the goddess who can send or frustrate dreams, picking up the last couplet (cf. T.3.4.9ff., Prop. 4.4.23, Stat. *Theb.* 9.626ff.); it may be a prayer to her as the goddess of the Underworld to spare Delia's life (cf. Prop. 2.28.47ff.); he may be addressing her as the goddess of witchcraft and asking for her magic aid (cf. e.g. Ov. *Met.* 7.194f.).

17–18 omnia persolvi: i.e. she regained health, the climax to all his efforts. Note the emphatic position and the intensifying prefix.

An abrupt switch to present unhappiness follows, whose effect is heightened by the asyndeton, the opposition of *alter* to *ipse ego*, the brevity in contrast to the length of the preceding passage, the chiastic *fruitur . . . amore / . . . precibus . . . utitur*, repeating the same idea for emphasis, the pathetic *felix* and the juxtaposition *ille meis*.

For the contrast between past and present see intro. essay. For the complaint cf. Ov. *Her.* 5.59f., 6.75, 12.173f. (Medea) *quos ego servavi, paelex amplectitur artus, / et nostri fructus illa laboris habet.*

fruitur: 'has the profit of' (cf. Ov. *Her.* 6.75 *vota ego persolvam? votis Medea fruetur!*).

utitur: 'enjoys the fruit of' (cf. Cic. *N.D.* 1.103 *utatur enim suis bonis oportet et fruatur qui beatus futurus est*).

19–36 *At mihi felicem vitam* picks up and contrasts with *felix . . . ille* (18), and *salva* continues the situation of the previous lines.

T.'s unrealized fantasy of a happy life in the country with Delia, should she recover. For the lover and his mistress together in the country see intro. essay to 1.1 and 1.2.71ff. Here T. concentrates on Delia's part, imagining her in the rôle of the traditional farmer's wife. As usual in T., the picture is optimistic, but this time there is less emphasis on *paupertas* and religion, and Messalla is introduced. T. produces a fresh and charming vignette, full of detail and liveliness (esp. the direct quotation and anaphora). The detail also indicates the extent of T.'s dreaming, and the lines are intended to make Delia pity the poet thwarted of his happiness and to show her how much he thought of her and what she is missing (some points seem particularly well aimed at the susceptibilities of the *domina*: e.g. the affectionate slave-child at 25f., the promise of supremacy at 29f. and the presence of T.'s eminent and famous patron at 31ff.). Lines 19f. and 35f. enclose the dream and provide a neat ring-structure (repetition of *fingebam* and the futility of the fantasy). The tone of the dream itself is hopeful and happy, but these two couplets give the whole section an air of pathos and poignant melancholy.

19–20 at mihi felicem vitam: i.e. *at me feliciter victurum esse.* For the apodosis (and protasis) expressed by means of a noun cf. Sall. *J.* 25.7 *timebat iram senatus, ni paruisset legatis* and Cic. *Tusc.* 1.32 (*sine magna spe*), 1.63 (*sine divino ingenio*) and Plat. *Phaed.* 99A (ἄνευ).

For the contrast between past and present see intro. essay.

fingebam demens, sed renuente deo: see Critical Appendix.

For *renuente deo* cf. Ov. *Met.* 8.325, Mart. 2.14.14, Sil. It. 10.49 (*fato renuente*). If any one god is intended here, it is probably Amor.

21–24 The change into direct quotation is frequent in poetry (see Dissen and cf. 1.6.51ff., 1.8.55ff., 1.9.17ff., 2.5.39ff.): here it gives T.'s fantasy more immediacy and pathos.

The particular province of the farmer's wife was the household, but her duties did extend to outside work, and her general rôle was that of an overseer (Xen. *Oec.* 7.35ff., 9.14ff.). It would not be usual, however, for the farmer's wife to perform the tasks mentioned in these lines. They are to be undertaken by Delia either in her eagerness to help (*mihi* in 23) or because T. is short of labour (cf. 1.1.31-2, 35-6 and notes).

area dum messes sole calente teret: like *musta* (24), *messes* may be plural for singular or, as Putnam suggests, T. may be thinking of repetitions of the events in the future.

For the personification cf. Hor. *S.* 1.1.45, Virg. *G.* 1.192, 298, Sen. *Thy.* 356f.

Threshing took place in July (Hes. *Opera* 597f., Col. *R.R.* 2.20) in the midday heat (Virg. *G.* 1.298 *et medio tostas aestu terit area fruges*). On threshing and the *area* see Cato *Ag. Cult.* 91, 129, Varro *R.R.* 1.51f., Virg. *G.* 1.178ff., Col. *R.R.* 2.19f.

aut mihi servabit plenis in lintribus uvas: for the vintage cf. Cato *Ag. Cult.* 23ff., Varro *R.R.* 1.54, T. 1.1.10, 1.7.35f., 2.1.45, 2.5.85f.

Lintribus refers to the troughs in which the grapes were put after the vintage (Serv. ad *G.* 1.262). Note the optimism in *plenis* (cf. 1.1.10).

pressaque veloci candida musta pede: for *pressa* used in the sense of *expressa* cf. 2.1.45, Virg. *G.* 3.85 (= Sen. *Epist.* 95.68), Luc. 4.317 *ac si quos palmite crudo / arboris aut tenera sucos pressere medulla.*

For white must see Plin. *N.H.* 14.78, 100, 18.102, 24.129, esp. 23.29 *musta differentias habent naturales has, quod sunt candida aut nigra aut inter utrumque.*

On the treading of grapes cf. Cato *Ag. Cult.* 25, Virg. *G.* 2.7f., T. 1.7.36, 2.1.45, 2.5.85, Col. *R.R.* 12.26-8, 37, and see esp. Varro *R.R.* 1.54 (and Tilly ad loc.). *Veloci* is a graphic touch here.

25–26 **consuescet numerare pecus**: performing this duty and similar ones was a way in which the farmer's wife helped outside: cf. Theoc. *Id.* 8.15f., Hor. *Epod.* 2.45f., Virg. *Ecl.* 3.33f. (possibly imitated here) *est mihi namque domi pater, est iniusta noverca, / bisque die numerant ambo pecus*, Ov. *Med. Fac.* 15.

consuescet amantis / garrulus in dominae ludere verna sinu: just as Delia will come to like the countryside and fit into its way of life, so its inhabitants will come to like her and grow accustomed to her. The change of subject also adds variety.

Dealing with slaves, esp. the household slaves, was the traditional duty of the wife (Xen. *Oec.* 7.35f.). *Garrulus* is a good point of detail here, and Delia's treatment of the child adds a homely touch (cf. 2.1.23f.), which represents her in the tradition of the best wives (e.g. Plut. *Cato Maior* 20.5). In general homeborn slaves seem to have been kindly treated by the Romans (Hor. *S.* 2.6.66f., Sen. *Prov.* 1.6 etc.).

27–28 The offerings here pick up the activities of the previous six lines and again indicate optimism. Religion was traditionally supervised by the farmer and his wife (Cato *Ag. Cult.* 143 of the bailiff's wife *rem divinam ni faciat neve mandet, qui pro ea faciat, iniussu domini aut dominae*).

deo . . . agricolae: see 1.1.13-14n. If any one god is meant, it is probably Silvanus: for the offering of first-fruits to him cf. Hor. *Epod.* 2.17ff., and for *daps* cf. Cato *Ag. Cult.* 83 (on *Marti Silvano* meaning *Marti et Silvano* see Pauly s.v. Silvanus). For Silvanus' protection of animals cf. Virg. *Aen.* 8.601 *arvorum pecorisque deo* (Vertumnus (see 1.1.13-14n.) is never found in this connection).

segete spicas: for the lengthening of the open, short syllable before two consonants see 1.6.33-4n.

dapem: for *daps* (and *dapes* with singular sense) used of a religious offering cf. 49-50n., Cato *Ag. Cult.* 50, 131, 132, Virg. *Aen.* 3.301ff. *sollemnis cum forte dapes . . . libabat cineri*, Paul. ex Fest. p.68M.

29–30 Delia is to be totally in charge of the house (emphasized by *illa . . . cunctos, illi . . . omnia* and the contrasting *in tota me nihil*), which would please T. (*at iuvet* in emphatic position) because it would show that she is an eager participant in his ideal life and because this was the traditional state of affairs: cf. Col. *R.R.* 12. *praef.* 4ff., esp. 7 *nam et apud Graecos, et mox apud Romanos usque in patrum nostrorum memoriam fere domesticus labor matronalis fuit, tamquam ad requiem forensium exercitationum omni cura deposita patribusfamilias intra domesticos penates se recipientibus.* For the sentiment cf. Xen. *Oec.* 7.42.

For the shift to the subjunctive see 1.1.21-4n.

cunctos: see 1.4.75-8n.

31–34 T. seems to become really carried away in his dreaming, and the inclusion of his patron (note the affectionate *meus*) is a natural (and pathetic) touch. Delia is to share T.'s regard for Messalla (*veneror* indicates deep reverence: elsewhere it is used of religious veneration) and is to react with old-fashioned hospitality – more than that, through her respect for him she is to perform herself (*ipsa ministra*) duties that a slave would normally do (cf. e.g. Plut. *Cato Maior* 21). Messalla is to receive special treatment (*dulcia poma, selectis . . . arboribus*), as befits one of his standing, but in harmony with the whole section this is to consist of rustic simplicity. Cf. Philodemus *A.P.* 11.44 and Hor. *C.* 1.20.

On the text of 33-4 see Critical Appendix.

Hunc is surely object to *curet* because of *huic paret* immediately following, and the idea of Delia attending to Messalla himself brings out well her envisaged respect for him. *Tantum* is the adjective, agreeing with *virum*. For the seemingly gratuitous pronouns beside *tantum . . . virum* see *Thes. L. L.* VI $_3$.2708.67ff., which cites alongside this passage Caes. *B. G.* 5.42.2 (where there are textual difficulties), 7.63.3 *nacti obsides . . . horum supplicio dubitantis territant, B. C.* 1.70.3 *nactus planitiem in hac contra hostem aciem instruit*, 3.40.3 *navis longas aggressus . . . IIII ex his abduxit*, Sen. *Ben.* 3.33.5 *si quis sapientiam consecutus hanc patri tradiderit.* Accordingly there is a sense-pause after *virum*.

Epulas goes with *paret* and *gerat*. The word seems rather grandiose for the rustic meal implied here (it usually denotes a sumptuous banquet), but is also applied to humble food at Hor. *Epod.* 2.61. It suggests pride in the meal provided.

The hexameter is a metrically curious line.

For the phenomenon of allowing syllables to remain closed before an initial vowel see 1.10.13-14n. This phenomenon normally occurs at the main caesura, but for 4S cf. Prop.2.28.29 *et tibi Maeonias inter heroidas omnis* (*inter heroidas omnis* NFLP: *omnis herodias inter* Δ). Housman (*JPh* 21 (1893), 174) claims that the order *omnis heroidas inter* is confirmed by Ov. *Tr.* 1.6.33 *prima locum sanctas heroidas inter haberes*, and says that the lengthening of *-er* is unexampled in Prop., but such a very late position of *inter* is without parallel in elegy or the elegiacs of Catullus, as is the placing of *inter* at the end of the line when it does not govern the words in the next line. The Δ reading may be a correction of a supposed fault or it may be a reminiscence of Ov. *Tr.* 1.6.33. In the case of T.1.5.33 the syllabic division is facilitated by the sense-pause.

On hiatus in elegy see Platnauer 57ff. Hiatus after interjections and 'Greek Hiatus' (see Platnauer 58f.) are common, but otherwise hiatus in elegy is rare and often accompanied by textual difficulties, as here. The probable instances are as follows. Firstly with open final vowels (i) Catull.99.7f. *multis diluta labella / guttis abstersti omnibus articulis* (*guttis abstersti omnibus* 0: *guttis astersi omnibus* X: *guttis abstersisti omnibus* Avantius[3]: *abstersti guttis omnibus* Ald.: *guttis abstersti mollibus* Lee). The line as it stands in 0 makes perfectly good sense. For the frequency in Catull. of the syncopated form in *-sti* see Kroll on 14.14: the X reading is best explained as due to confusion over this form (cf. 14.14, 77.3, 110.3). The emendations seem unlikely: difficulty with the syncopated form is more probable than difficulty with the common full form (*abstersisti*); *abstersti guttis* produces an inelegant heaping-up of ablatives; Lee's *mollibus* (see Quinn ad loc.) seems unlikely to be corrupted into *omnibus* and has less point than *omnibus*, while *molli . . . articulo* at Quint.11.1.70, cited by Quinn, is used metaphorically; (ii) Propertius 3.7.49 *sed Chio thalamo aut Oricia terebintho.* Here mss. variants do not affect the hiatus, which seems guaranteed by the reminiscence of Virg. *Aen.* 10.136 *inclusum buxo aut Oricia terebintho*; (iii) Ov. *Her.* 9.131 *forsitan et pulsa Aetolide Deianira* (all mss.). Palmer says that *Aetolide* is perhaps corrupt (Appendix I, p. 509), but there are no good grounds for suspicion. *Aetolide* is defended by Soph. *Trach.* 7f., where Deianira says *νυμφείων ὄκνον / ἄλγιστον ἔσχον, εἴ τις Αἰτωλὶς γυνή*. The fact that Planudes here has *τάχα δὲ καὶ ἐκβαλοῦσα ἡ Οἰχαλὶς Δηιάνειραν* is not significant: omissions (*Aetolide*) are not infrequent in Planudes (see Palmer's introduction p.xlix), and for the specification of the subject (in 132 Ovid has *uxor*) cf. *Her.* 6.1, where *carina* is rendered by Ἀργώ. Palmer's attempt to argue for the emendation *Calydonide* here, based on an emendation at 133, where the text is far from certain, is futile.

Secondly, hiatus with *-m*. (i) Prop.2.15.1 *o me felicem! o nox mihi candida! et o tu* (*nox o* Itali: *io . . . io nox . . . io tu* Housman: *o tu nox* Paley dub., Havet). *Nox o* is probably a correction to avoid the hiatus: the order *o nox* is supported by the positions of *o* elsewhere in the line and by the fact that in such triple repetitions in poetry *o* is not postponed (cf. Enn. *Ann.* 117V, *Trag.* 87 Jocelyn, Ter. *Ad.* 304, 790, Ov. *Met.* 1.351, Sil.It.13.749, esp. *Culex* 94 *o pecudes, o Panes, et o gratissima tempe*). The strong stop provided by the exclamation helps the hiatus, and emendation seems unjustified; (ii) Prop.2.32.45 *haec eadem ante illam impune et Lesbia fecit* (*illam iam* Vo.: *eademne* Lachmann). *Iam* here seems the merest stopgap, and, in any case, *iam ante* is the normal phrase. There seems no good reason why *-ne* should have dropped out, and the question form here seems inappropriate and less vigorous than the statement (cf. the *exempla* at 31ff., 57ff.).

In the above exx. hiatus in elegiacs occurs at the main caesura, although outside elegy hiatus at 4S is not uncommon (e.g. Virg. *Aen.* 1.16, 5.735, 9.291, 10.141, 12.31). It seems likely that at T.1.5.33 the pause in sense and metre helps.

5–36 The couplet recalls 19f. (esp. *fingebam*), but seems all the more pathetic here because the unhappiness of the present has been temporarily forgotten during the fantasy. For the contrast see intro. essay.

The idea of winds invalidating words by carrying them away goes back as far as Homer (*Od.* 8.408f.) and was very common in Greek and Latin (Otto *Sprichwörter* s.v. *ventus* 2, Nisbet & Hubbard on Hor. *C.* 1.26.2). T. achieves novelty here by the choice of significant concretes. The combination of Eurus and Notus is taken from storms in Homer: *Il.* 2.144ff., 16.765 (cf. also Eurus, Notus and others at Hom. *Od.* 5.295f., Virg. *Aen.* 1.85f., 2.416ff.). The winds are synonymous with a wild storm and signify the total destruction of his fantasy. Armenia is chosen as a mountainous, and therefore windy, region (Plin. *N.H.* 6.25ff.), and as a distant place, to show how far away T.'s dreams now are. The remoteness is also brought out by the exotic *odoratos*, which would suggest to a Roman the faraway regions from which perfumes were imported (1.3.5-8n.; Armenia produced amomum: Plin. *N.H.* 12.48f.).

There is no difficulty here over *Eurusque Notusque* not leading to Armenia: Latin poets in general are imprecise in terminology where winds are concerned (see Housman on Lucan 7.871), these particular winds are used by T. as a symbol and, in any case, *per* means 'through, all over', not 'to'.

The double *-que* here may well be a reminiscence of Homer. This use of *-que* . . . *-que* is a feature of epic style (thereby raising the tone here), not found in classical prose. It appears as early as Ennius and seems to have derived from Homer's τε . . . τε (Austin on Virg. *Aen.* 4.83, Williams on *Aen.* 5.92, Smith on 1.1.33).

37–46 Like the dream-section, this is another reminiscence, and the actions mentioned here chronologically succeed the fantasy.

Two couplets on his unsuccessful attempts to forget Delia are followed by three couplets on the reason for this lack of success. The appeal lies in the description of his suffering (esp. in contrast to the happy dream above) and in the acknowledgement of Delia's beauty and its effect on him (the failure on many occasions of two proven *remedia amoris*, the great compliments at 43ff.). The mood is pathetic helplessness.

37–38 saepe ego temptavi curas depellere vino: wine was a relief from troubles in general (Alcaeus 91, 96.3f.D, Plat. *Leg.* 666B, Hor. *Epod.* 9.37f., *C.* 1.7.17ff., 4.12.19f., T.1.7.39f., Sen. *Phaed.* 445) and esp. from troubles caused by love: cf. *A.P.* 11.49 (Evenus), 12.49 (Meleager), Alciphron 1.35, T.1.2.1f., 3.6.3ff., Prop.3.17, Ov. *Rem.* 805ff., Mart. 1.106.7ff. *suspiras, retices, gemis: negavit. / crebros ergo licet bibas trientes / et durum iugules mero dolorem. / quid parcis tibi, Rufe? dormiendum est.* The remedy also fails at Ov. *Her.* 16.231f.

Saepe is emphatic by position.

Curae are amatory 'cares', as often: see Smith and cf. also Catull. 64.72, Prop. 1.3.46, T.3.6.7, 37.

at dolor in lacrimas verterat omne merum: Smith interprets: 'the wine was tears when I came to drink it. Sorrow had turned it', and compares Calp. *Ecl.* 3.51f. *te sine, vae misero, mihi lilia nigra videntur / nec sapiunt fontes et acescunt vina bibenti* and Nemes. *Ecl.* 2.42f. *omnes ecce cibos et nostri pocula Bacchi / horreo* (cf. also, from the opposite point of view, Petron.93.5f. Baehrens). The choice of tears as a symbol for bitterness would also suggest the idea that the wine-cup held only sadness for T. With this interpretation this is a striking and original phrase for which there is no exact parallel.

Alternatively, on a more prosaic level, T. may have in mind a physiological process, i.e. the wine entered his bloodstream and came out as tears because of his anguish. For ancient theories on the relationship of food and drink to the bloodstream, and of the bloodstream to tears see Onians *Origins of European Thought* (Cambridge, 1954), 42f., 202, 218. T. may be thinking of the passing of liquid into the veins and bloodstream (Plin. *N.H.* 11.223, Sen. *Epist.* 122.6, Arnob. *Adv. Nat.* 5.6) and the idea of tears as a separation of watery liquid from the blood (Empedocles A78 Diels). Cf. also Celsus 6.6.14 (worry and food produce tears). For wine causing tears for lovers cf. *A.P.* 12.116 (anon.), 135 (Asclepiades). With this interpretation *verterat* is used for the perfect or imperfect (see Platnauer 112ff.).

On *dolor* see 1.2.1-2n.

39–40 saepe aliam tenui: for this remedy cf. Cic. *Tusc.* 4.75, Hor. *Epod.* 11.23ff., T.1.9.79ff., Prop.3.15.9f., Ov. *Her.* 19.104 *fitque novus nostri finis amoris amor, Rem.* 441ff.

For *teneo* with ref. to sexual intercourse cf. 2.6.52, Ov. *Am.* 3.7.3.

sed iam cum gaudia adirem: for *gaudia* of orgasm cf. Lucr.4.1106, 1196, T.2.1.12, Hor. *C.* 3.6.28.

admonuit dominae deseruitque Venus: cf. Prop.3.6.34 *noctibus illorum dormiet ipsa Venus*, T.4.13.14, Ov. *Am.* 1.4.66. For the idea of Venus affecting sexual performance cf. also Hdt.2.181, Ov. *A.A.* 2.419.

On *domina* see 1.1.45-6n.

41–42 See Critical Appendix.

tunc me discedens devotum femina dixit: for *devotum* 'bewitched' cf. 1.8.18, Ov. *Am.* 3.7.27, 80, *Her.* 6.91. For impotence caused by magic cf. Hdt.2.181, Ov. *Am.* 3.7.27ff., 79f., Petron. *S.* 129ff.

et pudet et narrat scire nefanda meam: for the situation and the woman's reactions cf. Ov. *Am.* 3.7.77ff.

For the change from impersonal to personal expression cf. Ov. *Rem.* 407, *Met.* 14.279, esp. *ExP.* 4.15.29 (see the discussion in the Critical Appendix): the implication here is that it is her shame that leads her to accusations of witchcraft.

There are various ways of taking *narrat*. The tense (and that of *pudet*) may be either genuine present or (picking up *dixit*) historic present. The woman may be speaking to T. alone (cf. Ov. *Am.* 3.7.77ff.), in which case *narrat* may be little more than a synonym for *dicit* (cf. Ter. *Hec.* 145, Cic. *Fin.* 2.13 *'omnibus laetitiis laetum' esse se narrat*), or, as *narro* is often used of relating a story at length or in detail (cf. Prop.4.7.67, Hor. *C.* 3.7.17f. *narrat paene datum Pelea Tartaro, / Magnessam Hippolyten dum fugit abstinens*), the idea may even be that the woman in the act of leaving is giving a quite detailed account of Delia's knowledge of witchcraft (cf. Ov. *Her.* 6.83ff.) with spiteful elaboration. Alternatively the woman may be speaking to others, spreading gossip about Delia's knowledge of magic (for *narro* used of gossip see Austin on Virg. *Aen.* 2.549, *OLD* s.v. 4). The reason for her gossiping could be simply that her shame has made her spiteful. Again, as there seems to be a danger of Ovid's experience with the girl being found out at *Am.* 3.7.83f., the woman's shame may be prompting her to get in first and exculpate herself before the story leaks out, or, if the story has already been found out, to defend herself.

Nefanda is a strong word and, as Smith points out, is impressively indefinite.

Meam means 'my girl'. This use of the possessive pronoun is common: cf. (*mea* / *meus*) 2.3.77, 2.6.52, 4.7.8, Prop.3.8.22, Ov. *A.A.* 1.322; (*tua* / *tuus*) 4.13.21, Prop.1.9.22, Ov. *Rem.* 573; (*sua*) 2.5.103, Prop. 1.3.30, 3.14.22.

Note the gloomy spondees here and the alliteration in the hexameter (carrying on from 40).

43–44 For *verba* of 'charms, spells' cf. Hor. *Epist.* 1.1.34, Ov. *Met.* 7.203, 248, 14.57, 301.

Speculations on whether magic inspired love, and, if not, what did enchant men first appear in Greek tragedy: cf. Eur. *Androm.* 205f. (character rather than beauty) οὐκ ἐξ ἐμῶν σε φαρμάκων στυγεῖ πόσις, / ἀλλ' εἰ ξυνεῖναι μὴ 'πιτηδεία κυρεῖς. This sentiment is picked up by Menander (646K). Afranius emphasized the physical aspect (380-381R *aetas et corpus tenerum et morigeratio, / haec sunt venena formosarum mulierum*). T. skilfully adapts Afranius by a logical introduction, concentration on the physical side and definition of the feminine charms. He also combines the two usual modes of expression (the antithesis between magic and the real attraction, and the metaphorical use of a word normally applied to magic). At 1.8.23ff. he is more explicit (see notes). Propertius (3.6.25ff.) picked up the character argument, and Ovid (*Her.* 6.83ff., *A.A.* 2.99ff., *Med. Fac.* 35ff.) typically combined both character and beauty (cf. also Plut. *Mor.* 141B-C).

Both the arm in general (Hor. *S.* 1.2.92, *C.* 1.13.3, Ov. *Met.* 1.501, Alciphron 3.67) and the upper arm in particular (Ov. *Met.* 1.501, *A.A.* 3.307ff.) were considered to have attractions. Here, as often, it is hard to tell whether *lacertus* refers to the upper arm or the whole arm. For the attraction of *lacerti* in general cf. Ov. loc. cit., *Am.* 1.5.19, and for *lacerti teneri* in particular cf. Prop.3.6.13, 4.3.23, where their attractiveness is implied.

This is one of the few places where T. is at all precise about Delia's appearance (cf. 66, 1.3.91f., 1.1.55). Blond hair was not common among the Greeks or Romans, and was admired by them (Gow on Theoc. *Id.* 8.3). It seems to have been popular among the elegists' mistresses, and was often achieved by dyeing (cf. Prop.2.2.5, Ov. *Am.* 1.14, 2.4.39, 3.7.23, Gow loc. cit. and Pease below). Apart from this, blond hair seems confined mainly to foreigners (1.7.11-12n.) or to persons of heroic or divine status (Pease on Virg. *Aen.* 4.590). So Delia's hair (along with her beauty in general, and her antipathy towards T.: 45-6n.) may have suggested the following *exemplum* (Homer mentions the beauty of Thetis' hair at *Il.* 18.407 Θέτι καλλιπλοκάμῳ, and Heliodorus says that her hair is blond at *A.P.* 9.485.1, 14, although it is blue according to Pindar *Paean*.6.84 Bowra). Note that although *flavis . . . comis* here suggests that T. is thinking of a blond-haired

Thetis at 45f., he may well not have pictured her in such detail, but be thinking of her simply as a goddess with beautiful hair in general.

For *flavus, flavere, flavescere, flavidus, sufflavus* see André *Étude sur les termes de couleur dans la langue Latine* (Paris, 1949), 128ff. The terms are applied to shades of yellow, brownish-yellow and reddish-yellow, and they are often used of hair (esp. *flavus*): of barbarians (1.7. 12, Lucan 1.402, 2.51, 3.78, Juv.13.164, Mart.6.61.3), deities (Virg. *G.* 1.96, Ov. *F.* 6.652, *Met.* 6.118) and Greeks and Romans (Catull.64. 63, Hor. *C.* 1.5.4, 2.4.14, 3.9.19, 4.4.4, Ov. *Am.* 2.4.43, *Met.* 9.307, Stat. *Theb.* 4.262, Suet. *Aug.* 79).

The designation of Delia at this stage as *nostra puella* is pathetic. The careful attention to sound in this couplet (same internal rhyme in hex. and pent. (see 1.1.53-4n.), *facit . . . facie, tenerisque lacertis, devovet et, nostra puella*) makes it a truly poetic tribute to Delia.

45–46 The mythological *exemplum*, esp. comparing the mistress to a goddess or heroine, was frequent in elegy (Catull.68.73ff., Prop.1.3. 1ff., 2.2.5ff., Ov. *Am.* 1.7.13ff., 1.10.1ff.), and similarly in Comedy women were often compared or identified with Venus (e.g. Plaut. *Rud.* 420, *Poen.* 278, *Bacc.* 217). Such an *exemplum* occurs here only in T., and so represents a great compliment to Delia.

The story of Peleus and Thetis was handled variously, but her beauty was generally agreed upon (e.g. Pind. *Isth.* 8.27ff., Catull.64.28). The most common version was that she was seized by him against her will (Hom. *Il.* 18.429ff., Pind. *Nem.* 3.35f., 4.62ff., Hdt.7.191, Apollod.3. 13.5, Paus.5.18.5, Ov. *Met.* 11.229ff.), and in some accounts she left Peleus afterwards (e.g. Ap.Rhod.4.866ff.).

Most obviously this pictorial *exemplum* refers to Delia's beauty, but the unwillingness of Thetis in many accounts suggests T.'s present difficulties with Delia. The idea is not openly stated (and we would not expect it to be in a παρακλαυσίθυρον), but, in view of Delia's attitude to T. in the rest of the poem and esp. in the lines immediately surrounding the *exemplum*, it seems a reasonable inference. It may be hinted at in 46, since in other refs. to Thetis riding to Peleus in similar fashion (presumably either based on this line or derived from a common source) her unwillingness is emphasized: cf. Ov. *Met.* 11.236ff. *quo saepe venire / frenato delphine sedens, Theti, nuda solebas. / illic te Peleus, ut somno vincta iacebas, / occupat, et quoniam precibus temptata repugnas, / vim parat*, Val.Fl.1.131ff. *Peleos in thalamos vehitur Thetis; aequora delphin / corripit, illa sedet deiecta in lumina palla / nec Iove maiorem nasci suspirat Achillem.*

Haemonium . . . Pelea: Haemon (son of Pelasgus) was the father of Thessalus, so that *Haemonius* means 'Thessalian' (Rhianus fr. 25 = Powell *Coll.Alex.* p.13). Peleus' kingdom was in Thessaly (Apollod. 3.13.1). Before here the adjective appears only in Propertius (1.13.

21, 1.15.20).

Nereis: the second syllable can be long or short, after Νηρηΐς or Νηρεΐς (see Smith).

vecta est frenato . . . pisce: so she is represented in art from the 5th century (see Brommer *Vasenlisten*², 241ff., 270ff.). Cf. also Ovid, Val. Flacc. above, Stat. *Ach.* 1.221f.

caerula: the epithet is also applied to Thetis at Hor. *Epod.* 13.16, Prop.2.9.15, Ov. *Met.* 13.288, Stat. *Ach.* 1.650. The precise ref. of the word is hard to pin down. *Caerul(e)us* is frequently applied to marine deities (*OLD* s.v. 3a), and so here it is probably used loosely as *epitheton ornans*, 'the sea-goddess Thetis' being the implication (the clothes (Ov. *Met.* 9.32), hair (Hor. *C.* 3.28.10, Ov. *A.A.* 1.224, *Met.* 13.960), eyes (Cic. *N.D.* 1.83) and body (Ov. *Met.* 13.895, 962) were usually of a blue-green colour in marine and river-deities). If there is any specific ref. in the adjective used not expressly of a part of the body, but with a proper name, it can refer to blue eyes (Hor. *Epod.*16.7) or blue skin (Mart.11.53.1, of the woad-stained Britons). The former is perfectly acceptable here, but the latter seems less likely. Even if T. is here thinking of Thetis as blond-haired (43-4n.), a poet may not have seen any difficulty in an implied combination of blue skin and blond hair, but the dark blue denoted by *caerul(e)us* (1.7.11-12n.) applied to Thetis' skin would hardly fit with the stock description of her as ἀργυρόπεζα (Hom.*Od.* 24.92 etc., Hes. *Theog.* 1006, *Hom. Hymn.* 3.319; cf. also *A.P.* 5.48.4 (Rufinus), Stat. *Ach.* 1.100) and would be without parallel. Moreover, in a comparison one would hardly expect a poet to bring out such an obvious point of dissimilarity between Thetis and Delia.

For the contrast with *flavis* (44) cf. 1.7.11-12n.

47–58 In 47 *haec* refers to Delia's charms and *nocuere* to their effect on T., as described above (see Critical Appendix on 47-8). The transition is also helped by the fact that *noceo* (cf. *devovet*, 44) is also used of the effects of magic (1.8.23, Ov. *Am.* 3.7.28 etc.).

T. now pronounces a curse on the *lena*, who is viewed as the root-cause of his troubles with Delia, followed by a single couplet which declares emphatically that the fulfilment of the curse has divine sanction. For the curse on the *lena* cf. Plaut. *As.* 127ff., T.2.6.53f., Prop.4.5.1ff., 75ff., Ov. *Am.* 1.8.113f.

The explanations of the curse given by previous commentators are generally vague, incoherent and unconvincing, and are often inadequately supported. The refs. throughout to details connected with magic are remarkable and seem too frequent to be merely coincidental. When this point is taken into consideration two interpretations of the curse are possible.

Firstly, it has been suggested to me that the *lena* is not now a witch and that the point of the curse is that she should have to earn her living through witchcraft rather than as a *lena* (because of hunger (53), presumably caused by poverty). The lines will bear this interpretation: at 49f. she may be partaking of victims in sacrifices to the gods of the Underworld, or in the form of a *strix vel sim*. enjoying a carnivorous repast, or consuming magic brews; at 51f. ghosts and *strix* may be her concomitants; at 53f. she may be seeking ingredients for her magic charms and concoctions; at 55f. she may be changed into an animal and be wandering with a train of dogs. In this case presumably *saga* is applied to her at 59 either as a synonym for *lena* (see Lewis and Short s.v. *saga* 2) or because T.'s vengeful imagination has determined to view her as a witch from line 49 on.

A different interpretation was suggested by Oppenheim (loc. cit. intro. essay). The *lena* is at present also a witch (59), and the curse makes her a victim of her own craft: she is forced (because of maddening hunger, 53) to consume the foul ingredients of her own magic offerings and concoctions (49f., 53f.), and the beings that she normally commands or uses turn against her (51f., 55f.). For fuller details see commentary below. Her hunger is presumably due to poverty, so that the punishment fits the crime: in her capacity as a *lena* who gives mercenary advice (59f.) she is cursed with poverty, and in her capacity as a witch her own craft is turned against her.

I favour Oppenheim's theory for the following reasons: *aspera* (56) suggests hostility; *semper* (52), *ipsa* and *furens* (53) now have more point; the curse thus exhibits more fully T.'s customary apt reversal of circumstances; the passage has a greater air of anger and is a more bitter attack on the *lena*; the lines are in general more frightening for Delia and represent a more terrible divine punishment for her benefit (see below); in elegy the *lena* is usually also a witch (1.2.41-2n.). Accordingly (with variations over details) I accept his interpretation in the commentary below.

Precision and certainty over points in the curse is often difficult. T.'s expression is at times unclear, and there is no good reason to suppose that he knew much about magic beyond literary refs., so that he may be vague and inexact in his own mind over the details. In fact, this indefiniteness tends to make the curse more mysterious, and so more awesome.

The mood is furious anger and bitterness. On the most obvious level T. gives vent to his feelings about the *lena*, and the intensity of the attack on her is an indication of the intensity of his love for Delia (whose estrangement the *lena* is supposed to have caused). The lines are also intended to undermine the influence of the *lena* on Delia – hence the terrible curse and the promise of divine support for it, to frighten his mistress and let her know the punishment that awaits such a character. In addition, although T. is careful to shift the blame from his mistress at 47f. and the curse is actually directed at the *lena*, the section also contains an indirect criticism of her for following the advice of the *lena* and a covert warning of divine disapproval for Delia herself (57-8n.).

Incidentally the curse does much to refute the conventional view of T. as a rather anaemic and gentle author.

47–48 See Critical Appendix.

After the sublime comparison comes the sordid present (for the contrast see intro. essay).

For a comparable change of ref. with forms of *hic* see 1.9.75 and notes.

Nocuere here looks like a deliberate echo of 13: T. saved Delia from harm, but her beauty harms him.

On the *dives amator* in elegy cf. 1.6.53-4n., 1.9.53, 2.3.59f., Prop. 4.5, Ov. *Am.* 1.8.23, 3.8. Cf. also Pyrgopolynices in Plaut. *Miles*, Polymachaeroplagides in Plaut. *Pseud.*, Therapontigonus in Plaut. *Curc.*, Stratophanes in Plaut. *Truc.*, Thraso in Ter. *Eun.*, Catull.69, Hor. *Epod.* 11, 15.

For the *lena* cf. Aristoph. *Thesm.* 505, Diph.43.22K, Cleareta in Plaut. *As.*, Syra and Melaenis in Plaut. *Cist.*, T.2.6.44ff., Prop.4.5, Ov. *Am.* 1.8. See also 59-60n.

On T.'s usage of the perfect forms in *-ere* and *-erunt* see Smith. More common is *-ere* (8: 4; *amarunt* at 2.3.69). This is no doubt for metrical convenience and because of the archaic tone (Williams on Virg. *Aen.* 5.580, Austin on *Aen.* 2.53).

For the forceful *exitium* cf. Prop.2.22.4, Ov. *Am.* 1.1.22.

49–50 sanguineas edat illa dapes: see Critical Appendix.

Explanations of *sanguineas . . . dapes* as raw meat or human flesh seem unlikely, since the rest of the curse is of a specifically magic nature and in other refs. to food she has to eat substances connected with her own craft. *Daps* is used of religious offerings (27-8n.), and it seems most probable that here she has to consume offerings to her own patron deities. For various bloody offerings to the gods of magic cf. 1.2.61f., Hor. *S.* 1.8.27f., Ov. *F.* 1.389, Plut. *Mor.* 277B, 280C, Paus. 3.14.9, Gow on Theoc. *Id.* 2.12. T. may be thinking in particular of Ἑκάτης δεῖπνα (dogs and dogs' entrails formed part of them: Plut. *Mor.* 290D, Rohde *Psyche* (trans. Hillis), p. 322 n. 88). Ἑκάτης δεῖπνα were set out at the places where three roads met and were frequently eaten by the poor (Ar. *Plut.* 596f., Lucian *Dial. Mort.* 331). This may in turn explain the visitations of 51f. and 55f., since the purpose of the δεῖπνα was to placate Hecate and spirits (Plut. *Mor.* 709A, Rohde *Psyche* loc. cit.), and those who interfered with them were liable to be punished (Petron. *S.* 134).

tristia cum multo pocula felle bibat: previous explanations of this substance as simply a substitute for wine or an equivalent of the lover's cup of gall are inadequate, and again there is reference to magic. *Poculum* may be used of drinks, draughts in general, so that the line could refer to liquids (including much gall) from the *dapes* above. *Poculum* can denote a magic brew (Hor. *Epod.* 5.38, 17.80), and so she may here have to consume her own brews (for gall in magic brews and remedies cf. Plin. *N.H.* 28.7, 91, 94, 30.82). *Poculum* can also refer to poison (Cic. *Clu.* 31), and the idea may even be that she should drink her own poisons (for gall as a poison cf. Ov. *Tr.* 5.7.16, *ExP.* 1.2.16; for the witch as poisoner see 1.2.41-2n.).

Tristia may mean 'bitter-tasting' (cf. Lucr. 4.634, Virg. *G.* 2.126) or, if the ref. is to magic brews or poison, 'baleful' (cf. Virg. *Aen.* 3.214, Ov. *Met.* 6.140).

This detail is particularly apt in the case of the *lena*, who was proverbially fond of wine (cf. Prop. 4.5.2 *et tua, quod non vis, sentiat umbra sitim*, Ov. *Am.* 1.8.3f., 114).

It is sometimes claimed that Call. fr. 530Pf. (χολῇ δ' ἶσα γέντα πάσαιο) is echoed here, but the fragment is too short for any certainty.

The couplet is forcefully expressed (*sanguineas* and *cruento, tristia* (all in emphatic positions) and *multo*).

51–52 **hanc volitent animae circum**: witches normally conjured and controlled ghosts, often sending them against others (1.2.45-8 and n., Apul. *Met.* 9.29, *P. Mag. Leid. V.* 7.10, Rohde op.cit., p. 326 n. 106, 107, Appendix 7).

sua fata querentes: the words may be simply a reminiscence of Homer's ὃν πότμον γοόωσα (*Il.* 16.857, 22.363). Alternatively the phrase may suggest that the ghosts are motivated by desire for vengeance, in which case they may be ghosts of lovers she has harmed by corrupting their mistresses or ghosts of people she has killed (for ghosts coming back to earth for revenge cf. esp. Hor. *Epod.* 5.92ff. *nocturnus occurram Furor, / petamque vultus umbra curvis unguibus, / quae vis deorum est Manium, / et inquietis adsidens praecordiis / pavore somnos auferam*, also Virg. *Aen.* 4.385f., Livy 3.58.11, *Ibis* 145ff., Suet. *Otho* 7, Val. Fl. 3.378ff.). For another possible reason for the visitation see 49-50n.

semper: doubly emphatic by position.

e tectis strix violenta canat: again one of her own creatures is to turn against her. Exact identity of the *strix* was uncertain (usually defined as a screech-owl), and it was the subject of some strange stories (Ov. *F.* 6.131ff., Plin. *N.H.* 11.232). It had definite connections with magic: it was used as an ingredient in magic charms etc. (Hor. *Epod.* 5.20, Prop. 3.6.29, Ov. *Met.* 7.269, Sen. *Med.* 733f.), witches could transform themselves into *striges* (Ov. *F.* 6.141f., Festus s.v. *strigem* =

p. 314M), could sound like them (1.2.47-8n.), and seem to have been on intimate terms with them (Prop.4.5.17 *consuluitque striges nostro de sanguine*).

The exact function of the *strix* here is uncertain. It may be heralding disaster for her (cf. Sen. *H.F.* 688 *omenque triste resonat infaustae strigis*, Stat. *Theb.* 3.511), as all owls do, esp. when on one's own roof (Ov. *Met.* 6.431f., Plin. *N.H.* 10.34f., Pease on Virg. *Aen.* 4.462). Alternatively, it may even be waiting to attack her, like the ghosts and dogs (for this habit of the *strix* cf. Plaut. *Pseud.* 820f., Ov. *F.* 6.131ff., Sil.It. 13.598 *sparsis strix sanguine pennis*).

Violenta may be fem. nom. sing., referring to the violent nature of the bird, or neut. acc. pl., referring to its prophecies of violence, or its strident cry (used adverbially, i.e. 'vehemently, loudly': see Page on Virg. *Aen.* 9.632 and cf. Sen. *Thy.* 1080 *omni parte violentum intona*).

53–54 ipsa fame stimulante furens: as at 49f., she is forced herself to devour substances connected with her craft. Note the emphasis in the collocation.

For *fame stimulante* cf. Ov. *Tr.* 1.6.9, Juv. 14.84. The long e in *fame* is the normal quantity (Kühner-Stegmann 1. p. 486).

herbasque sepulcris / quaerat: for such herbs used in magic concoctions and charms cf. Theoc. *Id.* 5.121, Hor. *S.* 1.8.22, *Epod.* 5.17f., Prop.4.5.11.

a saevis ossa relicta lupis: for bones touched or eaten by the wolf employed in magic cf. Lucan 6.551ff. *nec carpere membra / volt ferro manibusque suis, morsusque luporum / exspectat siccis raptura e faucibus artus*, 627ff., Plin. *N.H.* 28.178, 211 (cf. also Hor. *Epod.* 5.23). The adjective underlines the unnaturalness of the action.

The angry sigmatism (evident elsewhere in the curse) is esp. noteworthy in this couplet.

55–56 Again her own creatures turn against her: witches could turn into dogs (Apul. *Met.* 2.22), and dogs were sacred to Hecate and normally controlled by witches (49-50n., 1.2.51-2n., Sen. *H.O.* 460, Gow on Theoc. *Id.* 2.12, 35, Rohde op.cit., p. 324 n.99).

E triviis may go with *aspera turba canum* or with *post agat*. Either dogs from the *trivia* are to chase her (for crossroads as the haunt of dogs cf. Lucr.4.1203, Ov. *F.* 5.140 *compita grata cani*), or dogs are to chase her from the place where three roads meet, where she may be imagined as performing magic (as sacred to Hecate (15-16n.), this spot was considered efficacious for magic: Plato *Leg.* 933B, Plin. *N.H.* 32. 113) or after Ἑκάτης δεῖπνα (49-50n.).

In either case her howls are to be in terror (for *ululo* so used cf. Virg. *Aen.* 2.488; the frequency of u in 55 suggests her cries) and she is presumably to be bare-groined because her clothes are hitched up to run better or they are torn up to this point by the dogs.

Thus on a number of occasions she is to be driven through towns as a spectacle of ridicule for any onlookers: cf. Hor. *S.* 1.8.47ff. *at illae currere in urbem. / Canidiae dentes, altum Saganae caliendrum / excidere atque herbas atque incantata lacertis / vincula cum magno risuque iocoque videres.*

57–58 Divine approval for T.'s curse gives it weight and is intended to undermine the *lena*'s advice and frighten Delia (see below). Note the forcefulness in the four separate statements (the first three are short, sharp phrases) and in the placement of important words in emphatic positions.

sunt numina amanti: see 1.2.27-8n. for the lover's divine protection.

saevit et iniusta lege relicta Venus: *iniusta lege* is a difficult phrase. *Lex* is used of a contract and of a term of a contract or agreement, and so is applied to lovers' compacts (1.6.69-72n.). Thus the following meanings are possible: (i) 'Venus is angry when deserted because of (i.e. for) an unjust compact (with another)'; (ii) 'Venus is angry when abandoned and the (present) compact is improper, unfair (i.e. disregarded, broken)'; (iii) 'Venus is angry when abandoned and a term of the (present) compact is improper, unfair (i.e. disregarded, broken)'.

For lovers' compacts see 7-8n., 1.9.1-2n., and for Venus' anger when one party abandons another see 1.9.19-20n. The point of the remark, of course, is that Delia is supposed to have abandoned T. and to prefer a rich lover. On the surface the ref. here is to the *lena*, since she was apparently responsible (cf. Prop.4.5.65ff.), but the reference of the words is ambiguous, and the way in which T. moves on to address Delia immediately is a hint that divine wrath may be directed at Delia also. So the remark is a covert warning as well as a passing rebuke.

59–66 The theme of the mercenary *lena* is picked up by *sagae praecepta rapacis* (59), while the introduction of Delia has been prepared for by the mention of the lovers' compact and the ambiguity of reference in the previous couplet.

A general exhortation to Delia and attack on money used in love is followed by a recommendation of the lover who has no money. The recommendation is bound together by insistent anaphora of *pauper* (in emphatic positions), and there seems to be a chronological progression, representing the poor man's services at various times of day and night. The point is that the rich man may give presents, but he would never perform the tasks undertaken by the poor man: the former orders the girl about and has no feeling for her (cf. Ov. *Am.* 1.10. 43ff., 3.8.61f.), but the latter is a humble and faithful lover (cf. Prop. 2.24.39f., Ov. *Am.* 1.3.5ff., *A.A.* 2.161ff.). In fact, the poor lover's services here are those normally carried out by a slave. For *servitium amoris* see 5-6n., and for the lover performing servile tasks see 1.1.

55-6n.: new details in this connection are the early visit (61f.), making a way in the crowd (63f.) and removing the girl's sandals (66). Here T. is trying to undermine directly the advice of the *lena*, and obviously the implication is that he is prepared to perform all these services for Delia himself. The tone is one of humility and self-abasement.

59–60 at tu quam primum sagae praecepta rapacis / desere: for the greed of the *lena* cf. Plaut. *Cist.* 47ff., *As.* 177ff., Ter. *Heaut.* 233f. *mater quoius sub imperiost mala, / quoi nil iam praeter pretium dulcest*, Prop. 4.5.21ff., Ov. *Am.* 1.8.23ff.

Note the grave spondees and the (doubly) emphatic position of *desere*.

The expression may be based on Prop. 1.11.27 *tu modo quam primum corruptas desere Baias.*

nam donis vincitur omnis amor: 'for love is always destroyed by gifts' (*omnis* adjective for adverb). It is possible that the sense here is: 'for love is always destroyed by (consideration of) gifts', i.e. love is always destroyed in a girl when she sets to work assessing the value of the gifts and granting her favours to the man who gives her most. The remark then, however, would be somewhat abrupt and the point of the praise of the poor man that follows hard to see. It seems more likely that the sense is 'a man's love for a girl ends when he has to give gifts' (when the girl follows the instructions of the *lena*, as at 68). The threat of men ceasing to love Delia seems a stronger argument than the prospect of Delia ceasing to love others, and the remark now fits logically into T.'s argument here (the rich man's lack of love in pointed contrast to the poor man's devotion in the following lines). For the expression cf. 3.6.4 (to Liber) *saepe tuo cecidit munere victus Amor*, Ov. *Rem.* 260 *nec fugiet vivo sulphure victus Amor*, 462 *successore novo vincitur omnis amor* (based on this line). For the idea cf. e.g. Ov. *Am.* 1.10.43ff.

The phrase may be a variation on Virg. *Ecl.* 10.69 *omnia vincit Amor*, as Putnam suggests.

61–62 pauper erit praesto tibi semper: a general introduction to the poor lover's obsequious actions and servile tasks (for *esse praesto* of a slave cf. Plaut. *Men.* 982). Note the emphatic position of *semper*.

pauper adibit / primus: the fact that he arrives first (*primus* emphatic by position) shows his devotion (cf. Ov. *A.A.* 2.223f. *iussus adesse foro, iussa maturius hora / fac semper venias*), and the morning visit also suggests the client's obsequious *salutatio*.

in tenero fixus erit latere: like an attendant slave. In Ter. *Phorm.* the lover who performs such a duty (85f.) is called a slave (144f. *quid paedagogus ille qui citharistriam, quid rei gerit?*). Cf. also Ov. *Am.* 3.11.17f. *quando ego non fixus lateri patienter adhaesi, / ipse tuus custos, ipse vir, ipse comes?*

Tenero is a compliment (cf. 1.1.64, 68, 1.5.43, 1.6.33).

63–64 For making a way in the crowd (apparently in day-time), a vivid touch, cf. esp. Ov. *A.A.* 2.210 *ipse fac in turba, qua venit illa, locum*, and cf. also Theophr. *Char.* 2.5 (Ussher), Hor. *S.* 2.5.94f. This was a servile duty, often undertaken by clients (cf. Petron. *S.* 28, Mart. 2.18, 3.7.2, 10.74.3).

For the crowds in Rome see Juv.3.243ff.

subicietque manus: to push away the crowd, or possibly to support Delia.

The rhythm and sound of the pentameter suggest the lover's bustling activity.

65–66 T. seems to be thinking of the evening, whether the ref. is to a dinner or to an assignation.

pauper ad occultos furtim deducet amicos: there is no tautology (*furtim* refers to the desire for secrecy of the poor lover and his mistress, *occultos* to the attempt to avoid detection by the *amici*). The *amici* here may be friends (T.'s or Delia's), but the emphasis on stealth (esp. the juxtaposition) is more easily intelligible and T.'s conduct even more obsequious if they are Delia's lovers (for *amicus* meaning 'lover' cf. Prop.2.13.51, 3.20.9). T. is playing the rôle of attendant slave again (1.9.41-2, Ov. *A.A.* 2.227f. *nocte domum repetens epulis perfuncta redibit, / tunc quoque pro servo, si vocat illa, veni*).

vinclaque de niveo detrahet ipse pede: either at dinner (Hor. *S.* 2.8.77, Mart.3.50.3) or simply after her journey (Ter. *Heaut.* 124). In either case the removal of the sandals was a servile duty (Ter.loc.cit., Mart. 14.65) – hence *ipse*. Cf. Ov. *A.A.* 2.211f. *nec dubita tereti scamnum producere lecto / et tenero soleam deme vel adde pedi.*

Vincla is used of various fastenings, here of sandal-straps (cf. Virg. *Aen.* 4.518, 8.458).

Niveo is a compliment (1.4.11-12n.).

67–76 *Heu* (67) brings the reader up sharply, but the theme is still Delia's venality and T.'s attempts to overcome it.

In the first couplet T. states that his efforts to persuade Delia have failed, and in the final four couplets he warns his rival to beware of being ousted himself by a new man (there is a neat structure here: the two couplets on the new man are enclosed by two concerning T.'s present rival and containing statements of a proverbial nature on the likelihood of change). It is noticeable that there is no angry attack on his mistress even now: lines 67-8 are only an oblique complaint (a statement of fact, with reference made to the door rather than to Delia), and at 69ff., in a show of restraint and perhaps mindful of the possibility of eventual reinstatement (line 70 could yet refer to T. in the distant future), he still does not retract his obsequious attitude to his mistress, but contents himself with ironic and rather gloating advice to his rival that indirectly makes a parting shot at Delia. The tone here is sad, but also dignified and resigned.

Various words from the opening of the elegy are repeated here (see intro. essay).

67–68 **heu canimus frustra**: *heu* brings us suddenly to the present (see intro. essay and cf. 1.4.81).

For *canere frustra* cf. Virg. *Ecl.* 10.8, Prop.4.8.47, Livy 40.8.10.

nec verbis victa patescit / ianua: see 1.4.61-2n. T. transports us forcibly to Delia's door and shows us that the whole poem is a *παρακλαυσίθυρον* (see intro. essay).

For *verbis victa* cf. Prop.1.16.36, T.1.2.9, Ov. *Am.* 3.9.22 *carmine quid victas obstipuisse feras?*

Patesco is found only at Lucr.5.614 before here, and is rarely used of things actually opening (cf. Sen. *Phaed.* 384 *sed en, patescunt regiae fastigia*).

plena . . . manu: a vivid touch: cf. Hom. *Od.* 11.359, T.1.9.52 (cf. also *Od.* 10.42), and see Otto *Sprichwörter* s.v. *manus* 17. The hand is either to be full of coins or to hold some sort of material gift, such as jewels.

69–70 **at tu, qui potior nunc es**: for *potior* of a more favoured rival cf. Plaut. *Cas.* 112, Ter. *Phorm.* 533, Hor. *S.* 2.5.76, *Epod.* 15.13 *non feret adsiduas potiori te dare noctes, C.* 3.9.2. For the address to the rival, *coniunx*, mocker etc., often connected with nemesis (1.2.87-96n.), cf. Catull.15, 21, 40, 83, Hor. *Epod.* 15.17ff., Prop.1.5, 1.7, 1.9, 1.13, 2.25.21ff., T.1.2.87ff., 1.6.15ff., 1.9.53ff., Ov. *Am.* 2.19, 3.4.

mea fata timeto: see Critical Appendix.

The rival may soon be replaced by another man (mentioned at 71ff.). As usual, the punishment fits the crime, with the rival suffering the very same fate that T. has suffered. For the situation cf. Hor. *Epod.* 15.17ff., Prop.2.9.1f. and, from a different point of view, 1.9.79-80n.

For the imperative form see 1.8.49-50n.

versatur celeri Fors levis orbe rotae: Cic. *In Pis.* 22 (*ne tum quidem fortunae rotam pertimescebat*) is the first ref. to the wheel of fortune in Latin, but the idea goes back to Greek (Pind. *Ol.* 2.21f. ὅταν θεοῦ Μοῖρα πέμπῃ / ἀνεκὰς ὄλβον ὑψηλόν, Soph.fr.575, 871 Pearson). For the wheel of fortune in Augustan poetry cf. Ov. *Tr.* 5.8.7, *ExP.* 2.3.56, 4.3.31. See esp. Robinson *CPh* XLI (1946), 207ff.

For other exx. of wheels in an amatory context cf. Prop.2.8.8, Hor. *C.* 3.10.10.

The primary meaning of *levis* is 'fickle', but the connotations of 'light' and 'swift' (like *celeri*) underline the speed of change.

71–74 For Scaliger's transposition of 71-6 see Critical Appendix.

This is a vivid picture of the new man skulking about Delia's door: cf. *A.P.* 5.189 (Asclepiades), T.1.6.31f., Ov. *Am.* 2.19.39f. *incipe, quis totiens furtim tua limina pulsat, / quaerere, quid latrent nocte silente canes, Her.* 20.129f., *Tr.* 2.459f. In view of *iam nunc* in 71 (cf. 1.3.53,

2.3.3, 4.5.11) and *solus* in 74, either this is a process which T. has noticed already in existence, but which is not taking place at this particular point in time, or, if T. is thinking of the immediate present, possibly we are to imagine that T. has moved off and the other man has just arrived.

Note the solemn spondees and emphatic position of *non frustra* in 71.

exscreat: to attract attention (cf. Ov. *Her.* 21.24 *exscreat et ficta dat mihi signa nota, Tr.* 2.460; cf. also Ter. *Heaut.*373). For a similar stealthy signal see 1.2.31-2n. The verb is unusual (before here only at Plaut. *As.* 40, Varro *L. L.* 7.65).

75–76 furtivus amor: see 1.2.33-4n. for the expression.

utere quaeso, / dum licet: for *utor* with the object implied (here something like 'your opportunity', 'your affair' or 'your mistress') cf. 1.8.48, Prop.1.13.34, 4.5.60. *Utere* and *dum licet* are emphatic by position.

in liquida nat tibi linter aqua: see Critical Appendix.

In prose and poetry of the Republican and Augustan periods the word *linter* generally refers to a skiff used on rivers and lakes (see Serv. ad *G.* 1.262 *lintres: fluviales naviculas*, Caes. *B. G.* 1.53, Livy 21.26.8). The only exception is Ov. *F.* 2.864, but there too the main idea is of a smaller craft (cf. *F.* 1.4). Similarly the phrase *liquida . . . aqua* in these periods is applied mainly to rivers and running water (at Ov. *A.A.* 2.472 it is used of water in general). Most probably, then, the image here is a small boat on a river.

Liquida means 'running': i.e. 'there is a current that can sweep you away, you may be ousted' (for the effect of the current on these skiffs see Livy 21.27.8). A close parallel to this idea is found at Prop.2.4.19f. (of homosexual, in contrast to heterosexual, encounters) *tranquillo tuta descendis flumine cumba: / quid tibi tam parvi litoris unda nocet*? For other exx. of river imagery applied to love cf. Callimachus *A.P.* 12.139, Ov. *A.A.* 1.620. Note the emphatic position of *in liquida.*

6

Leo *Zu augusteischen Dichtern. Phil. Unters. 2* (Berlin, 1881), 41f.; Karsten *Mnemosyne* XV (1887), 306ff.; Williams *Tradition and Originality in Roman Poetry* (Oxford, 1968), 535ff.; Gaisser *AJPh* XCII (1971), 202ff.

The elegy shows T.'s relationship with Delia in a particularly bad state: their affair has been going on for some time (61f.), and still her *coniunx* has not found out, but Delia has now taken a new lover as well (5f.), and apparently is not averse to other admirers, esp. those with money (17ff., 39ff., 51ff.). 1.6 represents an attempt by T. to end Delia's infidelities.

1-14	Introduction of situation and main themes.
15-42	Attack on the *coniunx*: 15-24 list of deceits which may be practised on him; T.'s proposed guard on Delia; 25-42 list of deceits which have been practised on him; T.'s proposed guard on Delia.
43-56	Transition: the prophecy of Bellona's priestess.
57-86	Attack on Delia: 57-66 T.'s leniency due to Delia's mother; 67-76 exhortation to faithfulness; 77-84 punishment of unfaithful woman; 85-86 conclusion.

After the introduction all sections share the same purpose (to put a stop to his mistress' infidelities), and, although the poem falls into two main parts (attack on the *coniunx* and on Delia), transition is carefully made at 43-56. In addition, the following verbal reminiscences occur: (in connection with *praecepta*) *doceo* (9, 67) and *disco* (11, 52); (in connection with *furtivus amor*) *nox* (6, 32, 61), *tacitus* (6, 12, cf. 60), *servo* (16, 34, 37, 76) and *pecco* (16, 71); also deliberately repeated is *credo* (7, 23, 37).

1.6 is another treatment of the *praeceptor amandi* theme (see intro. essay to 1.4), but with marked differences: in the present elegy the subject of the teachings is heterosexual love, their purpose is to stop Delia's affairs with others, T. himself takes on the rôle of *praeceptor* throughout most of the poem, and the tone of *praeceptor* and *praecepta* is deadly serious.

The figure of the poet as *praeceptor amandi* and the people to whom T. addresses his *praecepta* are not new (see intro. essay to 1.4), but there is novelty in the elaboration and development of these addresses. T.'s main concern is with Delia and her *coniunx*, but the complaint to Love in the opening lines is an early indication of the professorial attitude of the rest of the poem. T.'s precepts for Delia's benefit take two main forms: the teaching of tricks to avoid detection in their affair (9ff.) and the exhortation to be abstinent from other men (67ff.). The latter precept had already been pressed on Cynthia by Propertius in 1.2 and 1.15, although the emphasis in T. is different, with a definition of the envisaged relationship (69ff.) and a ref. to the punishment of the unfaithful woman (77ff.). However, the idea of the poet teaching methods of deception to his mistress is entirely original, as are some of the tricks mentioned and their rebounding on the poet himself (9ff., see also intro. essay to 1.9). Similarly, the theme of the lover addressing learned and informed remarks to the *coniunx* had already appeared briefly in Catullus 83, but here (15ff.) it is much amplified and elaborated, while the topic of tricks which may be and have been practised on the *coniunx* is entirely new in this connection. Originality also lies in the combination of these addresses: in former versions of the theme the *praecepta* had always been addressed to one person or class of people (e.g. lovers in general) at a time, but here T. represents himself as so concerned to drive his point home that he lectures both Delia and her *coniunx*, and has remarks to make to Love as well.

Ovid noted the presence of the *praeceptor amandi* theme in this elegy and used it in his defence at *Tr.* 2.447ff.: 447-50 echoes lines 7-10; 451-2 lines 25-6; 453-4 lines 19-20; 455-8 lines 13-16; 459-60 lines 31-2 and 1.5.74.

At first sight 1.6 is a rather puzzling poem, whose exact tone and mood are hard to decide, and scholars have produced various interpretations and have often resorted to emendation (cf. Gaisser and Karsten loc.cit.). Close examination of the elegy is necessary and comparison with the poet's attitude and approach to Delia elsewhere is instructive. T. states that his mistress' behaviour has caused him unhappiness (9f.) and anger, although his anger is now subdued (58). So the overall mood of the poem is not furious rage (cf. e.g. Catull. 11, Prop. 3.25), but a cold anger, controlled, calculating and dignified. T. makes it clear that he does still love Delia (65), and that he does want their affair to continue (hence the whole poem), but certainly not as at present. In his attempt to secure this he employs a harsher method than that of 1.2 or 1.5, which seems prompted by the bad state of affairs. 1.6 takes the form of a two-pronged attack (on the incautiousness of the *coniunx*, which provides Delia with her opportunity, and on the inclinations of Delia herself). For the *coniunx* he shows supreme contempt: the man should ensure a proper guard on Delia, or, better still, entrust the task to T., and, it is implied, relinquish his position as *coniunx* in T.'s favour. The address to him is marked by insolence, callousness, impatience and insults, and, so far from concealing his position as Delia's lover, T. even plays on it. For the remainder of the elegy he completely ignores him and actually goes on to demand from Delia *castitas* for himself. To Delia he shows a harder tone than anywhere else. He gives her a stern talking to, warning her off her present conduct and making quite clear the strict, but fair, terms on which he wants to continue their relationship (67ff.). Under no illusions about her lies and infidelity, and not ignoring them either (7f., 15f., 35f., 66, 67), he threatens her with the prophecy of Bellona's priestess and the punishment of the unfaithful mistress, which are far more pointed and unpleasant than other parables for her benefit, he openly insults and criticizes her at 57ff. (see 57-66n.) and makes digs at her throughout the poem (see notes on 7f., 24, 52, 53, 56, 66, 67f., 86). Thus his manner towards his mistress is cool and severe. The elegy shows a different side to the poet. It is not without humour, of a rather callous sort, for the reader (esp. the rebound at 9ff. and the outrageous attitude to the *coniunx*), but above all it is a fine study in the measured insult, the literate gibe and cold intimidation, all of which stand out the more in contrast to the *obsequium* and *blanditia* of 1.5.

1–14 In this general introduction the background-situation is made clear (despite her *coniunx*, Delia is carrying on an affair with T., but at the same time has another lover), and the main themes of *furtivus amor* and erotic *praecepta* appear. The poet's mood also becomes evident (unhappiness, indignation and cold anger).

1–2 semper ut inducar blandos offers mihi vultus: for the brief lecture to Love see intro. essay.

Semper may refer to T.'s love-life in general or to his affair with Delia in particular (implying that her infidelities have been going on for a long time). The word (like *post* below) is given emphasis by its position.

Induco is used of luring into a snare (Ter. *Andr.* 180 (*id voluit nos sic necopinantis duci falso gaudio*) and Donatus ad loc. *vel induci, ut feras in retia*, Quint.5.7.11 *inducuntur in laqueos*), and so probably leads into the hunting-image in 4.

post tamen es misero tristis et asper, Amor: note the build-up of significant adjectives. For *tristis et asper* cf. 1.9.20, 2.3.33.

The sigmatism has an angry air.

3–4 quid tibi, saeve, rei mecum est: see Critical Appendix.

For the expression cf. Plaut. *Men.* 494, Ter. *Ad.* 177 (cf. also Plaut. *Aul.* 631, *Cas.* 97, *Men.* 370). The colloquial tone of the phrase here makes this rather an insulting way of addressing a god.

For Love's cruelty see 1.10.57-8n.

an gloria magna est / insidias homini composuisse deum: the application to love of imagery from hunting was common: see Kenney *Mnemosyne* XXIII (1970), 386-8 and cf. also Eur. *Bacc.* 459, *A.P.* 5.56.4 (Dioscorides), 12.102 (Callimachus), Plaut. *Truc.* 395, *As.* 215ff.; for elegy cf. T.1.9.46, Prop.2.32.19f. *nil agis, insidias in me componis inanis, / tendis iners docto retia nota mihi*, 3.8.37, Ov. *Am.* 2.4.12, *Her.* 20.45f., *A.A.* 1.89, 2.2, 3.554. For the unusual idea of Amor as a huntsman ambushing humans cf. Ibycus 7D, *A.P.* 12.132 (Meleager), Plaut. *Trin.* 237, Ov. *Her.* 20.45f. *ut partem effugias, non omnia retia falles, / quae tibi, quam credis, plura tetendit Amor.*

For the omnipotence of Amor see 29-30n., and for the complaint that the lover is only a mortal against a god cf. *A.P.* 5.10 (Alcaeus), 93 (Rufinus), 188 (Leonidas of Tarentum), 12.120 (Posidippus). The sarcasm with which the complaint is here made gives originality (cf. Virg. *Aen.* 4.93ff.). Note the contrast between *homini* and *deum* (in emphatic position).

The infinitive as subject with a substantive (or neuter adjective) as predicate occurs ten times in the *Corp. Tib.* (see Smith, and Gild.-Lodge 422). For *gloria* as predicate (with adjectives, such as *magna, nulla*) in this construction cf. Ov. *Am.* 2.9.6, Livy 22.25.15, Luc.8.110, Mart. 12.36.13.

For the hexameter ending see 1.3.5-8n.

5–6 **nam mihi tenduntur casses**: clarifies *insidias* (4): 'snares' (i.e. intrigues) are being laid against his love. The hunting-metaphor is usually employed to express the way in which the lover 'catches' the beloved: for this new usage cf. Prop.3.8.37 *at tibi, qui nostro nexisti retia lecto*. Cf. also 1.9.46, Prop.2.32.19f. (crafty plots described as 'snares').

The description of Delia's infidelity as a snare for T. is an early example of his complete disregard for the *coniunx*.

iam Delia furtim / nescio quem tacita callida nocte fovet: for *nescio quis* of an unknown rival cf. Prop.1.11.7, Ov. *Am.* 2.5.62, 3.11.11. This scansion of *nescio* is the only one possible in dactylic verse (cf. 1.5.75, 1.6.55). For other exx. of this short final o in the 1st pers. sing. of the present indicative see Platnauer 51f.

For *fovet* 'embraces' cf. Prop.2.18.9, 2.22.37, Ov. *ExP.* 4.10.13.

Note again the build-up of significant words (here to emphasize Delia's stealth and cunning).

7–8 **illa quidem tam multa negat**: see Critical Appendix.

Tam multa means 'ever so much' or 'ever so often'. For the adverbial use of *multa* see Williams on Virg. *Aen.* 3.610, and for *tam* joined to *multus* doing little more than strengthening it cf. Prop.1.4.1 *quid mihi tam multas laudando, Basse, puellas*, 2.20.27, 3.22.1 *frigida tam multos placuit tibi Cyzicus annos.*

sed credere durum est: reflects T.'s hardening of attitude (see intro. essay). This is a common complaint elsewhere in love-poetry (e.g. *A.P.* 5.52 (Dioscorides), 184 (Meleager), Catull.70, Prop.1.15).

For the hexameter ending see 1.3.5-8n.

sic etiam de me pernegat usque viro: a surprising and sardonic touch. *Pernegat usque* is stronger than *tam multa negat*: her denials to her *coniunx* are more emphatic and frequent, but just as false (*viro* here must refer to the *coniunx* of 15, as T. could not be expected to know whether she was making denials to the boyfriend of 6).

9–10 For the poet as *praeceptor* to his mistress see intro. essay. For the rebound of one's own skills on oneself see Smith and Rogers on Aristoph. *Av.* 808. The application of this idea to love particularly appealed to Ovid (*Am.* 2.19.34, *A.A.* 3.589f. *ponite iam gladios hebetes, pugnetur acutis; / nec dubito, telis quin petar ipse meis, Rem.* 501f.). The idea is first used in connection with the *praeceptor amandi* theme here.

Note the indignantly emphatic positions of *ipse* and *mea*.

Guards were a constant nuisance to the lover (*A.P.* 5.219 (Paulus

Silentiarius), T.1.2.5, Prop.2.23.9, 14, Ov. *Am.* 3.8.63 etc.), and refs. to duping them are frequent: Plaut. *Miles* 153, 467, T.1.2.15, 1.8.55f., 2.1.75f., 4.6.11f., Ov. *Am.* 1.6.7f., 2.12.3, 3.1.49, *Met.* 4.85, esp. *Am.* 2.2, *A.A.* 3.611ff.

11–12 fingere tunc didicit causas ut sola cubaret: cf. Ov. *Am.* 2.19.42 and see 1.3.25-6n. for the most common excuse mentioned in elegy.

cardine tunc tacito vertere posse fores: for the ancient door and its creaking see 1.2.9-10n. One way to silence the hinges was to pour water on them: cf. Aristoph. *Thesm.* 487f. (and schol.) ἐγὼ δὲ καταχέασα τοῦ στροφέως ὕδωρ / ἐξῆλθον ὡς τὸν μοιχόν, Plaut. *Curc.* 158ff. Cf. also 1.8.59-60n. Silence was, of course, essential in all such operations (1.2.20, 1.8.59f., 2.1.75ff., Prop.4.5.73f., Ov. *Am.* 1.6.7f., 3.1.51f.).

13–14 Love-bites are frequently mentioned in Roman literature: cf. Plaut. *Pseud.* 67, Catull.8.18, Cic. *Verr.* 2.5.32, T.1.8.38, Prop.3.8.21f., 4.3.25f., 4.5.39f., Ov. *Am.* 1.7.41f. *aptius inpressis fuerat livere labellis / et collo blandi dentis habere notam*, 1.8.98, 3.14.34, Hor. *C.* 1.13.12. Refs. to them are less common in Greek: cf. *A.P.* 5.244.2 (Paulus Silentiarius), Plut. *Pomp.* 2.2, Lucian *Dial.Mer.* 290, Ach. Tat.2.37.7.

For the various herbs and concoctions used to treat bites and bruises (first mentioned here in connection with the *praeceptor amandi* theme) cf. Pliny *N.H.* 13.125, 20.24, 23.18, 25.101, 31.129.

impresso . . . dente: for the expression cf. Hor. *C.* 1.13.12, Ov. *Am.* 1.7.41.

15–24 T. now turns to the *coniunx*, who has allowed the present situation to arise (*fallacis . . . puellae* and the deception at 17ff. pick up the previous section).

The first part of the attack on the *coniunx*: T. puts him on his guard against various tricks which may be practised on him by Delia (4 couplets), then suggests that he let T. himself guard Delia and gives a short description of how he would guard her (1 couplet). The fact that the final trick (the pretext of going to the temple of the Bona Dea: 21f.) might reasonably be expected to fool the stupid *coniunx* neatly allows T. to make his request at this point. This is an outrageous address, and the contempt for the *coniunx* which characterizes the whole attack on him is already evident here in the candour, insolence, ambiguity and play on the poet's position as Delia's lover (see intro. essay).

15–16 For the situation see 1.2.55-6n. On the address to the *coniunx* see 1.5.69-70n. and intro. essay (cf. esp. Ov. *Am.* 2.19.37ff.). There is open disdain for the *coniunx* here and insulting candour concerning Delia's conduct. Note the solemn spondees.

There is ambiguity in line 16, which may be deliberate (to goad the man). The problems are: the allusion in *me quoque*, the sense of *servato* and the form of the verb that *servato* represents (for the punctuation adopted at the end of 16 see Critical Appendix). There are two possible interpretations of the line: (i) *servato* is used in the sense of 'save', i.e. 'protect the interests of' (cf. Ter. *Heaut.*845). *Me quoque* then refers to the *coniunx* as well as T. With this interpretation *servato* is unlikely to be the imperative, as the *ut* clause would then give poor sense (Delia's fidelity could hardly be described as the purpose or consequence of their joint 'salvation': if anything, their joint 'salvation' would be the purpose or consequence of ensuring her fidelity). *Servato* in this sense is probably the perf. part. pass., forming an ablative absolute construction with *me quoque*. (ii) *servato* is used in the sense of 'guard' (cf. Ov. *Am.* 2.2.1). *Me quoque* then means 'me as well as Delia', since she is the one watched by the *coniunx* at 17ff. With this interpretation *servato* can be either the imperative (for the form see 1.8.49-50n.) or the perf. part. pass. The tone may be serious (T. says that he is actually prepared to be watched rather than tolerate a rival), or, more likely, this is a contemptuous aside, not meant seriously.

With either interpretation this is an insolent remark, candidly admitting T.'s interest and actually playing on his position (see intro. essay).

Me and *nihil* are emphatic by placement.

peccet: 'be unfaithful': cf. 71, 1.9.23, 4.14.1, Prop.2.19.10. The verb often has explicit sexual overtones (Ter. *Ad.* 725, Hor. *S.* 1.2.63, Ov. *Her.* 16.297 *nunc ea peccemus quae corriget hora iugalis*, T.4.7.9).

17–18 **neu iuvenes celebret multo sermone caveto**: most previous commentators interpret as 'frequent the company of and talk much with'. For *celebro* used in the sense of 'frequent the company of' cf. Tac. *Ann.* 11.16, Plin. *Epist.* 8.12.3. Apart from simply preventing prolonged contact, conversation would be prohibited because it was a means of starting an affair (Ov. *A.A.* 1.143) and of passing messages and hints (Plaut. *As.* 792f., Ov. *Am.* 2.5.19f.), or T. may be referring to the intimate conversations of lovers (Plaut. *Bacc.* 116, *Pseud.* 65). It is also possible that *celebro* here means *notum reddere, laudibus efferre* (*Thes. L. L.* III.746.52ff.). Such praise would, of course, be a sign of affection (Ter. *Eun.* 437ff., Hor. *C.* 1.13.1ff., Ov. *Am.* 2.7.7), and so provocative (Ov. *Am.* 2.4.19f.).

For the form of the imperative see 1.8.49-50n. The choice of the verb here is pointed (the *coniunx* is *incautus* at present).

neve cubet laxo pectus aperta sinu: *accumbo* is more usual of reclining at table, but for *cubo* so used see *OLD* s.v. 1d and cf. also Cic. *Mur.* 74. As Putnam seems to suggest, the echo of 11 here may be deliberate and *cubo* may have been chosen as a suggestive word (it is more often used of going to bed) for a suggestive action.

For the revealing of the breasts cf. Prop.2.22.7f. *interea nostri quaerunt sibi vulnus ocelli, / candida non tecto pectore si qua sedet*, 4.8.47, Ov. *Her.* 16.249f., *F.* 1.408.

The fact that Delia is not supposed to be wearing the *stola* here is another indication that she is not to be viewed as a married woman (see Introduction sect. 4). The ref. is to the *tunica*. Presumably Delia would not be wearing a *fascia* or *strophium* underneath (cf. Corinna in Ov. *Am.* 1.5), nor be concealed under a *pallium* (cf. Ov. *Am.* 1.4.41, 49f.). She would be wearing a *tunica* alone (for this garment worn at dinner cf. e.g. Prop.4.8.61, Ov. *Her.* 16.249), which, when loose, would naturally reveal the breasts of one in a reclining position: cf. Ov. *Her.* 16.249f. *prodita sunt, memini, tunica tua pectora laxa / atque oculis aditum nuda dedere meis.*

19–20 For nods see 1.2.21-2n.

For messages traced in wine (first mentioned here) see Ov. *Her.* 17. 87f. *orbe quoque in mensae legi sub nomine nostro, / quod deducta mero littera fecit, AMO, Am.* 1.4.20, 2.5.17f., *A.A.* 1.571, *Tr.* 2.453f., and cf. 1.10.29-32n.

mensae ... in orbe: round tables became common during the 2nd century B.C. (Livy 39.6.7).

21–22 exibit quam saepe, time: i.e. *quam saepe exibit, tam saepe time.*

seu visere dicet / sacra Bonae maribus non adeunda deae: on *seu* = *vel si* see Housman *CQ* VII.20.

This excuse is first found here. For such pretexts for going out cf. Prop.2.32.1ff., 4.8.1ff., Ov. *A.A.* 3.633ff., Juv.6.488f., and for a similar misuse of religion see 11-12n.

On the Bona Dea see Pauly s.v. and Wiseman *Cinna the Poet* (Leicester, 1974), chap. 7. In the books of the pontiffs the goddess was called *Bona, Fauna, Ops* and *Fatua* (Macrob. *Sat.* 1.12.21). She was identified with various goddesses, including Damia, Maia, Juno, Proserpina and Hecate (Macrob. loc. cit., Festus s.v. *Damium* = p. 68M), and was said to be the daughter, wife or sister of Faunus (Macrob. *Sat.* 1.12.24f., 27, Serv. ad *Aen.* 8.314, Plut. *Mor.* 268d-e, Lact. *Div. Inst.* 1.22.9). Similarly there is uncertainty as to her nature, although Labeo says that she was an earth-goddess (Macrob. *Sat.* 1.12.21ff.), and the idea of a goddess of bounty and fertility fits well with Damia and with the titles *Bona* and *Ops*. She had a temple on the Aventine from which men were prohibited (Ov. *A.A.* 3.244, 637, *F.* 5.147ff.). Her annual festival on the night of the 4th – 5th of December (Wiseman op. cit., p. 130) was celebrated at the house of a magistrate holding *imperium*, with his wife or mother in charge, assisted by the Vestal Virgins (Plut. *Caes.* 9, *Cic.* 19, Cic. *Att.* 1.13.3). All males were expelled from the house, and Clodius' presence in the disguise of a flute-girl caused a scandal in 62 B.C. (Plut. *Cic.* 28, and see 23-4n.). Of the actual celebrations little is known, except that there was a sacrifice on behalf of the people (Cic. *Att.* 1.12.3, 1.13.3, Dio 37.35.4), and music and wine were present (Plut. *Caes.* 9, *Mor.* 268e).

23–24 at mihi si credas, illam sequar unus ad aras: *at mihi* is emphatically placed. There seems to be deliberate, taunting ambiguity here. The purpose of the request is clear enough (to ensure a proper guard on Delia), but the exact position that T. wants for himself is not clear. On the surface he is asking to be made Delia's guard, an outrageous proposal which represents a piquant reversal of the usual situation and would itself give T. a pretext for being constantly in her company. But *credas* also suggests usurpation of the position of the *coniunx* himself (for *credo* used of entrusting a person to a lover cf. 1.4.9, Prop.1.20.52 *formosum Nymphis credere visus Hylan*, Ov. *Rem.* 451). Again T. shows disdain for the *coniunx* and plays on his rôle as Delia's lover (cf. 37-8n. and see intro. essay).

Ad aras is in emphatic position: it was forbidden for a man to go beyond the doors of the temple, and to go up to the altar itself would represent even greater sacrilege (cf. Prop.4.9.53ff.).

tunc mihi non oculis sit timuisse meis: for such sacrilege punished by blindness cf. Cic. *Dom.* 105, *Har.* 37, 38 (to Clodius, who had not been blinded) *an tibi luminis obesset caecitas plus quam libidinis?* There is cynicism here: T. need have no fears of being blinded because Delia is not going to the Bona Dea, as André points out.

The infinitive as subject without a substantive or neuter adjective as predicate (3-4n.) is not as rare as Smith maintains (cf. e.g. Virg. *Ecl.* 10.46 *nec sit mihi credere tantum*, Prop.1.20.13f., T.4.3.3, Ov. *A.A.* 1.619, Sil.It.6.488).

25–42 To demonstrate his suitability to guard Delia properly T. gives exx. of how he himself has frequently duped the *coniunx*, thereby indicating that he is wise to such deception, but the *coniunx* is not.

The second part of the attack on the *coniunx*: a list of tricks (4 couplets) is followed by a request to let T. guard Delia (3 couplets) and a description of how he would guard her (2 couplets). The structure resembles that of 15-24, but here the tone is more insolent and contemptuous: T. coolly lists tricks which he himself played on the *coniunx* (inserting an excuse that adds to the insult), leads into the request by means of impatient and callous argument, couches his request in more elaborately ambiguous terms, making greater play on his position as Delia's lover, and concentrates more on how he intends to guard Delia (forgetting the *coniunx* and turning to the serious danger – rivals). After this final taunt T. dismisses the *coniunx* for the rest of the poem (see intro. essay).

25–26 For this and similar pretexts for touching cf. Naevius fr. 78R *anulum dat alii spectandum*, Plaut. *As.* 778, Ov. *Her.* 20.139f., *Am.* 3.2.41f., *A.A.* 1.149ff. *utque fit, in gremium pulvis si forte puellae / deciderit,* *digitis excutiendus erit; / etsi nullus erit pulvis, tamen excute nullum.* Note the insolently emphatic position of *saepe* here (and in 27).

The elegists' mistresses seem to have been fond of jewelry (e.g. Prop. 3.6.12, 4.5.21f., 4.7.9, Ov. *Am.* 2.15). *Gemmas* refers to precious stones in rings or bracelets and *signum* to the device of a ring (often a portrait or mythological subject: Ov. *A.A.* 3.223f., *Tr.* 1.7.5f.).

eius: the form occurs elsewhere in elegy only at Prop. 4.2.35, 4.6.67, Ov. *Tr.* 3.4.27, *ExP.* 4.15.6 (in Catullus' elegiacs only at 84.5).

per causam: the phrase is frequent in prose, but in poetry it is first found here and elsewhere occurs only at Ov. *Her.* 20.140, *Tr.* 2.452 (see *Thes. L. L.* III.679.69ff.). Here it is used adverbially (as in Ovid), picking up 25.

27–28 For the situation cf. Plaut. *As.* 771ff. *tecum una postea aeque pocla potitet: / aps ted accipiat, tibi propinet, tu bibas, / ne illa minus aut plus quam tu sapiat*, Ov. *Am.* 1.4.51ff., 2.5.13f., Juv. 1.57.

For the use of neat wine to induce sleep see 1.2.1-2n.

On the combination of agent noun and finite verb (*bibebam / . . . victor*) to express the force of two verbs see 1.3.15-16n.

sobria: 'that make sober' (cf. 2.1.46, Stat. *Silv.* 5.1.121 *ipsa dapes modicas et sobria pocula tradit*).

victor: the metaphor is probably military (see 1.10.53-6n.).

29–30 iussit Amor: for the excuse that Love was really responsible cf. *A.P.* 12.117 (Meleager), 118 (Callimachus), Plaut. *Poen.* 140f., *Miles* 1287f., Ter. *Ad.* 469f., Ov. *Am.* 1.6.59f., Sen. *Phaed.* 184ff. *quid ratio possit? vicit ac regnat furor / potensque tota mente dominatur deus* etc.

contra quis ferat arma deos?: the stupidity and impiety of fighting against the gods was proverbial (see Smith and cf. also Hom. *Il.* 5.130, 6.129, Pind. *Pyth.* 2.88; see also 1.10.59-60n.). In particular no mortal (or god) stood much chance against the deities of love (Soph. *Trach.* 497, *Ant.* 781ff., Eur. fr. 430N, Aristoph. *Nub.* 1081f., Ov. *Am.* 1.2.37, *Her.* 9.25f. *quem non mille ferae, quem non Stheneleius hostis, / non potuit Iuno vincere, vincit amor*), who, like any other gods, had to be obeyed (Eur. *Hipp.* 5f., 443ff., Theoc. *Id.* 30.25ff., T. 1.3.21f., Ov. *Her.* 4.11 *quidquid Amor iussit, non est contemnere tutum*).

As a love-poet, T. may regard this as a valid plea, but this obviously defective argument (cf. Aristot. *Eth.Nic.* 3.3, Plaut. *Aul.* 745ff., Sen. *Phaed.* 195ff.) is probably used as a stock excuse or deliberate insult, in view of T.'s overall attitude to the *coniunx* (so too *ignosce fatenti* can hardly be meant seriously). In either case, the couplet implies a low opinion of the man's intelligence and prepares the way for an even greater confession (the actions of 25-8 are relatively harmless, but 31-2 implies an attempted, and possibly successful, secret meeting for obvious purposes).

This is the only case of *contra* so separated from its noun cited by *Thes.L.L.* IV.751.69 (cf. Catull.64.101 *saevum cupiens contra contendere monstrum*).

Throughout the couplet important words are placed in emphatic positions.

31–32 instabat tota cui tua nocte canis: see Critical Appendix.

For *instare* ('threaten, harass') applied to animals cf. e.g. Virg. *G.* 3.154 (gadfly), Prop.2.5.20 *verum etiam instanti laesa repugnat ovis*, Ov. *Tr.* 3.5.35 *at lupus et turpes instant morientibus ursi.*

The imperfect here (like *bibebam* in 27) probably denotes a number of occasions.

The dog was a constant irritation to the lover: cf. Aristoph. *Thesm.* 417, *A.P.* 5.30 (Antipater of Thessalonica), Hor. *Epod.* 5.58, *C.* 3.16.2, T.2.4.32, Prop.4.5.73f. *canis, in nostros nimis experrecta dolores, / cum fallenda meo pollice clatra forent*, Ov. *Am.* 2.19.40, *Tr.* 2.459.

33–34 Unless Delia is put under a close and continual surveillance, merely locking doors is insufficient, because locked doors present no obstacle to determined lovers (1.2.17f., 31f., 1.6.11f., 1.8.59f. and notes) and the woman may well find lovers within the house (Ov. *Am.* 3.4.8 *omnibus exclusis intus adulter erit*, Juv.6.346-8, O29-34).

For the use of *bona* here cf. Ov. *Am.* 2.5.29ff. *'quid facis?' exclamo, 'quo nunc mea gaudia differs? / iniciam dominas in mea iura manus. / haec tibi sunt mecum, mihi sunt communia tecum – / in bona cur quisquam tertius ista venit?'*

The callous contempt seems to be reinforced by the sigmatism and alliteration (esp. of hard sounds) in this couplet and the next.

The question of the syllabic lengthening in *servare* is a difficult one (see also Critical Appendix). There are two possible explanations of the phenomenon. Firstly, the sense-pause in arsis between *servare* and *frustra* may give the extra length to the syllable, but such a lengthening seems to be unparalleled. The alternative explanation (syllabic division shifts from / -re / frus- / to / -re f / -rus- / and lengthens by closing the previously short syllable) seems more likely. For such a lengthening of an open, short syllable before two consonants cf. (mute and liquid) *Propontida trucemve* (Catull.4.9), *impotentia freta* (Catull.4.18), *ultima Britannia* (Catull.29.4), *populea fruns* (Enn. *Ann.* 577V), *linea pluebant* (Stat. *Silv.* 1.6.10), and see further Müller 390f.; cf. also (before s and another consonant) 1.5.28, and see Müller loc.cit., Fordyce on Catull.17.24. Although there is only one other place in Augustan elegy where an open syllable is lengthened before a pair of initial consonants (1.5.28), the phenomenon is not entirely without parallel in elegy, and it is noteworthy that this other ex. occurs in T. himself. Similarly, although the majority of exx. involve s and another consonant, 5 exx. cited above involve mute and liquid, and 4 of these occur in T.'s precursors. The fact that none of these exx. involves a sense-pause raises more of a problem, but the pause here is not a strong one (cf. Platnauer 24, who does not regard commas as indicating sense-pauses at all).

D. S. Raven brings to my attention the very rare elision at 3w in the hexameter here (according to Platnauer 84, found elsewhere in elegy only at Ov. *F.* 5.247; 6.679).

35–36 The headache here is surely an excuse for refusing copulation, so that the ref. in *tenet* and *suspirat* is not to intercourse, as Smith implies, but must be to a simple embrace (for *teneo* so used cf. e.g. Ov. *Her.* 13. 157, 18.164) and sighs of love (cf. Cat.64.98 *in flavo saepe hospite suspirantem*, Ov. *F.* 1.417). The taunt is particularly unpleasant: the sighs which the *coniunx* fondly imagines are for himself are in fact not for him at all.

For the excuse of the headache cf. Ov. *Am.* 1.8.73, 2.19.11. The detail was probably inspired by Plaut. *Truc.* 632 *nam mihi de vento miserae condoluit caput.*

The simple accusative of person or thing sighed for is poetic and is first found here (accusative and infinitive at Lucr.2.1164f.): cf. 4.5.11, Ov. *Tr.* 1.1.27 *invenies aliquem, qui me suspiret ademptum, Lydia* 3, Juv.11.152, Prudent. *Cath.* 2.43f.

amores: 'the loved one' or, more insulting, 'loved ones' (see Smith and cf. also Catull.38.6, Ov. *Am.* 3.9.32 *altera cura recens, altera primus amor.*).

37–38 The same goading ambiguity is evident here as in the parallel proposal at 23, and again T. shows scorn for the *coniunx* and plays on his position as Delia's lover.

At first sight it appears that T. is asking to be made Delia's guard and claiming to be fully prepared to accept this servile post, and punishment, should he fail in his duties (*verbera . . . vincla*). The *vincla pedum* may denote the chains of the *ianitor* (1.1.55-6n.) or a form of punishment (e.g. Ov. *Am.* 2.2.47). However, picking up the implications of 33, the wording also suggests usurpation of the position of the *coniunx*: *servare* was applied to the *coniunx* at 34; *credo* can be used of entrusting someone to a lover (23-4n.); the ref. to flogging and chains may well be an allusion to *servitium amoris* (1.5.5-6n.): these two details (see 1.9.21-2n., 1.1.55-6n.) suggest the alternative meaning 'I am willing to be her devoted lover'.

at mihi: emphatic by position.

servandam credas: for the gerundive as predicate to the direct object of the verb see Roby 1401, Kühner-Stegmann 1. p.731. In general the usage is common and is found as early as Ennius (*Var.* 75V, with *do*), but, according to *Thes. L. L.*, this is the only ex. with *credo* in classical literature, and elsewhere it occurs only at Solin.12.7 (*delphina puer* *fragmentis panis primo illexit et in tantum consuetudo valuit ut alendum se etiam manui ipsius crederet*), although it is not rare with synonyms such as *do* and *trado.*

39–40 Excessive attention to the hair and wearing of the slack toga were characteristics of 'dandies' and generally considered effeminate. The point here is that this care over the appearance is to attract girls, and so T. is addressing potential lovers (cf. 1.8.9f., 2.3.78, Ov. *A.A.* 3. 433ff., *Rem.* 679f.).

For attention to the hair cf. also Plaut. *As.* 627, Cic. *Sest.* 18, Ov. *A.A.* 1.505ff. *sed tibi nec ferro placeat torquere capillos, / nec tua mordaci pumice crura teras; / . . . forma viros neglecta decet*, 3.434, 443, Mart.3.63.

For the slack toga cf. also Cic. *Cat.* 2.22 *quos pexo capillo, nitidos, aut imberbis aut bene barbatos videtis, manicatis et talaribus tunicis, velis amictos, non togis*, Macrob. *Sat.* 3.13.4.

41–42 On the corrupt pentameter see Critical Appendix. The general sense here seems to be: 'let anyone who meets us stand back, or I will suspect him (of trying to touch or communicate with Delia)'.

Line 42 may have contained a variation on the ritual injunction *procul, o procul este, profani* (Virg. *Aen.* 6.258, cf. Call. *Hymn.*2.2, Stat. *Silv.* 3.3.13), thereby leading into the Bellona-section.

43–56 The switch to the prophecy here is rather sudden and unexpected, but it is connected with the idea of the previous lines, a fact emphasized by the repetition of *sic.* See also 41-2n.

The section on the prophecy of Bellona's priestess. The first couplet provides a transition and introduction to the section, the next three couplets prepare for the prophecy by describing the ecstatic frenzy of the priestess inspired by the goddess, and the final three couplets give the prophecy itself. To give the warning weight, there is emphatic and solemn expression, a detailed description of the priestess' awesome behaviour (this is one of the fullest accounts extant), direct quotation of part of the prophecy (couched in proverbial and ritualistic language) and intimidating indefiniteness about the rest of it (concerning Delia). The warning appears initially to be directed at potential rivals, but is also aimed at Delia herself, who is actually mentioned in the final couplet (so Bellona is chosen as an impressive deity in general and in particular one who exerted influence on women: e.g. Juv.6.511ff.). The admonishment for Delia is pointed, and there are also some gibes at her in the section. Thus transition is made from the attack on the *coniunx* to the attack on Delia.

43–44 sic fieri iubet ipse deus: for such divine approval see 1.4.23-4n. *Deus* may refer to Amor (see 51) or to Bellona (see 45 and 50; for *deus* applied to a goddess see 1.2.87-8n.).

sic magna sacerdos / est mihi divino vaticinata sono: *magna sacerdos* (see below) and *divino . . . sono* (cf. Virg. *Aen.* 3.373 *divino ex ore*, 6.50 *nec mortale sonans*) are to add impressiveness.

Magnus may refer to actual size (cf. Virg. *Aen.* 6.49 and Serv. ad loc., Ov. *F.* 6.539f.), but without qualification it probably denotes might and power, a sense frequent in divine contexts (47-50n.). So elsewhere *magnus* with this meaning is applied to seers: Virg. *Aen.* 6.544, Sil.It. 13.756, and cf. also *Aen.* 6.11 (of prophetic inspiration), Sil.It.5.118f. *sat magnus in hostem / augur adest ensis.*

Bellona was usually served by male priests, and T. may be thinking here of a eunuch priest (cf. Val.Flacc.7.636 *exectos lacerat Bellona comatos*), although there is a ref. to a priestess at Strabo 12.575.

Note the forceful anaphora of *sic* and the emphatic positioning of *sic, deus, sic* and *sacerdos.*

45–46 For oriental gods in T. see intro. essay to 1.3. Bellona was originally a Roman war-goddess, but she was commonly identified with the Greek Enyo and in later times with Cappadocian Ma. The earliest mention of a priest of Ma-Bellona in Italy is in connection with Sulla (probably due to propaganda: Plut. *Sull.* 27.6, cf. also 9, Latte *Römische Religionsgeschichte* (München, 1960), 281f.). Ma-Bellona had a temple in Rome, the *aedes Bellonae Pulvinensis*, although the exact location is uncertain (see Wissowa *Religion and Kultus der Römer* (Munich, 1912), 349). Her priests, called *Bellonarii* or *fanatici* (Acro ad Hor. *S.* 2.3.222, Juv.4.123f.), were Asiatics and dressed in black (Tert. *Pall.* 4).

Physical anaesthesia reached in delirium was common in oriental religion: see esp. Nonn. *Dionys.* 14.381ff., Iamblichus *De Myst.* 3.4 (p.110 Parthey). For the insensibility to wounds of the *Bellonarii* see 47-50n. Immunity to fire is not connected elsewhere with the *Bellonarii* but is common enough in this type of cult (Eur. *Bacc.* 757f. and Dodds ad loc., Iamb.loc.cit.), and flagellation is not attributed to them elsewhere but was frequent among the priests of the Great Mother, with whom Bellona was often connected (see Bailey *Phases in the Religion of Ancient Rome* (London, 1932), 190f.).

Acrem and *torta* (1.9.21-2n.) are added here to increase the impressiveness. So too *acrem* and *flammam* are in emphatic positions.

haec, ubi Bellonae motu est agitata: *moveo* and *motus* (like *agito*) in this context denote both physical movement and mental agitation: cf. Ov. *Tr.* 4.1.43, Lucan 1.566 (predominantly mental) and Ov. *Met.* 6. 158 (predominantly physical). Both ideas seem to be present here.

nec . . . / . . . non: *nec* followed by *non* is rare (cf. 1.1.29-31, Prop. 3.2.13f., 4.1.15f.) and may be in imitation of the Greek οὔτε . . . οὐ (see Denniston *The Greek Particles* (Oxford, 1954), 510f.).

47–50 The priests of Bellona mutilated their arms and bodies with various weapons (Lucan 1.565f. *tum, quos sectis Bellona lacertis / saeva movet, cecinere deos*, Tert. *Apol.* 9.10, Lactant. *Fals.Relig.* 1.21), offered the blood to the goddess or the worshippers (Tert. *Apol.* 9.10 *hodie istic Bellonae sacratus sanguis de femore proscisso in palmulam exceptus et esui datus signat*, Minuc. Felix *Oct.* 30) and in a state of delirium gave prophecies (Lucan loc.cit., Juv.4.123f. *ut fanaticus oestro / percussus, Bellona, tuo divinat*). For prophecy on trivial matters, such as the present example, cf. Juv.6.511ff.

bipenne: for this rare form of the abl. see *Thes. L. L.* II.2001.24f.

inulta: 'with impunity, unharmed' (*OLD* s.v. 1).

deam: i.e. the statue of the goddess.

latus praefixa veru: *veru* may mean 'skewer' (e.g. Virg. *G.* 2.396), in which case the idea is that the surface skin is pierced, so that a little of the skewer is beneath and most of it in front. Alternatively, *veru* may mean 'spear' (e.g. Virg. *Aen.* 7.665), in which case the idea is probably that the priestess drives it in up to the point only and leaves the shaft sticking out (for the expression cf. Virg. *Aen.* 9.465f., Suet. *Iul.* 85).

dea magna: (cf. 43) to give solemnity. *Magnus* as an epithet of divinities refers to the power and might of the god (cf. Cic. *Dom.* 144). This application occurs from earliest times throughout Latin: of the gods themselves Enn. *Ann.* 207V, Plaut. *Aul.* 776, *Poen.* 1163, *Truc.* 701, Cic. *N.D.* 2.64, Hor. *S.* 1.7.33, 2.5.60, *Epod.* 15.3, *C.* 1.10.5, Virg. *Ecl.* 3.104, *G.* 1.338, 3.1, *Aen.* 3.104, 437, T.1.2.79, 3.4.16, 4.2.1, 4.5.9, 4.13.16; of their *numen* 3.6.22, Virg. *Aen.* 2.623, 3.264, 633f.; of their offspring 4.1.68. See Roscher *Lex. der griech. und röm. Mythologie* vol.7, INDEX s.v. *magnus*.

monet: 'prompts, inspires' (cf. Virg. *Aen.* 7.41 *tu vatem, tu, diva, mone*, Livy 26.19.4 etc.).

51–52 parcite quam custodit Amor violare puellam: for the dramatic change into direct quotation see 1.5.21-4n.

This use of *parco* is confined mainly to poetry and non-classical prose (Lewis & Short s.v. II B β). Elsewhere in the *Corp. Tib.* it occurs at 3.5.6.

On the divine protection of lovers see 1.2.27-8n. *Violare* is a strong word, used of physical violence (Ov. *ExP.* 3.5.45), including sexual connection (Varro *L. L.* 6.80, Cic. *Fam.* 9.22.1), and, the sense required here in view of *custodit Amor*, religious desecration (Caes. *B. G.* 6.23.9 *hospitem violare fas non putant: qui quacumque de causa ad eos venerunt, ab iniuria prohibent, sanctos habent*, Cic. *Verr.* 2.5.186, Virg. *Aen.* 11.591 (and Serv. ad loc.), Ov. *Met.* 8.741).

ne pigeat magno post didicisse malo: the old proverb of πάθει μάθος (cf. Hom. *Il.* 17.32, Hes. *Opera* 218, Aesch. *Ag.* 176f., Plat. *Symp.* 222B, Livy 22.39.10). The proverb is applied to love also at 1.8.5f., Prop. 1.9.7.

Magno . . . malo may well be a dig at Delia (cf. 53-4n.). The ablative is one of means or cause.

Disco is used absolutely to mean 'learn, acquire knowledge' (obviously that the girl is protected by Love, as Dissen, the ever-faithful Némethy, and André point out), here, as elsewhere, without a ref. to literal education (cf. Juv.6.66 *Thymele tunc rustica discit*).

53–54 The curse is esp. appropriate for a *dives amator* and suggests that this is what T. fears. There may well be a sting in the tail also: anyone who took up with Delia would lose his money because of her mercenary nature anyway (see Gaisser loc.cit.intro.essay). For the curse of loss of wealth cf. 1.9.11f. (and n.), 2.4.39f.

The flowing of the priestess' blood (understand *labitur* with *sanguis*) has already been mentioned, and the *cinis* here is most obviously ashes from the fire of 45f. Presumably shortly before she speaks or as she speaks the ashes are scattered into the wind, either by an attendant (cf. Thestylis in Theoc. *Id.* 2) or by the priestess herself. This type of solemn, symbolic parallelism was common in magic incantations, prayers, oaths, curses etc.: cf. Hom. *Il.* 3.299f., Soph. *Ajax* 1175ff., Virg. *Ecl.* 8.80f., Livy 1.24.8, 21.45.8, Gow on Theoc. *Id.* 2.17-63.

attigerit: sc. *eam*. For the omission of *si* see 1.10.11-12n. To restrict the verb to its sexual sense, as Putnam does, seems too limiting.

sanguis: on the quantity see 65-6n.

diripiturque: for the postposition of *-que* see 1.1.39-40n. (*quart. loc.* here only in T.).

For the present tense in such utterances, which is common (but see Livy 1.24.8, where the words precede the action), cf. Soph. *Ajax* 1179, Theoc. *Id.* 2.28, 30, Virg. *Ecl.* 8.80 *limus ut hic durescit et haec ut cera liquescit.*

55–56 nescio quas . . . poenas: on the scansion of *nescio* see 5-6n. The indefiniteness seems intended to frighten Delia.

si tamen admittas, sit precor illa levis: *admitto* is generally taken to mean 'commit' (i.e. a crime): for this rare absolute use cf. Livy 2.37.3, Sen. *Dial.* 3.19.6. But there may be some sneering word-play here: the verb could also mean 'admit', i.e. a lover (a common sense in elegy: cf. Prop.2.17.12, 3.21.7, Ov. *Am.* 1.6.72, 1.8.53, *A.A.* 3.605 and see *Thes. L. L.* I.749.56ff.), and there may even be a ref. to copulation (for *admitto* with this meaning see *Thes. L. L.* I.751.60ff.: in this sense it is normally applied to animals, which makes the tone here all the more unpleasant, but it is used of a human (a pervert) at Sen. *N. Q.* 1.16.5). *Illa* refers to Bellona.

57–66 The transition is effected by *non ego te propter parco tibi*, which picks up the previous line and callously corrects any possible misapprehensions arising from it.

The first part of the attack on Delia (for the precept see intro. essay) consists of praise of Delia's mother. The first couplet provides a transition and introduction to the section, the next two describe the mother's help in T.'s affair with Delia, and the last two consist in good wishes for and praise of the mother. The statement that his regard for Delia's mother is the reason for his leniency (and love, 65) constitutes a calculated insult to and criticism of his mistress, whose effect is heightened by repeating this statement at the beginning and end of the section and by dwelling on the justification (59-62) and expression (63-6) of this regard. The lines are cold and directly unpleasant, and this is the harshest thing T. ever has to say to his mistress.

Gaisser (loc.cit.intro.essay) maintains that a play on the sense of 'venal' in *aurea* (58) and the connotations of procuring in *adducit* (59) indicate irony, and that T. is here reminding Delia and her mother that they are in fact only courtesan and *lena*. This interpretation is possible, but is hard to prove (esp. in view of 63f.). If there is irony here, most probably it lies in the very pretence that Delia's mother is responsible for T.'s mercy and love.

57–58 mater: although this term is frequently applied to the *lena*, in view of 65f. and the characteristic attitude of the *lena* to T.'s poverty in 1.5, it seems probable that the ref. here is to Delia's mother, who did not act in the capacity of a *lena*. It may be Delia's mother who shows a similar regard for T.'s interests at 1.3.83f. (see n.).

aurea: commonly used (esp. in love-poetry) in a laudatory sense, i.e. 'splendid, excellent' (Nisbet & Hubbard on Hor. *C.* 1.5.9, André *Étude sur les termes de couleur dans la langue Latine* (Paris, 1949), 156).

Note the forceful alliteration and the emphatic positions of *mater* and *anus*.

59–62 The exact situation here is uncertain. Both couplets may refer to the same thing: (i) a secret meeting in the house of the *coniunx* (cf. 1.2.17f., 31f., Prop.2.6.37f., Ov. *Am.* 2.19.37ff.), the mother opening the door to admit T. (as for the noise made by T. at 61f. (heard from afar), presumably he becomes quiet when he reaches the house, or perhaps, unlike Delia's mother, he shows a disregard for secrecy because of his contempt for the stupid *coniunx*, cf. 31f.); (ii) an outside rendezvous nearby (cf. 1.9.41f., Prop.4.7.15ff.), the mother opening the door and taking Delia out (under these circumstances there is not so much need for stealth on T.'s part, as he will not be coming right up to the house or trying to gain entry). In either case, 61-2 will chronologically precede 59-60. The third possibility, which avoids this difficulty over chronology, is that T. is thinking of two separate situations. In this case, taken in isolation, probably the first couplet refers to a meeting inside (hence the excessive stealth of the mother) and the second to a meeting outside (hence the lack of stealth by T.).

59–60 haec mihi te adducit tenebris: an expressive collocation of pronouns. Most often the girl had to grope her way through the darkness on her own (1.2.19-20n.), so that the mother's action here is particularly helpful.

multoque timore: fear of detection was usual, and was actually recommended by Ovid (*Am.* 2.19.55). The mother's help despite her great fear underlines her kindness.

clam taciturna: note the emphatic juxtaposition. For similar tautology cf. 1.8.60, 1.10.34, 2.6.45f.

61–62 haec foribusque manet noctu me adfixa: the girl herself usually had to wait by the door (cf. 1.2.18, 31f., 1.9.43-4n.), thereby in danger of discovery. This is help indeed by the mother.

Adfixa goes with *foribus* ('rooted to the doorway'): cf. Virg. *Aen.* 10.160f. *Pallasque sinistro / adfixus lateri*, Val.Max.2.1.9 *affixi . . . valvis.*

proculque / cognoscit strepitus me veniente pedum: the recognition of T.'s footsteps suggests that she has performed this function before and that the affair has been going on for some time.

63–64 proprios ego tecum, / sit modo fas, annos contribuisse velim: for the wish (like *vive diu*, esp. apt for an old woman) cf. *Carm.Epig.* 995. 25f., Prop.4.11.95, Ov. *Met.* 7.168 *deme meis annis et demptos adde parenti, Tr.* 5.5.25f.

With *contribuo* in this sense the dative (e.g. Sen. *Dial.* 10.15.1 *suos* [sc. *annos*] *tibi contribuet*) is more usual than *cum* (here only). The *cum* expresses the idea of both bringing together their years and sharing them. *Cum* is commonly used with verbs of combining and sharing (*OLD* s.v. 5a, 13c). Quite similar is Caes. *B. C.* 1.60 (*Calagurritani, qui erant cum Oscensibus contributi*), where the verb is used of attaching one town to another (the mss.' *cum* makes perfectly good sense there and need not be suspected).

For *sit modo fas* cf. Cic. *Tusc.* 5.13.38, Catull.51.2, T.2.3.74, Ov. *Tr.* 5.3.27, *ExP.* 4.8.55.

65–66 Note the emphasis in the alliterative repetitions of *tu* and *tuus* and in the positions of the first *te* and *tuus*. The phrase *te propter* looks like a pointed echo of 57.

quidquid agit: again a gibe at Delia.

sanguis: the i of the final syllable of the word was originally long (Lindsay *The Latin Language* (Oxford, 1894), 377), and this quantity is not unusual in the classical period: cf. Lucr.4.1050, 6.1203, Virg. *Aen.* 10.487, Ov. *F.* 6.488, *Met.* 10.459, Lucan 2.338, 7.635, 9.702, 10.128, Sil.It.9.555, 10.23, Val.Fl.3.234, Sen. *Med.* 775. It seems to be a feature of more elevated styles, and the only other ex. of it in elegy is in Ovid's *Fasti*. For the more common short final syllable cf. 54 and see Neue 1.243.

67–76 The address to Delia's mother continues, and the implications of *quidquid agit* (66) are picked up.

The second part of the attack on Delia consists of an exhortation to keep away from other men. The first couplet acts as a transition and introduction to the section, the next two concern the terms for T. and the final two the terms for Delia proposed in their affair. The tone here is stern, but fair: T. is not prepared to let the present situation continue, but requires true *castitas* from Delia (emphasized by the repetition of *casta* at 67 and 75), making it quite clear that he wants faithfulness and love to be her motivation, not fear of a beating; he is willing to accept punishment if he is even suspected of doing wrong, and the implication is that Delia too must be above suspicion.

67–68 sit modo casta, doce: for *casta* 'abstinent from other men' see 1.3.83-4n. Delia's mother may appear in a similar rôle at 1.3.83f. (see n.).

quamvis non vitta ligatos / impediat crines nec stola longa pedes: this couplet shows clearly that Delia is not to be regarded as a married woman (see Introduction sect. 4). This looks like a tart reminder to his mistress of her social standing.

The *vitta* and *stola* were parts of the Roman matron's dress. The *vitta* was associated with *matronae* from as early as Plautus (*Miles* 791f. *eam huc ornatam adducas, ex matronarum modo, / capite compto, crinis vittasque habeat*; cf. also Serv. ad *Aen.* 7.403), although a different type of *vitta* could be worn by unmarried girls (Camps on Prop.4.11.34, Marquardt *Privatleben*, 44 n.6). The *stola* could only be worn by married women: cf. Hor. *S.* 1.2.94f. *matronae praeter faciem nil cernere possis, / cetera, ni Catia est, demissa veste tegentis*, Macrob. *Sat.* 1.6.13, Val. Max.6.1. For a description of the *stola* see Wilson *The Clothing of the Ancient Romans* (Baltimore, 1938), 155ff.

69–72 That there should be terms for T. also is only fair, but anger and jealousy on Delia's part would be welcomed by T. as an indication of her love, since these emotions are felt only by the real lover (1.10.57-8n., 1.10.61-4n., *A.P.* 5.306 (Philodemus), Lucian *Dial. Mer.* 8.1 (299), Ter. *Eun.* 434ff., Catull.83, Prop.3.8.9ff.) – so he is prepared to undergo punishment merely on the grounds of suspicious behaviour.

For jealousy and quarrels in the love-affair see 1.10.53-6n. For praise of another and suspicion of unfaithfulness as the causes cf. Aristoph. *Plut.* 1013ff., Lucian *Dial. Mer.* 8.1 (299), Ter. *Eun.* 437ff., Hor. *C.* 1.13, Prop.3.15, Ov. *Am.* 2.7. Such quarrels more often than not ended in violence. For angry women attacking the eyes cf. Ter. *Eun.* 648, 740 and Donatus ad loc. (*femineae minae sunt et in libidinosos quam maxime*); for them attacking the hair cf. Ter. *Eun.* 859f., Prop. 3.8.5, Ov. *Her.* 20.81, *Am.* 2.7.7, *A.A.* 2.451, *Met.* 2.476f. *dixit et adversam prensis a fronte capillis / stravit humi pronam.*

et mihi sint durae leges: see 1.9.1-2n. *Lex* is used of a contract (Cic. *Verr.* 2.1.143, *De Or.* 1.178) and of the terms of a contract or agreement (Cic. *Verr.* 2.3.19, Livy 9.5.3), the latter being the apposite meaning here. For a similar use of *lex* in amatory contexts cf. 2.4.52, Prop.3.

20.15f., 4.8.74ff.

ullam: substantive (cf. 2.1.9, 2.4.43, and see Seyffert on Cic. *Lael.* 15.52 = p. 356).

On the text of 71-2 see Critical Appendix.

peccasse: see 15-16n.

immerito pronas proripiarque vias: note the emphatic position of *immerito* ('even though I be undeserving / guiltless': cf. Hor. *C.* 3.6.1). *Pronas . . . vias* may denote a steep road or roads (cf. Ov. *Her.* 18.121, *Met.* 2.67), but it seems more likely that *pronas* is a transferred epithet (Lee translates: 'face down'). This is a bold usage for T. but not impossible (cf. Smith on 1.4.10).

This accusative of motion is found elsewhere in elegy (Smith cites 7 exx.), although it occurs here only in T. Such an accusative with *proripio*, however, appears nowhere else in classical literature.

73–74 **non ego te pulsare velim**: possibly in retaliation, but more likely in anger at infidelity by Delia (parallel to 69-72 and picked up in the next couplet).

The man usually had no qualms over using violence: cf. Theoc. *Id.* 14.34f., Herodas 2.68ff., Lucian *Dial.Mer.* 8.1 (299), *A.P.* 5.218 (Agathias Scholasticus), T.1.10.53ff., Hor. *C.* 1.17.24ff. *nec metues protervum / suspecta Cyrum, ne male dispari / incontinentes iniciat manus / et scindat haerentem coronam / crinibus immeritamque vestem*, Ov. *Am.* 1.7. The same sentiment occurs at 1.10.61-4 (see notes); cf. also Prop. 2.5.21ff., Ov. *A.A.* 3.567ff.

sed, venerit iste / si furor: a variety of meanings is possible. *Iste* may mean 'like yours' or simply 'this', and *furor* may mean 'anger', 'longing', 'violent behaviour' or 'madness'. Certainly any of the first three meanings of *furor* here would adequately describe the action, and 'like yours' would go well with these three meanings (picking up 69-72). However, 'madness' seems more likely here, as it brings out better T.'s abhorrence of the act (*furor* is used in this sense in a similar situation at Ov. *Am.* 1.7.2f.), in which case *iste* means 'this', since T. is hardly likely to describe as 'madness like yours' a course of action which he has just recommended at 69-72.

Venerit may be fut. perf. or perf. subj. (the perf. subj. in both protasis and apodosis is occasional but classical: cf. Plaut. *Truc.* 60ff., Ter. *Heaut.* 316, Cic. *Off.* 3.30).

optarim non habuisse manus: in early Latin there are 35 exx. (17 in apodosis) of the perfect subjunctive as potential (Bennett *Syntax of Early Latin* vol. 1 (Boston, 1910), 202f.). This usage is not common, but it is classical: cf. Cic. *Off.* 3.29, *Fin.* 2.59, Hor. *Epod.* 2.39ff., *C.* 4. 8.20ff., Livy 26.49.3, 27.27.12 (Handford *The Latin Subjunctive* (Methuen, 1947), 105f., 126f., Thomas *Recherches sur le subjonctif latin* (Paris, 1938), 103ff.).

For the expression cf. Ov. *Am.* 1.7.23f.

75–76 **nec saevo sis casta metu**: i.e. through fear of beatings, picking up *pulsare* in 73.

For *casta* 'abstinent from other men' see 1.3.83-4n.

mente fideli: / mutuus . . . amor: for a faithful heart and reciprocal love ensuring abstinence from other men cf. Prop.2.18.35 *ipse tuus semper tibi sit custodia lectus*, 3.12.15ff., Ov. *Am.* 3.4.1ff. *dure vir, imposito tenerae custode puellae / nil agis: ingenio est quaeque tuenda suo. / si qua metu dempto casta est, ea denique casta est; / quae, quia non liceat, non facit, illa facit. / ut iam servaris bene corpus, adultera mens est, / nec custodiri, ne velit, ulla potest* (T.'s reasoning here is similar).

absenti . . . mihi: for the temptations facing one partner when the other is away see 1.3.83-4n.

This is a carefully constructed couplet: the chiastic antithesis in 75 (*saevo . . . metu . . . mente fideli*), the expressive juxtaposition in 76 (*te mihi*) and the placing of important words in emphatic positions throughout.

77–84 For the transition see Critical Appendix on 77.

The third part of the attack on Delia concerns the punishment of the unfaithful woman. The first two couplets describe the actual tasks to which the woman is reduced, and the next two comment on the justice of the punishment.

For the theme of nemesis see 1.2.87-96n., and for the example of the unhappy old age of the cruel mistress see Nisbet & Hubbard on Hor. *C.* 1.25 and cf. also *A.P.* 5.23 (Callimachus), 28 (Rufinus), Ov. *A.A.* 3.69ff. In particular, *A.P.* 6.283 (anon.) seems to have inspired T.'s version (the epigram's date is probably about the time of Meleager: see Gow and Page *The Greek Anthology. Hellenistic Epigrams* 2.p.579): Ἡ τὸ πρὶν αὐχήσασα πολυχρύσοις ἐπ' ἐρασταῖς, / ἡ Νέμεσιν δεινὴν οὐχὶ κύσασα θεόν, / μίσθια νῦν σπαθίοις πενιχροῖς πηνίσματα κρούει. / ὀψέ γ' Ἀθηναίῃ Κύπριν ἐληΐσατο.

T.'s version is more pointed. The punishment fits the crime and there is an apt reversal of situations: the unfaithful woman is now poor after being mercenary (and probably rich); she is now unhappy and the young men (whom formerly she must have taken a delight in making miserable) are now happy; she is now a decrepit old woman and young men no longer run after her (formerly she must have allured them by her beauty). T.'s version is also more comprehensive, as he describes not just one but several unpleasant tasks, and he paints a black picture by means of some good points of detail (see below).

Spinning and weaving were occupations of the chaste, which adds piquancy here (there may also be an ironic echo of 1.3.83ff.: see Gaisser loc.cit.intro.essay), but were also tasks of the poor and entailed hard work: see 1.3.83-94n., *A.P.* 6.48 (anon.), 247 (Philippus), 288 (Leonidas). The obvious implication is that Delia has the same faults and will face the same punishment (cf. 2.4.39ff.). This is cold and severe intimidation.

77–**80** See Critical Appendix.

There is emphasis here on the woman's poverty (*inops* and the hired loom, for which cf. Juv.8.43) and decrepitude (*victa senecta* and *tremula*, underlined by the contrast with *firma*).

Three separate processes are alluded to: spinning (78), preparations for weaving (79) and cleaning and softening of the wool prior to spinning (80). For the description of spinning see 1.3.83-94n., and for a discussion of the subject in general see Wilson *The Clothing of the Ancient Romans* (Baltimore, 1938), 14ff.

ducit inops tremula stamina torta manu: the wool was rolled into a loose ball and the distaff inserted, held in the left hand; the fibres were drawn out with the right hand and at the same time spirally twisted, the thread so produced being wound upon the spindle: cf. Catull.64.311ff. *laeva colum molli lana retinebat amictum, / dextera tum leviter deducens fila supinis / formabat digitis, tum prono in pollice torquens / libratum tereti versabat turbine fusum.*

firmaque conductis adnectit licia telis: the upright (or vertical) loom was generally used by the Romans of the classical period, and for the sake of clarity this type will be referred to here. The basic process of weaving is the passing of a (horizontal) thread, the woof or weft, over and under the (vertical) threads known as the warp. First all the warp threads were attached to a crossbeam at the top of the loom, then alternate threads were brought forward and rested on the outer side of a rod towards the bottom of the loom. The remaining warp threads hung vertically. A movable rod (leash rod) was placed against the forward warp threads between the crossbeam at the top and the rod towards the bottom. To this leash rod were attached cords which ended in loops, called leashes (*licia*). Each of the vertically hanging warp threads was passed through one of these leashes (the process here described: attaching leashes (*licia*) to the warp threads (*telis*): cf. Virg. *G.* 1.285f. *licia telae / addere*, and Page ad loc.). The woof thread was passed through the space between the two sets of warp threads above the leashes. Then the leash rod was moved forward until it brought the vertically hanging warp threads in front of the other warp threads that rested on the rod at the bottom of the loom, and the woof thread was passed through the new space between the two sets of warp threads. The leash rod was then replaced in its original position and the process repeated. For a full discussion see Wilson op.cit.16ff.

tractaque de niveo vellere ducta putat: see Critical Appendix.

Tracta (the noun) is a technical word for 'flocks of wool' (Varro apud Nonius p.228M.; also used of pieces of dough at Cato *Ag. Cult.* 76.1, 4), and *ducta* agrees with it. Before spinning, the wool was softened by being drawn through the hands (*ducta*: cf. Ov. *Met.* 4.34, *Her.* 3.70 *est mihi, quae lanas molliat, apta manus*) and cleaned (*putat* (its rare literal sense): cf. Non. p.369M, Varro *R.R.* 2.2.18 *ne lana inquinetur, quo minus vel infici recte possit vel lavari ac putari*). Crude wool was generally cleaned before spinning by washing, plucking, carding and beating with sticks (Ar. *Lys.* 574ff., Claud. *In Eutrop.* 2.381ff., Forbes *Studies in Ancient Technology* vol. IV (Leiden, 1956), 21, 81).

81–84 For young men rejoicing in such exx. of nemesis cf. Hor. *C.* 1.25, 4.13.24ff. (of the Fates) *servatura diu parem / cornicis vetulae temporibus Lycen, / possent ut iuvenes visere fervidi / multo non sine risu / dilapsam in cineres facem.*

tot mala: brings out the woman's misery, like *flentem* (underlined by the contrast with *animo gaudente*).

senem: also occurs as an adjective at 1.2.90, 1.7.56, 1.10.44, but as an adjective the word is rarely found in the feminine (cf. Cic. *Leg.* 2. 4.9 *vis senior*). The word is given emphasis by its position and again points to the woman's decrepitude.

hanc Venus ex alto flentem sublimis Olympo / spectat: for Delia's benefit the couplet is intended to be awesome and impressive, and Venus is shown in a dignified and truly Olympian pose: cf. Hom. *Il.* 11.336f., Virg. *Aen.* 11.725f., Ov. *Am.* 1.2.39f., Sil.It.1.51. The expression suggests imitation of Virg. *G.* 1.95f. (*neque illum / flava Ceres alto nequiquam spectat Olympo*).

The primary meaning of *sublimis* is 'on high', but the connotations of 'proud' and 'eminent' may also be present (cf. Varro *R.R.* 2.4.9, Ov. *F.* 1.301, *Her.* 9.129 *dat vultum populo sublimis ut Hercule victo*).

et infidis quam sit acerba monet: i.e. Venus was responsible. For the harsh and punitive aspects of Venus see 1.9.19-20n. For *acerba* see 1.2.97-8n.

85–86 *Haec . . . maledicta* and *cana . . . coma* pick up the preceding lines, as T. makes clear the choice that faces Delia and closes the poem by stating the sentiment behind it.

haec aliis maledicta cadant: for the turning of evil on the heads of others see Fraenkel *Horace* (Oxford, 1957), 411.

nos, Delia, amoris / exemplum cana simus uterque coma: for the sentiment cf. Catull.109, Hor. *Epod.* 15.1ff., Prop.1.1.32, 2.16.22, T.4.5.15f., Mart.4.13.7ff. *candida perpetuo reside, Concordia, lecto, / tamque pari semper sit Venus aequa iugo: / diligat illa senem quondam, sed et ipsa marito / tum quoque, cum fuerit, non videatur anus.*

For the expression *amoris / exemplum* cf. Ov. *Tr.* 1.5.21, 4.4.71. *Uterque* is a pointed addition.

7

Postgate *CR* XVII (1903), 112ff.; Levy *SIFC* VII (1929), 101ff.; Schuster *Tibull-Studien*, 17ff.; Klingner *Eranos* XLIX (1951), 117ff.; Luck *The Latin Love Elegy*, chap.5; Elder *TAPhA* XCVI (1965), 97ff.; Gaisser *CPh* LXVI (1971), 221ff.; Cairns *Generic Composition in Greek and Roman Poetry* (Edinburgh, 1972), 95f., 167ff.; Bulloch *PCPhS* 199 (1973), 71ff.; Bright *GB* III (1975), 31ff.

The elegy takes the form of a celebration of T.'s patron on a private and public level. Privately it is in honour of Messalla's birthday. Publicly it praises his defeat of the Aquitanians, which fell on or near his birthday (3-4n.) and for which he celebrated a triumph, and his Eastern expedition. One of the places visited by Messalla on this expedition was Egypt, a fact which leads into the central Osiris-section. Messalla's repair of part of the *via Latina* with his share of the proceeds of the spoils from the Aquitanian triumph is also mentioned. Lines 1ff. and 49ff. suggest that the setting is a feast celebrating the birthday in Messalla's house.

1-12	Messalla's birthday, triumph and Aquitanian campaign.
13-22	Messalla's Eastern expedition.
23-28	Bridge: the Nile's nature and its identification with Osiris.
29-48	Osiris-section: 29-42 his inventions; 43-48 his attributes.
49-54	Bridge: worship of Genius-Natalis.
55-64	Birthday wishes for Messalla.

All parts of the poem are in some way relevant to Messalla's birthday and exploits (on the Osiris-section see below), and the progression of thought is generally logical and smooth (on this aspect I acknowledge a partial debt to Schuster op.cit.), although the transition at 49 is rather contrived. Sections are bound together by the following verbal repetitions: *cano* / *cantus* (1, 13, 27, 37, 44, 47, 61), *pubes* (5, 27), *caerul(e)us* (12, 14), *doceo* / *doctus* (20, 28, 33, 37), *arens* / *aridus* (21, 26), *Nilus* (22, 23), *Osiris* (27, 29, 43).

There is difficulty and disagreement over the genre(s) of 1.7. The piece is generally viewed as a combination of hymn (the Osiris-section), 'victory-poem' or 'triumphal ode' and birthday poem (with emphasis often placed on the last of these three), although Cairns (op.cit.) also talks vaguely of the paean and the dithyramb, and Bright (loc.cit.) advanced the bizarre and feebly supported theory that 1.7 is an 'epyllion' (despite the fact that it is in the elegiac metre and the poem as a whole could hardly be classed as a 'little epic' or a 'narrative of a heroic or mythological topic'). There are also problems over the relevance and function of the Osiris-section, which I think are of importance in determining the genre(s) of the whole elegy.

To explain the incorporation of the section on Osiris there has been much discussion and speculation. It does seem possible that Messalla may have come into contact with and grown interested in the cult of Osiris while he was in Egypt, and T. may be flattering one of his patron's interests here. Nor is it inconceivable that T. himself formed a liking for this god of wine, music and love. Again, Osiris, who was connected with agriculture and widely worshipped in Egypt (27-8n.), could be viewed as the incarnation of that fertile province, which may merit more mention than the other places visited by Messalla in view of its importance to Rome because of the corn-supply (so Messalla's deeds there may have been worthy of emphasis). It has also been claimed that Osiris should be viewed as the divine counterpart of Messalla (the semi-divine figure of Messalla as *triumphator* (5ff.) has prepared for this idea): both may be seen as the bringers of stability and happiness to men, and there are cross-references to connect the two (the crown at 7 and 45, *pubes* at 5 and 27, *te canit* at 27 echoed by *te canet* at 61).

All these suggestions seem to me possible reasons for T. placing more emphasis on Egypt than on the other areas connected with the Eastern expedition and for T. choosing to talk about Osiris in particular, but they do not make clear why he does this at such great length and in such an important (central) position, and so they leave unexplained the function in the poem of the Osiris-section. To solve this problem some scholars have recourse to T.'s supposed penchant for digressions or regard the lines on the Nile and Osiris as a continuation of the process of place-name accompanied by allusion (but here the allusion would be taken to such great lengths as to amount to a virtual digression).

It is my belief that there is a simple solution, which also does away with the rather ungainly and amorphous hodgepodge of genres posited for 1.7. I contend that the piece is an ἐπινίκιον (with elements of the birthday-poem infused) and that the Osiris-section represents the mythological portion of T.'s ἐπινίκιον (on the genre see e.g. Smyth *Greek Melic Poets* (London, 1906), lxxx ff., Jebb *Bacchylides* (repr.1967), 56ff.). My reasons for this contention are various. The background-situation of 1.7 is similar to that of the epinikion (Messalla has won a victory, which is being celebrated by the poet). The structure of 1.7 closely resembles that of the ἐπινίκιον: the personal and encomiastic portions are at the beginning and end, the mythological section is in the middle, and the conclusion also contains wishes and prayers. Similarly, over points of detail, the poet gives the victor's name and the scene of the victory, tells us the city rendered illustrious by the victory

(5) and mentions other achievements by the victor (all in the normal place in the epinikion). Nor is there anything in 1.7 that is esp. incompatible with this genre. Certainly there is no overt moralizing, but this was a common, not inevitable, feature of the ἐπινίκιον, and T. may well have considered it inappropriate or impolitic in the case of Messalla. Anyway, T.'s usual moralistic themes would hardly fit here, and the absence of such a feature helps to give T.'s epinikion its particular elegiac tone. In addition, the fact that in 1.7 T. imitates Callimachus fr. 383 and 384 Pf. (which are probably ἐπινίκια) may well be significant (see below). I would add here that I see nothing to necessitate the explanation of the Osiris-section as a hymn, nor do I see the point of wandering off into a hymn at this stage in the elegy. Rather it is a recountal in an epinikion of the deeds and attributes of a mythical personage (as at e.g. Pind. *Isth.* 4.52ff.), with an address at 43ff. to the subject of the myth (as at e.g. Pind. *Isth.* 6.19ff.). This interpretation alone, in my opinion, gives the whole poem real shape and unity.

Osiris is a good choice for the mythological portion. Normally in the ἐπινίκιον the myth had some connection, albeit a remote one, with the subject of the ode. Here Osiris is a god of Egypt, which was one of the places visited by Messalla on his Eastern expedition. The parallelism between the god and the man (see above) constitutes a further connection, and thematically Osiris, in view of his gay and festive aspect, provides a useful link between Messalla's Oriental expedition and his birthday.

The infusion of elements of the birthday-poem mentioned above occurs at the beginning and end (1f., 49ff.). These elements smoothly perform the function of the personal details, good wishes and prayers of the epinikion. The mention of Fate and the allusion to birth (1f.) are details found elsewhere in ἐπινίκια (cf. e.g. Pind. *Nem.* 7.1ff., 56ff., *Isth.* 6.16ff.). In particular the birthday-wishes (49ff.) fit in well: for the idea of sons worthy of their father (55f.) cf. Pind. *Pyth.* 10.22ff., and for the hope that the victor may win praise for his achievements and enjoy continued good fortune (57ff.) cf. Pind. *Ol.* 7.87ff., *Pyth.* 5.117ff., *Nem.* 2.24f., *Isth.* 1.64ff. The smoothness of the combination is facilitated by the fact that Messalla won his victory on (or near) his birthday (3-4n.).

With regard to the genres of 1.7 Alexandrian influence has been suggested (see esp. Luck op.cit.), but there are also signs of considerable originality on T.'s part. The ἐπινίκιον, it is true, was an ancient genre, but its revival here (in Latin) shows a degree of novelty. T.'s epinikion may have been inspired by Callimachus fr. 383 and 384 Pf. (T. was acquainted with these: see below), which look like ἐπινίκια, celebrating athletic victories by an unknown man at Nemea and by Sosibius (see Pfeiffer ad loc.). Callimachus may have provided the model for the revival and for the use of elegiacs (rather than the traditional lyric metres), but the employment of the genre to celebrate a military (rather than athletic) victory is entirely original. Elements of the birthday-poem (i.e. a poem celebrating the anniversary of the day on which a person was born) first appear here. The genre subsequently became common: cf. 2.2, 4.5, 4.6, Prop.3.10, Ov. *Tr.* 3.13, 5.5, Hor. *C.*4.11, Mart.4.1, 10.24, 12.60, and see further Bowerman *CJ* XII (1916-17), 310ff. Just possibly the idea of the birthday-poem was suggested by Callimachus fr. 202 Pf. (cf. also Hedylus in Athen.176D), although Callimachus' poem (and the ref. in Hedylus) concerns Greek celebrations connected with the actual birth of a child and there is no strong evidence of any specific imitation of fr. 202 in 1.7 (see below). At any rate, the introduction of the Genius-Natalis, the details of his worship and the birthday-wishes (also present in 2.2) are all Tibullan innovations and exerted considerable influence on subsequent versions. Finally, novelty is evident not only in the revival and invention of genre here but also in the fusion of these two genres.

The influence of Callimachus is evident in the language and expression of 1.7 (see Pfeiffer on Call. frags. 202, 383, 384 and 709, Luck op.cit., Bulloch loc.cit.). As Ernesti first pointed out, 28 is an almost direct translation of Call.fr.383.16Pf. εἰδ⌊υῖ⌋αι φαλιὸν τ⌊αῦ⌋ρον ἰηλεμίσαι. So too 22 has been compared with Call.fr.384.27Pf. θηλύτατον καὶ Νεῖλο[ς ἄ]γων ἐνιαύσιον ὕδωρ and 23f. with Call.fr.384.31-2Pf. (Nile speaking) ὃν οὐδ' ὅθεν ο⌊ἶ⌋δεν ὁδεύω / θνητὸ⌋ς ἀνήρ, where imitation seems likely in view of similarity in thought and because the lines are close together in both poems (both are victory-poems too). Similarly *Mopsopio* in 54, which is first found here in Latin, may be taken from Callimachus (see fr.709Pf.). Imitation is also claimed with far less justification at two other points in 1.7 where there is no close verbal similarity and many parallels for the thought exist. Lines 1-2 have been compared with Call.fr.202.9Pf. κά[λ]λιστα νήθουσαι (here the context is unclear and the exact meaning of κά[λ]λιστα uncertain) and *Hymn.* 5.103f. (Athena speaking to Chariclo) ἐπεὶ μοιρᾶν ὧδ' ἐπένησε λίνα, / ἁνίκα τὸ πρᾶτον νιν ἐγείναο, although the idea of the Fates spinning out the thread of a man's future life at his birth is as old as Homer (1-2n.). Again line 51 has been compared with Call.fr.7.12Pf. (of the Graces) ἀπ' ὀστλί⌊γ⌋γων δ' αἰὲν ἄλειφα ῥέει and *Hymn.*2.38 (of Apollo) αἱ δὲ κόμαι θυόεντα πέδῳ λείβουσιν ἔλαια, although this type of phrase itself is frequent (e.g. *Hom.Hymn.*24.3, T.2.2.7, 3.4.28, Sen. *H.F.*468f.), and the actual practice of anointing gods' heads was common (see Pfeiffer on Call.fr.7.12, Allen and Halliday on *Hom.Hymn.* 24.3).

As usual, T. adapts his sources: in 22 a simple fact is given point by the contrasts between the Nile's flood and the dry fields and between the life-giving Nile and destructive Sirius, while at 23-4 a statement by the Nile in Callimachus, which Luck reasonably calls 'a little chatty and fatuous', and in 28 the reminiscence of Callimachus are used by T. to invest the Nile with an air of solemnity and mystery. Quite possibly these Alexandrian refs. are designed to flatter Messalla's interest in literature (see Gaisser loc. cit.).

Imitation of other authors here by T. has also been claimed, but most of the exx. suggested seem to me improbable. Many have maintained that the opening of the poem was influenced by Catull. 64.303ff., and Elder (loc. cit.) cites the following specific parallels: 1 = Catull. 64.383 *carmina divino cecinerunt pectore Parcae* (the song of the Fates first appears in Homer, and the verbal similarity is neither extensive nor striking), 3 = Catull. 64.321 *talia divino fuderunt carmine fata* (comment is unnecessary) and 11 = Catull. 64.357 *testis erit magnis virtutibus unda Scamandri* (this use of *testis* occurs in Cicero and Ennius: see 9-10n.). Elder also claims that the colour-contrast in 12 is in imitation of Ennius *Ann.* 384-5V *verrunt extemplo placide mare: marmore flavo / caeruleum spumat sale conferta rate pulsum* (this is possible, but the same colour-contrast also occurs 1.5.44-6, which could hardly have been inspired by Ennius, and a similar one at 1.3.94).

Cartault compares Virg. *G.* 1.223 *committas semina* with line 31, and Putnam points out that *facta parentis* (55) also occurs in Virg. *Ecl.* 4.26 (both of these are possible cases of imitation, but may be simply coincidental).

No exact parallel exists for 1.7 in classical literature, and in particular it is a novel and extraordinary poem for Latin elegy at this stage in its development: there is nothing like it in Propertius I or elsewhere in T.'s own first book. The subject-matter, the 'official' character and the almost complete absence of love (except for 44) are hitherto unfamiliar in elegy, and this strangeness is underlined by the positioning between two love-poems. This is an original and experimental composition, and it is also a very individual amalgam. The piece contains a unique combination of genres, both of which appear here first in Latin, and one of which is entirely new. There is a mixture of themes too (public and private, war and peace, serious and gay, Genius and Osiris, Italy and abroad), including some outlandish details (exotic place-names, bizarre customs and the mysterious Nile). Unusually extensive and broad *doctrina* is also in evidence (geographical, religious and literary). The tone, in line with the epinikion genre, is generally stately: there is much that is lofty (and out of the ordinary) in the language, forms and expression, and various poetic devices (esp. anaphora, artistic placement of words and metrical effects) contribute to the elevation of style. Yet T.'s epinikion does also have a particular elegiac flavour due to the absence of heavy moralizing and the relief provided by some lighter touches in the personal details (9, 55f.), the rustic refs. and the worship of Genius-Natalis. I must admit that personally I find this the least attractive of T.'s poems, although I may be influenced by the prejudices of my own generation (it seems to have been a favourite of the Victorians). At any rate, 1.7 is an unusual elegy that shows the poet's versatility and adds variety to his first collection.

1–12 A solemn and stately opening concerns a prophecy made on the day of Messalla's birth that his victory over the Aquitanians was destined to fall on this day's anniversary (thus elements of the birthday-poem and ἐπινίκιον are combined: see intro. essay). Next T. briefly describes Messalla's triumph for this victory, and then he lists places that bear witness to T.'s presence on the campaign and to the glory won by Messalla. On the Aquitanian campaign see Introduction sect. 4.

Anaphora is in evidence (*hic* 1, 3; *qui* 3, 4; *testis* 10, 11), and care is taken to avoid monotony in the list (there is variety in the type of subject and in the number of subjects per couplet, refs. to tribes are added for interest, and a colour-contrast (12) also enlivens).

1–2 hunc cecinere diem Parcae fatalia nentes / stamina: the deities of fate spinning out the thread of a man's future life at his birth first appear in Homer (*Il.* 20.127f., 24.209f., *Od.* 7.196f.) For the prophetic song of the Fates cf. Plat. *Res.Pub.* 617C, Catull.64.320ff. Here their song is apparently on the day of Messalla's birth (cf. T.4.5.3f., Ov. *Met.* 8.451ff., *Tr.* 5.3.25f., Hygin. *fab.* 171).

On the perfect form see 1.5.47-8n.

For the suggested imitation here see intro. essay.

non ulli dissoluenda deo: for fate superior to the gods cf. Hom. *Od.* 3.236ff., Aesch. *P. V.* 517f., Hdt.1.91, Virg. *Aen.* 5.798, 12.147f., Ov. *Met.* 15.780f., *Tr.* 5.3.17f. Elsewhere Zeus can control Fate and intervene, and Fate appears as the will of Zeus (Hom. *Il.* 8.69ff., 16.434, 441f., Pauly s.v. *Fatum*).

For the scansion of the u in *dissoluenda* see Platnauer 70f. Such a scansion is not common in elegy and is mainly found with *solvo, volvo* and their compounds (elsewhere in T. at 40, 1.10.62).

3–4 hunc fore, Aquitanas posset qui fundere gentes: for the uncommon figure of the day doing all that is done on that day cf. Pind. *Pyth.* 9.68, Soph. *Ajax* 131, Prop.1.13.25 *una dies omnis potuit praecurrere amantis*, Hor. *C.* 3.8.9f. Apparently Messalla's victory over the Aquitanians took place on or very near his birthday (cf. Corn.Nep. *Timol.* 5).

The adjective *Aquitanus* is rare and first appears here. The precise ref. in the word is unclear: the borders of old Aquitania were the Garonne, the Pyrenees and the Bay of Biscay (Caes. *B.G.* 1.1), but other territory was added by Augustus to form new Aquitania (11-12n.).

On the suggested imitation here see intro. essay.

quem tremeret forti milite victus Atur: see Critical Appendix.

The Atur is the modern Adour (more commonly Aturus, but for this form cf. Vibius Sequester 20), a river in old Aquitania: it rises near the Pyrenees and flows into the Bay of Biscay near Bayonne (Luc. 1.420f., Auson. *Mosel.* 466f.).

Roman poets often identified a region or country by means of its chief river (cf. 11-14, 22). So they described military operations as undertaken against the country's river (Virg. *Aen.* 6.800, Prop. 3.11. 41f. *ausa Iovi nostro latrantem opponere Anubim, / et Tiberim Nili cogere ferre minas*), and representations of rivers were present in triumphal processions (cf. Ov. *A.A.* 1.219ff., *Tr.* 4.2.37, *ExP.* 2.1.39, 3.4.107f., Tac. *Ann.* 2.41).

5–8 For the triumph theme see Galinsky *WS* LXXXII (1969), 75ff., and for description and discussion of the triumph see Pauly s.v. *Triumphus*, Versnel *Triumphus* (Leiden, 1970).

evenere: the subject here may be the events prophesied in the previous lines (cf. 1.5.58) or the events that are described in the following lines. The distinction is a fine one, as the triumph is the proof and recognition of the victory. On the form of the perfect see 1.5.47-8n.

novos . . . triumphos: plural for singular. *Novus* here means 'fresh, further' (*OLD* s.v.5). Augustus had celebrated a triumph in 29 B.C. The suggestion that this is yet another triumph is a compliment to the Augustan régime.

pubes Romana: *pubes* for *populus* is mainly poetic (see Fordyce on Catull. 64.267 and cf. also 27, Virg. *Aen.* 7.219).

evinctos bracchia capta duces: *evincio* occurs only at Hem. *Hist.* 37 and Virg. *Ecl.* 7.32 before here and is in general uncommon (*Thes. L. L.* V_2.1041.35ff.). For the expression *bracchia capta* cf. Ov. *Am.* 1.14.45, *Met.* 13.667, *Tr.* 4.2.21, Mart. 14.26.2.

The principal captives in chains were included in the triumphal procession (Prop. 3.4.18, Ov. *A.A.* 1.215, *Tr.* 4.2.21f., *ExP.* 2.1.43f.).

at te victrices lauros, Messalla, gerentem: for *victrices lauros* 'the laurel of the victor' cf. Virg. *Ecl.* 8.13 and (*triumphalis laurus*) T.2.5.5, Ov. *Am.* 2.12.1. The general wore a laurel wreath on his head and carried a laurel bough in his right hand (2.5.117, Ov. *Am.* 2.12.1, *ExP.* 2.2.89f., Plut. *Aem. Paul.* 34.3, Plin. *N.H.* 15.127, 137 *ex ea triumphans postea Caesar laurum in manu tenuit coronamque capite gessit*). The spondees here add solemnity.

portabat nitidis currus eburnus equis: the general rode in a chariot adorned with gold and ivory (Hor. *Epod.* 9.21f., Ov. *ExP.* 3.4.35 *illa ducis facies in curru stantis eburno*) and drawn by four white horses (Prop. 4.1.32, Ov. *A.A.* 1.214 *quattuor in niveis aureus ibis equis*).

On T.'s use of *porto* see 1.3.93-4n. For the change in tense (to vivid imperfect) see 1.1.21-4n.

Nitidus here means 'brilliant, bright', perhaps with connotations of beauty and elegance. *Niteo, nitor* and *nitidus* are often found with *albus* and *candidus* (Hor. *C.* 2.5.18, Ov. *Med. Fac.* 52, *Tr.* 3.10.22) and are commonly used of white objects (1.4.64, Hor. *C.* 1.19.5, Ov. *Met.* 1.610f., 2.3, *Moretum* 106).

The form *eburnus* is confined to poetry and later prose (*Thes. L. L.* V_2.22.62ff.).

Note the assonance and internal rhyme in this line. At 5, 6 and 8 the final four words of the line are arranged in the same pattern.

9–10 **non sine me est tibi partus honos**: see Critical Appendix.

This is a brief mention of T.'s personal part in the Aquitanian campaign (see Introduction sect. 4) = 'I was with you when you won glory'.

Tarbella Pyrene / testis: see Critical Appendix.

The Tarbelli were a people of Aquitania (Caes. *B. G.* 3.27, Plin. *N.H.* 31.4), and *Tarbella Pyrene* is the part of the Pyrenees near the Tarbelli, viz. the south-west of old Aquitania. *Tarbellus* as an adjective is rare and first appears here.

The y in *Pyrene* is usually long, but for this scansion cf. *Pyrenaeae* at Lucan 4.83.

For this use of *testis* with geographical features cf. Cic. *Leg. Manil.* 30, *De Or.* 3.167 (quoting Ennius), Catull. 64.357, Hor. *C.* 4.4.38, Ov. *ExP.* 4.9.114 *officii testis Pontica terra mei.*

Oceani litora Santonici: the part of the Ocean near the Santones, i.e. above the mouth of the Garonne. This is the earliest occurrence of the adjective.

Note the alliteration (of t and p) and in the pentameter the internal rhyme.

11–12 See Critical Appendix.

The precise point of the geographical refs. in this couplet and the last is far from clear, and the situation is complicated by the fact that at an unknown date Augustus added territory to old Aquitania to form new Aquitania (see Strabo 177, 189f., Dio Cass. 53.12 and the discussions in Postgate and Elder loc.cit.intro.essay). Messalla's campaign may have been against the peoples of old Aquitania before new Aquitania was created, or even against those of new Aquitania (although this seems unlikely), and there is no reason why he could not have dealt with some of the Aquitanians (or minor disturbances by others also) outside the borders of (old or new) Aquitania. Thus the lines may refer to isolated victories at each of the places named, or T. may mean that the enemy were systematically driven on two fronts to their furthest natural boundaries (sea and mountains in 9f.) and elsewhere as far as the Arar, Rhodanus and Liger (11f.), which would form natural defences for Messalla. Again, Postgate maintained that 9f. refer to victories in old

Aquitania and 11f. to the subsequent formation of new Aquitania, since the rivers mentioned in 11f. 'form with the ocean what we may call the water-boundaries of the territory which . . . Augustus added to Aquitania'. Augustus' formation of new Aquitania may well have taken place at this time, and the Arar and Rhodanus, while not strictly forming the boundaries of the new territory, could readily suggest themselves as such to one more interested in poetry than the niceties of geography.

testis Arar Rhodanusque celer: see Critical Appendix.

On the suggested imitation here see intro. essay.

The Arar (Saône) was noted for its sluggishness: cf. Caes. *B.G.* 1.12 *flumen est Arar, quod per fines Aeduorum et Sequanorum in Rhodanum influit, incredibili lenitate, ita ut oculis, in utram partem fluat, iudicari non possit.* It runs southwards to join at Lyons the Rhodanus (Rhone), a very swift river which flows from the Alps to the Mediterranean (Lucan 1.433f., Plin. *N.H.* 3.33 *Rhodanus amnis ex Alpibus se rapiens per Lemannum lacum segnemque deferens Ararem*). So too the rivers are joined in the Latin (there is also an implicit antithesis in the juxtaposition).

magnusque Garunna: one of the chief rivers in Gaul (*magnus*), the Garonne flows from the Pyrenees into the Bay of Biscay (cf. Plin. *N.H.* 4.105, Mela 3.21, Strabo 190).

Carnutis et flavi caerula lympha Liger: the Loire formed the northern boundary of the territory added to old Aquitania (Caes. *B.G.* 7.5 *flumen Ligerim . . . quod Bituriges ab Aeduis dividit*). Cenabum on the Loire was the principal town of the Carnutes or Carnuti (for the scansion of *Carnutis* cf. Venantius Fortunatus *Vita S.Mart.* 3.153).

For the blond hair of the Gauls cf. Claud. *Ruf.* 2.110, *Cons.Stilich.* 2.240f., and for the use of *flavus* see 1.5.43-4n.

Caerul(e)us denotes esp. a dark blue (André *Étude sur les termes de couleur dans la langue Latine* (Paris, 1949), 162ff.). Commentators have been quick to point out that the Liger is not dark blue but clear (see e.g. Smith, who goes so far as to compare it to a mountain brook in Vermont). However, clear water appears a dark blue when viewed from any distance under a cloudless sky, as it reflects the colour of the sky (one of the primary uses of the adjective is of the sky: Lucr. 1.1090, André op.cit., p. 165). Ausonius applies the adjective to the clear Moselle (*Mosel.* 55ff.) at *Mosel.* 84. In any case, T. is not a geographer but a poet: *caerulus* seems a natural epithet for rivers in general, and particularly recommends itself here for the colour-contrast with *flavi* (on this colour-contrast see intro. essay).

Lympha is a poetic term for water (*OLD* s.v. 2).

Note the juxtaposition *flavi caerula*, the alliteration and the rhyme in -*nusque.*

13–22 The geographical list and the theme of Messalla's glory continue, but T. now moves on to his patron's Eastern expedition. The transition is helped by reference to a river in 13f., which picks up the rivers in 11f., and by *caeruleus* (14), which echoes *caerula* (12).

For the little that we know of this expedition see Introduction sect. 4. It would appear that T. was left behind at Corcyra, and so the point of these refs. is to give further exx. of Messalla's *honos* (9), not of T.'s presence with him (so the construction changes from *testis*). The events which earned his patron glory at the places mentioned by T. are unknown. There is a progression in the course of the list around the eastern curve of the Mediterranean, finally ending in Egypt at the furthest point from Rome in the expedition.

Again care is taken to avoid monotony in the list: there is an overall East-West contrast (with the earlier part of the list), a change to questions (taking different forms) and to one subject per couplet, variety in types of subject and in sentence-length, and a local tribe (16), a religious taboo (17f.) and an allusion to the discovery of navigation (19f.) are added for interest.

13–14 See Critical Appendix.

The Cydnus is a river in Cilicia running from Taurus (15-16n.) through Tarsus and flowing into a shallow lake near its outlet (Plin. *N.H.* 5.92, Strabo 672). Although swift in its upper course (cf. Lucian *Dom.* 1), it becomes slow in the lower part (Curtius 3.4.8). The river was noted for its coldness and clearness (Lucian loc.cit., Arrian *Anab.* 2.4.7, Curtius 3.4.8f., 3.5.2f.).

Tacitis . . . undis goes with *serpis*, and *placidis . . . aquis* goes with *vada* as a descriptive ablative. The ref. in *vada* is to the lake near the outlet of the Cydnus (for *vada* in this sense cf. Ov. *F.* 1.501 *fluminis illa latus, cui sunt vada iuncta Tarenti*). For the intrusion of *serpis* in the descriptive ablative (accompanied by another ablative) cf. Virg. *Aen.* 1.313, 12.165 *bina manu lato crispans hastilia ferro.*

For the emphasis on the quietness and slowness of the river in *tacitis qui leniter undis / . . . serpis* cf. Virg. *Aen.* 8.87f., Hor. *C.* 1.31.7f. *quae Liris quieta / mordet aqua taciturnus amnis*, Ov. *ExP.* 4.10.54, Sen. *H.F.* 712f.

Again commentators point out that the river is not dark blue (*caeruleus*): see 11-12n., and note that here the word may particularly recommend itself for artistic repetition and smoothness of transition (echoing *caerula*, 12).

There is no distinction in meaning between *caerulus* and *caeruleus*: both forms are found as early as Ennius and Plautus, and continue throughout Latin.

Note the rhyme in -is (1.1.53-4n.) and the extensive alliteration.

15–16 Taurus is a high mountain-range which stretches from Caria and Lycia to Armenia and Mesopotamia, extending the full length of northern Cilicia (Strabo 520f., Plin. *N.H.* 5.97f., Mela 1.15.81). Strabo (569) says that it was capable of cultivation in the midst of its heights (*alat*).

aetherio contingens vertice nubes: for the expression cf. Virg. *Aen.* 4.445f., Ov. *Met.* 1.316f. *mons ibi verticibus petit arduus astra duobus, / nomine Parnasus, superantque cacumina nubes, ExP.* 4.7.24. *Aetherius*, a word confined mainly to poetry and common in the loftier genres (*Thes. L. L.* I.1152.58ff.), is first applied to a mountain here (cf. Virg. *Aen.* 6.579, 8.319, 10.621, 11.867, Sil.It.3.480f.).

intonsos: see 1.4.37-8n.

17–18 For oriental religion in T. see intro. essay to 1.3. Doves were sacred to Astarte and regarded by the Syrians as holy and untouchable (cf. Xen. *Anab.* 1.4.9, Diod.2.4.6, Lucian *Dea Syr.* 14, 54, Euseb. *Praep. Evang.* 8.14.64).

ut: 'how' (also in indirect questions at 19, 1.8.57f., 2.1.15, 25, 2.5.72).

crebras: most probably means 'many', as *Thes. L. L.* and *OLD* quote no exx. of its absolute use meaning literally 'populous' or 'frequented' (Smith, Putnam).

Palaestino . . . Syro: *Syria* in classical authors was used of a wide area (cf. Plin. *N.H.* 5.66 *iuxta Syria litus occupat, quondam terrarum maxuma et plurimis distincta nominibus* etc.). The adjective is added to show precisely which region is meant (cf. Ov. *A.A.* 1.76, 416, Plin. *N.H.* 12.80).

Note the homoeoteleuton (see 1.1.53-4n.) and the internal rhyme in the pent.

19–20 Tyre was a Phoenician city built on an island, later connected to the mainland by Alexander (Strabo 757, Plin. *N.H.* 5.76). The lack of space meant that the city expanded upwards rather than outwards, and it was renowned for its high buildings (Strabo 757) and high fortifications (Arrian *Anab.* 2.18.2), both of which may be denoted here by *turribus*.

maris vastum . . . aequor: an original variation on the phrase *aequor(a) ponti* (which is common in poetry from Lucr. onwards): cf. esp. Virg. *Aen.* 2.780 *vastum maris aequor*, and also *Aen.* 3.495, Hor. *C.* 4.5.10, Claud. *Rapt. Pros.* 2.295. *Vastum* suggests emptiness and awesomeness as well as extent of space (Fordyce on Catull.64.156), and so highlights the danger and greatness of the achievement in 20.

prima ratem ventis credere docta Tyros: the Phoenicians were regarded as pioneers in navigation: cf. Plin. *N.H.* 5.67, 7.208f., Avien.3.1065f. (Holder) *primi docuere carinis / ferre cavis orbis commercia; sidera primi / servavere polo.* This line reflects the legendary navigational skills of the Phoenicians in general (Hom. *Od.* 15.415) and of the Tyrians in particular (Strabo 757, Curt.4.4.19f.).

On the theme of the inventor see 1.4.59-60n.

For *ratem ventis credere* cf. Germ. *Arat.* 14, Quint.12 *proem.* 2, *Anth.Lat.* 268R *crede ratem ventis.* The phrase brings out the hazards of seafaring (on *ratem* see 1.3.39-40n., on *ventis* see 1.3.37-8n.). See Smith for a quote from Shackerley Marmion.

The infinitive after adjectives, modelled on the Greek construction, is common in Augustan poetry and occurs elsewhere in T. at 28, 1.8.72 ('not knowing that . . . '), 1.9.37, 2.6.43. See Roby 1361 and Kühner-Stegmann 1.684ff.

21–22 arentes cum findit Sirius agros: on Sirius see 1.1.27-8n. For this description of midsummer heat cf. Catull.68.62 *cum gravis exustos aestus hiulcat agros*, Virg. *G.* 2.353, Ov. *Am.* 2.16.3, *Met.* 3.152, *Priap.* 63.2.

fertilis aestiva Nilus abundet aqua: for *fertilis* 'fertilizing' (active: see 1.1.7-8n.) cf. Val.Fl.7.607f. *pinguia Nili / fertilis arva*, Lucan 3.260 *fertilis Euphrates*, Plin. *N.H.* 18.43. The word appears here first in this rare active sense (*Thes.L.L.* VI_1.588.63ff.).

For various ancient explanations of the Nile's summer rise see Hdt. 2.19ff., Diod.1.36ff., Lucr.6.712ff., Lucan 10.219ff., Sen. *N.Q.* 4.1. 1ff., 6.8.3ff., Plin. *N.H.* 5.54ff. It lasts for about a hundred days, and the exact date, of course, varies from place to place. For T.'s reckoning of the date cf. Diod.1.19.1, Lucan 10.225f. *Nilus neque suscitat undas / ante Canis radios*, Plin. *N.H.* 5.56.

The dry fields in 21 contrast with the sea in the last couplet. Note also the internal contrasts between dry fields (21) and water (22) and between destructive Sirius (21) and the life-giving Nile (22).

See intro. essay for T.'s imitation here of Callimachus.

23–28 The continuation of the question form and of the subject of the Nile (*Nile* 23 picks up *Nilus* 22) and the return at 25f. to the fertilizing effect of its flood on the dry land (*arida* 26 echoes *arentes* 21) ensure a smooth transition.

These lines elaborate on the ref. to the Nile in the previous couplet, heightening the mystery by further remarks on its strange nature (its hidden source, the wonderful power of its inundation and the worship of it as Osiris by the outlandish Egyptians). The concentration here on the Nile may be explained by the fact that Egypt was esp. vital to Rome because of the corn-supply, and so Messalla's deeds there may have been particularly important and deserving of emphasis. The lines also form a bridge to the Osiris-section (29-48), making an effective transition: both the Nile and Osiris are Egyptian, the tone becomes more mystical and religious, the ref. to the fertilizing power of the Nile foreshadows Osiris' cultivation of the earth, and the actual identification of the Nile with Osiris (27) provides the verbal and thematic link.

23–24 For ancient discussion about the source of the Nile see Hdt.2.19ff.,

Diod. 1.37, Lucan 10.193ff., Sen. *N.Q.* 4.1.1ff., 6.8, Plin. *N.H.* 5.51ff., Claud. *Nilus* (= *Carm.Min.* 28), and cf. esp. Ov. *Met.* 2.254f. (as Phaethon scorches the world) *Nilus in extremum fugit perterritus orbem / occuluitque caput, quod adhuc latet*, Lucan 10.295ff. *arcanum natura caput non prodidit ulli, / nec licuit populis parvum te, Nile, videre, / amovitque sinus, et gentes maluit ortus / mirari quam nosse tuos.* Ramsay comments: 'The mystery of the sources of the Nile . . . has only been solved in our own day by our great countryman Livingstone . . . '

For *pater* used of rivers (esp. of the Tiber) cf. Enn. *Ann.* 54V, Livy 2.10.11.

quanam: elsewhere in Augustan poetry the word occurs only at 3.1.5. See intro. essay for T.'s imitation of Callimachus here.

25–26 **te propter nullos tellus tua postulat imbres**: for the idea that the Nile replaces rain in Egypt cf. Ap.Rhod.4.269ff., Lucan 8.444ff., Sen. *N.Q.* 4.2.1f. (at 4.2.2 he quotes part of line 26 and attributes it to Ovid) and Claud. *Nilus*.

Note the anaphora of *te* (also at 23 and 27).

For the postposition of *propter* see 1.1.21-4n.

arida nec pluvio supplicat herba Iovi: this unique and bold figure may have been suggested by the prayers of humans to Jupiter for rain (Petron. *S.* 44 *antea stolatae ibant nudis pedibus in clivum, passis capillis, mentibus puris, et Iovem aquam exorabant*) or possibly, as Vulpius thought, by a representation similar to that described at Paus. 1.24.3 (ἔστι δὲ καὶ Γῆς ἄγαλμα ἱκετευούσης ὗσαί οἱ τὸν Δία).

The epithet *pluvius* for Jupiter (probably after Ζεὺς ὑέτιος or ἰκμαῖος) is rare and first occurs here: cf. Stat. *Theb.* 4.758f., *Anth.Lat.* 395.46R (*pluvius*), *CIL* 9.234 (*pluvia*[*lis*]), Virg. *G.* 1.418 (*uvidus*), Apul. *Mund.* 37 (*imbricitor*).

The words are arranged on the pattern of the 'golden' line (cf. 34, 58, and see e.g. Williams on Virg. *Aen.* 5.46).

27–28 **te canit atque suum pubes miratur Osirim / barbara**: T. is here most probably identifying the Nile with Osiris. Unless *suum . . . Osirim* means 'as their Osiris', *te canit* is weak and isolated, and the transition to Osiris is very clumsy (see Klingner loc.cit.intro.essay). In addition this identification has support from Plutarch (*Mor.* 363D οὕτω παρ' Αἰγυπτίοις Νεῖλον εἶναι τὸν Ὄσιριν, 364A, 365B, 366A, 729B). The sense is either 'sings of you, and venerates you as their Osiris' or 'sings of and venerates you as their Osiris'.

Unelided *atque* is rare in elegy (Platnauer *CQ* XLII (1948), 90f.), but elsewhere in T. it also occurs at 2.2.8, 2.5.73 (see the discussion in Critical Appendix).

On *pubes* see 5-8n.

For *miratur* meaning 'venerates' cf. e.g. Virg. *Aen.* 8.517, Livy 1.7.8, Stat. *Silv.* 5.2.76.

For oriental religion in T. see intro. essay to 1.3. On Osiris see Witt *Isis in the Graeco-Roman World*, chap. 3, Frazer *Adonis, Attis, Osiris* 209ff., Roscher *Lex. der griech. und röm. Mythologie* s.v. Usire, Plutarch *De Iside et Osiride*, Diod.Sic.1.14ff. Osiris was the brother and husband of Isis (1.3.23-4n.), and was worshipped with her throughout Egypt (Hdt.2.42). In Egypt he was primarily a judge and god of the Underworld (Roscher loc.cit.), and he was also associated with fertility (Plut. *Mor.* 364, Roscher loc.cit.). He was supposed to be the founder of civilisation, teaching respect for the gods and law, and inventing the cultivation of the earth (Plut. *Mor.* 356, Diod.1.13ff.). Osiris was identified with various gods (Diod.1.11, 25, Roscher), esp. Dionysus (39-40n.). According to myth he was nailed in a coffin by his evil brother Set and thrown into the Nile. Isis recovered the body at Byblus, but Set tore it apart and scattered the pieces, which Isis later found and buried (Plut. *Mor.* 355D ff.).

Memphiten plangere docta bovem: Apis, the sacred bull, generally regarded as the incarnation of Osiris (Diod.1.85.4, Plut. *Mor.* 359B, 368C τὸν δ' Ἆπιν εἰκόνα μὲν Ὀσίριδος ἔμψυχον εἶναι), was kept in luxury at Memphis; at its death it was given a magnificent burial, and all the people and priests mourned, the priests seeking out a young bull with similar markings; when the new bull was found the mourning ceased, and the bull was taken to Memphis (see Smith, Lucian *Sacrif.* 15, Plut. *Mor.* 359B, 364E, Paus.1.18.4 and Frazer ad loc., Mayor on Juv.8.29).

This is the first occurrence of the rare adjective *Memphites.*

Plangere in the sense of 'mourn' first appears here with an accusative of the person (or thing) mourned for: this construction is mainly poetic (e.g. Stat. *Theb.* 11.117, Val.Fl.3.298, Claud. *Rapt.Pros.* 3.159, Mela 1.57).

For the infinitive after *docta* see 19-20n.

For T.'s imitation of Callimachus here see intro. essay.

29–48 *Osiris* (29) picks up *Osirim* (27). The bridge-section (23-8n.) has smoothed the transition to Osiris here, and the mention of oriental religion at 17f. and the theme of the inventor at 19f. have also helped to prepare the way.

See intro.essay for the relevance of this section and its function in the poem (= the central mythological portion of the ἐπινίκιον).

The section falls into two main parts (Osiris' inventions and attributes). In the first part (29-42) there is a couplet each on agriculture, arboriculture, viticulture and the vintage, while the final three couplets concern Osiris' gift of wine and his identification with Bacchus. There are chronological progressions: at 29-32 from ploughing to sowing and to picking, at 33-42 from cultivation of the vine to the vintage and to the drinking of wine and its effects. The bounty of Osiris' gifts is brought out here by underlining his knowledge and man's ignorance (*sollerti* 29, *inexpertae* 31 (see n.), *non notis* 32, *docuit* 33, *incultis* 36, *docuit* 37 and *nescia* 38). The next part (43-48), picking up 39-42, places emphasis on the gay and festive side of the god, thereby preparing the way for the ref. to birthday-celebrations at 49ff. There is extensive anaphora throughout the section (most of the words are emphatic by position): *primus* (29, 31, cf.35), *hic* (33, 34), *ille* (35, 37), *Bacchus et* (39, 41), *sed* and *et* (44ff.).

29–30 For the theme of the founding of civilisation see intro. essay to 1.3 (Ages), and cf. 1.10.45ff., 2.1.37ff. T.'s account corresponds at many points to Diod.1.14ff. (see below), and Lucr.5.933ff. lists the lack of similar inventions as a sign of the uncivilised world. On the inventor see 1.4.59-60n.

For Osiris and the invention of the plough see Serv. ad Virg. *G.* 1.19, 147 *Osirin vel Triptolemum aratrum invenisse.*

et teneram ferro sollicitavit humum: *tener* here, in view of *inexpertae . . . terrae* (31) and the general idea of the earliness of this period, probably denotes the soft soil of the young earth (for the idea cf. Lucr. 5.780f. *mundi novitatem et mollia terrae / arva*, 806), although the ref. may be to the alluvial soil of Egypt (e.g. Cic. *N.D.* 2.130). Note the juxtaposition of hardness in *ferro.*

Sollicito in the literal sense occurs mainly in poetry and post-Aug. prose (Lewis & Short s.v.I). For the verb used of 'disturbing' the earth by ploughing etc. cf. Virg. *G.* 2.418, Ov. *F.* 4.396.

31–32 For Osiris and the invention of sowing cf. Diod.1.14.1, 1.17.1.

For Osiris as the inventor of arboriculture and the discoverer of fruit cf. Diod.1.17.4f., 1.20.3, Plut. *Mor.* 356A.

inexpertae commisit semina terrae: the seed is a deposit, entrusted to the earth. For the expression cf. Virg. *G.* 1.223 *debita . . . sulcis committas semina*, 2.289, *Moretum* 70, Col. *R.R.* 2.8.4, Sen. *Ben.* 4. 9.2, and see intro. essay for the possibility of imitation here. For similar imagery cf. Cic. *Sen.* 51, Virg. *G.* 2.460, T.2.3.62, 2.6.21f.

Inexpertus here (in view of the emphasis in these lines on man's ignorance (29-48n.), and balancing with *non notis*) most probably means 'unknown, untried' (in this sense the word occurs only at Publil. *Sent.* G6 before here): cf. Ov. *Tr.* 3.8.3 *misit in ignotam qui rude semen humum.* Also possible, but less likely, is the meaning 'lacking experience of' (i.e. seeds): cf. Val.Fl.1.69f. *ignaras Cereris qui vomere terras / imbuit*. On the active force of verbal adjectives and participles in general see 1.4.11-12n., and for *inexpertus* (this would be its first appearance in this sense) cf. Sen. *Contr.* exc.6.8, Stat. *Theb.* 9.904.

33–34 For Osiris as the inventor of the vine and viticulture (N.B. his identification with Bacchus: 39-40n.) cf. Diod.1.15.8, 1.17.1, 1.20.4, 4.1.6f.

For the training of vines to props (vertical and horizontal, certain trees forming natural props) cf. Virg. *G.* 2.358ff., Varro *R.R.* 1.8 (and Tilly ad loc.), Col. *R.R.* 4, esp. 12f., 16ff., 5.5. For pruning cf. Cic. *Sen.* 52, Virg. *G.* 2.362ff., Col. *R.R.* 4, esp. 6ff., 21ff., 5.5. Training and pruning are specified as two of the more important and skilful processes.

dura: most obviously refers to the hardness of the *falx*, but also suggested is the idea that pruning must be done without pity (cf. Virg. *G.* 2.369f. *tum denique dura / exerce imperia et ramos compesce fluentis*).

Note the contrasts between hex. and pent. (*teneram* is opposed to *dura*, as joining is to cutting off) and the arrangement of words in the pent. on the pattern of the 'golden' line (25-6n.).

35–36 For Osiris as the inventor of wine see Diod.1.15.8, and on the treading of grapes see 1.5.21-4n.

incultis . . . pedibus: for *incultus* 'untrained, uncivilised' cf. Sall. *Cat.* 2.8 *sed multi mortales dediti ventri atque somno indocti incultique vitam sicuti peregrinantes transiere*, Livy 21.32.7, T.4.1.59.

The heavily spondaic nature of the lines may be intended to suggest a slow, uncertain treading.

37–38 There were various theories about the origin of song and dance (cf. e.g. Lucr.5.1379ff., Sen. *Epist.* 90.26, Plin *N.H.* 7.204, Plut. *Mor.* 974A, *De Musica*). For the idea that wine was responsible cf. Plato *Leg.* 653ff., esp. 672D οὐκοῦν καὶ ὅτι τὴν ῥυθμοῦ τε καὶ ἁρμονίας αἴσθησιν τοῖς ἀνθρώποις ἡμῖν ἐνδεδωκέναι τὴν ἀρχὴν ταύτην ἔφαμεν, Ἀπόλλωνα δὲ καὶ Μούσας καὶ Διόνυσον θεῶν αἰτίους γεγονέναι; For the obvious connection between wine, song and dance cf. e.g. Cic. *Mur.* 13, Athen. 37A, B. See also 43-4n., Maas *Hermes* XXXI (1896), 375ff.

ille liquor: for the ref. here see 49-50n.

inflectere: 'modulate': cf. *inflexus* at Cic. *Or.* 57 (*mira est enim quaedam natura vocis cuius quidem e tribus omnino sonis, inflexo, acuto, gravi, tanta sit et tam suavis varietas perfecta in cantibus*) and *inflectere* at Cic. *De Or.* 2.193 (of an actor modulating his voice, *inflexa ad miserabilem sonum voce*). This is a very rare use of the verb (see *Thes.L.L.* VII_1.1458.66ff.). *Flectere vocem* is also used of singing (Ov. *Am.* 2.4.25).

movit et ad certos nescia membra modos: for *moveo* used of movement in dancing cf. Lucr.4.789, Hor. *S.* 1.9.24, *Ars. Poet.* 232 *ut festis matrona moveri iussa diebus*. For *ad . . . modos* cf. 1.4.67-70n., Ov. *F.* 3.388, 6.692, Livy 7.2.4, Col. *R.R.* 12.2.4.

Note the antithetical juxtaposition (*certos nescia*). The assonance and alliteration make this an aptly musical line.

39–40 For the identification of Osiris with Bacchus here (see 49-50n.) cf. Hdt.2.42, 144 Ὄσιρις δέ ἐστι Διόνυσος κατὰ Ἑλλάδα γλῶσσαν, Diod. 1.13.5, 1.25.2, Plut. *Mor.* 364E, Serv. ad *Aen.* 11.287.

For wine as a relief from trouble and sadness see 1.5.37-8n. The ref.

here is probably to a rustic festival: cf. 1.10.51, 2.5.101, Hor. *Epist.* 2.1.139ff. *agricolae prisci . . . / condita post frumenta levantes tempore festo / corpus et ipsum animum spe finis dura ferentem.*

magno confecta labore: see 1.9.7-8n.

pectora tristitiae dissoluenda dedit: see Critical Appendix.

The genitive with verbs of separating etc. is a graecism for the ablative (for the abl. with *dissolvo* see Lucr.3.903). Such a genitive is not found elsewhere with *dissolvo*, but it does occur with *solvo* (e.g. Cic. *Leg.* 2.51, 53, Hor. *C.* 3.17.16), and it is in general a not uncommon construction (see Smith).

For the scansion of the u in *dissoluenda* see 1-2n.

Postgate *Selections* explains *dissoluenda dedit* as *fecit ut dissolverentur*, on the analogy of *do* meaning 'render, make' with the past participle (see *OLD* s.v. 24b). *Do* in this sense with the gerundive seems to be rare: Postgate cites only Plaut. *Cist.* 647f. *hanc ut habeo certum est non amittere; / nam hercle iam ad me adglutinandam totam decretum est dare* and Ov. *F.* 2.367f. *caestibus et iaculis et misso pondere saxi / bracchia per lusus experienda dabant* (where there is no idea of 'giving' present).

41–42 In view of the predominantly rustic tone of the passage so far and the connection with the preceding couplet, it seems likely that the ref. here is to slave-gangs that work the fields in chains (cf. 2.3.79f., Ov. *Tr.* 4.1.5) and that the occasion is the festival of 39-40. Rather similar to this couplet are 2.6.25f., Ov. *ExP.* 1.6.31f. (of Hope) *haec facit ut vivat fossor quoque compede vinctus, / liberaque a ferro crura futura putet.*

dura compede: the singular is mainly poetic in classical times (see *Thes. L. L.* III.2059.18ff.). *Durus* here may mean literally 'hard' or 'cruel'.

43–44 T. now starts to emphasize the festive side of the cult of Bacchus-Osiris: the details mentioned are characteristic of the joyful nature of the god himself, and are also suggestive of Dionysiac festivals and celebrations (e.g. Eur. *Bacc.* 370ff., Sen. *Oed.* 405ff.). There is continual alliteration in these final lines of the section.

In the pent. *aptus* is predicative, and in the hex. *apti* is to be supplied from *aptus.*

sed chorus et cantus: for this side of Osiris' nature cf. Diod. 1.18.4f., and for this characteristic of Bacchus see 37-8n. and cf. Virg. *Aen.* 1.734 *adsit laetitiae Bacchus dator*, Hor. *C.* 2.19.25f. *choreis aptior et iocis / ludoque.* On these details at Dionysiac festivals cf. e.g. Eur. *Bacc.* 378f.

Chorus meaning 'dancing' (often with some idea of singing also present) is mainly poetic: e.g. Naev. *Com.* 75R, Hor. *C.* 1.4.5, 2.12.17, Virg. *Aen.* 7.391, Suet. *Cal.* 37.2.

levis . . . amor: Osiris was a god of fertility (Plut. *Mor.* 365B-C, 371F); for Bacchus in this connection cf. Prop.3.17.5ff. Love was commonly associated with Dionysiac festivals (Eur. *Bacc.* 222f. and Dodds ad loc.).

The primary meaning of *levis* here is 'gay' (in contrast to *tristes*), but the connotations of 'fickle' and 'trifling' may also be present (cf. 1.1.73-4n.).

45–46 **sed varii flores**: for Bacchus' like of flowers cf. Ov. *F.* 5.345, Sen. *Oed.* 413 *te decet cingi comam floribus vernis*. Flowers were also worn by devotees (Dodds on Eur. *Bacc.* 108).

For the uncommon anaphora of *sed* cf. 1.8.25f., Ov. *Met.* 1.595f., 5.17f., Stat. *Silv.* 2.6.10, Tac. *Ann.* 1.10.

et frons redimita corymbis: cf. (of Bacchus) Prop.3.17.29, Ov. *F.* 1.393, 3.767ff., 6.483, Sen. *Oed.* 415f.; (of Osiris) Diod.1.17.4f.; (of devotees) Dodds on Eur. *Bacc.* 81.

Corymbus occurs only at Virg. *Ecl.* 3.39 before here.

fusa sed ad teneros lutea palla pedes: the traditional dress of Bacchus, also worn by worshippers at his festivals: cf. Aristoph. *Ran.* 46 (and Stanford ad loc.), Pollux 4.117, Prop.3.17.32, Sen. *Oed.* 418ff. *qualis iratam metuens novercam / creveras falsos imitatus artus, / crine flaventi simulata virgo, / lutea vestem retinente zona. / inde tam molles placuere cultus / et sinus laxi fluidumque syrma.*

This application of *fundo* to clothes first appears here and is not common (*Thes. L. L.* VI_1 .1568.20ff.).

Teneros suggests the youth (1.4.37-8n.) and effeminacy (Sen. *Oed.* 409) of the god (cf. Ov. *Am.* 3,2.53 *teneroque adsurgite Baccho*).

47-48 **Tyriae vestes**: cf. Ov. *Met.* 3.556 (of things dear to Bacchus) *purpuraque et pictis intextum vestibus aurum*, Sen. *Oed.* 413f. (to Bacchus) *decet . . . / te caput Tyria cohibere mitra*. Purple was a festal colour (Ov. *Tr.* 1.1.5f.). Tyrian was the best purple (1.9.69-70n.).

dulcis tibia cantu: commonly associated with Bacchus and his worship (cf. Eur. *Bacc.* 380, Catull.64.264 *barbaraque horribili stridebat tibia cantu*, Virg. *Aen.* 11.737, Ov. *Met.* 3.533, 4.392, 11.16, Val.Fl. 6.142). For the flute's connection with Egypt see Prop.4.8.39.

The ablative is of part or thing concerned (see Roby 1210), or after *dulcis.*

et levis occultis conscia cista sacris: the sacred objects were kept in a box or basket (originally of wicker-work) and carried in the procession: see Nisbet & Hubbard on Hor. *C.* 1.18.12 and cf. also Sen. *H.O.* 594f. *nos Cadmeis orgia ferre / tecum solitae condita cistis*. For the *sacra* of Bacchus (poppies, pomegranates and phallus) see Nisbet & Hubbard loc.cit.

Levis most obviously refers to the lightness of the basket (see above), but the word also suggests gaiety (cf. *levis . . . amor*, 44).

Conscius applied to a thing in the sense of 'sharing knowledge of' is first found here with a dative and is mainly poetic (see Smith and cf.

also Ov. *Met.* 6.588 *nox conscia sacris*).

49–54 The concentration on the gay and festive side of Bacchus-Osiris in the previous lines has prepared the way for the happy celebrations here, and the actual transition is made by asking the god, standing by metonymy for wine, to be present at them (49-50n.).

These lines act as a bridge from the Osiris-section to the birthday-wishes for Messalla (55-64). At 49f. Bacchus-Osiris (= wine) is invited to join in the worship of Messalla's Genius on his birthday (including an offering of wine), then Bacchus-Osiris is dropped, and further offerings to the Genius are mentioned and the Genius is summoned. Anaphora is again in evidence (*et*), and the sound of these lines (see 1.1.53-4n.) is striking (alliteration of c, t and m, rhyme in -is at 49 (picking up 48), in -ent in 51 and internal rhyme in -o at 50 and 51; cf. also *collo* in 52). In these lines and in the following section there is a combination of elements of the birthday-poem and the ἐπινίκιον (see intro.essay).

49–50 See Critical Appendix.

There is difficulty over the identity of the addressee here. The subject of the verbs can hardly be the Genius, and it is just as unlikely that it is Messalla (one does not invite a person to his own birthday-celebrations in his own house). The addressee in 43-48 is Osiris, and a change here, without specifying the name of the new subject, would be abrupt and obscure in the extreme, and would leave the Osiris-section as a lengthy and irrelevant digression entirely unconnected with the remainder of the elegy. Yet, it is hard to see why Osiris, or indeed any god, should be summoned to a feast worshipping the Genius of Messalla (esp. by a religious conservative like T.). Dissen comments: '*Nam Genius illustris viri est illustris deus, cuius sacris celebrandis provincialis deus recte advocari potuit*'. As we find Egyptian gods arrayed against Roman gods elsewhere in Augustan poetry (Virg. *Aen.* 8.698ff., Prop. 3.11.41), a tone of condescension towards a foreign and conquered deity would not be unreasonable, but in 1.7 such a tone is hardly in keeping with the favourable attitude elsewhere to Osiris, who is actually identified with Bacchus (39-40n.). Dissen cites no parallel for the invitation of even a *provincialis deus* to birthday-celebrations, and, in any case, it would hardly be politic to have a god worshipping the Genius of Messalla (rather than that of Augustus). Némethy comments: '*invitat Osirim (i.e. Bacchum), laetitiae datorem, ad natalem Messallae laete celebrandum, ut Dido in convivio Verg. Aen.* 1.734 *adsit laetitiae Bacchus dator*'. The quote from Virgil is hardly appropriate here, and again one wonders what Bacchus could have to do with the worship of Messalla's Genius. Other commentators are silent, as if there were no problem.

Since Osiris as a god is clearly inappropriate here, it seems likely that Bacchus-Osiris stands for wine by metonymy (see 1.2.3-4n.). T. here glides into metonymy: at 27-36 and 43-8 Osiris is deity, but at 37-42 there is a slight blurring which helps the change at 49. In 37 *ille liquor* most obviously picks up *iucundos . . . sapores* in 35, although it might mean 'he, as liquor', while at 39-42 *Bacchus* is most probably the deity, in view of the common identification of Bacchus with Osiris (39-40n.) and the way in which T. moves on in 43-8 to Osiris the god, but it is possible that *Bacchus* stands for wine.

The couplet, then, addresses wine, asking wine to be present, to honour the Genius by means of games and dances (which wine inspires) and to drench the temples of the Genius. In other words, at the birthday-celebrations T. wishes there to be wine to stimulate the dances and games in honour of the god and to soak the Genius' temples, and, in order to effect transition (albeit somewhat contrived) from Bacchus-Osiris, he expresses this wish by a series of imperatives addressed to wine.

For wine inspiring games, dances and festivity see 37-8n. and cf. Prop.3.10.21ff., Hor. *C.* 3.21.2. With regard to the personification cf. 37f., Otto *Sprichwörter* s.v. *vinum* and (addressed to an amphora) Hor. *C.* 3.21. In particular, for *huc ades* cf. Hor. *C.* 3.21.8 *descende*; for *concelebra* cf. 2.1.29, Prop.3.17.37f. *crater antistitis auro / libatum* (*libabit* Foster) *fundens in tua sacra merum* (perhaps no stranger than grass praying at 26); for the pleonasm in *funde mero* cf. Lucan 3.658 *eiectat saniem . . . sanguis*, and see Housman *CQ* XXVII (1933), 4, on Lucan 1.102, Manil.1.539, *addenda* to Manil.vol.V.p.129.

huc ades et centum ludis Geniumque choreis / concelebra: the Genius, connected with *genitus, gignere* (Aug. *C.D.* 7.13), in origin probably represented the male's virile powers, which meant the continuation of the family (Rose *CQ* XVII (1923), 57ff.). In classical times the Genius was something like a guardian spirit, and came into being with each man and attended him throughout his life (Apul. *Deo Soc.* 15, Censorin.3 *genius est deus cuius in tutela ut quisque natus est vivit*). A person's Genius was worshipped esp. on his birthday, generally as described here. The female counterpart was called Juno (3.6.48, 4.6.1, 4.13.15, Petron. *S.* 25, Sen. *Epist.* 110.1, Plin. *N.H.* 2.16). The Genius was one of the more homely gods which T. seems to like so much and was associated with the Lares (Censorin.3).

For birthday games cf. Ov. *ExP.* 4.9.115f., and for dances on the birthday cf. Prop.3.10.23.

The word *centum* is used, as often, of an indefinitely large number (see *Thes.L.L.* III.827.77ff).

On the scansion of *choreis* see 1.3.59-60n.

For the (uncommon) attachment of *-que* to the word preceding the one to which it would usually be joined cf. 1.1.51, 1.3.56, Hor. *C.* 1.30.5f. *solutis / Gratiae zonis properentque Nymphae*, 2.19.28 *pacis eras mediusque belli*, 32 *ore pedes tetigitque crura*, 3.4.11 *ludo fatigatumque somno, Carm.Saec.* 22 *ut cantus referatque ludos.*

Concelebro is first used here of worshipping a god. The usage is very rare, and the only other exx. cited by *Thes.L.L.* are Sil.It.8.221 (of the goddess Anna, cf. 210), Auson.317.9, Paulin.Nol. *Carm.* 27. 138, Arnob. *Nat.* 5.39, Ambros. *Abr.* 1.5.38. The prefix seems to express the idea of joining in worship. For the use of the simple *celebro* in this connection cf. e.g. 63, Virg. *Aen.* 8.76, Ov. *F.* 6.775.

et multo tempora funde mero: for the offering of wine to the Genius cf. 2.2.8, 4.6.14, Hor. *Epist.* 2.1.144. *Fundo* meaning 'drench with' is first found here and is not common (cf. 3.2.20, Mart.3.82.26).

51–52 The pronoun most obviously picks up *Geniumque* in 49, and the offerings mentioned in the couplet are commonly made to the Genius. It is unclear whether the precise ref. in *illius* is to a statuette of the Genius or to the god himself, and the distinction is often blurred.

illius et nitido stillent unguenta capillo: cf. 2.2.7, and see intro.essay (suggested imitation of Callimachus).

For the scansion of *illius* see 1.8.65-6n.

et capite et collo mollia serta gerat: cf. 2.2.6, Hor. *Epist.* 2.1.144 [*piabant*] *floribus et vino Genium memorem brevis aevi.*

Mollia refers to the soft flowers that compose the garlands (cf. Virg. *G.* 4.137 *ille comam mollis iam tondebat hyacinthi*). For the garland worn around the neck cf. Lucr.5.1399, Cic. *Verr.* 2.5.27, Hor. *S.* 2.3. 256, Ov. *F.* 2.739, Plut. *Mor.* 647E, Athen.674C.

53–54 sic venias, hodierne: see Critical Appendix.

Again there is difficulty over the addressee here. Most commentators take *hodierne* as adjective for adverb (*hodie*) attracted to the vocative. With such an interpretation the address can hardly be to the Genius (the progression from *illius* in 51 is highly improbable), but must be to Osiris. Yet *venias* is then repetitive (cf. *ades* in 49), and the presence of Osiris here is pointless (if Osiris = wine, the offerings are meaningless; if Osiris is a god, one may object to offerings made to him, as this is supposed to be a feast worshipping the Genius, and one may again ask what such a feast has to do with Osiris as god). Lines 63-4 suggest that here the Genius (= Natalis) is addressed, and the offerings should obviously be made to him.

Dissen records Voss' interpretation of *hodierne* as *tutelarem deum hodierni diei* (although Dissen disagrees), and more recently Lee prints *sic venias, hodierne*: and translates 'So come you, hodiernal:'. To take *hodierne* as an address to Natalis seems to me the most likely solution. It does not seem unreasonable that *hodierne*, 'you of today', could be an alternative for Natalis, 'you of the birthday' (for 'today' used of the birthday cf. 4.6.3 *hodie*, Prop.3.10.7 *hodierna luce*). Although there seems to be no parallel for *hodiernus* with ref. to Natalis, such an interpretation is scarcely more strange than taking *hodierne* to mean *hodie* (*Thes.L.L.* cites no parallel for such a usage, and there is no other ex. in T. of such an attraction to the vocative), and it at least means that the couplet now makes sense.

For the request to the Genius to attend cf. 2.5.5ff., and on the (mainly poetic) form of the command see 1.2.9-10n.

tibi dem turis honores: for the offering cf. 2.2.3, 4.5.9, Ov. *Tr.* 3.13.16, 23, Mart.10.24.5. For someone other than the person whose birthday it is making the offering cf. 4.5.9, Ov. *Tr.* 5.5.11f.

liba et Mopsopio dulcia melle feram: for the offering cf. 2.2.8, Ov. *Tr.* 3.13.17, Mart.10.24.4. *Liba* were sacrificial cakes (on the ingredients see Cato *Agr. Cult.* 75, Serv. ad *Aen.* 7.109).

The learned epithet *Mopsopius* means 'Attic', as Mopsopus was a legendary old king of Athens (Strabo 397, 443, Pfeiffer on Call.fr.709). The adjective is first found here in Latin and was possibly taken from Callimachus (see intro.essay). Attic honey was renowned for its quality (Plin. *N.H.* 11.32 *ibi optumus semper ubi optimorum doliolis florum conditur. fit Atticae regionis hoc et Siculae Hymetto et Hybla, apricis locis*).

55–64 With *at tibi* (55) in contrast to *tibi* (53), T. turns naturally from the Genius of Messalla to Messalla himself. It is strange that Messalla is not mentioned by name here, but it immediately becomes clear in the couplet whom T. is addressing, so that there is no real chance of ambiguity or obscurity. This section is also linked to the previous one by verbal reminiscences (*celebrande* 63, cf. *concelebra* 50; *veni* 64, cf. *venias* 53).

Birthday-wishes for Messalla. In the first couplet T. wishes that his patron's children may prove as illustrious as their father's deeds have made him, in the next three he gives an example of Messalla's deeds (his repair of part of the *via Latina*), expressing the hope that Messalla will receive due praise for this work, and in the final couplet he wishes his patron many happy returns of the day. With a neat ring-structure T. closes the elegy as it began (Messalla's glory, the ref. to his triumph (57-8n.) and his birthday).

55–56 at tibi succrescat proles: on *proles* see 1.4.7-8n.

For *succresco* meaning 'grow up to succeed' cf. Cic. *De Or.* 3.230 *non enim ille mediocris orator vestrae quasi succrescit aetati*, Livy 10.13.7.

Messalla's children were M. Valerius Messalla Messalinus (cf. 2.5.115), M. Aurelius Cotta Maximus (see Mayor on Juv.7.95) and Valeria Messalina (Forcellini *Onomasticon* s.v. Valerius = vol.2. p.750). Messalinus had been born by the time of the present poem, but the birth-dates of the other two children are not certain, so that T. may be wishing that Messalla will have more children (cf. 2.2.21f.).

quae facta parentis augeat: for sons worthy of their father (*augeat* in emphatic position, picked up by *veneranda*) cf. Pind. *Pyth.* 10.22ff.,

Cic. *Tusc.* 1.111, Hor. *Ars Poet.*24.

There are two possible meanings for *facta parentis / augeat.* Firstly 'add (their own deeds) to the deeds of their father': for *augeo* used of adding to the number of things belonging to someone else cf. esp. Prop.3.7.32 *fortunae miseras auximus arte vias*, Ov. *F.* 1.613 *augeat imperium nostri ducis, augeat annos*, and see in general *Thes. L. L.* II. 1345.71ff. Postgate *Selections* suggests another interpretation of *augeat*: '"enhance", the greatness of the sons' achievements redounds upon the father's' (comparing Sil.It.3.708 *Sidonios augebis avos*). Cf. also Cic. *Balb.* 31, *Pis.* 32, *Dom.* 19, Sil.It.3.595 (*nomen*), and see *OLD* s.v.5.

On the possibility of imitation here see intro. essay.

senem: (emphatic by position) i.e. may Messalla have a long life (cf.63f.).

57–58 monumenta viae: *monumentum* is used of any memorial, esp. of public works. For its application to a road cf. Cic. *Mil.* 17, 37, Quint. *Inst.* 5.10.41. *Viae* is a genitive of definition.

For a full discussion of the ref. here see McCracken *AJPh* LIII (1932), 344ff. Augustus himself rebuilt the *via Flaminia* as far as Ariminum, and assigned the rest of the highways to generals who had celebrated triumphs, the cost to be covered by their prize-money (Suet. *Aug.* 30, Cass.Dio 53.22, *Mon.Anc.* c.20). Triumphing generals often spent their share of the prize-money on public works (e.g. Suet. *Iul.*26), and *opibus . . . tuis* (59) shows that Messalla did this, thus linking up this section with the Aquitanian triumph. Messalla repaired a section of the *via Latina*, at least from Rome to Tusculum and the Alban Hills (for its route see Strabo 237). Other parts of the same road were repaired by C. Calvisius Sabinus (*CIL* x. 6895) and L. Arruntius (*CIL* x. 5055).

quem . . . / . . . detinet: keeps from Rome, most probably on business in the country. Lee's suggestion (p. 109) that there is here a ref. to the *Feriae Latinae* on the Alban Mount is possible, but they were only held annually.

Tuscula: the adjective (poetic for *Tusculanus*) first appears here.

candidaque . . . Alba: Alba is not the town, which was destroyed much earlier and never rebuilt (Livy 1.29). Possibly the ref. is to the region (cf. Porph. ad Hor. *Epist.* 1.4.2) or the Mons Albanus (cf. Lucan 1.198 *et residens celsa Latialis Iuppiter Alba*, 3.87).

Candida is a play on Alba. If there is any particular significance in the word, it probably does not refer to the native rock of the region: there seems to be no evidence for limestone deposits there, and the area was most famous for peperino, a greyish-brown tufa (Tac. *Ann.* 15. 43, Plin. *N.H.* 36.167). There may be a ref. to white villas (cf. Hor. *Epod.* 1.29 *superni villa candens Tusculi*), which were found in the region (Hor.loc.cit., Strabo 239, Cic. *Att.* 4.11.1) and would be visible from Rome (cf. Strabo 238 ἐν ὄψει δ' εἰσὶ τοῖς ἐν Ῥώμῃ Τίβουρά τε καὶ Πραίνεστος καὶ Τοῦσκλον). For *candidus* so used cf. Prop. 3.16.3 and Camps ad loc.

The words in the pentameter are arranged on the pattern of the 'golden' line (25-6n.)

59–60 T. here seems to be referring to two types of road (*hic* . . . / . . . *hic*), the *via glarea strata* and the *via silice strata* (Ulp. *Dig.* 43. 11.2). For the former see Livy 41.27.5, for the latter see Stat. *Silv.* 4.3 and Vitruvius 7.1 (it differs from the pavement only in the top layer, which was blocks of stone or lava). It would appear that Messalla's section of the *via Latina* was partly gravel and partly *silex* (cf. Livy 41.27.5): materials varied with local conditions, and volcanic rock would be abundant in the region of Alba.

sternitur: the technical word for 'laying' a road (e.g. Livy 8.15.8, 10.23.12 *semitamque saxo quadrato . . . straverunt*, 41.27.5).

silex: the word is applied to various types of volcanic rock, esp. basalt (see Monro on Lucr.1.571, Bailey on Lucr.6.683, Plin. *N.H.* 36.174).

61–62 te canet agricola, a magna cum venerit urbe: see Critical Appendix.

For the (rare) elision cf. esp. 1.2.59, 2.4.21, and see Platnauer 82f.

For *magna* . . . *urbe* cf. 2.5.56. Here the phrase seems to reflect the rustic naiveté of the farmer in the 'big city'.

inoffensum rettuleritque pedem: *inoffensus* occurs only at Varro *Men.* 288 before here and is not common in the classical period. Here the word means 'without stumbling': cf. Ov. *Am.* 1.6.8 *inoffensos dirigit ille pedes, Tr.* 3.4.33.

As there was no street-lighting (1.9.41-2n.), the farmer would be all the more likely to stumble in the dark (hence the emphasis on *serus*). On the difficulties of travelling on roads in a worse condition than Messalla's see e.g. Stat. *Silv.* 4.3.27ff.

63–64 *Natalis* refers to the Genius (2.2.1, 5, 21, 4.5.9, 19).

T. makes two wishes: that Messalla may live to celebrate many more birthdays (cf. Ov. *Tr.* 5.5.23f. *vivat . . . / consumatque annos, sed diuturna, suos*, Mart.4.1.3ff., 10.24.6ff.) and that each birthday may be more joyous and fortunate than the last (cf. Mart.4.1.4 *semper et hoc voltu vel meliore nite*).

For this use of *candidus* see 1.3.93-4n. and cf. Ov. *Tr.* 5.5.14. On the emphatic positioning and repetition of *candidior* see 1.1.77-8n.

8

Wimmel *Der frühe Tibull* 49ff.

T. has discovered that some sort of an affair is going on between Marathus and a young girl called Pholoe. The boy is completely infatuated, but is having little success, and is reduced to tears by the girl's behaviour. Pholoe demands presents and torments him by refusing to let him go to see her and breaking her promise to go to see him. Apparently her excuse for these actions is that she is guarded (see 35f., 55; it is not entirely clear whether Marathus or Pholoe is supposed to be under guard, but at 75f. T. puts Marathus in the position of an *exclusus amator*, and, although the locked door mentioned there could be merely a general ex. of *fastus*, almost all points at 71ff. correspond with the boy's present situation (see notes ad loc.), so that the guard is probably on Pholoe). Marathus does not think much of this excuse. At this juncture comes T.'s poem, which advises the girl to mend her ways, or she will be punished for her arrogance (the form of the poem suggests that T. ranges the pair before him and addresses each in turn; on this dramatic situation cf. also 35-6n., 67-78n., 67-68n.). These background-circumstances are not made clear at once, but are revealed gradually (cf. Wimmel). For this process see intro.essay to 1.4.

1-26	T.'s knowledge of the affair:	(to Marathus)	1-8	establish existence of affair.
			9-16	define the lover's part.
			17-26	decide cause of infatuation.
27-66	Advice to girl:	(to Pholoe)	27-28	transition.
			29-48	attack on her venality.
			49-66	attack on her cruelty.
67-78	Threats for girl:	(to Marathus)	67-68	transition: T.'s advice ignored.
		(to Pholoe)	69-78	threats of punishment and an ex. of punishment for same crime.

The progression of thought is smooth enough, as T. reveals that he knows about the affair, advises the girl on how to behave, and, when she seems to be unmoved by his advice, threatens her with retribution. All his remarks are addressed to one or other of the pair before him.

Unity is also ensured by thematic cross-references: *furtivus amor* in the first section (1f., 7) recurs in the second (35ff., 55ff.); the uselessness of Marathus' attention to his appearance in the first section (9ff.) is paralleled in the second by the uselessness of the old woman's attention to her appearance (41ff.); the hints of nemesis in the second section (39-40n.) are picked up in the third (69ff., 77-8n.); Pholoe's maltreatment of Marathus in the second section corresponds with his maltreatment of his former lovers in the third (71ff. and notes). Verbal reminiscences also bind together the poem: see notes on 71-8 and cf. also (furtiveness) *lenis* (2, 57), *sonus* / *sonare* (2, (22), 58, 66), *dissimulo* (7, 44), *furtim* / *furtivus* (35, 57); (unhappiness) *lacrima* / *lacrimare* (54, 67, 73), *miser* (23, 53, 61, 71); (the gods, generally in connection with the above) *deus* (3, 7, 56, 72), *Venus* (5, 28, 35, cf. 57).

In 1.8 we see again T. in his pose as instructor in love (see intro. essays to 1.4 and 1.6). From the start (1-26n.) T. establishes himself in this rôle, and throughout the poem he exhibits appropriate knowledge and experience not only in the amatory sphere, by his observations and advice, but also in other fields, by his informed refs. to magic (17ff.), beauty-treatment (43ff.) and divine nature (69f.).

1.8 is a variation on the poem addressed to a friend in love: cf. *A.P.* 5.130 (Maecius), 12.49 (Meleager), 71 (Callimachus), 72 (Meleager), Catull.6, 55, Prop.1.5, 1.9, 2.34, Hor. *C.* 1.27. Common features of the genre occurring here are the friend infatuated, but unhappy in his love, and the poet recognizing the signs and seeing through concealment (1-2n.). In the present elegy the influence of Propertius 1.9 is evident. Propertius shows similar amusement at his friend's plight, which is also viewed as an example of nemesis, and he too assumes fully the rôle of *praeceptor amandi*. In addition, there are verbal and thematic reminiscences of 1.9 (5-6n., 7-8n., 9-10n.).

There are, however, definite differences between T. and Prop. The circumstances vary to a significant extent and are revealed far more slowly in 1.8. So Prop.'s mirth is seen at once to be prompted by the fact that his friend Ponticus used to laugh at lovers but is now in love himself, whereas T. eventually tells us that his amusement (which is all-pervasive and expressed with more irony) is due to Marathus being punished for his cruelty to his lovers by suffering similar cruelty at the hands of Pholoe. The actual exx. of retribution differ, and the theme receives a more extensive and complex treatment in T. (see below). T.'s amatory precepts are addressed both to a girl and to a *puer delicatus* (an original combination in this connection).

There are three further points which distinguish the present poem from Prop.1.9 and also represent original contributions to the whole genre: T. gives his usual long, detailed treatment; he addresses the girl, and, more important, reserves most of his attention and advice for her;

the friend here is more than just a friend – he is a boy with whom T. himself is supposed to be involved.

The influence of the epigram is also evident in 1.8. The genre of the poem may be traced back to epigram (see above). The *puer delicatus* is a common figure in epigram, where the idea of the boy in love with a girl first occurs (*A.P.* 12.109 (Meleager), T.1.9.39ff., cf. Prop.1.20; see also Gow on Theoc. *Id.* 7.118 for the beloved becoming a lover). However, the boy's lack of success and suffering are entirely new details, and T. is the first to exploit the situation at length. It is made clear at the end of the poem that the girl's maltreatment of Marathus is supposed to be his punishment for his former cruelty to his own lovers. So the whole poem can be viewed as an amplification of the common epigrammatic theme of nemesis, in particular the example of the scorner scorned. Again there is elaboration in the length of the treatment, and novelty in the handling of the theme (71-2n). So too T.'s description at 39ff. of the unhappy old age of the woman who has money but who has grown ugly and is scorned by men is strongly suggestive of another theme frequent in epigram, the punishment of the cruel mistress (39-40n.), and the hint that this may be Pholoe's punishment, if she does not stop being cruel to Marathus, is confirmed at the end of the elegy (77-8n.). This treatment of the punishment of the cruel mistress shows more subtle allusiveness than is found anywhere in epigram. It also gives a novel twist to the first ex. of nemesis. Normally we find only the scorner scorned, but T. gives the conventional situation added complexity by implying that Pholoe, the scorner of the scorner scorned (Marathus), will herself be scorned in turn. For similar complexity see 1.2.87-96n., *A.P.* 5.300 (Paulus Silentiarius).

The subtlety and cleverness of 1.8 have been generally overlooked or misunderstood. Sober, serious-minded scholars have been perplexed by the apparent absence of any concern here at Marathus' attachment to another and have missed the point of the elegy. In fact, the attitude in the poem seems to be that this attachment is a harmless diversion (cf. 1.9, where there is similar unconcern at the boyfriend's liaison with a girl (41ff.), but anger is shown at his affair with another man), and, more important, that it has a distinctly humorous side (a *puer delicatus* of all people infatuated, unsuccessful and badly treated!). So there is gentle banter, irony and amusement over the boy's predicament and his exaggerated reaction to it. The humour reaches its climax in the final section, in which T. states that Marathus' present suffering is his punishment for the very similar suffering that he caused his own lovers (that T. would be included among Marathus' wronged lovers (71-2n.) gives the particular grounds for amusement), and then goes on to hint that unless Pholoe stops maltreating the boy she herself will be punished by being similarly maltreated. T. is also deftly exploiting the technical literary possibilities of the rather bizarre circumstances. A deliberately slow revelation of these circumstances teases the reader (1-26n.) and makes the most of the element of surprise. His application of the idea of nemesis to the situation produces a twist to that theme that is both clever and entertaining (see above). So too T. is savouring the somewhat complex inversions and contradictions of the standard rôles of three elegiac figures: the mistress is sought not by the poet but by the *puer delicatus*, and is addressed by the poet not on his own but on the boy's behalf; the boyfriend is not the usual uninvolved and even amused character but is involved and unhappy, and he is not up to his normal tricks of tormenting his lover and asking for presents, but is himself being tormented and asked for presents; the poet, instead of being earnest and miserable, is detached and quite gleeful, and, instead of arguing with and threatening the mistress on his own behalf, is doing so on the boy's behalf. T. plays his part in all this with panache, making observations and giving advice with a deliciously mock-solemn tone, as a rather superior, if not unsympathetic, *praeceptor*. Amused and amusing, this is a witty and accomplished elegy.

–26 The section acts as a general introduction: 1-8 state that T. has discovered the existence of an affair, despite attempts at concealment; 9-16 show further knowledge: the addressee is infatuated, but unsuccessful, and the addressee's beloved is naturally good-looking; 17-26 decide the cause of the infatuation (sexual attraction). The circumstances are cleverly revealed, as T. exploits the infrequency of paederasty in elegy at this stage and the extreme rarity of the love of a *puer delicatus* for a girl (see intro. essay). At 1f. (and again at 7f.) he states that a furtive affair is in progress, but does not make clear the sex of the addressee. The reader most naturally assumes that a woman is addressed, and the attention to appearance at 9ff. tends to strengthen this assumption (esp. the details at 9-11). So at 15 it comes as an amusing surprise to learn that the addressee's beloved is female. In retrospect 9ff. suggest that the person addressed is a *puer delicatus*. Hence T.'s ironic suggestion at 17ff. (a *puer delicatus* so infatuated with a girl! – is he bewitched?), finally corrected at 23ff.

In this opening section T.'s sly humour is already evident, and the bantering tone is helped by the extensive use of anaphora, balance and contrast, and by the mock-seriousness of T.'s remarks in his rôle as *praeceptor* (the dissection into three groups of lines dealing with various aspects of the affair fits in with this pose).

–2 For nods see 1.2.21-2n. For whispered words cf. Hes. *Theog.* 203ff., Theoc. *Id.* 2.141, 27.68, Prop. 1.11.13, Hor. *C.* 1.9.19.

These covert actions, intended to conceal the affair, are common phenomena, and so indicate to the keen observer that an affair is in progress. For the poet seeing through concealment and recognizing signs cf. *A.P.* 5.130 (Maecius), 12.71 (Callimachus), Catull.6, 55, and see intro. essay.

celari: *celare* with a double accusative (of thing concealed and of person from whom it is concealed) is common, and in the passive the person naturally becomes nominative. However, the thing concealed, when expressed as an indirect question, is rare with an accusative of person (cf. Cic. *Off.* 3.52, Val.Max.5.9.4).

ferant: 'mean' (cf. Ov. *Am.* 3.5.32, Sen. *Oct.* 711 *quid pallor iste, quid ferant lacrimae, doce*).

miti . . . sono: rather ambiguous. *Mitis* here may mean 'mild, gentle' (Cic. *Sen.* 28, Tac. *Ann.* 2.34, 4.47) or 'compliant' in the amatory sense (1.4.53-6n.). *Sonus* may refer to the sound of the *lenia verba*, or to their tone and character (Cic. *Opt.Gen.* 1.1, *Brut.* 26.100), or the word may mean 'utterance' (1.6.44, Sen. *Troad.* 190).

3–4 **nec mihi sunt sortes nec conscia fibra deorum**: for lot see 1.3. 11-12n. *Extispicium* consisted of an examination of the entrails of sacrificed animals, with particular attention to their markings, size, colour and shape (Aesch. *P.V.* 493ff., Cic. *Div.* 2.28ff., Halliday *Greek Divination* (Chicago, 1967), 187ff.).

Conscia . . . deorum is an aptly mysterious phrase. The meaning seems to be 'acquainted with the will of the gods', with the genitive, as elsewhere, indicating the object of knowledge (*Thes.L.L.* IV.370.32ff.). For *deorum* = *deorum voluntatis* cf. Prop.4.1.104 *aut sibi commissos fibra locuta deos*, and for the idea cf. 2.1.26, Prop.loc.cit., Ov. *Met.* 15.794f.

Various meanings for *fibra* are possible here. The word is often used by poets for *exta* or *iecur*. As a technical term it is applied to a liver's division (Celsus 4.1.5), extremity (Serv. ad *G.* 1.120, *Aen.* 10.176, Varro *L.L.* 5.79), filament (Serv. ad *G.* 1.120) and protuberance (Serv. ad *Aen.* 6.600). In general see Thulin *Die etrusk. Disciplin*.II.42-4, Pease on Cic. *Div.* 1.16.

praecinit eventus nec mihi cantus avis: there were five kinds of augury: *ex caelo, ex avibus, ex tripudiis, ex quadrupedibus, ex diris* (Festus s.v. *quinque genera*). *Aves* were divided into two classes, *alites*, who gave auguries by flight, and *oscines*, whose voice was observed. Among *oscines* were the owl, the raven and the crow. The omen varied according to their note and the place from which they sang (Cic. *Div.* 1.120, Festus s.v. *oscines*). For *praecinit* 'foretell' cf. Cic. *Har.Resp.* 20, T.2.5.74.

5–6 There is humour here, since the interpretation of such nods and whispers hardly necessitates the skill of prophecy, simply some experience in love. However, T. elevates his pose as instructor by representing himself not as an interpreter of divine will but in touch with Venus herself (*ipsa Venus* in emphatic position).

This contrast between prophecy and erotic experience was inspired by Prop.1.9.5ff. *non me Chaoniae vincant in amore columbae / dicere, quos iuvenes quaeque puella domet. / me dolor et lacrimae merito fecere peritum.* T. adapts and expands upon his model: he makes a contrast between agents of the gods and contact with the goddess herself, gives broader exx. of divination and expresses the pain of love in emphatic terms (the intensifying *per*-, litotes, addition of *multis* and position of *verberibus*) and by means of an image which has additional connotations. Cf. also Prop.1.10.19f., 2.21.3, 3.8.17, Ov.*A.A.* 1.25ff., *Tr.* 1.9.49ff., Petron. *S.*126.3.

T.'s education came about while he was the slave of Venus, bound and beaten by her, i.e. while he was in love and suffering its hardships (Prop.'s *dolor et lacrimae*). For *servitium amoris* see 1.5.5-6n. (servile punishment is a Tibullan innovation). The idea of the lover as the slave of Venus (1.2.97-8n.) is here given novelty by the full treatment and the combination with the figure of Venus as teacher (1.2.19-20n.). The bonds signify love: a man in love is often described as 'bound' (e.g. 1.9.79), esp. by Venus or Amor (*A.P.* 12.98.1 (Posidippus), Plaut. *Trin.*658, Prop.3.24.14, Ov. *Rem.* 529). The floggings signify the pain and sufferings of love: the lover is frequently beaten (1.9. 21-2n.; by Venus at Hor. *C.* 3.26.11, Mart.6.21.9f.). For the proverb of πάθει μάθος and its application to love see 1.6.51-2n.

The image of binding here is esp. effective because of the ancient practice of tying a person up before a beating (Plaut. *Aul.* 347, *Poen.* 146, Cic. *Verr.* 2.5.161, 163), but there is difficulty over the 'magic' knot.

None of the common uses of knots in magic seems appropriate here (e.g. in connection with amulets, *devinctiones* or κατάδεσμοι, the 'knot of Hercules': see Pauly s.v. *nodus*). It has been suggested that T. is here attributing the knot used in love-magic to Venus, who is occasionally found with magic powers (e.g. Pind. *Pyth.* 4.213ff.), but the idea of Venus as a witch seems irrelevant and inappropriate here. It has also been suggested that the point to *magico* is that Venus' bonds, like magic knots, are difficult to loose, and that *magicus* here means 'indissoluble' (see e.g. Smith), but there is no parallel for such a use of *magicus*.

In an image it seems natural to expect figurative usage, and so the phrase may well mean little more than that T. is 'bewitched' by love. So the effects on the lover of a woman's lips and breasts (Paulus Silentiarius *A.P.* 5.270), voice (Philodemus *A.P.* 5.121), character (Eur. *Andr.* 207f., Menand.646K) and beauty (Afran.381R) are described as 'magic'. T. elsewhere applies terms from magic to love (1.5. 43-4n., 1.5.47-8n., 1.8.25), and for such a use of *magicus* cf. Philodemus *A.P.* 5.121.1ff. μικκὴ καὶ μελανεῦσα Φιλαίνιον, ἀλλὰ σελίνων /

οὐλοτέρη, καὶ μυοῦ χρῶτα τερεινοτέρη / καὶ κεστοῦ φωνεῦσα μαγώτερα.

7–8 deus crudelius urit, / quos videt invitos succubuisse sibi: *deus* may refer to Amor, or to Venus, as she is mentioned in the previous couplet (for *deus* used of a goddess see 1.2.87-8n.).

As Marathus has submitted and is in love (cf. *placet*, 15, *amor*, 52, *amantem*, 61), the perfect infinitive has its full force here, i.e. 'those that he/she sees have submitted to him/her against their will'. The attempt at concealment would be taken as a sign of unwillingness (cf Ov. *Am.* 1.2.17f.).

T. shows his experience by aptly quoting an old amatory precept: cf. Eur. *Hipp.* 5f., 443ff., fr.340, 665N, Catull.61.198ff., Ov. *Am.* 1.2. 17f., and esp. Prop.1.9.33f., which probably inspired this couplet (see intro. essay) *quare, si pudor est, quam primum errata fatere: / dicere quo pereas saepe in amore levat*. Hence the frequent advice that it is best to yield to Love (1.6.29-30n.).

The (mock-) solemnity seems reinforced by the alliteration in the couplet.

9–10 The pains taken by the lover over his appearance show his eagerness to attract the girl (2.3.77f., Prop.2.4.5f., Paulus Silentiarius *A.P.* 5.228) and his effeminacy (1.9.15-16n.). The contrast between three couplets on the lover's comprehensive, but unavailing, efforts (literally from head to toe) and merely one couplet on the girl's success despite her lack of attention (15-16) suggests amusement.

For hair-care see 1.6.39-40n., 1.9.67-8n. Excessive attention to the hair was considered unmanly, and the frequent alterations (emphatic *saepeque*) of the arrangement of the hair here are particularly effeminate and fastidious (Call. *Hym.* 5.22, of the vain Aphrodite, πολλάκι τὰν αὐτὰν δὶς μετέθηκε κόμαν, Ov. *A.A.* 1.306 *quid totiens positas fingis inepta comas*?).

quid tibi nunc molles prodest coluisse capillos: probably imitates Prop.1.9.9 (*quid tibi nunc misero prodest grave dicere carmen*), in view of the influence of that poem in these opening lines.

Nunc (cf. *iam*, 13) suggests mirth at the failure of the lover's normally successful methods of attracting (men) in the present situation.

Mollis is also applied to flowing hair at Virg. *Aen.* 2.683, Ov. *ExP.* 3.3.17 (cf. Hor. *Ars Poet.* 33 and Brink ad loc.). Here, as Marathus was a *puer capillatus* and his hair has not yet been cut, the primary meaning of *mollis* is 'soft to the touch', although the connotation of 'effeminate' is also present.

11–12 quid fuco splendente genas ornare: cosmetics were commonly used by women in Greece and Rome (e.g. Ussher on Aristoph. *Eccl.* 878, Ov. *Med. Fac.*) and by effeminate men (Petron. *S.* 23, 126, Athen.542D).

Fucus (φῦκος) was primarily a water (esp. sea) plant from which red or purple dye was made (Plin. *N.H.* 13.136, 26.103, Pauly s.v. *fucus*), and here probably refers to rouge. For *splendente* cf. *splendor* of *coccum* at Plin. *N.H.* 33.121, and on the use of rouge by men see Athen.loc.cit.

quid ungues / artificis docta subsecuisse manu: manicure was usually done by a barber (Plaut. *Aul.*312, Mart.3.74.3, Val.Max.3.2.15), but here apparently the foppish lover does this himself – and with skill (note the juxtaposition *artificis docta*). Failure to take care of the nails was regarded as slovenly (Hor. *Epist.* 1.1.104, Ov. *A.A.* 1.519), but here the lover's attention is another ex. of his womanly fastidiousness and studied elegance (cf. Paulus Silentiarius *A.P.* 5.228, Theophr. *Char.* 26.4 Ussher).

Subseco is not common and is only found at Varro *R.R.* 1.23.2, 1.49.1, 1.50.1 before here (of mowing). For its use in this connection cf. Ov. *F.* 6.230 *non ungues ferro subsecuisse licet.*

13–14 frustra iam vestes, frustra mutantur amictus: *vestes* may refer to clothes in general and *amictus* to styles of dressing (*OLD* s.v.3; for an ex. of a dandified style see 1.6.39-40n.). Alternatively, *vestes* may refer to the inner, *amictus* to the outer garments (Virg. *Aen.* 5.421, Sen. *Ben.* 7.9.5). The reason for the change of clothes may be that they have become dirty or disarrayed (cf. Mart.2.41.10, 3.63.10, Macrob. *S.* 3.13.5), or the lover may be trying various sets of extravagant clothes in his attempts to attract the girl (cf. Paulus Silentiarius *A.P.* 5.228). Over-attention to dress was considered effeminate (Macrob. *S.* 3.13.4, Aul.Gell.1.5, and see 1.6.39-40n.): for the correct attitude see Ov. *A.A.* 1.514 *sit bene conveniens et sine labe toga.*

ansaque compressos colligat arta pedes: *ansa* is first used here of the loop on a sandal (cf. Plin. *N.H.* 35.85).

Too large a shoe was regarded as inelegant (Aristoph. *Eq.* 321, Theophr. *Char.* 4.1 Ussher, Hor. *S.* 1.3.31f., Ov. *A.A.* 1.516), but the difficulties of too small a shoe were also noted (Hor. *Epist.* 1.10.42f.). The lover here (note the emphasis in *arta* and the repeated prefix) seems to be trying deliberately to make his feet appear small (cf. Lucian *Amores* 41), since large feet were considered unattractive (Hor. *S.* 1.2.93, Ov. *Am.* 3.3.7 *pes erat exiguus – pedis est artissima forma*, *A.A.* 1.622). Excessive attention to footwear was foppish (Quint. 11.3.137).

15–16 The girl's lack of adornment directly picks up the lover's attentions at 9-11 (note also *inculto*, 15, in contrast to *coluisse*, 9, and *arte*, 16, in contrast to *artificis*, 12). The couplet is a humorous application of the idea that natural beauty is superior to the artificial (see Smith and cf. also Paulus Silentiarius *A.P.* 5.270.1f., Philostr. *Ep.* 27).

placet: for the amatory use of the verb see 1.4.11-12n.

venerit: the verb may be a synonym for *esse* (1.2.75-6n.) or may be used of coming to an assignation (1.9.43, Prop.2.18.30, 2.22.43, 46).

nec nitidum tarda compserit arte caput: *nitidum* may be proleptic, but probably the hair (like the face) was naturally beautiful.

For the time taken by a woman over her appearance cf. Ter. *Heaut.* 239f., Prop.1.15.6. The point here is that the girl has not taken a long time, but the lover has (cf. Mart.7.83 *Eutrapelus tonsor dum circuit ora Luperci / expingitque genas, altera barba subit*, 8.52).

On the arrangement of words here see 1.7.25-6n.

17–18 The lover's odd behaviour (the excesses at 9ff. and the whole idea of a *puer delicatus* so in love with a girl) might suggest the influence of witchcraft, as it was thought that love-magic could cause excessive infatuation and derangement (cf. Ov. *Her.* 6.83ff., *A.A.* 2.106 *philtra nocent animis vimque furoris habent*, Juv.6.610ff., Suet. *Cal.* 50). But there is irony in the suggestion of a mental disorder (*nocuisse*, 23) and the influence of magic, esp. when the real reason for the lover's actions is clear (23-6).

To inspire love by magic use was made of herbs, potions, charms, sympathetic magic and the ἴυγξ (see esp. Theoc. *Id.* 2, Virg. *Ecl.* 8.64ff., Hor. *Epod.* 5, Lucian *Dial.Mer.* 4).

pallentibus herbis: either 'pale herbs', or, more likely, 'herbs that make pale' (cf. Ov. *A.A.* 2.105, Pers.5.55 *rugosum piper et pallentis grana cumini*): the lover's pallor is really caused by love (51-2n.).

devovit tacito tempore noctis anus: for the witch see 1.2.41-2n. Magic ceremonies were normally conducted in silence (Gow on Theoc. *Id.* 2.38) and at night (1.2.61-2n.). The periphrasis (= *silentio noctis*) seems mock-solemn.

19–22 T. increases the irony by citing exx. of the power of magic in other fields in support of the suggestion that the lover may be bewitched. The humour is heightened by the apparent seriousness of the remarks (note the preponderance of spondees). For the list of magic feats see 1.2.41-64n. It is possible that these lines were inspired by Virg. *Ecl.* 8, where similar phenomena are described in similar language and form (69ff. *carmina vel caelo possunt deducere lunam, / carminibus Circe socios mutavit Ulixi, / frigidus in pratis cantando rumpitur anguis*, and 99 *atque satas alio vidi traducere messis*). Note the structure: one couplet on earth (19 moving the immovable, 20 stopping the moving) is followed by one couplet on heaven (21 magic, 22 counter-magic). The knowledgeable refs. to magic also fit in with T.'s pose as instructor (see intro. essay).

19–20 For the transference of crops by magic incantation (banned in the Twelve Tables) cf. Plin. *N.H.* 28.17, Sen. *N.Q.* 4.7.2, Nemes. *Ecl.* 4.71. For the same feat without specific reference to incantation see Smith.

The powers of magical incantation over snakes included splitting them (Lucil.575 Marx, Virg. *Ecl.* 8.71, Ov. *Am.* 2.1.25, *Med.Fac.* 39,

*Met.*7.203, Nemes. *Ecl.*4.70, Plin. *N.H.*28.19), summoning them (Sen. *Med.*684f., Plin. *N.H.*28.19), putting them to sleep (Ap.Rhod. 4.145ff., Virg. *Aen.*7.754, Val.Fl.8.68, Sil.It.8.498) and halting them (Petron. *S.* 134 *iussi stare dracones*, Sen. *Med.* 688ff.).

iratae . . . anguis: the adjective suggests that the magic here is apotropaic and emphasizes the difficulty of the feat.

For the uncommon feminine gender of *anguis* cf. Cic. *N.D.* 1.101, *Div.* 2.62, Varro of Atax fr.8B, Ov. *Med.Fac.*39, *Met.* 4.594, Tac. *Ann.* 11.11, Val.Max.1.6.4, 1.8.19, and see Charisius 90.13ff. K, who quotes this line. For the use of *anguis* see 1.4.35-6n.

1–22 For the power of incantation to bring down the moon cf. Nonn. *Dionys.*36.347, Virg. *Ecl.*8.69, Hor. *Epod.*5.45f., 17.77f., Ov. *Am.* 2.1.23, Petron. *S.* 134, Luc.6.499ff., Claud. *Ruf.* 1.146f. The feat was esp. connected with Thessalian witches (Aristoph. *Nub.* 749, Plat. *Gorg.* 513A, Hor. *Epod.*5.45f., Lucan loc.cit., Plin. *N.H.* 30.7, Sen. *H.O.* 525f., Claudian loc.cit.). The purpose was to make the moon drop poisonous foam (Luc.6.506, 669, Stat. *Theb.*2.284f., Val.Fl.6.447, Apul. *Met.* 1.3). As Smith points out, it would appear that this power attributed to incantation was an explanation of eclipses: cf. schol. ad Ap.Rhod.3.533, 4.59-61, Plin. *N.H.* 2.54 *in defectibus siderum scelera aut mortem aliquam pavente . . . aut in lunae veneficia arguente mortalitate et ob id crepitu dissono auxiliante.* So brass is clashed in both instances (see below).

et faceret, si non aera repulsa sonent: for the mixed construction see 1.4.63-4n. *Faceret* stands for *deduceret*: this use of *facio* ('to do so', with the meaning taken from another verb) is common throughout Latin (see *Thes.L.L.* VI_1.107.31ff.).

For *aera repulsa* used of the beating of cymbals or other brass objects cf. Ov. *Met.* 3.532f., *F.* 4.184 *aeraque tinnitus aere repulsa dabunt.*

This beating of brass was done in the case of eclipses (Livy 26.5.9, Ov. *Met.* 4.332f., Tac. *Ann.* 1.28.2) and of witchcraft (Ov. *Med.Fac.* 41, *Met.* 7.207, Mart.12.57.16f., Juv.6.442f., Sen. *Med.* 795f., Stat. *Theb.* 6.686f.). The purpose was supposedly to scare off the evil forces causing the phenomenon: cf. Plin.loc.cit., Alexander Aphro. *Prob.* 2.46 κινοῦσι δὲ χαλκὸν καὶ σίδηρον ἄνθρωποι πάντες, ὡς τοὺς δαίμονας ἀπελαύνοντες. Brass was often so used in other connections also (see Pease and Austin on Virg. *Aen.* 4.513, schol. ad Ap.Rhod. 2.526, Ov. *F.* 5.441f.).

Aes for an instrument made of *aes* occurs as early as Ennius and, although found in prose, is more common in poetry (*Thes.L.L.* I.1073. 48ff.).

3–24 The anticlimax in the realism, the irony in *heu misero* and the mocking echo of 17 in the hexameter suggest amusement, and so the metre becomes more dactylic.

On this contrast between magic and less sinister charms (here explicitly sexual: 25f.) see 1.5.43-4n. The learned apophthegm in the pentameter (*forma* in emphatic position) befits T.'s pose as *praeceptor*.

For *noceo* used of magic see 1.5.47-8n.

25–26 For a similar effect of these actions cf. *A.P.* 5.96 (Meleager), 5.129.7f. (Automedon), 5.305 (anon.), 12.133 (Meleager), Ov. *Am.* 2.5.51f.

On anaphora of *sed* see 1.7.45-6n.

nocet: for this play on the use of the verb of magic see 1.5.47-8n.

femori conseruisse femur: see Critical Appendix. For the phrase cf. *A.P.* 5.129.7f. (Automedon), Catull.69.2, Ov. *Am.* 1.4.43, 3.7.10, 3.14.22, *Her.* 2.58. The precise implications here are not clear. From 35-8 it appears that at present the girl will not allow the lover to have intercourse with her. The reference here may be simply to touching (cf. Ov. *Am.* 1.4.43). Alternatively, the phrase may refer to actual intercourse (cf. Catull.69.2, Ov. *Her.* 2.57f. *turpiter hospitium lecto cumulasse iugali / paenitet, et lateri conseruisse latus*), if the perfect infinitives have their full force (the girl has now ceased to grant her favours, but the 'harm' has already been done).

27–48 T. now turns to address the girl, following up the suggestion of her power over the lover at 25f. and her lack of compliance at 9ff. (*tristia*, 28, picks up *misero*, 23).

The first couplet introduces the whole section, T.'s advice to the girl (27-66). Lines 29-48 form the first part of the advice, an attack on her venality. The basic idea advanced here is the superiority of youth and beauty to old age and money, and the idea is given a comprehensive treatment, viewed from two different angles in symmetrical 10-line groups. Lines 29-38 point out that the lover's youth and beauty are preferable to the old age of another man, even if he does have money, and the girl is advised to enjoy herself with the lover. The appeal is to her sensuality with concentration on youth (the lover's). Lines 39-48 point out that her own youth and beauty are preferable to the old age which she may herself suffer, even if she does have money, and advise her to enjoy her youth, while she can. Here the appeal is to the vanity of the girl with concentration on old age (the girl's).

T. betrays amusement at several points during these lines, but humour is esp. evident in the bizarre circumstances: a *puer delicatus* finds his partner uncompliant and is asked for gifts, while the poet recommends his boy to another and uses on the boy's behalf arguments similar to those he would usually employ on his own behalf (expressed forcefully and with apparent seriousness).

27–28 nec tu difficilis puero tamen esse memento: for *difficilis* 'uncompliant' in the amatory sense cf. Ov. *A.A.* 2.566, Hor. *C.* 3.7.32, 3.10.11 *non te Penelopen difficilem procis*.

The use of *puer* here (rather than *iuvenis*, as at 31) seems intended to bring out the lover's childishness, and so arouse pity in the girl (cf. 49f.).

persequitur poenis tristia facta Venus: note the intensifying *per-* prefix. This is the first appearance in the poem of the nemesis theme (71-2n.). For the punitive aspect of Venus see 1.9.19-20n.

Tristia here may mean 'unkind, unpleasant' (cf. Ov. *Met.*9.4) or 'cruel' (cf. Virg. *Aen.*2.548 *illi mea tristia facta / degeneremque Neoptolemum narrare memento*).

29–30 For other refs. to venality in T. see 1.4.58, 1.5.67f., 1.6.53-4n., 1.9 (passim), 2.1.73, 2.3.49, 2.4.14. The girl's mercenary nature is a new detail. Note the emphasis in the position and repetition of *munera.*

det munera canus amator: again the pose of the *praeceptor*: T. is aware of all the practical realities and the way in which they can be used to the best effect (cf. 50). An old man is naturally repulsive to a girl (cf. Mimnerm. 1.9-10D, Anac.5D, T.1.9.67ff., Prop.2.18, Paulus Silentiarius *A.P.* 5.264) – hence the necessity for gifts.

The *canus amator* here may be envisaged as a particular person ('your old lover'), but, in view of the general ref. to *veteres . . . senes* in the parallel couplet (49f.), it seems more likely that the phrase means 'some old lover'.

ut foveat molli frigida membra sinu: see Critical Appendix.

For the man as subject of the verb cf. Catull.68.29, Sen. *Prov.* 3.5 *in sinu amicae foveret manum.*

Canus amator (merely warming himself and not performing any sexual act) is in contrast to the lover below. Humorously the remainder of the pent. gives the lie to the sexual sense of *fovere* (e.g. 1.6.6). So too *frigida* also has connotations of lack of passion (*Thes.L.L.* VI_1. 1329.73ff.).

The bosom was an obvious source of warmth (Ov.*Her.* 3.114, *A.A.* 2.360, Phaedr.66.3). It is not clear whether here T. is thinking of the bosom of clothes (1.6.18) or of the person (Ov.*Her.* 1.45).

Putnam points out that in the word-order the cold limbs are enclosed by the soft bosom. Note too the pattern of initial consonants (f and m).

31–32 carior est auro: this type of phrase was proverbial (see Smith and cf. also Aristot.ap.Athen.696C, Cic. *Res Pub.* 3.5.8), but is neatly applied here, since T. is talking of venality.

iuvenis: a difficult word here. Elsewhere in this elegy the lover is described as a *puer*, and the normal progression is from *puer* to *adulescens.* However, the progression from *puer* to *iuvenis* is found (Cic. *Sen.* 33, Hor. *Ars Poet.* 161), and *adulescens* and *iuvenis* were interchangeable terms (Introduction sect.2). In any case, *adulescens* is rare in verse (Axelson 58f.). *Puer* and *iuvenis* are applied to the same person at Virg. *Aen.*7.531, 575, Ov. *F.* 1.367, 371. Here the relative clause mentioning the absence of beard makes it clear that *iuvenis* is applied to one who is really a *puer*. The lover seems to be approaching an intermediate age, so that *iuvenis* can also be applied to him. *Puer* technically was used of someone up to the age of 14 or 15 (Varro ap.Censorin.14, Isid. *Orig.* 11.2.3), while *iuvenis* was applied to someone as young as 16 (Hor. *Ars Poet.* 161 and Brink ad loc.). *Iuvenis* presumably is employed here to bring out the sexual maturity of the lover, suggesting that he too is an adult, like *canus amator*, but a more desirable one.

cui levia fulgent / ora nec amplexus aspera barba terit: *fulgent* (in contrast to the gleam of gold) suggests the light colour and shining appearance of beardless cheeks (cf. Irenaeus Referendarius *A.P.* 12.249, Stat. *Silv.* 3.4.65). A smooth face was considered attractive in a boy (Theogn.1327f., Lucian *Amores* 10), and the advent of the beard ruined his good looks (*A.P.* 12.10 (Strato), 25, 26, 27 (Statyllius Flaccus), 31 (Phanias), 186, 220 (Strato), 1.9.13-14n.).

For the realistic detail of the beard rasping cf. Theoc. *Id.* 15.130, Plaut. *Cas.* 929, Mart.11.39.3f. *iam mihi nigrescunt tonsa sudaria barba / et queritur labris puncta puella meis*, Longus 1.16.

For *amplexus* = *te amplectentem* cf. Ov. *F.* 3.496 and see 1.2.11-12n.

33–34 This couplet is virtually a restatement of the last in more emphatic terms (note the solemn spondees).

huic tu: an expressive juxtaposition.

candentes: note the compliment (1.4.11-12n.).

et regum magnae despiciantur opes: in earlier exx. of the rejection of the wealth and power of kings a humbler station in life is usually the chosen alternative (Archiloch.22D, Anac.8D, Pind. *Pyth.* 11.52f., Eur. *Ion* 621ff., *Hipp.*1013ff.). For the preference of love cf. Prop.1.14.13, 23f. *quae mihi dum placata aderit, non ulla verebor / regna vel Alcinoi munera despicere*, Hor. *C.* 2.12.21ff., T.3.3.23f., 29. See also 1.2.75-6n.

35–36 See Critical Appendix.

The purpose of these lines is to answer or forestall an imaginary excuse by the girl that she cannot see the boy because she is afraid of detection (hence *furtim*: see intro.essay). Perhaps we are to imagine that the girl has just shown signs of protest. For *at* introducing a refutation of an imaginary objection see Kühner-Stegmann 2.86f., and for this use of *at* with an unexpressed objection cf. e.g. Ov. *Her.* 12.1 *at tibi Colchorum, memini, regina vacavi* (best taken as an answer to a refusal by Jason to listen to her: see Palmer ad loc.).

Venus invenit puero concumbere: for Venus as an instructress in love see 1.2.19-20n. The use of *puer* again suggests an appeal to the girl.

The gnomic perfect is mainly poetic: in Latin it first appears at Catull. 62.42 and was common in Augustan poetry (e.g. Virg. *G.* 4.43, Hor. *Ars Poet.* 343, 373, Prop.3.11.6, T.1.4.17f., 1.8.56, 2.1.73f.).

For the infinitive with *invenio* cf. Virg. *G.* 1.140, Plin. *N.H.* 17.67,

35.153, Sil.It.12.90f. The construction is probably due to the Greek usage of εὑρίσκω with the infinitive (Soph. *O.T.* 120 and Jebb ad loc.).

teneros conserit usque sinus: Smith's explanation of this phrase as an agricultural metaphor (of sexual intercourse) seems highly improbable: the metaphor is usually made clear by the addition of *arva* or a similar word, *sinus* so used is not common, and it is hard to believe that the lover would be capable of continuous intercourse (*usque*). It seems best to take *conserit* as 'joins' (as in 26), and the ref. then is to embraces. For the construction cf. Virg. *Aen.* 9.741, Stat. *Silv.* 1.6.60. For similar expressions of the close embrace cf. Prop.4.7.19, Ov. *Her.* 15.191, 19.62, *Met.* 2.604f. *illa suo totiens cum pectore iuncta / . . . pectora.* The words are reminiscent of phrases such as *pugnam, manus conserere*, and so lead into the military idea in *pugnantibus* (37).

37–38 For 'french-kissing' (or, as Némethy would have it, '*genus osculorum infame*') cf. Aristoph. *Nub.* 51, *A.P.* 5.129.7 (Automedon), Ov. *Am.* 2.5.23f. *improba tum vero iungentes oscula vidi – / illa mihi lingua nexa fuisse liquet*, 57f., 3.7.9, 3.14.23, *Her.* 15.129f., Ach.Tat. 2.37.8. Note the collocation of vivid details (*anhelanti pugnantibus umida linguis*).

For love-bites see 1.6.13-14n.

39–40 non lapis hanc gemmaeque iuvant: T. may mean jewels of all kinds (Hor. *C.* 3.24.48), or a distinction may be intended, in which case *lapis* most probably refers to ear-rings and necklaces, and *gemmae* to rings (1.6.25, Ov. *A.A.* 1.432, *Med.Fac.* 20ff., Mart.11.50.4 *gemma vel a digito vel cadit aure lapis*). Jewels may be an ex. of wealth in general, or of the *munera* of 29 in particular (cf. e.g. Prop.2.16.15ff., Ov. *Am.* 2.15). For the uselessness of wealth without love see 1.2.75-6n.

quae frigore sola / dormiat et nulli sit cupienda viro: often the deserted lover is described as experiencing cold (Ov. *Am.* 3.5.42, *A.A.* 3.70, *Her.* 1.7, 19.69 *cur ego tot viduas exegi frigida noctes?*).

Being scorned by lovers and growing ugly in old age (elaborated in the following lines) were details commonly found in the punishment of the cruel mistress (1.6.77-84n.). T. is here using these details ostensibly to lead into the exhortation of 47f., but, in view of the warning of nemesis at 28, it seems probable that he is hinting indirectly that such will be the girl's punishment, if she does not change her ways. Verbal echoes at the end of the poem confirm this hint (see 77-8n.). The nemesis theme is thus used far more subtly than by any of T.'s predecessors. He concentrates on the unpleasantness of such an old age, adding details that have special ref. to the girl's best features (see below). Note also the emphatic position of *sola* here and the juxtaposition (*frigore sola*).

41–42 The couplet has particular point, since the girl has beautiful hair (16 – hence the concentration on hair-care below). Note the emphatic expression: the initial exclamation, repetition of *sero*, concentration on old age (*vetus, senecta*) and white hair (*infecit . . . caput, cana*).

For *inficio* used of old age turning hair white cf. 2.2.20, Ov. *Tr.* 4.8.2 *inficit et nigras alba senecta comas.* However, the word is properly used of dyeing the hair: the refs. here to old age 'dyeing' the hair and in the next couplet to the woman dyeing her hair a different colour underline the the unpleasant humour of the situation.

43–44 The refs. to beauty-care fit in with T.'s overall pose as instructor (see intro. essay). The use of dye to conceal white hairs was generally regarded as futile and ridiculous: cf. Antiphilus of Byzantium *A.P.* 11.66, Lucian *A.P.* 11.408, Mart.3.43, 4.36, Tert. *Cult.Fem.* 2.6. For the use of nuts in this connection cf. (acorns and walnuts) Marc. Emp.7.10, Plin. *N.H.* 15.87, (gall nuts) *N.H.* 24.10 *omnis capillos denigrat.*

tum studium formae est: the girl will lose her beauty (*forma*, 24). *Studium* suggests eagerness and application to study.

For the emphatic anaphora of *tum* (also in 45) cf. 1.10.3f., 2.1.43f.

viridi cortice: for the phrase cf. Virg. *Ecl.* 5.13, Ov. *A.A.* 2.649. The adjective literally means 'green', but aptly the connotation of youth is also present.

45–46 tollere tum cura est albos a stirpe capillos: for the plucking of white hairs cf. Prop.3.25.13, Macrob. *S.* 2.5.7, Phaedr.2.2. *Tollere* can be used simply of 'removing', but is also used of 'killing' and 'destroying', and *a stirpe* may refer to plucking out hair 'by the root', but can also mean 'utterly' (of destruction etc.: e.g. Sall. *Cat.*10.1): this accessory notion humorously suggests the desperation of the old woman.

et faciem dempta pelle referre novam: again the words have esp. point, since the girl has a lovely face (15).

Dempta pelle is a very curious phrase, which has no parallel. In context it must mean 'with the facial defects removed'. *Pellis* is used of old skin (doubtless due to its resemblance to a hide) at Hor. *Epod.* 17.22, Juv.10.192, and of discoloured skin at Pers.3.95. Here, in view of *dempta*, the word must stand not for the skin itself, but for the various defects which earn it the name of *pellis* (e.g. wrinkles, hardness, discolouring, spots). The phrase *dempta pelle* is made clear by the contrast with *faciem . . . novam*, and, as Dissen suggests, was possibly derived from the ugly snake's sloughing of its skin (1.4.35-6n.; *pellis* is used of a snake's skin at Ov. *A.A.* 3.77, *Met.* 9.266). The expression indicates amusement at the situation.

Various substances were used for removing facial blemishes: cf. Plin. *N.H.* 11.238 *Poppaea . . . quingentas per omnia secum fetas trahens balnearum etiam solio totum corpus illo lacte macerabat, extendi quoque cutem credens*, 21.127, 23.85, 24.43, 26.163, 28.183f., 30.30, Seren. Sammon. 154.

47–48 For T.'s advice here see 1.4.27-8n.: note the solemnity (underlined by the spondees) and the emphasis (positions of *at tu, utere* and *non tardo*).

at tu: in contrast to those who behave in a different fashion to the one T. would advise, and who suffer the unpleasantness described above.

dum primi floret tibi temporis aetas: the first indication that the girl also is young. *Aetas* (defined by *primi . . . temporis*) means 'youth': cf. Prop.2.8.17, 2.10.7.

For blooming youth cf. Hes. *Theog.* 988 τόν ῥα νέον τέρεν ἄνθος ἔχοντ' ἐρικυδέος ἥβης, *Hom. Hym.* 4.375, Catull.68.16, Virg. *Ecl.* 7.4.

49–66 The second part of the advice to the girl (27-66) consists of an attack on her cruelty. The first couplet is parallel to 29-30 (*neu* picks up *ne* (29), the same sense-pause occurs in the hexameter, and here too T. exhorts her to reserve harsher treatment for the old). Again the theme of youth is present, but here the emphasis is on the boy's childishness, and the appeal is to the girl's pity. The first three couplets are a request to spare the boy because of the effect she is having on him; the next six quote the boy's own complaint that, although he knows how to conduct a secret affair, she still scorns him (three couplets on his expertise are balanced by three on his lack of success).

Again the poet uses on the boy's behalf the type of argument that he would normally employ on his own behalf, and there is also humour in the *puer delicatus* being tormented by another and in his rather exaggerated reactions. During the course of these lines it is stated that the boy is none other than Marathus, and that he is reduced to tearful bewilderment by her cruelty.

49–50 neu Marathum torque: for effect the boy's name is not given until now. There seems to be a deliberate (ironical) echo of 1.4.81 here. Exactly how the girl torments him is not made clear until later (55-6n.).

puero quae gloria victo est?: *puero* (emphatic by position) again suggests an appeal. For the sentiment cf. 1.6.3-4n., *Hom. Hym.* 4.330f., Ov. *Met.* 3.654f., 12.292f. *puero quae gloria fuso / parta tibi est?*

Victo is probably an ex. of *militia amoris* (1.10.53-6n.): so *gloria* is frequently used in a military context (cf. Hor. *C.* 3.26.2), and *veteres* (50) and *sontica causa* (51) have military connotations (see below).

For the hex. ending see 1.3.5-8n.

in veteres esto dura, puella, senes: cf. 29-30 (and notes).

Durus is frequently used of a cruel mistress: cf. 2.6.28, Prop.1.1.10, 1.7.6, Ov. *Am.* 1.9.19, Hor. *C.* 3.7.31f. *et te saepe vocanti / duram, difficilis mane.*

Veteres and *senes*, by increasing the contrast with *puero* (49) and *tenero* (51), underline Marathus' youth. The adjective here means 'experienced': cf. Tac. *Ann.* 6.12, 44, Ov. *A.A.* 3.565 *ille vetus miles sensim et sapienter amabit.* In this sense it is applied esp. to veteran soldiers (Lewis & Short s.v. 1B), so that the military metaphor probably continues here. For the veteran in love's warfare cf. Hor. *C.* 3.26, Ov. *Am.* 2.9.23, *A.A.* 3.565, *Rem.* 4.

Esto has a solemn and archaic ring: this imperative form was used in legal language from the time of the Twelve Tables (Neue 3.213ff., Kühner-Stegmann 1.196ff.). It occurs elsewhere in the *Corp. Tib.* at 1.2.87, 1.5.69, 1.6.16 (possibly: see n.), 17, 1.10.67, 4.2.3, 4.5.9.

51–52 non illi sontica causa est: the following is the evidence for *sonticus* and *sontica causa*. Firstly, *sontica causa*: Festus 290M (s.v. *sonticum morbum*) *sonticam esse oportet causam, quam ob rem perdas mulierem* and 344M (s.v. *sontica causa*) *sontica causa dicitur a morbo sontico, propter quem, quod est gerendum, agere desistimus. M. Porcius . . . 'A. Atili, quid dicam causae extitisse, timidus ne sis. an impedimento tibi causam sonticam fuisse?'* It would appear that the phrase meant a 'just' or 'valid excuse' (cf. Paul. ex Fest. 291M, where *sonticum* is glossed by *iustum*). A *morbus sonticus* provided such an excuse, properly for not appearing at some proceedings: cf. Gell. 16.4.4 (of enrolled soldiers who had to appear on an appointed day, with the following exceptions) *funus familiare feriaeve denicales . . . morbus sonticus*, 20.1.25ff., esp. 27 (of the law that a mount be provided for an aged man or one suffering from a less serious disease who is called into court) *ceteroqui morbum vehementiorem, vim graviter nocendi habentem, legum istarum scriptores alio in loco non per se morbum sed morbum sonticum appellant.* Further evidence for *morbus sonticus* is Festus p. 290 *sonticum morbum in XII significare ait Aelius Stilo certum cum iusta causa; quem nonnulli putant esse qui noceat, quod sontes significat nocentes*, p. 111 *insons, extra culpam, a quo dici morbus quoque existimatur sonticus, qui perpetuo noceat*, Iavolenus *lib.* 14 ex Cassio, Ulp. *Dig.* 50.16.113 *morbus sonticus est qui cuique rei nocet*, Iulianus *id.* 42.1.60 *sonticus autem existimandus est qui cuiusque rei agendae impedimento est.*

The precise derivation of *sonticus* is disputed: all connect it with *sons*, but some maintain that *sons* is the archaic present part. of *esse* (cf. Stilo in Festus p. 290), others that *sons*, on the analogy of *insons*, = *nocens* (cf. Gell. 20.1.27, Festus p. 290, 111, Ulp. *Dig.* 50.16.113). However, the term *morbus sonticus* clearly denotes a dangerous disease.

In the present case, *sontica causa* can hardly have its usual meaning of a 'just' or 'valid excuse', as this would give the sense: 'spare the boy: he cannot offer a just/valid excuse (for being spared), but his infatuation for you is making him pale'. Surely his pallor caused by infatuation would be described as a 'just/valid excuse'.

It is more likely that *sontica causa* is a variant on *sonticus morbus*, as Dissen suggests (for *causa* meaning 'medical symptoms, a medical case' see *OLD* s.v. *causa* 13). This gives the more natural sense: 'spare the boy: he does not have a dangerous disease, but it is excessive love for you that causes his pallor'. T. may be basing his appeal here on the fact that Marathus' extreme pallor (so marked that one might imagine it was caused by a serious disease) is caused by his infatuation for the girl. Alternatively, he may be (ironically) suggesting that the reason why the girl is avoiding contact with Marathus is because his pallor makes her think that he has a dangerous (contagious) disease, and so he points out to her the real cause of his pallor (cf. Lee: 'No need to isolate his sickness'). Pointing out the reason for the lover's pallor is, of course, in line with T.'s pose as *praeceptor*.

The application of this (unique) variant on this old, technical phrase from Roman law to such a trivial situation suggests amusement on T.'s part.

The military metaphor in the last couplet perhaps remains with *sontica causa*: according to *Thes.L.L.* III.702.6ff. *caus(s)arius* is (i) *in re medicina i.q. morbo affectus*, and (ii) *in re militari de militibus aegrotis, invalidis, qui propter valetudinem arma ferre non possunt*: cf. Livy 6.6.14, Ulp. *Dig.* 3.2.2.2 (*missio*) *est causaria, quae propter valetudinem laboribus militiae solvit* (*militem*), Pauly s.v. *causarius* (= III.1812).

For the hexameter ending see 1.3.5-8n.

sed nimius luto corpora tingit amor: see Critical Appendix.

Lutum was a plant used for dyeing yellow, and hence the colour yellow (Virg. *Ecl.* 4.44, *Ciris* 317).

Marathus' pallor is described as 'yellow' because olive-skinned people turn pale yellow rather than pale white (see Smith, Fordyce on Catull. 81.4 and cf. also Ov. *A.A.* 3.703ff., *Met.* 4.134f., 11.417f. *buxoque simillimus ora / pallor obit*).

For the traditional pallor of lovers cf. Sappho 2.14D, Theoc. *Id.* 2.88, Prop.1.1.22, 1.5.21, 1.9.17, 1.13.7, 3.8.28, 4.3.28, Ov. *Am.* 3.6.25, *A.A.* 1.729f., Hor. *C.* 3.10.14.

53–54 **vel miser absenti maestas quam saepe querellas / conicit**: see Critical Appendix.

Vel means 'for instance' (giving an ex. of Marathus' *nimius . . . amor*, his reaction when he is deprived of her company). When so used the word is often found with an exclamation: cf. Ter. *Hec.* 60, *Heaut.* 567, Cic. *Fam.* 2.13.1 *raras tuas quidem . . . sed suaves accipio litteras; vel quas proxime acceperam, quam prudentes!*

The dative with *conicio* is not common: cf. Virg. *Aen.* 7.347, 456, 11.194, Sil.It.14.305f.

The purpose of the emphasis on Marathus' unhappiness, excessive complaints and tears (below) is on the surface to arouse sympathy in the girl, but the exaggeration also suggests amusement.

lacrimis omnia plena madent: for the expression cf. Ov.*Her.* 8.75f., 12.64, *F.* 4.537 *luctus videt omnia plena*, Stat. *Theb.* 11.417.

55–56 T. increases the pathos by quoting Marathus' own words, the complaints to the absent girl which T. represents himself as having overheard (1.5.21-4n.). The sight of the boy, formerly so sure of his sophistication, but now reduced to tearful and childish reproaches, is on the surface intended to move pity, but again suggests amusement.

poterat custodia vinci: there are two possible explanations of the imperfect here. (i) 'The indicative (of certain verbs) is used to express positively the existence of power, possibility, duty, convenience etc. in contrast to particular acts . . . The imperfect of present time or of a continuous state in past time, the action being regarded as no longer possible . . . Often the suppressed condition is 'if the occasion arose' . . . and the like.' (Roby 1535-6). Here the imperfect would probably be in contrast to the present state of affairs, in view of *spernis* (i.e. 'the watch could be defeated'): cf. Cic. *Fin.* 2.18.57, Ov. *Tr.* 5.1.49 *'at poteras' inquis 'melius mala ferre silendo'.* The imperfect is similarly used at 1.9.46. (ii) *Poterat* may have the sense 'most certainly can', in imitation of the Greek use of the imperfect (with or without ἄρα): cf. Prop. 1.13. 34, Hor. *Epist.* 1.4.6 *non tu corpus eras sine pectore*, and see Fraenkel *Horace* (Oxford, 1957), p. 324 n.3.

These words answer *quid me spernis?* and indicate that the girl's excuse was the guard (35-6n.). It seems probable that the guard is on the girl (see intro. essay). It becomes clear later that she will not allow Marathus to try to elude the guard (59-60) and she will not try to elude it herself (63-66). On eluding guards see 1.6.9-10n.

ipse dedit cupidis fallere posse deus: with *fallere* understand *custodiam*. The infinitive after *dare* meaning 'grant' or 'allow' is first found in Lucr. and is common in Augustan poetry. For the double infinitive cf. Lucr.6.1227f., T.3.4.48, Ov. *A.A.* 2.28, *Met.* 12.556-8, 14.843f., *Tr.* 1.1.34, 3.1.23f.

The perfect is gnomic, as in the parallel passage (35-6n.).

Deus refers to Amor (cf. 1.2.19-20 and n.).

57–58 venus furtiva: cf. Ov. *Am.* 2.8.8, *A.A.* 1.275, and see 1.2.33-4n.

For soft breathing and silent kissing (realistic details first found here) cf. Ov. *F.* 1.425ff. *surgit amans animamque tenens vestigia furtim / suspenso digitis fert taciturna gradu. / ut tetigit niveae secreta cubilia nymphae / ipsa sui flatus ne sonet aura, cavet*, Ach.Tat.2.7.5.

For snatched kisses see 1.4.53-6n. Here also the ref. may be to teasing playfulness, but probably is to the furtive haste necessary under such circumstances (cf. Paulus Silentiarius *A.P.* 5.219).

59–60 possum media quamvis obrepere nocte: Némethy's suggestion that *quamvis* stands for *quamvis puellam* (governed by *obrepere*) is unlikely, as this would hardly be a very diplomatic or persuasive remark to pass on to the girl, and the substantival form *quamvis* is unparalleled in the *Corp. Tib.* It seems better to take *quamvis* as the adverb, modifying *media . . . nocte*, a use of the word common in prose and poetry (Kühner-Stegmann II.445f.). The word is added because in the middle of the night (rather than earlier, as at Ov. *Am.* 2.19.38) the feat would be esp. difficult due to the complete silence and pitch blackness. Thus it brings out well the skilfulness and stealth.

strepitu nullo clam: such collocations are not unusual in T., but here the words suggest the excitement and exaggerated emphasis of Marathus' claim.

reserare fores: as the guard seems to be on the girl (see intro. essay), it seems likely that Marathus here means opening doors from the outside: for *resero* so used cf. Ov. *Met.* 10.384. A method of locking and opening doors from the outside occurs as early as Homer (*Od.* 1.441f., 21.46ff., Aristoph. *Thesm.* 421ff., Apul. *Met.* 4.10). For lovers opening doors from the outside cf. *A.P.* 5.242 (Eratosthenes Scholasticus), Prop.4.5.73f. *et canis, in nostros nimis experrecta dolores, / cum fallenda meo pollice clatra forent*, Lucian *Dial.Mer.* 12.3 (314). For other exx. of lovers tampering with doors see 1.2.17-18, 1.6.11-12n., and cf. Ov. *Am.* 3.1.49f., *A.A.* 3.643.

61–62 Marathus' lack of success despite his skills recalls 1.4.81ff. Note the self-pity in *miserum* and the reproach in *saeva*.

63–64 promittit: also used absolutely at Catull.110.5 and Ov. *A.A.* 3.461. Usually *venerem* or *noctem* is expressed (e.g. 2.6.49, Prop.4.5.33, Ov. *A.A.* 2.523, *Rem.* 400). The word is vague, but the following lines show that she is promising here to visit Marathus (*promissum* seems to be so used at Prop.2.17.1).

subito sed perfida fallit: for the situation cf. *A.P.* 5.7, 150 (Asclepiades), 152 (Meleager), 265 (Cometas Chartularius), 279 (Paulus Silentiarius), 12.201 (Strato), Hor. *S.* 1.5.82ff., Prop.2.17, 2.22.43ff., Ov. *Her.* 19, Mart.11.73.

nox . . . evigilanda: in this connection cf. *A.P.* 5.152.3 (Meleager), 279.4 (Paulus Silentiarius), Ov. *Her.* 19.39ff., esp. Prop.2.22.45ff. *hic unus dolor est ex omnibus acer amanti, / speranti subito si qua venire negat. / quanta illum toto versant suspiria lecto, / cum recipi quod non venerit illa vetat, / et rursus puerum quaerendo audita fatigat, / quem, quae scire timet, quaerere fata iubet.* So the lover cannot sleep when parted from his mistress for some other reason or troubled by her behaviour towards him (1.2.75ff., Prop.4.3.29ff., 4.7.5f., Hor. *C.* 3.7.7f.).

Evigilo occurs here only in the sense of *pervigilo* or *vigilo*, i.e. 'stay awake through' (transitive).

multis . . . malis: again Marathus is feeling sorry for himself.

65–66 For the lover imagining that he hears his mistress' approaching footsteps (a realistic detail first found here) cf. Ov. *Her.* 19.53f. *auribus incertas voces captamus, et omnem / adventus strepitum credimus esse tui.* For similar exx. of the lover hopefully seizing on anything cf. *A.P.* 6.333 (Marcus Argentarius), Virg. *Ecl.* 8.105ff., Ov. *Am.* 1.6.49f.

venturam: either a participle, or *esse* is to be supplied.

quodcumque movetur: cf. Cic. *In Cat.* 1.18 *quidquid increpuerit, Catilinam timeri.*

illius: the second i can be long or short in classical verse (e.g. short at Catull.64.348, Lucr.4.1062, Hor. *S.* 2.5.29, Virg. *Aen.* 1.16, Ov. *Am.* 1.4.34, *Aetna* 400; long at Catull.67.23, Lucr.3.520, Hor. *S.* 1.10.57, Virg. *Aen.* 1.683, Ov. *Am.* 1.13.44, *Aetna* 392). In the *Corp. Tib.* the i is short at 1.7.51, 2.4.52, 2.6.33, 36, 4.2.5, and long at 1.8.66, 2.2.7, 2.6.31, 4.1.81.

67–78 It seems that we are to imagine a pause after 66, during which it becomes apparent that the girl is unmoved. Thereupon T. turns to Marathus and tells him to stop crying, since (like T.'s words) the boy's tears that have accompanied his advice (67-8n.) are having no effect on her arrogant obstinacy, and then T. proceeds to warn the girl that this kind of behaviour is liable to nemesis.

The final section of the poem consists of threats. The first couplet acts as a transition and introduction, and in the next five couplets threats of punishment for the girl's arrogance (69f., 77f.) enclose an ex. of punishment for a similar crime (71–6). T. continues to use on the boy's behalf the love-poet's own arguments in (mock-) solemn form, and saves a few final revelations and surprises for the end of the poem (he tells us the girl's name, gives the particular reason for his amusement at the situation and closes with a humorous twist to the theme of nemesis).

67–68 desistas lacrimare, puer: it would appear that T.'s advice to the girl has been accompanied by tears from Marathus, in an attempt to win her over (the pentameter implies that the crying has been going on for quite some time).

non frangitur illa: in humorous contrast to Marathus the girl is hard. The words also suggest that Marathus is using the trick of crying to get his own way (1.9.29-30n., 1.10.53-6n., cf. 1.9.37f.) and that T. in line with his pose as instructor is fully aware of this trick.

et tua iam fletu lumina fessa tument: Marathus is addressed as if he were a girl (cf. 1.1.67f., 2.6.43, Plaut. *Amph.* 530, Ov. *A.A.* 1.129). For the effeminacy of the *puer delicatus* see 1.9.15-16n. The eyes were a criterion of beauty in the boyfriend (*A.P.* 12.5.3f. (Strato) *οὐδὲ κόρας ξανθὰς παραπέμπομαι· ἀλλὰ περισσῶς / τοὺς μελανοφθάλμους αἰγλοφανεῖς τε φιλῶ*, 110 (Meleager), 130 (anon.), 144 (Meleager),

Catull.48, Hor. *C.*1.32.11f. *Lycum nigris oculis nigroque / crine decorum*).

69–70 oderunt, Pholoe, moneo, fastidia divi: proverbial (esp. in love: see below): cf. e.g. Theogn.151f. ὕβριν, Κύρνε, θεὸς πρῶτον κακῷ ὤπασεν ἀνδρί / οὗ μέλλει χώρην μηδεμίην θέμεναι, Pind. *Pyth.* 2.51, Aesch. *Pers.*827ff., Soph. *O.T.*872ff. The veiled threat of punishment is picked up at 77f. Note the (mock-) solemnity and emphasis (positions of *oderunt* and *divi*). The ref. to divine nature fits in with T.'s pose as instructor (see intro. essay).

At last T. states the girl's name (see Introduction sect. 4).

nec prodest sanctis tura dedisse focis: i.e. it is no use trying to appease the gods, if you are arrogant (which is an offence against the gods): cf. Plat. *Alc.* 2.149E, *Leg.* 4.716E, Cic. *Leg.* 2.9.22, 2.16.4.

71–72 The couplet gives at last the particular reason for the amusement at the situation: Marathus himself used to behave exactly as Pholoe is now doing (1.4.81ff. suggest that T. himself would be included among these *miseros . . . amantes*). The boy as an ex. of nemesis is a rather surprising choice, but a good one (Pholoe can see for herself the effect on him of his punishment).

For the theme of nemesis see 1.2.87-96n. The punishment of the cruel lover was very common. For the cruel mistress see 1.6.77-84n. The scornful and arrogant male was usually punished by loss of beauty (1.9.13-14n.) or, as here, by falling in love himself and being similarly maltreated (cf. Theogn.1329ff., *A.P.* 5.300 (Paulus Silentiarius), 12.12 (Flaccus), 193 (Strato), Prop.1.13). The lover's arrogance is described in more detail than is usual, as is his punishment (Pholoe's treatment of him throughout the poem). So the way in which the punishment fits the crime is brought out at greater length than elsewhere: Pholoe's treatment of him corresponds more or less exactly with his former behaviour to his own lovers (see below). For the extra twist given to this nemesis theme at the end see 77-8n.

miseros ludebat amantes: Marathus is now in this position himself (the phrase echoes 61, and Marathus is described as *miser* at 23 and 53 also).

nescius ultorem post caput esse deum: for the infinitive after the adjective see 1.7.19-20n. The sure punishment of the gods (1.9.3-4n.) is a clear hint for Pholoe (cf. 28, 69).

The idea of pursuit from behind in such contexts goes back as far as Homer (*Il.* 9.512), but novelty is achieved here by the expression, which seems to be a variant on the common *ad / super / supra caput* and for which there is no exact parallel (Putnam cites Hor. *C.* 3.1.40 *post equitem sedet atra Cura*).

73–74 saepe etiam lacrimas fertur risisse dolentis: so now Pholoe is unmoved by Marathus' tears: cf. 53-4 (esp. *saepe* and *lacrimis*) and 67-8.

Fertur means that he had a reputation for this behaviour.

For *doleo* in an amatory context see 1.2.1-2n. André points out the juxtaposition *risisse dolentis*, which highlights the boy's cruelty.

et cupidum ficta detinuisse mora: compare Pholoe's treatment of Marathus and her excuse at 35-6 (see notes) and 55ff. (see 55-6n., and cf. esp. *cupidis* in 56). The invented delay was either due to mere cruelty or intended to inflame the lover's passion (*A.P.* 5.233.1ff. (Macedonius the Consul), Prop.4.5.29f., 33f., Ov. *Am.* 1.8.73ff., *A.A.* 3.473f. *postque brevem rescribe moram: mora semper amantes / incitat, exiguum si modo tempus habet*). Here, in view of the hexameter, Postgate ('kept a lover waiting') gives the primary sense, but Lee's interpretation ('kept desire on edge') is also implied.

75–76 Note the emphatic anaphora of *nunc* (cf. 1.3.49f., 1.9.29f., 2.5. 3f., 7f.), in contrast to *quondam* (71), and the preponderance of spondees. Again there are clear hints for Pholoe.

fastus: Pholoe is haughty (cf. 69 *fastidia*, 77).

quaecumque opposita est ianua dura sera: suggests that Marathus is an *exclusus amator* and that the guard is on Pholoe (see intro. essay). The obvious implication is that he used to lock out lovers himself, and so the locked-out lover often prays that the beloved may suffer a similar fate (*A.P.* 5.23 (Callimachus), 164 (Asclepiades), Prop.3.25.15f., esp. *A.P.* 12.193.5f. (Strato) μνησθήσῃ τούτων, ὑπερήφανε· καὶ οὐ φιλήσεις / καὶ κωμῳδήσεις τὴν Ἀποκλειομένην.

The door is made of wood, but is *dura* esp. because it is closed against him (1.1.55-6n.).

77–78 at te poena manet, ni desinis esse superba: *at* may introduce a threat (*OLD* s.v. 11e) or simply a change of character (Critical Appendix on 1.6.77). T. returns to the idea of 69f. (Pholoe's arrogance) and closes the poem with an open threat of nemesis.

quam cupies votis hunc revocare diem: the form of punishment is not specified, but the similarity between the crimes of Marathus and Pholoe suggests that their punishments will be the same, and she too will be scorned. The echo in *revocare* here of *revocatur* in 41 (in lines on an old woman scorned, used as a hint of nemesis for Pholoe: see 39-40n.) tends to confirm this suggestion, and so *poena* (77 and 28) and *cupies* (78, cf. *cupienda*, 40) direct the reader back to the same section and theme. Thus subtly and humorously T. closes the poem with an extra (and new) twist to the conventional situation: normally we find only the scorner scorned, but here T. implies that the scorner (Pholoe) of the scorner scorned (Marathus) will herself be scorned in turn (see intro. essay).

9

Dawson *AJPh* LXVII (1946), 1ff.; Wimmel *Der frühe Tibull* 81ff.

T.'s liaison with the boy of this poem (probably Marathus: see Introduction sect. 4) is supposed to have been going on for some time: T. says that he frequently helped him in his affair with a girl, he used to write poetry in his praise, he repeatedly warned him not to let himself be seduced by money, and the boy in reply used to swear that he would not sell himself at any price (17-18n.). However, despite his repeated oaths and despite all that T. has done for him, the boy is supposed to have taken up with a diseased old man, whose only possible attraction could be his money, and to have slept with him. In the poem T. recounts the boy's deceits and ingratitude, curses his seducer and threatens the boy with various punishments, stating in the final lines that he is contemplating a separation from him. There is a gradual revelation of these circumstances, to hold the reader's interest and give the end of the poem its maximum impact (see Wimmel loc.cit., Dissen and cf. intro. essay to 1.4).

1-16	Introduction:	1-4	The boy's perjury and its inevitable punishment by the gods.
		5-16	Pleas for divine mercy leading into less serious punishment.
17-52	Complaints to the boy:	17-30	T.'s advice not to succumb to money.
		31-38	The boy's false oaths not to let himself be seduced.
		39-46	His use of T. in his affair with a girl.
		47-50	T.'s misplaced praise of the boy.
		51-52	Dismissal of the boy.
53-74	Attack on the seducer:	53-58	His wife's future affairs.
		59-64	His wife to surpass his sister's excesses.
		65-74	His wife's present misdemeanours.
75-84	Conclusion:		T.'s separation from the boy.

The progression of thought within sections is sometimes abrupt (deliberately: see below), but care is taken over the transitions. The main themes of the poem (deceit, venality and punishment) appear in all sections, and words connected with these themes recur: (punishment) *poena* (4, 13, 81); (deceit) *celo* (3, 23), *dolus* (24, 54), *fallere* (37, cf. *fallax*, 83), *stultus* (45, 65); (venality) *munus* (11, 12, 43), *aurum* (17, 18, 31, 69, cf. *aureus*, 82), *vendere* (32, 51, 77), *pretium* (33, 52).

The poem contemplating or announcing the end of an affair was for obvious reasons not as common as some other types: see *A.P.* 5.107 (Philodemus), 175, 12.128 (Meleager), 237 (Strato), Catull.8, 11, 76, Hor. *Epod.* 15, Prop.2.5, 3.24, 3.25, Ov. *Am.* 3.11a. As the circumstances obviously vary, no rigid pattern emerges, but a number of features in 1.9 occur in many of the other exx. For instance, the complaint of perjury is also found in *A.P.* 5.175 (Meleager), 12.237 (Strato), Hor. *Epod.* 15, Ov. *Am.* 3.11a, and the recollection of past details in the affair in *A.P.* 5.107 (Philodemus), Catull.8, 76, Hor. *Epod.* 15, Prop. 3.24, 3.25, Ov. *Am.* 3.11a. So too the idea of the poet taking up with another lover also occurs in *A.P.* 5.107 (Philodemus), 12.128 (Meleager), Hor. *Epod.* 15, Prop.2.5.

In particular, as Wimmel (loc.cit.) points out, the influence of Hor. *Epod.* 15 is evident in 1.9. Wimmel, however, tends to exaggerate this influence. In both poems there is a recollection of the beloved's oath with a complaint of perjury (1ff., 31ff., cf. *Epod.* 15.1ff.), and both poets address their rival (53ff., cf. *Epod.* 15.17ff.), and threaten to take another lover (79ff., cf. *Epod.* 15.13f.). There is also definite verbal reminiscence at 5f. (cf. *Epod.* 15.3f. *cum tu, magnorum numen laesura deorum, / in verba iurabas mea*). But beyond this there are no similarities in language. The address to the rival is an Horatian innovation in this type of poem, but in 1.9 this address is longer and more bitter in tone, while the rival's fate is different (in Horace the beloved is to leave him for another) and appears in a different position in the poem (in Horace it is at the end). The threat to take another lover is not an Horatian innovation (see above), and in 1.9 there is variation in the inclusion of *servitium amoris* and the offering with inscription. In addition, there are certain definite differences from Horace: *Epod.* 15 is concerned with a heterosexual affair but 1.9 with a homosexual liaison (rare in 'separation-poems': cf. Meleager *A.P.* 12.128, Strato 12.237), and the situation is different (in T. the rival is supposed to be a diseased old man), as is the poet's reaction to it (the conflict of emotions discussed below; for this conflict cf. Catull.8, 76, Prop.2.5).

There are also a number of features in 1.9 which first appear here in the 'separation-poem': the multiplicity of punishments proposed for the beloved is a novelty in this connection; 1.9 is the longest ex. of a 'separation-poem' and contains a much more detailed description of past events and deceits in the affair than others do; the slow revelation of the circumstances is also novel and gives the threat of separation at the end of the poem more impact than it has in other versions.

Dawson (loc.cit.) claims that 1.9 was influenced by Call. *Iamb.* 3, but there are no close verbal similarities between the two poems, and the themes of the venal boy (*A.P.* 12.44 Glaucus, 148 Callimachus, 212, 237 Strato) and the unfaithful boy (Theogn.1311ff., Theoc. *Id.* 29, *A.P.* 12.237 Strato, Catull.24, 81) are by no means restricted to *Iamb.* 3.

1.9 presents convincingly the emotional outburst of a man hurt by the behaviour of the boy he loves, and hardly able to believe or understand what the boy has done. For the old man who seduced his boyfriend T. shows supreme hatred and contempt, and curses him in a long and angry passage (which, incidentally, is hardly in accord with the standard evaluation of T. as a quiet and rather anaemic writer). His feelings concerning the boy himself are mixed. Certainly there is anger (see esp. 17-52), along with shame, self-pity and incredulous dismay. So too the recurrence of nemesis throughout and the rather unexpected return to the boy's behaviour and punishment at 75ff. suggest obsession with these details. But T. also shows a lingering affection for his boyfriend. He is still conscious of his attractions (6, 13ff., 30, 51). Despite what has happened he refers to him as *meus / noster puer* (11, 75) and seems to view him more as a victim (11, 53, cf. 19), reserving his deepest anger and greatest bitterness for the seducer. He proclaims sympathy for the boy's plight (3), and hastily deprecates the serious punishment at the hands of the gods that an incensed and disgusted lover would normally pray for (5ff.). In addition, he betrays uncertainty over his own reaction to the threatened separation (81f.). These traces of affection, found side by side with anger and shame, represent a conflict of emotions that forms an undercurrent throughout the elegy. Suitably enough, there is little attention to *doctrina* or neatness of structure, and the progression of thought is sometimes abrupt (esp. 1ff., 39f.).

On the face of it 1.9 is a poem of powerful emotions. But there is more to it than that. The elegy gains greatly in subtle humour by its position immediately after 1.8, firmly and amusingly re-establishing T. in the rôle of the wronged and unhappy lover. In contrast to the detachment and humour in 1.8, we find here involvement and anger. After his superior amusement at Marathus' unhappiness in love in 1.8, now T. himself is unhappy in love. So too in 1.9 the poet has been duped by his boy, although at 1.8.1f. he maintained that he could not be taken in (*celare* at 1.8.1, 1.9.3, 23). Similarly T. himself being deceived in 1.9 represents an entertaining rebound of 1.8.35ff., where he recommends such deception (to Pholoe), and the seduction of the boy in 1.9 by the gifts of an old man is a rebound of the poet's advice to the girl success in 1.9 contradicts T.'s claim of the sexual frustration of old age at 1.8.39ff. But the most diverting contrast is that between the poet's pose as an expert in love in 1.8 and his complete naivety in 1.9. T. openly admits his lack of sophistication at 37f. and 45f., and elsewhere in the elegy shows absence of perception to a degree surprising in a love-elegist: the bewildered question at 1f., the lack of suspicion at the extravagant oaths at 31ff. (contrast 1.4.21ff.), falling for the trick of crying at 37f. (contrast 1.8.67f.) and the dismay at the boy's contact with the repulsive old man (contrast 1.8.29f.). So too it is probably correct to see lack of amatory erudition in T.'s claims that lovers' perjuries are punished (3f., contrast 1.4.21ff.) and that god reveals furtive affairs (23ff., contrast 1.8.35ff., 56).

Apart from creating this amusing antithesis, the juxtaposition of 1.8 and 1.9 also produces neatness in the overall arrangement of T.'s paederastic elegies, whereby in the conjunction of 1.8 and 1.9, as in 1.4 itself, T. makes an entertaining contrast between uninvolved precepts and personal involvement.

1–16 A general introduction to the main themes (deceit, venality and punishment) and background-situation, although we are told here only that the boy has broken faith with T. and has been seduced by gifts. In effect T. is saying here that he wants the boy to be punished for his perjury, but, instead of the usual manifestations of divine wrath, he envisages less serious (but very apt) punishments for him. However, the progression of thought is jerky, and T. moves from perjury and its inevitable punishment (1-4) to a plea for mercy (5-11), then (in the same line) back to punishment (11-16). Such jerkiness befits the conflict of feelings shown in the elegy and esp. visible in this section, as anger and self-pity struggle with affection for the boy and awareness of his attractions. In keeping with the poet's seriousness and attempt to frighten the *puer delicatus* the lines are solemn (esp. the legal imagery at 1ff., the grim picture of *Poena* in 4, the mysterious punishment at 13ff.), although the naivety that characterizes T.'s attitude throughout the poem is also evident.

1–2 For the naive opening question see intro. essay. The interruption of the basic question *quid mihi foedera per divos dabas?* by remarks on the boy's intended infidelity suggests well emotional disturbance. Note too the self-pity in *miseros.*

The idea of sexual unions other than marriage as compacts of partnership (for this use of *foedus* see 1.5.7-8n.) originated in Latin with Catullus (76.3, 109.5f., 87.3f. *nulla fides ullo fuit umquam foedere tanta / quanta in amore tuo ex parte reperta meast*). The elegists took up this idea and added a number of details and technical expressions: for the terms of the contract see 1.6.69-72n.; see also Prop.3.20.15ff.

(terms, seal, witness), 4.8.73ff. (exx. of terms). So T. is here using technical language (*foedera; dare*, cf. Sall. *Iug.* 104.5, Livy 23.5.9; *violo*, cf. Cic. *Res Pub.* 1.19.31, Livy 28.44.7).

For the complaint of perjury see intro. essay and cf. also *A.P.* 5.7 (Asclepiades), 8 (Meleager), 52 (Dioscorides), 184 (Meleager), 279 (Paulus Silentiarius), Prop. 1.15, Ov. *Am.* 3.3, Hor. *C.* 2.8.

fueras . . . laesurus amores: for *laedere amorem* of faithlessness cf. Ov. *Her.* 7.59, *Tr.* 2.387f. (of Medea) *tingueret ut ferrum natorum sanguine mater, / concitus a laeso fecit amore dolor.*

The future participle with *sum* in the past tense denotes an action which was intended in the past. Although *fueras* may be used merely as an alternative for *eras*, here it probably places the boy's intention to deceive prior to the swearing (see Smith, Roby 1494).

3–4 a miser: as Smith points out, *a* is rare in books 1 and 2, and therefore emphatic (only at 1.10.59, 2.1.79 elsewhere). For the compassion here see intro. essay.

sera tamen tacitis Poena venit pedibus: i.e. 'comes late, but comes none the less' (cf. Virg. *Ecl.* 1.27 *libertas, quae sera tamen respexit inertem*, Prop. 3.15.35 and Camps ad loc.).

The slow but sure punishment of the gods is an idea found from earliest times: see Smith, Dodds on Eur. *Bacc.* 882, Ogilvie on Livy 3.56.7, Otto *Sprichwörter* s.v. deus (11), and cf. also Hes. *Opera* 333f., Theogn. 203f., Stat. *Theb.* 5.688f., 23-4n.

On *Poena* see Critical Appendix. *Poena* (also found in the plural) was the personification of retribution: cf. esp. Aesch. *Choeph.* 935f. ἔμολε μὲν δίκα Πριαμίδαις χρόνῳ / βαρύδικος ποινά, Hor. *C.* 3.2.31f., Stat. *Theb.* 5.59f. *movet et caelestia quondam / corda dolor lentoque inrepunt agmine Poenae*. Cf. also Paus. 1.43.7, Plut. *Mor.* 564E-F, *Culex* 376f., Luc. 6.695, Val. Fl. 1.790ff.

Usually of course lovers' perjuries were supposed to go unpunished (1.4.21-2n.): see intro. essay. Note the forceful alliteration (t and esp. p, also in *parcite*, first word in 5).

5–6 For similar compassion in T. cf. 1.1.67f., 1.8.49f., 1.10.59ff., 2.6.41 and see intro. essay. The appeal rests on three grounds: (i) he is beautiful, (ii) he only did it once (*semel* in emphatic position), (iii) he is no worse than the rest of mankind (see on 7-10).

For (i) cf. Theogn. 1279ff., Prop. 2.28.1f. *Iuppiter, affectae tandem miserere puellae: / tam formosa tuum mortua crimen erit*, 49f., Ov. *Am.* 3.3.11f., 25f., 41ff.

For (ii) cf. Ter. *Eun.* 852f., *Phorm.* 141f., Cic. *Quinct.* 16.52, Ov. *Am.* 2.14.43, Petron. *S.* 49, Quint. 7.4.31 *est enim domestica disceptatio, in qua et semel peccasse et per errorem et levius, quam obiciatur, absolutioni nonnunquam sufficit.* See Smith for a quote from Rip at 1.8.29f. (*munera* at 1.8.29, 1.9.11, 12). Again, the ugly old man's

Van Winkle.

aequum est impune licere: keeps up the legal image.

numina formosis laedere vestra semel: for *formosis* see 1.4.3-4n. The word here shows that T. is still aware of the boy's attractions (see intro. essay).

On *numen* see Bailey *Religion in Virgil* (Oxford, 1935), 60ff. The word may denote the will of a god or the god himself seen as a power or spirit. Here *numina . . . vestra* may well be little more than a dignified periphrasis for *vos* (see Bailey op.cit.65, who cites *Aen.* 1.48, 3.437, 543; see also Austin on *Aen.* 4.204).

For the use of *laedo* in this connection cf. Hor. *Epod.* 15.3 (see intro. essay), T.1.3.79, 3.4.16, 3.6.26.

7–**10** At first sight these lines seem odd, as no connection between them and the preceding lines is immediately apparent. Their purpose is to show that all men have a mercenary nature, but the fact that this point is made first aims at more inclination to leniency by the time the case of the boy is reached (cf. the order at 1.4.3ff.). The repetition of *lucra* (in emphatic positions) with a form of *peto* binds the couplets together, and the contrast between land- and sea-occupations makes the argument more comprehensive. Note also the gradation: trading is less reputable (poetically) than farming and more dangerous – hence the idea that man will do anything for money, and the likelihood of greater clemency by line 11.

For the excuse cf. Sen. *Contr.* 2.4.10, Petron. *S.* 49, Donatus ad Ter. *Phorm.* 245 *quod a precatoribus dici solebat communia esse et posse fieri.*

Farming and trading (and a few other occupations) were often used to show the diversity of aspirations and to indicate by contrast the poet's preference: cf. Bacchyl. *Epinik.* 10.35ff. Snell, Soph. *Ant.* 332ff., Virg. *G.* 2.490ff., Hor. *S.* 1.1, *C.* 1.1, T.1.1, 1.2.65ff., 1.10. At the time of T. and elsewhere in T. the occupations are usually contrasted to show the superiority of life in the country. Here T. emphasizes the inherent similarity, in that the incentive of each occupation is the pursuit of gain (cf. Solon 1.41ff.D, Pind. *Ol.* 2.63ff., *Isth.* 1.47ff.). For greed for wealth see esp. intro. essay to 1.1.

7–**8** A realistic approach is evident in the statement that gain is the aim of farming (cf. Solon, Pindar loc.cit., Hes. *Opera* 17ff., 298ff., Virg. *G.* 2.513ff.) and in the mention of the hard work involved (cf. Virg. *G.* 1.121ff., 2.401f., T.1.7.39).

durum terrae rusticus urget opus: 'the rustic toils at the hard work of the land' (i.e. ploughing). For *urgeo* so used cf. Hor. *Epist.* 1.14.26f., Virg. *Aen.* 9.488f., esp. Ov. *Met.* 4.390, and for *opus* of agricultural labour cf. Cic. *Sen.* 7.24. On the expression *terrae . . . opus* cf. Virg. *Aen.* 8.516 *grave Martis opus*.

The frequency of u in the pentameter is striking, and the sound perhaps brings out the toil of the rustic.

9–10 For the dangers of navigation see 1.3.37-8n. (here well expressed by *instabiles* and the emphasis on passivity – sea obeys winds, ships are led by stars). For greed as its motive see 1.3.39-40n.

instabiles . . . rates: for the application of the adjective cf. Caes. *B.G.*4.23 *ut maritimae res postularent, ut quae celerem atque instabilem motum haberent*, Virg. *G.*4.195, Ov. *Met.* 2.164, Curt.4.2.9, 8.13.11.

sidera certa: most obviously the adjective means 'fixed, sure', in contrast to *instabiles* (see 1.4.19-20n.), but there is an accessory notion of 'trustworthy' for navigating by (Hor. *C.* 2.16.3f., Ov. *Her.* 18.155, Luc.3.218f. *has ad bella rates non flexo limite ponti / certior haud ullis duxit Cynosura carinis*).

11–12 muneribus meus est captus puer: confirms the suggestion in the previous lines that the boy has been seduced by gifts. *Muneribus* picks up *lucra* but also points to the lower level on which the *puer delicatus* operates. For the venality of boys see intro. essay.

For *capio* see 1.4.3-4n. The word suggests that the boy is a victim (see intro. essay).

For the use of *meus . . . puer* despite what has happened see intro. essay.

On the rare sense-pause see Platnauer p.25.

at deus illa / in cinerem et liquidas munera vertat aquas: on *at* in curses see 1.3.33-4n. This curse and the punishment of the following lines are less severe than the usual manifestations of divine wrath, but are also very apt (the boy's beauty led to the offer of gifts, which he accepted: he is, therefore, to lose both the gifts and his beauty). For the curse here cf. Hom. *Il.* 7.99, Plaut. *Rud.* 1257 *si aurum si argentum est, omne id ut fiat cinis*, Prop.2.16.43ff., Ov. *Am.* 3.8.65f. See also 49-50n.

Liquidas may be *epitheton ornans* here, but I am inclined to agree with Dissen *'diffluant [munera], ait, ut liquida est aqua'.*

13–14 The exact ref. here is not immediately apparent and seems to have been left deliberately vague, to make the punishment more frightening. Some commentators compare 1.4.41ff. (the lover's services) and maintain that the boy's seducer will force him to accompany him everywhere and that the boy will thus lose his beauty. However, there has been no mention so far of the seducer, and he would hardly spoil the boy's beauty in this way, since he would presumably find it attractive himself. There is also a considerable element of exaggeration at 1.4.41ff. (see notes ad loc.).

It seems more likely that the present passage is parallel to 1.4.67-70, but with a different emphasis. The crime is the same (1.4.67 *vendit amorem*, cf. 1.9.32, 51, 77) and the punishment is similar (1.4.68f. a long journey on foot, cf. 1.9.16; 1.4.70 physical disfigurement, cf. the loss of beauty here).

In any case, the point is that the *puer delicatus* is to lose his beauty (*decorem* in emphatic position). For the theme of nemesis see 1.2. 87-96n. This punishment for the cruel lover usually took the form of the advent of hairs (cf. *A.P.* 12.33 (Meleager), 35 (Diocles), 39 (anon.), 174 (Fronto), 186, 229 (Strato), Hor. *C.* 4.10 etc.). T.'s list is more comprehensive (literally from head to toe) and has real point, since he mentions the details of appearance that a *puer delicatus* would prize (as is clear from 1.8.9ff.). Note the forcefulness of expression (the intensifying prefix in *persolvet*, the alliteration of p and d (13f.), the emphatic repetition and positions of *uro* in 15). Note too that the poet is still aware of the boy's attractions (see intro. essay).

pulvisque decorem / detrahet: dust would affect both his person and his dress (cf. 1.8.13f.): e.g. Cic. *Inv.* 1.30.47, Virg. *G.* 4.96f., Stat. *Theb.* 3.326.

et ventis horrida facta coma: (in contrast to the elaborate hair, e.g., of 1.8.9f.) a sign of ugliness: cf. Cic. *Sest.* 8.19 *capillo ita horrido, ut Capua . . . Seplasiam sublaturus videretur*, T.2.3.23f.

The phrase is the subject of *detrahet* along with *pulvisque*. For the homoeoteleuton see 1.1.53-4n.

15–16 uretur facies: his fair complexion (1.4.11-12n.) will be spoiled by sunburn: cf. Mart.2.41.12, Nemes. *Ecl.* 4.44f. *tu quoque, saeve puer, niveum ne perde colorem / sole sub hoc.*

urentur sole capilli: T. returns to the boy's hair, because he would prize its appearance (e.g. 1.8.9f.). The sun will bleach or dry and take the sheen from his hair or make it woolly (Strabo 695, Plin. *N.H.* 2.189). In any case it will have an unpleasant appearance (cf. Prop.4.9.45f. *sin aliquem vultusque meus saetaeque leonis / terrent et Libyco sole perusta coma*).

invalidos . . . pedes: for the *puer delicatus* and his attention to his feet cf. 1.8.14. As Smith points out, the boy is treated as if he were a woman: cf. Virg. *Ecl.* 10.49, Prop.1.8.7, Ov. *Am.* 1.4.44 *nec tenerum duro cum pede iunge pedem, A.A.* 1.162, 2.212, 534. The *puer delicatus* was noted for his delicacy and effeminacy: cf. Anac.4D, Hor. *Epod.* 11.23ff., T.1.4.9, 14, 58, 1.8.9ff., 67f., 1.9.30, *A.P.* 12.175 (Strato).

Invalidus is borrowed from Virgil (the word is found only at *G.* 3.128, 189, 4.498 before here).

The pentameter may contain an inversion of Lucr.1.315f. (*strataque iam vulgi pedibus detrita viarum / saxea conspicimus*), as Putnam suggests.

17–52 Complaints to the boy. At first sight the transition seems a little abrupt, but the poet's first complaint is that the boy ignored T.'s advice not to sell his charms and thereby make himself liable to punishment, and so the themes of venality, the boy's beauty and nemesis are continued. The transition is also helped by verbal echoes (*formam*, 17, cf. *formosis*, 6; *divitiis captus*, 19, cf. *muneribus . . . captus*, 11).

Throughout the section there is a progression in passion, as fresh instances of the deceitfulness of the *puer delicatus* and the poet's own naivety are recalled. Again there is an undercurrent: although T. now repudiates his former devotion, he still betrays consciousness of the boy's charms (30, 51). T. begins by stating the advice which he gave so often to the boy (17-30): the first six couplets are a (rather pathetic) quotation of his words, and a final couplet describes T.'s present shame at the entreaties which accompanied the advice. The recollection then moves to the boy's answering oaths not to let himself be seduced and the way in which T. was taken in (31-38). Anger at this deception leads to a sudden remembrance of the boy's affair with a girl (39-46): this situation suggests to T. in the first couplet a very apt punishment (that the girl should be as fickle towards the *puer delicatus* as he was towards T.); T. then elaborates on the boy's fickleness in two couplets on his help to him with the girl and a final couplet on the way in which the boy only used him. A final reminiscence concerns the poetry which T. composed in praise of the boy (47-50): here the anger mounts, and one line only recalls his poetry, while the remaining lines concern his shame at and desired destruction of the verse. The last couplet of the section represents a climax in which as a result of these reminiscences T. curtly dismisses the boy.

During these complaints we are told a new detail in the background-situation (the *puer delicatus* is also in love with a girl), and in the final couplet there is a hint that T. may be contemplating a separation from the boy.

17–18 For the change to direct speech see 1.5.21-4n. Note the emphasis in the strong word *polluo* (cf. *violo* in 19), the repetition of *auro*, the positions of *saepe* and *mala* and the sigmatism in the pentameter (and below). T.'s advice was expressed forcefully.

quotiens: throughout the section there is emphasis on the frequency of T.'s kindness and of the boy's deceit (*usque* 38, *quotiens* 41, *saepe* 43, the imperfects at 29, 31, 37, 38, 46, 47).

subesse: 'lurk unseen': cf. Lucr.3.273 *nam penitus prorsum latet haec natura subestque*, Tac. *Ann.* 2.41, *Hist.* 4.16.

19–20 **divitiis captus**: cf. 11 and see 1.4.3-4n.

violavit: see 1.6.51-2n.

asperaque est illi difficilisque Venus: for the harsh and punitive aspects of Venus see 1.2.37-40n., 1.8.7-8n., 1.10.57-8n., Nisbet & Hubbard on Hor. *C.* 1.19.1 *mater saeva Cupidinum*. Cf. also Eur. *Hipp.* 5f. (Aphrodite) τοὺς μὲν σέβοντας τἀμὰ πρεσβεύω κράτη, / σφάλλω δ' ὅσοι φρονοῦσιν εἰς ἡμᾶς μέγα, Theoc. *Id.* 20.44f., *A.P.* 5.280

(Agathias Scholasticus), T.1.5.58, 1.6.83f., 1.8.28, 4.13.23f., Prop. 4.5.65f., Ov. *A.A.* 2.397f., *Met.* 14.693f. The point is underlined by the use of two adjectives here.

21–22 Some commentators maintain that these lines are addressed to Venus and that T. is asking her to direct her wrath against himself rather than the *puer delicatus*. However, the couplet comes between direct addresses to the boy at 17 and 23, and there has been no indication of a change of addressee, while the nature of the attack clearly suggests *servitium amoris*. It seems most likely that the lines are addressed to the *puer delicatus* and that T. is asking the boy to take him as his abject slave and treat him as he wishes, rather than sell himself. The couplet takes the form of an impassioned interjection, which by its extreme nature greatly adds to the impact of the preceding lines.

Note the emphasis in the group of three punishments, a Tibullan innovation in *servitium amoris* (1.5.5-6n.).

ure meum potius flamma caput: see 1.5.5-6n.

pete ferro / corpus: shackles (cf. 2.6.26) may be meant (see 1.1. 55-6n.), or T. may even be thinking of mutilation (cf. Suet. *Cal.* 32.2), which would be an entirely original detail in the figure.

intorto verbere terga seca: for this common servile torture (e.g. Ov. *Her.* 20.77) in *servitium amoris* cf. 1.6.37f., 1.8.5-6n., 2.3.80, Ov. *A.A.* 2.533f. *nec maledicta puta nec verbera ferre puellae / turpe.*

Seca (cf. Hor. *Epod.* 4.11, Mart. 10.5.14) and *intorto* bring out the savagery (for the phrase *intorto verbere* cf. 1.6.46, Virg. *G.* 3.106, *Aen.* 7.378, Ov. *Ibis* 159: the idea is of a lash made of twisted thongs, like the twisted ropes at Catull. 64.235).

The pattern of initial letters from the third word of the couplet to the tenth is remarkable.

23–24 For the common idea that sins cannot be concealed, but are found out in the course of time or by divine intervention see Smith, Otto *Sprichwörter* s.v. *tempus* 5, and cf. also Eur.fr.441N χρόνος διέρπων πάντ᾽ ἀληθεύειν φιλεῖ, *Trag. Graec. Frag. Adesp.* 511N χρόνος τὰ κρυπτὰ πάντα εἰς φάος ἄγει, Diog. 10.151, Aelian *Var. Hist.* fr.62 (Hercher). See also 3-4n. T. cites realistic exx. for illustration below. For the contrast with 1.8 see intro. essay.

peccare: the whole passage is general, so strictly *peccare* should be taken to mean 'sin' in general, but the particular ref. here is clear (1.6.15-16n.).

deus: a general term, and so more impressive.

dolos: again a generalization, but again the particular ref. here is obvious (53-4n.).

Note the vigorous alliteration here.

25–26 An application of the proverbial *in vino veritas* (see Gow on Theoc. *Id.* 29.1, Otto *Sprichwörter* s.v. *vinum* 2). For wine as a betrayer of secrets see Smith, Nisbet & Hubbard on Hor. *C.* 1.18.16 and cf. also *A.P.*12.135 (Asclepiades).

ipse deus tacito permisit lene ministro: see Critical Appendix.

With *lene* it seems obscure and unnecessary to understand *merum* from *mero* in 26. *Lene* is most probably the adverb (cf. Sen. *Phaed.* 509, Calp. *Ecl.* 7.25, Nemes. *Ecl.* 4.47). *Ministro* is a slave who has witnessed something, and *tacito* means normally silent (i.e. through fear of his master: cf. Hor. *S.* 2.7.1f.). However, most slaves like to gossip (Sen. *Epist.* 47.3f., Macrob. *S.* 1.11.15), so *permisit lene* (i.e. 'indulgently': cf. Cic. *Fam.* 5.2.9, *Rosc.Am.* 154, Ov. *Tr.* 5.2.36) means that god, like a kind master, has allowed the slave to follow his natural inclinations, under the influence of wine (26). So *permisit lene* is in opposition to *iussit . . . invitos* (28), the contrast emphasizing the power of god.

libera verba: 'free' words from a slave is a good touch.

For the same internal rhyme in hex. and pent. see 1.1.53-4n.

27–28 The repetition of *ipse deus* emphasizes the idea of god's personal intervention, and the juxtaposition *tegenda loqui* brings out his power.

For the revelation of secrets in sleep cf. Cic. *Top.* 20.75, Lucr. 4.1018f., 5.1158ff., Tac. *Ann.* 4.60 *ne nox quidem secura, cum uxor vigilias somnos suspiria matri Liviae atque illa Seiano patefaceret.*

29–30 For shame at one's former behaviour towards a lover cf. 47f., Prop. 2.24.16, 3.24, Ov. *Am.* 2.18.7f., 3.11.

flevisse . . . / . . . ad teneros procubuisse pedes: on *teneros . . . pedes* see 15-16n. and intro. essay. For these methods of entreaty cf. Prop. 4.8.72, Ov. *Her.* 16.272, *Am.* 1.7.61 *ter tamen ante pedes volui procumbere supplex, A.A.* 1.659f. *et lacrimae prosunt; lacrimis adamanta movebis: / fac madidas videat, si potes, illa genas.* Another charge against the boy is that he ignored these entreaties.

31–34 The exaggeration of these protestations might have seemed suspicious (see intro. essay). For the division of wealth into riches and land see 1.1.1-2n. For the combination of gold and jewels cf. Prop. 1.8.39 *hanc ego non auro, non Indis flectere conchis*, 1.14.11f., Hor. *C.* 2.16.7f., 3.24.48.

divitis auri: see 1.10.7-8n. The adjective highlights the extravagance of the claim.

Campania terra: a volcanic plain in central Italy, noted for its fertility: cf. Prop. 3.5.5, Livy 7.38.6f., Plin. *N.H.* 3.60ff., 18.111, esp. Cic. *Leg. Agr.* 2.35.95 *Campani semper superbi bonitate agrorum et fructuum magnitudine.*

Bacchi cura: for the idea and the expression cf. 3.4.43, Ov. *Am.* 3.9.17, Hor. *C.* 2.6.19f., Stat. *Silv.* 2.2.4. The phrase makes the region seem even more desirable.

Falernus ager: a region in Campania at the foot of Mt. Massicus, famous for its wines (*Bacchi cura*): cf. Hor. *C.* 3.1.43, Plin. *N.H.* 14.62, esp. Varro *R.R.* 1.2.6 *contra quid in Italia utensile non modo non nascitur, sed etiam non egregium fit? Quod far conferam Campano? . . . Quod vinum Falerno?*

Note the progression from the most fertile district in Italy to that district's own best wine-producing area.

The positions of the negatives (note esp. repeated *non*) give emphasis.

35–36 For this expression of deception and persuasiveness cf. Titinius 100R, Ov. *Met.* 11.313f. *nascitur Autolycus furtum ingeniosus ad omne, / candida de nigris et de candentibus atra / qui facere adsuerat*, Juv.3.30. It represents T. as supremely credulous (cf. Petron. *S.* 37 *mero meridie si dixerit illi tenebras esse, credet*, possibly Prop.4.1.143).

eriperes: 'take away my belief that'. This is the only case of *eripio* with an accusative and infinitive. For the infinitive alone cf. Sil.It. 14.131f.

sidera caeli: 'the stars of (i.e. in) heaven' (cf. e.g. Virg. *G.* 2.1, 4.58, *Aen.* 1.259, 8.141, 10.176, 11.878, Petron. *S.* 123 v.201f.).

puras fulminis esse vias: see Critical Appendix.

Purus, when applied to celestial phenomena, primarily means 'free from clouds' (e.g. 4.1.10), which implies that the light of these phenomena is of the same brilliance as usual (see Acron ad Hor. *C.* 2.5.19), and so the word occasionally means 'undimmed' in general, i.e. 'clear, bright'. So Virgil (*Aen.* 2.589f.) of the appearance of Venus to Aeneas: *cum mihi se, non ante oculis tam clara, videndam / obtulit et pura per noctem in luce refulsit*, where *pura* is virtually synonymous with *clara*. Similarly Ovid (*A.A.* 3.55f.) after an interview with Venus says *purior aether / fulsit*, where there has been no mention of clouds. When Horace speaks of the dazzling beauty of Glycera (*C.* 1.19.5f.) he compares it to Parian marble, and the point of the comparison is the brilliance of the marble: *urit me Glycerae nitor, / splendentis Pario marmore purius.*

Vias most probably means the 'paths' or 'tracks' of the thunderbolt. This is the meaning of the word at Sen. *Thy.* 358f. *quem non concutiet cadens / obliqui via fulminis* (cf. *iter* at Sen. *N.Q.* 2.58.2). So *via* is also applied to a star's path at Virg. *Aen.* 2.696-8 (*pace* Austin) and the path of an arrow compared to a shooting star at *Aen.* 5.525ff.

37–38 For the trick of crying cf. 1.8.67f. and see 29-30n., 1.10.53-6n. For T.'s attitude see 1.8.67-8n. On T.'s naivety here and his admission of it see intro. essay.

non ego fallere doctus: see 1.7.19-20n. for the infinitive after the adjective.

umentes: the form (pres. part.) is first found here. It is also applied to tears at Ov. *Met.* 11.464, Sil.It.9.30 *sed vos, quorum oculos atque ora umentia vidi. Umidus* is more common in prose and poetry, while *umens* is restricted to poetry and post-Aug. prose. Even in poetry *umens* is very rare apart from the loftier genres: it never occurs in lyric, comedy or satire (nor in Lucr. or Sen. *Trag.*), and only appears with any real frequency in later authors. Virgil prefers *umidus* (17: 4), in Lucan and Val.Fl. the two words are about equally popular, Statius prefers *umens*, and Sil.It. shows a marked preference for *umens* (17: 1). In elegy *umens* occurs elsewhere only at Ov. *Am.* 1.14.34, and *umidus* is generally more common (in T. *umidus* 1 (1.8.37): *umens* 1; Prop. 3: 0; Ovid 9: 1). Metre, of course, is relevant: *umidas* would not go here, and both words are obviously necessary to supply forms that can go into dactylic verse for all the cases.

9–40 quid faciam, nisi et ipse fores in amore puellae?: see Critical Appendix.

Quid faciam is a rhetorical question which serves the function of an apodosis, the *nisi* clause coming as an afterthought and showing that he has just realized a fitting punishment: 'I do not know what to do (to punish you) – but no, you yourself are also in love, so (40) I pray that the girl proves as fickle as you'. In other words, the recollection of the lies and tricks in the previous lines led T. to desire some punishment for the boy, but he could not think of one, until he suddenly remembered the boy's love for the girl. The broken syntax and rapid change of thought suggest well an emotional and confused state of mind.

Smith explains *et ipse fores in amore puellae* as 'you yourself are in love with a girl in spite of your other affair', but this interpretation seems unlikely, since *ipse* would then be redundant, and this explanation of *et . . . in amore puellae* implies that the boy was in love with the seducer, whereas there is no suggestion that he finds anything attractive in him other than his money. It seems best to interpret the words as 'you yourself are also in love (with a girl)', i.e. 'you are in love with a girl, as I am in love with you' (hence the aptness and effectiveness of the punishment). For the *puer delicatus* in love with a girl see intro. essay to 1.8.

Fores stands for *esses* (see Smith), and *puellae* is an objective genitive.

sit precor exemplo sit levis illa tuo: for *exemplo . . . tuo* cf. Ov. *Am.* 1.4.46, *A.A.* 1.658, and for the rebound (underlined by the juxtaposition *illa tuo*) cf. 1.6.9-10n. Note the vigorous repetition of *sit.*

1–42 These lines pick up the idea of the boy's fickleness towards T. (in his affair with the girl). The exact situation here is not clear. The meetings between the boy and the girl (implied in *verbis*, i.e. *sermo amatorius*: cf. 1.8.2) may have been so skilfully arranged that simply by replacing the lantern-bearer T. ensured absolute secrecy, or he may have acted as a look-out at the meetings as well as lighting the way. The stealth is either due to a natural desire for privacy or because of a jealous lover.

For the nocturnal rendezvous cf. 1.2.24ff., 1.6.5f., 61f., 1.8.59, 64, 2.6.49, Prop.1.3.37, Ov. *Am.* 1.8.67.

For T. 'playing gooseberry' cf. Prop.1.10, 1.13, and for his helpful attitude to the boy cf. 1.8.

Because there was no regular street-lighting people had either to grope their way around or to have their way lighted by lanterns and torches at night (1.2.36, Juv.3.282ff., Petron. *S.* 79). This function was normally performed by slaves (Mart.8.75, Suet. *Aug.* 29.3 *per nocturnum iter lecticam eius fulgur praestrinxisset servumque praelucentem exanimasset*, Val.Max.6.8.1), so that T.'s action here is an ex. of *servitium amoris* (1.5.5-6n.). For this type of task (first found here in the figure) cf. 1.5.65-6n.

T. underlines his devotion by *o quotiens, ipse* (emphatic position) and *multa . . . nocte* ('late at night': cf. Cic. *Q. Frat.* 2.7.2, Caes. *B.G.* 3.26.6).

43–44 It seems likely that T. is thinking of one situation here. In this case *clausas post . . . fores* indicates that the girl is inside a house, while *latuit* and *adoperta* make it clear that she is trying to escape detection. The fact that she is hiding behind a door means that she must be trying to escape detection from those outside (in any case, if she were trying to be undetected by persons also within, *post* would be inappropriate and the covering of the head would be ineffectual). It seems unlikely that she has come to the house where the boy lives, since, once admitted, there would be no need for her to lurk behind the door in particular to escape the notice of people outside. Most probably, then, the action is supposed to be taking place in the house in which she lives.

Two situations are suggested. *Insperanti venit tibi* implies that the boy has already arrived at her house, although without much hope of success. Then possibly the girl makes her way to the door and hides there until the coast is clear to admit him (for the situation cf. 1.2.18ff., 2.1.75ff.). Alternatively, the pent. may precede the hex. chronologically: she hides behind the door and then comes out to him when the coast is clear (for the situation and the chronological displacement cf. 1.6. 59-62n.).

It is also possible that T. is thinking of two different situations in this couplet, *venit* being a general ref. to meetings and *latuit* etc. referring to the girl hiding behind her door ready to admit the boy (for similar ambiguity see 1.6.59-62).

Whatever the exact circumstances, *munere nostro* will mean that T. has persuaded the girl or told her how to handle the operation. For *munere nostro* (i.e. 'assistance') cf. Ov. *Met.* 7.93. The contrast with the *munera* of the seducer (11f.) is deliberate: this was T.'s 'gift'.

T.'s kindness is brought out by *insperanti*, and by *saepe* and *nostro* in emphatic positions.

adoperta: see 1.1.69-70n.

45–46 tum miser interii: for *intereo* used of the effects of deception cf. Plaut. *Aul.*713, *Most.*1031, *Pers.*780 *perii, interii. pessumus hic mi dies hodie inluxit corruptor, / ita me Toxilu' perfabricavit itaque meam rem divexavit. / vehiclum argenti miser eieci*. The boy's deceit consisted in pretending to love T., so that he would help him in his affair with the girl, while he did not love T. at all but was merely using him for his services. Note the self-pity in *miser.*

stulte confisus amari: according to *Thes.L.L.* IV.208.69ff. *confido* with a present infinitive is first found in Cicero. The construction is found occasionally in poetry (e.g. Lucr.5.390), but is more common in prose. For the omission of *me* cf. Lucr.loc.cit.

On T.'s admission of his naivety here see intro. essay.

nam poteram ad laqueos cautior esse tuos: explains *stulte*. For this use of the imperfect indicative see Roby 1535-6 and 1.8.55-6n. Here the ref. is to the past ('I could have been . . .').

For the imagery see 1.6.3-4n., 1.6.5-6n.

Cautus with *ad* is rare apart from late authors: see *Thes. L. L.* III.642. 35f., and cf. also Livy 24.32.3. The usage is not confined to very late authors, as Smith maintains (cf. Quint.6.1.20, Aul.Gell.13.28.4).

47–48 attonita laudes tibi mente canebam: *attonitus* probably comes from Virgil (before here it is found only at Sall.*Hist.* fr.1.136, Virg. *G.* 2.508, 3.545). Properly it means 'struck by thunder', but it is applied to various violent emotional disturbances. For its amatory application cf. Ov. *Her.*16.135f. *ut vidi, obstipui praecordiaque intima sensi / attonitus curis intumuisse novis, A.A.*2.296, *Met.*10.154, Sen. *Contr.* 10.3.10, Fronto 20.1N. Lee (p.110) points out three meanings possible here ('spellbound', 'inspired', 'crazy'); also possible is the sense 'fascinated, absorbed' (see *OLD* s.v. 2d, 3, 4, 5).

In *laudes . . . canebam* the ref. may be to general complimentary remarks in his poetry (Prop.2.25.1ff., 3.24.1ff., Ov. *Am.* 3.12), or to private poems sent to the boy (cf. Ov. *A.A.*2.273ff.), or possibly to poems in praise of the boy addressed to the girl (e.g. 1.8).

at me nunc nostri Pieridumque pudet: see Critical Appendix.

Nostri stands for *mei* (1.2.11-12n.) and *Pieridum* stands for 'poetry' (1.4.61-2n.).

For shame at one's behaviour see 29-30n., esp. Prop.3.24.3f. *noster amor tales tribuit tibi, Cynthia, laudes: / versibus insignem te pudet esse meis.* The halting monosyllables and the alliteration seem to underline the gravity of T.'s feelings.

49–50 Compare 11-12n. The destruction of one's poems by such methods was a common literary motif: see Nisbet & Hubbard on Hor. *C.*1.16.3 and cf. also Mart.1.5 *do tibi naumachiam, tu das epigrammata nobis: / vis, puto, cum libro, Marce, natare tuo*, 3.100 *cursorem sexta tibi, Rufe,* *remisimus hora, / carmina quem madidum nostra tulisse reor: / imbribus inmodicis caelum nam forte ruebat. / non aliter mitti debuit ille liber.* The combination of both methods and the adjectives *rapida* and *liquida* emphasize the totality of destruction desired.

Vulcanus: 'fire' (Plaut. *Amph.* 341, Virg. *Aen.* 7.77 etc.).

For the same internal rhyme in hex. and pent. see 1.1.53-4n.

51–52 The passage reaches a climax and T. curtly dismisses the *puer delicatus* (until 75). This is a vague hint that T. may be contemplating a definite separation.

formam: T. is still aware of the boy's attractions (see intro. essay).

cura est: for the hex. ending see 1.3.5-8n.

plena . . . manu: a vivid touch. For the phrase see 1.5.67-8n.

53–74 *At te* picks up *tu* (51), as T. moves from angry address to the corrupted to angry address to the corrupter.

The attack on the boy's seducer is a vicious and bitter passage, full of slander, insults and malicious gossip (implicit and explicit), which are expressed in carefully chosen language and presented in graphic detail. The point of the curse (53-64) is that the seducer's wife is to prefer other men to him, just as the boy is supposed to have preferred the seducer to T.: the first three couplets describe her future infidelity with a number of lovers and the seducer's ignorance of it; three balancing couplets extend the insults by describing the lustfulness and drunkenness of the seducer's sister and praying that his wife will surpass her. The final five couplets (65-74) return to the present and with callous candour and sarcasm point out that the process is already under way. The supreme insult is reserved for the final couplet, in which T. fully exculpates the wife on the grounds of the seducer's physical repulsiveness. During the course of this attack T. incidentally reveals that the seducer is a married man, and that he is old and diseased.

53–54 For the address to the seducer see 1.5.69-70n. and intro. essay. For the theme of nemesis see 1.2.87-96n. The punishment fits the crime (53-74n.): for the curse cf. 3.6.12, Ov. *Ibis* 353ff. *tam quoque di faciant possis gaudere fideli / coniuge quam Talai Tyndareique gener: / quaeque parare suis letum patruelibus ausae / Belides assidua colla premuntur aqua. / Byblidos et Canaces, sicut facis, ardeat igne, / nec nisi per crimen sit tibi fida soror*, *Priap.* 47.

puerum . . . corrumpere es ausus: again the boy is seen as a victim (see intro. essay). For the uncommon elision see Platnauer p.85.

rideat adsiduis uxor inulta dolis: the wife is to be unfaithful – repeatedly (for *doli* cf. 24, 3.6.12, Prop.4.7.16, Ov. *Am.* 2.19.44), and, fool that he is, the seducer is not to realize (see 1.2.55-6n.). The idea of his own wife laughing at him is an unpleasant detail. An ablative with *rideo* in this sense occurs here only, although it is not uncommon with *derideo* (e.g. Petron. *S.* 92, 106).

For *uxor* see 1.4.73-4n.

55–56 et cum furtivo iuvenem lassaverit usu: i.e. her lust is to be so great that she tires out even her virile young lover (cf. Ov. *Am.* 3.11.13f.). *Iuvenis* (cf. 71) has particular point, as the word suggests vigour and her husband is an old man (73f.).

Lasso is found only at *Trag.Incert.* 241R before here: for its use in this connection cf. Juv.6.130.

Usus is applied to intercourse first here (cf. Ov. *Am.* 3.7.3, *Rem.* 357, *F.* 4.657 and *usura corporis* at Plaut. *Amph.* 108). In this sense *uti* of a woman is odd and rare (cf. Ov. *A.A.* 3.786 *ut celer aversis utere Parthus equis*): women did not normally take the initiative.

languida: i.e. finally sated, she will want no more sexual encounters: cf. Ov. *Am.* 3.7.80, *A.A.* 2.692 *langueat, et tangi se vetet illa diu*, Mart. 12.97.6f.

interposita . . . veste: to prevent her husband's advances. This is a realistic detail. *Vestis* may refer to the coverlet (Agathias Scholasticus *A.P.* 5.294.3) or to the wife's clothes (Prop.2.15.6, 17, Lucian *Dial.Mer.* 309).

57–58 Note the pointed juxtaposition *externa tuo* (the fact that this is happening in his own bed (and house) makes things even worse) and the emphasis in the repeated *semper* and *pateat . . . aperta.*

vestigia: the 'marks' of a lover: see Shackleton Bailey *Propertiana* 82 and cf. also Cic. *Verr.* 3.34.79, Livy 1.58.7, Aristaenet.2.22 (of an adulteress on her husband's arrival) *τὴν στρωμνὴν ἐνετάραξε, παντελῶς συγχέουσα τὸ ἔρεισμα τοῦ δευτέρου σώματος, ὅτι κατηγόρει μηνύματα συζυγίας.*

cupidis: i.e. 'lovers' (cf. 1.8.56, 74). Note the progression to more than one lover.

59–60 nec lasciva soror dicatur plura bibisse / pocula: it is not clear whose sister is meant here, but there would be more point if it was the seducer's sister. *Dicatur* (cf.61 *ferunt*) means that the women are both to be infamous, so that the seducer's reputation and standing will suffer.

Excessive drinking by women was considered disgraceful (Juv.6. 300ff., Sen. *Epist.* 95.21, Athen.440D). This remark is esp. insulting, since it classes the sister and the wife with types such as *lenae* and *meretrices* (see Nisbet & Hubbard on Hor. *C.* 1.36.13, and cf. also Prop.4.5.2, Ov. *Am.* 1.8.3, 114).

plures emeruisse viros: *viros* may refer to men in general, or her own boyfriends, or other women's husbands / boyfriends, which would be even more of an insult.

The accusative of person with *emereo* is rare (= 'procure the favour / regard of': see *OLD* s.v. 3, *Thes.L.L.* V_2.472.72ff.), and the word is first used here in the erotic sense (cf. Ov. *Am.* 3.11.14 and *Am.* 2.8.24 *unum est e dominis emeruisse satis*, where there seems to be a play on this sense). It may well contain a hint at *meretrix*.

61–62 The couplet expands on *plura bibisse / pocula* (59f.).

ducere: 'prolong' (Lucr.3.1087f. *nec prorsum vitam ducendo demimus hilum / tempore de mortis*, Caes. *B.C.* 2.37.5, 6).

dum rota Luciferi provocet orta diem: drinking all night was esp. disgraceful: cf. Ov. *Am.* 1.8.3f., Mart.1.28, Claud. *Eutrop.* 2.84f. *inter quae tumidus leno producere cenas / in lucem, foetere mero.*

As Smith points out, the grandiloquence is satirical (cf. Ov.loc.cit.). Lucifer, the planet Venus (called Lucifer in the morning and Vesper at evening), was variously represented in antiquity, first here with a chariot: cf. Ov. *Am.* 1.6.65, *Eleg. in Maec.* 1.132, Mart.8.21.1ff. *Phosphore, redde diem: quid gaudia nostra moraris? / Caesare venturo, Phosphore, redde diem. / Roma rogat. placidi numquid te pigra Bootae / plaustra vehunt, lento quod nimis axe venis?* Lucifer is always the herald of the day, as here: cf. Hom. *Il.* 23.226f., Virg. *Ecl.* 8.17, *Aen.* 2.801f., Ov. *Met.* 4.629f., 8.1f., *F.* 5.548, *Tr.* 3.5.55f., Sen. *Oed.* 507.

For *rota* standing for 'chariot' cf. Prop.4.10.42, Ov. *A.A.* 2.230, *Met.* 2.312.

63–64 This couplet expands on *plures emeruisse viros* (60).

queat: not part of the curse: the subjunctive is potential ('no one could . . .').

melius consumere noctem: sneering double entendre. There is no distinction between the tenses of this infinitive and of *disposuisse* (1.1.29-30n.). *Melius* goes with both verbs.

aut operum varias disposuisse vices: for *opus* of the act of copulation cf. Plaut. *As.* 873 *ille operi foris faciendo lassus noctu ⟨ad me⟩ advenit*, Hor. *Epod.* 12.16, Ov. *Am.* 1.4.48, 2.10.36, *A.A.* 2.480, 730, *Rem.* 399, Mart.11.104.11.

Vices are 'variations' in posture (I can find no parallel for the word in this sense; more usual is *modus* or *figura*: e.g. Ov. *A.A.* 2.679f.). For *dispono* in this connection cf. Ov. *Am.* 3.7.64 *quos ego non finxi disposuique modos!* This is a good point of detail and brings out her lust well: such behaviour was the mark of a lascivious woman and a whore (Aristoph. *Vesp.* 500f., Mart.9.67; hence the slander at Juv. 6.406). For an interesting list of positions see Ov. *A.A.* 3.769ff.

65–66 **at tua**: sc. *uxor*.

perdidicit: i.e. the accomplishments mentioned above. Note the insult in the intensifying prefix (and in the following superlative).

nec tu, stultissime, sentis: for the situation cf. 54, 1.2.55-6n. Note the hissing sigmatism.

cum tibi non solita corpus ab arte movet: see 1.5.3-4n. for *ab arte*. Some commentators take the ref. here to be to gait (i.e. to attract: cf. Ov. *A.A.* 3.301ff.). This interpretation is possible, but in view of the allusion in *perdidicit* the line could also refer to sexual intercourse (cf.

*Priap.*83.23), the implication being that she has learnt refinements from her lover (cf. Ov.*Am.*2.5.53ff., of kisses, *torqueor infelix, ne tam bona senserit alter, / et volo non ex hac illa fuisse nota. / haec quoque, quam docui, multo meliora fuerunt, / et quiddam visa est addidicisse novi*). In this way the idea of the curse already nearing completion would be brought out well (cf. 54f.). Another possibility is that the wife is already growing cold towards her husband and not showing her usual expertise for his benefit. The ambiguity may be deliberate, to goad the seducer.

67–68 For attention to the appearance to attract the lover see Prop.1.2, Ov.*A.A.*3.129ff., and cf. 1.8.9-10n.

disponere crines: for the arranging of hair see 1.8.9-10n. For some of the many hair-styles in fashion see Ov.*A.A.* 3.137ff. More elaborate styles involved the use of hair-nets and jewels (Ov.*Am.* 3.13.25, Petron. *S.* 67, Plin.*N.H.*9.117). In general see Balsdon *Roman Women* (London, 1962), 255ff.

tenues . . . comas: a sign of beauty (Ov. *Am.* 1.14.5 *quid, quod erant tenues, et quos ornare timeres?*).

denso . . . dente: for *dens* used of the teeth of a comb cf. Varro *L.L.* 5.113 (weaving), Mart.12.82.9, 14.25.2. *Dente* is a poetic singular, accompanied, as often, by an adjective indicating plurality. For *densus* so used cf. Ov. *Am.* 3.13.7, *F.* 2.165, Juv.1.120, Stat. *Silv.* 1.2.74f. *hunc egomet tota quondam – tibi dulce – pharetra / improbus et densa trepidantem cuspide fixi.*

Combs were made of various materials, including tortoiseshell (Ov. *A.A.* 3.147), boxwood (*A.P.* 6.211 (Leonidas), Mart.14.25) and ivory (Claud. *Epithal.Nupt.Hon.Aug.* 102f.).

The repetition of initial t, p and d seems to reinforce the sarcasm.

69–70 ista haec persuadet facies: see Critical Appendix.

Haec here is probably not fem. sing., as the collocation *iste hic* and the attachment of these two demonstratives to one noun is in general doubtful in the classical period (*Thes.L.L.* VI$_3$.2743.11ff.) and would be entirely without parallel in elegy. It is most likely that *haec* is neut. acc. plural, either prospective to the subjunctives (see *OLD* s.v. 12b), or referring to the actions of 67-8 (cf. Cic. *Phil.*2.10.24, Ov.*Her.*19.187 for the direct object), with the construction in the second half of the line changing to subjunctive (with *ut* omitted). The omission of *ut* with *persuadeo* is very rare (cf. Sall. *Iug.* 35.2 and see 1.2.25a-26n.).

Facies sharpens the sarcasm in *pro te* (67).

auroque lacertos / vinciat: i.e. with a gold bracelet or bracelets (cf. Ov.*Her.*9.59). Gold bracelets are, of course, her best and most expensive ones (cf. Petron. *S.* 32, 67) – hence the position of *auro*.

Tyrio prodeat apta sinu: for *sinus* of clothes cf. Ov. *Her.* 13.36, *F.* 2.310, 5.28. *Tyrio* refers to Tyrian dye, one of the finest and most costly purple dyes (Ov. *A.A.* 3.169ff., Plin. *N.H.* 9.135, 137), which was often used as a symbol of wealth and luxury (1.2.75, 2.3.58, 2.4.28, 4.2.15f., Prop.2.16.18, Hor. *S.* 2.4.84, *Epist.* 1.6.17f.).

For *prodeat* meaning 'go out' cf. Hor. *C.* 2.8.7, Ov. *A.A.* 3.131, *F.* 4.309.

Tyrio . . . apta sinu is an odd phrase. Normally *apta* is taken in the sense of 'fitted with, provided with', i.e. here 'arrayed in, attired in' (see *Thes.L.L.* II.328.44ff., *OLD* s.v. 4). There is no exact parallel for *aptus* in this sense of a person attired in clothing: the nearest exx. are Ov. *Met.* 14.765 *forma deus aptus anili* (*forma* M), Livy 3.27.6 *non itineri magis apti quam proelio*.

Luck's translation 'elegant mit einem Bausch aus tyrischem Stoff' is also perhaps just possible, although elsewhere in the sense of 'neat, orderly' with ref. to persons the word seems to be confined to speakers and writers in respect of style (*OLD* s.v.6).

As *aptus* of women has some currency in an amatory context (e.g. Ov. *Am.* 2.8.4, *A.A.* 1.44), the words are also capable of a different interpretation: *Tyrio . . . sinu* could still be taken with *apta*, or it could be an ablative of accompaniment going with *prodeat* (cf. Cic. *Pis.* 93), while *apta* could be used to mean 'prepared, ready' (*OLD* s.v.5) or 'fitting, suitable' (*OLD* s.v.9), i.e. for a man. In view of the sarcasm in 67f. and the blunt outspokenness of 71ff., the latter interpretation is perhaps most likely here, or, at least, the ambiguity is deliberate.

71–72 **iuveni**: see 55-6n. for the point of this word.

bella: rare in Augustan elegy (elsewhere only at 3.4.52, 4.13.5, Ov. *Am.* 1.9.6). The usual literary word for 'beautiful' was *pulcher*, and *bellus* is very seldom used in formal or elevated language. The adjective belongs to common speech: it is found mainly in comedy (in Plautus 27 times; in the more polished Terence once), satire (Lucil.3, in all Horace only at *S.* 1.4.114, Persius 2, Petronius 10, not in Juv.), Catullus (14; *pulcher* 7, but only twice in the shorter poems: see Fordyce on 3.14) and Cicero's letters (28). The colloquial tone of the word perhaps adds to the insult here.

devoveat pro quo remque domumque tuam: i.e. 'your fortune' ('wealth and property': cf. Hor. *Epist.* 1.2.51). For the sentiment see 1.2.75-6n., 1.8.33-4n.

Note the emphatic position of *devoveat*: for displacement in T. (*pro quo*) see 1.1.21-4n., 1.1.39-40n., 1.4.23-4n.

73–74 **corpora foeda podagra**: a realistic detail. The disease may be gout or any pains in the feet, and was generally caused by excesses or senile decay (see Celsus, ed. Spencer (Loeb Library), vol.1, p.463ff.).

Foeda may refer to the repulsive manifestations of the disease itself, e.g. the disfigurement caused by the knotting and hardening of joints, esp. in the fingers (cf. Lucil.331 Marx *quod deformis, senex arthriticus ac podagrosus*, Ov. *ExP.* 1.3.23, Lucian (?) *Podagra* 287, Apul. *Met.* 5.10), or to the disgusting treatments for the disease (cf. Lucian (?) *Podagra* 149ff., Plin. *N.H.* 26.100ff., Apul.loc.cit., Serv.ad. *G.* 3.299), which included filthy plasters and rags, stinking poultices and the use of lappago, seaweed, mud, axle-grease and human excrement.

et senis amplexus culta puella fugit: note the pointed contrast between *senis* and *puella*. For the sentiment see 1.8.29-30n.

Cultus means 'refined, sophisticated', with regard to appearance (Prop.1.2.26, T.4.2.1, Ov. *Am.* 2.4.37) and intellectual accomplishments (Ov. *A.A.* 2.175, 3.51). Here there seems to be some irony: the wife is well-dressed (69f.), but her 'accomplishments' are rather special (65f.).

75–84 *Huic* picks up *senis* (74), and T.'s dismay at the behaviour of the *puer delicatus* seems natural after the preceding couplet and is in line with the naivety shown throughout the poem (see intro. essay). In addition, *vendere es ausus* (77) echoes *corrumpere es ausus* (53).

The conclusion of the elegy. The return here to the boy's venality, infidelity and punishment is psychologically convincing, in so far as it suggests obsession with these points. The poet shows angry incredulity, but again there is a conflict of feeling evident in the use of *noster puer* in 75 and the subjunctives at 81f. (see intro. essay). The first two couplets express dismay that the boy could have demeaned himself by sleeping with such a creature (at last making clear the boy's exact relationship with the seducer). The final three couplets describe the most serious punishment for the boy yet (as far as T. is concerned). Here for the first time T. states clearly that he is considering a definite separation from the boy and is contemplating taking up with another boy.

75–76 See Critical Appendix.

Accumbo used sexually, as here, is rare. The verb also takes the dative at Prop.2.3.30, 3.15.12.

The change of ref. is abrupt and at first sight a little ambiguous, but *huic* must refer to the *senex* and *hunc* to the boy. There is a comparable change of ref. with forms of *hic* at 1.5.47, and cf. also Plaut. *Curc.* 716f. *libera haec est, hic huius frater est, haec autem illius soror, / haec mihi nubet: tu huic argentum redde. hoc iudicium meum est*, Ter. *Heaut.* 276f. *haec ubi aperuit ostium, / continuo hic se coniecit intro*, *Ad.* 650ff. *haec virgo orbast patre; / hic meus amicus illi genere est proxumus: / huic leges cogunt nubere hanc*, Catull.24.8f. *sed bello huic neque servos est neque arca. / hoc tu quam lubet abice elevaque*, Cic. *Mil.* 99 *haec tu mecum saepe his absentibus*, *Pro Clu.* 30 *vos, quaeso, memoria teneatis non mihi hoc esse propositum, ut accusem Oppianicum mortuum, sed cum hoc persuadere vobis velim, iudicium ab hoc non esse corruptum, hoc uti initio ac fundamento defensionis, Oppianicum hominem sceleratissimum et nocentissimum esse damnatum*, Livy 1.43.2 *arma his imperata galea . . . haec ut tegumenta corporis essent*, 42.62.10f. *haec legati. summotis his cum consultarent. . .*

For the use of *noster puer* despite what has happened see intro. essay.

cum trucibus venerem iungere posse feris: an ex. of the impossible, probably an adaptation of the strange matings of animals in the ἀδύνατα (Nisbet & Hubbard on Hor. *C.* 1.29.10): cf. Aristoph. *Pax* 1076f., Virg. *Ecl.* 8.27, Hor. *Epod.* 16.30ff. *novaque monstra iunxerit libidine / mirus amor, iuvet ut tigres subsidere cervis, / adulteretur et columba miluo, C.* 1.33.7f. *sed prius Apulis / iungentur capreae lupis, Ars Poet.* 12f.

This particular form of expression (if something is true, then something contrary to nature is also true) was very common, esp. in Latin: e.g. Eur. *Supp.* 520f., *A.P.* 5.19 (Rufinus), Hor. *C.* 1.29.10ff., Prop. 2.1.65ff., Juv. 13.64ff., Claud. *Eutrop.* 1.350ff.

Trucibus emphasizes the impossibility of the union.

For *venerem iungere* cf. Ov. *A.A.* 2.679, *Rem.* 407f., *Ibis* 351, and see 1.1.69-70n.

77–78 For blandishments see 1.2.91-4n.

meas . . . / . . . mea: 'that are mine by right' (cf. Prop. 1.3.37, Ov. *Am.* 1.4.40, 2.5.29, *Her.* 20.145 *iste sinus meus est! mea turpiter oscula sumis!*).

vendere es ausus: for the elision see 53-4n.

Note the careful arrangement (*meas aliis tu . . . / tune aliis . . . mea*).

79–80 Again the theme of nemesis (1.2.87-96n.) appears: cf. *A.P.* 5.107 (Philodemus), Virg. *Ecl.* 2.73, Prop. 2.5.3ff., 4.8.27f. *cum fieret nostro totiens iniuria lecto, / mutato volui castra movere toro*. As often in T., the punishment fits the crime: just as the seducer supplanted T. in the affections of the *puer delicatus*, so another boy will supplant this *puer delicatus* in T.'s affections. Note also the reversal of the present situation (*tum flebis* and *tua tum me poena iuvet*, 81).

vinctum: for chains in *servitium amoris* see 1.1.55-6n.

et geret in regno regna superba tuo: for the figure of the beloved as a ruler cf. *A.P.* 12.56.5f., 128.6 (Meleager), Hor. *C.* 3.9.9, T. 4.5.4, Ov. *Am.* 2.17.11, 2.19.33, *Rem.* 15 *at siquis male fert indignae regna puellae.* So Love often rules (Soph. *Trach.* 443f., Eur. *Hipp.* 538, Ov. *Am.* 1.1.13, 26, 2.9.52, *Her.* 4.12), and occasionally even the lover does (2.3.59, Prop. 2.16.28). The verbal play here gives some novelty (*regno* means 'kingdom' and *regna* means 'reign'). *Regna gero* (cf. Ov. *Am.* 2.9.52, Sen. *Oed.* 264) is a variation on *gero magistratum, imperium* etc. (*CIL* 1.582.19, Cic. *Phil.* 5.52, Sall. *Iug.* 85.1).

This figure (esp. *superba*) and *servitium amoris* represent T. as completely dominated by the new boy, thereby reminding the addressee of what he will lose and implying a contrast to his present relationship with the seducer as a hired lover likely to be ordered about (1.5.59-66n.).

81–82 **iuvet . . . / . . . notet**: the subjunctives are normally translated as future indicatives, but the evidence for the use of the independent subjunctive to express simple futurity is slight and disputed (Handford *The Latin Subjunctive* (London, 1947), p. 83). Most probably, in keeping with the conflicting emotions evident elsewhere in the poem, the subjunctives are jussive or express wish, and indicate uncertainty about T.'s own reaction to the threatened separation.

merenti: because Venus will have set him free from the boy (83). The word is common in connection with votive inscriptions (e.g. Ov. *F.* 3.268).

aurea palma: Dissen notes an earlier view that *palma* is an alternative spelling of *parma* (= *clipeolus*), but there seems to be no good evidence and no modern support for this notion. T. is here talking of the palm, which is used as a symbol of victory. T.'s victory will consist of his release from bondage to his present boy and the boy's discomfiture.

The palm as a prize in athletic and other contests seems to have become common in the 4th cent. B. C. in Greece, and was later adopted by the Romans (Tarbell *CPh* III (1908), 264ff., Pauly s.v. *Phoinix*). For the dedication of the prize in a contest cf. *A.P.* 6.49 (anon.), and for gold in dedications cf. *A.P.* 6.60 (Palladas), 214 (Simonides), 292 (Hedylus), 332 (Hadrian). It is not clear why T.'s palm is supposed to be golden: the idea may be that T. will win (and dedicate) a golden palm as a prize (cf. Plin. *N.H.* 21.6, 33.54, Stat. *Silv.* 3.5.28f., 4.2.65ff.), or that he will win a palm as a prize, and dedicate a golden replica of this palm (for the dedication of representations cf. *A.P.* 6.40 (Macedonius), 149 (Callimachus), Gow *JHS* LXXX (1960), 92). In view of the refs. to gold at 17, 18 and 31 the golden palm is a neat twist here.

For the palm as a symbol of victory in an amatory context cf. Prop. 2.9.40, 4.1.140, Hor. *C.* 3.20.12. For the motif of dedication cf. *A.P.* 5.191 (Meleager), 199 (Hedylus), Hor. *C.* 3.26, Prop. 2.14.25ff. *magna ego dona tua figam, Cytherea, columna, / taleque sub nostro nomine carmen erit: / has pono ante tuas tibi, diva, Propertius aedes / exuvias, tota nocte receptus amans.*

83–84 The votive inscription was a common elegiac motif: cf. Prop. 2.14.27f., 4.3.72, Ov. *Am.* 1.11.27f., 2.13.25, *Her.* 15.183f. *grata lyram posui tibi, Phoebe, poetria Sappho: / convenit illa mihi, convenit illa tibi.*

RESOLUTUS: cf. *vinctum* (79) and see 1.2.59-60n. Paradoxically not until he is chained a second time will T. be free – from *fallax amor.*

GRATA SIS, DEA, MENTE ROGAT: two senses are possible for the adjective here: (i) 'gracious' (as T. will have already experienced Venus' favour in his release from bondage, he will simply ask for the continuation of her kindness, and the dedication will be a thank-offering with no apparent ulterior motive: cf. *A.P.* 6.34 Rhianus, 36 Philippus of Thessalonica); (ii) 'grateful' (again T. will ask Venus to show him further favour, but favour specifically prompted by the dedication: cf. *A.P.* 6.42 anon.).

For the omission of *ut* with *rogo* see 1.2.25a-6n.

10

Grimal *Fondation Hardt Entretiens* VII, 274ff.; Wimmel *Der frühe Tibull*, 121ff.; Pillinger *CJ* LXVI (1971), 204ff.

Of the background-situation the only definite clues come at 13 (*nunc ad bella trahor*), where T. says that he is to go to war, and at 25, *aerata . . . tela*, which suggests that the enemy will be barbarians (25-6n.). *Trahor* in 13 may mean that T. is part of someone's train (cf. Livy 30.9.10, Vell.2.112.4), or it may simply express reluctance. The campaign in the poem seems to be T.'s first campaign, since at 15f. when he appeals to the Lares for protection in the coming fighting he bases his appeal on their care for him as a child, not in some other battle. The fact that he does not mention Messalla or Delia here (contrast 1.1), although capable of other explanations, may also suggest an early date for the poem (before he knew them).

The poem contains a description of the ideal existence which T. would like to lead in contrast to the soldier's life which he is now to endure. T. dwells on four aspects of this ideal and contrasts them with four features of the soldier's life (see structure below). These aspects combine to form a coherent whole: T. wishes for a long life of old-fashioned piety and morality in the country; this will involve hard work and a low standard of living, but the activities will be peaceful and the way of life carefree; above all, war in all aspects is to be absent, and even the fights of lovers are to be restrained.

1-14	Golden Age:	1-10	Greed and bellicosity of present age contrasted with peace and *paupertas* of Golden Age.
		11-14	Peace of Golden Age preferred to hazards of present age.
15-32	Piety:	15-24	Appeal to Lares and description of early piety.
		25-28	Appeal to Lares and description of T.'s own piety.
		29-32	Piety preferred to military glory.
33-44	Rustic Life:	33-38	Soldier's early death rejected because

			of unpleasant after-life.
		39-44	Old rustic's late death and pleasant life preferred.
45-68	Peace:	45-52	Invention and blessings of Peace.
		53-64	Amatory violence rejected for more gentle conduct.
		65-68	Violence left to the soldier and rejected by T. for Peace.

The progression of thought is logical and the transitions are smooth throughout. Each section emphasizes a different aspect of T.'s ideal life, but the aspects come together to form a coherent picture (see above). In addition, there is a certain amount of run over: in every section the rustic nature of T.'s ideal is mentioned and a distinct contrast is made with the soldier's way of life; the theme of *paupertas* is present in the first three sections; line 8 (see 7-8n.) may well prefigure and lines 51-2 do recall the piety section. Verbal echoes also help bind together the poem: (in connection with war) *mors* (4, 33), *dux* (10, 30), *tristis* (11, 49), *arma* (12, 29, 50), *telum* (14, 25), *gero* (14, 28, 66), *miles* (32, 50), *occupo* (40, 50); (in connection with T.'s ideal) *ovis* (10, 41), *priscus* (17, 44), *rusticus* (26, 51), *merum* (32, 48), *uxor* (42, 52); see also 45-6n. (*primus*, 1, *primum*, 45).

The similarities between the present poem and 1.1 are extensive. Firstly, the situations are similar: although there are differences in the exact circumstances, both poems are set shortly before a campaign. So T.'s reaction is similar in both elegies: he describes various aspects of his ideal existence in contrast to various aspects of the soldier's life. Again there is the full treatment and the combination of a number of themes. In particular, some of the actual details of the ideal are the same (a life of rustic *paupertas* and old-fashioned piety), and in both 1.1 and 1.10 military glory is rejected.

In addition, a large number of minor details are common to both poems: simple cups (8, cf. 1.1.38), freedom from care (10, cf. 1.1.25, 48, 77), the trumpet (12, cf. 1.1.4, 75), the protection of the Lares (15f., 25, cf. 1.1.19f.), shame at humble worship (17, cf. 1.1.37f.), first fruits (21, cf. 1.1.13f.), garlands of corn-ears (22, cf. 1.1.15f.), a rustic *hostia* (26, cf. 1.1.22), the contrast between T.'s ideal and the desires of another (29ff., cf. 1.1.1ff., 49f.), the unnoticed approach of Death (34, cf. 1.1.70), inactive old age (40, cf. 1.1.71), *militia amoris* and broken doors (53ff., cf. 1.1.73ff.), the symbols of iron and stone (59, cf. 1.1.63f.) and the idea of the lover happy at his mistress' tears (63f., cf. 1.1.61f.). This extensive correspondence between 1.10 and 1.1 gives the whole of the first book unity and balance.

Despite these many similarities there are also certain definite differences in emphasis and treatment of the main theme of rustic life being preferable to warfare (for this theme see intro. essay to 1.1), which ensure that 1.10 has originality of its own. For instance, in 1.10 T. picks out three different aspects of the soldier's life for rejection (his perils, early death and violence). Love plays a less important rôle this time, with no mention of the poet's own mistress, so that the unconventional element in this poem is less marked (see intro. essay to 1.1), and T. seems more aware of the hard work involved in country life (42, cf. 49). So too there are two different aspects of his own ideal existence in the present elegy (the Golden Age and Peace).

For the theme of the Golden Age see intro. essay to 1.3. T. here shows originality in the discussion of the cause of war in this connection, the suggestion that the invention of the sword may have been responsible and the eventual conclusion that greed was really to blame (1-8 and notes). For the theme of the praise of Peace see the passages cited by Smith (1.10.45-63n.), and cf. also Hesiod *Opera* 225ff., Aristophanes *Pax*, fr.294K, Menander fr.719K. The theme was very common in Greek poetry, but is first treated at length in Latin poetry in the present elegy (Lucretius 1.28ff. is a prayer for peace rather than a description of the blessings of peace). Originality is again evident in the designation of Peace as the inventor of agriculture (45-6n.) and in the emphasis on love in peace-time (53-6n.). The presence of the themes of the Golden Age and the praise of Peace ensures a difference between 1.10 and 1.1, while the novel treatment of these themes and the combination of them with the themes of rustic *paupertas* and piety (for these see intro. essay to 1.1) represent an original variation on the whole theme of rustic life being preferable to warfare.

A further difference between the two poems lies in the fact that, whereas in 1.1 T. had definite models, in 1.10 no distinct source is evident. Certain scholars have suggested various models for 1.10 as a whole. Cartault (p. 120) claims that the poem was inspired by Virgil *G.* 2.458ff. Certain sentiments are common to both these passages, but the main theme of 1.10 is a frequent one (see intro. essay to 1.1), and there are no details peculiar to Virgil taken up by T. and no close verbal similarities. Of the various echoes of Hesiod suggested by Grimal (loc.cit.) I find only two at all likely (see 11-12n., 35-6n.). Similarly, despite the many versions of the praise of Peace, various passages have been singled out as a source for this section (45ff.). Ponchont (p. 72f.) suggests Aristoph. *Pax* 1127-90, Smith (on 1.10.45-63) Bacchylides fr.4 Snell, Wimmel (op.cit., p. 145) and Pillinger (loc.cit.) Lucr.1.28ff., Grimal (loc.cit.) Hes. *Opera* 228-31, while Wimmel (op.cit., p. 144) cites a number of minor points in common with Virg. *G.* 2, ranging from *bidentibus* at line 400 (cf. 49) to *interea* at line 429 (cf. 45), whose imagined relevance escapes me. Again there are no close verbal similarities and no repetition of details peculiar to any one of these passages to justify the claim of imitation here.

1.10 is a convincing picture of the feelings of a poet writing on the eve of a campaign. After the initial anger at the invention of the sword and the start of war we see at several points strong antipathy to military life in disparaging and sarcastic remarks. A consonant tenderness is shown by the criticism of similar violence in lovers' quarrels. We see too T.'s gloomy trepidation at the coming fighting and his horror of death and the Underworld courted by the soldier, but evident above all is his touching wistfulness for an alternative way of life. In line with his simple ideal the elegy itself is kept on a simple level. The non-military subject-matter is homely, and, aptly, the expression is for the most part unostentatious, with little *doctrina* and a general plainness of vocabulary and grammar. So too the overall structure is neat, but straightforward and unambitious. The poem is enlivened by some good points of detail (12, 14, 31f., 34, 37, 44); also noteworthy are the pleasantly musical lines at 15ff. (see notes for most striking exx.) and the many charming touches (esp. the shepherd sleeping among his sheep at 9f., the poet as a child running about at the feet of the Lares at 16, the little daughter carrying the honeycomb at 24, the old rustic with his son tending the flock, and his wife preparing hot water for him at 41f.). This really is artistic simplicity.

1–14 T. informs us that he is to go to war but is unhappy with the existence of the soldier, and here dwells on one aspect of the life that he would prefer to lead, opposing the ideal of the Golden Age to the dangers that he faces as a soldier. T. does not specify the early period that he is thinking of here, but it is probably the Golden Age, since the absence of the sword and warfare, the pastoral existence and the opposition to the warlike present are features found in his account of the Golden Age in 1.3 (see notes below), and there are a number of verbal echoes of that account (1-3, cf. 1.3.47f.; 4, cf. 1.3.50; 9, cf. 1.3.47; 10, cf. 1.3.46). So again he recognizes only two ages (1.3. 49-52n.).

The section contains a variety of emotions. In 1-10 T. contrasts the greed and bellicosity of the present age with the peace and *paupertas* of the Golden Age, as a consideration of the cause of war leads to a description of the period before war. The opening (1-4) is angry. The attribution of responsibility for the start of war to the inventor of the sword seems natural (hence the frequency of curses on the inventor: see 1.4. 59-60n.) and may have been suggested by the fact that previous accounts of the Ages had described the discovery of the sword as the concomitant of war (1-4n.). However, at 5f. the tone becomes more calm and rational, as T. wonders if he may have maligned the inventor. In 7-10 he accepts the validity of this doubt and states that gold is the real reason for war, and in wistful lines cites as evidence the fact that in the Golden Age when there was no gold there was no war. At 11-14 T. repeats the contrast between the Golden and present ages (in reverse order), stating his longing for the Golden Age and (at last) the reason for it (he is to go to war and is afraid). The mention of weapons and war at the beginning and end of the section (1, 3, 12, 13, 14) gives a neat ring-structure.

1–4 An angry start: note the forceful adjectives (1 *horrendos*, 2 *ferus, ferreus*, 4 *dirae*), the frequency of f, s, r and p in 1f., the exclamation in 2 and the anaphora of *tum* in 3f., driving home the evil effects of the invention.

For the inventor and the cursing of the inventor see 1.4.59-60n. On the invention of the sword see 1.3.47-8n. In previous versions of the Ages this invention normally accompanied the start of war: here for the first time it is suggested that the invention brought about war and the cause of war is explained in connection with the Ages theme.

quis fuit: 'who was he?' or 'what sort of man was he?'.

protulit: 'made known, invented' (see Brink on Hor. *Ars Poet*.130, Enk on Prop.2.6.31 and cf. also Cic. *Acad.*2.1.2 *pollicenti cuidam se artem ei memoriae quae tum primum proferebatur traditurum*).

enses: see 1.3.47-8n.

ferus et vere ferreus: for the phrase see Cic. *Q. Frat*.1.3.3, and cf. also Enn. *Ann.* 183-4V *feroque / ornatur ferro*. Here, because the phrase is applied to the inventor of the sword, *ferreus* suggests iron-hearted, like the iron sword he invented. As the sword was supposed by some to have originated in the Iron Age (e.g. Cic. *N.D.* 2.159), *vere ferreus* may also mean iron-hearted and so 'truly a man of the Iron Age': cf. Ov. *A.A.* 2.277f. *aurea sunt vere nunc saecula: plurimus auro / venit honos: auro conciliatur amor.*

tum brevior dirae mortis aperta via est: for the expression and the idea see 1.3.49-50n. For the pent. ending see 1.4.3-4n.

Dirus as an epithet for death is unusual and first occurs here (see *Thes. L. L.* V_1.1273.51ff.).

5–6 Note the contrasts between *nos* (emphatic position) and *ille* and between *feras* (emphatic position) and *mala nostra*; the position of *nihil* and the adjectives *miser* and *saevas* (underlines the need for the sword) also help exonerate the inventor. The alliteration of n and m in 5 is striking.

The doubts raised here show the influence of philosophers and moralists. For the view that natural causes were responsible for inventions see Bailey on Lucr.5.1028-90 and 1448-57. In particular the influence of wild animals was noted: Lucretius mentions the trouble caused by them to early man (5.982ff.), and Plato (*Polit.* 274B-D) and Diod.

Sic.(1.8) attribute the growth of crafts and speech to this factor. So wild animals were supposed to have played an important part in the start of violence: cf. Ov. *Met.* 15.106f., Sen. *Epist.* 90.41, Rutil. *Red. Suo* 1.365ff. *saecula semideum, ferrati nescia Martis, / ferro crudeles sustinuere feras: / humanis manibus non sufficit usus inermis, / si non sint aliae ferrea tela manus.* The Parthenius fragment ὅστις ἐπ' ἀνθρώπους ἔξυσεν αἰγανέην (Meineke *Analect. Alex.* p.263) may reflect this idea, but the line is without context.

For the misuse of gifts cf. Plato *Gorg.* 456Dff., Cic. *N.D.* 3.69ff., Sen. *N.Q.* 5.18.4, 13ff., Plin. *N.H.* 2.157 *verum fateamur: terra nobis malorum remedium genuit, nos illud vitae fecimus venenum; non enim et ferro, quo carere non possumus, simili modo utimur?*

7–8 The idea that greed was the cause of war was common, esp. in philosophy (cf. Plato *Res Pub.* 373D, *Phaedo* 66C, Lucr. 3.70f., 5. 1423f., Virg. *G.* 2.505f., Hor. *Epod.* 1.23ff., *C.* 1.29, T.1.1.1ff., 49f., 75f., 1.2.65ff., 2.3.37ff., Prop. 3.4, 3.5 and see Shackleton Bailey *Propertiana* p.222). In particular the influence of Lucretius is evident here, since he included this idea in his account of the growth of civilization at 5.1113f. *posterius res inventast aurumque repertum / quod facile et validis et pulchris dempsit honorem* and at 5.1418ff. T. here is the first to apply this idea of greed as the cause of war to the Ages theme (cf. Ov. *Am.* 3.8.53f., *Met.* 1.139ff., Sen. *Phaed.* 540ff., *Oct.* 417ff.). For the attack on wealth in general see intro. essay to 1.1.

divitis . . . auri: for the phrase cf. 1.9.31, 3.3.11, Manil. 5.16, *Laus Pis.* 219. The adjective here brings out the greed and has real point (hence its position).

nec bella fuerunt, / faginus astabat cum scyphus ante dapes: for the absence of war in the Golden Age see 1.3.47-8n.

Faginus, emphatic by position, is in contrast to *auri*. For the antiquity and simplicity of the beech-cup cf. Virg. *Ecl.* 3.36ff., Ov. *F.* 5.522, Plin. *N.H.* 16.185, Sen. *H.O.* 653, Sil.It. 7.187ff. *subito, mirabile dictu, / fagina pampineo spumarunt pocula suco, / pauperis hospitii pretium.* Beech cups are first mentioned here by T. in connection with the Golden Age.

The phrase *faginus . . . scyphus* is unusual and seems to be an adaptation of Virg. *Ecl.* 3.36f. *pocula . . . / fagina* (before T. the adjective is only found here and at *G.* 3.172). This is the only appearance of *faginus* in elegy and the word is in general rare (*Thes. L. L.* VI_1.172.47ff.). *Scyphus* (= σκύφος) is also uncommon, esp. in verse (e.g. never in Terence, Lucr., Catull, Prop., Ovid, Persius, Sil.It.; once in Plautus, Virgil, Val.Flacc.; twice in Horace). On *scyphus* see also Nisbet & Hubbard on Hor. *C.* 1.27.1.

Dapes may refer to a banquet, but perhaps more likely is the interpretation of Dissen and Lee ('sacrificial feast'), which connects *paupertas* with religion, as often in T., and prefigures the next section (on the meanings of *dapes* see 1.5.27-8n., 1.5.49-50n.).

9–10 non arces, non vallus erat: sophisticated warfare was absent from the Golden Age (1.3.47-8n.), esp. siege-craft (cf. Ov. *Met*.1.97), since men did not even live in cities then (1.3.43-4n.).

somnumque petebat / securus varias dux gregis inter oves: a contrast to the soldier (cf. 11f., and see 1.1.3-4n., 1.1.25-6n.). *Dux gregis* here refers to the shepherd (cf. *Culex* 175, Ov. *F.* 4.786), although elsewhere this type of phrase is applied to the leading animal (e.g. 2.1.58). For the carefree pastoral existence in the Golden Age see 1.3.45-6n., and for the charming sketch of the sleeping shepherd cf. *Culex* 157ff. *pastor, ut ad fontem densa requievit in umbra, / mitem concepit proiectus membra soporem, / anxius insidiis nullis, sed lentus in herbis / securo pressos somno mandaverat artus.*

Note that in the word-order the *dux gregis* is surrounded by his *varias . . . oves*.

On *somnum petere* see 1.1.47-8n. *Peto* is frequently used in a military connection (e.g. 'attack', 'march to') and so probably underlines the contrast with the soldier here. So *dux gregis* suggests that the shepherd was the only type of 'commander' then (cf. *duces*, 30).

On *varias* see Critical Appendix. There are two possible meanings for the adjective here. It may denote a flock of sheep in which each individual is of a different colour to her fellows (cf. the fabulous sheep of Virg. *Ecl.* 4.43ff.). Alternatively, and more likely, it may mean 'spotted'. *Varius* was the technical term for spotted sheep: cf. Varro *R.R.* 2.2.4, Plin. *N.H.* 31.13, Col. *R.R.* 7.3.1, and (of a pig) Petron. *S.* 45. Sheep of one colour were more valuable and prized than spotted ones: Varro loc.cit. (of the ram) *animadvertendum quoque lingua ne nigra aut varia sit, quod fere qui eam habent nigros aut varios procreant agnos*, Virg. *G.* 3.387ff., Col.loc.cit., Pall.8.4.2. So the *variae oves* here are indicative of *paupertas.*

11–12 tunc mihi vita foret: on *foret* for *esset* see Smith on 1.9.39. The subjunctives in the couplet may express wishes (both the imperfect and pluperfect subjunctive are used in wishes that refer to the past: see Woodcock 116, 117). Alternatively, *tunc mihi vita foret* may be the protasis of a condition (for the omission of *si* cf. 1.6.53, and see Gild.-Lodge 598). On the use of the imperfect subjunctive in past unreal conditions see Woodcock 199: as he points out, the sense 'was destined to' is usually evident.

Dawson (*AJPh* LXVII (1946), 14 n.27) suggests that this couplet was inspired by Call.fr.193.1Pf. ε⌊ἴ⌋θ' ἦν, ἄ⌊ναξ⌋ ὦπολλον, ἡνίκ' οὐκ ἦα, but Grimal's suggestion (loc.cit. intro. essay) that Hesiod *Opera* 174f. was the inspiration here seems more likely, since in Hesiod the wish is found in connection with the Golden Age and its opposition to the present age, as here. Cf. also 1.3.35ff., 2.3.74f.

vulgi nec tristia nossem / arma: see Critical Appendix.

Vulgus is often used of the rank and file (Nepos. *Alcib.* 8.2, Ov. *Met.* 13.1, Livy 22.30.7, Tac. *Hist.* 1.25, Curtius 7.2.33), sometimes containing just the note of disparagement required here and to be found in the parallel phrase *tristia duri / militis... arma* at 49f.: cf. Virg. *Aen.* 12.223, Livy 7.8.1 *volgus aliud armatorum, velut delegata primoribus pugna, eventum suum in virtute aliena ponit*, 44.34.4.

For *tristia . . . arma* cf. 49f., Prop. 1.7.2.

nec audissem corde micante tubam: a vivid detail. *Mico* is first used here of the palpitating heart: cf. Ov. *A.A.* 3.722, *F.* 3.36 *terreor admonitu, corque timore micat*, 331, 6.338, Manil. 5.224, Apul. *Met.* 11.13.

For the motif of the trumpet see 1.1.3-4n.

13–14 **nunc ad bella trahor**: T. is to go to war himself (see intro. essay). For the opposition of the warlike present to the Golden Age see 1.3. 49-50n. *Nunc* is in strong contrast to *tunc* (11).

For the phenomenon of allowing syllables to remain closed before an initial vowel in the *Corp. Tib.* cf. 1.4.27, 44, 1.5.33 (and n.), 2.2.5, 4.2.3. Elsewhere in elegy, as here, this phenomenon occurs most frequently at the main caesura (Platnauer 59f.). Here the syllabic division is facilitated by the sense-pause. Note also that the o in *trahor* was not always short, so that we may here have an ex. of archaising prosody. The Old Latin prosody was *trăhō*, which became *trăhŏ* in Classical Latin by virtue of *brevis brevians*, but Classical Latin poets could still avail themselves of Old Latin prosody, if it suited them to do so (cf. Platnauer 50ff.). So *trahor* might involve long o (cf. Lindsay *Early Latin Verse* 123f.).

iam quis forsitan hostis / haesura in nostro tela gerit latere: the (very human) trepidation seems to be an elegiac equivalent of the Homeric idea of death in battle being fated (e.g. *Il.* 22.208ff.).

Quis for *aliquis* in a principal sentence is rare in classical authors, esp. with an appositive (see Smith). The present indicative with *forsitan* is also rare (elsewhere in elegy only in Ovid (9 times): see Leo *Sen. Trag.* 1.63f. and cf. also Ov. *Her.* 19.57).

For *haesura* here (another vivid detail) cf. e.g. Virg. *Aen.* 4.73 *haeret lateri letalis harundo*, Ov. *Tr.* 1.1.43f.

Nostro stands for *meo* (1.2.11-12n.).

Tela may be plural for singular, or T. may be (pessimistically) thinking of more than one weapon.

The side was the soldier's most unprotected part and often the location of a mortal wound: cf. Virg. *Aen.* 10.314, 12.507f. *excipit in latus et, qua fata celerrima, crudum / transadigit costas et cratis pectoris ensem*, Ov. *Met.* 9.412, Sen. *H.O.* 1165f.

15–32 Transition is made by means of an appeal to the Lares to protect T. in the fighting, which seems natural enough after the trepidation in 13f. The transition is also helped by the details of *paupertas* at 19f.

T. moves on to another aspect of the life he would prefer to lead, piety. At 15-24 he makes his first appeal to the Lares, basing it on two grounds: (i) they should continue caring for him, as they did when he was a child; (ii) they should not take amiss their humble adornment, since they were contented with this type of simple piety in the time of his ancestor. The affectionate way in which T. dwells on this early piety suggests that he views it as an ideal, and so he compares his own piety to it (17ff.). At 25-28 T. again makes an appeal to the Lares, this time based on the promise of votive offerings, and again compares his piety to that of his ancestor's time, thematically (the simple rustic offerings, the personal performance of the rites and the repayal of the vow: cf. 21ff.) and verbally (*pura*, 27, cf. *purum*, 24; *sequar*, 27, cf. *postque comes*, 24; *geram*, 28, cf. *ferebat*, 23; *ipse*, 28, cf. *ipse*, 23). At 29-32 T. contrasts his piety-ideal with military glory in a mock-heroic sketch of the soldier.

15–16 sed patrii servate Lares: the appeal to the Lares here is in line with the regard shown for them elsewhere in T. (1.1.19-20n.) and keeps the poem on a simple, homely level.

The protection of the household gods extended beyond the home to war: cf. Prop.3.3.11, Ov. *Tr.* 4.8.21f., Paul. ex Fest. p.102M *Hostiliis Laribus immolabant, quod ab his hostes arceri putabant.*

See 1.3.33-4n. for *patrius* applied to the Lares. This epithet and *prisco* (17) help prepare the way for the shift to the past that follows.

aluistis et idem, / cursarem vestros cum tener ante pedes: children were under the care of the Lares – hence the dedication to them of the *bulla* on reaching manhood (Petron. *S.* 60, Pers.5.30f. *cum primum pavido custos mihi purpura cessit / bullaque subcinctis Laribus donata pependit*).

For the delightful picture in 16 cf. 2.2.22. As Putnam points out, *curso* (rather than *curro*) suggests the constant running about of a child.

17–18 neu pudeat prisco vos esse e stipite factos: i.e. 'do not refuse me because I have not made you new and expensive statues' (as at Petron. *S.* 29). For humble adornment and the apology for it see 1.1.37-8n.

sic veteris sedes incoluistis avi: the exact point here is made clear in the following lines ('I maintain the simple but true piety of my ancestor, which you were contented with in his day'). Wooden statues were generally connected with ancient simplicity: cf. 20, 2.5.28, Prop. 4.2.59f., Plin. *N.H.* 34.34 *mirumque mihi videtur, cum statuarum origo tam vetus Italiae sit, lignea potius aut fictilia deorum simulacra in delubris dicata usque ad devictam Asiam, unde luxuria.*

19–20 For this description cf. the early days of Rome at 2.5.23ff., Prop.

4.1.1ff., Ov. *F.* 1.197ff. Here, as often, the simple but geniune piety and morality of this period is brought out (see above and cf. also 1.1.39-40n.). The criticism of contemporary immorality is implicit, but brief. Note the emphasis on humble *paupertas* in *paupere* and (juxtaposed) *exigua ligneus.*

exigua . . . aede: the *lararium* (Juv.8.110f.), later enlarged by some (e.g. Petron. *S.* 29). For the original cramped quarters of the gods cf. Prop.4.1.5f. *fictilibus crevere deis haec aurea templa / nec fuit opprobrio facta sine arte casa*, Ov. *F.* 1.201 *Iuppiter angusta vix totus stabat in aede.*

ligneus . . . deus: i.e. Lar.

Note the assonance (i, e and u) in the pentameter.

21–22 For humble offerings see 1.1.37-8n. The offerings to the Lares varied: cf. e.g. Plaut. *Aul.Prolog.* 23f. (quoted in 23-4n.), Cato *Ag. Cult.* 143 *Lari familiari pro copia supplicet*. They included lambs, heifers and pigs (1.1.21f., 1.10.26, Plaut. *Rud.* 1208, Hor. *S.* 2.3.164f., *C.* 3.23.4), incense (1.3.33-4n.), *liba* (1.10.23, Dio. Hal. 4.14.3) and, as here, firstfruits (Hor. *S.* 2.5.12ff., Porph. ad loc., *C.* 3.23.3f.). For firstfruits see also 1.1.13-14n.

placatus: adjectival.

spicea serta: see 1.1.15-16n.

The sigmatism and assonance (a, e and ae) in the pentameter are striking.

23–24 **liba ipse ferebat**: for *liba* as offerings to the Lares see 21-2n., and on their ingredients see 1.7.53-4n.

On the personal performance of the ceremony cf. 27f. and see 1.1. 35-6n.

postque comes purum filia parva favum: for the charming detail cf. Ov. *F.* 2.652, and for the worship of the Lares by the daughter cf. Plaut. *Aul. Prolog.* 23ff. (Lar speaking) *huic filia una est. ea mihi cottidie / aut ture aut vino aut aliqui semper supplicat, / dat mihi coronas.*

See 1.3.25-6n. for ritual purity.

The pentameter contains an intricate pattern of initial consonants and word-endings.

25–26 **aerata . . . tela**: as Postgate *Selections* remarks, these words suggest barbarian enemies, since the Romans used iron weapons (Plin. *N.H.* 34.138).

For the lacuna after line 25 see Critical Appendix. The missing lines contained the verb required for 26, and probably made a further ref. to the dangers and a more detailed mention of the rustic offering.

porcus: for the pig as a victim for the Lares see 21-2n. This was a common thank-offering for a safe return from war (Macrob. *S.* 6.9.4, Gell.16.6.7 *Mars, tibi facturum voveo, si umquam redierit, / bidenti verre*).

27–28 **hanc pura cum veste sequar**: *hanc* probably refers to the *hostia* of

26, which goes in front (cf. 2.1.15f.).

For ritual purity see 1.3.25-6n., and cf. esp. 2.1.13.

myrtoque canistra / vincta: the basket was used for carrying the offerings (Ov. *F.* 2.650f. *stat puer et manibus lata canistra tenet. / inde ubi ter fruges medios immisit in ignis*). For the adornment of the basket cf. Ov. *Met.* 2.713 *pura coronatis portabant sacra canistris*. On the use of myrtle in connection with the Lares cf. Hor. *C.* 3.23.16. Note the echo in *myrto vinctus.*

29–32 sic placeam vobis: i.e. as a pious man rather than a soldier. Note the emphatic sense-pause and the contrasting *alius sit fortis . . . / . . . Marte favente.*

The brief sketch of the soldier given by T. here is mock-heroic, the sarcasm perhaps reinforced by the sigmatism. He performs epic deeds: he does not kill ordinary soldiers, but, like the heroes in Homer and Virgil, he kills opposing leaders; *Marte favente* (cf. Ov. *Her.* 3.88) suggests the divine aid given to heroes in epic; he recalls his exploits like Odysseus in Hom. *Od.* 9-12 and Aeneas in Virg. *Aen.* 2-3 (although here there is a suggestion of boasting). This idea is also evident in the language: *fortis in armis* has an epic ring (Sil.It.17.262 *fortis . . . dextera in armis*, and cf. also Virg. *Aen.* 12.107, 938); *sternat* is a strong word, used of great carnage (e.g. Livy 24.38.7, Virg. *Aen.* 10.119); *miles*, nominative in apposition and in emphatic position, means 'a real soldier.'

mihi potanti: drinking is the lighter side of T.'s ideal existence (cf. 51). In contrast to the soldier T. quietly drinks.

in mensa pingere castra mero: for this use of wine, an original and good point of detail, cf. Ov. *Her.* 1.29ff., and see 1.6.19-20n.

33–44 The transition is smooth: T. continues with his rejection of the soldier's way of life, and now moves to his early death, picking up the mention of death in war in the previous sentence (30). *Vinea culta* (35) may also be intended to recall *mero* (32).

T. here dwells on another aspect of his ideal, country-life. The mood changes from horror and gloom to delight and longing in a section of extensive contrast. In the first three couplets he describes the soldier's invitation of death in war as madness because of the after-life in the Underworld. In the final three couplets he contrasts the life of *paupertas* and hard work of the rustic who reaches old age, and states his preference for such an existence.

33–34 quis furor est atram bellis accersere Mortem?: *quis furor est* (cf. 4.3.7, Ov. *Am.* 3.14.7, *A.A.* 3.172, *Met.* 6.170) and *atram* express well T.'s horror.

For *ater* of Death, and darkness as an attribute of Death see 1.3.3-4n.

Lee translates: 'What madness to join forces with sombre Death in war!' As *acceso* is used of summoning troops (*OLD* s.v. *arcesso* 1bβ), there may be verbal play here.

imminet et tacito clam venit illa pede: a vivid touch. For Death always beside us and unnoticed until the end see 1.1.69-70n., Mimnerm. 2.5-7D, Lucr.3.959, Prop.2.27.11f. Note the emphatic juxtaposition (*tacito clam*).

35–36 non seges est infra, non vinea culta: cf. Plato *Res Pub.* 621A πορεύεσθαι ἅπαντας εἰς τὸ τῆς Λήθης πεδίον διὰ καύματος τε καὶ πνίγους δεινοῦ· καὶ γὰρ εἶναι αὐτὸ κενὸν δένδρων τε καὶ ὅσα γῆ φύει, Sen. *H.F.* 697ff. (in contrast to T.'s ideal life: cf. 21f., 45ff.). Fertile Elysium (1.3.61-2n.) is ignored in these lines.

Infra is used here only of the Underworld (like the Greek κάτω): the word is used of places under ground at *Aetna* 317, Sen. *N.Q.* 3.16.4, Stat. *Silv.* 4.4.83.

audax / Cerberus: for Cerberus see 1.3.71-2n. The adjective seems to be a reminiscence of Hes. *Theog.* 311f. Κέρβερον . . . / . . . ἀναιδέα (cf. also *improbus* at Prop.4.11.25), and may be onomatopoeic, the sound suggesting barking, as Lee points out.

Stygiae navita turpis aquae: Charon was the ferryman of the Styx (Virg. *Aen.* 6.385, 391). He is usually represented as an old man of grim and dirty appearance: cf. Virg. *Aen.* 6.298ff., Prop.3.18.24, Juv.3.265f. *iam sedet in ripa taetrumque novicius horret / porthmea*, Paus.10.28.2. *Turpis* here may well apply to character as well as appearance, as Smith suggests, and so heighten the contrast with the more appealing figures at 39ff.

37–38 pertusisque genis ustoque capillo: see Critical Appendix.

Ustoque capillo refers to the effects of the pyre. *Pertusisque* means 'bored through', and the ref. is to the eyes devoured by the pyre (for *pertundo* used of fire cf. Col. *R.R.* 12.19.5) or by worms after burial (for the verb used of worms cf. Juv.7.26). Disfigured corpses here add a particularly grotesque and unpleasant element.

Propertius alludes to this idea at 4.7.7ff.: *eosdem habuit secum quibus est elata capillos, / eosdem oculos: lateri vestis adusta fuit, / et solitum digito beryllon adederat ignis, / summaque Lethaeus triverat ora liquor.* So the dead show the marks of the wounds by which they were killed (Hom. *Od.* 11.40f., Virg. *Aen.* 6.494ff., Ov. *Met.* 10.49, Sil. It.12.547, Tac. *Ann.* 1.65). For the notion that the dead are affected by what happens to them after death see also 1.1.67-8n., 1.4.60.

errat ad obscuros pallida turba lacus: note the juxtaposition (*obscuros pallida*): the Underworld was generally supposed to be dark (Hom. *Il.* 15.191, *Od.* 11.57 etc.), but its inhabitants pale (Virg. *Aen.* 4.26, 242f., 6.480).

On the wandering ghosts see 1.3.69-70n.

For the sluggish rivers of the Underworld described as 'lakes' cf. Aristoph. *Ran.* 137f. εὐθὺς γὰρ ἐπὶ λίμνην μεγάλην ἥξεις πάνυ / ἄβυσσον, T.2.6.40, Virg. *Aen.* 6.134, 323, Ov. *A.A.* 3.322, *Met.* 1.737.

39–40 To underline the contrast with the soldier T. uses words with definite military connotations: *laudo* (see 1.1.57-8n.), *paro* (Caes. *B.G.* 3.9.3, 5.42.5), *occupo* (Caes. *B.C.* 3.111.1, Livy 36.16.8), *piger* (Livy 21.25.6, Hor. *Epist.* 2.1.124) and in 42 *comparo* (Caes. *B.G.* 8.6.2, Livy 42.30.11). So too *fessus* (42) is very often used in a military context (Sall. *Iug.* 53.5, Livy 2.26.3, Virg. *Aen.* 2.109).

For the theme of an old age of rustic *paupertas* cf. Virg. *G.* 4.125ff., Claudian *Carm. Min.* XX.

hic: for the scansion (also found in comedy, Lucr. and Virgil) see *Thes. L. L.* VI_3.2696.46ff., Müller p.425.

prole parata: cf. the next couplet. The family that forms an important part of the rustic's life is in opposition to the inhabitants of the Underworld (35-38). For children among the blessings of country-life cf. Hor. *Epod.* 2.39f., Virg. *G.* 2.523 *interea dulces pendent circum oscula nati*, T.2.1.23f., 2.5.91ff.

For *proles* see 1.4.7-8n.

occupat in parva pigra senecta casa: for the inactivity of old age see 1.1.71-2n., and for the expression cf. Ov. *Met.* 10.396 *non est mea pigra senectus*, 1.2.29-30n. Old age overtakes the rustic, unlike the soldier who summons death (33).

For the homoeoteleuton Smith compares Prop.4.10.20, Virg. *G.* 4.366. See also 1.1.53-4n. Two of the final a's are long and two short, which gives variety. The alliteration of p in this couplet is also noteworthy.

41–42 ipse suas sectatur oves, at filius agnos: the old man with the sheep balances the son with the lambs (for the young tending lambs cf. Eur. *Cycl.* 27f.). These animals are in contrast to Cerberus (36).

et calidam fesso comparat uxor aquam: this water contrasts with the water in the Underworld (36, 38). For the wife's task here cf. Hor. *Epod.* 2.43f. *sacrum vetustis extruat lignis focum / lassi sub adventum viri.*

For *uxor* see 1.4.73-4n.

For the husband's hard work cf. Hor. loc. cit., and see 1.9.7-8n.

43–44 caput candescere canis: in contrast to the burnt hair of the ghosts in the Underworld (37). This is a striking phrase for emphasis: before T. *candesco* appears only at Lucr.1.490 (of heated metal), and *cani* as a noun only at Cic. *Sen.* 18.62. The striking alliteration of c (cf. s in *sic ego sim*) seems intended to help drive home T.'s point.

temporis et prisci facta referre senem: for old men talking of the past, a realistic detail, cf. Homer's Nestor, Aristot. *Rhet.* 2.13.12, Cato (passim) in Cic. *Sen.*, T.3.5.26, Hor. *Ars Poet.* 173f. Note the emphatic position of *senem*. The echo of 31 makes a clear contrast with the soldier telling of his exploits.

45–68 *Interea*, picking up 43f., provides the transition (1.1.69-74n.), and the continuation of the rustic setting along with the mention of the son (48, cf. 41) also help. In addition, *candida* (45) echoes *candescere* (43).

T. moves on to the final feature of his ideal life, peace. In the first four couplets he praises the invention and blessings of Peace: the contrast with the weapons, violence and devastation of war, elsewhere implicit, is made explicit at 49f. The next six couplets concern love, one of the blessings of Peace, or, to be more precise, lovers' quarrels: six lines describe the man's violence in such quarrels and a balancing six deplore such behaviour and recommend more gentle conduct. The quarrel may be a general feature of peacetime (*tunc*, 53), but the transition to it is even smoother if it is due to drinking at a festival (51f.), as is the case at 2.5.101f. (for the activities of 53ff. taking place in the country see intro. essay to 1.1). So too the recommendation at 59-64 has a general application, but is more relevant if T. is there still thinking primarily of the countryside: in his ideal existence he would wish even lovers' fights to be restrained (N.B. rustic girls could take care over their appearance, as at 61f.: see Theoc. *Id.*27.53). The obvious similarities between the violent lover and the soldier are underlined by the use of *militia amoris*. So this inner contrast mirrors the overall contrast between peace and violence, and the passage on love reflects the sentiments of the section as a whole. The final two couplets link closely the amatory passage with the rest of the section, as T. openly identifies the violent lover with the soldier and states his preference for Peace.

The final couplet echoes the opening of the section and provides a neat ring-structure: *Pax* (67), cf. *Pax* (45ff.), *alma* (67), cf. the function of Peace at 45ff. (esp. *aluit*, 47), *candidus* (68), cf. *candida* (45).

45–46 See Critical Appendix.

For the blessings of Peace see intro. essay. In former versions Peace had connections with agriculture (e.g. Aristoph. *Pax* 530, 589f., Menand. 719K, Theoc. *Id.*16.88ff.), but T. gives his version originality by ascribing to Peace the invention of agriculture. This discovery had formerly been ascribed to Ceres (Call. *Hymn.* 6.19f., Virg. *G.* 1.147f.), with whom Peace was closely connected (Call. *Hymn.* 6.137, Ov. *F.* 1.704 *pax Cererem nutrit, pacis alumna Ceres*). By the mention of this beneficial invention T. makes a sharp contrast with the inventor of the sword (1ff.). For the inventor theme see 1.4.59-60n. Note the emphatic anaphora of *Pax* in this couplet and the following lines.

candida: for this application of the adjective cf. Ov. *A.A.* 3.502 *candida pax homines, trux decet ira feras*, Calp. *Ecl.* 1.54. Line 68 suggests that here T. is thinking primarily of white clothes, but the connotations of beauty and good fortune (1.3.93-4n.) may also be present.

iuga curva: cf. Ov. *A.A.* 1.318, *ExP.* 1.8.54, Sen. *Oed.* 300, 721, Claud. *Rapt. Pros.* 1.12f.

47–48 Pax aluit vites et sucos condidit uvae: cf. Aristoph. *Pax* 308 τὴν θεῶν πασῶν μεγίστην καὶ φιλαμπελωτάτην, 520 ὦ πότνια βοτρυόδωρε, 535ff., 596ff., fr.387K.

As Postgate *Selections* points out, the idea in the pent. is that the wine is so plentiful in peace that it is even sufficient for the next generation.

49–50 For the punctuation of the parenthesis see Critical Appendix (on 51-2).

This couplet states openly the contrast between the implements and activities of peace and the weapons and activities of the violent soldier: the well-used, shining farm-implements are opposed to the unused, rusty weapons in a dark corner (cf. Ov. *F.* 4.927f. *sarcula nunc durusque bidens et vomer aduncus, / ruris opes, niteant: inquinet arma situs*). The farm-implements shine with use (cf. Virg. *G.* 1.46 *sulco attritus splendescere vomer*).

The disuse of weapons is a frequent theme: cf. Bacchyl. *Paean.* 4.69ff. Snell, Eur. Fr. 369N, Theoc. *Id.* 16.96f., Hor. *S.* 2.1.43, Ov. *F.* 4. 928ff., Sen. *Thy.* 565f., Sil.It.7.533ff. *longum / detergete situm ferro multoque cruore / exsatiate, viri, plenos rubiginis enses.*

For *tristia . . . / . . . arma* and *duri / militis* see 11-12n. Note the emphatic juxtaposition *tristia duri.*

Occupo is often used in a military connection (39-40n.), so that there is neat word-play here.

51–52 There is no need to assume a lacuna before this couplet: see Critical Appendix.

For the scene cf. Livy 5.40.9.

On the postposition of *-que* see 1.1.39-40n. and cf. esp. Prop. 3.21.16. For *male* used as a negative see Austin on Virg. *Aen.* 4.8.

The reference in *lucoque* is to a sacred grove, possibly surrounding a temple (cf. Hor. *C.* 1.4.11, Virg. *Aen.* 11.740, Serv. ad *Aen.* 1.446). For religious rites and festivals among the blessings of peace cf. Bacchyl. *Paean.* 4.64f. Snell, Aristoph. *Pax* 530f., Philemon 71.9K. Drunkenness was usual at such festivals: cf. 2.1.29f., 2.5.101f., Ov. *F.* 3.523ff., esp. 541f. *occurrit nuper (visa est mihi digna relatu) / pompa: senem potum pota trahebat anus*. For the attendance by all the community cf. Virg. *G.* 1.343 *cuncta tibi Cererem pubes agrestis adoret.*

For children among the blessings of Peace cf. Hes. *Opera* 228, Eur. *Bacch.* 419f., *Supp.* 489f., Philemon 71.9K.

uxor: see 1.4.73-4n.

53–56 For love in peace-time cf. Aristoph. *Pax* 439f., 1138f. As a love-poet, T. considerably expands this detail, and so gives his version of the blessings of Peace further originality. He omits the pleasant side of love and concentrates on the quarrel and its violence, to bring out the similarities to war (see 45-68n.).

On quarrels in the love-affair cf. 1.6.69-72n., and see below. For violence to the girl cf. Theoc. *Id.* 14.34f., Prop.2.5.23f., Ov. *Am.* 1.7, *A.A.* 3.568. For the breaking down of doors cf. Theoc. *Id.* 2.127f., Ter. *Ad.* 102f., T.1.1.73, Prop.2.5.22, Hor. *C.* 3.26.6ff., Ov. *Am.* 1.9.20, *A.A.* 3.567 etc. The girl frequently cries and arouses remorse (note the balancing *flet . . . / flet*): cf. Ter. *Andr.* 556ff. *dum tempus datur / dumque eius lubido occlusast contumeliis, / priu' quam harum scelera et lacrumae confictae dolis / redducunt animum aegrotum ad misericordiam / uxorem demu'*, Prop.3.25.5ff., Ov. *Am.* 1.7.57ff. On the trick of crying see also 1.8.67-8n., 1.9.29-30n.

calent: 'flourish' (e.g. Cic. *Phil.* 5.4.11). The heat of battle (cf. Virg. *G.* 3.46, Livy 24.45.4) and the fires of love (*OLD* s.v. *caleo* 6) are also suggested.

conqueriturque: for the postposition of *-que* see 1.1.39-40n.

subtusa: see Critical Appendix.

As in words such as *subdulcis* and *subirascor*, the prefix here denotes 'a little, somewhat'. Lewis & Short translate *tundo* as 'beat, strike, thump, buffet with repeated blows', so that *subtusa* here may mean 'thumped about a bit', although it may be objected that the verb in this sense hardly lends itself to gradations of intensity. *Tundo* is also used of less violent actions (e.g. Lucr.4.265 *lapidem digito cum tundimus*), so that the compound here may denote a still less violent action and mean something like 'slapped about a bit'. Whatever the precise force of *subtusa*, it suggests some gradation of violence, which is to be expected in the man's fight with his girl (in contrast to the violence that would be employed against another man, or that is used on Rufa at Catull. 59.5 *ab semiraso tunderetur ustore*). The word is extremely rare (elsewhere possibly only at Boeth. *Geom.* 1. p.1180: see Critical Appendix).

To emphasize the similarities between the violent lover and the soldier, T. uses words with military connotations: 53 *bella*, 54 *perfractas . . . fores* (for the similarities to military situations see Ov. *Am.* 1.9.20, Livy 26.46.6; for *foris* cf. Livy 25.30.10, 28.6.5; for *perfringere* cf. Caes. *B. G.* 7.85.3, Tac. *Hist.* 3.20, 29) and 55 *victor*.

On *militia amoris* see Murgatroyd *Latomus* XXXIV (1975), 59ff. *Militia amoris* is first found in Greek lyric and elegy in very basic form (Sappho 1.28D, Anacreon 34D, Theognis 1285f.). The figure became more common in Greek tragedy (Aesch. *Choeph.* 598ff., Soph. *Ant.* 781, Eur. *And.* 631), but first became really frequent in the Alexandrians: Ap.Rhod.3.296f., *A.P.* 5.199.3ff. (Hedylus), 12.37.1f. (Dioscorides), 12.120 (Posidippus). The Alexandrian features were picked up and often elaborated by the Roman poets of the Republic (Caecil.66-7 Ribb.[3], Plaut. *Pers.* 231f., Ter. *Eun.* 59ff., Catull.66.13f.), but the figure reached the peak of its development in the hands of the Roman elegists, who employed it frequently and at great length, with the addition of many clarifying details. With them it rose above the level of a mere conceit, since they used it to reinforce their concept of the humility of the lover (Ov. *A.A.* 2.197, 233-42) and incorporated it within their general philosophy by stating their preference for love's warfare rather than real warfare (1.1.75-6n.).

For the battles of love (*veneris . . . bella*) see 1.3.63-4n., and for a victory won by one of the lovers (*victor*) cf. Theogn.1286, Lucil.1181 Marx, T.1.4.40, 1.6.28, 1.8.49, Prop.2.14.23f., Ov. *Her.* 4.14, *Am.* 1.7.35ff., and see my article (cited above) p.62 n.11. In book 2 the figure occurs at 2.1.71ff., 2.3.33f., 2.5.106, 2.6.1ff., but in books 3 and 4 never. Original points of detail added by T. are the use of the term 'general' at 1.1.75, the camp at 2.3.33f. and the picture of Amor as a general with standards at 2.6.1ff.

57–58 A pictorial couplet, possibly inspired by an actual painting, as Némethy suggests. Note the careful positioning of *lentus* (placed next to the contrasting *iratum* and (like Amor) between *iratum . . . utrumque*).

The gods of love were traditionally cruel (1.9.19-20n., Meleager *A.P.* 5.57, 178, T.1.6.2, 2.4.4f., 2.6.15) and unconcerned, even amused, by mortals in love (Meleager *A.P.* 5.176, 179, Hor. *C.* 1.33.10ff.).

The lack of concern here may also be due to the consideration that quarrels are indicative of love (1.6.69-72n., 1.10.61-4n.) and beneficial to it (Ter. *Andr.* 555), and, in any case, quarrels are short-lived (Menand. 797K *ὀργὴ φιλούντων ὀλίγον ἰσχύει χρόνον*, T.2.5.101ff.).

59–60 a lapis est ferrumque: for the images cf. line 2, and see 1.1.63-4n. The interjection *a* is rare in T.1 and 2, and is therefore emphatic (1.9.3-4n.), as is the combination of images.

suam quicumque puellam / verberat: for the displacement see 1.4.23-4n. Note the emphasis given to *verberat* by its position and the sense-pause.

e caelo deripit ille deos: expresses very strong disapproval: the mistress is equivalent to a divinity (cf. *A.P.* 5.137 (Meleager), Catull.68.70, Ov. *Am.* 1.7.28, 32, 3.2.60).

For the impiety of fighting against the gods cf. 1.6.29-30n. The allusion here is to the Titans or Giants, who tried to dethrone the Olympians (Hes. *Theog.* 617ff., Ov. *Met.* 1.151ff.) and became proverbs of brute force and impiety (Plato *Leg.* 3.701C, Plaut. *Pers.* 26f. *quid ego faciam? disne advorser? quasi Titani cum is belligerem / quibu' sat esse non queam?*, Cic. *de Sen.* 5 *quid est enim aliud gigantum modo bellare cum dis nisi naturae repugnare?*).

For the sentiment cf. Plut. *Cato Maior* 20.3, Ov. *Am.* 1.7.6, 31f. *pessima Tydides scelerum monimenta reliquit. / ille deam primus perculit – alter ego!*

61–64 T. recommends more gentle behaviour in contrast to the violence of 53ff. For similar gentleness see 1.6.73-4n., 1.9.5-6n.

sit satis e membris tenuem rescindere vestem: for tearing the girl's clothes see Enk on Prop.2.5.21. Here the idea is that violence is better directed at the clothes than the person (*scissosque capillos*, 53), and to tear the clothes from the body is preferable to harming the body itself (*subtusa genas*, 55). This action would still be effective, in view of the fine clothes (*tenuem*: cf. 1.6.17-18n.).

The verb itself does not imply lack of violence, as Smith suggests (cf. e.g. Caes. *B.G.* 1.7, Virg. *G.* 1.280, Claud. *B.Gild.* 1.136): this idea of lack of violence is brought out by the fact that clothes (rather than hair) are torn, and, since the clothes are *tenuem*, not much force would be required to tear them.

sit satis ornatus dissoluisse comae: rather than tearing the hair (*scissosque capillos*, 53). Again this action would be effective, in view of the care taken over the hair (cf. 1.9.67-8n.).

There is no distinction between the tenses of *rescindere* and *dissoluisse* (1.1.29-30n.). For the scansion of the u see 1.7.1-2n.

sit lacrimas movisse satis: the perfect infinitive seems to have its full force here, i.e. 'be content with having made her cry', rather than prolonging the tears (as at 57f.). The tears here are caused by the actions above, not by the violence of 53ff., so that the man need not cry himself through remorse (55f.).

quater ille beatus: this type of phrase originated in epic (Hom. *Od.* 5.306, Virg. *Aen.* 1.94), but was by no means confined to that genre (e.g. Aristoph. *Pax* 1333, *A.P.* 5.195.5, 12.52.3 (Meleager), Prop. 3.12.15, Hor. *C.* 1.13.17, T.3.3.26, Ov. *A.A.* 2.447f., *Tr.* 3.12.25, *ExP.* 4.9.34), and does not suggest any lack of seriousness here, as Smith maintains.

quo tenera irato flere puella potest: if the girl was not in love with him, she would not be moved to tears (Ov. *A.A.* 2.447ff., cf. 1.6.69-72n.). Here it is emphasized that the tears are caused by angry actions, rather than the mad violence of 56.

Propertius seems to make a criticism of this whole passage (and possibly of 1.1.73f. also) at 2.5.21ff. (see Solmsen *Philologus* 105 (1961), 273ff.). In similar circumstances at *Am.* 1.7.45ff. Ovid thinks that shouting and tearing of the dress should have been enough, but at *A.A.* 2.169ff. he refers to torn dresses and disordered hair-styles as expensive and unbecoming (cf. Prop.4.5.31f.), and at *A.A.* 3.565ff. he refers to such behaviour as that of a learner.

65–66 sed manibus qui saevus erit: i.e. as at 53ff. (esp. *dementes . . . manus*, 56). The vigorous rejection of such violence seems to be reinforced by the sigmatism in the hexameter.

scutumque sudemque / is gerat: i.e. 'he should be a soldier' (cf. Hor. *Epod.* 9.11f. *Romanus eheu – posteri negabitis – / emancipatus feminae /*

fert vallum et arma, T.2.6.2).

miti: also used of Venus at 2.3.72. Note the contrast with *saevus.*

67–68 This description of Peace is similar to representations of her in art and on coins (cf. e.g. Mattingly and Sydenham *Roman Imperial Coinage* vol.2 index 3, s.v. *Pax*, and vol.5, part 2 index 4, s.v. *Pax*).

alma: cf. 45ff. (esp. 47 *aluit*).

teneto: on the form see 1.8.49-50n.

perfluat et pomis candidus ante sinus: see Critical Appendix.

There is no exact parallel for the verb in the sense required here ('overflow'), but it is used of someone leaking secrets at Ter. *Eun.* 105 (*plenus rimarum sum: hac atque illac perfluo*) and of someone dripping with sweat at Apul. *Met.* 1.13 (*haec ego ut accepi, sudore frigido miser perfluo*). The *per-* brings out well the idea of abundance.

For *candidus sinus* cf. *candida*, 45 (and notes).

CRITICAL APPENDIX

The terms 'n.', 'see n.' and 'see intro. essay' refer the reader to the notes or introductory essay in the commentary on the appropriate line or poem.

The *sigla* most frequently referred to are those of Postgate's *Oxford Classical Text* (2nd ed., 1915), as printed below. Occasionally it has been necessary to make reference to the *sigla* of Lenz and Galinsky (see Lenz & Gal., p.33ff.), where there is discussion of readings not recorded in Postgate.

SIGLA

CODICES:

A	=	Ambrosianus R.sup.26	saec. xiv
V	=	Vaticanus 3270	saec. xv
g	=	Guelferbytanus MS. Aug.82, 6 fol.	saec. xv
Cui.	=	Cuiacianus, quondam Iac. Cuiacii nunc Samuelis Allen liber a. 1466 vel 1467 scriptus	
ψ	=	codicum aliorum lectiones vel Italorum saec. xv reperta	

EXCERPTA:

Fr.	=	Frisingensia Excerpta in codice Monacensi 6292 exstantia	saec. x
Par.	=	Parisina Excerpta secundum duos codices Paris. 7647 (Par. 1) et 17903 (Par. 2) citata	saec. xi

EDITIONES:

Plant.	=	editio Plantiniana Antuerpiae a. 1569 emissa	

1.1.2 **et teneat culti iugera multa soli,**
multa Par.Fr.Diomedes p.484K: *magna* codd.

Despite the spirited defence of Lee (loc.cit.intro.essay), if *iugera* here is taken in the sense of fixed measures of land, there is no exact parallel for the phrase *iugera magna*, and *Thes.L.L.* VIII.127.82ff. offers no real support for such an application of *magnus* here. *Iugera* can also be used *'latius de quolibet spatio amplo'* (*Thes.L.L.* VII_2.628.70ff.), but this usage is uncommon and seems to be confined to Silver and Late Latin, while *iugera* in this sense is nowhere else accompanied by an adjective indicating size. *Iugera multa* has support from 2.3.42, 3.5.5 and esp. Ov. *F.* 3.192 *iugeraque inculti pauca tenere soli*, a clear allusion to this line, where *pauca* is the deliberate opposite of *multa*, as *inculti* is of *culti.*

1.1.6 **dum meus adsiduo luceat igne focus.**
adsiduo] *exiguo* Par.

Adsiduo here has real point (see n.). *Exiguo* takes the idea of *paupertas* too far: a small farm (22) and a small flock (33) are reasonable enough, but a small fire would be of little use in general and esp. in the storm of 45ff. In any case, an abundance of firewood would be a natural benefit of living in the country (see West *Reading Horace* (Edinburgh, 1967), 4ff. and cf. Virg. *Ecl.* 7.49f., T.2.1.22). *Exiguo* may be due to a misguided attempt to avoid repetition of *adsiduus* from 3 or to stress the notion of poverty, or the scribe's eye may have wandered to *exigui* (22) or *exiguo* (33).

1.1.25-32 These lines are transposed to follow line 6.

With the line-order as given in the mss. the themes of this half of the poem are hopelessly entangled and the progression of T.'s ideas is repetitious and erratic, whereas elsewhere T. takes great care over logic and structure. The work in 7f. is mentioned with a brevity bordering on parenthesis, and seems odd and abrupt so soon after the wish for *inertia* in 5. So too the wish in 25 is no less odd and abrupt so close to the prayer of 24, as T. suddenly leaves the theme of piety for that of work in the country, which he has already considered at 7f. Then at 35 he abruptly drops this theme and returns to piety. Finally, at 37 he prays to deities whom he has not mentioned for twelve lines (apart from Pales).

Transposition seems necessary, and the most likely is that suggested by Richter, which gives the order 1-6, 25-32, 7-24, 33ff. The wish of 25 goes better here, following that of 5f. and continuing the sentiment of the opening lines. Lines 27f. continue the idea of *inertia*, while 29 provides a gradual transition to some work in the country. *Ipse* in 7 picks up *pudeat* and *pigeat* (29 and 31). Similarly 33f. pick up the mention of the lamb and of *paupertas* in 19-24 (*exiguo*, 33, cf. *exigui*, 22), and .Pales at 35f. forms a natural part of the list of gods to whom offerings are made. Finally, the prayer at 37 is now addressed to deities who have been mentioned recently.

.1.25 **iam modo iam possim contentus vivere parvo**

iam modo iam possim Fris.: *iam modo non possum* OEs.PQ.: *iam modo nunc possum* ce: *quippe ego iam possum* Flor.: *iam mihi iam possim* Schneidewin (*sigla* of Lenz & Gal.).

Iam modo iam possim is the only text from the mss. and Excerpts that makes sense here: for the (most appropriate) repetition of *iam* and for the use of *modo* in a wish see n. Emendation seems unnecessary.

.1.9 **nec spes destituat**

The ref. here is not to the goddess, and so *spes* should not be spelt with a capital, as Fisher *Hermes* XCVII (1969), 378f. has demonstrated. The point that T. is making here and in the following lines is that his work should be rewarded with success because of his piety towards the country gods (hence *nam* in 11). As Spes the goddess is not one of these rustic deities, if we understand the goddess here and write *Spes*, it is on her that T. is dependent for his success, so that *nam* in 11 and the subsequent list of gods are meaningless.

.1.15-18 **flava Ceres, tibi fit nostro de rure corona**
spicea, quae templi pendeat ante fores;
pomosisque ruber custos donatur in hortis
terreat ut saeva falce Priapus aves.

fit Lambinus: *sit* codd. *donatur* Lambinus: *ponatur* codd.

At 11ff. T. is explaining why his hopes for his work's success are justified (because of his piety towards the rustic gods). This explanation is expressed in a series of present indicatives which have a continuous force. However, in the middle of this series the mss. have two subjunctives which interrupt the flow of thought and transfer to the vague future actions which T. is at pains to emphasize are habitual. In addition, in the midst of the list of offerings to the gods with the text in the mss. Priapus would be given no offering but merely be set up, which seems esp. odd coming immediately before *vos quoque . . . / . . . fertis munera vestra, Lares* (19f.). Priapus would also be placed in the gardens when they are full of fruit, but it would be strange if T. did not intend to have a Priapus in his gardens before then, not only in view of his habitual piety, but also because Priapus normally resided in gardens all year round (1.4.5f.) and gave his protection to other produce which came to maturity at various times in the year (*Priap*.84.1f., 85.6ff.).

In an attempt to remedy the situation Postgate *Selections* transposed lines 15-18 to follow 10, which not only ignores the last of my objections but also places the emphasis here on T.'s success rather than on his piety, thereby weakening the rejection of soldiering on moral grounds. Moreover, this order gives the sense: 'may I give a harvest-offering (15f.) . . . for I give a harvest-offering (13f.)'.

The emendations *fit* and *donatur* remedy all the above objections and are palaeographically sound (confusion between f and s is common, and *ponatur* could have been due to the letter p elsewhere in the couplet or to the presence of *ponitur* in 14).

1.1.35-36 hic ego pastoremque meum lustrare quot annis
et placidam soleo spargere lacte Palem.

hic A: *hinc* Postgate: *hunc* Dietrich: *hoc* Richter: *ipse* Leonhard: *hic ego pastor ovemque* Nitzsch.

Emendation is unnecessary, as Dissen and Fisher (*Hermes* XCVII (1969), 379f.) have shown. Just as 9f. is explained by 11ff., so 33-4 is explained by 35f. (see n.).

1.1.38 and 40 Since I regard 39f. not as an interjection but as the first of two excuses (39-40n., 41-44n.), I omit Postgate's dashes here.

1.1.47-48 aut, gelidas hibernus aquas cum fuderit Auster,
securum somnos igne iuvante sequi!

igne A: *imbre* Par.

The only valid parallel for rain (rather than running water, which is quite different) causing sleep from the list given by Westendorp-Boerma (*Mnemosyne* Ser.4 Vol.4 (1951), 308ff.) is Livy 24.46.5, where it is noteworthy that Livy qualifies *imber* with the words *lentior deinde aequaliorque accidens*. Here there is no such qualification, and, in any case, the calmer aftermath of the storm (which Westendorp-Boerma would have us believe is implied in the lone, unqualified *imbre*) would not cause particular discomfort to the soldier, and so is not to the point here, since at 49f. T. makes it clear that he is thinking about the type of bad weather which the soldier must endure but he avoids. In fact, T. refers to the rain in this passage as *tristes . . . pluvias* (50), and Auster is present in his traditional rôle as a cold and stormy wind (see n.). Such being the case, the rain would hardly be soporific (cf. e.g. Plin. *Epist.* 2.17.22).

Enk (*Mnemosyne* Ser.4 Vol.14 (1961), 180f.) provides a parallel for a Roman heating his bedroom (Plin. *Epist.* 2.17.23) and makes the valid observation that there is no reason at all why a Roman should not light a fire there on a cold night. Moreover, the pleasure of enjoying the warmth of a fire indoors while the weather is bad outside is a poetic theme (see 45-6n.). In addition, *igne*, unlike *imbre*, performs a valuable function in the couplet from the point of view of contrast, and seems like a deliberate echo from line 6 (see n.). The reading *imbre* was probably suggested by the picture in 47, and a similar confusion of the two words is to be found at Catull.62.7.

1.1.55 me retinent vinctum formosae vincla puellae,

vinctum] *victum* ψ.

Victum is highly improbable, as neither T. nor any other poet ever mixes *militia amoris* with *servitium amoris* in this fashion. The purpose of *vinctum* is to emphasize the poet's slavery (see n.).

.1.60 **te teneam moriens deficiente manu.**

te ψ: *et* A.

As Cartault points out, A has *et* in 59 and 60, which in 59 is impossible and in 60 is probably a repetition of the mistake. T. is fond of the repeated pronoun (e.g. 1.6.63ff., 1.9.65ff.), and it performs a useful function here (see n.). Ovid in his adaptation of this line at *Am.* 3.9.58 makes Nemesis say *me tenuit moriens deficiente mànu*, which is more pointed if T. said here *te teneam* etc. to Delia.

.1.74 **rixas inseruisse iuvat.**

inseruisse] *conseruisse* ψ.

Rixas inseruisse is a difficult phrase, but it does make sense (see n.), and so should be retained. *Rixas conseruisse* is easier and leads well into the military imagery of 75 as another variation on a military phrase (e.g. *manum, pugnam, proelia* etc. *conserere*). The presence of *conseruisse* here is probably due to a failure to understand *inseruisse* or to the fact that *conseruisse* does lead into 75 so well.

.1.78 **despiciam dites despiciamque famem.**

despiciam dites Flor.BG: *dites despiciam* OCHPQY (*sigla* of Lenz & Gal.).

A delicate decision. The order *dites despiciam* does place *dites* in an emphatic position, and it does provide a heavy spondaic first foot. However, the order *despiciam dites* is in accordance with Tibullan practice (1.4.82, 1.7.64, 2.5.100, 105), and this is not a particular case to justify variation from the norm (Cartault's argument that *dites* should be first word answering to *divitias* (1) is invalidated by the fact that in 41 and 49 *divitias* and *dives* are not placed first).

.2.3 **multo percussum tempora baccho**

percussum OBHPde: *perfusum* Es.Qrecc. (*sigla* of Lenz & Gal.).

The use of a verb of pouring in connection with getting drunk is found, and the metaphor of being drenched or wet with wine is very common (e.g. *vino madere, tingui, udus, irrigatus esse, proluere se, fundi*). This probably explains the presence of *perfusum* here. There is a similar confusion of the two words in the mss. at Juv.10.149. *Percussum* is preferable because it is a more violent metaphor in line with the forcefulness of expression and military imagery of line 2. The same use of *percutio* is found at Plaut. *Cas.* 640, and for similar imagery see n.

.2.7 **ianua difficilis domini, te verberet imber,**

domini] *dominae* ψ: *domino* Illmann: *dominis* Postgate: *densus* Helm.

Dominae seems unlikely here. It cannot be a genitive with *difficilis* in agreement, since to describe Delia as *difficilis* would not agree with the attitude to her in the rest of the poem and would hardly be fair (at 5 and 15 T. says that she is under guard, and her fear of the *coniunx* at

41 makes it likely that he has put her under guard, while one would expect a few lines complaining of her cruelty, if she had locked T. out). *Dominae* could be a genitive standing on its own (*difficilis* agreeing with *ianua*), but the word then seems solitary and weak. *Dominae*, if taken as a dative, would give a most unusual viewpoint: elsewhere it is always to the *exclusus amator* rather than to the girl inside that the door is 'difficult'.

Both *domino* and *dominis* are improbable corrections: in view of the presence elsewhere in the couplet of *imperio, difficilis* and *Iovis*, corruption to these conjectures seems more likely than corruption of them to the mss. readings, and, in any case, *dominus* would then have to mean 'lover', a usage of the word not found until Ovid.

Even more improbable is *densus* (with a comma after *difficilis*), which could hardly have been corrupted into the mss. readings.

Domini, the majority mss. reading, makes much better sense. It is unlikely to go with *imber. Domini* on its own would not refer esp. to Jupiter, since the word is applied to various gods (*Thes.L.L.* V_1.1931. 39ff.). Leo (*Zu augusteischen Dichtern.Phil. Unters.II* (Berlin, 1881), 35.17) maintains that the ref. is made clear in line 8, but clarification is usually supplied at an earlier stage, and the change in construction from *domini . . . imber* to *Iovis imperio . . . missa* tends to obscure rather than clarify. It seems best to place a comma after *domini*, taking it to mean 'householder', qualified by *difficilis* (see n.). Otherwise *domini* is solitary and weak. Leo (loc.cit.) holds that then the complaint is not directed against the door, but, in fact, *difficilis domini* is little more than an aside, and the *imber* and *fulmina* at any rate are directed against the door.

1.2.19 **molli furtim derepere lecto,**

derepere Fris.: *decedere* OBPQc: *discedere* e: *deducere* H: *descendere* Douza, Markland (*sigla* of Lenz & Gal.).

The suitability of *derepere* is shown by the use of *obrepere* in a similar situation at 1.8.59, and this reading emphasizes better the stealth necessary in such circumstances. On the reference in the verb here see n. For other compounds of *repo* in T. see 1.1.71, 1.2.85, 1.8.59. *Derepo* is rare (*Thes.L.L.*V_1.629.27ff.), and the application of compounds of *repo* to the lover is not common (see n.), so that the other readings are probably attempts to substitute a more usual word.

1.2.25 This line is joined to 25a without a gap in AV, but a lacuna is shown in *unus Foroiuliensis* (see Lenz & Gal.). Various spurious lines fill the gap in other mss.: *ille deus certae dat mihi signa viae, usque meum custos ad latus haeret amor* (cf. Johnson *Latin MSS.*, 82), *securum in tenebris me facit esse venus, praesidio noctis sentio adesse deam* (see Lenz & Gal.). Something has obviously dropped out. The sense requires no more than a pentameter, saying something like 'Venus protects me from danger', and from the point of view of structure the loss of more than one line seems unlikely, since the two other parts of this section are only 10 and 8 lines each.

1.2.40 **is Venerem e rabido sentiet esse mari.**

rabido ψ: *rapido* A^{Fr}.

Both *rapidus* ('swift-flowing, surging': cf. Catull.63.16, 64.358, Ov. *Her.*7.142) and *rabidus* ('raging, furious': see n.) are used as epithets for the sea, but *rabidus* is a stronger word, and so has more point here, as it brings out better the goddess' cruelty. *Rapidus* appears below in 44, and there seems little point in repeating the adjective within so few lines. The two words are often confused in the mss. (see Lenz & Gal.), and the scribe's eye may well have wandered to line 44.

1.2.65-66 **ferreus ille fuit qui, te cum posset habere,**
maluerit praedas stultus et arma sequi.

fuit] *fuat* Scaliger. *posset* g: *possit* A.

Cartault objects to *fuit* and *posset* on the grounds that *possit* remains unexplained and that T. cannot be talking of a rival, since it is the beginning of the affair, nor of Delia's *coniunx*, since the rest of the poem shows that he is at Rome. He therefore accepts *possit* and *fuat*.

However, *posset* could have been corrupted to *possit* under the influence of *fuit* or *maluerit*. *Fuit* may itself refer to an imaginary person (see n.). There is no reason why it could not refer to a rival (the existence of rivals has been suggested by 9 and 57f.). Nor is there any reason why *fuit* may not refer to the *coniunx*: there is no definite indication in the poem that he is either present or absent (see intro. essay), and the reference here may be to an expedition from which he has returned or is on the point of returning (see n.). In fact, it seems most likely that T. is referring to the *coniunx* here (see n.).

.2.87-88 **at tu, qui laetus rides mala nostra, caveto**
mox tibi: non uni saeviet usque deus.

at tu, qui laetus] *qui nimium letus* Par.: *lentus* Broukhusius. *non uni* ψ: *non vanus* H (Lenz & Gal.): *non unus* A: *et iratus* Par.

At tu, qui laetus gives good sense, and *qui nimium letus* has no connecting link, where T.'s characteristic *at tu* is necessary. *Lentus* is an unnecessary emendation, and *laetus* brings out better the joyful malevolence and spite of ἐπιχαιρεκακία.

Non vanus and *non unus* do not make sense, and *et iratus* looks like a violent correction. *Non uni* (i.e. 'not against me alone') makes excellent sense and could easily have been corrupted into *non unus* (under the influence of *usque deus*, or by dittography becoming *non unis*, and then *non unus*). The dative with *saevio* is rare but not without parallel (see n.).

With these readings the best punctuation seems to be that in Postgate

(OCT), as printed above. Lee (*PCPhS* 200, n.s.20 (1974), 53) places a colon after *caveto* and takes the pentameter as one sentence ('later the god will rage against *you*, he will not always rage against one person'). I feel that this lessens the emphasis of *mox tibi* and *non uni* (see n.), and it produces a rather clumsy construction for which there is no certain parallel in T. (at 2.5.59f. *Solis* need not go with *ortus* as well as *equos* (see Postgate *Selections* ad loc.), as Lee suggests).

1.2.89 **vidi ego qui iuvenum miseros lusisset amores**
lusisset] *dampnasset* Par.

The ex. of nemesis is for the benefit of the person in 87 who laughs at T.'s misfortunes, so 'mocked' seems more appropriate here than 'condemned' or 'censured'.

1.2.95 **hunc puer, hunc iuvenis turba circumterit arta,**
curcim(n)terit OHPQY: *circumstetit* e et i.m.V^2: *circumstitit* d: *circumdedit* Flor. (*sigla* of Lenz & Gal.).

Circumterit ('press on all sides') makes good sense, although the verb is found only here (for a similar use of *tero* see n.). The other readings substitute more usual words. Metrical considerations (1.3.5-8n.) favour *circumterit* written as one word.

1.3.4 **abstineas avidas Mors modo nigra manus.**
Mors modo nigra OBg.HMP: *Mors precor atra* GQ^2Yd: *Mors precor nigra* unus cod. (Hiller ad 2.1.67): *Mors violenta* Qc: *Mors violanda* e (*sigla* of Lenz & Gal.).

Mors precor nigra is unmetrical, and *violenta* and *violanda* look like violent corrections. *Mors precor atra* could easily be due to the scribe's eye wandering to the line below or to a deliberate attempt at symmetry, but, although *nigra* could be a gloss on *atra*, the presence of *modo* is not so easy to explain. In fact, as Cartault points out, *modo* has real point: T. has resigned himself to not joining Messalla and the *cohors*, and prays only (*modo*) that Death spare him. This interpretation seems better than taking *modo* to refer to time; *modo* can hardly go with *Mors . . . nigra*, since the phrase *Mors modo nigra* would then imply *Mors modo non nigra* or something equally inane; if *modo* = *dummodo*, it is hard to see the apodosis: T.'s captivity in Phaeacia could hardly be said to depend on Death withholding her hand (cf. Ov. *Am.* 3.9.47f.), and it would be scarcely less strange if his sickness were said to depend on the same condition. For *modo* meaning 'only, just' in commands or requests see n. (often a particular state of affairs in another clause seems to depend on the fulfilment of the clause containing *modo* (clearly inappropriate here), but for exx. where this is not the case see n.). The position of *modo* here may seem odd, but *modo* is similarly separated from its verb at 3.6.9, and for the intrusion between the two vocatives cf. 1.2.71. *Niger* is found elsewhere as an epithet of *Mors* (see n.), and there seems no reason why T. in the next line should not change the epithet to *ater* (and add *precor*) for greater intensity.

1.3.12 **rettulit e triviis omina certa puer.**

triviis A: *trinis* Muretus. *omina* A (*manu altera in ras.*): *omnia* V (*ut videtur*).

The much-maligned *triviis* does make sense: the boy reported clear omens that he had picked up at the *trivia* (see n.). *Omina* is preferable here. *Omnia* provides poor sense and is probably due to *omnes* in 10, and, as the comprehensiveness of Delia's consultations in 10 is emphasized, one might expect more than just *sortes* in this couplet. The verdict of the *sortes* is given in 13, as is the verdict of the gods consulted (10), and there is no difficulty over *omina dira* in 17 following *omina certa* here, as the omens of 17 are presumably different ones.

Trinis, then, seems an unnecessary correction, and, in any case, if it were accepted (referring to the *sortes* of 11), *rettulit* would then have to mean something like 'made answer', but there is no parallel for a *puer* acting as *interpres*, and the idea seems unlikely.

1.3.13-14 **tamen est deterrita numquam**
quin fleret nostras respiceretque vias.

numquam] *nusquam* V. *quin* ed. Aldina 1502: *cum* A. *respiceretque*] *respueretque* ψ: *despiceretque* Ber.PQ (Lenz & Gal.): *despueretque* Haupt.

On *numquam* see n. *Nusquam* is clearly inferior and probably came from *usquam* in 9 or a misreading of the abbreviation *nūquam* for *numquam.*

Cum seems suspicious in view of *cuncta* above in 13, and, if it were accepted, *numquam* (best taken with 10ff.) would have to refer to 14. *Quin* is not uncommon with *deterreo* (see n.), and the corruption of *quin* to *quom* is easy (esp. under the influence of *cuncta*).

Respiceretque ('view with alarm': see n.) makes perfectly good sense and is preferable to *despiceretque* and *respueretque*, since it picks up the idea of anxiety in *fleret*. Emendation seems unjustified.

.3.17 **aut ego sum causatus aves aut omina dira**

aves aut ψ: *aves dant* A.

The A reading is unlikely, as there is no parallel for *causor* introducing a direct statement, and the change to the indirect statement in 18 governed by the same verb is improbable. Note also that there is punctuation after *aves* in A (see Ponchont). *Aut* removes these difficulties (the first *aut* goes with the second *aut*). *Dant* is due to a misreading of *aut* or to a misunderstanding of the syntax.

.3.18 **Saturnive sacram me tenuisse diem.**

Saturnive quidam apud Broukhusium: *Saturni* A: *Saturni aut* ed. Reg. (Lenz & Gal.).

The asyndeton provided by the A reading does not seem possible, esp. in as fastidious an author as T. Something has dropped out, and *-ve* seems most likely here. If accepted, *Saturnive* makes *sacram* an iambus before the main caesura, but this structure occurs five times in T. and is not rare elsewhere in elegy (W.Meyer *Zur Gesch. des griech. und lat. Hexam.* (SB Akad. Münch.1884), 1032f.). If *aut* were accepted, this would be the only case in T. where the first syllable of *sacram* is long and the only ex. in T. of the rare elision of i before au (Platnauer 77). In addition, the postponement of *aut* elsewhere in T. occurs only at 2.5.112 and is in general uncommon (Platnauer 94, Norden *Aeneis Buch VI*^{3} (Leipzig, 1926), 404).

1.3.50 **nunc mare, nunc leti mille repente viae.**

repente ψ: *reperte* AV: *multa reperta via* ψ: *multa reperta via est* L.Mueller: *mille patentque viae* Leo.

Reperte is obviously wrong, but *repente* gives good sense (see n.) and is palaeographically probable (the same corruption of the word is found at *Aetna* 281, and in general confusion between n and r is common). Other readings and emendations involve alteration of words not in doubt.

1.3.64 **adsidue proelia miscet Amor.**

The love-god is more likely (and more usual) in this connection than *amor.*

1.3.69 **Tisiphoneque impexa feros pro crinibus angues**

impexa] *implexa* ψ.

With *implexa* the meaning would be 'with fierce plaited snakes in lieu of hair'. *Impexa* fits better with the wild figure of Tisiphone, unkempt here as elsewhere (e.g. Ov. *Met.* 4.474): the word may mean 'entangled, unkempt' or 'uncombed' (see n.). *Implexa* is either simply a mistake (there is similar confusion between the two words at Virg. *G.* 4.482) or perhaps a reminiscence of Virg. *G.* 4.482 (*caeruleosque implexae crinibus anguis*).

1.4.9 **ne fuge te tenerae puerorum credere turbae:**

ne fuge te exc. Perrei: *o fugite* Fris.: *o fuge te* ω: *o fugito* Housman (*sigla* of Lenz & Gal.).

O fugite is unmetrical, and elsewhere in the speech the second person singular is used for address.

O fuge te . . . most obviously means 'forbear to entrust yourself to the young band of boys'. This is a strange remark in the mouth of the lascivious Priapus, and this recommendation of avoidance of involvement hardly agrees with the mood and tone of the remainder of the speech. After such a remark *sed* in 15 and the advice of the following lines do not make sense: at 9ff. the addressee is warned to avoid boys, but at 15ff. the addressee is given advice as though he is having an affair. It seems unnecessary and unjustified to assume a lacuna (= 'but if you do fall in love with a boy'). *O fuge te . . .* can hardly mean 'do not entrust yourself to a lot of boys at once': this interpretation of *turbae* is unlikely in view of the qualification *tenerae*, the elaboration at

11-14 seems then excessive, not to say irrelevant, and the logic of the connection by *sed* in 15 is hard to see.

Ne fuge te . . . provides excellent sense ('do not forbear . . . ' = 'do entrust yourself to the young band of boys'). For *credo* reflexive in the general sense of 'entrust' see *OLD* s.v. 1d, and for *credo* in the particular context of entrusting oneself to a lover cf. Prop.1.20.52, Ov.*Rem.* 451. It may be objected that this recommendation is absurd, given that the enquirer has no intention of doing anything but put himself in the hands of boys. However, the enquiry, as represented by T. in the opening lines, contains no such implication: Priapus is simply asked what his technique is for catching young boys. Note also that T. later represents himself as having asked on behalf of Titius, and it is dangerous to speculate about the intentions of a blind (73-4n.). In addition, since T. does not make clear the manner in which he is supposed to have represented this enquiry as coming from Titius, there are no grounds for assuming that Priapus could have any idea as to what Titius' intentions might be.

In any case, this brief recommendation of παιδικὸς ἔρως seems a natural enough introduction to a series of precepts on that topic, and, in fact, may be modelled on the openings of other didactic works (see 9-14n.). The sentiment fits well with the next line and entirely justifies the elaboration at 11-14, while the lasciviousness of the remark is perfectly in harmony with the character of Priapus. Probably *ne* dropped out and *o* was inserted as a stop-gap (cf. 1.9.45).

O fugito, then, would appear to be an unnecessary emendation, and, if it were accepted, the sense would be 'do not trust boys' (again the qualification *tenerae* makes the interpretation 'do not trust all boys' unlikely), but the elaboration at 11-14 then seems excessive and irrelevant, while the connection at 15 (*sed*) is hard to follow.

1.4.27-28 **at si tardus eris errabis; transiet aetas:**
quam cito non segnis stat remeatque dies.

transiet] *transiit* ψ. *remeatque*] *remeatve* ψ.

Some editors place heavy stops after *quam cito* and *dies*, while others put a heavy stop after *transiet aetas* and a comma after *dies*. The above punctuation seems preferable. With punctuation after *quam cito* there is a sense-pause in the pent. at 1d (frequency in elegy only 2.7%: see Platnauer 26) and the anaphora of *quam cito* is spoiled (a frequent device in this speech: cf. esp. 11ff., 65f.). With a comma after *dies* the statement of the basic precept in this section does not occupy a couplet (invariably the case until the abandonment of the calm and reasoned attitude at 57ff.). The above punctuation removes these difficulties, and, although it gives the tautologous *quam cito non segnis*, there is similar tautology elsewhere in T. (e.g. 2.1.80), and here such tautology actually suits the exaggerated emphasis found throughout the speech of Priapus.

Probably *transiet* is another ex. of the rare forms in Priapus' speech (see n.), while *transiit* looks like an attempt to remove this unusual form.

The decision between *-que* and *-ve* is a delicate one. However, I see no very strong reason for challenging *-que* here: *-que* itself may stand for *-ve* (see Austin on Virg. *Aen.* 2.37, Fordyce on Catull.45.6f.), while the emendation of *-que* to *-ve* by ψ at 1.6.25 (from Ov. *Tr.* 2.451) tends to throw suspicion on *-ve* here.

1.4.30 **quam cito formosas populus alta comas.**

alta] *alba* ψ.

Alta fits in well with the idea of the similarity between this natural ex. and the human situation (see n.). In view of this parallelism (throughout the couplet) *alba* seems unlikely: the white poplar, although beautiful, has white foliage (Plin. *N.H.* 16.85f.), but white hair is obviously not a sign of beauty or youth in humans, and hair turning white may well be the human parallel to the poplar's loss of its foliage (see n.). *Alba* may be simply a mistake, or a misguided attempt to pick up *purpureus* in 29, or due to the frequency of the phrase *alba populus* (Hor. *C.* 2.3.9, Ov. *Her.* 9.64, Plin. *N.H.* 16.85, 87, 17.143 etc.).

1.4.43-44 **quamvis praetexens picta ferrugine caelum**
venturam admittat imbrifer arcus aquam.

picta] *picea* d. *caelum*] *tellum* P. *admittat* Hyde: *amiciat* ABBer.PQc: *amitiat* M: *annutiat* V: *annuntiet* recc. *imbrifer*] *nimbifer* Itali: *nubifer* recc. *arcus*] *Eurus* Huschke (*sigla* of Lenz & Gal.).

We can immediately accept *caelum* in 43 (*tellum* is nonsense) and *arcus* in 44 (there is no reason for suspicion, and *praetexens* (43) strongly suggests a rainbow's stripe, while Hieronymus Balbus *C.* XX (see Lenz & Gal.) is not close enough elsewhere to suggest any need for emendation here). It is now clear that the couplet refers to the stripe of a rainbow in the sky.

Ferrugo in 43 denotes dark colours (see n.). The word could well describe the hue of a stormy sky and, although not so used elsewhere, is applied to other celestial phenomena (cf. e.g. Virg. *G.* 1.467, Ov. *Met.* 15.789), while *piceus* obviously fits in well (of the sky and clouds at e.g. Ov. *Met.* 11.549, Val.Fl.2.115, 517). *Picea ferrugine* would make sense as an ablative of description with *caelum* ('the pitch-black sky'). On the other hand, *ferrugine* could refer to the rainbow itself, if T. were envisaging a rainbow in which the darker colours of the spectrum were predominant, and *pictus* is elsewhere used in connection with a rainbow (see n.). *Picta ferrugine* would then go with *praetexens.* Both readings make sense, but *picta* seems the more likely. *Piceus* is not found elsewhere in T., whereas *pictus* is (1.2.77, 1.3.28), and *picta* is the *lectio difficilior* (the phrase *picta ferrugine* seems odd at first sight, but *picea ferrugine* seems perfectly natural in view of the application to *ferrugo* of similar adjectives, e.g. *ater* at Ov.*Met.* 15.789 and *obscurus* at Virg. *G.* 1.467, Ov.*Met.* 5.404).

In 44 *annutiat* is senseless and *annuntiet* unmetrical, while the scansion of *amiciat* / *amitiat* is impossible for dactylic metres, and, even if the first syllable could be lengthened, the word would give an expression unparalleled in classical literature (on the rare occasions when clothing or covering is mentioned in connection with a rainbow, rather than the rainbow described as covering or clothing for the water, the rainbow itself is covered, e.g. with clothes at Ov. *Met.* 11.589f., girdle of clouds at Sil.It.9.471). However, *admittat* gives good sense (see n.) and seems palaeographically likely (written as *amittat* it could have given rise to the corruptions *amiciat* and *anutiat*).

Imbrifer is found before T. and is elsewhere applied to rainbows (see n.). If the word is accepted here, the final syllable of *admittat* would remain closed before an initial vowel, but the scansion *admittāt* here does seem admissible (see n.). Neither *nimbifer* nor *nubifer* is found before T., and the words are not elsewhere applied to rainbows. They are probably due to misguided attempts to correct the metre.

1.4.45-48 Since I believe the ref. in 47-8 is to the boating-trip mentioned in 45-6 (see 47-8n.), I punctuate with a comma at the end of 46 and a full stop at the end of 48.

1.4.54 **pugnabit, sed tibi rapta dabit.**

tibi rapta Santen: *tamen apta* A.

The kisses of 53, 54 and the first half of 55 are all of the same type, i.e. stolen kisses prior to *post adferet* etc. In the A reading *apta* (*oscula*) are usually explained as 'french-kisses' (cf. Ov. *Her.* 15.129f.), but it is difficult to see how such kisses can be snatched. Even if *apta* has another meaning (such as 'fitting', i.e. in view of the lover's obsequiousness), with the A reading the boy would be giving the kisses unsnatched in 54, despite the fact that in 53 and the first half of 55 he is only letting them be snatched. This spoils the typical cleverness of the climax in 53-6 and the triple repetition of *rapio*, while *rapta dabit* in 55 seems clumsy after *apta dabit*. *Tamen apta* is probably due to a misguided attempt to avoid repetition, and *tibi rapta* provides the most likely solution.

1.4.71 **blanditiis vult esse locum Venus ipsa:**

ipsa] *illa* Heyne.

The mss.' *ipsa* here has real point, because, if money rules love, what Venus herself wishes (the use of the love-poet's traditional method) is impossible, i.e. the very goddess of love is thwarted (see n.). Heyne's *illa* (with the colon after *Venus*) does not provide this necessary emphasis. For the phrase *ipsa Venus* cf. 1.2.16, 1.8.5 (cf. also *ipse deus* 1.6.43, 1.8.56, 1.9.25, 27 and *Pater ipse* 1.4.23). The sense-pause produced by reading *ipsa* is rare (and emphatic), but not much more unusual than that produced by *illa* (Platnauer 25).

1.5.3 **namque agor ut per plana citus sola verbere turben**

turben Charisius p.145.8K: *turbo* codd.

For the rare form *turben* see n. It seems likely that scribes have introduced the usual form *turbo* here. T. will have chosen *turben* either for variety, because it is so unusual, or perhaps in imitation of its use by a previous author in a passage which has not survived (e.g. possibly Catullus, mentioned by Servius on *Aen.* 7.378). Certainly the analogistic grammatical theory cannot be cited in favour of *turbo* here (see Axelson 130, Introduction sect. 7).

1.5.14 **somnia, ter sancta deveneranda mola;**

deveneranda] *devenerata* ψ Guyet.

The gerundive provides good sense here (see n.). *Devenerata* seems unnecessary and unlikely (in view of *velatus* and *solutis* in 15, the corruption of gerundive to participle is more probable than the reverse process).

1.5.20 **fingebam demens, sed renuente deo.**

sed A: *et* Santen.

The fact that T.'s dream was mad or foolish does not necessarily mean that it could not have come true. Actually *demens* is virtually an interjection. What really affected the outcome was *renuente deo.* Emendation is unnecessary.

1.5.33-34 **et, tantum venerata virum, hunc sedula curet,**
huic paret atque epulas ipsa ministra gerat.

hunc . . . / huic] *nunc . . . / nunc* ψ: *tunc . . . / tunc* ς (Hiller).

With the hexameter as it stands in the majority of mss. there is difficulty over the final syllable of *virum* remaining closed before an initial vowel and over the hiatus between *virum* and *hunc*, and there are problems over the function of *hunc* and the punctuation to be adopted (Postgate (OCT) punctuates as above, whereas Lenz & Gal. place a comma after *curet* but do not punctuate after *et* and *virum*). In the light of the discussion in the commentary (see n.) I think that *hunc . . . / huic* with the above punctuation is just defensible. The alternative readings are improbable (*huic* in 34 could hardly be a corruption of *nunc* or *tunc*, and it supports *hunc* in 33) and look like misguided attempts to correct supposed faults in the metre.

1.5.41-42 **tunc me discedens devotum femina dixit,**
et pudet et narrat scire nefanda meam.

et pudet et narrat codd.: *a pudet, et narrat* Mueller: *et, pudet a, narrat* Baehrens: *ei pudet, et narrat* O. Richter: *et, pudet, enarrat* Gruppe: *et pubi narrat* Drenkhahn: *et, pudet ei, narrat* Scaliger: *et, pudet id, narrat* Havet: *et putet et narret* Rigler.

The above conjectures have been prompted by a number of considerations: as the text stands in the mss. there is an abrupt shift from impersonal to personal expression; there are problems over the relationship of the mss. reading to the verb in the hexameter, and at first sight there may seem to be difficulty in the change of tenses; the triple *-et* appears to have caused suspicions; many have baulked at the idea of the girl feeling shame.

Certainly one might expect *pudet* to refer to the poet's shame (cf. Ov. *Am.* 3.7.19f., 37f., 72), but with the mss. reading *pudet* surely refers to the woman's shame, and the idea of shame on her part is not unparalleled (in a similar situation Ovid also refers to the shame of the girl and her suspicion of the influence of witchcraft at *Am.* 3.7.77ff.).

In defence of the phraseology Smith cites three passages from Ovid (which also contain triple *-et*). The first two (*Rem.* 407f. *et pudet et dicam: Venerem quoque iunge figura, / qua minime iungi quamque decere putas* and *Met.* 14.279 *(et pudet et referam) saetis horrescere coepi*) are not so pertinent, since the phrases there are of a parenthetic nature, combine present and future tenses and *et pudet* in those passages has a concessive force which is inappropriate here (rather the implication is that it is her shame that leads her to accusations of witchcraft). The third passage, where *et pudet* has no concessive force, is a better parallel: *ExP.* 4.15.29f. *et pudet et metuo semperque eademque precari, / ne subeant animo taedia iusta tuo. Pudet* at *ExP.* 4.15.29 may or may not be used absolutely, but it certainly is used absolutely in the two former passages from Ovid.

There is little real difficulty in the change from perfect to presents in the couplet: the presents may be genuine (see n.) or historic (cf. e.g. in a similar situation Ov. *Am.* 3.7.73-84).

There remains the question of the relation of these verbs to *dixit* in 41. Lenz & Gal. group all three verbs together with no punctuation, while Smith and Putnam place a comma at the end of 41, thus separating *dixit*. I follow Smith and Putnam, since there is no satisfactory parallel for the triple grouping with this use of *pudet*, while the group of two has support from Ovid.

1.5.47-48 haec nocuere mihi, quod adest huic dives amator:
venit in exitium callida lena meum.

Postgate (OCT) and other editors punctuate with a full stop after *mihi* and a comma after *amator.* Although *haec nocuere mihi* is found at Ov. *Met.* 9.613 as a sentence on its own, to take the phrase here as such leaves an abrupt transition in the middle of the line. The transition to the curse-section is smoother if one takes *haec* to refer to Delia's charms (mentioned in 43-6) and *nocuere* to their effect on T. (described at 37ff.), and punctuates as above: 'her beauty has had this iniurious effect on me (rather than stimulating me) because she has a rich lover: it is a crafty *lena* who is to blame for my trouble'.

1.5.49 **sanguineas edat illa dapes**
edat] *edit* Francken.

In a discussion of the subjunctive of *edo* Postgate (*CR* XVI (1902), 111f.) concludes that the forms *edim, edis* etc. lived on 'into the late Republic and early Empire, when they were ousted by *edam, edas* etc.' Before the present passage he observes two exx. of *edam, edas* etc. (Plaut. *Stich.* 554, *Poen.* 534). Other exx. of this form cited by *Thes. L. L.* V_2.98.73ff. include Ov. *Met.* 14.194, *Ibis* 604, Sen. *Thy.* 278, *Dial.* 10.12.5, 12.10.3, *Epist.* 19.10, Cels. 3.12.4. At Hor. *S.* 2.8.90 and Virg. *Aen.* 12.801 the mss. disagree over the form.

The exx. from Plautus should perhaps not be pressed: Postgate thinks that 'it seems incredible that the two forms of the subjunctive struggled together for existence for two centuries before the strife was decided in favour of one of them' (N.B. Plautus elsewhere has *edim, edis* etc.: see Neue 3.309ff., Postgate loc.cit.), while A is present for neither passage. However, there are no good grounds for challenging the exx. from Ovid and Seneca, and neither author uses *edim, edis* etc. (Celsus is less sure, as *edit* is the reading at 5.28.7). Given this situation there seems no reason why T. should not introduce the *edam edas* etc. form here. Postgate (p. 112) admits that the form *edit* normally escaped corruption, and, in view of *venit* and *exitium* immediately above in 48, corruption of *edat* to *edit* actually seems more likely than the reverse process.

1.5.69 **at tu, qui potior nunc es, mea fata timeto:**
fata Muretus: *furta* codd.

If *mea furta* were accepted, it would have to mean 'intrigues on my part', and *quidam* (71) would then refer to T., the idea being that T. himself will supplant his rich rival. This idea, however, does not fit the situation of the poem: as T. remarks at 67f., for the present Delia is unlikely to receive T. because of his lack of money, while at 67 he describes his own efforts as *frustra*, but at 71 the efforts *iam nunc* of the *quidam* are *non frustra*. It has been claimed that Ovid attributes the actions of 71ff. to T. at *Tr.* 2.459f., but there are textual difficulties in the Ovidian passage (see below on 71-6). In any case, Ovid is there combining two passages from T., and, even if he does assign these actions to T., the discrepancy could be due to artistic variation or deliberate exaggeration (to make his point that other Roman love-poets have not been punished for their misdemeanours). *Furta* could easily have come from 65, 75 or even 1.6.5. Muretus' *fata* is the easiest and most likely emendation, the idea being that another man is now on the scene and may soon oust Delia's present lover, as T. himself was ousted.

1.5.71-76 Scaliger proposed the transposition of these lines to follow 1.6.32, based on Ov. *Tr.* 2.459f., where a reminiscence of line 74 is found immediately after a reference to 1.6.32 (*scit, cui latretur, cum* *solus obambulet, ipsas (ipse / ipsa) / cui (qui / cur) totiens clausas excreet ante fores*). If the transposition were accepted, it would leave 1.5 with an abrupt ending, and 1.6.33ff. would not follow on logically from 1.5.75-6. There is no reason why Ovid should not be combining two very similar situations from two adjoining poems of T.

1.5.76 **in liquida nat tibi linter aqua.**

nat g: *nam* A: *nunc* Rossberg: *non* Cartault: *stat* Guyet. *aqua*] *aqua est* Deutsch.

It seems probable that the image here is a small boat on a river (see n.). To take *liquida . . . aqua* as translucent, and therefore tranquil, water necessitates emendation. But the mss. give perfectly good sense if *liquida* is taken to mean 'running', as at 1.9.50 (see n.). In such river-imagery the verb is most often expressed, and, in any case, postposition of *nam* is very rare in the *Corp. Tib.* (with certainty only at 3.4.43).

1.6.3 **quid tibi, saeve, rei mecum est?**

saeve, rei Postgate: *sevicie* A: *saeve puer* ψ.

The phrase *quid tibi saevitiae mecum est* is without parallel, and the defence of it on the analogy of *quid tibi rei / negotii mecum est* is not convincing. *Saeve puer* has the look of an interpolation and may have come from Ov. *Am.* 1.1.5. The corruption to *sevicie* of *saeve, rei*, however, does seem likely (see Postgate *CR* XIX (1905), 213), and the phrase *quid tibi rei mecum est* is well enough attested elsewhere and gives good sense here (see n.).

1.6.7 **illa quidem tam multa negat, sed credere durum est:**

tam multa A: *iurata* Heyne.

Heyne's emendation is based on Ov. *Tr.* 2.447 *credere iuranti durum putat esse Tibullus* and has been accepted by a number of editors. Certainly the precise force of *tam* is difficult to see immediately, and the presence of *nam* and *iam* in 5 might give grounds for suspicion. However, *tam multa* is defensible if taken in the sense of 'ever so much' or 'ever so often' (see n.), and with this meaning the phrase is further defended by the progression to *usque* in the pent. (cf. *negat* and *pernegat*). In any case, there is no need to expect the same word here as in Ovid, since there are numerous discrepancies between the two passages.

1.6.15-16 **at tu, fallacis coniunx incaute puellae,**
me quoque servato, peccet ut illa nihil,

Whatever the interpretation of line 16 (for the possibilities see n.), the above punctuation, as in Postgate (OCT), seems preferable to that of most other editors (full stop after *nihil*). If *servato* is perf. part. passive (in the sense of 'protect the interests of' or 'guard'), this is the only punctuation possible (the main verb of the sentence begun in 15 does not appear until the end of 17 in *caveto*). If *servato* is the imperative (in the sense of 'guard'), then *me quoque* means 'me as well as Delia', and, as no mention is made of guarding her until 17, a comma after *nihil* makes the ref. more easily understood (*neu . . . caveto* in 17, i.e. *et ne . . . caveto*, will be the continuation of the imperative).

Platnauer (27ff.) puts the frequency of enjambment in T. at 9%, and, although usually only two couplets are so linked, a run-over into a third couplet, as here (15-20), occurs at 1.3.5ff., 1.7.17ff., 43ff., 2.1.51ff., 2.4.55ff., 2.5.27ff., 113ff., 2.6.35ff., and even longer periods occur elsewhere in elegy (e.g. 3.4.51-60, Prop. 2.1.71-8).

1.6.32 **instabat tota cui tua nocte canis.**

instabat] *latrabat* Baehrens.

Baehrens called *instabat* 'ungeheuerliche' and based his emendation on Ov. *Tr.* 2.459 (quoted in Critical Appendix on 1.5.71-6). He may also have had in mind Hor. *Epod.* 5.58, Ov. *Am.* 2.19.40, where *latro* is used in similar contexts. Certainly this would be the only ex. of *instare* in T. I and II, and with the meaning required here ('threaten, harass') the word is normally used of persons or things. However, *instabat* is defensible, as the verb in this sense is applied to animals elsewhere (see n.). In any case, there are numerous words that occur only once in T. I and II, and there are in general many discrepancies between the Ovidian passage and T., while in the particular instance of 459f. Ovid is combining two passages of T. (1.6.31f. and 1.5.74), so that his *latretur* is probably used as a convenient alternative for *instabat*.

1.6.33-34 **quid tenera tibi coniuge opus? tua si bona nescis**
servare, frustra clavis inest foribus.

post *servare* add. *ah* vel *heu* vel *ac* vel *et* recc. (Lenz & Gal.).

On the basis of the discussion in the commentary (see n.) I feel that the syllabic lengthening in *servare* here is just defensible. In any case, the additions in recc. seem improbable. *Et* and *ac* are undesirable, since it seems most natural to take *frustra* etc. as the logical consequence of *tua si* etc., rather than as a secondary reason for the *coniunx* not needing a girl or a final comment on the whole couplet. Similarly, out of 8 exx. in T. I and II, with one exception (1.8.23) *a* and a single *heu* are always placed first in the line, while a tone of real pity or sadness is highly inappropriate here, and irony seems actually to lessen the impatient and cutting callousness. These additions are probably attempts to remedy an imagined fault in the metre.

1.6.42 **†stet procul aut alia stet procul ante via†.**

The line as it stands in most mss. does not make sense (the *atque* of the Itali for *aut* does not help) and is obviously corrupt. Various emendations have been tried, but none is fully convincing. Statius proposed *stet procul ante, alia stet procul ante via,* but this gives poor sense and repetition of *ante* has little point. Others have concentrated on the second *stet procul*: e.g. Müller's *sit procul aut alia stet precor ante via*, Rabus' *stet procul aut alia se occulat ille via*, Helm's *stet procul aut alia se ferat ante via*, Havet's *stet procul aut alia se trahat ante via*, Cartault's *stet procul aut alia det mihi terga via*, Lee's *stet procul aut alia transeat ille via*, and Calonghi's *stet procul aut alia det cito terga via*. These corrections are arbitrary and violent, and presume that the second *stet procul* is due to dittography or that it has been added to fill a gap in the line. But, as Eden points out, the repetition may be a perfectly genuine variation on the phrase *procul, o procul este, profani* (see Lenz & Gal.), so necessitating emendation elsewhere. Eden himself suggests *hinc* for *aut*, but the corruption of *hinc* to *aut* seems unlikely. As none of the many conjectures is fully convincing and it is unclear which words require emendation, the only course open is to obelize.

1.6.71-72 **et si quid peccasse putet, ducarque capillis**
immerito pronas proripiarque vias.

putet Qrecc.: *putat* OBPYc: *puter* Itali: *putor* de: *putem* H. *ducarque* Ber.[2]HQe: *ducorque* OBPYcd: *ducatque* ed.min. 1472: *ducterque* ψ or Scaliger. *immerito* codd.: *immerito in medias* Rothstein: *in medias praeceps* Belling: *in medium, praeceps* Helm. *pronas* G[2]recc.: *proprias* OBCHQ: *propria* P: *properans* G: *pronus* Francken. *proripiarque* Ber.[2]H: *proripiorque* OBcd: *proprior atque* P: *proripiatque* Qed.min. 1472: *proripiasque* e: nnm *per rapiarque?. vias*] *manus* HQ (*sigla* of Lenz & Gal.).

In lines 69-70 and 73-4 T. is talking about a hypothetical state of affairs in the future, so that the subjunctive is clearly required in 71-2. Accordingly, in 71 the indicatives *putat* and *putor* are inappropriate. *Putem* is senseless. Of the two remaining readings *putet* is preferable: in view of the frequency of r in this couplet the corruption of *putet* to *puter* seems more likely than the reverse process.

The indicative *ducorque* is inappropriate. *Ductare* is mainly ante- and post-class. and is not found elsewhere in T. or other Augustan authors, while the sense of the verb in the classical period ('to lead', of troops) is not to the point here. *Ducatque* probably came from *putet* (or *putat*) and seems odd with the passive in 72. *Ducarque* seems most likely and balances well with *proripiarque*.

In 72 *vias* is obviously correct (*manus* from 74), as is *proripiarque* (the indicative is inappropriate, *proprior atque* is nonsense, *proripiasque* is probably due to the frequency of *-as* in the line and would involve an unlikely change to address, and *proripiatque* repeats the mistake of *ducatque* above).

Proprias and *propria* are nonsense, while *properans* is probably an attempt to make sense out of these readings, and, in any case, is otiose and redundant. *Pronas* seems much better, and *pronus* is a prosaic and unnecessary conjecture. *Pronas* may refer to the steepness of the *viae*, but it seems more likely that it is a transferred epithet (see n.). This is the only ex. in T. of such an accusative of motion (but see Smith for similar usage elsewhere in elegy), and the only ex. in classical lit. of *proripi* with this accusative instead of a preposition, but the lines make perfectly good sense, and similar anomaly in T. is not rare enough to justify suspicion here.

At the beginning of 72 *immerito* is described by Postgate (OCT) as '*vix sanum*', but emendation seems unjustified. In fact, *immerito* continues the idea of *et mihi sint durae leges* (69). The word means 'even though I be undeserving / guiltless' (cf. Hor. *C.* 3.6.1 *delicta maiorum immeritus lues*). Just as in 69f. T. has committed no actual offence but has merely behaved suspiciously, so here regardless of his innocence he is to be punished on grounds of suspicion alone. T. would not care about being innocent because such behaviour on Delia's part would be indicative of love (see n.).

1.6.77 Postgate (OCT) marks a lacuna before this line and in his *Selections* maintains that one or more couplets describing the happy old age of the faithful woman have dropped out. Certainly there is a bit of a lurch in passing directly from youthful years of faithful devotion to the old age of infidelity. However, the sense runs on well enough in the text as we have it: transition by contrast to the faithful figure of Delia depicted in 75f. (for *at* used to make transition from one character to another cf. 1.5.19, 1.7.7, 1.8.77 (see n.), 2.3.33, 2.4.45). The lurch here is no greater than that at 1.8.39, where T. makes a similar transition (from injunctions to give in to the boy to description of the unhappy old age of the mistress). Similarly Propertius (3.25) and Julianus (*A.P.* 5.298) pass directly into the girl's old age. In fact, such a description of the faithful woman's declining years as Postgate requires seems otiose and unlikely here: the implications of 77ff. are perfectly obvious, and it is not T.'s custom to include such 'companion-pictures' with exx. of nemesis, nor are they found in any other versions of this particular ex. (see 77-84n.).

1.6.80 **tractaque de niveo vellere ducta putat.**

ducta] *dente* ψ Statius.

Dente seems unlikely here: in view of *gaudente vident* immediately below in 81, the corruption of *ducta* to *dente* seems more likely than the reverse process, and the heaping-up of ablatives that *dente* would produce is inelegant.

1.7.4 **quem tremeret forti milite victus Atur.**

Atur Scaliger: *Atax* codd.

The Atax was the principal river of the Province and had been in Roman hands for nearly a hundred years. This fact led Scaliger to propose *Atur*, a river in old Aquitania. Postgate (loc.cit.intro.essay) tried to defend *Atax* by suggesting an invasion of the Province and occupation of the Atax by the Aquitanians (*forti milite victus*), which necessitated Messalla's despatch. However, since with the reading *quem* the Atax should rejoice rather than 'tremble' at Messalla's day of victory, for the line to make sense he was reduced to emending the inoffensive *quem* to *cum*. Even if this emendation is accepted, in a poem in praise of his patron's achievements one would expect T. to refer to victories won by Messalla rather than his opponents, and to describe as 'brave' Messalla's troops rather than the enemy. In addition, there is no evidence of such an invasion of the Province, a serious and alarming occurrence which surely would have merited some mention elsewhere.

Ramsay suggested that the Atax 'may well have been the scene of some preliminary victory, as its valley affords the natural access to Aquitania.' Reference to any kind of minor battle in 4 would make the line decidedly anticlimactic, and sudden abandonment of allegiance to Rome by the Atax (cf. *tremeret, victus*) seems most unlikely.

Scaliger's *Atur* gives excellent sense and seems plausible, *Atax* being due to a scribe's confusion over the geographical names.

1.7.9 **non sine me est tibi partus honos:**

non sine me est tibi codd.: *non sine Marte ibi* Baehrens: *non sine re* Housman.

There seems no reason to suspect the mss. reading here. Postgate (loc.cit.intro.essay) claimed that there is no indication elsewhere in his poetry that T. ever went to Aquitania, but by the same token there is also no indication in his poetry that he did not. The *vita* tells us that T. was present on the campaign (*cuius [Messallae] et contubernalis Aquitanico bello militaribus donis donatus est*), and there is no particular reason for doubting the credibility of the *vita* (see Introduction sect. 1). Postgate also claimed that by these words the shy, retiring T. is thrusting himself forward in the celebration of his patron. On the contrary, this seems merely a brief, simple allusion to his own part in the war, *non sine me* meaning 'I was with you' (cf. 1.3.1 *sine me*). It seems only natural that T. should wish to associate himself in some small way with his patron here, as at 53f., while these personal refs. indicate T.'s particular reason for writing the poem and help relieve what would otherwise be a rather impersonal elegy (in a similar way T. introduces the personal element into 2.5 at 109ff.).

Tarbella Pyrene

Tarbella Scaliger: *tua bella* A.

The A reading is nonsense and probably due to the scribe's failure to recognize the geographical name. *Tarbella* is palaeographically sound and gives good sense (see n.).

1.7.11 Postgate (loc.cit.intro.essay) maintained that before this line there has dropped out a couplet to facilitate transition from Messalla's deeds in war to those in peace. However, it is by no means certain that 11-12 refer to deeds in peace (see n.), and, even if they do, *honos* (9) is such a vague term that T. would probably see no need to differentiate between military and peaceful glory but would prefer a smooth transition by the repetition of *testis* and the continuation of the geographical list.

testis Arar Rhodanusque celer

Arar Rhodanusque] *Atur Duranusque* Scaliger.

Scaliger objected to *Arar Rhodanusque* because those rivers do not fit in with the idea of an Aquitanian victory and nothing else. However, it seems unlikely that *Atur* should be repeated from 4, and the form *Duranus* is not elsewhere attested. In any case, there are feasible explanations of the ref. to the Arar and Rhodanus here (see n.).

1.7.13-14 **an te, Cydne, canam, tacitis qui leniter undis**
caeruleus placidis per vada serpis aquis,

tactis . . . *ulvis* Lachmann: *tractis* . . . *undis* Némethy: *caeruleis placidus* Statius: *placidae*. . . *aquae* Voss: *caeruleae placidus*. . . *aquae* Huschke.

The mss. reading here has often been questioned: the repeated *-is* forms have aroused suspicion of corruption, and it has been objected that *tacitis* . . . *undis* and *placidis* . . . *aquis* are both ablatives of precisely the same type hanging on one and the same verb (*serpis*), and that this construction is unlikely, without parallel and leaves the lines open to charges of pleonasm.

However, the couplet as it stands in the mss. is grammatically correct if one takes *tacitis* . . . *undis* with *serpis* and *placidis* . . . *aquis* as a descriptive ablative with *vada* (see n.). With this interpretation there is no pleonasm. For the repetition of the *-is* ending cf. esp. 1.5.43f. Emendation does not seem justified.

1.7.27 **te canit atque suum pubes miratur Osirim**

atque] *utque* Platnauer.

The rarity of unelided *atque* in elegy prompted the emendation (*CQ* XLII (1948), 90f.; see also Lee *PCPhS* 200 (1974), 55). However, the line makes sense as it stands in the mss. (see n.), and there are two other exx. of unelided *atque* in T.: 2.5.73 is supported by the analogy of Virg. *Ecl.* 5.23 (*atque deos atque astra vocat*), as Lee points out, while the arguments against and emendations of 2.2.8 by Platnauer (p.93) and Lee (p.56) do not convince me. In addition, as Lee admits, there is no parallel in T. for such a use of *ut*.

1.7.40 **pectora tristitiae dissoluenda dedit:**

tristitiae] *laetitiae* Muretus.

The mss. reading involves two oddities (*tristitiae* as a graecism for *tristitia* with *dissolvo*, and *dare* in the sense of 'render, make' with a gerundive). *Laetitiae* (supported by Housman *CR* XVII (1903), 309) is obviously much easier, but the poem contains many unusual expressions and usages, and on the basis of the discussion in the commentary I feel that *tristitiae* is just defensible here.

1.7.49-50 **huc ades et centum ludis Geniumque choreis / concelebra**

et centum A: *ad cantum* Francken. *centum ludis Geniumque* ψ: *centum ludos Geniumque* A: *Genium ludis Geniumque* Y^2 recc. (Lenz & Gal.): *Genium ludis centumque* Ramsay: *Genium ludo Geniumque* Markland: *sanctum ludo Geniumque* Guyet: *centum ludos Genioque* Rigler. *choreis* codd.: *choreas* Rigler.

The A reading involves a harsh zeugma, and wine (the probable addressee: see n.) could hardly be asked to celebrate dances. Of the other two mss. readings ψ is the *lectio difficilior* (because of the displacement of *-que*), but does make sense. *Centum* (= an indefinitely large number: see n.) harmonizes with *multo* in 50, and a large number of games and dances brings out well the festivity of the occasion (cf. Prop.3.10.23 *tibia nocturnis succumbat rauca choreis*). The displacement of *-que* is uncommon, but not without parallel (see n.). *Ludis* was probably corrupted to *ludos* because of the following accusative *Geniumque*. *Genium* (Y^2 recc.) is probably due to an attempt to remove a supposed difficulty over the position of *-que* (although it may simply be a misreading of *centum*), and is less vigorous and pointed than *centum*.

Emendation, then, is not required, but, in any case, Ramsay's transposition is unnecessary, suspicions of *centum* (Francken, Guyet) seem unwarranted, Markland's *Genium* is less pointed than *centum*, and his singular *ludo* seems odd next to *choreis* (cf. *ludis* at Ov. *ExP.* 4.9.116), while Rigler alters the unoffending *choreis* and produces the unlikely invitation to wine to celebrate games and dances.

1.7.53 **sic venias, hodierne: tibi dem turis honores,**

tibi dem] *deus, tibi* Francken: *Geni tibi* Postgate.

With the text as it stands in the mss. and with the usual interpretation of *hodierne* as standing for *hodie*, the address here must be to Osiris, which is inappropriate (see n.). The above emendations were intended to make the address to the Genius, but they are unconvincing, and unnecessary, if one takes *hodierne* as a true vocative referring to the Genius (see n.), and so punctuates with a comma after *venias*.

1.7.61 **te canet agricola, a magna cum venerit urbe**

a Baehrens: *e* Itali: om. A.

The evidence for the lengthening of a short final vowel at the caesura is flimsy (Housman *CQ* XXI (1927), 1ff.). The omission of *a* by haplography seems likely (more so than omission of *e*), and *a* provides a more usual construction. The elision so produced is rare, but not unparalleled in T. (see n.).

1.8.26 **femori conseruisse femur.**

femori codd.: *femini* Statius.

Statius' emendation was prompted by Charisius (87.3f., 130.36-7K), who attributes the words *implicuitque femur femini* to T. However, Charisius' words simply do not agree with this line. Either he has only half-remembered it, or he is referring to another (lost) passage in T., or he is confusing T. with another author. In any case, up to the time of Suetonius singular forms in *femin-* are less common than those in *femor-* (according to *Thes.L.L.* VI$_1$.470.50ff., 15: 19), and the dative singular *femini* occurs only at Plin. *N.H.* 28.217. Note also that in the three Ovidian reminiscences of this phrase *femori* occurs (*Am.* 1.4.43, 3.7.10, 3.14.22).

1.8.30 **ut foveat molli frigida membra sinu.**

foveat] *foveas* ψ.

Usually the girl is the subject of *fovere* in such circumstances, but there is a parallel for the man as subject (see n.). *Foveas* may be an attempt to give the verb its more usual subject, or it may be due to the influence of *poscas* in 29.

1.8.35-36 **at Venus invenit puero concumbere furtim,**
dum timet et teneros conserit usque sinus,

at] *ac* Baehrens: *et* Drenkhahn. *invenit* A: *inveniet* ψ. *concumbere*] *súccumbere* C (Lenz & Gal.). *timet*] *tumet* ψ. *et . . . conserit*] *et . . . conseret* P (Lenz & Gal.): *et . . . conserere* Heyne: *ut . . . conserat* Müller.

At is difficult, as the word usually introduces an objection, not a reply to an objection. However, the use of *at* here to answer or forestall an imaginary excuse by the girl is possible (see n.), and emendation seems unnecessary.

Invenit gives excellent sense as a gnomic perfect (see n.), which is found in the parallel passage at 55f. and in a similar general statement at 2.1.73f. *Inveniet* is probably due to a misunderstanding of the perfect or to the influence of *timet* in 36.

Concumbere seems more apt, as *succumbere* in the sexual sense usually has an unpleasant tone: Varro *R.R.* 2.10.9, Catull.111.3 (of promiscuous intercourse), Ov. *F.* 2.810 (rape), Petron. *S.* 126 (with a slave), Mart.14.201 (of a homosexual); at Mart.13.64.1 the verb is applied to a hen.

Timet provides good sense, picking up *furtim* (for the fear of detection usually present in such circumstances see 1.6.59-60n.). *Tumet* seems unlikely. Smith claims that the word is used of erection, but it seems too explicit a word for T., and for this sense to fit in here Smith is forced to give a highly unlikely explanation of *teneros conserit usque sinus* (see n.). Dissen explains *dum tumet* as 'while he is still young', but this is a later use (Virg. *G.* 2.324 may be an early ex., but is not pertinent here), generally restricted to females, and applied to virginity, years etc. rather than people themselves (e.g. *tumeo* at Stat. *Ach.* 1.292, *tumidus* at *Theb*.2.204, *tumesco* at Claud. *Epithal.Pallad.* 125). The word may also be used of anger or pride, but these emotions are irrelevant here. In view of the proximity of *dum*, the corruption of *timet* to *tumet* seems likely.

In the remainder of the pentameter clearly *conseret* is inappropriate (from *timet et*), but *et . . . conserit* makes sense (referring to embraces (see n.), a natural reaction of the boy during the encounter). Heyne's *et . . . conserere* leaves *dum timet* very isolated and produces an elision not found elsewhere in T. (Platnauer 89), while the corruption of *conserit* to *conserere* seems more likely than the reverse process, in view of the presence of three infinitives in the immediate context. Müller's *ut . . . conserat* is prosaic and pedestrian: as a consecutive clause it is otiose, as a purpose clause it is inappropriate, and as a negative fear clause it is irrelevant.

1.8.52 **sed nimius luto corpora tingit amor.**
luto ψ: *luteo* A.

If scanned *lŭtĕō*, the A reading does not make sense, as the word is then an adjective and refers to a muddy colour. If scanned *lūtēō*, the reading is hardly less unlikely, as the synizesis is unparalleled and the word is not at all common as a noun until Pliny (*N.H.* 30.141 etc.). *Luto* gives perfectly good sense (see n.). The corruption was probably due to the rarity of *lutum*.

1.8.53-54 **vel miser absenti maestas quam saepe querellas / conicit**
vel] *ut* de: *vae* Itali: *heu* Camps (*sigla* of Lenz & Gal.).

Vel gives good sense (see n.) and is, in any case, more vigorous than *vae* (not found elsewhere in the *Corp. Tib.*) and *heu* (see Lee p.102), while *ut* probably came from *luto* in 52 or from *ut* in 57 or 58.

1.9.4 In agreement with Postgate (OCT), I have printed *Poena* with a capital because the goddess fits better with the personification of *tacitis . . . pedibus* and would be more awesome for the boy.

1.9.25 **ipse deus tacito permisit lene ministro**
lene Ber.[2]HQV[2]V_5de[2]: *laene* G: *leve* OP: *laeva* Yce: *lena* vel *s(a)eva* recc. (*sigla* of Lenz & Gal.).

Lene gives excellent sense here. Of the other readings only *lena* makes sense (see Dissen), but it gives an unusual word-order and necessitates taking *deus* as Amor, where *deus* seems to be a more general term. As Lenz suggests (*Mnemosyne* Ser.4 vol.22 (1969), 380f.), *lene* is most probably the adverb (see n.). There is no reason to suppose that *tacito* implies that the *minister* does not want to speak and that this couplet, like the next, is an ex. of duress, as Postgate maintained (*CR* XXIII (1909), 186). In fact there seems to be a deliberate contrast between the two couplets (see n.). In 27f. god is commanding the unwilling to speak, but in 25f. he is allowing one who would like to speak to do so (a gossipy slave, who is normally silent through fear of his master, has witnessed something: seen n.). The many alternative readings (and emendations) are due to the rarity of the adverb and a misunderstanding of its application.

1.9.36 **puras fulminis esse vias.**

puras codd.: *pronas* Heyne: *rubras* Postgate. *fulminis* Bg.de et ex corr.G: *fluminis* OBHPQ (*sigla* of Lenz & Gal.).

As T. is here talking of immutable, universal laws, such as that stars shine in the sky, *fluminis* is clearly incorrect, since not all rivers are clear (there is no reason for suspecting the mss. reading *puras* here, as it makes perfectly good sense (see n.), and the emendations are unnecessary). *Fluminis* is due to a misplacement of the l. *Fulminis* gives good sense, and the ref. is to the brightness and clearness that is a universal property of the tracks or paths of thunderbolts (see n.).

1.9.39 **quid faciam, nisi et ipse fores in amore puellae?**

faciam Oce: *facerem* Cu.HP: *faceres* BGQV_5d et i.m. V^2 (*sigla* of Lenz & Gal.).

The imperfect subjunctive, if deliberative, refers to the past, which is clearly inappropriate. If taken as the apodosis of a condition, *faceres* would mean 'loving a girl you broke your oath - what would you do if you were not in love with a girl?' However, it is difficult to envisage anything that the *puer delicatus* could do that would seem worse to T. than breaking his oath, which is the whole reason for the poem. It is also hard to see how the girl, if she did not prevent him from breaking his oath, could have prevented him from doing anything worse. *Facerem* as the apodosis of a condition does make sense, but the broken syntax of *quid faciam*, suggesting an emotional state (see n.), seems preferable to the comparatively calm condition. *Quid faciam* is also the *lectio difficilior*, and the alternative readings were probably attempts to make the tense of *facere* square with *fores* through a misunderstanding of the syntax.

1.9.48 **at me nunc nostri Pieridumque pudet.**

at ψ: *et* A.

If *et* is read here, then *quin etiam* in 47 must apply to the whole sentence, and it is then difficult to see what the phrase picks up. If *at* is read, *quin etiam* applies only to the hexameter (i.e. another ex. of his stupidity, picking up the previous lines), and the pentameter shows his present reaction (cf. the contrast in 29f.). The corruption of *at* to *et* is an easy one and was probably helped by *etiam* immediately above.

1.9.69 **ista haec persuadet facies,**

ista h(a)ec Ber.GHPQc et i.m. V^2: *ista* AV: *istane* Postgate: *istaec* Lachmann: *isthaec* Vahlen-Helm: *ista ita* Havet (*sigla* of Lenz & Gal.).

Ista is unmetrical, but *ista haec* makes perfectly good sense (see n.). The loss of *h(a)ec* is easy enough to credit here, and, although one cannot be sure that *ista haec* is not an emendation, it seems more likely than the conjectures of modern scholars. The form *isthaec* (with aspirate) is not attested, and *istaec* seems improbable, as the adjective *istic* is not found elsewhere in Augustan elegy. *Ista ita* seems prosaic and weak, and *ita* does not occur elsewhere in the *Corp. Tib*. *Istane* is initially attractive (the *-ne* dropping out before the pe- in *persuadet*), but, I think, stretches coincidence a little too far. The full form *-ne* occurs at only three other places in T. (*viden* appears at 2.1.25), and all these instances are in lines nearby (67, 77, 78). It seems a shade unlikely that we should have yet another rare *-ne* within so few lines and another pair of questions with repeated *-ne* at 67-70, as at 77-8.

1.9.75-76 huic tamen accubuit noster puer: hunc ego credam
cum trucibus venerem iungere posse feris.

huic ψ: *hunc* A: *hic* Cartault: *cui* Luck. *hunc* codd.: *illum* Lee. The purpose of the conjectures is to remove the change of ref. with forms of *hic* produced by the mss. readings. However, despite a little initial ambiguity, the sense of the line is clear enough (see n.), and the change of ref. here seems just defensible on the basis of the parallels cited in the commentary. So I read *hunc* in the second half of the hexameter.

In the first half of the line *huic* seems more likely than *hunc*. *Accumbo* in a sexual sense takes the dative in Propertius (see n.). The accusative with the verb is found at Plaut. *Men*. 476, 1142, *Bacch*. 1189, but the word is probably not used sexually there, and, in any case, Propertius is a better authority for Augustan usage. The A reading probably came from the *hunc* later in the line.

Emendation, then, is unnecessary, but, in any case, the conjectures proposed are not convincing (see Lee *PCPhS* 200 (1974), 55f.). Cartault suggested *hic* as the pronoun and understood *ei* with *accubuit*, but, as Lee points out, the absence of the dative here seems awkward. Lee's suggestion that *hic* may be taken as the adverb (= *in senis amplexibus*) seems unlikely, as *in amplexibus accumbere* is an odd phrase and one for which he can produce no parallel. Luck's *cui* seems prosaic, and is ambiguous, in that *cui* may seem to be picked up by *hunc* later in the line, as Lee remarks. Lee himself suggests *illum* (for *hunc*), but he admits that he can cite no parallel for the elision produced by this conjecture.

1.10.9-10 somnumque petebat
securus varias dux gregis inter oves.

varias ω: *sparsas* recc. (Lenz & Gal.).

There are two possible interpretations of *sparsas*. Firstly, 'spotted': in this sense *sparsus* is usually qualified in classical authors (cf. e.g. Virg. *Ecl*. 2.41, Livy 41.21.13), and, in any case, *varius* is the technical term in this connection (see n.). Secondly, the word may mean 'scattered': cf. Lenz & Gal. '*dux gregis, i.e. pastor, non aries, somnum petebat securus et furum vel luporum incuriosus, quamquam oves sparsae erant et quod non habebat quod eas colligeret'*. However, the idea of freedom from care (not a major motif in these lines) is already given full expression in *somnumque petebat / securus*, and the detail of thieves or wolves is inappropriate (surely more serious cares are in point here: cf. Dissen *'Securus, non timens hostes'*).

Varias gives excellent sense. Most probably it denotes spotted sheep, which are another example of *paupertas* (see n.), so that the present couplet balances 7-8 with the idea of the absence of war when there was *paupertas* (the main point to these lines).

Sparsas may be an alteration by a scribe wishing to emphasize the shepherd's freedom from care (as D.S. Raven suggests to me), or it may be a gloss or part of a gloss on *varias* (cf. Donatus ad Ter. *Heaut.* 1062 for *sparsus* taken to mean 'spotted'), or, just possibly, *securus sparsas* may be a misreading of *securus varias* (cf. Lenz & Gal.).

1.10.11-12 vulgi nec tristia nossem / arma

vulgi A: *dulcis* V_5 (Lenz & Gal.): *Valgi* Heyne: *vulgo* Haupt-Vahlen: *vigili* Postgate: *facilis* Reid.

Dulcis is weak and superfluous here, but *vulgi* gives excellent sense (see n.), and there is no need for emendation.

1.10.25-26 at nobis aerata, Lares, depellite tela,

. . . .

hostiaque e plena rustica porcus hara.

The text as it stands in most mss. presents some difficulties. The pentameter cannot be taken as a second subject with *Lares*, since such a juxtaposition of Lares and pig would be ridiculous, the stretch of sense involved would be unusual for T. (the pig itself does not actually ward off the weapons) and *porcus* is not in the vocative. Nor can the pentameter be taken as the apodosis of a conditional sentence with *-que* meaning 'and then', as some have suggested. There is no parallel for a protasis consisting of an imperative, followed by an apodosis consisting of mere nominatives with no verb expressed. *Hostia erit* (V_5 Lenz & Gal.) does not help. It leaves 26 with no connecting link and an unusual ablative without *e*. The corruption of *erit* to *-que e* is very unlikely, while the reverse procedure would naturally be an attempt to make sense out of nonsense. There seems to be no reason to suspect 26, so the lacuna after 25 marked in ψ must be correct. As the sense here is barely interrupted, it is likely that only two lines have dropped out (the first of which possibly began with *hostis* or *hasta*, which would explain the lacuna).

1.10.37-38 illic pertusisque genis ustoque capillo

errat ad obscuros pallida turba lacus.

pertusisque Livineius: *perscissisque* Par.: *percussisque* A: *perculsisque* recc. (Lenz & Gal.).

Perscissisque is obviously wrong, since it has no sense or application in this context. *Percussisque* and *perculsisque* most probably refer to the ghosts of soldiers or men who have been murdered. However, it seems strange that in a general description of the Underworld, when covering the dead, T. should confine himself to these people and that he should mention wounds to the cheeks or eyes, which would not necessarily prove fatal, rather than wounds to the breast or side. It seems far more likely that *pallida turba* refers to the dead in general and line 37 to certain characteristics common to all of them (in which case *percussisque* and *perculsisque genis* in this sense must be wrong, since comparatively few of the dead would share this disfigurement). Similarly, the alternative interpretation (cheeks struck in grief) seems unlikely, since not all of the dead would behave so, and, in any case, the detail seems irrelevant and inappropriate here (esp. in conjunction with *ustoque capillo*: see below).

Ustoque capillo must refer to the effects of the pyre, which many would show (see n.). Livineius' conjecture fits in excellently with this idea: it means 'bored through', and the ref. is to the effect on the eyes of the pyre or worms after burial (see n.). The conjecture is also palaeographically sound, since its rarity and its alternative spelling (*pertussisque*) may well explain the mss. readings here. For all these reasons it seems more likely than the numerous other emendations here (see Lenz & Gal., O'Neil *A Critical Concordance of the Tibullan Corpus* (Ithaca, 1963), p.7).

1.10.45-47 I have printed *Pax* each time with capitals in these lines, since *Pax* is fully personified and the ref. is most probably to the goddess (so *candida* is applied to her at 45 (cf. 68), and she is described as an inventor: see n.). At 49 the construction and the ref. change (*pace* = 'in peacetime').

1.10.51-52 rusticus e lucoque vehit, male sobrius ipse,
uxorem plaustro progeniemque domum.

Haupt placed a lacuna before this couplet, and editors who follow him usually suppose that the earlier part of a description of a rustic festival has dropped out. The lacuna is unnecessary. If *at tristia duri / militis in tenebris occupat arma situs* in 49f. is taken as a brief antithetical parenthesis (punctuated as in my text), then this couplet continues smoothly from *pace bidens vomerque nitent* in 49, keeping up the rustic setting and referring to other blessings of peace-time (see n.). In addition, the present couplet makes perfectly good sense in itself and needs no further explanation (see n.), while in the middle of a passage in praise of Peace a longer ref. to a rustic festival (in honour of another deity) would be inappropriate.

1.10.55 flet teneras subtusa genas:
subtusa] *subscisa* P (Lenz & Gal.): *suffusa* Scaliger: *obtusa* Némethy.

Subscisa is nonsense, but *subtusa*, although odd, is probably right. The word does make sense, if taken to mean 'thumped about a bit' or 'slapped about a bit' (see n.). Although the verb in either sense would be unique in Latin, and may be unique in any sense (elsewhere it occurs only at Boeth. *Geom* 1.p.1180, of an angle, meaning 'obtuse', and may there be corrupt, since Lucr. (4.355) talks of an *angulus obtusus*), yet anomaly is not rare enough elsewhere in T. to justify suspicion here. Emendation does not seem necessary.

1.10.68 perfluat et pomis candidus ante sinus.

perfluat ψ: *profluat* g: *prefluat* A.

The choice between the readings is difficult, since, whatever word is read, its sense here is not its usual one. However, the ψ reading is the most likely, as *perfluo* is the only word that is found with a meaning similar to the one required here (see n.).

INDEXES

INDEX NOMINUM

INDEX VERBORUM

INDEX RERUM

www.ingramcontent.com/pod-product-compliance
Lightning Source LLC
Chambersburg PA
CBHW060228100726
47907CB00003B/547
9781853991752